03

EVERYMAN'S UNITED NATIONS

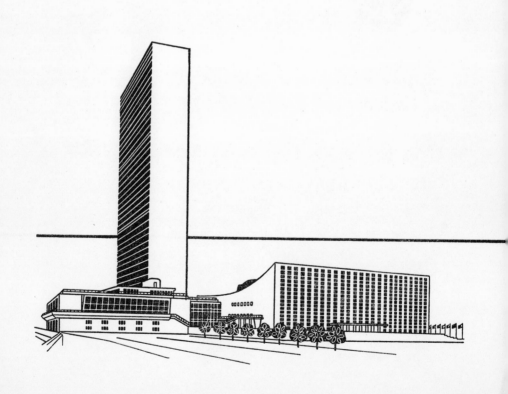

Everyman's
UNITED
NATIONS
1945-1955

A Ready Reference to the Structure,
Functions and Work of the United Nations
and its Related Agencies
during the Ten Years ending December 31, 1955

FIFTH EDITION

Published by the United Nations
Department of Public Information

NEW YORK, 1956

First Edition 1948
Second Edition 1950
Third Edition ....April, 1952
Second Printing ....August, 1952
Third Printing ......December, 1952
Fourth Edition ....August, 1953
Second Printing ....April, 1954
Third Printing ....March, 1955
Fifth Edition ....September, 1956

UNITED NATIONS PUBLICATIONS • 1956 • I • 13

Price: $1.50 (U.S.A.); 11/0 stg.; 6.50 Swiss francs
(or equivalent in other currencies)

FOREWORD

This fifth revised edition of *Everyman's United Nations* summarizes the activities and achievements of the United Nations and the related specialized agencies for the decade ending December 31, 1955. The steps leading to the adoption of the United Nations Charter are also described briefly.

On October 24, 1955, the United Nations completed its first ten years. The Organization was the outgrowth of a war alliance and was born of a determination to "save succeeding generations from the scourge of war." It provides the machinery through which its Member nations may combine their efforts to preserve peace and to promote world-wide human betterment.

The United Nations has been faced with many grave and difficult problems in these first ten years. There have been achievements and there have been disappointing setbacks. In the perspective of a decade, however, the reader will find in the pages of this volume that there has been progress in many fields toward the great purposes and principles which the United Nations was created to serve. In seeking to meet the many challenges which the first ten years produced, the Members of the United Nations have also gained experience which may help to strengthen the Organization for the responsibilities and the new challenges that lie ahead.

The United Nations cannot acquire maximum vitality without the support of the world's peoples. Unless they are fully informed of its aims and activities, they cannot be expected to support it. *Everyman's United Nations*, a concise account of the aims, structure and work of the United Nations family, is intended to help the peoples become so informed.

AHMED S. BOKHARI
Under-Secretary of the
United Nations

TABLE OF CONTENTS

PART I. THE UNITED NATIONS

PART II. THE WORK OF THE UNITED NATIONS

8

PART I **THE UNITED NATIONS**

INTRODUCTION

The deep-felt needs and intentions which inspired the founding of the United Nations are proclaimed in the preamble of the Charter, signed at San Francisco on the twenty-sixth day of June 1945. The preamble reads:

WE THE PEOPLES OF THE UNITED NATIONS DETERMINED to save succeeding generations from the scourge of war, which twice in our lifetime has brought untold sorrow to mankind, and to reaffirm faith in fundamental human rights, in the dignity and worth of the human person, in the equal rights of men and women and of nations large and small, and to establish conditions under which justice and respect for the obligations arising from treaties and other sources of international law can be maintained, and to promote social progress and better standards of life in larger freedom,

AND FOR THESE ENDS to practice tolerance and live together in peace with one another as good neighbors, and

to unite our strength to maintain international peace and security, and to insure, by the acceptance of principles and the institution of methods, that armed force shall not be used, save in the common interest, and

to employ international machinery for the promotion of the economic and social advancement of all peoples,

HAVE RESOLVED TO COMBINE OUR EFFORTS TO ACCOMPLISH THESE AIMS. Accordingly, our respective Governments, through representatives assembled in the city of San Francisco, who have exhibited their full powers found to be in good and due form, have agreed to the present Charter of the United Nations and do hereby establish an international organization to be known as the United Nations.

PURPOSES

The four purposes of the United Nations are:

1. to maintain international peace and security;
2. to develop friendly relations among nations based on respect for the equal rights and self-determination of peoples;
3. to cooperate in solving international problems of an economic, social, cultural or humanitarian character, and in promoting respect for human rights and fundamental freedoms for all; and
4. to be a centre for harmonizing the actions of nations in attaining these common ends.

PRINCIPLES

To fulfil the purposes for which it was established, the United Nations acts in accordance with the following principles:

1. the Organization is based on the principle of the sovereign equality of all its Members;

2. Members are to fulfil in good faith the obligations they have assumed under the Charter;

3. they are to settle their international disputes by peaceful means;

4. they are to refrain in their international relations from the threat or use of force in any manner inconsistent with the purposes of the United Nations;

5. they are to give the United Nations every assistance in any action it takes in accordance with the Charter, and to refrain from giving assistance to any state against which the Organization is taking preventive or enforcement action;

6. the United Nations is to insure that non-Members act in accordance with these principles so far as is necessary for maintaining international peace and security;

7. the Organization is not to intervene in matters essentially within the domestic jurisdiction of any state. This provision does not apply, however, when enforcement action is taken with respect to threats to the peace, breaches of the peace, and acts of aggression.

FINANCES

The United Nations is financed by contributions from Member States. How much each Member shall pay is determined by the General Assembly. *(For percentage contribution, see pages 338-340.)*

STEPS TO THE CHARTER

London Declaration

Signed on June 12, 1941, at St. James's Palace by the representatives of Great Britain, Canada, Australia, New Zealand and the Union of South Africa, and of the exiled Governments of Belgium, Czechoslovakia, Greece, Luxembourg, the Netherlands, Norway, Poland, Yugoslavia and of General de Gaulle of France. The document declares against separate peace and states:

"The only true basis of enduring peace is the willing cooperation of free peoples in a world in which, relieved of the menace of aggression, all may enjoy economic and social security;

"It is our intention to work together, and with other free peoples, both in war and peace, to this end."

Atlantic Charter

Signed on August 14, 1941, by President Roosevelt and Prime Minister Winston Churchill. Clause 6 reads:

"After the final destruction of the Nazi tyranny, they hope to see established a peace which will afford to all nations the means of dwelling in safety within their own boundaries, and which will afford assurance that all the men in all the lands may live out their lives in freedom from fear and want."

Clause 8 reads:

"They believe that all of the nations of the world, for realistic as well as spiritual reasons, must come to the abandonment of the use of force. Since no future peace can be maintained if land, sea, or air armaments continue to be employed by nations which threaten, or may threaten, aggression outside of their frontiers, they believe, pending the establishment of a wider and permanent system of general security, that the disarmament of such nations is essential. They will likewise aid and encourage all other practicable measures which will lighten for peace-loving peoples the crushing burden of armaments."

Clause 5 declares the signatories' desire to bring about the fullest collaboration between all nations in the economic field with the objective of securing, for all, improved labor standards, economic advancement and social security.

United Nations Declaration

Signed by the representatives of 26 states on January 1, 1942, at Washington, D. C. The Declaration reads:

"The Governments signatory hereto,

"Having subscribed to a common program of purposes and principles embodied in the Joint Declaration of the President of the United States of America and the Prime Minister of the United Kingdom of Great Britain and Northern Ireland dated August 14, 1941, known as the Atlantic Charter,

"Being convinced that complete victory over their enemies is essential to defend life, liberty, independence, and religious freedom, and to preserve human rights and justice in their own lands as well as in other lands, and that they are now engaged in a common struggle against savage and brutal forces seeking to subjugate the world,

DECLARE:

"(i) Each Government pledges itself to employ its full resources, military or economic, against those members of the Tripartite Pact and its adherents with which such government is at war.

"(ii) Each Government pledges itself to cooperate with the Governments signatory hereto and not to make a separate armistice or peace with the enemies.

"The foregoing declaration may be adhered to by other nations which are, or may be, rendering material assistance and contributions in the struggle for victory over Hitlerism."

Signatories were:

The United States of America	Australia	Greece	Nicaragua
	Belgium	Guatemala	Norway
The United Kingdom of Great Britain and Northern Ireland	Canada	Haiti	Panama
	Costa Rica	Honduras	Poland
	Cuba	India	Union of South Africa
The Union of Soviet Socialist Republics	Czechoslovakia	Luxembourg	Yugoslavia
	Dominican Republic	Netherlands	
China	El Salvador	New Zealand	

Later adherents to the Declaration were:

Mexico	Iran	Peru	Turkey
Philippines	Colombia	Chile	Egypt
Ethiopia	Liberia	Paraguay	Saudi Arabia
Iraq	France	Venezuela	Syria
Brazil	Ecuador	Uruguay	Lebanon
Bolivia			

(Note: France and Denmark were generally regarded as having been identified with the United Nations from the beginning, as the French authorities abroad had carried on hostilities, and the Danish Minister in Washington had signified the adherence of all free Danes to the Allied cause. As the Declaration was signed by

16

governments, they could not at that time, however, formally adhere to it.

(France, when the French National Committee was constituted as a government, adhered formally to the Declaration. Denmark, which was not liberated until after the opening of the San Francisco Conference, was admitted as one of the United Nations by the Conference.)

Moscow and Teheran Conferences

On October 30, 1943, a declaration was signed in Moscow by Vyacheslav Molotov, Anthony Eden, Cordell Hull, and Foo Ping Shen, the Chinese Ambassador to the Soviet Union. Clause 4 of the Moscow Declaration on General Security proclaims that:

"they [the four Governments] recognize the necessity of establishing at the earliest practicable date a general international organization, based on the principle of the sovereign equality of all peace-loving states, and open to membership by all such states, large and small, for the maintenance of international peace and security."

In December of the same year, Roosevelt, Stalin and Churchill, meeting at Teheran, declared:

"We are sure that our concord will win an enduring peace. We recognize fully the supreme responsibility resting upon us and all the United Nations to make a peace which will command the goodwill of the overwhelming mass of the peoples of the world and banish the scourge and terror of war for many generations."

Dumbarton Oaks and Yalta Conferences

The first blueprint of the Organization was prepared at a conference held at a mansion known as Dumbarton Oaks in Washington, D.C. The first phase of the conference was between the representatives of the U.S.S.R., the United Kingdom and the United States from August 21 to September 28, 1944, and the second phase between the representatives of China, the United Kingdom and the United States from September 29 to October 7. (This arrangement served to respect U.S.S.R. neutrality in the war against Japan.) At the end of the conference, proposals for the structure of a world organization were published. Extensive public discussion followed in Allied countries.

According to the Dumbarton Oaks proposals, the key body in the United Nations for preserving world peace was to be the Security Council on which the "Big Five"— China, France, the U.S.S.R., the United Kingdom and the United States—were to be permanently represented. However, the proposals did not specify the voting procedure in the Council. This was discussed at Yalta at a conference between Roosevelt, Churchill and Stalin. On February 11, 1945, the conference announced that this point had been settled. The three leaders then declared:

"We are resolved upon the earliest possible establishment with our Allies of a general international organization to maintain peace and security. . . .

"We have agreed that a Conference of United Nations should be called to meet at San Francisco in the United States on the twenty-fifth April 1945, to prepare the charter of such an organization, along the lines proposed in the informal conversations of Dumbarton Oaks."

The United Nations Conference on International Organization

Delegates of 50 nations met at San Francisco between April 25 and June 26, 1945. Working on the Dumbarton Oaks proposals, the Yalta agreement, and amendments proposed by various governments, the Conference hammered out the Charter of the

United Nations and the Statute of the new International Court of Justice. The Charter was passed unanimously and signed by all the representatives.

It came into force on October 24, 1945, when China, France, the U.S.S.R., the United Kingdom and the United States and a majority of the other signatories had filed their instruments of ratification. October 24 is now observed as United Nations Day.

MEMBERS

The original Members of the United Nations are those states which took part in the San Francisco Conference or had previously signed the Declaration by United Nations, and which signed and ratified the Charter.

They are:

Argentina	Denmark	Lebanon	Syria
Australia	Dominican Republic	Liberia	Turkey
Belgium	Ecuador	Luxembourg	Ukrainian Soviet Socialist
Bolivia	Egypt	Mexico	Republic
Brazil	El Salvador	Netherlands	Union of South Africa
Byelorussian Soviet	Ethiopia	New Zealand	Union of Soviet Socialist
Socialist Republic	France	Nicaragua	Republics
Canada	Greece	Norway	United Kingdom of Great
Chile	Guatemala	Panama	Britain and Northern
China	Haiti	Paraguay	Ireland
Colombia	Honduras	Peru	United States of America
Costa Rica	India	Philippines	Uruguay
Cuba	Iran	Poland[1]	Venezuela
Czechoslovakia	Iraq	Saudi Arabia	Yugoslavia

Membership in the United Nations is open to all peace-loving states which accept and, in the judgment of the Organization, are able and willing to carry out the obligations of the Charter. Any state desiring to become a Member must submit an application containing a declaration that it accepts the obligations contained in the Charter.

New Members are admitted by a two-thirds vote of the General Assembly upon the recommendation of the Security Council. Membership becomes effective on the date on which the Assembly takes its decision on the application.

The following additional Members had been admitted as of January 1956, bringing the total of Members to 76.

	Date of Admission		Date of Admission
Afghanistan	November 19, 1946	Israel	May 11, 1949
Iceland	November 19, 1946	Indonesia	September 28, 1950
Sweden	November 19, 1946	Albania	December 14, 1955
Thailand	December 16, 1946	Austria	December 14, 1955
(formerly Siam)		Bulgaria	December 14, 1955
Pakistan	September 30, 1947	Cambodia	December 14, 1955
Yemen	September 30, 1947	Ceylon	December 14, 1955
Burma	April 19, 1948	Finland	December 14, 1955

---

[1] Poland did not attend the San Francisco Conference because the composition of her new government was not announced until June 28—too late for the Conference. A space, however, was left for the signature of Poland, one of the original signatories of the Declaration by United Nations. Poland signed the Charter on October 15, 1945, thus becoming one of the original Members.

Date of Admission		Date of Admission	
Hungary	December 14, 1955	Libya	December 14, 1955
Ireland	December 14, 1955	Nepal	December 14, 1955
Italy	December 14, 1955	Portugal	December 14, 1955
Jordan	December 14, 1955	Romania	December 14, 1955
Laos	December 14, 1955	Spain	December 14, 1955

The General Assembly, upon the recommendation of the Security Council, may suspend a Member against which preventive or enforcement action has been taken by the Security Council, and may expel a Member which has persistently violated the principles of the Charter.

PRINCIPAL ORGANS

The United Nations has six principal organs: the General Assembly, the Security Council, the Economic and Social Council, the Trusteeship Council, the International Court of Justice, and the Secretariat.

LANGUAGES

In all the organs of the United Nations, other than the International Court of Justice, the official languages are Chinese, French, English, Russian and Spanish, and the working languages are English and French. In the General Assembly and the Economic and Social Council, Spanish is also a working language. Speeches made in one of the working languages are interpreted into the other working languages. Speeches made in one of the other official languages are interpreted into the working languages. If a speaker uses still another language, he himself provides for interpretation into a working language.

The official languages of the International Court of Justice are French and English.

AMENDMENTS TO THE CHARTER

The Charter can be amended by the General Assembly or by a General Conference of Members of the United Nations. A General Conference may be held at a date and place decided upon by a two-thirds vote of the Assembly and a vote of any seven members of the Security Council. Each Member of the United Nations has one vote in the Conference.

As a General Conference had not been held before the tenth annual session of the Assembly, the proposal to call such a Conference was automatically placed on its agenda. The Assembly in November 1955, decided that a General Conference of the Members of the United Nations to review the Charter should be held at "an appropriate time." It set up a committee consisting of all the Members of the United Nations to consider, in consultation with the Secretary-General, the question of fixing a time and place for the Conference, and its organization and procedures. The Security Council in December 1955 expressed its concurrence in the General Assembly's decision (*see pages 72-74*).

A two-thirds vote in the General Assembly or in the General Conference is required for the adoption of amendments. Amendments thus adopted take effect for all Members of the United Nations when they are ratified by two thirds of the Members, including all the permanent members of the Security Council.

THE GENERAL ASSEMBLY

The General Assembly is the centerpiece of the United Nations. It is the one organ in which all Member States are represented; it has powers and functions with respect to all other United Nations bodies; it elects by itself or with the Security Council some or all members of other organs; and it has the right to discuss all matters within the scope of the Charter. The Security Council, the Economic and Social Council, the Trusteeship Council, and the Secretary-General submit annual and special reports to the Assembly, which considers them. It also controls the budget of the Organization and the contributions of Member States. The Assembly's decisions are framed as "recommendations" to Member States, the other organs, or the specialized agencies related to the United Nations. While these recommendations are not binding and may be ignored by the parties concerned, they do have the moral persuasion of the majority of the world's governments behind them.

Functions and Powers

The functions and powers of the General Assembly may be grouped under the following headings:

MAINTENANCE OF INTERNATIONAL PEACE AND SECURITY

Although the Security Council is entrusted with the primary responsibility for international peace and security, including plans for the regulation of armaments, the Assembly may consider the general principles of cooperation in the maintenance of peace and security, including those governing disarmament and the regulation of armaments. It may make recommendations with regard to such principles to the Members or to the Security Council, or to both.

The Assembly may discuss any question relating to the maintenance of international peace and security brought before it by any Member, by the Security Council, or by a non-Member state which accepts the obligations of pacific settlement provided in the Charter. The Assembly may make recommendations to the state or states concerned or to the Security Council on any such question, except when the Security Council is exercising its functions in that matter (unless the Council so requests).

The Assembly may recommend measures for the peaceful adjustment of any situation, regardless of origin, which it considers likely to impair the general welfare or friendly relations among nations, including a situation resulting from a violation of the principles and purposes of the United Nations, provided the Security Council is not exercising its functions on the matter.

The Assembly may call the attention of the Security Council to situations which are likely to endanger international peace and security. It initiates studies and makes recommendations to promote international cooperation in the political field, and to encourage the progressive development of international law and its codification.

If the Security Council, because of lack of unanimity of the permanent members, fails to exercise its primary responsibility for the maintenance of international peace and security in any case where there appears to be a threat to the peace, breach of the peace, or act of aggression, the Assembly, under its "Uniting for Peace" resolution of November 3, 1950, will consider the matter immediately with a view to making appropriate recommendations to Members for collective measures to maintain or restore international peace and security. In the case of a breach of the peace or act of aggression, such measures might include the use of armed force when necessary.

INTERNATIONAL ECONOMIC AND SOCIAL COOPERATION

Responsibility for discharging the functions and powers of the United Nations with respect to international economic and social cooperation rests with the General Assembly and, under its authority, with the Economic and Social Council.

Agreements negotiated by that Council to bring specialized inter-governmental organizations in the economic, social, cultural and health fields into relationship with the United Nations are subject to approval by the Assembly. The Assembly may make recommendations for coordinating the policies and activities of these specialized agencies.

INTERNATIONAL TRUSTEESHIP SYSTEM

The Assembly, with the assistance of the Trusteeship Council, exercises the functions of the United Nations with regard to all Trust Territories not designated as strategic. It approves the terms of the Trusteeship Agreements and their alteration or amendment.

INFORMATION ON NON-SELF-GOVERNING TERRITORIES

The Assembly considers the Secretary-General's summaries and analyses of information transmitted by Members administering non-self-governing territories not placed under the Trusteeship System, and is assisted in this consideration by a Special Committee established by it for the purpose.

BUDGETARY POWERS

The Assembly controls the finances of the United Nations. It considers and approves the budget and apportions the expenses among the Members. It also is empowered to examine the administrative budgets of the specialized agencies and to make recommendations to those agencies.

Voting Procedure

Each Member of the United Nations has one vote in the General Assembly.

Decisions on "important questions" are made by a two-thirds majority of the Members present and voting. As defined in the Charter, "important questions" include: recommendations concerning international peace and security, election of members of the Councils, admission and expulsion of Members and suspension of the rights and privileges of Membership, questions relating to the operation of the Trusteeship System, and budgetary matters. Other matters, including additional categories of questions to be determined by two-thirds majority, are decided by simple majority of the Members present and voting.

In the election of Judges of the International Court of Justice, those candidates who obtain an absolute majority of votes in the General Assembly and in the Security Council are elected.

A Member which is in arrears in its financial contributions to the Organization has no vote in the Assembly if its arrears equal or exceed the contributions due from it for the preceding two full years. But the Assembly may permit such a Member to vote if it is satisfied that the failure to pay is due to conditions beyond the Member's control.

Sessions

The Assembly meets every year in regular session beginning on the third Tuesday in September. Special sessions may be called at the request of the Security Council, a majority of the Member States, or one Member with the concurrence of a majority.

If, because of a lack of unanimity of the permanent members of the Security Council, the Council fails to act on a threat to the peace, breach of the peace, or act of aggression, an emergency special session of the Assembly may be called within 24 hours of a request by the Council on the vote of any seven of its members, or by a majority of the United Nations Members.

Organization

The General Assembly adopts its own rules of procedure, including rules governing the public character of its proceedings. It elects its President and Vice-Presidents, for each session; it may establish such subsidiary organs as it considers necessary.

The Assembly does most of its work in committees, of which there are four types: main committees, procedural committees, standing committees, and *ad hoc* committees.

MAIN COMMITTEES consider agenda items referred to them by the Assembly, and prepare recommendations for submission to its plenary meetings. Every Member has the right to be represented on each of the Main Committees.

There are six:

First Committee (Political and Security, including the Regulation of Armaments),
Second Committee (Economic and Financial),
Third Committee (Social, Humanitarian and Cultural),
Fourth Committee (Trusteeship, including Non-Self-Governing Territories),
Fifth Committee (Administrative and Budgetary),
Sixth Committee (Legal).

At each session since the second, the Assembly has established as well an *ad hoc* Political Committee of full membership to share the work of the First Committee in dealing with the large number of political questions on its agenda.

PROCEDURAL COMMITTEES deal with the organization and conduct of the Assembly's business. There are two: General Committee composed of the President and seven Vice-Presidents of the Assembly, the Chairmen of the six Main Committees. and beginning with the seventh session, the Chairman of the *ad hoc* Political Committee; and Credentials Committee (nine members).

STANDING COMMITTEES deal with continuing problems. Two provided for in the Assembly's rules of procedure are: Advisory Committee on Administrative and Budgetary Questions (nine members), and Committee on Contributions (ten members).

OTHER STANDING BODIES established by the Assembly are: the Board of Auditors (three members), Investments Committee (three members), and United Nations Staff Pension Committee (nine members).

AD HOC COMMITTEES. The Assembly or any of its committees may appoint committees for special purposes. Examples of such *ad hoc* committees set up by the Assembly are: Advisory Committee on the International Conference on the Peaceful Uses of Atomic Energy, United Nations Commission for the Unification and Rehabilition of Korea, United Nations Korean Reconstruction Agency, United Nations Conciliation Commission for Palestine, United Nations Relief and Works Agency for Palestine Refugees in the Near East, Committee on Information from Non-Self-Governing Territories, Collective Measures Committee, and Office of the United Nations High Commissioner for Refugees.

INTERIM COMMITTEE. The Interim Committee, popularly known as the "Little Assembly," was originally set up by the Assembly in November 1947, for an experimental period of one year. A subsidiary organ of the Assembly, it was to assist the latter in carrying out its functions. Each Member State had the right to appoint one representative to it. In 1948, the Assembly decided to continue the life of the Interim Committee for another year, and, in 1949, reestablished it for an indefinite period, to meet when the Assembly is not actually in regular session.

Subsidiary to the Assembly is a permanent body, the International Law Commission, composed of fifteen members (*see page 313*).

Another subsidiary body is the Peace Observation Commission (fourteen members).

Relations with other Organs

Election. The Assembly elects the non-permanent members of the Security Council, the members of the Economic and Social Council, and the elective members of the Trusteeship Council.

On the recommendation of the Security Council, it appoints the Secretary-General.

The Assembly and the Security Council, voting independently, elect the judges of the International Court of Justice.

* *Reports.* The Assembly receives annual and special reports from the Security Council and reports from the other organs. The Secretary-General reports annually on the work of the Organization as a whole.

International Court of Justice. The Assembly, on the recommendation of the Security Council, determines the conditions on which a state not a Member of the United Nations may become a party to the Statute of the International Court. The Assembly may request the Court to give an advisory opinion on any legal question, and may authorize the other organs (apart from the Security Council, which itself has this right), as well as the specialized agencies, to request advisory opinions on legal questions.

Other Organs. The Economic and Social Council and the Trusteeship Council operate under the authority of the General Assembly. The regulations under which the staff of the Secretariat is appointed are established by the Assembly.

THE SECURITY COUNCIL

Composition

The Security Council consists of eleven Members of the United Nations. China, France, the U.S.S.R., the United Kingdom and the United States are permanent members.

In electing the six non-permanent members, the General Assembly pays due regard, first, to their contribution to the maintenance of international peace and security and to other purposes of the United Nations, and also to equitable geographical distribution. Each member is elected for a term of two years and, on retirement, is not eligible for immediate reelection.

The non-permanent members in 1956 were: Belgium, Iran and Peru (January 1, 1955–December 31, 1956); Australia, Cuba and Yugoslavia (January 1, 1956–December 31, 1957).

Each member has one representative.

Any Member of the United Nations which is not a member of the Council may participate, without vote, in any discussion in the Council if the Council considers that the interests of that Member are especially affected.

Any state, whether a Member of the United Nations or not, which is a party to a dispute being considered by the Council, must be invited to participate, without vote, in the discussions.

Functions and Powers

Members of the United Nations have conferred on the Security Council the primary responsibility for maintaining international peace and security. For this purpose, they have agreed that it is acting for all of them and that they will accept and carry out its decisions.

The Council is to act in accordance with the purposes and principles of the United Nations. Its specific powers are laid down in Chapters VI, VII, VIII and XII of the Charter.

PACIFIC SETTLEMENT OF DISPUTES

Parties to a dispute, the continuance of which is likely to endanger international peace and security, are first of all to seek a solution by negotiation, inquiry, mediation, conciliation, arbitration, judicial settlement, resort to regional agencies or arrangements, or other peaceful means. The Security Council may call on states to settle their disputes by such means.

The Council may investigate any dispute or situation to see if its continuance is likely to endanger international peace and security. Such a dispute or situation may be brought to its attention by any Member or, if it accepts in advance the obligations of pacific settlement contained in the Charter, by any non-Member.

The General Assembly may call the attention of the Council to situations which are likely to endanger international peace and security. Likewise, the Secretary-General may bring to the Council's attention any matter which he thinks may threaten the maintenance of peace and security.

During the course of a dispute the Council may recommend procedures or methods of adjustment. It may also recommend terms of settlement if it finds that continuance of the dispute is in fact likely to endanger the maintenance of peace and security. If all the parties to a dispute so request, it may make recommendations with a view to pacific settlement.

PREVENTIVE OR ENFORCEMENT ACTION

The Council determines the existence of any threat to the peace, breach of the peace, or act of aggression. It makes recommendations or decides to take enforcement measures to maintain or restore international peace and security. Before doing so, it may call on the parties to a dispute to comply with provisional measures.

The Council may take enforcement action as follows:

1. Measures not involving the use of armed force. It may call on Members to apply such measures as complete or partial interruption of economic relations and of rail, sea, air, postal, telegraphic, radio, and other means of communication, and the severance of diplomatic relations.

2. Action by air, sea or land forces. The Council may also take action that may include demonstrations, blockade, and other operations by air, sea or land forces of Members of the United Nations.

The Council decides if the action necessary to carry out its decisions is to be taken by all or by some of the Members of the United Nations. Members are to take this action either directly or through the appropriate international agencies of which they are members.

Members have agreed to help each other in carrying out the Council's decisions. If any state, whether a Member or not, is faced with special economic problems arising from the carrying out, against another state, of preventive or enforcement measures decided on by the Council, it may consult the Council on how these problems can be solved.

AGREEMENTS ON ARMED FORCES. All Members have undertaken to make available to the Council on its call, in accordance with special agreements to be negotiated on the initiative of the Council, the armed forces, assistance and facilities, including rights of passage, necessary for maintaining international peace and security. Under the Charter, the Council is required to plan application of armed force with the assistance of the Military Staff Committee *(see below)*.

TRANSITIONAL ARRANGEMENTS. Pending the coming into force of these agreements, the Charter provides that China, France, the U.S.S.R., the United Kingdom and the United States, after consultation, are to take joint action on behalf of the United Nations for maintaining peace and security.

RIGHT OF SELF-DEFENCE. The Charter provides that Members, if attacked, may defend themselves, either individually or acting together, until the Council takes action. They must, however, report to the Council what measures they have taken, and the Council may then take any action it considers necessary.

REGIONAL AGENCIES AND ARRANGEMENTS. The Council is to encourage the development of pacific settlement of local disputes through regional arrangements or by regional agencies.

Where appropriate, the Council will utilize such regional agencies or arrangements for enforcement action under its authority. The Council, however, must authorize such enforcement action, except when it is taken against ex-enemy states (of the Second World War) by the governments responsible for such action. These agencies or arrangements and their activities must be consistent with the purposes and principles of the United Nations, and all action undertaken or contemplated for maintaining international peace and security through them must be reported to the Council.

STRATEGIC AREAS UNDER THE TRUSTEESHIP SYSTEM. The Security Council is responsible for all functions of the United Nations under the Trusteeship System with regard to Trust Territories classed as "strategic areas." It is assisted in certain matters by the Trusteeship Council *(see page 34)*.

REGULATION OF ARMAMENTS. In order to promote the establishment and maintenance of international peace and security with the least diversion for armaments of the world's human and economic resources, the Security Council is also responsible for formulating plans for regulating armaments. In this work, it is assisted by the Military Staff Committee and other bodies *(see page 40)*. The plans for establishment of a system for such regulations are to be submitted to Members of the United Nations.

Voting Procedure

Each member of the Security Council has one vote. Decisions on procedural matters are made by an affirmative vote of any seven members. Decisions on other (that is, substantive) matters are made by an affirmative vote of seven members, including the concurring votes of the permanent members, except that any member must abstain from voting in decisions concerning the pacific settlement of a dispute to which it is a party. (A negative vote by a permanent member on a matter of substance is popularly referred to as a "veto." In practice, a permanent member's abstention from voting on a substantive question is not regarded as a "veto.")

In the election of Judges of the International Court of Justice, those candidates who obtain an absolute majority of votes in the General Assembly and in the Security Council are elected. Any vote in the Security Council for the election of Judges of the International Court, is taken without any distinction between permanent and non-permanent members of the Council.

Sessions

The Security Council is so organized as to be able to function continuously— at the seat of the United Nations or at other places if this will facilitate its work.

It is also required by the Charter to hold periodic meetings at which each of its members may, if it wishes, be represented by a member of the government or by some other specially designated representative.

Organization

The Presidency of the Council is held monthly in turn by the Member States in English alphabetical order. The Council decides its own rules of procedure, and may establish what subsidiary organs it considers necessary.

Subsidiary organs reporting to the Council are: the Military Staff Committee, the Disarmament Commission (established by the General Assembly and reporting to both the Council and the Assembly), and various standing committees, *ad hoc* committees and commissions.

THE MILITARY STAFF COMMITTEE consists of the Chiefs of Staff (or their representatives) of the permanent members of the Council. It advises and assists the Council on all questions relating to the Council's military requirements for maintaining international peace and security, the employment and command of forces placed at its disposal, the regulation of armaments, and possible disarmament. It is to be responsible under the Security Council for the strategic direction of any armed forces placed at the Council's disposal.

THE DISARMAMENT COMMISSION, established by the General Assembly on January 11, 1952, under the Security Council, has the same membership as the Council, and in addition, Canada, when that country is not a member of the Council. The Commission replaced the former Atomic Energy Commission and the Commission for Conventional Armaments. The Disarmament Commission was directed to prepare proposals to be embodied in a draft treaty (or treaties) for the regulation, limitation and balanced reduction of all armed forces and all armaments; for the elimination of all major weapons adaptable to mass destruction; and for effective international control of atomic energy to insure the prohibition of atomic weapons and the use of atomic energy for peaceful purposes only. When preparing these proposals, the Commission is to formulate plans for the establishment within the framework of the Security Council of an international control organ (or organs) to insure the implementation of the treaty (or treaties), and it is to consider from the outset plans for progressive and continuing disclosure and verification of all armaments and armed forces. A conference of all states is to be convened to consider the Commission's proposals when any part of its program is ready for submission to governments.

There are two standing committees, each consisting of representatives of the eleven members of the Council:

COMMITTEE OF EXPERTS, which studies and advises the Council on rules of procedure and other technical matters;

COMMITTEE ON THE ADMISSION OF NEW MEMBERS, which examines such applications for membership in the United Nations as may be referred to it by the Council.

The Security Council also makes use from time to time of *ad hoc* committees and commissions, for example, the United Nations Commission for Indonesia, and the United Nations Representative for India and Pakistan.

Relations with other Organs

The Security Council makes annual and special reports to the General Assembly. It may request the assistance of the Economic and Social Council.

It has the assistance of the Trusteeship Council in performing duties relating to political, economic, social and educational matters in Trust Territories which are designated as strategic areas.

The Security Council and the General Assembly, voting independently, elect the judges of the International Court of Justice. The Council may ask the Court for an advisory opinion on any legal question. If any party to a case fails to perform the obligations incumbent on it under a judgment by the Court, the other party may have recourse to the Council which, if it deems it necessary, may make recommendations or decide on measures to give effect to the Court's judgment. The Council recommends to the Assembly the terms on which a state which is not a Member of the United Nations may become a party to the Statute of the Court. Subject to the provisions of treaties in force, the Council lays down the conditions on which the Court is to be open to a state which is not a party to its Statute.

In the election of Court Judges, those candidates who obtain an absolute majority of votes in the General Assembly and Security Council are elected.

It is on the Security Council's recommendation that the General Assembly appoints the Secretary-General.

THE ECONOMIC AND SOCIAL COUNCIL

Composition

The Economic and Social Council consists of eighteen members elected by the General Assembly, six of whom are elected each year for a three-year term. Retiring members are eligible for immediate reelection. Each member of the Council has one representative.

The members of the Council in 1956 and their terms of office were: Czechoslovakia, Ecuador, Norway, Pakistan, the U.S.S.R., the United Kingdom (January 1, 1954—December 31, 1956); Argentina, China, the Dominican Republic, Egypt, France, the Netherlands (January 1, 1955—December 31, 1957); Brazil, Canada, Greece, Indonesia, the United States, Yugoslavia (January 1, 1956—December 31, 1958).

The Council may invite any Member State not a member of the Council to participate, but without a vote, in discussions of any matter of particular concern to that Member.

It may arrange for representatives of specialized agencies to participate without vote in discussions of the Council and its commissions. It may also be represented at the deliberations of the specialized agencies.

Further, it may arrange for observers from non-governmental organizations having consultative status (*see below*) to attend its meetings.

Functions and Powers

The Economic and Social Council is responsible under the authority of the General Assembly for promoting:

higher standards of living, full employment, and conditions of economic and social progress and development;

solutions of international economic, social, health and related problems;

international cultural and educational cooperation; and

universal respect for, and observance of, human rights and fundamental freedoms for all without distinction as to race, sex, language or religion.

The Council is also empowered to perform the following more specific functions:

make or initiate studies and reports on international economic, social, cultural, educational, health and related matters; and to make recommendations on such matters to the General Assembly, to United Nations Members, and to the specialized agencies concerned;

make recommendations to promote respect for, and observance of, human rights and fundamental freedoms;

prepare draft conventions on matters within its competence and submit these to the General Assembly;

call international conferences on matters within its competence.

The Council shall perform such functions as fall within its competence to carry out the recommendations of the Assembly. The Council has also to assist the Security Council at that organ's request. It may furnish information to the Security Council.

With the approval of the General Assembly, the Council may also perform services at the request of Members of the United Nations. It may, in addition, obtain reports from Members on steps taken to give effect to its recommendations, and those of the Assembly on matters which fall within its competence.

Relations with Specialized Agencies

The Charter provides for relating the various inter-governmental agencies with wide responsibilities in economic, social, educational, health and other fields to the United Nations as "specialized agencies." This is done through the Economic and Social Council, which negotiates agreements subject to approval by the General Assembly.

The Council is responsible for coordinating the activities of the agencies. This it may do through consultations with them and through recommendations to the agencies, to the Assembly, and to Members of the United Nations. It may receive regular reports from these agencies, including reports on measures taken to give effect to its recommendations and to those of the Assembly on matters within its competence. The Council may communicate its observations on these reports to the Assembly. Further, it may perform services at the request of the agencies, if it has the Assembly's approval.

Relations with Non-Governmental Organizations

The Council arranges for consultation with international non-governmental organizations concerned with matters within its competence. It may make similar arrangements with national non-governmental organizations, after consulting the Member State concerned.

Non-governmental organizations may be granted consultative status in one of two categories or placed on a register for *ad hoc* consultations.

Voting Procedure

Each member of the Council has one vote, and decisions are made by a majority of the members present and voting.

Sessions

The Council normally holds at least two sessions a year.

Organization

The Economic and Social Council adopts its own rules of procedure, elects its President and Vice-Presidents, and establishes such commissions and committees as it considers necessary.

Regional Economic Commissions

The Economic and Social Council deals with problems of general concern to all or most Member States. It soon found, however, that several economic problems could best be dealt with on a regional basis, and decided to set up regional economic commissions. These consist of United Nations Members in the areas concerned and other Members having special interests there. Non-Member states and territories of the regions may be elected to participate as associate members. So far, three such commissions have been established as follows:

ECONOMIC COMMISSION FOR EUROPE (ECE). Set up in 1947, this has 28 members. In addition, European States, non-Members of the United Nations, participate in a consultative capacity in the work of the Commission. Subsidiary bodies include committees on coal, electric power, industry and materials, inland transport, manpower, steel, timber, the development of trade, and agricultural problems.

ECONOMIC COMMISSION FOR ASIA AND THE FAR EAST (ECAFE). Set up in 1947, the Commission has 22 members and two associate members. Its subsidiary bodies include: a Committee on Industry and Trade, with sub-committees on iron and steel, on electric power, on mineral resources development and on trade; and an Inland Transport Committee with sub-committees on railways, inland waterways and highways. A Bureau of Flood Control and Water Resources Development forms part of the Secretariat.

ECONOMIC COMMISSION FOR LATIN AMERICA (ECLA). Set up in 1948, this has 24 members. In addition, Italy and Spain are invited to attend sessions of the Commission in a consultative capacity. It has established a Committee on Economic Cooperation in Central America, with a Sub-Committee on Central American Trade. The Commission also convenes technical meetings, for example, a meeting of experts on iron and steel industry and on the pulp and paper industry in Latin America, and maintains a training program for economists.

A proposal for the establishment of an Economic Commission for the Middle East has also been made to the Council but no decision has so far been taken on this proposal.

Functional Commissions and Sub-Commissions

The Economic and Social Council is aided in its work by several expert bodies called functional commissions and sub-commissions. These subsidiary bodies keep international problems in their respective fields under continuous review. They maintain close contact with the work of the Secretariat in their fields, study the problems and proposals referred to them by the Council, and submit to it detailed reports and recommendations.

The Council has eight functional commissions and one sub-commission, as follows:

(a) Transport and Communications Commission (fifteen members);
(b) Statistical Commission (fifteen members);
(c) Population Commission (fifteen members);
(d) Social Commission (eighteen members);
(e) Commission on Human Rights (eighteen members);
       Sub-Commission on Prevention of Discrimination and Protection of Minorities (twelve members);
(f) Commission on the Status of Women (eighteen members);
(g) Commission on Narcotic Drugs (fifteen members); and
(h) Commission on International Commodity Trade (eighteen members).

The first six of the functional commissions are composed of representatives from States Members of the United Nations elected by the Council. With a view to securing a balanced representation in the various fields covered by the Commissions, the Secretary-General consults with the governments so elected before the representatives are finally nominated by those governments and confirmed by the Council.

The Commission on Narcotic Drugs and the Commission on International Commodity Trade are composed of representatives of States Members of the United Nations directly nominated by their respective governments.

The Sub-Commission is composed of persons selected by the Commission on Human Rights, in consultation with the Secretary-General, and subject to the consent of the governments of which the persons are nationals.

Standing Committees

Technical Assistance Committee (consisting of all eighteen Council members).

Committee on Negotiations with Inter-Governmental Agencies (consisting of the Council President and eleven members).

Council Committee on Non-Governmental Organizations (consisting of seven Council members).

Interim Committee on Program of Meetings (consisting of five members).

Ad Hoc Committees

Established from time to time by the Council as it considers necessary.

Special Bodies

Under this heading may be grouped:

Permanent Central Opium Board (eight members).

Drug Supervisory Body (four experts), concerned, as is the Central Opium Board, with control of narcotic drugs.

United Nations Children's Fund (UNICEF) (twenty-six countries are represented on its Executive Board).

Administrative Committee on Coordination (consisting of the Secretary-General of the United Nations as Chairman, and the executive heads of the specialized agencies).

Interim Coordinating Committee for International Commodity Arrangements (four members).

Technical Assistance Board (consisting of an Executive Chairman and the Executive Heads, or their representatives, of the Organizations participating in the Expanded Program of Technical Assistance).

Specialized Agencies

AGENCIES IN RELATIONSHIP WITH THE UNITED NATIONS

International Labor Organization (ILO).
Food and Agriculture Organization of the United Nations (FAO).
United Nations Educational, Scientific and Cultural Organization (UNESCO).
International Civil Aviation Organization (ICAO).
International Bank for Reconstruction and Development.
International Monetary Fund.
International Telecommunication Union (ITU).
Universal Postal Union (UPU).
World Health Organization (WHO).
World Meteorological Organization (WMO).
[Another specialized agency, the International Refugee Organization (IRO), created in December 1946, ceased operations at the end of 1951.]

AGENCY WITH WHICH AGREEMENT HAS BEEN NEGOTIATED BUT WHICH WAS NOT YET IN FORCE BY THE END OF 1955

Inter-Governmental Maritime Consultative Organization (IMCO). (The agreement with IMCO has already been approved by the General Assembly of the United Nations, and will come into force when approved by the Assembly of IMCO.)

AGENCY WITH WHICH NEGOTIATION FOR AGREEMENT HAS BEEN AUTHORIZED BY THE COUNCIL

International Trade Organization (ITO) or its Interim Commission.

The Havana Charter called for 20 acceptances to bring the International Trade Organization (ITO) into existence, but at the end of 1955, only two countries had accepted, one of them conditionally. Nevertheless, one of the main objectives of that Charter has been embodied in an international commercial treaty, known as the General Agreement on Tariffs and Trade (GATT). A permanent Organization for Trade Cooperation to administer the General Agreement is to come into being when it has been accepted by countries which account for a high proportion of world trade.

Non-Governmental Organizations (NGO's)

Non-governmental organizations (NGO's) may be consulted by the Economic and Social Council on questions with which they are concerned. The Council recognizes that these organizations should have the opportunity to express their views, and that they often possess special experience or technical knowledge which will be of great value to the Council in its work.

There are two categories (A and B) of NGO's which have been granted consultative status.

Organizations in Category A are those which have a basic interest in most activities of the Council, and are closely linked with the economic or social life of the areas which they represent.

Organizations in Category B are those with a special competence, but which are specifically concerned with only a few of the fields of activity covered by the Council.

In addition, there are other organizations placed on a register for *ad hoc* consultations.

All these organizations may send observers to public meetings of the Council and its commissions. Those in Categories A and B may submit written statements for circulation as documents of these United Nations bodies, and may also present their views orally. Category A organizations may propose items for possible inclusion in the Council's provisional agenda. Such proposals must first be submitted for a decision to the Council Committee on Non-Governmental Organizations—a standing committee which also advises the Council on which organizations are to be given consultative status. Category A organizations, however, may propose items directly for the provisional agenda of the commissions.

In addition, all three groups of non-governmental organizations can consult with the United Nations Secretariat on matters of mutual concern.

NON-GOVERNMENTAL ORGANIZATIONS IN CATEGORY A. The following ten organizations had been granted consultative status in Category A by the end of 1955:

International Chamber of Commerce; International Confederation of Free Trade Unions; International Cooperative Alliance; International Federation of Agricultural Producers; International Federation of Christian Trade Unions; International Organization of Employers; Inter-Parliamentary Union; World Federation of Trade Unions; World Federation of United Nations Associations; and World Veterans Federation.

NON-GOVERNMENTAL ORGANIZATIONS IN CATEGORY B. The following 110 organizations had been granted consultative status in Category B by the end of 1955 (those followed by the name of a country are national non-governmental organizations):

Agudas Israel World Organization; All India Women's Conference (India); All Pakistan Women's Association (Pakistan); Anti-Slavery Society, The (United Kingdom); CARE (Cooperative for American Remittances to Everywhere, Inc.) (U.S.A.); Carnegie Endowment for International Peace (U.S.A.); Catholic International Union for Social Service; Chamber of Commerce of the United States of America (U.S.A.); Commission of the Churches on International Affairs, The; *Confédération internationale du crédit populaire;* Consultative Council of Jewish Organizations; Coordinating Board of Jewish Organizations for Consultation with the Economic and Social Council of the United Nations; Friends World Committee for Consultation; Howard League for Penal Reform (United Kingdom); Indian Council of World Affairs (India); Inter-American Council of Commerce and Production; Inter-American Federation of Automobile Clubs; Inter-American Press Association; Inter-American Statistical Institute; International Abolitionist Federation; International African Institute; International Air Transport Association; International Alliance of Women—Equal Rights, Equal Responsibilities; International Association of Juvenile Court Judges; International Association of Penal Law; International Automobile Federation; International Bar Association; International Bureau for the Suppression of Traffic in Persons; International Catholic Child Bureau; International Catholic Migration Commission; International Catholic Press Union; International Commission Against Concentration Camp Practices; International Commission on Irrigation and Drainage; International Committee of Schools of Social Work; International Committee of Scientific Management; International Committee of the Red Cross; International Conference of Catholic Charities; International Conference of Social Work; International Congresses for Modern Architecture; International Cooperative Women's Guild; International Council for Building Research, Studies and Documentation; International Council of Women; International Criminal Police Commission; International Federation for Housing and Town Planning; International Federation for the Rights of Man; International Federation of Business and Professional Women; International Federation *"Amies de la jeune fille";* International Federation of Journalists; International Federation of Newspaper Publishers (Proprietors) and Editors; International Federation of Settlements; International Federation of University Women; International Federation of Women Lawyers; International Fiscal Association; International Institute of Administrative Sciences; International Institute of Public Finance; International Islamic Economic Organization; International Labor Assistance; International Law Association, The; International League for the Rights of Man, The; International Movement for Fraternal Union Among Races and Peoples; International Organization for Standardization; International Road Federation; International Road Transport Union; International Social Service; International Society for Criminology; International Society for the Welfare of Cripples; International Society of Social Defence; International Statistical Institute; International Thrift Institute; International Touring Alliance; International Union for Child Welfare; International Union for Inland Navigation; International Union for the Protection of Nature; International Union for the Scientific Study of Population; International Union of Architects; International Union of Family Organizations; International Union of Local Authorities; International Union of Marine Insurance; International Union of Official Travel Organizations; International Union of Producers and Distributors of Electric Power; International Union of Public Transport; International Union of Railways; International Union of Socialist Youth; Junior Chamber International; League of Red Cross Societies; Liaison Committee of Women's International Organizations; Lions International—The International Association of Lions Clubs; National Association of Manufacturers (U.S.A.); *Nouvelles équipes internationales—Union des démocrates chrétiens;* Pacific South-East Asia Women's Association; *Pax Romana*—International Movement of Catholic Students; International Catholic Movement for Intellectual and Cultural Affairs; Rotary International; Salvation Army, The; *Société belge d'études et d'expansion* (Belgium); Society of Comparative Legislation (France); South American Petroleum Institute; Women's International League for Peace and Freedom; World Assembly of Youth; World Confederation of Organizations of the Teaching Profession; World Council for the Welfare of the Blind; World Federation of Catholic Young Women and Girls; World Jewish Congress; World Movement of Mothers; World Power Conference; World's Alliance of Young Men's Christian Associations (World's YMCA); World's Woman's Christian Temperance Union; World's Young Women's Christian Association (World's YWCA); World Union for Progressive Judaism; World Union of Catholic Women's Organizations; Young Christian Workers.

NON-GOVERNMENTAL ORGANIZATIONS ON REGISTER. An additional 163 organizations had been placed on the register by the end of 1955.

TRUSTEESHIP AND NON-SELF-GOVERNING TERRITORIES

Non-Self-Governing Territories

The Charter contains a "Declaration on Non-Self-Governing Territories." In this, Members of the United Nations administering territories which are not fully self-governing have accepted as "a sacred trust" the obligation to promote to the utmost the well-being of the inhabitants of those territories. To this end, they have undertaken to observe the following provisions:

(a) To insure the political, economic, social and educational advancement of the inhabitants, with due regard to their culture, and to insure their just treatment and protection against abuses;

(b) To develop self-government, and assist the peoples in developing their own free political institutions according to the particular circumstances of each territory and the stage of advancement of its peoples;

(c) To further international peace and security;

(d) To promote constructive measures of development, to encourage research, and cooperate with each other and with specialized international bodies to achieve the social, economic and scientific purposes contained in the Declaration; and

(e) To transmit to the Secretary-General for information purposes, subject to such limitations as are necessary for security and constitutional reasons, statistical and other technical information relating to economic, social and educational conditions in non-self-governing territories which are not placed under the International Trusteeship System.

Member States also agree, according to Article 74, that their policy in respect to these territories be based on the general principle of good neighborliness, with due account of the interests and well-being of the rest of the world.

The information transmitted under Article 73e is summarized and analyzed by the Secretary-General, and his analyses and summaries are considered by the General Assembly. The Assembly is aided in its consideration by a committee composed of the seven Members of the United Nations transmitting information and an equal number of Members elected by the Assembly's Fourth Committee on as wide a geographical basis as possible.

The Special Committee was first established in 1947 on a yearly basis. In 1949, the Assembly renewed the Committee for a term of three years and, in 1952 and 1955, extended its mandate for a further three years.

International Trusteeship System

Apart from the provisions of the Declaration Regarding Non-Self-Governing Territories, the Charter set up a system for international supervision and administration of certain territories, the International Trusteeship System, and established a principal organ for this purpose—the Trusteeship Council.

Member States which administer a non-self-governing territory may place it within the System by submitting a draft Trusteeship Agreement. This document has to be agreed upon "by states directly concerned" and approved by the General Assembly, whereupon the territory becomes a Trust Territory. The agreement stipulates the terms and conditions on which the territory is to be administered. It has, of course, to state who is to administer the territory—one or more states, or the United Nations itself.

In submitting the draft agreement, a state may designate all or part of a territory as "strategic," in which case the agreement has to be approved by the Security Council. The Council exercises all United Nations functions in respect to these territories but it avails itself of the assistance of the Trusteeship Council to perform functions relating to political, economic, social and educational matters.

Objectives of the Trusteeship System

The objectives of the International Trusteeship System are:

To further international peace and security;

To promote the political, economic, social and educational advancement of the inhabitants of the Trust Territories, and their progressive development toward self-government or independence, in accordance with the circumstances of each Territory and the wishes of its people;

To encourage respect for human rights and fundamental freedoms for all, and to encourage recognition of the interdependence of the peoples of the world; and

To insure equal treatment in social, economic and commercial matters for all Members of the United Nations and their nationals, and equal treatment for the latter in the administration of justice, provided this does not conflict with the attainment of the other objectives of the Trusteeship System.

THE TRUSTEESHIP COUNCIL

Composition

The Trusteeship Council consists of Member States administering Trust Territories; permanent members of the Security Council which do not administer Trust Territories, and enough other non-administering countries elected by the Assembly for three-year terms to insure that the membership is equally divided between administering and non-administering members.

ADMINISTERING MEMBERS. The members (January 1956) were: Australia, Belgium, France, Italy, New Zealand, the United Kingdom, and the United States.

PERMANENT MEMBERS OF THE SECURITY COUNCIL NOT ADMINISTERING TRUST TERRITORIES. China and the U.S.S.R.

OTHER MEMBERS. Burma (date of retirement—December 31, 1958); Guatemala (December 31, 1958); Haiti (December 31, 1956); India (December 31, 1956); and Syria (December 31, 1958).

Each member of the Trusteeship Council designates one specially qualified person to represent it therein.

Functions and Powers

The Trusteeship Council, under the authority of the General Assembly, carries out the functions of the United Nations with regard to Trust Territories except in those areas which are designated as "strategic." The Security Council exercises the functions of the United Nations in "strategic areas," with the assistance of the Trusteeship Council in political, economic, social and educational matters.

The Trusteeship Council considers reports submitted by the Administering Authority on the basis of a questionnaire prepared by the Council, and examines petitions in consultation with the Administering Authority. It provides for periodic Visiting Missions to Trust Territories at times agreed upon with the Administering Authority, and takes other actions in conformity with the terms of the Trusteeship Agreements.

Voting Procedure

Each member of the Trusteeship Council has one vote, and decisions are made by a simple majority of the members present and voting.

Sessions

The Trusteeship Council meets twice a year, generally in January and in June. It may meet at other times by its own decision, or on the request of a majority of its members, or the General Assembly or the Security Council. The Economic and Social Council or any member of the Trusteeship Council may likewise request a special session of the latter; if a majority of the members of the Trusteeship Council concur in the request, then a special session is held.

Organization

The Council adopts it own rules of procedure, including the method of selecting its officers. A new President and Vice-President are elected at the beginning of the Council's regular session each June.

The Trusteeship Council avails itself, when appropriate, of the assistance of the Economic and Social Council and of the specialized agencies in regard to matters with which they are respectively concerned.

THE INTERNATIONAL COURT OF JUSTICE

The International Court of Justice is the principal judicial organ of the United Nations, and functions in accordance with its Statute. This is based upon the Statute of the Permanent Court of International Justice, which it superseded, and is an integral part of the United Nations Charter.

Composition

PARTIES TO THE STATUTE

All Members of the United Nations are automatically parties to the Statute of the International Court. A state not belonging to the United Nations may become a party to the Statute on conditions to be determined in each case by the General Assembly on recommendation of the Security Council. (*See also page 292.*)

MEMBERS OF THE COURT

The fifteen members of the Court (that is, the judges) are chosen without regard to nationality, but no two may be nationals of the same state. They must be persons of high moral character, who possess the qualifications required in their respective countries for appointment to the highest judicial offices, or are jurisconsults of recognized competence in international law.

The judges are elected by the General Assembly and the Security Council, voting independently. The Assembly and the Security Council are enjoined by the Statute to make sure that the main forms of civilization and the principal legal systems of the world are represented in the Court.

Judges serve for nine years and are eligible for reelection. At the first election in 1946, however, the terms of five judges were limited to three years, and of five more to six years. The period each judge was to serve was decided by lot. In order to fill the vacancies which would occur on the expiration of the terms of office of five judges at the end of every three years, the second election took place in 1948, the third in 1951, and the fourth in 1954. Separate elections also took place in 1951, 1953 and 1954 to fill the vacancies caused by the resignation of one judge and by the death of two judges. A judge elected in such a case holds office for the remainder of his predecessor's term.

The present judges (December 1955) were:

ELECTED FOR NINE YEARS, TO SERVE UNTIL FEBRUARY 5, 1958. Abdel Hamid Badawi (Egypt), *Vice President;* Hsu Mo (China) (deceased June 28, 1956); John E. Read (Canada); Bohdan Winiarski (Poland); Milovan Zoricic (Yugoslavia).

ELECTED FOR NINE YEARS, TO SERVE UNTIL FEBRUARY 5, 1961. E. C. Armand-Ugón (Uruguay); Green H. Hackworth (United States), *President;* Helge Klaestad (Norway). (Judge Sergei Aleksandrovich Golunsky, who was also elected for nine years, resigned on July 25, 1953. At the eighth session of the General Assembly, Feodor Ivanovich Kojevnikov (U.S.S.R.) was elected to serve the balance of the term). (Judge Benegal N. Rau (India), who was also elected for nine years, died on November 30, 1953. At the ninth session of the General Assembly, Mohammad Zafrulla Khan (Pakistan) was elected to serve the balance of the term).

ELECTED FOR NINE YEARS, TO SERVE UNTIL FEBRUARY 5, 1964. Jules Basdevant (France), Roberto Córdova (Mexico), José Gustavo Guerrero (El Salvador), Hersch Lauterpacht (United Kingdom), Lucio M. Moreno Quintana (Argentina).

Competence of the Court

Only states may be parties in cases before the Court, which is open to all states that are parties to its Statute. It is open to other states on conditions laid down by the Security Council. Such states deposit with the Court's Registrar a declaration accepting the Court's jurisdiction in accordance with the United Nations Charter and the Statute and Rules of the Court, undertaking to comply in good faith with the Court's decisions and accepting the obligations of a Member of the United Nations under Article 94 of the Charter. Such declarations may be particular, accepting the Court's jurisdiction with respect to a particular case which has arisen; or they may be general, accepting jurisdiction with respect to all disputes, or particular classes of disputes, which have arisen or may arise.

The Security Council has reserved the right to amend these conditions.

Jurisdiction

The jurisdiction of the Court comprises all cases which the parties refer to it, and all matters specially provided for in the Charter or in treaties or conventions in force.

In the event of a dispute as to whether the Court has jurisdiction, the matter shall be settled by the decision of the Court.

To preserve continuity with the work of the Permanent Court of International Justice, the Statute of the International Court of Justice stipulates that whenever a treaty or convention in force provides for reference of a matter to the Permanent Court, the matter is to be referred to the International Court.

States are not forced to submit cases to the Court. The Charter provides that Members of the United Nations may entrust the solution of their differences to other tribunals which are already in existence or may be concluded in the future.

Compulsory Jurisdiction

Those states which are parties to the Statute may at any time declare that they recognize as compulsory, *ipso facto* and without special agreement, in relation to any state accepting the same obligation, the jurisdiction of the Court in all legal disputes concerning: (1) the interpretation of a treaty; (2) any question of international law; (3) the existence of any fact which, if established, would constitute a breach of an international obligation; and (4) the nature or extent of the reparation to be made for the breach of an international obligation.

States which thus choose to accept compulsory jurisdiction may do so either unconditionally or on condition of reciprocity on the part of other states, or for a certain time.

The Statute of the Permanent Court of International Justice provided for similar declarations of acceptance of compulsory jurisdiction. Under the Statute of the International Court of Justice any such declaration still in force shall be deemed to be acceptance of the compulsory jurisdiction of the International Court.

Application of International Law

The Court, whose function is to decide in accordance with international law such disputes as are submitted to it, applies: (1) international conventions, whether general or particular, establishing rules expressly recognized by the contesting states; (2) international custom, as evidence of a general practice accepted as law; (3) the general principles of law recognized by civilized nations; and (4) judicial decisions and the teachings of the most highly qualified publicists of the various nations, as subsidiary means for the determination of the rules of law.

The Court may decide a case *ex aequo et bono* (that is, according to the principles of equity) if the parties agree to this.

Decisions and Voting Procedure

Each Member of the United Nations undertakes to comply with the decisions of the Court in any case to which it is a party. If any party to a case fails to perform its obligations under the judgment rendered by the Court, the other party may have recourse to the Security Council, which may make recommendations or decide upon measures to give effect to the judgment.

The Court may indicate any provisional measures which, in its judgment, should be taken to preserve the respective rights of either party.

Decisions have no binding force, except between the parties concerned and in respect of a particular case. The judgment of the Court is final and without appeal.

All questions before the Court are decided by a majority of the judges present, the quorum being nine. In the event of an equality of votes, the President or the judge who acts in his place has a casting vote. The judgment must state the reasons on which it is based, and must include the names of the judges who have taken part in the decisions. Any judge is entitled to deliver a separate opinion. The judgment of the Court must be signed by the President and Registrar. It must be read in open Court after due notice has been given to the agents of the parties to the case.

Advisory Opinions

The General Assembly or the Security Council may request the Court to give an advisory opinion on any legal question. Other organs of the United Nations and specialized agencies, when authorized by the Assembly, may also request advisory opinions on legal questions arising within the scope of their activities. The Assembly has authorized the following organs and specialized agencies to request advisory opinions: Economic and Social Council; Trusteeship Council; Interim Committee of the General Assembly; International Labor Organization; Food and Agriculture Organization of the United Nations; United Nations Educational, Scientific and Cultural Organization; International Bank for Reconstruction and Development; International Civil Aviation Organization; International Monetary Fund; International Telecommunication Union; World Health Organization; Inter-Governmental Maritime Consultative Organization; International Refugee Organization; and World Meteorological Organization.

Sessions

Except for judicial vacations, the Court is permanently in session at The Hague. It may sit elsewhere when needed.

Organization

The Court elects its own President and Vice-President for three years; they may be reelected. It appoints its Registrar and such other officers as may be necessary.

The Court forms annually a chamber of five judges which may hear and determine cases by summary procedure. From time to time, it may establish one or more chambers of three or more judges to deal with particular categories of cases. A judgment by any of the chambers is considered a judgment by the Court.

THE SECRETARIAT

Composition

The Secretariat consists of a Secretary-General and such staff as the United Nations may require.

Secretary-General

The Secretary-General is the chief administrative officer of the United Nations. He is appointed by the General Assembly on the recommendation of the Security Council. The Secretary-General's term of office is five years. The first Secretary-General was Trygve Lie, whose term expired on February 1, 1951. He was continued in office by the fifth session of the General Assembly for a further three years. On November 10, 1952, he tendered his resignation to the seventh session of the Assembly (*see page 74*). On April 7, 1953, Dag Hammarskjold, Swedish Minister of State, became the Organization's second Secretary-General.

The Secretary-General acts in that capacity at all meetings of the General Assembly, the Security Council, the Economic and Social Council, and the Trusteeship Council, and performs such other functions as are entrusted to him by these organs. He is required to submit an annual report to the General Assembly on the work of the United Nations.

The Secretary-General may bring to the attention of the Security Council any matter which in his opinion may threaten international peace and security.

Organization

The Secretariat is divided into six offices, five departments and one administration. The principal officers of the Secretariat (January 1956) were:

EXECUTIVE OFFICE OF THE SECRETARY-GENERAL—Executive Assistant to the Secretary-General: Andrew W. Cordier (*United States*)

OFFICE OF LEGAL AFFAIRS—The Legal Counsel: Constantin A. Stavropoulos (*Greece*)

OFFICE OF THE CONTROLLER—Controller: Bruce R. Turner (*New Zealand*)

OFFICE OF PERSONNEL—Director of Personnel: J. A. C. Robertson (*United Kingdom*)

OFFICE OF UNDER-SECRETARIES WITHOUT DEPARTMENT—Under-Secretary: Ralph J. Bunche (*United States*)
Under-Secretary: Ilya S. Tchernychev (*U.S.S.R.*)

DEPARTMENT OF POLITICAL AND SECURITY COUNCIL AFFAIRS—Under-Secretary: Dragoslav Protitch (*Yugoslavia*)

DEPARTMENT OF ECONOMIC AND SOCIAL AFFAIRS—Under-Secretary: Philippe de Seynes (*France*)
Deputy Under-Secretary: Martin Hill (*United Kingdom*)

DEPARTMENT OF TRUSTEESHIP AND INFORMATION FROM NON-SELF-GOVERNING TERRITORIES—Under-Secretary: Benjamin Cohen (*Chile*)

DEPARTMENT OF PUBLIC INFORMATION—Under-Secretary: Ahmed S. Bokhari (*Pakistan*)
Deputy Under-Secretary: Alfred G. Katzin (*Union of South Africa*)

DEPARTMENT OF CONFERENCE SERVICES—Under-Secretary: Victor Hoo (*China*)

OFFICE OF GENERAL SERVICES—Director: David B. Vaughan (*United States*)

TECHNICAL ASSISTANCE ADMINISTRATION—Director-General: Hugh L. Keenleyside (*Canada*)

Deputy Director-General: Gustavo Martínez Cabañas (*Mexico*)

UNITED NATIONS CHILDREN'S FUND (UNICEF)—Executive Director: Maurice Pate (*United States*)

TECHNICAL ASSISTANCE BOARD—Executive Chairman: David Owen (*United Kingdom*)

Staff

The staff of the United Nations is appointed by the Secretary-General under regulations established by the General Assembly. Appropriate staffs, which form part of the Secretariat, are permanently assigned to the Security Council, the Economic and Social Council, the Trusteeship Council, and, as required, to other organs of the United Nations.

The "paramount consideration" in employing staff and in determining conditions of service is, the Charter lays down, the necessity of securing the highest standards of efficiency, competence and integrity. Due regard must be paid to the importance of recruiting on as wide a geographical basis as possible.

International Character of the Secretariat

Article 100 of the Charter provides that the Secretary-General and the staff, in the performance of their duties shall not seek or receive instructions from any government or any authority outside the United Nations. They must also refrain from any act which might reflect on their position as international officials responsible only to the United Nations. For its part, each Member of the United Nations is bound by the Charter to respect the exclusively international character of the responsibilities of the Secretary-General and the staff, and not to seek to influence them in the discharge of their responsibilities.

PART II **THE WORK OF THE UNITED NATIONS**

POLITICAL AND SECURITY QUESTIONS

Atomic Energy and Disarmament

The work of the United Nations in the fields of atomic energy and disarmament—two of the major political questions dealt with by the Organization from its inception—is described below.

DISARMAMENT

ESTABLISHMENT OF THE ATOMIC ENERGY COMMISSION. By its first resolution, the General Assembly on January 24, 1946, unanimously established the Atomic Energy Commission and instructed it to make specific proposals: (a) for extending between all nations the exchange of basic scientific information for peaceful ends, (b) for control of atomic energy to the extent necessary to insure its use only for peaceful purposes, (c) for the elimination from national armaments of atomic weapons and of all other major weapons adaptable to mass destruction, and (d) for effective safeguards by way of inspection and other means to protect complying states against the hazards of violations and evasions. The Commission was composed of the states represented on the Security Council and Canada, when Canada was not a member of the Council.

The Commission began its work on June 14, 1946. At the first meeting, the United States proposed the creation of an International Atomic Development Authority to which should be entrusted all phases of the development and use of atomic energy. At the next meeting the U.S.S.R. proposed a draft convention to forbid the production and use of atomic weapons and procedures for working out a system of control.

The Commission proceeded to consider these two proposals, setting up appropriate committees for the purpose. Among other things, the Commission requested its Scientific and Technical Committee to report whether effective control of atomic energy was possible. On September 26, the Committee reported that it found no basis in the available scientific facts for supposing that effective control was not technologically feasible.

Matters then were carried forward in Committee 2, which proceeded to study and report upon the problem of safeguards. Meanwhile the Commission decided to submit to the Security Council by the end of the year a report of its proceedings, findings and recommendations. A number of general findings and recommendations were proposed by the United States, based upon the principles of its original proposals, and were incorporated in the report. On December 30, the Commission adopted its first report.

GENERAL ASSEMBLY DECISIONS OF DECEMBER 14, 1946. During the second part of its first session, the General Assembly had before it the question of the general reduction of armaments and related matters: the presence of troops of the United

Nations on non-enemy territories and information on armed forces of the United Nations. In a resolution unanimously adopted on December 14, 1946, the General Assembly recognized the necessity of an early regulation and reduction of armaments and armed forces, and recommended that the Security Council give prompt consideration to formulating appropriate practical measures for inclusion in international agreements. The resolution also urged expeditious fulfilment by the Atomic Energy Commission of its terms of reference, and prompt consideration by the Council to the working out of proposals to provide practical and effective safeguards in connection with the control of atomic energy and the general regulation and reduction of armaments.

In the same resolution, the Assembly recommended the progressive and balanced withdrawal of the occupation forces in ex-enemy territories and the withdrawal without delay of forces stationed on the territories of Members without the latter's consent.

In a companion resolution, the Assembly called on the Security Council to determine, as soon as possible, the information which Members should be called upon to furnish in order to give effect to those recommendations.

ESTABLISHMENT OF THE COMMISSION FOR CONVENTIONAL ARMAMENTS. Pursuant to these resolutions, the Security Council decided on February 13, 1947, to set up the Commission for Conventional Armaments with instructions to prepare proposals for the general regulation and reduction of armaments and armed forces, and for practical and effective safeguards in that connection.

SECOND REPORT OF THE ATOMIC ENERGY COMMISSION. The Security Council then turned to the consideration of the first report of the Atomic Energy Commission, and on March 10 resolved to request the Atomic Energy Commission to continue its inquiry into all phases of the problem of the international control of atomic energy, and to submit a second report before the next session of the Assembly.

During the ensuing months, the Commission pursued three main lines of discussion: it examined the areas of disagreement, as reflected in amendments and additions submitted by the U.S.S.R. to the first report; it considered proposals presented on June 11, 1947, by the U.S.S.R. containing basic provisions for an international agreement on atomic energy control; and it drew up a list of principal subjects to be incorporated in the specific proposals for the international control of atomic energy, and prepared specific proposals on a number of those subjects.

In its second report, adopted on September 11, 1947, the Commission stated that consideration of the U.S.S.R. amendments to the first report had not led it to revise its general findings and recommendations. With regard to the U.S.S.R. proposals of June 11, the report recorded the Commission's resolution of August 15 to the effect that, as then constituted, they did not provide an adequate basis for the development of specific proposals for an effective system of international control.

The report also contained the specific proposals worked out by the Commission under the title "Operational and developmental functions of the international control agency". These proposals rested on the following basic principles: (1) decisions concerning the production and use of atomic energy should not be left in the hands of individual nations; (2) policies that substantially affect world security should be defined by treaty, and the agency should be awarded the necessary powers and functions to carry out those policies; (3) nations should grant to the agency, subject to appropriate procedural requirements, rights of inspection in any part of their territory; and (4) international agreement to outlaw the national production, possession and use of atomic weapons, to be effective, should be embodied in a treaty providing for a comprehensive system of international control.

THIRD REPORT OF THE ATOMIC ENERGY COMMISSION. Following the second session of the General Assembly, during which disarmament questions were not debated, the Atomic Energy Commission resumed its work. It gave further study to the U.S.S.R. proposals of June 11, 1947, and continued with the list of subjects in its program of work. The Working Committee, to which the former task was entrusted, concluded on April 5, 1948, that the U.S.S.R. proposals did not provide an adequate basis for the effective international control of atomic energy and the elimination from national armaments of atomic weapons, and that no useful purpose could be served by further discussion of them. Committee 2 approached the subject of the organization and administration of the international agency, but on March 30 concluded that it was first necessary to agree on the functions and powers of the agency.

The Commission accordingly met to consider the situation and on May 17 adopted its third report, which stated that it had reached an impasse and could not then prepare a draft treaty incorporating its ultimate proposals.

WORK OF THE COMMISSION FOR CONVENTIONAL ARMAMENTS 1947-1948. The Commission for Conventional Armaments began its work on March 24, 1947, and proceeded to plan its work program, which was approved by the Security Council on July 8. The Working Committee of the Commission first considered the question of jurisdiction, and on September 9 adopted a resolution to the effect that all armaments and armed forces fell within its jurisdiction except atomic weapons and weapons of mass destruction, including atomic explosive weapons, radioactive material weapons, lethal chemical and biological weapons, and any future weapons having characteristics comparable in destructive effect.

The Working Committee then turned to the discussion of general principles, and on July 26, 1948, adopted a resolution approving principles including the following: (1) a system for the regulation and reduction of armaments and armed forces should provide for the adherence of all states and initially all states having substantial military resources; (2) the system could only be put into effect in an atmosphere of international confidence and security, but would itself increase such confidence and justify further measures; (3) armaments and armed forces should be limited to those indispensable to the maintenance of international peace and security; (4) an adequate system of safeguards was necessary; and (5) there should be provision for effective enforcement action in the event of violations.

GENERAL ASSEMBLY DECISIONS OF 1948. The General Assembly considered the three reports of the Atomic Energy Commission at its third session, and on November 4, 1948, approved the general findings and recommendations of the first report and the specific proposals of the second report as constituting the necessary basis for establishing an effective system of international control of atomic energy to insure its use only for peaceful purposes and for the elimination from national armaments of atomic weapons. The Assembly also expressed its concern at the impasse in the Commission, and requested the six permanent members of the Commission to meet together and consult in order to determine if there existed a basis for agreement.

At the same time, the Assembly rejected a U.S.S.R. proposal to recommend the preparation of a draft convention on the prohibition of atomic weapons and a draft convention on the establishment of effective international control, both to be signed and brought into operation simultaneously.

Also at the third session, the U.S.S.R. submitted an item entitled "Prohibition of the atomic weapon and reduction by one-third of the armaments and armed forces of the permanent members of the Security Council". The draft resolution of the U.S.S.R. proposed that the permanent members of the Council, as a first step towards the reduction of armaments and armed forces, should reduce by one-third during one year all existing land, naval and air forces; that atomic weapons should be prohibited as weapons intended for aggression and not for defence; that there should be established, within the framework of the Security Council, an international control body for the purpose of supervision of and control over the implementation of those measures; and that full official data on the armaments and armed forces of the five great Powers be submitted to this body.

On November 19, 1948, the General Assembly rejected the U.S.S.R. proposal, and adopted a resolution recommended by the First Committee. That resolution recommended that the Security Council should pursue the study of the regulation and reduction of conventional armaments and armed forces through the agency of the Commission for Conventional Armaments, and proposed that the Commission, in carrying out its plan of work, should devote its first attention to formulating proposals for the receipt, checking and publication, by an international organ of control within the framework of the Security Council, of full information supplied by Member States with regard to their effectives and conventional armaments.

ATOMIC ENERGY COMMISSION AND CONSULTATIONS OF ITS PERMANENT MEMBERS. The Atomic Energy Commission reconvened on February 18, 1949. The U.S.S.R. laid before it a proposal to begin the preparation of two draft conventions, relating to prohibition and control, both to be concluded and put into effect simultaneously, as it had proposed in the Assembly. After considering that proposal, the Commission concluded that, as no new material had been submitted, there was no useful purpose to be served by further discussion of those proposals. With regard to the remainder of its program, the Commission concluded that the impasse as analyzed in its third report still existed, and that further study would not be useful until the six permanent members had reported that there existed a basis for agreement.

The Security Council directed the Secretary-General to transmit the Commission's conclusions to the Assembly. A Soviet proposal requesting the Commission to continue its work was rejected.

Consultations among the six permanent members of the Commission (Canada, China, France, the U.S.S.R., the United Kingdom and the United States) began on August 9, and ten meetings were held between then and October 13, when it was decided to inform the General Assembly of the course of the consultations. No conclusions on the questions under consideration had been reached. However, in a joint statement to the Assembly, Canada, China, France, the United Kingdom and the United States declared that the consultations had served to clarify some points on which there was disagreement.

FURTHER PROPOSALS OF THE COMMISSION FOR CONVENTIONAL ARMAMENTS. The Security Council discussed the General Assembly resolution of November 19, 1948, during February 1949, and resolved to transmit it to the Commission for Conventional Armaments for action according to its terms. The Commission proceeded to meet and in its Working Committee considered a French plan for a census and verification of the armed forces and conventional armaments of the Member States of the United Nations. That plan was adopted on August 1, 1949, by the Commission.

The census plan was considered by the Security Council, which on October 18, failed to adopt it because of the negative vote of the U.S.S.R. At the same meeting, the Council rejected a U.S.S.R. proposal which would have recognized as essential, for the elaboration of measures for the reduction of armaments, the submission by states of information both on conventional armaments and on atomic weapons. The Council then decided to transmit to the General Assembly the records of the discussions in the Commission for Conventional Armaments and in the Security Council.

GENERAL ASSEMBLY DECISIONS OF 1949. On November 23, 1949, the General Assembly urged all nations to join in a peaceful cooperative development and use of atomic energy; it called upon governments to facilitate, by the acceptance of effective control, the effective prohibition and elimination of atomic weapons; it requested the permanent members of the Commission to continue their consultations; and it recommended that all nations, in the use of their rights of sovereignty, should join in mutual agreement to limit the individual exercise of those rights in the control of atomic energy to the extent required for the promotion of world security and peace, and recommended that all nations should agree to exercise such rights jointly.

On December 5, 1949, the General Assembly approved the census plan of the Commission for Conventional Armaments as the necessary basis for carrying out the recommendations it had made at the third session. And it recommended that the Security Council, despite the lack of unanimity of its permanent members, should continue its study of the regulation and reduction of conventional armaments and armed forces through the agency of the Commission, in order to make such progress as might be possible.

CONCLUSION OF DISCUSSIONS IN THE TWO COMMISSIONS. The six permanent members of the Atomic Energy Commission resumed their consultations after the end of the fourth session. The consultations were, however, suspended on January 19,1950, over the question of the representation of China (*See page 98*).

The General Assembly resolution relating to conventional armaments was transmitted by the Security Council to the Commission for Conventional Armaments. When the Commission met on April 27, 1950, a U.S.S.R. proposal concerning the representation of China was rejected, and the U.S.S.R. representative left the meeting. The Commission, however, continued to hold discussions on the question of safeguards and on August 9, adopted a report to the Security Council. The Council, however, took no action.

COMMITTEE OF TWELVE. At the fifth session of the General Assembly, the President of the United States, addressing a plenary meeting on October 24, 1950, proposed in general terms an examination of the possibility of making progress through some means of coordinating the work of the Atomic Energy Commission and the Commission for Conventional Armaments. A draft resolution to that effect was sponsored jointly by Australia, Canada, Ecuador, France, the Netherlands, Turkey, the United Kingdom and the United States. The U.S.S.R., however, proposed that the Atomic Energy Commission be instructed to resume its work and prepare two draft conventions, on prohibition and on control, both conventions to be concluded and brought into effect simultaneously.

On December 13, the General Assembly adopted the eight-Power proposal and rejected the U.S.S.R. draft resolution. By that decision the Assembly established a Committee of Twelve, consisting of the members of the Security Council and Canada, to consider and report to the sixth session on ways and means whereby the work of the two Commissions might be coordinated, and on the advisability of their functions being merged and placed under a new and consolidated disarmament commission.

The Committee of Twelve considered the problems assigned to it between February 14 and September 28, 1951, when it approved its report to the General Assembly. It recommended the establishment of a new commission to carry forward the tasks assigned to the Atomic Energy Commission and the Commission for Conventional Armaments, which would be dissolved.

ESTABLISHMENT OF THE DISARMAMENT COMMISSION. At the sixth session, the General Assembly considered concurrently the report of the Committee of Twelve and an item submitted jointly by France, the United Kingdom and the United States entitled "Regulation, limitation and balanced reduction of all armed forces and all armaments". The three Powers presented a proposal for the establishment of a new Disarmament Commission and providing terms of reference for it. The U.S.S.R. submitted an amendment relating to the directives and principles in the three-Power draft. A sub-committee of the four Powers was formed under the chairmanship of the President of the General Assembly and discussed the differences at ten meetings. The members then reported in a memorandum by the President, surveying the areas of agreement, possible agreement, and disagreement.

The matters on which there appeared to be either agreement or the possibility of agreement included certain of the general objectives of the draft resolution and the amendment, the machinery to be used in attaining those objectives, and some of the tasks that had to be performed. Points of importance on which there was fundamental divergence of views included the specific means of attaining the general objectives of the tripartite and U.S.S.R. proposals, and the principles to be established for the guidance of the new Commission.

After the U.S.S.R. amendment had been rejected on January 11, 1952, the General Assembly adopted, with modifications that did not affect its main substance, the three-Power proposal. That decision provided for the establishment of a Disarmament Commission under the Security Council to prepare proposals to be embodied in a draft treaty or treaties for the regulation, limitation and balanced reduction of all armed forces and all armaments, and for the effective international control of atomic energy to insure the prohibition of atomic weapons and the use of atomic energy for peaceful purposes only.

The Commission was to be guided by certain principles, including: (1) that there should be progressive disclosure and verification on a continuing basis of all armed forces and all armaments, including atomic; (2) that the verification should be based on international inspection; (3) that unless a better or no less effective system was devised, the United Nations plan for the international control of atomic energy and the prohibition of atomic weapons should continue to serve as a basis for international control; and (4) that there should be a system of safeguards to insure observance and detect violations, with a minimum of interference in the internal life of each country.

The Commission was directed to consider from the outset plans for disclosure and verification, the implementation of which was recognized as a first and indispensable step in the disarmament program. Regarding its plan for regulation, limitation and balanced reduction, the Commission was directed to formulate criteria of general application; to formulate proposals for each state, taking into account the criteria, for determining over-all limits and restrictions on armed forces and armaments; and to consider methods whereby states could agree among themselves concerning the allocation of the permitted national armed forces and armaments.

FIRST YEAR OF THE DISARMAMENT COMMISSION. The Disarmament Commission held its first meeting in Paris on February 4, 1952, and disposed of procedural matters. Continuing its meetings in New York, it adopted a program of work which would deal with all matters under three headings: (1) disclosure and verification of all armaments and armed forces, (2) regulation of all armaments and armed forces, and (3) procedure and timetable for giving effect to the disarmament program.

At the second meeting, the U.S.S.R. representative asked the Commission to consider, with reference to charges of the use of bacterial weapons in Korea and China, the question of the violation of the prohibition of bacterial warfare so as to prevent its further use and to bring the violators to account. The United States representative repudiated the charges as did the representatives of other countries which had forces in Korea, and said his Government had asked the International Committee of the Red Cross for an impartial investigation. (See under "Question of a Request for Investigation of Alleged Bacterial Warfare".) Eventually the discussion of the charges was ruled out of order in the Commission.

The Commission had before it a number of proposals: (1) proposals made by the U.S.S.R. at the sixth session of the General Assembly on the prohibition of atomic weapons, the reduction of armed forces and armaments by one-third, the submission of official military data, the establishment of an international control organ, and the convening of a world conference (see under "Measures to combat the threat of a new world war and to strengthen peace and friendship among the nations"); (2) a United States working paper entitled "Proposals for progressive and continuing disclosure and verification of armed forces and armaments"; (3) a United States proposal entitled "Essential principles for a disarmament program"; and (4) a working paper submitted jointly by France, the United Kingdom and the United States, setting forth proposals for fixing numerical limitations on all armed forces, and a later supplement thereto. In addition, the representative of France presented suggestions regarding the schedule and timetable for giving effect to the disarmament program.

The proposals by France, the United Kingdom and the United States regarding armed forces suggested that numerical ceilings for China, the U.S.S.R. and the United States should be fixed at between 1,000,000 and 1,500,000 effectives, and for France and the United Kingdom at between 700,000 and 800,000 effectives. For other states having substantial armed forces, ceilings should be fixed with a view to avoiding a disequilibrium of power. They would normally be less than one per cent of the population and less than current levels.

The French suggestions concerning the schedule for giving effect to the disarmament program would synchronize the operations of disclosure and verification, of the reduction of armed forces and conventional armaments, and of the prohibition of atomic and other weapons of mass destruction.

The Commission did not reach conclusions on any of the foregoing matters and submitted its second report, which was a comprehensive summary of its discussions, on October 9, 1952.

DECISION OF THE SEVENTH SESSION OF THE GENERAL ASSEMBLY. The report of the Disarmament Commission was considered by the seventh session of the General Assembly. On April 8, 1953, the Assembly adopted a resolution which, after taking note of the Commission's report, reaffirmed its resolution establishing the Commission and requested the Commission to continue its work for the development by the United Nations of comprehensive and coordinated plans providing for: (1) the regulation, limitation and balanced reduction of all armed forces and armaments; (2) the elimination and prohibition of all major weapons, including bacterial, adaptable to mass destruction; and (3) the effective international control of atomic energy to insure the prohibition of atomic weapons and the use of atomic energy for peaceful purposes only; the whole program to be carried out under effective international control and in such a way that no state would have cause to fear that its security was endangered. The resolution also requested the Commission to report again no later than September 1, 1953.

In the paragraph-by-paragraph voting on the resolution, the only negative votes cast were in connection with the clause reaffirming the resolution adopted at the sixth session. The U.S.S.R. representative stated that he could not vote to reaffirm a resolution of which parts had been unacceptable to his Government.

THIRD REPORT OF THE DISARMAMENT COMMISSION. Between the adoption of the foregoing resolution and the opening of the eighth session, the Disarmament Commission met once only, in order to adopt a report. That report expressed the hope that recent international events would create a more propitious atmosphere for the reconsideration of the disarmament question, whose capital importance in conjunction with other questions affecting the maintenance of peace was recognized by all. The report was adopted unanimously.

DECISIONS OF THE EIGHTH SESSION OF THE GENERAL ASSEMBLY. At the eighth session, a joint proposal was submitted by Brazil, Canada, Chile, China, Colombia, Denmark, France, Greece, Lebanon, New Zealand, Pakistan, Turkey, the United Kingdom and the United States. After several revisions and the inclusion of a number of amendments, notably that of India suggesting the establishment of a sub-committee, the main points of the proposal were that the General Assembly should: (1) recognize the general wish and affirm its earnest desire to reach agreement as early as possible on a comprehensive and coordinated plan under international control for the regulation, limitation and reduction of all armed forces and armaments, for the elimination and prohibition of atomic, hydrogen, bacterial, chemical and all such other weapons of war and mass destruction, and for the attainment of these ends through effective measures; (2) take note of the third report of the Disarmament Commission; (3) request the Commission to continue its efforts to reach agreement on the problems with which it was concerned, taking into consideration proposals made at the eighth session of the General Assembly, and to report again to the Assembly and to the Security Council not later than September 1, 1954; (4) call on all Member States and particularly the major Powers to intensify their efforts to assist the Commission in its tasks, and to submit to it any proposals which they might have to make in the field of disarmament; and (5) suggest that the Commission should study the desirability of establishing a sub-committee, consisting of representatives of the Powers principally involved, which should seek in private an acceptable solution and report to the Commission as soon as possible in order that the latter might study and report on such a solution to the Assembly and to the Council not later than September 1, 1954.

The U.S.S.R. submitted amendments to the fourteen-Power proposal, which would, in part, have had the following effect: (1) to substitute for clause (1), above, a provision that the General Assembly should recognize that the use of atomic and hydrogen weapons of aggression and mass destruction was contrary to the conscience and honor of the peoples and incompatible with membership in the United Nations, and declare that the government which was the first to use the atomic, hydrogen or any other instrument of mass destruction against any other country would commit a crime against humanity and would be deemed a war criminal; and (2) to substitute for clause (3), above, a provision that the Disarmament Commission should be requested to submit to the Security Council, not later than March 1, 1954, proposals providing in the first place for a substantial reduction in the armaments of the five great Powers and for the prohibition of atomic, hydrogen and other types of weapons of mass destruction, together with the simultaneous establishment of strict international control over the observance of that prohibition.

On November 28, 1953, the Assembly rejected the U.S.S.R. amendments, and adopted the revised fourteen-Power proposal. No negative votes were cast against the operative clauses of the resolution.

ESTABLISHMENT OF THE SUB-COMMITTEE OF THE DISARMAMENT COMMISSION. The Disarmament Commission met in April 1954, to consider its tasks under the foregoing General Assembly resolution. The United Kingdom proposed that the Commission, taking note of the Assembly resolution and of the communiqué on disarmament agreed by the Foreign Ministers of France, the U.S.S.R., the United Kingdom and the United States at Berlin on February 18, 1954, should decide to establish a Sub-Committee consisting of Canada, France, the U.S.S.R., the United Kingdom and the United States and recommend that the Sub-Committee meet forthwith and report by July 15.

The U.S.S.R. proposed enlarging the membership to include the People's Republic of China, Czechoslovakia and India. The majority were opposed to the inclusion of those States on the general ground that members of the sub-committee should be members of the Commission. On April 19, the United Kingdom proposal was adopted.

PROCEEDINGS IN 1954 OF THE SUB-COMMITTEE OF THE DISARMAMENT COMMISSION. The Sub-Committee met in secret at Lancaster House in London from May 13 to June 22, 1954, when the Sub-Committee approved its report for submission to the Disarmament Commission.

During the course of nineteen meetings in that period, various proposals, draft resolutions, memoranda and working papers were submitted to the Sub-Committee, including: (1) a U.S.S.R. draft resolution presenting proposals for diminishing the threat of a new world war and strengthening the peace and security of the nations; (2) a United Kingdom memorandum concerning what weapons and armed forces and other matters should be covered by a disarmament convention; (3) a United States working paper on methods of implementing and enforcing disarmament programs and the establishment of international control organs with appropriate rights, powers and functions; (4) a U.S.S.R. draft resolution concerning the assumption of a solemn and unconditional obligation not to employ atomic, hydrogen or other weapons of mass destruction; (5) a U.S.S.R. proposal on basic provisions of a draft international convention for the prohibition of atomic, hydrogen and other weapons of mass destruction, for a substantial reduction in armaments and armed forces, and for the establishment of international control over the observance of the convention; and (6) a memorandum presented jointly by France and the United Kingdom on June 11 containing proposals submitted as a possible basis for compromise (for particulars of this memorandum, see below under "Discussion at the ninth session of the General Assembly").

After considering the Sub-Committee's report, the Disarmament Commission expressed, in its own report unanimously adopted on July 29, the hope that circumstances would facilitate the continued and fruitful consideration of the question of disarmament. The Commission transmitted to the General Assembly with its report, together with the report of the Sub-Committee, proposals concerning the hydrogen bomb and a "standstill" agreement on test explosions made by the Prime Minister of India on April 2, 1954.

DISCUSSION AT THE NINTH SESSION OF THE GENERAL ASSEMBLY. At its ninth session, the General Assembly considered the above report, together with an item submitted by the U.S.S.R. entitled "Conclusion of an international convention (treaty) on the reduction of armaments and the prohibition of atomic, hydrogen and other weapons of mass destruction".

With the request for the inclusion of the item, the U.S.S.R. had submitted a draft resolution, according to which the Assembly would instruct the Commission to prepare, for confirmation by the Security Council, a draft international convention providing for the prohibition of atomic, hydrogen and other weapons of mass destruction and their elimination from the armaments of states, a substantial reduction in armaments and the establishment of international control over the implementation of these decisions on the basis of the proposals contained in the memorandum submitted to the Sub-Committee of the Disarmament Commission on June 11, 1954, by France and the United Kingdom.

The main proposals in the memorandum referred to in the U.S.S.R. draft resolution, which had been presented by France and the United Kingdom to the Sub-Committee as a possible basis for compromise, were to the following effect:

(1) The States members of the Sub-Committee should regard themselves as prohibited, in accordance with the terms of the Charter, from the use of nuclear weapons except in defence against aggression.

(2) The draft disarmament treaty prepared by the Commission would be approved by a world disarmament conference and would enter into force on ratification by specified states. It would include provisions covering the following: (a) the total prohibition of the use and manufacture of nuclear weapons of mass destruction of every type, together with the conversion of existing stocks of nuclear weapons for peaceful purposes; (b) major reductions in all armed forces and conventional armaments; and (c) the establishment of a control organ with rights and powers and functions adequate to guarantee the effective observance of the agreed prohibitions and reductions.

(3) The treaty should provide that the disarmament program be carried out as described below.

(4) After the constitution and positioning of the control organ, and its reporting that it was able effectively to enforce them, the following measures should enter into effect: (a) over-all military manpower should be limited to December 31, 1953, levels; (b) over-all military expenditure, both atomic and non-atomic, should be limited to amounts spent in the year ending December 31, 1953.

(5) As soon as the control organ reported that it was able effectively to enforce them, the following measures should enter into effect: (a) one half of the agreed reductions of conventional armaments and armed forces should take effect, and (b) on completion of (a) the manufacture of all kinds of nuclear weapons and all other prohibited weapons should cease.

(6) As soon as the control organ reported that it was able effectively to enforce them, the following measures should enter into effect: (a) the second half of the agreed reductions of conventional armaments and armed forces should take effect; and (b) on completion of (a): (i) the total prohibition and elimination of nuclear weapons and the conversion of existing stocks of nuclear materials for peaceful purposes should be carried out; and (ii) the total prohibition and elimination of all other prohibited weapons should be carried out.

The U.S.S.R. draft resolution went on to propose that the international convention to be drafted by the Disarmament Commission should contain the following basic provisions:

(1) The following measures should be taken simultaneously: (a) in six months or one year, states should reduce their armaments and armed forces (from the December 31, 1953, strength) and budgetary appropriations for military requirements (from the 1953 amount) by 50 per cent of agreed levels; and (b) to supervise the reduction, a temporary international control commission should be established, under the Security Council, with the right to require states to provide the necessary information on the measures taken by them to reduce armaments and armed forces. The commission should take the necessary steps to supervise the fulfilment by states of the obligations assumed by them in connection with the reduction of armaments, armed forces and appropriations for military requirements. States should periodically supply the commission with information concerning the implementation of the measures provided for in the convention.

(2) On completion of the measures referred to in paragraph (1), the following measures should be taken simultaneously: (a) in six months or one year, states should reduce their armaments, armed forces and budgetary appropriations for military requirements by the remaining 50 per cent of the agreed levels; (b) a complete prohibition of atomic, hydrogen and other weapons of mass destruction should be carried into effect, the production of such weapons should be discontinued and they should be entirely eliminated from the armaments of states; all existing atomic materials should be used only for peaceful purposes. These measures should be completed not later than the measures taken for the reduction of armaments and armed forces referred to in paragraph (2) (a), and the production of atomic and hydrogen weapons should cease immediately, as soon as a start was made with the reduction of armaments, armed forces and appropriations for military requirements in respect of the remaining 50 per cent of the agreed standards; and (c) states should institute a standing international organ for the supervision of the disarmament measures. This international organ should have full powers of supervision, including the power of inspection on a continuing basis to the extent necessary to insure the implementation of the convention by all states.

The draft resolution further provided that the Disarmament Commission should be instructed to study and submit recommendations on the proposal concerning the prohibition of the "use of nuclear weapons except in defence against aggression" contained in the Franco-British memorandum of June 11, 1954.

The General Assembly adopted unanimously on November 4, 1954, a resolution sponsored by Canada, France, the U.S.S.R., the United Kingdom and the United States, which provided that the Assembly should:

(1) conclude that a further effort should be made to reach agreement on comprehensive and coordinated proposals to be embodied in a draft international disarmament convention providing for: (a) the regulation, limitation and major reduction of all armed forces and all conventional armaments; (b) the total prohibition of the use and manufacture of nuclear weapons and weapons of mass destruction of every type, together with the conversion of existing stocks of nuclear weapons for peaceful purposes; and (c) the establishment of effective international control, through a control organ with rights, powers and functions adequate to guarantee the effective observance of the agreed reductions of all armaments and armed forces and the prohibition of nuclear and other weapons of mass destruction, and to insure the use of atomic energy for peaceful purposes only; the whole program to be such that no state would have cause to fear that its security was endangered; (2) request the Disarmament Commission to seek an acceptable solution of the disarmament problem, taking into account the various proposals referred to in the preamble of the resolution and any other proposals within the Commission's terms of reference; (3) suggest that the Disarmament Commission should reconvene its Sub-Committee; and (4) request the Disarmament Commission to report as soon as sufficient progress had been made.

PROCEEDINGS OF FEBRUARY-MAY 1955 OF THE SUB-COMMITTEE OF THE DISARMAMENT COMMISSION. On November 19, 1954, the Disarmament Commission met and agreed that the Sub-Committee should reconvene. The Sub-Committee held 28 meetings at Lancaster House between February 25 and May 18, 1955, when it adjourned to give the five Governments an opportunity to consider the situation then reached and the progress made since the beginning of the talks.

The discussions in London were principally concerned with the proposals in the Franco-British memorandum of June 11, 1954, and in the U.S.S.R. draft resolution of September 30, 1954. On March 8, 1955, Canada, France, the United Kingdom and the United States submitted a joint draft resolution incorporating the proposals contained in the Franco-British memorandum. On March 19, the U.S.S.R. submitted a draft resolution incorporating and elaborating upon its proposals of September 30. In particular, the U.S.S.R. draft added provisions for a limitation of armaments and armed forces as a first step; for a major reduction on the part of the great Powers; for a world conference; for the application of simple agreed criteria in establishing the norms for reduction; and for unrestricted access for the inspectors of the control organ, within the limits of the supervisory functions they would exercise, to all establishments subject to control.

SUPPLEMENTARY WESTERN PROPOSALS IN THE SUB-COMMITTEE. In response to questions raised by the U.S.S.R. during the discussions, the four Powers presented amendments to their March 8 proposals. These had the following effect: (1) to provide that the disarmament treaty should establish time limits applicable to the various limitations, reductions and prohibitions in the program, subject to any extension of time which might be essential in any phase to permit states to complete the measures; (2) to include conventional armaments in the "freeze"; and (3) to make explicit provision that the reductions in armed forces and armaments should be accompanied by consequent reductions in over-all military expenditures.

In addition to those four-Power amendments, France and the United Kingdom submitted, conditionally, an amendment concerning the timing of the complete prohibition of nuclear weapons and the elimination of all stockpiles. They proposed that, on the completion of the third quarter of the agreed reductions of conventional armaments and armed forces, a complete prohibition on the use of atomic, hydrogen and other weapons of mass destruction should come into force. Simultaneously, the elimination of those weapons and the final quarter of the agreed reductions on the conventional side should begin; and both processes should be completed within the time limit laid down in the disarmament treaty. All atomic materials should then be used for peaceful purposes only. This amendment was conditional upon agreement being reached on two essentials in the disarmament program: drastic reductions in the armed forces and conventional armaments of the great Powers, as suggested in an earlier joint proposal, and the institution of an effective system of control which would operate throughout the whole disarmament program.

The proposal referred to above concerning the drastic reductions in the armed forces of the great Powers was contained in another joint Franco-British memorandum. In that, they stated that they were each prepared to reduce their over-all armed forces to a total of 650,000 men, as part of a general scheme of reductions which would provide that: (1) there should be a uniform ceiling for the three other permanent members of the Security Council which should be fixed at between one and one and a half million men; (2) the forces permitted to other states should be substantially lower than the levels for the five Powers; and (3) no state should be entitled to increase its armed forces above existing levels, except that special arrangements would have to be made for certain specified states.

The four Powers also tabled jointly: a proposal respecting basic principles on the question of reductions in armed forces and conventional armaments, a proposal on nuclear disarmament, and a draft resolution on the principles of controls.

U.S.S.R. PROPOSALS OF MAY 10, 1955. Following extensive discussion of questions raised in the foregoing proposals and documents, the U.S.S.R. submitted on May 10, 1955, a proposal consisting of three parts.

The first part consisted of a Declaration, in which the U.S.S.R. took note of various factors contributing to international tensions and mistrust, and expressed the view that the cessation of the "cold war" would help to bring about the relaxation of tensions and the creation of international confidence. That in turn would create the requisite conditions for the execution of a broad disarmament program implemented under international control. The U.S.S.R. accordingly put forward a number of specific proposals which the General Assembly might adopt in order to relax international tensions.

The second part of the U.S.S.R. proposal contained the provisions of the suggested convention on the reduction of armaments and the prohibition of atomic weapons.

It proposed that the following measures, constituting the first of two stages, should be taken in 1956: (1) The states parties to the convention should undertake not to increase their armed forces and conventional armaments above the level obtaining on December 31, 1954. They should also undertake not to increase their appropriations for armed forces and armaments, including atomic weapons, above the level of the expenditures effected for those purposes during the year ended December 31, 1954. These measures should be carried out within two months of the entry into force of the agreement. The United States, the U.S.S.R., China, the United Kingdom and France should furnish the Disarmament Commission, within one month after the entry into force of the Convention, with full official figures of their armed forces, conventional armaments and military expenditures. (2) The five Powers should undertake to reduce the strength of their armed forces so as not to exceed the following figures: for China, the U.S.S.R. and the United States, 1,000,000 to 1,500,000; for France and the United Kingdom, 650,000. The five Powers should undertake also to reduce their conventional armaments correspondingly. The five Powers should in the course of one year effect a reduction in their armed forces and armaments by 50 per cent of the difference between the level of their armed forces and armaments obtaining on December 31, 1954, and the agreed reduced level. Appropriations by states for armed forces and conventional armaments should be reduced correspondingly. (3) There should be convened, not later than during the first half of 1956, a world conference, with a view to determining the size of the reduction of the armaments and armed forces of the other states and to prohibiting atomic weapons. The strength of the armed forces authorized for other states should in all cases be considerably lower than the levels established for the five Powers. (4) As one of the first measures for the execution of the program for the reduction of armaments and the prohibition of atomic weapons, states possessing atomic and hydrogen weapons should undertake to discontinue tests of these weapons. With a view to supervision of the fulfilment by states of that obligation, an international commission should be set up which would submit reports to the Security Council and the General Assembly. (5) Simultaneously with the initiation of measures for the reduction of the armaments and armed forces of the five Powers by the first 50 per cent and before the entry into force of the agreement on the complete prohibition of atomic weapons, states should assume a solemn obligation not to use nuclear weapons, except for purposes of defence against aggression, when a decision to that effect was taken by the Security Council. (6) States possessing military, naval and air bases in the territories of other states should undertake to liquidate such bases. The question of the bases to be liquidated during the first stage should be agreed upon.

For the second stage, to be carried out in 1957, the U.S.S.R. proposed the following: (1) The production of atomic and hydrogen weapons should be discontinued immediately, and budgetary appropriations of states for military requirements reduced correspondingly. (2) The United States, the U.S.S.R., China, the United Kingdom and France should, in the course of one year, reduce their armed forces and armaments by the remaining 50 per cent of the agreed reductions and correspondingly reduce their appropriations for armed forces and conventional armaments. Reductions fixed for other states at the world conference should also be completed. (3) After the reduction of armed forces and conventional armaments had been carried out to the extent of 75 per cent of the total reduction laid down in the convention, a complete prohibition on the use of atomic, hydrogen and other weapons of mass destruction should enter into force. The elimination of these weapons from the armaments of states and their destruction, and the reduction of armed forces and conventional armaments by the final 25 per cent of the agreed reductions should begin simultaneously; and both these processes should be completed within the time-limits in 1957. All atomic materials should thereafter be used exclusively for peaceful purposes. (4) Measures for the liquidation of all foreign military, naval and air bases on the territories of other states should be completed.

The U.S.S.R. proposed that the General Assembly should decide to institute a permanent international control organ having the following rights and powers: (1) During the first stage of execution of the measures for the reduction of armaments and the prohibition of atomic weapons: (a) In order to prevent a surprise attack by one state upon another, the international control organ should establish on the territory of all the states concerned, on a basis of reciprocity, control posts at large ports, at railway junctions, on main motor highways and in aerodromes. The task of these posts would be to see to it that there was no dangerous concentration of military land forces or of air or naval forces. (b) The control organ should have the right to require from states any necessary information on the execution of measures for the reduction of armaments and armed forces. (c) The control organ should have unimpeded access to records relating to the budgetary appropriations of states for military needs, including all decisions of their legislative and executive organs on the subject. States should periodically, within specified time-limits, furnish the control organ with information on the execution of the measures provided for in the convention. (2) During the second stage of execution of measures for the reduction of armaments and the prohibition of atomic weapons the control organ would continue to have the rights and powers it exercised in the first stage, but would also have the following additional powers: (a) To exercise control, including inspection on a continuing basis, to the extent necessary to insure implementation of the convention by all states. The control organ should exercise these functions, while also enjoying the right to require from states the necessary information on the execution of measures for the reduction of armaments and armed forces. Staff recruited to carry out the work of inspection should be selected on an international basis. (b) To have permanently in all states signatories to the convention its own staff of inspectors having, within the bounds of the control functions they exercise, unimpeded access at all times to all objects of control. (3) The control organ should make recommendations to the Security Council on measures of prevention and suppression with regard to violators of the convention on the reduction of armaments and the prohibition of atomic weapons.

PROCEEDINGS, AUGUST-OCTOBER 1955, OF THE SUB-COMMITTEE. The Sub-Committee reconvened in New York on August 29, 1955, to continue its work, taking into account the directive issued by the four Heads of Government of France, the U.S.S.R., the United Kingdom and the United States, at the conclusion of their conference in Geneva on July 23, 1955. The discussions continued for eighteen meetings, until October 7.

To a large extent the discussions were concerned with the proposals on disarmament made by the four Heads of Government at the Geneva meeting, which were laid before the Sub-Committee for its consideration, some in an elaborated form.

France submitted a "Draft agreement on the financial supervision of disarmament and the allocation for peaceful purposes of the resulting funds", in addition to an extract from the statement of July 18, of the Prime Minister of France and the French memorandum of July 21. The United States submitted the statement on disarmament made by the President of the United States on July 21, and an "Outline plan for the implementation of the July 21, 1955, Presidential proposal at Geneva regarding disarmament". The U.S.S.R. circulated the proposal submitted by the Chairman of the Council of Ministers of the U.S.S.R. on July 21, together with his statement on that date concerning the reduction of armaments and the prohibition of atomic weapons. The United Kingdom circulated the proposal by its delegation at Geneva and the related statement of the Prime Minister on July 21.

At Geneva, France had proposed that the limitation of armaments should be linked with assistance to under-developed regions. The Prime Minister had pointed out that by that method, control would become easier, since it would be of the financial and budgetary type, while sanctions would consist of an automatic penalization by a sum equal to the amount of the infraction for the signatory maintaining its military potential higher than the agreed level. The draft agreement, added to the foregoing on August 29, had for its purpose the institution of financial supervision of military expenditure, together with a system of penalties, for the purpose of encouraging disarmament, and to provide for the allocation of the resulting funds to the improvement of levels of living and the development of under-developed areas. It consisted of three articles, concerning the powers of the proposed International Fund for Development and Mutual Assistance, the collection of resources, and the allocation of resources.

Also at Geneva, the President of the United States had stated that no sound and reliable disarmament agreement could be made unless there was control to support every portion of it. He noted, however, that there had not yet been found any scientific or other inspection method which would make certain the elimination of nuclear weapons, although useful checks might be found. He proposed, therefore, to take a practical, immediate step to provide against the possibility of a surprise attack, thus lessening danger and relaxing tension and making more easily attainable an effective system of inspection and disarmament. That step consisted in an exchange between the United States and the U.S.S.R. of a complete blueprint of their military establishments, and the provision of reciprocal facilities for aerial reconnaissance and photography.

In the outline plan for implementing the foregoing, the United States defined the term "blueprint of military establishments" as consisting of the identification, strength, command structure and disposition of personnel, units and equipment of all major land, sea and air forces, including organized reserves and para-military, and a complete list of military plants, facilities and installations with their locations. It proposed that ground observers be stationed at key locations to certify the accuracy of the data exchanged and to give warning of surprise attack; and that aerial reconnaissance be unrestricted. The data would be exchanged in agreed progressive steps and would concern: (a) weapons and delivery systems suitable for surprise attack, (b) transportation and telecommunications, (c) armed forces and their structure and positioning, and (d) additional facilities as mutually agreed.

The proposal circulated by the U.S.S.R. made by the Chairman of the Council of Ministers of the U.S.S.R. at Geneva, embodied the following points: (a) the level of the armed forces of the United States, the U.S.S.R. and China should be established at 1,000,000 to 1,500,000 men for each; that of the United Kingdom and France at 650,000 for each; that of other states should not exceed 150,000 to 200,000 and should be agreed at an appropriate international conference; (b) after 75 per cent of the agreed reductions of armed forces and armaments had been carried out, a complete prohibition of nuclear weapons should come into effect; (c) the four Powers should solemnly pledge themselves not to use nuclear weapons, the pledge to be simultaneous with the initiation of measures for the reduction of armaments, and exceptions would be permitted for purposes of defence against aggression when a decision to that effect was taken by the Security Council; (d) states possessing nuclear weapons should pledge themselves to discontinue tests of those weapons; (e) an effective international control over the implementation of measures for the reduction of armaments and the prohibition of atomic weapons should be established; and (f) pending the conclusion of the disarmament treaty, the four Powers should undertake not to be the first in the use of atomic weapons against any nation and should call upon all states to join that declaration.

The proposal made by the Prime Minister of the United Kingdom at Geneva was to the effect that a system of joint inspection of the forces confronting each other in Europe should be established as a means of increasing mutual confidence on that continent. He had indicated that the project would provide opportunity for the practical test on a limited scale of international inspection of forces in being and would provide valuable experience and lessons for use over a wider field in the future.

In addition, the Sub-Committee considered the question of the objects of control. The United Kingdom submitted a memorandum on the methods, objects and rights of inspection and supervision of the control organ, making proposals as to the kind of information which states should furnish to the control organ. The memorandum also made proposals as to the stage in the program at which the data should be submitted and the methods which the control organ might use to verify the data, exercise control, and supervise the measures of disarmament at each stage.

France submitted two memoranda dealing with the same general questions. They also dealt with procedures governing the timing of the various stages of the program and the enlargement of the powers of the control organ. In a further memorandum, France presented proposals concerning the structure of the international disarmament organization.

TENTH SESSION OF THE GENERAL ASSEMBLY. At its tenth session, the General Assembly considered the proceedings of the Sub-Committee, the report of which had been forwarded by the Disarmament Commission on November 25, 1955. Concurrently, the Assembly considered an item proposed by the U.S.S.R. entitled "Measures for the further relaxation of international tension and development of international cooperation".

After extensive debate, a proposal submitted jointly by Canada, France, the United Kingdom and the United States was revised, particularly in response to amendments proposed by the U.S.S.R. and by India, and on December 16 was adopted.

Under the terms of that resolution, the General Assembly urged that the states concerned and particularly those on the Sub-Committee should continue their endeavors to reach agreement on a comprehensive disarmament plan in accordance with the goals set out in the Assembly's resolution of November 4, 1954, and should, as initial steps, give priority to early agreement on and implementation of both (1) such confidence-building measures as President Eisenhower's plan for exchanging military blueprints and mutual aerial inspection and Marshal Bulganin's plan for establishing control posts at strategic centers, and (2) all such measures of adequately safeguarded disarmament as are now feasible. It suggested that account should also be taken of the proposals of the Prime Minister of France for exchanging and publishing information regarding military expenditures and budgets, of the Prime Minister of the United Kingdom for seeking practical experience in the problems of inspection and control, and of the Government of India regarding the suspension of experimental explosions of nuclear weapons and an "armaments truce". The resolution further called for study of the French proposal for the allocation of funds resulting from disarmament for improving standards of living, particularly in the less-developed countries. It also recommended that scientific search should be continued for methods that would make possible thoroughly effective inspection and control of nuclear weapons material, in order to facilitate the solution of the problem of comprehensive disarmament. And it suggested that the Disarmament Commission reconvene its Sub-Committee and that both should pursue their efforts to attain these objectives.

INTERNATIONAL COOPERATION IN DEVELOPING THE PEACEFUL USES OF ATOMIC ENERGY

On December 8, 1953, the President of the United States, addressing the eighth session of the General Assembly, proposed that governments jointly contribute normal uranium and fissionable materials to an international atomic energy agency to be set up under the aegis of the United Nations. The U.S.S.R. agreed to enter into private negotiations with the United States on the matter with the proviso that during the negotiations, as a means of assisting the use of atomic energy only for peaceful purposes, there would be considered at the same time the U.S.S.R. proposal for the assumption of an unconditional obligation not to use the atomic, hydrogen or any other weapon of mass destruction.

Communications exchanged between the United States and the U.S.S.R. in subsequent months on the question of international cooperation in developing the peaceful uses of atomic energy included a United States memorandum outlining an international atomic energy agency and proposing certain functions for it, such as the receipt and storage of atomic energy materials and the allocation of such materials to participating states, as well as information and service activities.

At the request of the United States, the General Assembly considered at its ninth session, the question of "International cooperation in developing the peaceful uses of atomic energy". Australia, Belgium, Canada, France, the Union of South Africa, the United Kingdom and the United States put forward proposals concerning an international atomic energy agency and an international conference on the peaceful uses of atomic energy. With the incorporation of a number of revisions and suggestions advanced during the discussion, the resolution was unanimously adopted on December 4, 1954.

The resolution expressed the hope that the agency would be established without delay, and suggested that it should then negotiate an appropriate form of agreement with the United Nations, and transmitted the record of the discussions to the States participating in its creation (the Powers sponsoring the proposal, together with Portugal); and it decided that an international technical conference should be held under the auspices of the United Nations to explore means of developing the peaceful uses of atomic energy through international cooperation and, in particular, to study the development of atomic power and to consider other technical areas, such as biology, medicine and radiation protection, most suitable for effective international cooperation. The Secretary-General was requested to organize and convene the conference with the assistance of an advisory committee composed of Brazil,

Canada, France, India, the U.S.S.R., the United Kingdom and the United States.

The Secretary-General and the Advisory Committee proceeded in January 1955, with the organization of the Conference, preparing the topical agenda and rules of procedure, providing for officers and staff and making other necessary arrangements.

The Conference met in Geneva from August 8 to 20, 1955. Seventy-three states and eight specialized agencies were represented by official delegations totalling 1,428. In addition, there were 1,334 observers in attendance, principally from non-governmental organizations, academic institutions and industrial concerns. Altogether, 1,067 scientific papers were received from 38 governments, from specialized agencies and the Department of Economic and Social Affairs of the United Nations Secretariat. Of these, 450 were selected for oral presentation and formed the basis of the Conference program. The organization of the Conference included an initial series of plenary sessions, three parallel series of section meetings dealing with technical and specialized matters, and a concluding plenary session. A series of public evening lectures was presented by a group of eminent scientists. Official exhibits were provided by Belgium, Canada, Denmark, France, Norway, Sweden, the U.S.S.R., the United Kingdom and the United States.

With regard to the agency, the negotiating Powers drew up a draft statute for its establishment which was circulated to other governments at the end of August 1955, for their consideration and comment.

At the tenth session, the General Assembly considered, under the heading "Peaceful uses of atomic energy", the Secretary-General's report on the Conference and reports of governments on progress in developing international cooperation for the peaceful uses of atomic energy. The United Kingdom and the United States introduced a draft resolution with which, in the course of its amendment and revision, the following also associated themselves as cosponsors: Australia, Belgium, Brazil, Canada and the Union of South Africa; Israel and Mexico; the Netherlands; Argentina, Norway and Peru; Denmark, Iceland and Sweden; Turkey and Luxembourg. In its final form, the proposal was adopted unanimously on December 3, 1955.

In its decision, the General Assembly noted the impressive results achieved by the International Conference in facilitating the free flow of scientific knowledge on the peaceful uses of atomic energy. It recommended that a second such conference be held under the auspices of the United Nations in two to three years' time and requested the Secretary-General, acting upon the advice of the Advisory Committee, to undertake once again the organizing and convening of the conference.

The resolution also noted with satisfaction that substantial progress had been made toward negotiation of a draft statute establishing an International Atomic Energy Agency. It welcomed the intention of the sponsoring governments to hold a general conference on the final text of the statute and further welcomed the invitations to Brazil, Czechoslovakia, India and the U.S.S.R. to participate in the negotiations on the statute. And it recommended that the negotiating governments take into account the views expressed during the debate as well as comments on the statute transmitted directly, and that all possible measures be taken to establish the agency without delay.

EFFECTS OF ATOMIC RADIATION

On August 4, 1955, the United States requested the inclusion in the agenda of the tenth session of the General Assembly of the item "Coordination of information relating to the effects of radiation upon human health and safety", and suggested in an accompanying memorandum that the United Nations was the appropriate agency for the systematic assembly and international dissemination of the large amount of existing data in order to provide all nations with a basis for their own evaluation of the problems. On August 31, India requested the addition to the agenda of the item "Dissemination of information on the effects of atomic radiation and on the effects of experimental explosions of thermonuclear bombs". These two items were considered in the First Committee under the general heading "Effects of atomic radiation".

Upon the initiative of Australia, Canada, Denmark, Iceland, Norway, Sweden, the United Kingdom and the United States, the General Assembly on December 3, 1955, decided unanimously to establish a scientific committee consisting of Australia, Brazil, Canada, Czechoslovakia, France, India, Japan, Sweden, the U.S.S.R., the United Kingdom and the United States for the purpose of: (a) receiving and assembling radiological information furnished by Members of the United Nations or of the specialized agencies on observed levels of ionizing radiation and radioactivity in the environment, and on scientific observations and experiments relevant to the effects of ionizing radiation on man and his environment; (b) recommending uniform standards with respect to procedures for sample collection and analyses; (c) compiling reports on observed radiological levels; (d) collating and evaluating the national reports; (e) making yearly progress reports and developing a summary of the reports received, together with the evaluation; and (f) publishing these documents and evaluations from time to time.

General Resolutions Relating to the Problems of Reducing International Tension and Strengthening Peace and Friendship Among Nations

MEASURES TO BE TAKEN AGAINST PROPAGANDA AND THE INCITERS OF A NEW WAR

At the second session of the Assembly, held in 1947, the U.S.S.R. introduced a draft resolution by which the Assembly would: (1) condemn criminal propaganda for a new war such as was carried on in Greece, Turkey and the United States; (2) call upon all governments to prohibit the carrying on of war propaganda in any form, on pain of criminal penalties; and (3) affirm the necessity for speedy action on the reduction of armaments, and the exclusion from national armaments of atomic and all other weapons for mass destruction.

The First Committee considered the U.S.S.R. draft resolution and a number of amendments. After rejecting the U.S.S.R. proposal, the Committee unanimously adopted a substitute draft resolution sponsored by Australia, Canada and France.

As unanimously adopted by the General Assembly, this resolution condemned all forms of propaganda, wherever conducted, which was either designed or likely to promote or encourage any threat to the peace, breach of the peace or act of aggression. Members were requested to take appropriate steps within their constitutional limits to promote friendly relations among nations, based on the purposes and principles of the Charter, by all available means of publicity and propaganda, and to encourage the dissemination of all information designed to give expression to the undoubted desire of all peoples for peace. The Assembly further directed that the resolution should be communicated to the Conference on Freedom of Information, to be held in the spring of 1948.

APPEAL TO THE GREAT POWERS

During the third session of the Assembly in 1948, Mexico submitted a draft resolution appealing to the Great Powers to redouble their efforts to achieve the final settlement of the Second World War and the conclusion of all the peace treaties.

Following consideration of the question by the First Committee, the General Assembly unanimously adopted a resolution which recalled and endorsed the Yalta declarations and expressed the conviction that the Great Powers would conform to the spirit of those declarations. It further recommended that the Powers and subsequent adherents of the Moscow Agreements of December 24, 1945, should redouble their efforts, in a spirit of solidarity and mutual understanding, to secure in the briefest possible time the final settlement of the war and the conclusion of all the peace settlements. The States which had subscribed and adhered to the Washington Declaration of January 1, 1942, should be associated in the performance of that noble task. The resolution took into account the fact that the United Nations could not fully attain its aims so long as the war remained in the process of liquidation and the peace treaties had not been put into force, as well as the fact that the disagreement between the Great Powers in a matter of vital importance to the United Nations, namely the conclusion of the peace treaties, was at that time the cause of deepest anxiety among the peoples of the world.

Following the adoption of this resolution, the Assembly President and the Secretary-General, in a communication to the delegations of the Great Powers, drew attention to the resolution, and urged as a first step toward carrying it out that the Powers concerned undertake immediate conversations and all other necessary steps toward the solution of the Berlin question (*see page 144*), thus opening the way to a prompt resumption of negotiations on the remaining peace treaties.

ESSENTIALS OF PEACE

In 1949, the U.S.S.R. asked the Assembly at its fourth session to consider an item on the condemnation of the preparations for a new war and the conclusion of a five-Power pact for the strengthening of peace, and submitted a draft resolution whereby the Assembly would condemn war propaganda, the armaments race, the establishment of foreign military bases and the organization of military blocs; regard the use of atomic and other means of mass destruction as incompatible with membership of the United Nations; and express the wish that the five permanent members of the Security Council would conclude a pact for the strengthening of peace.

During the First Committee's consideration of this matter, a draft resolution was submitted by the United Kingdom and the United States called "Essentials of Peace". The Committee rejected the U.S.S.R. draft resolution and recommended to the Assembly the one proposed by the United Kingdom and the United States.

As adopted by the General Assembly, the resolution declared that the United Nations Charter, the most solemn pact of peace in history, had laid down basic principles necessary for an enduring peace, that disregard of those principles was primarily responsible for the continuance of international tension, and that it was urgently necessary for all Members to act in accordance with them. The Assembly called upon all nations to refrain from the threat or use of force contrary to the Charter, and from any threat or act aimed at impairing the independence of any state or at fomenting civil strife, as well as to carry out in good faith their international agreements. All nations were asked to cooperate fully with the United Nations, promote freedom for the peaceful expression of political opposition, and promote religious freedom and respect for other fundamental human rights. It called on all Members to join fully in United Nations work, and on the permanent members of the Security Council to broaden their cooperation and to exercise restraint in the use of the veto. Finally, it called for cooperation to attain international regulation of armaments and atomic energy.

TWENTY-YEAR PROGRAM FOR ACHIEVING PEACE THROUGH THE UNITED NATIONS

In 1950, the Secretary-General circulated to all Member States a memorandum which he had discussed with the Heads of Government and with the Foreign Ministers of France, the United Kingdom, the U.S.S.R. and the United States during the spring of that year. The memorandum contained a series of ten points for consideration in developing a twenty-year program for achieving peace through the United Nations. Among the points suggested for study were: inauguration of periodic meetings of the Security Council attended by Heads of Governments or foreign ministers; renewed attempts to establish international control of atomic energy, other weapons of mass destruction and conventional armaments, and to agree on the armed forces to be made available to the Security Council; progress toward universality of membership; and continued and more vigorous use by Members of United Nations agencies in such fields as technical assistance for economic development, higher standards of living, respect for and observance of human rights and fundamental freedoms, advancement towards a status of equality of dependent, colonial or semi-colonial peoples, and the development of international law.

This memorandum was considered by the General Assembly at its fifth session, when two draft resolutions were introduced. One, sponsored by Canada, Chile, Colombia, Haiti, Lebanon, Pakistan, the Philippines, Sweden and Yugoslavia, provided that the Assembly, noting that progress had already been made with regard to certain points contained in the memorandum, would commend the Secretary-General for his initiative, and call upon the appropriate organs of the United Nations to consider those parts of the program with which they were particularly concerned. The other draft resolution, sponsored by the U.S.S.R., enumerated certain other considerations considered essential in further developing the program, such as the participation of the representative of the People's Republic of China in periodic meetings of the Security Council and unconditional prohibition of atomic weapons.

The Assembly adopted the joint draft resolution and rejected the U.S.S.R. proposal.

The Secretary-General transmitted the text of the Assembly resolution and of his memorandum to the Presidents of the organs of the United Nations and to several subsidiary bodies. At the sixth session of the Assembly in 1951, he submitted a progress report and noted that still greater determination and effort were required to give even a minimum assurance of peace. The Assembly again adopted a resolution, pursuant to a draft resolution submitted by the same nine States as at the previous session, which requested the appropriate organs to continue to give consideration to those parts of the memorandum with which they were particularly concerned, and to inform the Assembly of the results.

DECLARATION ON THE REMOVAL OF THE THREAT OF A NEW WAR AND THE STRENGTHENING OF PEACE AND SECURITY AMONG THE NATIONS

(Assembly Resolutions on Peace through Deeds and Condemnation of Propaganda against Peace)

In 1950, the U.S.S.R. asked that the fifth session of the Assembly consider an item entitled "Declaration on the removal of the threat of a new war and the strengthening of peace and security among the nations". The U.S.S.R. submitted a draft resolution in the First Committee, among other things, condemning propaganda in favor of a new war and urging all states to prohibit it, declaring that the use of atomic weapons should be unconditionally prohibited and control instituted to insure the observance of that prohibition, declaring that the first government to use such weapons would commit a crime against humanity, and desiring that the permanent members of the Security Council should conclude a pact for the strengthening of peace and reduce their armed forces by one-third.

Following consideration by the Committee and by the Assembly of a large number of alternative draft resolutions and amendments, two resolutions were eventually adopted on November 17, 1950.

In a resolution entitled "Peace through Deeds", originally sponsored by Bolivia, France, India, Lebanon, Mexico, the Netherlands, the United Kingdom and the United States, the Assembly, condemning intervention by a state in the internal affairs of another in order to change its legally established government by the threat or use of force, reaffirmed that whatever the weapons used, any aggression, whether committed openly or by fomenting civil strife in the interest of a foreign power, or by other means, was the gravest of all crimes against peace and security throughout the world. The Assembly determined that for lasting peace it was indispensable that prompt united action be taken to meet aggression and that every nation agree to accept effective international control of atomic energy, to strive for control and elimination of all other weapons of mass destruction, to regulate all armaments and armed forces and to strive towards development of resources for the general welfare. These goals could be attained if all the Members of the United Nations demonstrated by their deeds their will to achieve peace.

In the second resolution, entitled "Condemnation of Propaganda against Peace", originally submitted by Chile, the Assembly condemned all propaganda against peace and recommended the free exchange of information and ideas. The resolution declared that the propaganda in question included incitement to conflicts or acts of aggression, measures tending to isolate the peoples from contact with the outside world, and measures tending to silence or distort the peace activities of the United Nations or prevent peoples from knowing the views of other Member States.

DUTIES OF STATES IN THE EVENT OF THE OUTBREAK OF HOSTILITIES

In 1950, Yugoslavia submitted, for consideration at the fifth session of the Assembly, a draft resolution which provided that, if a state became engaged in hostilities with another state, it should within 24 hours publicly proclaim its readiness to order a cease-fire and to withdraw its forces from the territory or territorial waters of the opposing state, and should at midnight of the same day put the cease-fire order into effect and begin the withdrawal of its armed forces, to be completed within 48 hours. Any state which failed to make the specified statement or to effect the cease-fire and withdrawal should be considered an aggressor and should be held responsible for the breach of the peace.

In the course of the debate in the First Committee on this proposal, the U.S.S.R. submitted a draft resolution on the definition of aggression, which the Committee eventually decided to refer to the International Law Commission for study and report. The Committee also approved the Yugoslav draft resolution in revised form, providing additionally that the states engaged in hostilities should immediately inform the Secretary-General and invite appropriate United Nations organs to dispatch the Peace Observation Commission to the area of the conflict. Moreover, the resolution stated, the conduct of the states concerned in relation to the recommendations embodied in the resolution should be taken into account in any determination by the appropriate United Nations organs of the responsibility for the breach of the peace.

The resolution was adopted by the Assembly on November 17, 1950, and was subsequently transmitted to the Peace Observation Commission for its information.

MEASURES TO COMBAT THE THREAT OF A NEW WORLD WAR AND TO STRENGTHEN PEACE AND FRIENDSHIP AMONG THE NATIONS

In November 1951, the U.S.S.R. requested inclusion of this item in the agenda of the General Assembly, and submitted a draft resolution covering a number of questions and including a proposal that atomic weapons should be unconditionally prohibited and a strict international control for the enforcement of such prohibition established. The draft resolution further recommended that the permanent members of the Security Council reduce their armaments and armed forces by one-third within one year and that all states, not later than one month after the adoption of prohibition of the atomic weapons and the one-third reduction of military forces, submit official data on all their armaments and armed forces including atomic weapons and military bases on foreign territories. An International Control Organ within the framework of the Security Council was to be established with the right to conduct inspection on a continuing basis without interfering in the domestic affairs of states. A world conference on disarmament was to be convened not later than July 15, 1952.

Other parts of the U.S.S.R. draft resolution would declare participation in the "aggressive" Atlantic Bloc and establishment of bases on foreign territories incompatible with membership in the United Nations and would recognize as essential that the countries taking part in the Korean war should immediately cease their military operations, conclude an armistice and withdraw their forces from the 38th parallel within ten days, while all foreign troops and volunteers should be withdrawn from Korea within three months. The Assembly would further call on the five great Powers to conclude a peace pact.

The General Assembly on January 19, 1952, decided to refer those parts of the U.S.S.R. draft resolution dealing with the disarmament question to the Disarmament Commission, together with any other proposals made during the session on matters falling within the terms of reference of the Commission.

The remaining parts of the draft resolution were rejected.

MEASURES TO AVERT THE THREAT OF A NEW WORLD WAR AND TO STRENGTHEN PEACE AND FRIENDSHIP AMONG THE NATIONS

The inclusion of this item in the agenda of the General Assembly was requested by Poland in October 1952. In April 1953, the delegation of Poland submitted a draft resolution dealing mainly with means of ending the Korean war, but also containing a number of other proposals similar to those made in the U.S.S.R. draft resolution submitted in 1951. As to Korea, the Assembly would recommend the immediate cessation of military operations and resumption of truce negotiations; the withdrawal of foreign troops, including the Chinese volunteers, within a period of from two to three months; and the peaceful settlement of the Korean question on the principle of unification of Korea. The unification would be achieved by the Koreans themselves under the supervision of a commission with the participation of the parties immediately interested and of other states, including states which had not taken part in the war in Korea.

A Brazilian draft resolution was submitted providing that the General Assembly should, *inter alia:* (1) note with deep satisfaction that an agreement had been signed in Korea on the exchange of sick and wounded prisoners of war; (2) express the hope that the exchange would be speedily completed and that further negotiations would result in an early armistice; and (3) decide to recess the seventh session, and request the President of the General Assembly to reconvene the session to resume consideration of the Korean question upon notification of the signing of an armistice agreement or when, in the view of a majority of Members, other developments in Korea required consideration of the question.

The Polish representative later declared that in view of the fact that negotiations were in progress at Panmunjom regarding an armistice, he would not press for a vote on his proposal at that time but would support the Brazilian draft resolution, which was adopted unanimously. (*See section on the Korean question, page 86*).

MEASURES TO AVERT THE THREAT OF A NEW WORLD WAR AND TO REDUCE TENSION IN INTERNATIONAL RELATIONS

In September 1953, the U.S.S.R. requested inclusion of this item in the agenda of the General Assembly and submitted a draft resolution under which the General Assembly would declare atomic, hydrogen and other weapons of mass destruction unconditionally prohibited and would instruct the Security Council to prepare and implement an international agreement insuring the establishment of strict international control over observance of that prohibition; would recommend to the permanent members of the Security Council that they reduce their armed forces by one-third within a year, and that the Council, as soon as possible, should call an international disarmament conference; would further recommend that the Security Council should take steps for the elimination of military bases in the territories of other states; and would finally condemn propaganda inciting hatred among nations and call on all governments to put a stop to such propaganda.

The majority of speakers in the debate expressed opposition to the U.S.S.R. draft resolution on the ground that it was similar to those submitted in previous years and consistently rejected by the Assembly as spurious. All the operative paragraphs of the Soviet draft resolution were rejected by separate votes.

STRENGTHENING OF PEACE THROUGH THE REMOVAL OF BARRIERS TO FREE EXCHANGE OF INFORMATION AND IDEAS

In October 1954, Czechoslovakia requested inclusion in the agenda of the General Assembly of an item entitled "Prohibition of propaganda in favor of a new war" and submitted a draft resolution under which the Assembly would call upon all governments to observe strictly the resolution of November 3, 1947, condemning all forms of propaganda likely to provoke or encourage a threat to the peace.

Australia, Brazil, Cuba, France, Honduras, Iraq, Pakistan, the Philippines, the United Kingdom and the United States submitted jointly amendments to replace most of the Czechoslovak proposal by provisions whereby the Assembly would recall its resolutions of November 3, 1947, and November 17, 1950, regarding the condemnation of propaganda against peace, and its resolution of December 1, 1949, on the essentials of peace. The joint amendments would also have the Assembly call on all nations to remove the barriers denying to people the free exchange of information and ideas. The heading of the resolution was also to be changed in accordance with this last provision.

The resolution as thus amended was adopted on December 11, 1954.

MEASURES FOR THE FURTHER RELAXATION OF INTERNATIONAL TENSION AND DEVELOPMENT OF INTERNATIONAL COOPERATION

In September 1955, the U.S.S.R. requested inclusion of this item in the agenda of the General Assembly, and submitted a draft resolution to the effect that the Assembly would note with satisfaction the efforts made for the relaxation of international tension, particularly at the Geneva Conference of the four Heads of Governments and at the Bandung Conference. The Assembly would further note that it attached particular importance to all disarmament proposals, among others, those of the Soviet Government submitted on May 10 and July 21, 1955, and also those submitted by the President of the United States and by the United Kingdom and by France at the Geneva Conference.

The Political Committee discussed this item together with the report of the Disarmament Commission, and after having adopted a draft resolution on the disarmament question, decided not to vote on the U.S.S.R. draft resolution. The U.S.S.R. draft resolution was not pressed to a vote when the Assembly discussed the report of the First Committee.

Questions Relating to United Nations Procedures and Organs

UNITED NATIONS ARMED FORCES

On February 16, 1946, the Security Council directed the Military Staff Committee to examine from the military point of view Article 43 of the Charter, which contemplates agreements between the Council and Member States for making armed forces and assistance available to the Council. On April 30, 1947, the Committee presented a report on the general principles to govern the organization of the armed forces, drawn up under 41 articles. Most of the 25 articles agreed in the Committee were also accepted by the Council, but the area of agreement was not extended.

The Council then, on June 25, 1947, asked the Committee to submit an estimate of the over-all strength of the armed forces to be made available, indicating the strength and composition of the land, sea and air components, and the proportion of this strength to be provided on the basis of equality by the permanent members. France, the United Kingdom (China concurring) and the United States each provided the Security Council with provisional estimates. The U.S.S.R. considered that it was first necessary to resolve general principles, but in the Committee submitted estimates for preliminary and informal discussion. The exchange of views in the Committee on the question of over-all strength and composition of the forces continued during 1947 and the first half of 1948 without unanimity being achieved.

On July 2, 1948, the Committee informed the Council that it was not able to make further progress in the matter until agreement had been reached in the Council on the general principles previously reported upon. The Council did not discuss the problem and the Committee, after failing to agree on the possibility of studying other aspects of the matter and so reporting on August 6 and 16, 1948, has held no further discussion on the subject of United Nations armed forces.

INTERIM COMMITTEE OF THE GENERAL ASSEMBLY

On November 13, 1947, the General Assembly established the Interim Committee as a subsidiary organ which would function between the Assembly's regular sessions.

According to the terms of the Assembly resolution establishing it, the Committee was to consider and report on: (a) matters referred to it by the Assembly; (b) any dispute or any situation which, in virtue of Articles 11 (2), 14 or 35 of the Charter, had been proposed for inclusion in the agenda of the Assembly or brought before the latter by the Security Council, provided the Committee previously determined (by a two-thirds majority, unless the matter was one brought by the Council, in which case a simple majority was sufficient) the matter to be both important and requiring preliminary study; and (c) methods to be adopted to give effect to that part of Article 11 (para. 1) which deals with the general principles of cooperation in the maintenance of international peace and security, and to that part of Article 13 (para. 1.a) which deals with the promotion of international cooperation in the political field. It was also to consider, in connection with any matter under discussion by the Interim Committee, whether occasion might require a special session of the Assembly. It was empowered to conduct investigations and appoint commissions of inquiry within the scope of its duties, provided that decisions to do so be made by a two-thirds majority and that an investigation or inquiry elsewhere than at United Nations Headquarters should not be conducted without the consent of the state or states on whose territory it was to take place. Finally, the Committee was to report to the next session of the Assembly on the advisability of establishing a permanent committee to perform the duties of the Interim Committee. The Assembly stipulated that the Interim Committee should at all times take into account the responsibilities of the Security Council for the maintenance of international peace and security, as well as the duties of other bodies.

The Interim Committee was prolonged for one year in December 1948, its terms of reference being extended to include the right to request advisory opinions of the International Court of Justice on legal questions arising within the scope of its activities. On November 21, 1949, it was reestablished for an indefinite period.

The Interim Committee held no meeting from September 18, 1950, until March 17, 1952, during which time the General Assembly remained in session.

On March 17, 1952, the Interim Committee met and elected its officers. It then adjourned *sine die*. It did not meet during 1953 and 1954 because the Assembly remained in session. It convened on January 28, 1955, to elect its officers, for one year, and adjourned *sine die* immediately thereafter.

The Byelorussian S.S.R., Czechoslovakia, Poland, the Ukrainian S.S.R. and the U.S.S.R. have regarded the creation of the Interim Committee as contrary to the Charter and have never attended any of its meetings.

In 1948, the Interim Committee examined the following political matters: (a) the problem of voting in the Security Council (*see page 67*), (b) consultation by the Temporary Commission on Korea (*see page 83*), and (c) methods for promoting international cooperation in the political field.

In 1949-1950, the Committee considered: (a) the report of the United Nations Commission for Eritrea (*see page 131*); (b) the procedure to delimit the boundaries of the former Italian Colonies insofar as they were not already fixed by international agreement (*see page 132*); and (c) the question of threats to the political independence and territorial integrity of China and to the peace of the Far East, resulting from Soviet violations of the Sino-Soviet Treaty of Friendship and Alliance of August 14, 1945, and from Soviet violations of the Charter of the United Nations (*see page 98*).

The General Assembly referred to the Committee in 1950, the item on its agenda concerning the establishment of a Permanent Commission of Good Offices. It also intimated that the Committee was to continue its systematic examination of machinery for the pacific settlement of disputes.

APPOINTMENT OF RAPPORTEURS OR CONCILIATORS BY THE SECURITY COUNCIL

Among the recommendations made to the Assembly in the report of the Interim Committee to the third session in 1948, was a resolution containing suggestions to the Security Council concerning the performance of conciliation functions by a rapporteur or conciliator of the Council. Following consideration of this suggestion at the second part of its third session, the Assembly on April 28, 1949, adopted a resolution recommending that the Security Council, after a situation or dispute had been brought to its attention in accordance with its rules of procedure, and not later than immediately after the opening statements on behalf of the parties concerned, should invite the parties to meet with the President of the Council, and should attempt to agree upon a representative of the Council to act as rapporteur or conciliator for the case. The representative so agreed upon might be the President or any other representative on the Council, who would thereupon be appointed by the President to undertake the function of rapporteur or conciliator. If a rapporteur or conciliator were appointed, it would be desirable for the Council to abstain from further action on the case for a reasonable interval, during which actual efforts at conciliation would be in progress. The rapporteur or conciliator so agreed upon and appointed should attempt to conciliate the situation or dispute and should in due course report to the Security Council.

When the Security Council considered the matter in May 1950, it adopted a draft resolution which had been submitted by France and which, taking note of the Assembly's resolution, stated that the Council had decided to base itself, should an appropriate occasion arise, on the principles set forth in the Assembly resolution. The resolution was adopted unanimously, with one member (U.S.S.R.) absent.

PANEL FOR INQUIRY AND CONCILIATION

In its report to the third session of the Assembly in 1948, the Interim Committee recommended the adoption of a resolution relating to the establishment of a panel for inquiry and conciliation. The Assembly in April 1949, decided to invite each Member to designate from one to five persons who, by reason of their training, experience, character and standing, were deemed to be well fitted to serve as members of commissions of inquiry or of conciliation and who would be disposed to serve in that capacity.

In accordance with Article 2 of the annex to the resolution, the Secretary-General has from time to time communicated lists of persons nominated for inclusion in the panel of Member Governments. As of the end of 1955, panel members had been designated by the Governments of Afghanistan, Australia, Bolivia, Brazil, Burma, Canada, China, Colombia, Cuba, Denmark, the Dominican Republic, Ecuador, El Salvador, Greece, Haiti, India, Israel, the Netherlands, Norway, Pakistan, Sweden, Syria, the United Kingdom and the United States.

UNITED NATIONS GUARD, UNITED NATIONS FIELD SERVICE, AND PANEL OF FIELD OBSERVERS

In 1948, the Secretary-General submitted a proposal to the first part of the third session of the Assembly, for the creation of a United Nations Guard to assist United Nations missions in the field. While such a Guard might comprise several thousand persons, he proposed that to meet the immediate need it should be established 800 strong, consisting of a nucleus permanent establishment of 300, located and trained at United Nations Headquarters or at an appropriate European location, plus a volunteer reserve cadre of up to 500 men recruited multi-nationally and held in reserve at their homes at the call of the Secretary-General as and when required.

After a number of representatives had expressed their views on this proposal in the course of the second part of the third session of the Assembly, held in the spring of 1949, a Special Committee was appointed with instructions to study the proposal of the Secretary-General in all its technical aspects, together with such other proposals which might be made with regard to other similar means of increasing the effectiveness of the services provided to United Nations missions.

In the light of the discussions held in the Assembly, the Secretary-General submitted a revised proposal to the Special Committee, in which he suggested the establishment of two units, a United Nations Field Service consisting of 300 men seconded from national governments to provide certain technical services to field missions, and a Field Reserve Panel composed of a list of names of qualified persons to be called for service in response to a specific decision by the Assembly or the Security Council for such purposes as observation of truce terms, protection of neutralized places, or the supervision of polling places during a plebiscite.

In its report to the fourth session of the Assembly, the Special Committee stated that the majority of its members favored the establishment of a Field Service with the functions set forth by the Secretary-General, and held that those functions were not those of an international military force, but rather amounted to a systematization of the regular functions of the Secretariat. The majority also were in favor of the establishment of the proposed Panel of Field Observers. A minority report was also submitted setting forth objections to the two proposals, which were held to exceed the powers conferred upon the Secretary-General and infringe on the functions of the Security Council.

At its fourth session, the Assembly, on November 22, 1949, adopted the draft resolutions which had been recommended by the Special Committee. Under the first part the Assembly, considering that the Secretary-General had authority to establish the United Nations Field Service subject to the normal Assembly supervision, took note of his intention to establish that unit in a form modified by the observations contained in the report of the Special Committee. The second part of the resolution took note of the Secretary-General's intention to undertake the administrative arrangements for the proposed United Nations Panel of Field Observers with due regard to the observations contained in the report of the Special Committee, and requested him to establish and maintain a list of persons qualified to assist United Nations missions in the functions of observation and supervision.

ESTABLISHMENT OF A PERMANENT COMMISSION OF GOOD OFFICES

At the fifth session of the Assembly in 1950, Yugoslavia submitted a draft resolution which envisaged the creation of a commission, to be a permanent subsidiary organ of the Assembly, with the purpose of facilitating the opening of direct negotiations between parties in conflict before such a conflict assumed a character of danger to international peace and security.

At the suggestion of Lebanon and Uruguay, the Assembly decided to refer the question to the Interim Committee of the Assembly with the recommendation that that Committee, in continuing its systematic examination of machinery for the pacific settlement of disputes, should study the question in connection with the establishment of a permanent organ of conciliation, taking into account the suggestions contained in the draft resolution which had been submitted by Yugoslavia.

VOTING IN THE SECURITY COUNCIL

Article 27 of the Charter provides that, with two exceptions, decisions of the Security Council on non-procedural matters must be made by an affirmative vote of seven members, "including the concurring votes of the permanent members". The negative vote by a permanent member in such a case is popularly called the "veto". Many delegations had expressed concern at the effect which application of the veto was having on the work of the Council during its first year, and the question was raised in the General Assembly at the end of 1946.

RECOMMENDATIONS ADOPTED BY THE GENERAL ASSEMBLY AT THE SECOND PART OF
ITS FIRST SESSION. The General Assembly considered together three items dealing
mainly with the method of voting in the Security Council (*see "Charter Review"*,
page 72). On December 13, 1946, the Assembly adopted Resolution 40 (I.2) whereby: (1) it requested the permanent members of the Council to make every effort to
insure that their special voting privilege would not impede the Council in reaching
decisions promptly; (2) it recommended that the Council adopt practices and procedures designed to reduce the voting difficulties and to insure prompt and effective
exercise of its functions; and (3) that, in so doing, the Council consider the views
expressed in the Assembly.

The Council discussed the matter on August 27, 1947, and decided to refer it to
its Committee of Experts. The Committee was instructed to submit to the Council
its recommendations on the measures that the latter should adopt in view of the
Assembly's recommendations. The Committee of Experts of the Council found itself
unable to agree on recommendations to be submitted to the Council.

RESOLUTION ADOPTED BY THE GENERAL ASSEMBLY AT ITS SECOND SESSION. Two items
relating to the problem of voting in the Security Council were placed on the agenda
of the second regular session of the General Assembly. The first, requested by
Argentina, proposed the convocation of a General Conference of Members to amend
the privilege of the veto. The second, requested by Australia, concerned the extent
to which the recommendations contained in Assembly Resolution 40 (I.2) in relation to the exercise of the veto had been carried out.

On November 21, 1947, the General Assembly adopted Resolution 117 (II)
providing, in the first place, that the question of voting procedure in the Council
should be referred to the Interim Committee and requesting the latter to consult
with any committee which the Council might designate to cooperate with it in the
study of the problem. Secondly, Resolution 117 (II) invited the permanent members of the Council to consult with one another in order to secure agreement on
measures to insure the prompt and effective functioning of the Council.

On December 19, 1947, the Council decided that the letter from the Secretary-
General conveying Assembly Resolution 117 (II) "be received by the Security
Council".

RECOMMENDATIONS ADOPTED BY THE GENERAL ASSEMBLY AT ITS THIRD SESSION.
The Interim Committee examined the question of voting procedure in the Security
Council from March 15, 1948, until July 9, 1948, when it approved its report to
the General Assembly. At the first part of the third regular session of the Assembly,
the report of the Interim Committee and an item proposed by the representative of
Argentina for the convocation of a General Conference under Article 109 of the
Charter to study the question of the veto, were combined under the general agenda
item "The problem of voting in the Security Council". The Interim Committee's
report formed the basis for Assembly Resolution 267 (III) adopted on April 14,
1949, whereby the Assembly recommended that the members of the Council should
consider as procedural 35 types of decisions enumerated in an annex to the Resolution and that the permanent members of the Council should seek agreement among
themselves upon what decisions they might forbear to exercise their veto, when
seven affirmative votes had already been cast in the Council.

To avoid impairment of the usefulness and prestige of the Council through
excessive use of the veto, the Assembly further recommended that the permanent
members of the Council should consult together whenever feasible upon important
decisions to be taken by the Council or before a vote was taken if their unanimity
was essential to effective action, and where unanimity was not possible that they

exercise the veto only when they considered the question of vital importance, taking into account the interests of the United Nations as a whole, and that they state on what ground they considered this to be so.

Resolution 267 (III) finally recommended to the Members of the United Nations that, in agreements whereby they would confer functions on the Security Council, they should exclude the application of the rule of unanimity to the greatest extent feasible.

On October 18, 1949, the President of the Council stated, on behalf of the five permanent members, that no agreement had been reached on the Assembly's recommendation that the permanent members seek agreement on possible decisions by the Council on which they might forbear to exercise their veto. However, the consultations had indicated that agreement in principle existed on the practice of consultation before important decisions were to be taken.

RECOGNITION BY THE UNITED NATIONS OF THE REPRESENTATION OF A MEMBER STATE

In January 1950, the Security Council referred to its Committee of Experts two proposals submitted by India with a view to amending Rule 13 of its provisional rules of procedure. One of those proposals dealt with representation; the other, with credentials. In essence, the proposed amendment on representation would have provided that, once the right of a person to represent his country was called in question, the President of the Council should ascertain the views of all other Member States before the Council took a decision.

The majority of the Committee of Experts considered the question of such a nature that the General Assembly should be the organ to initiate study of, and seek uniformity and coordination with respect to, the procedure governing representation and credentials. However, the Committee agreed that the right of the Council to deal with any issue relating to the representation or credentials of its members was not open to question. It recommended that, for the moment, the Council take no action regarding the amendment. In this the Council concurred. (The Council adopted an amendment to Rule 13 of its provisional rules of procedure, specifying by whom the credentials of its members should be issued.)

Inclusion of the question of representation of a Member State in the agenda of the General Assembly was requested by Cuba in July 1950. Two proposals submitted to the *Ad Hoc* Political Committee by Cuba and the United Kingdom respectively, were referred for study and report to a sub-committee. The latter recommended the adoption of a draft resolution which would have provided that, in case of controversy, the question of the right of an authority to represent a Member State be considered in the light of the Principles and Purposes of the Charter and the circumstances of each case, as well as on the basis of a series of factors such as: (1) the extent of its effective control over the territory of the state and of its acceptance by the population, (2) the willingness of the authority to accept responsibility for the carrying out by the Member State of its obligations under the Charter, and (3) the extent to which the authority had been established through internal processes. It was also recommended that such questions, when they arose, should be considered by the Assembly, or by its Interim Committee if the Assembly were not in session.

The factors enumerated in the draft resolution were deleted as the result of the adoption of an amendment submitted by Egypt. The draft resolution as amended was approved by the General Assembly on December 14, 1950. Several delegations, including that of the U.S.S.R., declared that it was unacceptable. The use of such criteria as were left in the resolution would lead to arbitrary and discriminatory measures in respect of certain Member States and would open the way to interference in the internal affairs of Members. They also stated that the issue of representation should be decided independently by each organ of the United Nations, in accordance with its own rules of procedure.

UNITED ACTION FOR PEACE: THE PEACE OBSERVATION COMMISSION AND THE COLLECTIVE MEASURES COMMITTEE

At its fifth session, the General Assembly, under the item "United Action for Peace", considered proposals advanced by the United States to enable the Assembly to perform more effectively the functions entrusted to it by the Charter in the field of international peace and security. After revision and amendment during an extended debate, three resolutions were adopted on November 3.

Resolution A included provision for: (1) emergency special sessions of the General Assembly on 24 hours' notice on the vote of any seven members of the Security Council or a majority of the Members of the United Nations if the Security Council, because of a lack of unanimity among the permanent members, failed to act in any case where there appeared to be a threat to the peace, breach of the peace, or act of aggression; (2) establishment of a Peace Observation Commission composed of representatives of fourteen Members, including the five permanent members of the Security Council, to be utilized by the General Assembly, the Interim Committee or the Security Council to observe and report on the situation in any area where international tension threatened international peace and security; (3) maintenance by Member States of elements of their national armed forces for prompt availability as United Nations units; and the appointment by the Secretary-General of a panel of military experts to give technical advice to Member States on request; and (4) establishment of a Collective Measures Committee composed of representatives of fourteen Members to study and report on methods which might be used collectively to maintain and strengthen international peace and security.

Resolution B recommended the Security Council: (1) to take the necessary steps to insure that the provisions of the Charter, in particular, Chapters V, VI and VII, were implemented in connection with threats to the peace, breaches of the peace or acts of aggression and the peaceful settlement of disputes or situations likely to endanger the maintenance of international peace and security; and (2) to devise measures for the earliest application of Articles 43, 45, 46 and 47 of the Charter. The resolution stipulated that these recommendations should in no manner prevent the General Assembly from fulfiling its functions under resolution A.

Resolution C recommended that the permanent members of the Security Council should meet and discuss, collectively or otherwise, and, if necessary, with other states concerned, all problems likely to threaten international peace and hamper the activities of the United Nations, with a view to resolving fundamental differences and reaching agreement in accordance with the spirit and letter of the Charter.

The discussion centered principally on the constitutionality of the proposals in resolution A. The majority argued that the inability of the Security Council to discharge its primary responsibility for maintaining international peace and security, demonstrated by the experience of the previous five years, during which the veto had been used nearly 50 times, demanded the proposed more effective implementation of the residual right of the Assembly to make recommendations on any matters within the scope of the Charter, except disputes or situations with which the Council was dealing.

The minority, led by the U.S.S.R., insisted that the purpose of the proposal was to relieve the Security Council of its primary responsibility for maintaining peace and security and to eliminate the principle of unanimity, and was tantamount to changing the Charter. They disputed the argument that, under Article 11, the General Assembly could make recommendations involving action. They argued that it was the efforts of the Anglo-American majority in the Council to push through decisions in their own interests which had caused the minority in self-defense to use the veto, its only guarantee of independence and freedom of action. The minority viewed the provisions relating to the setting up of armed forces of the United Nations as an attempt to usurp the rights of the Security Council. Certain specific provisions of the resolution were accepted, including those establishing the Peace Observation Commission, but not those relating to the Collective Measures Committee.

Peace Observation Commission. The resolution constituted the Peace Observation Commission for 1951 and 1952 as follows: China, Colombia, Czechoslovakia, France, India, Iraq, Israel, New Zealand, Pakistan, Sweden, the U.S.S.R., the United Kingdom, the United States and Uruguay. This membership has been renewed at two-year intervals, except that in 1955, Colombia was replaced by Honduras.

On January 23, 1952, pursuant to a request of the General Assembly in its resolution of December 7, 1951, on the Greek Question (*see page 142*), the Commission established, by 12 votes to 2, a Balkan Sub-Commission composed of Colombia, France, Pakistan, Sweden and the United States. At the request of Greece, the Sub-Commission decided, on January 31, to conduct observation in the frontier areas of Greece. In quarterly reports, the observers appointed reported through a principal observer on conditions and incidents along the Greek-Bulgarian and Greek-Albanian borders. The Sub-Commission did not find it necessary to report to the Peace Observation Commission. On August 1, 1954, the observer group was discontinued at the suggestion of Greece.

Collective Measures Committee. The Collective Measures Committee, composed of Australia, Belgium, Brazil, Burma, Canada, Egypt, France, Mexico, the Philippines, Turkey, the United Kingdom, the United States, Venezuela and Yugoslavia, began meeting on March 5, 1951. Its studies were concentrated on the problems of the preparedness of states and on techniques, machinery and procedures relating to the coordination of national and international action in the fields of political, economic and financial, and military collective measures.

In its report to the sixth session of the General Assembly, the Committee set down the results of its studies under these three main classifications. Political measures might include appeals to the parties, the denunciation of an offending state, its suspension or expulsion from the United Nations or the specialized agencies, and the non-recognition of changes brought about by the threat or use of force. Economic and financial measures might involve the total severance of all economic and financial relations with an offending state, or selective measures (embargoes on exports, embargoes on imports, refusal of credits or loans, etc.). On military matters, the Committee dealt with both the organization of United Nations resources, and the coordination and utilization of a United Nations armed force. In respect of collective military measures, as well as of economic and financial measures, the Committee felt that further study was needed.

The General Assembly considered the matter under the title "Methods which might be used to maintain and strengthen international peace and security in accordance with the purposes and principles of the Charter: report of the Collective

Measures Committee". On January 12, 1952, the Assembly recommended that the various actions on the part of governments recommended in the resolution of November 3, 1950, be continued and broadened, and that the Committee continue its studies for another year.

The second report of the Collective Measures Committee elaborated the matters dealt with in the first report. It included three lists of materials to which selective embargoes could be applied: armaments; items of primary strategic importance; and strategic items which might be of vital importance, including industrial equipment and raw materials. The Committee had also studied the problem of the equitable sharing of the economic and financial burdens involved in collective measures. In the military field, the Committee gave preliminary consideration to a proposal of the Secretary-General for the establishment of a United Nations volunteer reserve.

By resolution of March 17, 1953, the General Assembly decided to continue the Committee for two years.

The Committee submitted its third report to the ninth session of the General Assembly. That report included a statement of the principles of collective security based on the Assembly's resolutions regarding collective measures and on the two previous reports of the Committee. In particular, the Organization should be guided by the following principles: (1) contributions to the collective effort should be made by states in accordance with their constitutional processes and to the extent they judged possible; (2) in the event of collective action against aggression, a primary objective should be to secure a maximum contribution of effective military forces, not only by direct contributions of forces but also by logistic and ancillary support; (3) the United Nations should take appropriate steps in conformity with the Charter to make effective any action in exercise of the right of self-defense under Article 51 or within the framework of regional arrangements covered by Chapter VIII, and states should seek all possible support for collective measures undertaken by the United Nations; and (4) collective economic and financial measures against aggression should include all practicable assistance to the victim and to the cooperating states.

On November 4, 1954, the General Assembly adopted a resolution which noted with approval the statement of principles of collective security, and directed the Committee to remain in a position to pursue such further studies as it might deem desirable.

CHARTER REVIEW

PROPOSALS SUBMITTED IN 1946. At the second part of its first session, the General Assembly referred to the First Committee three items dealing mainly with the method of voting in the Security Council. Two of those items submitted by Cuba proposed the calling of a general conference under Article 109, in order: (1) to eliminate the veto privilege, and (2) to review the Charter. The third item submitted by Australia dealt exclusively with the application of Article 27 of the Charter. The First Committee considered the three items together. Several draft resolutions presented by China, Argentina and Cuba were rejected by the First Committee. The resolution eventually adopted by the General Assembly dealt only with the voting procedure in the Security Council. (*See "Voting in the Security Council", page 67.*)

PROPOSALS SUBMITTED IN 1953. At its eighth session, the General Assembly considered three items dealing with a possible review of the Charter. The items, submitted respectively by Argentina, the Netherlands and Egypt, concerned the publication of documents and preparatory studies in connection with a possible Charter review.

The Sixth Committee considered the three items jointly. Three draft resolutions were introduced. Two were subsequently withdrawn; the third draft resolution submitted jointly by Argentina, Canada, Cuba, the Netherlands, New Zealand and Pakistan was adopted by the Sixth Committee after it had been substantially amended by the deletion of a provision whereby Member States would be invited to submit their preliminary views with regard to the possible revision of the Charter.

Some delegations opposed the proposals for preparatory work which, in their opinion, prejudged the question of the revision of the Charter and would, therefore, only increase international tension.

General Assembly resolution 796 (VIII), adopted on November 27, 1953, in its operative part requested the Secretary-General to prepare and circulate among the Member States during 1954 or shortly thereafter: (a) a systematic compilation of the documents of the United Nations Conference on International Organization not yet published, (b) a complete index of the documents of that Conference, and (c) a repertory of the practice of United Nations organs appropriately indexed.

Most of the documentation requested by the General Assembly was prepared by the Secretariat and circulated to the Member States before and during the tenth session of the Assembly.

PROPOSAL TO CALL A GENERAL CONFERENCE OF THE MEMBERS OF THE UNITED NATIONS FOR THE PURPOSE OF REVIEWING THE CHARTER—IN 1955. In conformity with Article 109 (3), the question of the convening of a General Conference for the purpose of reviewing the Charter appeared on the agenda of the tenth session of the General Assembly.

A draft resolution submitted jointly by Canada, Ecuador, Iraq, Thailand, the United Kingdom, the United States and Uruguay provided that the General Assembly would decide in principle to hold a General Conference to review the Charter and would appoint a committee which, after consultation with the Secretary-General, would report to the Assembly at its twelfth session on the question of fixing an appropriate time and place for the Conference, as well as its organization and procedure. Moreover, the Secretary-General would be requested to complete and continue the publication program undertaken pursuant to resolution 796 (VIII).

Two amendments were submitted; the first by Syria, the second jointly by Egypt and India. The first amendment would limit the terms of reference of the proposed committee to examination of the question whether the convening of a General Conference was desirable. The second amendment proposed enlargement of the membership of that committee.

A majority of the Assembly favored the adoption of the joint draft resolution and opposed the Syrian amendment. Most representatives urged caution in the matter of possible review of the Charter and stressed the danger of drastic or premature changes. Many held that the time was not appropriate for the holding of a successful Review Conference. Other representatives, though not objecting to the principle of a review of the Charter, thought that the decision to hold a General Conference should be postponed. Consequently, they supported the Syrian amendment.

Finally, some representatives opposed the joint draft resolution and any review of the Charter. In their opinion, a review of the Charter designed to change its fundamental provisions would hinder the strengthening of trust in the relations between states; if serious defects had developed in the operation of the United Nations, this was the result not of imperfections of the Charter, but of the fact that some of the most important of its provisions had been violated.

Shortly before the draft resolution was put to the vote, its sponsors declared that they accepted the Indian-Egyptian proposal to enlarge the Committee so that it would be composed of all the Members of the United Nations.

The Syrian amendment was rejected, and the joint draft resolution was adopted on November 21, 1955.

After the vote, the representatives of the U.S.S.R. and Poland stated that their delegations would not be able to take part in the work of the Committee or in any action aimed at reviewing the Charter.

On December 16, 1955, the Security Council adopted by 9 votes to 1, with 1 abstention, a resolution in which it expressed its concurrence in the General Assembly's decision. (According to Article 109 (3) of the Charter, a decision to hold a General Conference for the purpose of reviewing the Charter must be taken by a majority vote in the General Assembly and by a vote of any seven members in the Security Council.)

STRATEGIC AREAS UNDER TRUSTEESHIP

On February 17, 1947, the representative of the United States requested the Secretary-General to include in the provisional agenda of the Security Council, at an early date, the text of a draft trusteeship agreement for the Pacific islands formerly under Japanese mandate, which the Government of the United States was submitting for the approval of the Security Council, in accordance with Article 83 of the Charter.

On February 26, 1947, the question was put on the agenda. General discussion on the question started at that meeting and continued on March 7 and 12. On March 17, the President, in conformity with a previous decision of the Council, invited the representatives of Canada, India, the Netherlands, New Zealand and the Philippines to the Council table, to participate in the consideration of the draft trusteeship agreement. The terms of this agreement were considered in detail, and the Council, after approving several amendments, adopted the trusteeship agreement, as a whole, by a unanimous vote on April 2, 1947.

On November 7, 1947, the Secretary-General drew attention to the need for formulating procedures to govern the detailed application of Articles 87 and 88 (concerning the functions and powers of the Trusteeship Council) to this strategic area. The matter was referred to the Committee of Experts by the Security Council on November 15, 1947. On the basis of the report of the Committee, and after consultation between a Committee of the Council and a Committee of the Trusteeship Council, the Security Council, on March 7, 1949, defined the ways in which it could avail itself of the assistance of the Trusteeship Council in the performance of functions of the United Nations under the trusteeship system relating to political, economic, social and educational matters. (See also pages 268-274.)

APPOINTMENT OF THE SECRETARY-GENERAL OF THE UNITED NATIONS

On January 30, 1946, pursuant to Article 97 of the Charter, the Security Council at a private meeting by secret ballot decided to recommend to the General Assembly the appointment of Trygve Lie, of Norway, as Secretary-General of the United Nations. On February 1, the General Assembly, upon this recommendation, appointed Mr. Lie as its first Secretary-General.

On November 10, 1952, Secretary-General Trygve Lie tendered his resignation before a plenary meeting of the General Assembly. Reading a letter he had handed earlier that day to Assembly President Lester B. Pearson, he announced that he had decided, after lengthy consideration over many months, to submit his resignation. Three days later, the Assembly placed on its agenda the item "Appointment of the Secretary-General of the United Nations".

At six private meetings between March 11 and 31, 1953, the Security Council met to consider the recommendation which it should make to the General Assembly. On March 11, Brigadier General Carlos P. Romulo, of the Philippines, Stanislaw Skrzeszewski, of Poland, and Lester B. Pearson, of Canada, were proposed as Secretary-General by, respectively, the representatives of the United States, the Soviet Union and Denmark. Put to the vote by secret ballot on March 13, none of the three proposals was adopted. At the request of the Council, the permanent members then held consultations regarding the recommendation to be made and reported, but without any recommendation, to subsequent meetings of the Council. On March 19, a proposal by the representative of the Soviet Union to recommend Mrs. Vijaya Lakshmi Pandit, of India, was voted upon and not adopted. Finally on March 31, the Council, voting by secret ballot, adopted a proposal by the representative of France recommending to the General Assembly that Dag Hammarskjold, of Sweden, be appointed Secretary-General.

On April 7, the General Assembly dealt with this recommendation after the President had announced that the Assembly accepted, with very great regret, the resignation of Trygve Lie. After deciding that the terms of appointment of the second Secretary-General should be the same as those of the first, the Assembly by secret ballot adopted the Council's recommendation.

Mr. Hammarskjold was installed as Secretary-General at a meeting of the General Assembly on April 10, 1953.

Admission of New Members

APPLICATIONS FOR MEMBERSHIP AND STATES ADMITTED—
JANUARY 1, 1946, TO DECEMBER 31, 1955

Application	Date of Submission of Application	Date of Admission to Membership
Albania	January 25, 1946	December 14, 1955
Mongolian People's Republic	June 24, 1946	—
Jordan (Transjordan)	June 26, 1946	December 14, 1955
Afghanistan	July 2, 1946	November 9, 1946
Ireland	August 2, 1946	December 14, 1955
Portugal	August 2, 1946	December 14, 1955
Iceland	August 2, 1946	November 9, 1946
Thailand (Siam)	August 3, 1946[2]	December 15, 1946
Sweden	August 9, 1946	November 9, 1946
Hungary	April 22, 1947	December 14, 1955
Italy	May 7, 1947	December 14, 1955
Austria	July 2, 1947	December 14, 1955
Romania	July 10, 1947	December 14, 1955
Yemen	July 21, 1947	September 30, 1947
Bulgaria	July 26, 1947	December 14, 1955
Pakistan	August 15, 1947	September 30, 1947
Finland	September 19, 1947	December 14, 1955
Burma	February 27, 1948	May 11, 1949
Ceylon	May 25, 1948	December 14, 1955

[2] **Formal** application—an earlier communication regarding membership had been sent by Thailand (Siam) on May 20, 1946.

Application	Date of Submission of Application	Date of Admission to Membership
Republic of Korea	November 29, 1948	May 11, 1949
Israel	January 19, 1949	–
Democratic People's Republic of Korea	February 9, 1949	–
Nepal	February 13, 1949	December 14, 1955
Indonesia	September 25, 1950	September 28, 1950
Vietnam	December 17, 1951	–
Libya	December 24, 1951	December 14, 1955
Democratic Republic of Vietnam	(1) November 22, 1948[3] (2) December 29, 1951	–
Cambodia	June 15, 1952	December 14, 1955
Japan	June 16, 1952	–
Laos	June 20, 1952	December 14, 1955
Spain	September 22, 1955	December 14, 1955

BRIEF OUTLINE OF CONSIDERATION OF THE QUESTION OF ADMISSION OF NEW MEMBERS IN THE SECURITY COUNCIL AND IN THE GENERAL ASSEMBLY FROM 1946 TO DECEMBER 31, 1955. As a result of the deliberations of the Security Council on this question in 1946, Afghanistan, Iceland, Sweden and Thailand (Siam) were recommended by the Council and were admitted to membership by the General Assembly. Albania, the Mongolian People's Republic, Jordan (Transjordan), Ireland, and Portugal failed to obtain the recommendation of the Council, in the first two cases because the application did not obtain the requisite majority, and in the other three because of the negative vote of a permanent member of the Council (U.S.S.R.).

A similar situation resulted from reconsideration of these applications in 1947, in accordance with a request made by the General Assembly on November 19, 1946. Of the eight new applications received in 1947, Pakistan and Yemen obtained the recommendation of the Council, while of the remaining six, Hungary, Romania and Bulgaria failed to obtain the requisite majority; and Italy, Austria and Finland were not recommended because of the negative vote of a permanent member of the Council (U.S.S.R.). At its second regular session, on November 17, 1947, the General Assembly determined that in its judgment Ireland, Portugal, Jordan (Transjordan), Italy, Finland and Austria were peace-loving States within the meaning of Article 4 of the Charter and should therefore be admitted to membership. It requested the Council to reconsider those applications in the light of that determination and at the same time requested the permanent members of the Council to consult with a view to reaching agreement on the admission of the applicants which had not been recommended hitherto, and to submit their conclusions to the Council. The Assembly also requested the International Court of Justice to give an advisory opinion on whether a Member of the United Nations was juridically entitled to make its consent to the admission of a new Member dependent on conditions not expressly provided in the Charter—in particular, whether it could make its consent subject to the condition that other states be admitted at the same time.

On May 28, 1948, the Court decided, by a vote of 9 to 6, that a Member was not so entitled. (*See also page 308.*)

Reconsideration of the various pending applications in 1948 revealed no change in the positions of the members of the Security Council. However, of three new applications submitted in 1948, that of Burma obtained the recommendation of the Council. Ceylon failed to obtain the recommendation of the Council because

---

[3] Not circulated as a Council document until September 17, 1952.

of the negative vote of a permanent member (U.S.S.R.). The application of Israel, although it failed to obtain a recommendation in December 1948 when first considered, subsequently obtained the Council's recommendation in 1949.

At the first part of its third regular session in 1948, the General Assembly approved a number of resolutions on the admission of new Members, recommending that members of the Security Council and of the General Assembly in voting on applications for admission, should act in accordance with the advisory opinion given by the International Court of Justice. The Assembly requested the Council to reconsider individually the twelve pending applications, and also requested the Council to reconsider the applications of Finland, Ireland, Italy, Portugal and Jordan (Transjordan) in the light of the Court's advisory opinion and of the Assembly's determination that these countries fulfiled the requirements of Article 4 and should therefore be admitted. The Assembly also reaffirmed the view that opposition to those applications had been based on grounds not included in Article 4. It requested the Council to reconsider the application of Ceylon at the earliest possible moment in the light of the unanimous opinion revealed in Committee discussions that Ceylon fulfiled the requirements of the Charter and should be admitted.

The Council reconsidered the application of Ceylon on December 15, 1948, but failed to adopt a recommendation owing to the negative vote of a permanent member (U.S.S.R.).

None of the three new applications received in 1949 obtained the recommendation of the Council. The applications of the Republic of Korea and Nepal failed to obtain that recommendation owing to the negative vote of a permanent member (U.S.S.R.), while that of the Democratic People's Republic of Korea was not voted upon as such by the Council, which rejected a U.S.S.R. proposal to refer it to the Council's Committee on the Admission of New Members. Reexamination of the other pending applications in the course of 1949, revealed that the position of the members of the Council had not changed.

At its fourth session in 1949, the General Assembly once again requested the Council to reconsider nine applications which had obtained seven or more votes in the Council in the light of its determination or reaffirmation that they were qualified for admission and should be admitted. It requested the Council to keep under consideration the pending applications of all states which had not gained admission, and asked the permanent members of the Council to refrain from the use of the veto on recommendations of states for membership.

The Assembly also requested the International Court of Justice to give an advisory opinion on whether the admission of a state to membership could be effected by a decision of the General Assembly when the Security Council had made no recommendation because the candidate had failed to obtain the requisite majority or because of the negative vote of a permanent member.

By 12 votes to 2, the Court gave its opinion on March 3, 1950, that the admission of a state could not be so effected (*see also page 309*).

The only application discussed by the Council in 1950 was that of Indonesia, which obtained the Council's recommendation.

At its fifth session in 1950, the Assembly adopted a resolution recalling its previous resolutions and noting that no recommendations had been received from the Council for the admission of any of the other pending applications. It then asked the Council to keep the applications under consideration in accordance with the terms of the resolutions adopted in 1949.

The Council did not discuss the question of admission again prior to the sixth session of the General Assembly in 1951. At this session, the Assembly adopted, on December 7, 1951, a resolution on the question of the full participation of Italy in the work of the Trusteeship Council, in which it recommended that the Security Council urgently consider the question with a view to recommending Italy's immediate admission.

The Security Council took up this and previous resolutions at meetings held in December 1951 and in February 1952. A French draft resolution to recommend admission of Italy was not adopted because of the negative vote of a permanent member (U.S.S.R.). A U.S.S.R. draft resolution to recommend the simultaneous admission of fourteen applicants, including Italy, failed to obtain the necessary majority.

At the end of its sixth session, on February 1, 1952, the Assembly adopted two resolutions on the question of admission. Under the first, it declared that the judgment of the United Nations on the admission of new Members ought to be based exclusively on the conditions contained in Article 4, recommending that the Council reconsider all pending applications, taking into account such facts and evidence as applicants might present, and base its action exclusively on the conditions contained in the Charter and on the facts establishing the existence of those conditions; and requested the permanent members of the Council to confer with a view to assisting the Council to come to positive recommendations. Under the second resolution, the Assembly requested the Council to report to it at its seventh session on the status of applications still pending.

In the course of 1952, the Security Council considered six new applications, three of which were submitted in December 1951 and the remainder in 1952. Draft resolutions to recommend admission of Japan, Libya, Vietnam, Cambodia and Laos failed to obtain the recommendation of the Council owing to the negative vote of a permanent member (U.S.S.R.), and a draft resolution to recommend admission of the Democratic Republic of Vietnam failed to obtain the requisite majority. Consultations between the permanent members of the Council did not result in any change of position with regard to the other pending applications, and the Council again rejected a U.S.S.R. draft resolution to recommend the simultaneous admission of fourteen applicants. In its report to the General Assembly, the Council stated that it had not reconsidered two of the pending applications, those of the Republic of Korea and of the Democratic People's Republic of Korea. At the end of 1952, 21 applications were still pending.

At its seventh session, on December 21, 1952, the Assembly adopted seven resolutions on the admission of new Members, five of which requested the Council to take note of its determination that Japan, Vietnam, Cambodia, Laos and Libya were qualified for admission and should be admitted, while a sixth resolution reaffirmed a similar determination concerning Jordan.

By the other resolution the Assembly established a special committee, composed of representatives of nineteen Member States, which it instructed to make a detailed study of the problem of admission.

The Special Committee reviewed various proposals and suggestions advanced for solution of the question, but indicated in its report to the Assembly, approved on June 15, 1953, that it had appeared that none of them had been likely to secure general acceptance among its members.

The Security Council did not discuss the question of admission in 1953 or 1954.

At its eighth session, on October 23, 1953, the General Assembly unanimously adopted a resolution establishing a Committee of Good Offices, consisting of representatives of Egypt, the Netherlands and Peru, which it empowered to consult with members of the Council with the object of exploring the possibilities of reaching an understanding which would facilitate the admission of new Members in accordance with Article 4.

The Committee of Good Offices stated in its report, submitted on September 3, 1954, that although there appeared to be no fundamental change from formerly held positions by members of the Security Council, it did not consider that all possibilities of reaching an understanding had been exhausted, and considered that the Assembly should continue its efforts to facilitate a solution.

As a result of discussion at its ninth session, on December 11, 1954, the General Assembly adopted unanimously a resolution taking note of the Committee's views; sending back to the Security Council the pending applications for membership for further consideration and positive recommendations; and requesting the Council and the Committee of Good Offices to report to it during the ninth session if possible, and in any event, during the tenth session.

The Committee of Good Offices submitted a preliminary report on September 19, 1955. Although the positions of the permanent members of the Council remained the same, the Committee said, they had conveyed the impression that adherence to those positions was not necessarily immutable. The Committee also noted that there might be further improvements in the international atmosphere during the next few months and expressed its readiness to continue its efforts during the course of the tenth session.

At its tenth session, the General Assembly, on December 8, 1955, adopted a resolution by which, believing that a broader representation in the membership of the United Nations would enable the Organization to play a more effective role in the current international situation, it requested the Council to consider, in the light of the general opinion in favor of the widest possible membership of the United Nations, the pending applications for membership of all those eighteen countries about which no problem of unification arose, and further requested the Council to report on those applications during the tenth session.

The Security Council examined the recommendations adopted by the Assembly at its ninth and tenth sessions, as well as the application of Spain, at meetings held in the middle of December 1955. The Council voted first on a joint draft resolution embodying the Assembly's recommendation and listing the eighteen countries in question, namely, Albania, the Mongolian People's Republic, Jordan, Ireland, Portugal, Hungary, Italy, Austria, Romania, Bulgaria, Finland, Ceylon, Nepal, Libya, Cambodia, Japan, Laos and Spain. The Council decided that a Chinese amendment to include the Republics of Korea and Vietnam in this list should be voted upon immediately before the remainder of the list. These two countries were not included, since in each case negative votes were cast by a permanent member of the Council (U.S.S.R.). The Council then proceeded to vote individually on the inclusion of each of the other eighteen listed applicants. Albania, Hungary, Romania and Bulgaria were included. The remaining applicants were not included, owing to the negative vote of a permanent member (China, in the case of the Mongolian People's Republic, and the U.S.S.R. in the case of the others). The paragraph containing the list was then voted upon as modified and was not adopted.

On December 14, the Council voted on a similar draft resolution, submitted by the U.S.S.R., recommending to the General Assembly the admission of sixteen of the above eighteen listed applicants, and omitting the Mongolian People's Republic and Japan. A United States amendment to add the name of Japan was not adopted owing to the negative vote of a permanent member (U.S.S.R.). In the course of separate votes, each of the sixteen listed applicants was approved and the draft resolution as a whole was adopted.

On the same day, the General Assembly considered the recommendation of the Council, in the form of a joint draft resolution submitted by 42 Member States, which listed the sixteen countries recommended by the Council. Each of those countries was admitted by a separate vote, but the draft resolution was not put to the vote as a whole. Since there was no objection, the President declared the resolution adopted, note being taken of Cuba's abstention.

The Security Council continued, in the course of several meetings in December 1955, to discuss the applications of the Mongolian People's Republic and Japan. A United States draft resolution to recommend that Japan be admitted at the eleventh regular session of the Assembly was not adopted, owing to the negative vote of a permanent member (U.S.S.R.). A U.S.S.R. draft resolution to recommend that the Mongolian People's Republic and Japan be admitted at the eleventh session failed to obtain the necessary majority.

Questions Relating to Asia

THE INDONESIAN QUESTION

UKRAINIAN APPLICATION. The situation in Indonesia first came before the Security Council on January 21, 1946, when the Ukrainian S.S.R. charged that military action against the local population by British and Japanese forces threatened international peace and security. A Ukrainian proposal for an investigating commission was rejected, as was an Egyptian draft resolution declaring that British troops should not be used against the Indonesian national movement, and should be withdrawn after the complete surrender of the Japanese and the liberation of Allied prisoners of war and internees.

INDIAN AND AUSTRALIAN APPLICATION. On July 30, 1947, Australia and India drew the Council's attention to fighting between the Netherlands and the Republic of Indonesia. The Council, on August 1, called on both parties to cease hostilities. Shortly thereafter the parties issued cease-fire orders. Some fighting continued, however, and, on August 25, the Council called for joint reports by the consuls of its members in Batavia. It also offered its good offices in settling the political dispute through a committee, to consist of one Council member selected by each of the parties and a third chosen by these two. The members chosen were Australia (by the Republic of Indonesia), Belgium (by the Netherlands), and the United States (by Australia and Belgium).

As a result of negotiations conducted by this Good Offices Committee, the Netherlands and the Republic signed a truce agreement on January 17, 1948, and agreed on eighteen principles as the basis for a political settlement.

Subsequently, however, there were continuing difficulties in the negotiations, which were suspended. On November 15, the Committee notified the Council that there had been no progress toward a settlement; indeed, there had been an increase in political tension, and a rising strain on the truce.

On December 18, the Netherlands denounced the truce agreement and commenced military operations against the Republic. Meeting in emergency session, the Security Council on December 24, called for a cessation of hostilities forthwith and the immediate release of the President of the Republic of Indonesia and other political prisoners taken since the renewal of hostilities. Four days later, it again called on the Netherlands to release the President and the other political prisoners at once.

On January 28, 1948, the Council repeated its call to cease all military operations and for the release, immediately, of all political prisoners. It recommended the establishment of a federal, independent and sovereign United States of Indonesia at the earliest possible date (with transfer of sovereignty not later than July 1, 1950), and also converted the Committee of Good Offices to a United Nations

Commission for Indonesia, with power to assist the parties in implementing this resolution.

On March 2, the Netherlands notified the Council that it had lifted restrictions on the liberty of movement of the Republican leaders, and it proposed a Round Table Conference at The Hague as soon as possible to arrange for hastening the transfer of sovereignty.

Three weeks later, the Council directed the Commission to assist the parties in implementing the January 28 resolution and on arranging the time and conditions of the Conference. Accordingly, at the Commission's invitation, the Netherlands and Republican delegations met at Batavia, from April 14 to August 1, 1948, and agreed on the return of the Republican Government to Jogjakarta, on measures to be taken to halt guerrilla warfare and restore peace, on discontinuance of military operations by the Netherlands and the immediate and unconditional release of all political prisoners, and on the holding of a Round Table Conference.

Republican leaders returned to the capital on July 6. Evacuation by Dutch troops and occupation by Republican forces were completed under the observation of United Nations military observers. Orders to cease hostilities became effective on August 10 in Java, and on August 14 in Sumatra.

ROUND TABLE CONFERENCE AND SUBSEQUENT EVENTS. The Round Table Conference met at The Hague from August 23 to November 2, 1949. Participating were representatives of the Netherlands, the Republic of Indonesia, the Federal Consultative Assembly (representing areas of Indonesia other than the Republic), and the United Nations Commission for Indonesia.

The Conference drew up a Charter of the Transfer of Sovereignty, which stated that the Netherlands unconditionally and irrevocably transferred complete sovereignty over Indonesia to the Republic of the United States of Indonesia, and recognized the Republic as an independent and sovereign state. New Guinea, however, was to continue under the Netherlands, but within one year its political status was to be determined through negotiation between the Republic and the Netherlands.

The Conference also adopted a Statute establishing the Netherlands-Indonesian Union, the purpose of which was to insure the cooperation of Indonesia and the Netherlands, particularly in matters of foreign relations and defence and, as far as necessary, finance and economic and cultural questions. This cooperation would be on the basis of free will and equality in status, with equal rights.

The General Assembly in December 1949 welcomed the results of the Round Table Conference.

The agreements reached at the Round Table Conference were ratified by both Houses of the Netherlands States-General and by all Parliaments and representative bodies of the states and territories which were to become the Republic of the United States of Indonesia. The formal transfer of sovereignty to the Republic took place on December 27, 1949.

In the months that followed, the United Nations Commission continued to observe the implementation of the Hague agreements.

On September 28, 1950, on recommendation of the Security Council two days earlier, the General Assembly admitted the Republic of Indonesia to membership in the United Nations.

Then on April 6, 1951, the Commission informed the Security Council that, since no items remained on its agenda, it was adjourning *sine die*, while continuing to hold itself at the disposal of the parties.

THE QUESTION OF WEST IRIAN (West New Guinea)

On August 17, 1954, Indonesia requested the inclusion of "The question of West Irian (West New Guinea)" in the agenda of the General Assembly. In an explanatory memorandum, it was stressed that, historically as well as constitutionally, West Irian had always been an integral part of Indonesia and that, under Article 2 of the Charter of Transfer of Sovereignty by which the Netherlands had transferred "complete sovereignty over Indonesia", it had been agreed that the *status quo* of the residency of New Guinea should be maintained with the stipulation that, within a year following the transfer of sovereignty, the question of the political status of New Guinea should be determined through negotiations between the Republic of Indonesia and the Netherlands. Negotiations so far had been abortive, and finally in July 1954, the Netherlands had definitely refused even to enter into negotiations on the question. Indonesia considered the question a latent threat to the peace and security of that part of the world if it remained unsolved.

During the debate, the Netherlands stressed that its administration of West New Guinea constituted a peaceful endeavor to create conditions for the self-determination of the population. A threat to the peace could occur only if Indonesia were to resort to aggressive action. Furthermore, there was no provision in the Charter of Transfer of Sovereignty to the effect either that Netherlands sovereignty over the territory should cease at the end of the one-year period for negotiations, or that a change in the *status quo* should take place in case the negotiations did not result in an agreement. The Netherlands had negotiated beyond its obligations under the Charter of Transfer of Sovereignty, and had proposed a number of solutions, which had been rejected. The Netherlands had then come to the conclusion that the possibilities of further negotiations had been exhausted.

On November 30, 1954, the First Committee adopted a joint draft resolution which provided that the Assembly would: (1) express the hope that Indonesia and the Netherlands would pursue their endeavors to find a solution to the dispute in conformity with the principles of the United Nations Charter, and (2) request the parties to report progress to the Assembly's tenth session. The vote on the draft resolution was 34 to 14, with 10 abstentions.

The General Assembly voted on the draft resolution on December 10. As none of the parts of the draft resolution obtained the required two-thirds majority, it was not put to the vote as a whole, and the General Assembly took no decision with regard to the item.

The question was reintroduced at the tenth session by Afghanistan and fourteen other Members, on the ground that a second examination by the Assembly would assist the parties in reaching a peaceful solution.

The General Assembly on October 3, 1955, included the item in its agenda.

On December 16, the General Assembly adopted a resolution originally sponsored by Ecuador, India, New Zealand, Norway and Syria, by which it expressed the hope that the negotiations which would commence shortly between the Governments of Indonesia and the Netherlands would be fruitful.

THE KOREAN QUESTION

THE PROBLEM OF THE INDEPENDENCE OF KOREA (1947-1949). The problem of the independence of Korea was brought before the General Assembly by the United States in September 1947.

At the Cairo Conference in 1943, the independence of Korea was first stated formally as a war aim. After the surrender of Japan, Korea had been occupied by the

United States and the U.S.S.R. with the 38th parallel forming an artificial dividing line. Under the Moscow Agreement of December 1945, the occupying Powers established a Joint Commission to set up a "Provisional Korean Democratic Government". Thereafter the Joint Commission, with the participation of that Government, was to work out measures for a four-Power (the U.S.S.R., China, the United Kingdom and the United States) trusteeship of Korea for a period of up to five years. The Joint Commission's negotiations in 1946 and 1947 having reached a deadlock, the United States submitted the problem to the United Nations.

On November 14, 1947, the Assembly created a Temporary Commission on Korea of nine Member States to facilitate the establishment of a National Government of Korea by means of duly elected Korean representatives, and to provide for early withdrawal of the occupation forces. The U.S.S.R. and five other delegations did not participate in the voting which followed rejection of U.S.S.R. proposals to invite elected representatives from Southern and Northern Korea to take part in the discussion, and to recommend the simultaneous withdrawal of the United States and the U.S.S.R. troops, thereby leaving to the Korean people itself the establishment of a national government. The Ukrainian S.S.R. did not take its seat on the Commission.

Unable, because of the negative attitude of the U.S.S.R. to enter North Korea and so fulfil its task of observing Korea-wide elections, the Commission consulted, in February 1948, the Interim Committee, which directed it to implement the Assembly's program in such parts of Korea as were accessible to it. Accordingly, on May 10, 1948, in South Korea only, it observed elections which led on August 15, to the establishment of a government in South Korea. In September, a separate government came into being in North Korea.

After considering the Commission's report, the Assembly on December 12, 1948, declared that there had been established in South Korea a lawful government (the Government of the Republic of Korea), based on elections which expressed the free will of the electorate of that part of Korea, and that this was the only such Government in Korea.

The Assembly also recommended that the occupying Powers withdraw their forces, and since the objective of unification of all Korea had not been attained, set up a Commission on Korea of seven Member States to lend its good offices to that end.

On July 28, 1949, the Commission reported to the Assembly that it had not been able to make any progress toward unifying North and South Korea. It declared that without a new effort by the U.S.S.R. and the United States to reach agreement on Korea, no substantial progress could be made. It had observed the withdrawal in June 1949, of the United States occupation forces, but not the reported withdrawal of those of the U.S.S.R. in December 1948.

On October 21, 1949, the Assembly continued the Commission, with the added task of observing and reporting developments which might lead to military conflict in Korea. The Assembly had already rejected the proposal of the U.S.S.R. supported by five other Member States, to terminate the Commission, the creation of which they had opposed in 1948, and to recognize that the unification of Korea was the task of the Korean people itself, and that the establishment of the Commission was contrary to the right of the people to self-determination.

COMPLAINT OF AGGRESSION AGAINST THE REPUBLIC OF KOREA—1950. On June 25, 1950, the Secretary-General was informed both by the United States and the United Nations Commission on Korea that North Korean forces had that morning invaded the Republic. The United States considered the attack an act of aggression, and the

Commission reported that the situation was assuming the character of a full-scale war, endangering the maintenance of international peace and security. In its subsequent report to the fifth session, the Commission characterized the invasion as an act of aggression initiated without warning and without provocation in execution of a completely prepared plan.

That same day, the Security Council determined, by a vote of 9 to none, with 1 abstention (Yugoslavia), and 1 member (the U.S.S.R.) absent, (The U.S.S.R. had withdrawn in January 1950, stating that it would not recognize as legal any decisions of the Council until "the representative of the Kuomintang Group had been removed." The U.S.S.R. returned, however, on August 1, 1950.) that the armed attack was a breach of the peace, called for immediate cessation of hostilities, withdrawal of troops, and the assistance of Members in carrying out its resolution.

Two days later, on June 27, the Council adopted a United States draft resolution noting that the authorities in North Korea had neither ceased hostilities nor withdrawn their armed forces, and recommending that Members furnish such assistance to the Republic of Korea as might be necessary to repel the armed attack and restore international peace and security in the area. The vote was 7 to 1 (Yugoslavia), with 1 member (U.S.S.R.) absent, and with Egypt and India not voting, but later indicating their respective positions as abstention from and acceptance of the resolution.

ACTION TAKEN BY MEMBER STATES AND CREATION OF THE UNIFIED COMMAND. On June 27, the United States had announced that its air and sea force had been ordered to give cover and support to the troops of the Korean Government. Its fleet had been ordered to prevent any attack on Formosa, and the Chinese Government on Formosa had been called on to cease all air and sea operations against the mainland. The Council was further informed on June 30, that the United States had ordered a naval blockade of the Korean coast, and authorized the use of ground forces as a further response to the June 27 resolution.

While 51 Members subsequently expressed general support for the stand taken by the Council, five including the U.S.S.R., together with the People's Republic of China and the Korean People's Democratic Republic, shared the view that the June 27 resolution of the Council was illegal, since it had been adopted in the absence of two permanent members, the People's Republic of China and the U.S.S.R. The Soviet Union also declared that the events in Korea were the result of an unprovoked attack by South Korean troops, and demanded the cessation of American intervention.

On July 27, the Council, by 7 votes to none, with 3 abstentions (Egypt, India and Yugoslavia), 1 member being absent (the U.S.S.R.), requested all Member States providing military forces in pursuance of the Council's resolutions to make them available to a unified command under the United States. The next day President Truman of the United States designated General Douglas MacArthur as Commanding General. Subsequently combatant units were provided by the following sixteen Member States: Australia, Belgium, Canada, Colombia, Ethiopia, France, Greece, Luxembourg, the Netherlands, New Zealand, the Philippines, Thailand, Turkey, the Union of South Africa, the United Kingdom and the United States. In addition, five nations—Denmark, India, Italy, Norway and Sweden—supplied medical units. The Republic of Korea also placed all its military forces under the Unified Command.

ESTABLISHMENT OF THE COMMISSION FOR THE UNIFICATION AND REHABILITATION OF KOREA (UNCURK). The capital of Korea, Seoul, fell on June 28, and in August, the United Nations forces were confined within the small Taegu-Pusan defence perimeter in south-east Korea, but by October, a surprise amphibious landing at Inchon reoccupied Seoul and enveloped the North Korean forces south of the 38th parallel. By mid-October almost all territory formerly comprising the Republic of Korea had been secured, and forces of the United Nations Command were advancing far into North Korea.

Meanwhile, on October 7, during consideration of the question of the independence of Korea (*see page 88*), the General Assembly adopted a resolution which recommended that "all appropriate steps be taken to insure conditions of stability throughout Korea", established the United Nations Commission for the Unification and Rehabilitation of Korea (UNCURK) of seven Member States to represent the United Nations in bringing about the establishment of a unified independent and democratic government of all Korea, and recommended that the United Nations forces should not remain in Korea otherwise than so far as necessary for the objectives stated, and that all necessary measures be taken to accomplish the economic rehabilitation of Korea. (*See page 89.*)

CHINESE INTERVENTION AND GENERAL ASSEMBLY ACTION. On November 6, a special report from the United Nations Command informed the Security Council that United Nations forces were in contact in North Korea with Chinese Communist military units. A representative of the People's Republic of China participated in the Council's subsequent combined discussion of complaints of armed aggression against the Republic of Korea and of armed invasion of Taiwan (Formosa) (*for the latter, see page 102*). On November 30, because of the negative vote of a permanent member, the Council did not adopt a resolution calling on all states and authorities to refrain from assisting the North Korean authorities and to prevent their nationals from giving assistance, and affirming that it was the policy of the United Nations to hold the Chinese frontier with Korea inviolate and fully to protect legitimate Chinese and Korean interests in the frontier zone. The Council rejected by a vote of 1 (U.S.S.R.) to 9, with India not participating, a draft resolution condemning the United States for armed aggression against Chinese territory and armed intervention in Korea, and demanding withdrawal of its forces.

During the previous August and September, following the return to the Council on August 1 of the representative of the U.S.S.R., the Council failed after lengthy debates to reach any substantive decisions on the Korean question. A United States proposal to condemn the North Korean authorities for continued defiance of the United Nations failed because of the U.S.S.R. negative vote. The Council rejected various U.S.S.R. proposals concerning invitations to representatives of the Chinese People's Republic and the Korean people, withdrawal of foreign troops from Korea, and cessation of United States bombing of Korean towns and the territory of China.

Against this background, the Council, on January 31, 1951, unanimously removed from its agenda the item "Complaint of aggression upon the Republic of Korea", since the General Assembly, which already had on its agenda the continuing item "The problem of the independence of Korea", had on December 6, 1950, admitted to its agenda the item "Intervention of the Central People's Government of the People's Republic of China in Korea". Thereafter the Assembly dealt with items relating to Korea covering the military, economic and political aspects of the United Nations action there, including efforts for a cessation of hostilities and the peaceful settlement of the Korean and related problems.

In its December discussions, the First Committee of the General Assembly gave priority to an Asian-Arab thirteen-Power draft resolution adopted on December 14, which established a three-man Cease-Fire Group (the President of the Assembly, Canada and India) to recommend satisfactory cease-fire arrangements in Korea.

On January 13, it transmitted to the People's Republic of China the Cease-Fire Group's program which aimed at achieving by successive stages a cease-fire in Korea.

After discussion of the Chinese reply, the Assembly on February 1, 1951, adopted a resolution which noted that the Chinese People's Government had not accepted the United Nations proposals to end hostilities, and found that it had engaged in aggression in Korea, called on it to cause its forces and nationals to withdraw from Korea, requested a committee (the Additional Measures Committee) to consider additional measures for meeting the aggression, reaffirmed the policy of achieving United Nations objectives in Korea by peaceful means, and created a Good Offices Committee (the President of the Assembly, Sweden and Mexico) to further those ends.

In the absence of a satisfactory progress report from the Good Offices Committee, the Assembly on May 18, on the basis of a report from the Additional Measures Committee, recommended that every state should apply an embargo on the shipment to areas under the control of the Chinese Central People's Government and of the North Korean authorities of arms, ammunition and implements of war, items useful in their production, petroleum, and transportation materials.

The U.S.S.R. and four other Members did not participate in the voting on the ground that the matter was exclusively within the jurisdiction of the Security Council.

ARMISTICE NEGOTIATIONS, 1951-1953. Subsequent to the appearance of the Chinese communist troops, the United Nations Command had been forced to withdraw south of Seoul, but by March 1951, had again advanced to a line across central Korea near the 38th parallel.

On June 23, 1951, in a radio address in New York, the representative of the U.S.S.R. suggested discussions between the belligerents as a first step towards a settlement of the armed conflict in Korea. By July 10, delegations representing the United Nations Command and the Chinese-North Korean Commanders had opened negotiations.

On October 18, 1952, the Unified Command informed the Assembly that in the fifteen months of negotiations a tentative draft armistice agreement covering all agreed points had been worked out by both sides. The differences preventing the conclusion of an armistice had been narrowed by April 1952, to one question whether all prisoners of war should be returned, by force if necessary. The United Nations Command was willing to return all except those who would violently resist repatriation. The North Koreans and Chinese, however, had insisted on the return of all prisoners. A total of about 132,000 prisoners were involved—121,000 held by the United Nations Command and 11,500 reported by the other side. On October 8, the truce negotiations had recessed indefinitely.

Meanwhile the forces of sixteen Members of the United Nations and the Republic of Korea had been engaged in operations against an army of more than 1,000,000 men, mainly Chinese, which had at its disposal more than 2,000 planes mostly based in Manchuria from which, the Command said, they attacked United Nations aircraft operating within Korea. Neither side, it was said, had undertaken sustained offensive action since the opening of armistice negotiations. However, there had been constant and often heavy military contact. In an August 1953 report to the Security Council concerning the Armistice Agreement, the Unified Command estimated the casualties of the 37 months of fighting in Korea as in excess of 300,000 casualties for the armed forces of the Republic of Korea, some 141,000 for the United States, and 14,000 for the other fifteen Member States, while casualties of the other side were estimated between 1,500,000 to 2,000,000.

In the face of the deadlocked negotiations, the lengthy Assembly debate at the seventh session centered on a draft resolution submitted by India presenting a formula, finally accepted, on December 3, 1952, as a just basis for an immediate cease-fire. It consisted of two basic affirmations, and an implementing course of action. First, the release and repatriation of prisoners should be in accordance with the Geneva Convention of 1949, and the principles of international law, and second, force should not be used against the prisoners "to prevent or effect" return to their homelands. U.S.S.R. amendments were rejected, including one eliminating the provision that force should not be used to prevent or effect the return of prisoners to their homelands.

Within two weeks, the Chinese and North Koreans had rejected the proposals. Finally, an agreement on the exchange of sick and wounded prisoners in April 1953, led to reopening of negotiations and settlement on June 8, 1953, of the larger question of repatriation of all prisoners. The prisoner-of-war agreement which was incorporated in the Armistice Agreement provided for a United Nations Repatriation Commission of Czechoslovakia, India (Chairman), Poland, Sweden and Switzerland to take custody of all prisoners who did not exercise their right to be repatriated; to arrange within 90 days for explanation to the prisoners, by representatives of their home countries, of their rights of repatriation; to refer then the question of prisoners who had not exercised their right of repatriation to a political conference, recommended in the Armistice Agreement, which would try to settle the question within 30 days; to release to civilian status 120 days after assumption of custody any prisoners who had not exercised their right to be repatriated and for whom the conference had agreed on no other disposition; and to assist any prisoners who wished to go to neutral nations. No force or threat of force was to be used against the prisoners.

The unilateral release on June 18, of 27,000 prisoners by the Republic of Korea Government from prisoner-of-war camps on the South Korean mainland delayed the armistice until that Government had assured the Unified Command that it would not obstruct its implementation. The Armistice Agreement was signed on July 27, 1953, by the Commanders of the United Nations Command, the Korean People's Army and the Chinese People's Volunteers, and hostilities ceased. The Agreement established a demarcation line and demilitarized zone; provided that no reinforcing personnel or combat equipment be introduced except on a replacement basis; set up a Military Armistice Commission of representatives from the two sides to supervise and settle any violations of the Agreement, and a Neutral Nations Supervisory Commission of four, Sweden and Switzerland appointed by the United Nations Command, and Czechoslovakia and Poland by the other side, to observe and investigate troop withdrawals and weapons replacement; recommended to the Governments of the countries concerned a political conference within three months to settle through negotiation the question of the withdrawal of all foreign forces from Korea, the peaceful settlement of the Korean question, etc.; and, declared that the agreement would remain in effect until superseded by mutually acceptable changes or by provision in an agreement for a peaceful settlement at a political level between both sides.

Shortly thereafter, the sixteen Powers contributing forces to United Nations action in Korea affirmed their determination to carry out the Armistice Agreement, and promptly to resist in case of renewal of armed attack, the grave consequences of which it would probably not be possible to confine within Korea.

THE QUESTION OF A POLITICAL CONFERENCE. On August 28, 1953, the General Assembly reaffirmed that the objective of the United Nations remained the achievement by peaceful means of a unified, independent and democratic Korea under a representative form of government, and the full restoration of peace in the area, and recommended that on one side of the political conference envisaged in the Armistice Agreement should participate those Member States and the Republic of Korea contributing armed forces under the Unified Command. The participation of the U.S.S.R. in the Conference was also provided for. The Assembly rejected a U.S.S.R. proposal for a conference of broader composition.

In September, the People's Republic of China and North Korea rejected the Assembly's proposal. Subsequent negotiations on the conference between the two sides at Panmunjom broke down in December. On February 23, 1954, however, it was announced, following a meeting in Berlin of the Foreign Ministers of France, the U.S.S.R., the United Kingdom and the United States, that they would convene a conference at Geneva, for the purpose of reaching a peaceful settlement of the Korean question, of representatives of their governments, the People's Republic of China, North and South Korea, and other countries whose armed forces had participated in the Korean hostilities.

The Conference failed to find an agreed solution to the Korean question. On November 11, fifteen of the sixteen Members of the United Nations which had participated in the Korean action and had been present at Geneva reported that the failure of the Conference did not prejudice the Armistice which remained in effect. The report included a declaration, to which the Republic of Korea was an additional signatory, of two principles: (1) The United Nations, under its Charter, is fully and rightfully empowered to take collective action to repel aggression, to restore peace and security, and to extend its good offices in seeking a peaceful settlement in Korea. (2) In order to establish a unified, independent and democratic Korea, genuinely free elections, under United Nations supervision, should be held to constitute the Korean National Assembly, in which representation should be in direct proportion to the indigenous population in Korea. So long as the other side rejected those principles, further consideration of the Korean question at the Conference was futile.

No progress has yet been reported in solving the impasse reached at Geneva, but the Armistice Agreement remains in effect. Meanwhile, the Republic of Korea has continued to allege a military build-up in North Korea, and to criticize the Armistice Agreement and the Neutral Nations Supervisory Commission (NNSC) which it states has been rendered impotent in the north. The build-up has been denied by the other side, which has insisted that the Armistice Agreement and the NNSC be maintained.

THE QUESTION OF THE INDEPENDENCE OF KOREA (1950-1955). During the continuation of the Korean conflict, the General Assembly took a number of decisions on the question of Korean independence which had been before it since 1947. (*See above.*)

The Commission on the Unification and Rehabilitation of Korea (UNCURK), consisting of seven Member States, was set up on October 7, 1950, to represent the United Nations in bringing about the establishment of a unified independent and democratic Government of all Korea, to exercise certain responsibilities in connection with the economic rehabilitation of Korea, and to assume the functions of the former Commission on Korea.

In subsequent annual reports, UNCURK informed the Assembly that the changed circumstances resulting from the intervention of the Chinese People's Volunteers in the autumn of 1950, made impossible the achievement of the Assembly's fundamental objectives, and thus narrowed the scope of the Commission's activities. In its 1954 and 1955 reports, the Commission declared that it was unable to contribute to the realization of the unification of Korea. It continued to represent the United Nations in Korea, to observe and report political and economic developments in the Republic of Korea, and to advise the United Nations Korean Reconstruction Agency (UNKRA) (*see below*). With a view to adapting its procedures to current circumstances, the Commission decided to establish as of January 1, 1956, a committee of four of its members to act on its behalf when the full Commission was not meeting.

While deferring consideration of the question at its sixth and eighth sessions, the Assembly adopted resolutions at its seventh, ninth and tenth sessions. On each occasion, the Republic of Korea was invited to participate, but proposals by the U.S.S.R. and some other members to invite the People's Republic of China and the Democratic People's Republic of Korea to participate were rejected. U.S.S.R. proposals to terminate UNCURK, which it deemed illegally established and useless, were rejected at the seventh and ninth sessions.

In its resolution of November 29, 1955, the Assembly, recalling that in December 1954 it had approved the report of the fifteen Governments participating in the Geneva Conference on behalf of the United Nations, reaffirmed the intention expressed at the ninth session to seek an early solution of the Korean question in accordance with the expressed objectives of the United Nations.

At the ninth and tenth sessions, the U.S.S.R., among others, considered the Geneva Conference report biased and incapable of serving as a basis of a solution. They supported a program for unification calling for free elections, under international supervision, in the whole of Korea on the basis of an agreement between North and South Korea to be concluded at an all-Korean conference, and the withdrawal of all foreign troops before the elections.

RELIEF AND REHABILITATION OF KOREA. Following the resolve of the United Nations to repel aggression in Korea, and as a consequence of the hostilities that ravaged the country, the task of rehabilitating Korea became a United Nations responsibility. Furthermore, relief to several hundreds of thousands of refugees seeking protection within areas controlled by the United Nations Command had to be provided.

On July 31, 1950, the Security Council inaugurated an emergency program for civilian relief through the Unified Command, with the Secretary-General and later the Agent-General of UNKRA acting as clearing agents for requests and offers of assistance. With contributions valued at nearly $50,000,000 from some 32 Member States, seven non-member states, specialized agencies and non-governmental organizations, and, in particular, assistance valued at over $400,000,000 from the United States, the Unified Command carried out by September 1953, through a Civil Assistance Command, a large-scale civilian and refugee relief program.

On December 1, 1950, the Assembly established the United Nations Korean Reconstruction Agency (UNKRA), under an Agent-General, responsible for a broad relief and rehabilitation program estimated by the Economic and Social Council to require not less than $250,000,000 for an initial period of somewhat more than twelve months from January 1, 1951. To finance the program, a Negotiating Committee was created to ascertain available voluntary contributions, and an Advisory Committee to advise the Agent-General, who was also to consult with and be guided by UNCURK on certain policy questions.

In a June 1953 report on the work of UNKRA since February 1951, the Agent-General stated that the continuance of hostilities had made it impossible for the Agency to carry out adequately its mandate. The Agency had been organized and a limited operational program had been carried out up to September 1952, and longer-term planning undertaken. The Agency had agreed with the United Nations Command to assume full responsibility six months after cessation of hostilities. A $70,000,000 relief and rehabilitation program had been approved by the Advisory Committee for the period ending June 30, 1953, but only some $50,000,000 had been obligated by that date, because of delay in the availability of funds. In a September report to the eighth session of the Assembly, the Agent-General announced that after the Armistice a coordinated plan of reconstruction consistent with UNKRA's responsibilities to the United Nations had been developed in which the Republic of Korea, the Unified Command and UNKRA would participate. Fields of responsibility had been assigned under which UNKRA was charged, broadly speaking, with long-term reconstruction, while the Civil Assistance Command continued largely responsible for health, transportation, communications, the provision of food, fertilizer and other essential raw materials. The report estimated the total cost of eventual Korean rehabilitation at more than $1,000,000,000 in external aid.

At the eighth session, the Agent-General appealed for more funds, stating that of $207,000,000 pledged, some with certain percentage limitations, only $88,000,000 had been received. On December 7, 1953, the Assembly approved the UNKRA program, and urged payment of pledges already made and contributions from those which had not already made them. In December 1954, the Assembly commended the excellent progress made by the Agency, and make a similar appeal for funds.

In further progress reports to the ninth and tenth sessions of the Assembly, the Agent-General described the achievements of the UNKRA program in its first two years of effective operations, and their very substantial contributions to the economy of the Republic of Korea. By June 30, 1955, out of the $139,000,000 received in contributions, some $121,000,000 had been obligated, and another $12,000,000 allocated under the 1953, 1954 and 1955 programs. UNKRA's areas of responsibility had had to be considerably reduced because of shortage of funds. Operational activity, however, had been brought to full tide, and a timetable for the completion of all projects established, with the majority to be finished by the end of 1956, and a few larger ones to carry on possibly into 1958.

Much of the planning, procurement and technical assistance of past years had borne fruit, and, because of emphasis on capital investment, had provided a considerable addition to Korean production, particularly in the fields of coal mining, cement, textiles, fisheries, and also to the Korean health and educational systems. Sustaining commodity imports, including food, fertilizer and raw materials, had been designed to finance local currency costs of its investment project program.

More than half of the projects on over 3,800 sites in all provinces in South Korea had been completed. The broad range of its activity included cement plants; a flat glass plant; important textile industry assistance making Korea self-sufficient; substantial coal-mining equipment and engineering aid to expand production; a mineral assay laboratory and a metal mine school; transportation and electric power facilities; irrigation and flood control; lumber; equipment; refrigeration and canning facilities and new trawlers for the fishing industry; pilot housing projects employing the earthblock construction process; the rehabilitation and restoration of schools, laboratories and experimental stations; orphanages; a large textbook printing plant; a teacher-training and vocational educational program; medical colleges and hospital restoration and technical medical aid; health, sanitation and welfare work in cooperation with the United Nations Civil Assistance Command; a community development employment program; and assistance to the useful work of voluntary agencies.

In October 1955, the Assembly commended UNKRA for the excellent progress made in assisting the Korean people to relieve their sufferings and to repair the devastation caused by aggression, and stressed that its program should be expeditiously implemented to the maximum extent possible within available funds.

OTHER MATTERS RELATED TO KOREA CONSIDERED BY THE SECURITY COUNCIL AND THE GENERAL ASSEMBLY (1950-1955). During and after the hostilities in Korea, the United Nations dealt with several questions related to the United Nations action.

The Security Council on July 7, 1950, authorized the Unified Command at its discretion to use the United Nations flag in the course of operations against North Korean forces concurrently with the flags of the various nations participating.

The General Assembly on December 12, 1950, requested the Secretary-General to arrange with the Unified Command for the design and award of a distinguishing ribbon or other insignia for personnel which had participated in Korea in the defence of the Principles of the Charter of the United Nations.

In December 1952, the Assembly rejected a U.S.S.R. draft resolution condemning the United States for the criminal acts involved in the alleged mass murder in prison camps, by American guards, of Korean and Chinese prisoners of war who were demanding repatriation.

The alleged use of bacteriological warfare by the United Nations forces in Korea was discussed in the summer of 1952 by the Security Council, and at its seventh and eighth sessions by the General Assembly. No investigation took place. (*See page 105.*)

At the request of the United States, the eighth session of the Assembly also discussed the question of alleged atrocities committed in Korea, contrary to the Geneva Conventions, against some 38,000 military and civilian victims by Chinese and North Korean forces. The Assembly in December 1953, expressed grave concern at reports of inhuman practices employed against soldiers of the United Nations Command and against the civil population of Korea, and condemned the commission by any governments of any such acts as a violation of international law and of the basic standards of morality.

In February 1954, the Neutral Nations Repatriation Commission, appointed under the Armistice Agreement, submitted a final report on its operations. This report and a subsequent one from the United Nations Command were circulated to all Member States.

By September 23, 1953, the commission had assumed custody from the United Nations Command and that of the Korean People's Army and the Chinese People's Volunteers of, respectively, 22,604 and 359 prisoners who had not exercised their right of repatriation. Because, at the end of the 90-day period allotted for explanation of the right of repatriation, the Political Conference envisaged in the Armistice Agreement had not materialized, the Commission referred to the two Commands the question of disposition of those prisoners who had not exercised their right of repatriation. Before the Commission dissolved itself on February 21, 1954, the Custodial Force, India, had restored to the United Nations Command on January 21, 21,805 prisoners, some two-thirds Chinese and one-third Korean, without, however, declaring their civilian status. On January 23, that Command released these former prisoners to civilian status. On January 28, the Custodial Force released to Red Cross representatives the 347 South Korean and United Nations Command prisoners who had refused to return to the control of that Command. Eighty-eight prisoners elected to proceed to neutral countries and were sent to India to remain under that Government's protection pending a decision on their final disposition.

At the request of India, that problem was discussed at the tenth session of the Assembly, which on November 29, 1955, adopted a resolution noting with appreciation that Argentina and Brazil had offered to resettle as many of the ex-prisoners who so opted and requesting other Member Governments to accept for settlement those not covered by present offers.

On December 4, 1954, the United States Government, as the Unified Command of the United Nations forces in Korea, complained of detention and imprisonment of United Nations military personnel in violation of the Korean Armistice Agreement. A memorandum explained that in January 1953 a United States aircraft had been shot down and its crew of eleven taken prisoner, and sentenced to long imprisonment in November 1954 by a Chinese Communist military tribunal. On December 10, the Assembly resolved that the detention and imprisonment of the eleven American airmen and of all other captured personnel of the United Nations Command desiring repatriation was a violation of the Armistice Agreement and asked the Secretary-General to seek their release.

After establishing in January 1955 personal contact in Peking with the Foreign Minister of the People's Republic of China, the Secretary-General continued his efforts. On September 9, his report to the Assembly on the question referred to messages he had received from the Foreign Minister announcing the release in May and August of groups of four and eleven American airmen.

On December 15, 1955, the General Assembly decided that the cemetery at Tanggok, near Pusan, in the Republic of Korea, should be established and maintained as a United Nations Memorial Cemetery in Korea in honor of the dead.

THE INDIA-PAKISTAN QUESTION

On January 1, 1948, India reported to the Security Council that tribesmen and others had been invading the State of Jammu and Kashmir and that extensive fighting was taking place.

Jammu and Kashmir was an Indian princedom which, under the scheme of partition and the Indian Independence Act of 1947, became free to accede to India or Pakistan. It borders on both India and Pakistan. After the invasion had begun, the Maharajah of the State requested accession to India, which India accepted on the understanding that, once normal conditions were restored, the question of accession "should be settled by a reference to the people."

India complained that Pakistan was assisting and participating in the invasion and thus was guilty of aggression. Pakistan contended that it had done everything short of war to discourage the tribal movement and declared that the accession to India was illegal. Both agreed that the situation between them might lead to a breach of international peace.

SECURITY COUNCIL ACTION. On January 20, the Council established a Commission of three members for investigation and mediation, to act first on the Jammu and Kashmir situation and, when so directed by the Council, on other situations complained of by Pakistan.

India subsequently nominated Czechoslovakia to the Commission, and Pakistan nominated Argentina. When these two States failed to agree on the third member, the President of the Council (on May 7) designated the United States. Meanwhile, on April 21, the Council decided to increase the membership to five and added Belgium and Colombia two days later.

In addition to the meetings of the Council to consider the question, numerous private consultations were held by the delegations of India and Pakistan at the instigation of the Council and under the guidance of its successive monthly Presidents. Finally, on April 21, the Council adopted a resolution, despite opposition to many of its provisions by both India and Pakistan, declaring that the dispute of Jammu and Kashmir was likely to endanger international peace and security. It therefore recommended what it regarded as appropriate measures to stop the fighting, and to create proper conditions for a free and impartial plebiscite. To assist in carrying out these measures, it instructed its Commission "to proceed at once to the Indian sub-continent and there place its good offices and mediation at the disposal of the Governments of India and Pakistan."

In the meantime, the Council heard statements by India and Pakistan on other matters included in the Pakistan complaint, and on June 3 it directed the India-Pakistan Commission to proceed without delay to the areas of dispute with a view to "accomplishing in priority" the duties assigned to it in connection with Jammu and Kashmir; and, further, to study and report, when it considered it appropriate, on the other matters.

WORK OF THE COMMISSION. The Commission arrived on the sub-continent on July 7, 1948, and on August 13, proposed that both Governments issue cease-fire orders at the earliest possible date to apply to all forces under their control in Jammu and Kashmir, and to accept certain principles as the basis for a truce agreement. These included: (1) that Pakistan would withdraw its troops recently stationed in the State and do its best to secure the withdrawal of tribesmen and Pakistan nationals not normally resident there; (2) that, pending a final solution, the territory evacuated by the troops would be administered by the local authorities under the surveillance of the Commission; (3) that, when the Commission notified India that Pakistan was complying with these terms, India would begin to withdraw the bulk of its forces in stages to be agreed on with the Commission; and (4) that, pending the acceptance of conditions for final settlement, the Indian Government would maintain within the lines existing at the moment of cease-fire those forces considered necessary to assist local authorities in observing law and order.

India, after a clarification of certain points, accepted the resolution. Pakistan, however, informed the Commission that it could not accept without certain reservations, in particular concerning the organization of a plebiscite. The Commission reported in September that it had temporarily exhausted possibilities of further negotiations.

The Security Council considered the report on November 25 in Paris, informed the Commission of its full support, and endorsed its appeal to India and Pakistan to refrain from any action which might aggravate the situation. Informal conversations with the parties then took place on the conditions and basic principles which should govern the plebiscite.

As a result, the Commission proposed to the Governments that the accession of the State would be decided by a free and impartial plebiscite; that the Secretary-General would nominate, in agreement with the Commission, a Plebiscite Administrator who would be a person of high international standing and who would derive from the Government of Jammu and Kashmir the powers which the Administrator considered necessary to organize and conduct a free and impartial plebiscite.

Both Governments accepted the proposals, with clarifications and understandings, and ordered a cease-fire as from January 1, 1949. On January 5, the Commission adopted a formal resolution embodying the proposals. It then appointed observers from various nations to report on the observance of the cease-fire agreement. On July 27, an agreement was reached on a cease-fire line, which was ratified by India and Pakistan a few days later.

Meanwhile, Fleet Admiral Chester W. Nimitz, U.S.N., was nominated Plebiscite Administrator by the Secretary-General in March. He was to be formally appointed by the Government of Jammu and Kashmir when the details of the plebiscite were settled after the acceptance of a truce agreement.

On April 15, the Commission presented simultaneously to both Governments its proposals for implementation of the truce agreement, emphasizing withdrawal on the entire cease-fire line, including the line in the northern frontier areas. After considering the replies, the Commission on April 28 presented its final terms and asked for unreserved acceptance. The replies did not constitute acceptance, however. Resorting to another procedure, then, the Commission later invited India and Pakistan to joint meetings at ministerial level, but abandoned the idea in the face of disagreement on the agenda.

As a final effort, the Commission asked the parties whether they would agree to submit the points at issue to arbitration, but this was not acceptable to India. In the circumstances, the Commission decided to report to the Council.

The Commission recommended that the Council designate an individual rather than a five-member body to bring the two Governments together on all unresolved issues. A minority report by the Czechoslovak member favored a new mediation effort by a Commission consisting of all the members of the Council.

After considering the Commission's report, the President, as instructed by the Council on December 17, 1949, held informal discussions with the parties, during which he submitted proposals calling for an agreed program of progressive demilitarization preparatory to the plebiscite, to be supervised by a United Nations Representative appointed by the Secretary-General in agreement with the two Governments. When the program was accomplished to the satisfaction of the Representative, the Plebiscite Administrator was to exercise the functions assigned to him. The proposals were still unacceptable to the Governments of India and Pakistan, and the now former President reported in February 1950 that no useful purpose could be served by continued activity on his part.

APPOINTMENT OF UNITED NATIONS REPRESENTATIVE. On March 14, the Council called on India and Pakistan to prepare and execute within five months a program of demilitarization based on the proposals. A United Nations Representative (Sir Owen Dixon, of Australia, was later appointed) was to assist in the realization of this program. Among other things, he was to exercise the powers of the United Nations Commission and, at the appropriate stage of demilitarization, to arrange for the Plebiscite Administrator to assume his functions.

On September 15, 1950, Sir Owen reported that no agreement had been reached on demilitarization and on preparations for the holding of a plebiscite. He recommended that the Council should press for a reduction in the military strength holding the cease-fire line to the normal protection of a peacetime frontier, as he considered the continued maintenance of such armies to be fraught with dangerous possibilities. He asked also to be relieved of his position.

After resuming consideration of this question on February 21, 1951, the Council provided on March 30, that a new Representative (Dr. Frank P. Graham of the United States was later appointed) should, after consultation with India and Pakistan, effect demilitarization on the basis of the Commission resolutions of August 13, 1948, and January 5, 1949. If, within three months of his arrival on the sub-continent, he had not done so or had not obtained the agreement of the parties to a plan for doing so, he should then report to the Council those points of difference regarding the interpretation and execution of the Commission resolutions which he considered had to be resolved for demilitarization to be carried out.

Further, the Council called on the parties, in the event of failure to reach full agreement, to accept arbitration on all outstanding points of difference. The arbitrator or panel of arbitrators would be appointed by the President of the International Court of Justice after consultation with the parties.

In a later development, on May 29, the Council approved the transmission of a cablegram to India and Pakistan recalling the March 30 resolution, and expressing the hope that they would do everything in their power to insure that the authorities in Kashmir did not disregard the Council, or act in a manner which would prejudice the determination of the future accession of the State in accordance with the procedures provided for in the resolutions of the Council and of the Commission. This decision followed representations by Pakistan regarding press reports that a proclamation had been issued on April 30 for convoking a Constituent Assembly in the State, and a reported statement by the Prime Minister of Jammu and Kashmir that that Assembly was being convened to decide the future of Kashmir and that no power could veto its decision.

THE TWELVE PROPOSALS. Dr. Graham arrived on the sub-continent on June 30, 1951, and personally presented his report to the Council on October 18. The report showed that twelve draft proposals had been submitted to the two Governments. Both Governments had accepted the general principles set forth in the first four proposals—reaffirmation of their determination not to resort to force over Kashmir, agreement to take measures to avoid warlike statements regarding that question, reaffirmation of their will to observe the cease-fire, and reaffirmation of their acceptance of the principle that the question of the accession of the State would be decided through a free and impartial plebiscite under the auspices of the United Nations.

Agreement had not been reached on the fifth proposal providing that the demilitarization of the State contemplated in the United Nations Commission in India and Pakistan (UNCIP) resolutions of August 13, 1948, and January 5, 1949, should be effected in a single, continuous process, nor on the remaining seven proposals setting forth the principles for a plan of demilitarization to be completed during a period of 90 days.

Dr. Graham analyzed the main differences on those eight points and concluded that, although he did not underestimate the difficulties, "the possibility of arriving at a basis of agreement between the two Governments is not excluded."

Dr. Graham's recommendations were that the Council should call on the two Governments to take measures to improve relations by avoiding any increase of military potential in the State and by curbing warlike statements; that the Council should consider a renewed effort to bring about agreement and, if it decided on this, it might instruct the Representative to continue negotiations for six weeks, to take place in Paris.

In Paris, in November 1951, the Council instructed Dr. Graham to continue his efforts to obtain agreement on a plan for demilitarization and to report within six weeks.

SECOND REPORT. In a second report on December 18, 1951, Dr. Graham said that the parties had agreed to four more proposals dealing with the process of demilitarization. These were designed to insure that the demilitarization would not involve a threat to the cease-fire agreement; that representatives of the two Governments would meet, under the auspices of the United Nations, to draw up the demilitarization program in accordance with agreed provisions; that completion of demilitarization would be without prejudice to the functions and responsibilities of the

Representative's Military Adviser, and, if disagreement continued, to the Representative, whose decision would be final.

Agreement had not been reached, however, on the four most basic proposals, Dr. Graham reported.

After discussion at three meetings of the Security Council, the President of the Council stated on January 31, 1952, that it was the sense of the Council, with the exception of the representative of the U.S.S.R., that the United Nations Representative, acting under the Council's resolutions of March 30 and November 10, 1951, was authorized, without any new decisions by the Council, to continue his efforts to fulfil his mission and to submit a report, which the Council hoped would be final, within two months.

THIRD REPORT. On April 22, 1952, Dr. Graham transmitted a third report which dealt with discussions held with representatives of India and Pakistan up to the time of his departure from the sub-continent on March 25. He reported that the chief remaining obstacle was the difference over the number and character of the forces to be left on each side of the cease-fire line at the end of the period of demilitarization. Pakistan had accepted, with certain qualifications regarding the character of the forces to be demilitarized, all twelve proposals. India had maintained that, if agreement could be reached on the issues of the number and character of the forces to be left on each side of the cease-fire line, the other two remaining differences, concerning the period of demilitarization and the induction into office of the Plebiscite Administrator, could be solved without difficulty.

Substantial withdrawals of forces from the State had been made by both sides since the cease-fire. Pointing out that further reductions of troops were directly related to the preparation of a plebiscite, the United Nations Representative considered it necessary that the Plebiscite Administrator-Designate should be associated with him in studies and in the consideration of common problems.

FOURTH REPORT. On May 29, 1952, Dr. Graham informed the President of the Council that, in agreement with the two Governments, the negotiations had been renewed, and that he would report at the appropriate moment on the outcome. He reported on September 16.

The negotiations, first in New York and later, at the ministerial level, in Geneva, had concluded on September 10, with no agreement reached on the most important points.

NEGOTIATIONS ON SPECIFIC PROPOSAL URGED. Dr. Graham gave the Council his personal appraisal of the situation at a meeting on October 10, in which he explained that the remaining difference was related to the differing reiterated conceptions of the two Governments on the status of the State, the nature of the responsibilities of the appropriate authorities on each side of the cease-fire line after demilitarization, and the obligations of the two Governments under the provisions of the UNCIP resolutions for a plebiscite.

The Council adopted a resolution on December 23, 1952, urging India and Pakistan to negotiate immediately under the auspices of Dr. Graham on the specific number of forces to remain on each side of the cease-fire line at the end of the period of demilitarization. That number, the resolution provided, should be between 3,000 and 6,000 on the Pakistan side and between 12,000 and 18,000 on the Indian side, and should be arrived at bearing in mind the principles or criteria proposed by Dr. Graham.

The Council endorsed the general principles on which Dr. Graham had sought to bring about agreement between the parties, recorded its gratitude for his great efforts to achieve a settlement, asked him to continue to make his services available to the two Governments, and requested him to keep the Council informed. It asked India and Pakistan to report within 30 days. The resolution was adopted (Pakistan, as a party to the dispute, did not vote).

Prior to the adoption of the resolution, India had declined to accept it as a basis for further talks. India was prepared, as always, to cooperate in and to persevere in the exploration of all peaceful procedures for the settlement of the problem. However, any consideration of that problem "must proceed on the clear and unequivocal recognition of the authority of the Jammu and Kashmir Government over the entire territory of the State; of the fact that the State, by virtue of its accession to India, became a part of the territory of the Indian Union; and of the Government of India's responsibility for the security of the State against external aggression. This leads inevitably to the conclusion that all armed forces must be removed from the Pakistan side of the cease-fire line and that Pakistan should exercise no authority whatsoever over the area which it has invaded."

For its part, Pakistan was prepared to continue the negotiations on the basis of the resolution, although it felt that the numbers of troops suggested were not fair to Pakistan.

On January 23, 1953, the United Nations Representative informed the President of the Security Council that India and Pakistan had agreed that a meeting of representatives of the two Governments at the ministerial level should be held under his auspices in Geneva beginning February 4, 1953.

FIFTH REPORT. The Representative transmitted on March 27, 1953, his fifth report to the Council, in which a summary was given of the negotiations in Geneva, as well as of meetings held with the representatives of the parties in New York in January 1953. It had been agreed that the negotiations in Geneva should proceed on the basis of the Commission's resolutions of August 13, 1948, and January 5, 1949, "bearing in mind the assurances, clarifications and elucidations given to the Governments of India and Pakistan" by the Commission. That basis was to be without prejudice to a further consideration, if necessary, of the twelve proposals originally submitted by the United Nations Representative on September 7, 1951.

The Representative stated in his report that it had not been possible to reach accord on a truce agreement based solely on part II of the Commission's resolution of August 13, 1948, as the same difficulties that had existed since 1949 were still the main obstacles to the carrying out of the commitments embodied in part II. In accordance with the agreed terms of reference, further consideration of his twelve proposals had therefore ensued. On February 14, 1953, he had presented proposals that forces on each side of the cease-fire line at the end of the period of demilitarization would be 6,000 on the Pakistan side and 21,000 on the India side, with no armor or artillery on either side. However, as before, both India and Pakistan were unable to agree on the number and character of the forces to be left on each side of the cease-fire line at the end of the period of demilitarization.

After further conversations, the United Nations Representative had felt that there was no ground left at that stage on which to continue the conversations and, therefore, in agreement with the two representatives, he had decided to conclude the conference.

THE HYDERABAD QUESTION

On August 21, 1948, the Government of the Nizam of Hyderabad brought a complaint before the Security Council that India threatened it with invasion and economic blockade.

On September 12 and 13, the Government reported, first the threat of invasion, then the outbreak of hostilities.

At the Council's discussion, the representative of India argued that Hyderabad was never an independent State and was therefore not competent to bring a question before the Council. India, he said, had been obliged to enter Hyderabad to suppress lawlessness.

Later, the representative of India told the Council that the Nizam of Hyderabad desired to withdraw the complaint. The Nizam confirmed this message. The validity of the credentials of the representative was then discussed, but no decision was taken. There was further debate by the representatives of Pakistan and India in May 1949. No further meetings have been held on the question.

POLITICAL INDEPENDENCE AND TERRITORIAL INTEGRITY OF CHINA

In September 1949, China submitted to the General Assembly the question of "threats to the political independence and territorial integrity of China and to the people of the Far East, resulting from Soviet violations of the Sino-Soviet Treaty of Friendship and Alliance of August 14, 1945, and from Soviet violations of the Charter of the United Nations".

The U.S.S.R., the Byelorussian S.S.R., Czechoslovakia, Poland and the Ukrainian S.S.R. announced that they would neither take part in the debate nor be bound by any decisions taken.

The representative of China called on the Assembly to pronounce judgment on the Soviet Union for obstructing the efforts of the Chinese National Government in Manchuria and to recommend that all Member States refrain from giving further military and economic aid to the Chinese communists.

The General Assembly, on December 8, 1949, called on all states to: (1) respect the political independence of China and to be guided by the principles of the United Nations in their relations with China, (2) respect the right of the people of China to choose freely their political institutions and to maintain a government independent of foreign control, (3) respect existing treaties relating to China, and (4) refrain from seeking to acquire spheres of influence or to obtain special rights or privileges within the territory of China.

The Assembly also asked its Interim Committee to keep the matter under examination. After the Interim Committee in 1950 had reported that it had not taken up this question, the Assembly adopted two resolutions on December 1, 1950. The first instructed the Interim Committee to continue its inquiry, and the second drew the attention of all states to the necessity of complying faithfully with the previous year's resolution.

After discussion at the sixth session, the Assembly on February 1, 1952, adopted another resolution. Submitted originally by China and amended by Thailand, this determined that the U.S.S.R., in its relations with China since the surrender of Japan, had failed to carry out the Treaty of Friendship and Alliance. The discussion had been marked by charges and denials of preparations for aggression in Southeast Asia.

THE QUESTION OF THE REPRESENTATION OF CHINA ON UNITED NATIONS BODIES

On November 18, 1949, the Foreign Minister of the Central People's Government of the People's Republic of China informed the President of the General Assembly and the Secretary-General that his Government repudiated the legal status of the delegation under T. F. Tsiang, and held that it had no right to speak for the Chinese people in the United Nations.

On December 29, 1949, the U.S.S.R. and the Ukrainian S.S.R. endorsed this position in the Security Council.

On January 8, 1950, the Foreign Minister of the People's Republic of China informed the Security Council that his Government considered that the presence of the delegation under Dr. Tsiang in the Council was illegal, and that it should be expelled.

The U.S.S.R. then proposed that the Council decide not to recognize the credentials of Dr. Tsiang and to exclude him.

The President (Dr. Tsiang) ruled that a meeting of the Council should be called to consider the U.S.S.R. proposal, which ruling was upheld.

The representative of the U.S.S.R. then said that he would not participate in the Council's work or take part in that meeting until the delegation under Dr. Tsiang had been expelled. Accordingly, he left the Council chamber.

When the U.S.S.R. draft resolution was discussed on January 12, the representative of Cuba presided at the request of the President (Dr. Tsiang).

On January 13, the U.S.S.R. draft resolution was rejected. The representative of the U.S.S.R. then declared that his delegation would not participate in the Council's work until the delegation under Dr. Tsiang had been removed. The U.S.S.R. would not recognize as legal any decision adopted with the participation of Dr. Tsiang, and would not be bound by such decisions. Accordingly, he left the Council chamber. (He did not return until August 1, 1950.)

This withdrawal was followed during succeeding months by similar withdrawals, by representatives of the U.S.S.R. and of certain other states, from other organs and bodies of the United Nations of which China was a member.

The question of the representation of China was raised again on August 1, 1950, when, at a meeting of the Council, the President (the representative of the U.S.S.R.) ruled that Dr. Tsiang did not represent China, and therefore could not take part in the Council's meetings.

After discussion, the Council adopted a proposal to overrule the ruling of the President.

Two days later, the Council rejected a U.S.S.R. proposal to include in the agenda an item entitled "Recognition of the representative of the Central People's Government of the People's Republic of China".

PROCEEDINGS IN THE GENERAL ASSEMBLY. By cablegram to the Secretary-General on August 26, 1950, the Minister for Foreign Affairs of the Central Chinese People's Government recalled his Government's previous notes and requested that the necessary arrangements be made for the delegation of the People's Republic of China to attend the fifth session of the General Assembly.

At the opening meeting of the session on September 19, the Assembly had before it four draft resolutions. One sponsored by Canada, together with an amendment by Australia, which Canada accepted, was adopted. This noted the differences of view concerning the representation of China, and provided for the establishment of a special committee of seven members to consider the question and to report, with recommendations, to the fifth session when consideration of the question of recognition by the United Nations of the representation of a Member State (*see page 69*) had been completed. Pending a decision on the report of the special committee, the representatives of the National Government of China were to be seated with the same rights as other representatives.

Later, on December 12, on the nomination of the President, the Assembly elected

Canada, Ecuador, India, Iraq, Mexico, the Philippines and Poland by secret ballot to serve on the special committee.

This special committee on October 16, 1951, rejected a Polish draft resolution calling on the Assembly to exclude the representatives of the National Government of China, and to invite the representatives of the Central People's Government. The committee authorized the Chairman to inform the Assembly that in existing circumstances it had been unable to make any recommendation on the question of the representation of China. The Assembly "noted" this report on the final day of its fifth session, November 5, and rejected a U.S.S.R. draft resolution providing that, since the special committee had not adopted any recommendations, the question should be referred to the sixth session.

On November 6, the U.S.S.R. proposed that the representation of China should be included in the agenda of the sixth session. Considering, however, that, as recently as the previous day, the Assembly had decided not to refer the matter for consideration to the sixth session, thereby expressing the sense that consideration was not "opportune or appropriate", the General Committee recommended that the Assembly reject the request. Also it recommended that, for the duration of the session in Paris, the Assembly postpone consideration of any further proposals to exclude representatives of the National Government of China from the Assembly, or to seat representatives of the Central People's Government to represent China. On November 13, the Assembly approved these recommendations.

Later, on December 7, when it took up the report of its Credentials Committee, the Byelorussian S.S.R. proposed that the Assembly regard the credentials of the representatives of the "Kuomintang Chiang Kai-shek Government" as invalid on the ground that they did not satisfy rule 27 of the rules of procedure requiring that they be issued either by the Head of a state or government or by the Minister for Foreign Affairs. This draft resolution was regarded as a proposal to reconsider the question of Chinese representation, and was rejected. The report of the Credentials Committee, finding that the governments of all Member States represented at the session had submitted satisfactory credentials, was then adopted.

At the seventh session of the General Assembly, the U.S.S.R. proposed in the Credentials Committee that the Assembly should regard as invalid "the credentials of the representatives of the so-called Kuomintang Government since these credentials do not satisfy the requirements of rule 27 of the rules of procedure". However, on the motion of the United States, the Committee adopted a resolution: (1) recommending that the General Assembly should postpone for the duration of its seventh session consideration of all proposals to exclude the representatives of the Government of the Republic of China, and to seat representatives of the People's Republic of China; and (2) finding that the credentials of the representatives of the Government of the Republic of China conformed with the provisions of the General Assembly's rules of procedure.

When the report of the Credentials Committee came before the General Assembly on October 25, 1952, the U.S.S.R. resubmitted its draft resolution.

The General Assembly adopted the report of the Credentials Committee, together with the recommendations contained therein. The Assembly also decided that it was neither necessary nor appropriate to vote upon the U.S.S.R. draft resolution.

At the opening meeting of both the eighth and the ninth sessions of the General Assembly, the U.S.S.R., on a point of order, raised the question of the representation of China in the United Nations, and submitted similar draft resolutions at both sessions that the Assembly should consider it necessary that the representatives of the People's Republic of China should take the lawful seat of China in the United Nations.

At both sessions, on the motion of the United States, the Assembly decided to postpone, for the duration of the respective sessions, consideration of all proposals to exclude the representatives of the Republic of China, and to seat representatives of the People's Republic of China. At both sessions, it was decided not to vote on the U.S.S.R. draft resolution.

At the opening meeting of the tenth session of the General Assembly on September 20, 1955, the U.S.S.R. once more submitted a draft resolution providing for the seating of representatives appointed by the Central People's Government of the People's Republic of China. In support of this draft resolution, the U.S.S.R. cited the Geneva Conference, and the more favorable conditions then existing for the solution of urgent, outstanding international problems, and the People's Republic's participation in the Bandung Conference, as well as in other international developments. The U.S.S.R. further stated that the participation of the People's Republic as a full-fledged Member of the United Nations was indispensable for the promotion of international peace and security.

This draft resolution was opposed on the ground that it would be unwise to vote on an issue on which the Assembly was so deeply and so evidently divided. Consequently, the Assembly adopted a United States resolution not to consider, at its tenth session, any proposals to exclude the representatives of the Republic of China or to seat representatives of the People's Republic of China.

The question of the representation of China has been raised on several other occasions in other organs and bodies of the United Nations.

COMPLAINT OF ARMED INVASION OF TAIWAN (FORMOSA)

The Foreign Minister of the Central Chinese People's Government cabled the Security Council on August 24, 1950, that the United States was committing aggression against Chinese territory. The movement of the United States Seventh Fleet toward the Strait of Taiwan, the arrival in Taiwan (Formosa) of contingents of the United States Air Force, and the prevention by armed force of the liberation of Taiwan by the Chinese People's Liberation Army constituted aggression, he contended, since Taiwan was an integral part of China, as stipulated in the Cairo Declaration of 1943 and the Potsdam communiqué of 1945.

The United States replied on August 25, that it had taken an impartial neutralizing action, addressed both to the forces on Taiwan and on the mainland, in order to keep the peace and to protect the security of United Nations troops in Korea—not to acquire a special position. The future status of Formosa could be settled only by international action. The United States would welcome United Nations consideration of the case and would approve full investigation at Headquarters or on the spot.

The Security Council voted on August 29, to include the item in its agenda and rejected a U.S.S.R. proposal to invite a representative of the Chinese People's Government.

On September 2, the U.S.S.R. proposed that the Council should condemn the action of the United States and should propose that it immediately withdraw all its forces.

On September 28, the Council voted on three proposals. The first was a Chinese motion that the Council should cease consideration of the item while the General Assembly was considering a comparable item.

The second was an Ecuadorian amendment to the Chinese motion to defer consideration until the first Council meeting after November 15, and to invite a representative of the People's Government to attend the discussion of its declaration regarding invasion of Taiwan.

The third was, for a second time, the U.S.S.R. draft resolution to invite a representative of the People's Republic.

The Chinese and U.S.S.R. draft resolutions were rejected, as was also the Ecuadorian amendment. The next day, however, the latter was reintroduced as a new draft resolution and was adopted.

On November 27, 1950, the Council decided to consider together the items entitled "Complaint of armed invasion of Taiwan (Formosa)" and "Complaint of aggression against the Republic of Korea" (*see page 83*).

COMPLAINT BY THE U.S.S.R. REGARDING AGGRESSION AGAINST CHINA BY THE UNITED STATES

The U.S.S.R., on September 20, 1950, proposed that the question of United States aggression against China be included in the agenda of the General Assembly's fifth session. The U.S.S.R. recalled that, on June 27, 1950, the President of the United States had stated that he had issued orders which had been followed immediately by the blockade of Taiwan by United States armed forces. These actions, said the U.S.S.R., represented gross interference in the internal affairs of China, a direct encroachment upon its territorial integrity and political independence, and a direct act of aggression against it.

On November 27, 1950, the Chairman of the First Committee, in pursuance of a resolution adopted on the proposal of the U.S.S.R., invited the representative of the Central Chinese People's Government to take part in the discussion.

On that day, the U.S.S.R. submitted a draft resolution to note the facts of the infringement of Chinese territorial integrity and the inviolability of its frontiers by naval and air units of the United States, and to request the Security Council to take the necessary steps to insure the immediate cessation of aggression against China by the United States.

On February 2, 1951, the United States representative denied that United States forces had blockaded and invaded Taiwan or had violated Chinese air space. Five days later, the Committee rejected the U.S.S.R. draft resolution. This being the only draft resolution under discussion, the Committee had no recommendation to submit to the Assembly.

On February 13, 1951, the Committee report came before the Assembly, which, in the absence of a recommendation, took no decision. At that meeting, the U.S.S.R. reintroduced its draft resolution, which was rejected.

THE QUESTION OF FORMOSA

On September 20, 1950, the United States requested that the question of Formosa be included in the agenda of the General Assembly. An explanatory note recalled the Cairo Declaration of 1943, the Potsdam Proclamation of 1945, and the Japanese surrender terms by which Japanese forces on Formosa surrendered to Generalissimo Chiang Kai-shek. The United States also recalled the circumstances of President Truman's order to the Seventh Fleet to neutralize Formosa, and his statement that determination of Formosa's future status must await the restoration of security in the Pacific, a peace settlement with Japan, or consideration by the United Nations. The note added that the United States had no territorial ambitions in Formosa and sought no special position or privilege; it suggested that the General Assembly should study the general situation with respect to Formosa with a view to formulating appropriate recommendations.

The U.S.S.R. objected to inclusion of the item on the ground that Taiwan was already clearly part of Chinese territory and that the reason the United States raised the question was that there had been a change of political regime in China and the United States intended to make a strategic base of Formosa.

The Assembly referred the question of Formosa to the First Committee, which decided, on November 15, to postpone the discussion until after consideration of other items, and, on February 7, 1951, to adjourn the discussion *sine die.*

COMPLAINT OF BOMBING BY UNITED STATES MILITARY AIRCRAFT OF THE TERRITORY OF CHINA

On August 28, 1950, the Minister for Foreign Affairs of the Central People's Government of the People's Republic of China charged that, on August 27, military aircraft of the United States forces had flown over Chinese territory and had killed a number of persons. He asked the Security Council to condemn the United States aggression forces and to take immediate measures to bring about the withdrawal of all United States forces from Korea.

The United States replied that the instructions under which aircraft were operating under the Unified Command in Korea strictly prohibited them from crossing the Korean frontier into adjacent territory. No evidence had been received to indicate that these instructions had been violated, but the United States Government would welcome an investigation on the spot by a commission appointed by the Security Council. (Later, the United States representative said an investigation by the United States military authorities had indicated that, by mistake, one aircraft might have strafed a Chinese airstrip on August 27.)

On August 31, the U.S.S.R. proposed a resolution to condemn the illegal acts of the United States and to call on that Government to prohibit such illegal acts.

This was followed by another U.S.S.R. proposal to invite a representative of the Chinese People's Republic to meetings on the question.

The United States proposed establishment of an investigation commission, composed of one member appointed by India and one by Sweden.

On September 10, 1950, the Foreign Minister of the People's Republic of China claimed, by cable, the right to participate in the consideration of the question.

On September 11, 1950, the Security Council rejected the U.S.S.R. proposal to invite a representative. The next day, seven votes were cast in favor of the United States draft resolution and 1 (U.S.S.R.) against, with 2 abstentions (India and Yugoslavia) and one member (China) not participating. Because of the negative vote of the U.S.S.R., the draft resolution was not adopted. The U.S.S.R. proposal was rejected by a vote of 1 to 8, with 1 abstention (Yugoslavia), one member (China) not participating.

FURTHER CHARGES OF UNITED STATES VIOLATIONS OF CHINESE TERRITORY

The Central Chinese People's Government charged on September 24, 1950, that United States military aircraft had bombed the city of Antung. It asked the General Assembly to recommend that the Security Council take effective measures to condemn "the aggressive crimes of the United States and bring about promptly the withdrawal of the United States forces in Korea".

On September 26, the United States reported to the Security Council that a plane of the United States Air Force might inadvertently have violated Chinese territory and dropped bombs in the vicinity of Antung on September 22. The United States deeply regretted any violations of Chinese territory and remained willing to pay compensation through the United Nations for any damages established by an impartial investigation on the spot.

A further complaint of the Chinese People's Government was on stoppage and illegal inspection of a Chinese merchant ship.

The Foreign Minister cabled on October 17, claiming the right to participate as "the sole legal Government representing the Chinese people".

The First Committee discussed the item in February 1951. The U.S.S.R. proposed a resolution condemning the United States, placing full responsibility on it for the acts charged, and recommending that the Security Council take immediate action to prevent such acts by the United States.

The United States submitted that all the alleged bombings occurred at Yalu River crossings and proved only that the United States Air Forces had bombed the Yalu River bridges across which Chinese communist troops had entered Korea. United States aircraft had, on two occasions, dropped bombs on Manchurian territory, by error. A neutral commission had been proposed to investigate the facts and assess the damages, and the proposal had been rejected because of the negative vote of the U.S.S.R.

On February 7, the Committee rejected the U.S.S.R. draft resolution.

On February 13, 1951, the U.S.S.R. reintroduced its draft resolution in the Assembly, which also rejected it.

GENEVA PROTOCOL FOR THE PROHIBITION OF THE USE OF BACTERIAL WEAPONS

In June 1952, at the request of the U.S.S.R., the Security Council considered the question of an appeal to states to accede to the Geneva Protocol of 1925 for the prohibition of the use of bacterial weapons, along with a U.S.S.R. draft resolution providing for the Council to make such an appeal. Only six states among those which had acceded to the Protocol had not yet ratified it, the Soviet Union pointed out. These were the United States, Japan, Brazil, Nicaragua, El Salvador and Uruguay. The signatory states not only had agreed on the prohibition of the use of gases and bacterial methods of warfare, but also had undertaken solemn international obligations to exert every effort to induce other states to accede to the Protocol.

The United States pointed out that the Protocol had been withdrawn from the United States Senate in 1947, together with other treaties which had become just as obsolete in view of changes in the world situation. Citing the reservations made by the U.S.S.R. to the Protocol, the United States said that, by charging the United Nations Command in Korea with the use of bacterial weapons, the U.S.S.R. had set the stage for using the weapons itself should it decide to declare that the states resisting aggression in Korea were its enemies.

The United States had never used germ warfare in the Second World War or at any other time. It had not used and was not using germ warfare of any kind in Korea. The United States proposed the absolute elimination of weapons of mass destruction through the establishment of an effective system which would render their use impossible, and that the U.S.S.R. draft resolution be referred to the Disarmament Commission.

Others, too, considered that the U.S.S.R. text could not be considered separately from recent U.S.S.R. charges relating to the alleged use of bacterial weapons in Korea.

On June 26, only the U.S.S.R. voted in support of its draft resolution, while the other ten members abstained. The proposal thus was not adopted. The United

States then withdrew its motion for reference of the draft resolution to the Disarmament Commission.

QUESTION OF A REQUEST FOR INVESTIGATION OF ALLEGED BACTERIAL WARFARE

In the course of the Security Council's consideration of the question concerning the Geneva Protocol, on June 20, 1952 (*see page 104*), the United States representative stated that the Council had an obligation to concern itself with the false charges raised by the U.S.S.R. alleging the use of germ warfare by the United Nations forces in Korea.

He submitted a draft resolution which noted the concerted dissemination by certain governments and authorities of the grave accusations, recalled that the United Nations Command had immediately denied them, and had requested the International Committee of the Red Cross to investigate and to report the results to the Council. The proposal then called on all governments and authorities concerned to accord to that Committee full cooperation.

On June 25, the item proposed by the United States was included in the Council's agenda. Previously, the Council had rejected a U.S.S.R. draft resolution to invite, simultaneously with the inclusion of the item in the agenda, representatives of the People's Republic of China and of the People's Democratic Republic of Korea to the meetings of the Council, on the ground that this would represent an imposition of a condition on the adoption of the agenda.

On July 1, the U.S.S.R. draft resolution, which was resubmitted in a revised form, was rejected.

The U.S.S.R. delegation then stated that, in the absence of representatives of the People's Republic of China and of the People's Democratic Republic of Korea, it was unable to take part in the consideration of the item and would vote against the United States draft resolution. Two days later, the United States proposal failed of adoption in view of the negative vote of the U.S.S.R.

The United States thereupon submitted a new draft resolution to conclude, from the refusal of the governments and authorities making the charges to permit an impartial investigation, that the charges must be presumed to be without substance and false.

As in the first instance, the U.S.S.R. did not participate in the discussion of this second United States draft resolution, which, after debate, was put to the vote on July 9. Because of the negative vote of a permanent member (U.S.S.R.), the proposal was not adopted.

At the request of the United States, the General Assembly considered the "Question of impartial investigation of charges of use by United Nations forces of bacteriological warfare" at its seventh session. In an explanatory memorandum, it was stated that, since February 1952, the world had been exposed to a false campaign to the effect that United Nations forces fighting in Korea had resorted to the use of bacterial warfare. The charges had been categorically denied as false and unfounded by the responsible officials of the United States and also of the Unified Command. The offer of the International Committee of the Red Cross and the World Health Organization to assist in investigating the charges had been rejected. An impartial investigation by the Security Council had been thwarted, but, nevertheless, the charges had been reiterated before the Assembly by Poland and the U.S.S.R.

On April 23, 1953, the General Assembly adopted a revised joint draft to establish, after the President of the Assembly had received an indication from all the governments and authorities concerned of their acceptance of the proposed investigation, a commission composed of Brazil, Egypt, Pakistan, Sweden and Uruguay, to carry out immediately an investigation of the charges; to call upon the governments and authorities concerned to enable the commission to travel freely throughout such areas of North and South Korea, the Chinese mainland, and Japan, as the commission might deem necessary, and otherwise to facilitate the task of the commission; and to direct the commission to enlist the aid of scientists of international reputation.

On July 28, 1953, the President of the Assembly notified Members that the proposal to establish the commission of investigation had been accepted by the United States, the Republic of Korea and Japan, and that no other replies had been received.

After the General Assembly had decided to include the item in the agenda of its eighth session, the United States on October 26, 1953, transmitted to the Secretary-General sworn statements by officers of the United States armed forces repudiating confessions regarding bacterial warfare which they had made while prisoners of war, and charging that the confessions had been extorted from them by their captors.

The U.S.S.R. submitted a draft resolution to the First Committee by which the Assembly would call upon all states which had not acceded to or ratified the Geneva Protocol of June 17, 1925, for the prohibition of the use of bacterial weapons, to accede to that Protocol or ratify it. Those representatives supporting the U.S.S.R. draft resolution said that it was hardly surprising that nothing had come of the proposal for an investigation of the charges of bacterial warfare, since the item had been considered at the previous session of the Assembly without the participation of representatives of the People's Republic of China and of the Democratic People's Republic of Korea. Moreover, this one-sided consideration had resulted in a proposal for an investigation which could not have been objective. It was further asserted that the charges that the testimony of American airmen regarding their use of bacterial weapons had been secured under duress and torture were without foundation. It was not the task of the General Assembly to inquire into those matters, however, but rather to invite those states which had not yet signed or ratified the Geneva Protocol of 1925 to do so as soon as possible, as that Protocol was a major norm of international law.

A joint draft resolution submitted by Canada, Colombia, France, New Zealand and the United Kingdom provided that the Assembly would refer the U.S.S.R. draft resolution to the Disarmament Commission for such consideration as was deemed appropriate under the Commission's plan of work and terms of reference, and would decide also to transmit to the Commission for its information the records of the discussion of the item in the First Committee. According to those supporting the draft resolution, who comprised the majority of representatives taking part in the debate, failure by the Chinese and North Korean originators of the germ warfare charges to accept the investigation proposed in the Assembly resolution of the previous session clearly indicated that they feared the presence of impartial investigators because they knew that their charges were false. Moreover, the repudiation by the American airmen of their alleged confessions and their charge that those confessions had been extorted under pressure had undermined the most important and publicized feature of the case. The U.S.S.R. draft resolution, in their view, was not connected with the item under discussion. Furthermore, they maintained that, in existing circumstances, only limited security could be provided by the Geneva Protocol, since its value obviously depended on the good faith of the signatories.

The First Committee approved the five-Power draft resolution, and then decided not to put the U.S.S.R. draft resolution to a vote.

The U.S.S.R. introduced in the Assembly a draft resolution similar to that submitted to the First Committee. However, the General Assembly adopted the draft resolution recommended by the First Committee, and adopted a motion of the United Kingdom not to vote upon the U.S.S.R. proposal.

On November 6, 1953, the Secretary-General transmitted the text of the resolution adopted by the General Assembly to the Chairman of the Disarmament Commission, together with the records of the First Committee's debates on the item.

COMPLAINT BY THE UNITED STATES REGARDING AN ATTACK ON ITS AIRCRAFT

On September 8, 1954, the United States informed the Security Council that, on September 4, a United States Navy aircraft, on a peaceful mission over international waters, had been attacked without warning and destroyed by two MIG-type aircraft with Soviet markings. The United States Government had protested to the Government of the U.S.S.R. and reserved all rights to claim damages for loss of property and life and for other circumstances. Believing that the incident was of a type which might endanger the maintenance of international peace and security, the United States requested an early meeting of the Council to consider the matter.

At a meeting of the Council on September 10, the representative of the U.S.S.R. opposed consideration of the question. The facts, as determined by the U.S.S.R. Government, were that the United States aircraft had violated the frontier of the U.S.S.R. and had opened fire on Soviet fighters which had approached the United States aircraft to advise it to withdraw immediately from U.S.S.R. air space. The Council decided to include the question in its agenda.

During the debate in the Council, reference was made to various other aerial incidents and the representative of the United States emphasized his Government's readiness, in the absence of negotiated settlements, to bring such incidents before the International Court of Justice for adjudication.

At the close of the debate on the item, the President stated that the list of speakers was exhausted and that the Council would be reconvened to consider the item if and when any delegation so requested.

The Council has subsequently received the texts of diplomatic notes exchanged between the Governments of the U.S.S.R. and of the United States on various incidents cited in its discussion.

COMPLAINT OF VIOLATION OF THE FREEDOM OF NAVIGATION IN THE AREA OF THE CHINA SEAS

On September 30, 1954, the U.S.S.R. requested that the General Assembly consider the item "Complaint of violation of the freedom of navigation in the area of the China seas."

Three draft resolutions were submitted to the *Ad Hoc* Political Committee during its consideration of the question from December 13 to 15, 1954. One, submitted by the U.S.S.R., provided that the Assembly condemn piratical raids on merchant vessels on the high seas committed by naval vessels based on Taiwan (Formosa) and controlled by United States authorities. The second draft resolution, presented by Syria, proposed that the General Assembly call upon all concerned to resolve their differences by peaceful means, and call upon all Members, in strict adherence to the principle of freedom of navigation on the high seas, to abstain from acts which could be considered contrary to that principle. Under the third draft resolution, submitted jointly by Cuba, the Philippines and the United States, the Assembly, after recalling its resolution 899 (IX) of December 14, 1954, which requested the International Law Commission to complete its final report concerning the regime of the high seas, the regime of territorial waters and related problems in time for the Assembly to consider those matters at its eleventh session, would decide to transmit to the Commission the relevant records and documents of the *Ad Hoc* Political Committee, including the Syrian draft resolution.

In the course of the debate, the representatives of Czechoslovakia, Poland and the U.S.S.R. described a number of cases in which, they stated, vessels belonging to their respective countries had been seized, their cargoes looted and the crews detained and mistreated unless they betrayed their countries. Certain of the ships had, before being attacked, been located by aircraft bearing United States Air Force markings, which had even fired on them, and then apparently reported their location to the Kuomintang naval authorities. Therefore, the United States could not disclaim responsibility for the piratical acts which occurred in the area of the China seas.

The representative of China stated that his Government had never refused to enter into negotiations in connection with incidents involving *bona fide* neutral merchant vessels and a great many complaints had, in fact, been settled. However, his country was entitled to intercept any war contraband. The charges that his Government had subjected the crews of seized vessels to inhuman treatment had been disproved by investigations on the spot by the French *Chargé d'Affaires* in Taipei.

The representative of the United States declared that his country was not occupying Taiwan and that the small contingent of Americans stationed there at the request of the Chinese Government could not and did not exercise any control over the latter. The Seventh Fleet was in the China seas only for the purpose of maintaining peace and stability in the area, and United States aircraft were acting legitimately when they identified all vessels in order to detect the presence of ships hostile to the mission of the Seventh Fleet.

The majority of speakers expressed opposition to the U.S.S.R. draft resolution, and towards the end of the debate, the representative of the U.S.S.R. declared that he would not insist on a vote on his draft resolution and would instead support the Syrian draft resolution. The Committee decided to give priority in voting to the three-Power draft resolution. Following the Committee's approval of the joint draft resolution, the representative of Syria said that he would not press for a vote on his draft resolution.

On December 17, 1954, the General Assembly adopted the draft resolution recommended by the *Ad Hoc* Political Committee.

COMPLAINT OF ACTS OF AGGRESSION AGAINST THE PEOPLE'S REPUBLIC OF CHINA AND RESPONSIBILITY OF THE UNITED STATES NAVY FOR THOSE ACTS

On October 15, 1954, the U.S.S.R. brought to the attention of the General Assembly the item: "Complaint of acts of aggression against the People's Republic of China and responsibility of the United States Navy for those acts."

In the *Ad Hoc* Political Committee, the U.S.S.R. representative described aggressive actions committed against the Chinese mainland by the forces of Chiang Kai-shek, and maintained that the United States was also responsible for those acts because it had exercised full control over Taiwan since June 1950. By the unilateral decision of the United States to take Taiwan under its protection, which constituted a violation of the territorial integrity of the People's Republic of China, and by concluding in 1954 a Mutual Defense Treaty with Chiang Kai-shek, the United States had violated the Cairo and Potsdam Declarations and other international treaties to which it was a party.

The U.S.S.R. introduced a draft resolution to condemn the acts of aggression committed against China by armed forces controlled by the United States, and to recommend that the United States should take the necessary steps to put an end to these acts of aggression and to piratical attacks on merchant vessels.

The United States stated that, since the aggression against the Republic of Korea, the United States had taken steps to prevent another act of aggression against Taiwan and to maintain stability in the area. A series of facts were enumerated which, they said, showed who were the true aggressors in Asia, such as the handing over of stocks of Japanese arms to the Chinese Communists in 1945, the building up of an important Communist army in North Korea, and the sending of more than a million so-called Chinese volunteers to Korea.

The representative of China declared that the so-called United States occupation of Taiwan by force was a fabrication made up for propaganda reasons; there were not more than 1,200 Americans stationed in Taiwan, and they were there at the express request of the Government of the Republic of China. Hostilities along the coast of China had been started on September 3, 1954, by the Chinese Communists when they bombarded the island of Quemoy. Therefore, it was not surprising that the Republic of China had retaliated against the aggressors.

On December 10, the Committee voted on the U.S.S.R. draft resolution; it was not adopted. It was reintroduced in the plenary meeting on December 17, 1954, and was again rejected.

QUESTION CONCERNING CERTAIN ISLANDS IN THE COASTAL AREA OF CHINA

On January 28, 1955, New Zealand requested that the Security Council consider the question of armed hostilities between the People's Republic of China and the Republic of China in the area of certain islands off the coast of the mainland of China.

On January 30, the U.S.S.R. requested that the Security Council consider the question of acts of aggression by the United States against the People's Republic of China in the area of Taiwan (Formosa) and other islands of China. At the same time, the U.S.S.R. transmittted a draft resolution which provided that the Council, considering that a number of acts committed by the armed forces of the United States or those controlled by it constituted aggression against the People's Republic of China, would: (1) condemn such acts of aggression; (2) recommend that the United States Government take immediate steps to put an end to these acts of aggression and intervention in the internal affairs of China; (3) further recommend that the United States Government should immediately withdraw all its naval, land and air forces from the island of Taiwan and other territories belonging to China; and (4) urge that no military action be permitted in the Taiwan area by either side, so that the evacuation from the islands in that area of all armed forces not controlled by the People's Republic of China might be facilitated.

On January 31, the Security Council included both items in its agenda and decided to conclude its consideration of the New Zealand item before taking up the U.S.S.R. item.

A proposal that the Council invite a representative of the People's Republic of China to participate in the discussion of the item was adopted.

On February 3, the Minister for Foreign Affairs of the People's Republic of China, in reply to the invitation to participate, charged that the aggression of the United States against the Chinese territory of Taiwan was the source of tension in the Far East, and supported the U.S.S.R. proposals for putting an end to United States aggression. Since the liberation of its own territory was a sovereign right of the Chinese people and entirely an internal affair, it was a violation of the Charter for the Council to consider the New Zealand item. So long as the People's Republic, which represented the 600,000,000 people of China, should still be deprived of its legitimate position and rights in the United Nations, it would be impossible for a representative of the People's Republic to take part in the discussion of questions concerning China in the United Nations; it would consider all decisions taken by the Council concerning China as being null and void. It could agree to participate in the Council's deliberations only for the purpose of discussing the draft resolution proposed by the U.S.S.R., and only when its representative attended in the name of China and the other occupant of China's seat had been expelled.

On February 14, 1955, the majority of members considered that the Council should adjourn its consideration of the New Zealand item pending further study and consultation among members. A proposal by the representative of the U.S.S.R. that the Council proceed to discuss the item submitted by his delegation was rejected, and the Council adjourned for the time being its consideration of the New Zealand item.

COMPLAINT BY THE UNION OF BURMA REGARDING AGGRESSION AGAINST IT BY THE GOVERNMENT OF THE REPUBLIC OF CHINA

At the request of Burma, the General Assembly on March 31, 1953, included in the agenda the item "Complaint by the Union of Burma regarding aggression against it by the Government of the Republic of China".

The situation, as described by Burma, was that early in 1950, some 1,700 Kuomintang troops had crossed the border into Burma. They had refused to submit to disarmament and internment, and engagements had taken place between them and the Burmese army. The number of the troops was estimated to be about 12,000. The commanding general, General Li Mi, had been moving between their headquarters at Mongshat and Formosa. The troops had also interfered in the internal political affairs of Burma, and, by the middle of 1952, about 1,000 Kuomintang troops had been fighting with the insurgents in the areas in which the Karen rebellion had been still active. Since 1950 Burma, through the good offices of friendly governments, particularly the United States, had made repeated demarches to the Government of Formosa with which Burma had severed diplomatic relations. In the opinion of the Burmese Government, the Kuomintang troops were being directed and supported in their illegal activities by the Government of Formosa. The Government of Burma submitted a draft resolution by which the General Assembly would note that "armed troops of the Kuomintang Government of Formosa have committed acts of infringements against the territorial integrity" of Burma and "acts of violation of its frontiers", and would recommend to the Security Council that it "condemn the Kuomintang Government of Formosa for the said acts of aggression" and "take all necessary steps to insure immediate cessation" of such acts.

The representative of China declared that the idea of aggression against Burma had never entered the mind of the Chinese Government, and that the army led by General Li Mi was no longer part of the regular forces of the Republic of China. Although the influence of the Government of China over General Li Mi varied from time to time, it promised to use whatever influence it might have to further the wishes of Burma. The Chinese Government would also try to stop the collection of funds for this army among free Chinese, had given assurances that it would not give clearance to any aircraft taking off from Formosa to fly to the border region, and would give the United Nations the utmost cooperation in order to get the troops in question out of Burma.

On April 23, the General Assembly adopted a resolution by which the Assembly: (1) deplored the presence of foreign forces in Burma and condemned their hostile acts against that country; (2) declared that these foreign forces must be disarmed and either agree to internment or leave the Union of Burma forthwith; (3) requested all states to respect the territorial integrity and political independence of Burma; (4) recommended that the negotiations then in progress through the good offices of certain Member States should be pursued, in order to put an end to the existing serious situation; (5) urged all states to afford the Government of Burma, on its request, all assistance in their power to facilitate by peaceful means the evacuation of those forces from Burma; and to refrain from furnishing any assistance to those forces which might enable them to continue their hostile acts against Burma; and (6) invited the Government of Burma to report on the situation to the General Assembly at its eighth session.

Pursuant to this resolution, Burma submitted a report on September 10, 1953, in which it described the establishment of the Joint Military Committee, composed of representatives of the United States, Thailand, Burma and the Republic of China to discuss the means for evacuating the irregular Chinese troops. The report indicated why Burma had withdrawn from the Committee, and concluded by expressing the view that any withdrawal of the Chinese troops from Burma would be only a "token" withdrawal.

On December 4, the General Assembly adopted a resolution which: (1) noted that limited evacuation of foreign forces in Burma had begun on November 7; (2) expressed concern that few arms had been surrendered by them; (3) expressed appreciation of the efforts of the United States and Thailand in striving for the evacuation of the forces; (4) urged that efforts should be continued for the evacuation or internment of the forces and the surrender of all arms; (5) reaffirmed the General Assembly resolution of the previous year; (6) urged all states to refrain from furnishing assistance to the forces which might enable them to remain on Burmese territory or to continue hostile acts against that country; and (7) invited the Government of Burma to report on the situation as appropriate.

On March 17, 1954, the representative of China reported to the Secretary-General that in two stages of evacuation, completed by December 9, 1953, and March 13, 1954, respectively, a total of 4,237 troops and 269 dependents had been evacuated.

On August 20, 1954, Burma again requested that its complaint be included in the agenda. The report of Burma, submitted on September 27, described the phases of the evacuation from Burma of 5,328 Chinese troops and 1,142 dependents since 1953. About the same number still remained. The Government had agreed to cease-fire arrangements in certain areas, but had at times been obliged to resort to military action. It had also agreed that surrendered arms should be flown out of Burma. A substantial number of irregulars had found their way back from Thailand to Burma, and there had recently been an attempt at reorganization of these troops, to which anti-Communist Chinese organizations overseas were reported to have decided to allocate $600,000 worth of aid. The situation, therefore, had merely been eased, but the danger had not been eradicated.

The final report of the Joint Military Committee composed of delegates from China, Thailand and the United States, was submitted on September 28. It gave details on the negotiations and operations which had resulted in the evacuation of a total of 6,986 persons. Since there was no evidence of any desire by the remaining forces to evacuate, the Joint Military Committee was formally dissolved on September 1.

In the *Ad Hoc* Political Committee the representative of Burma stated that a considerable task still remained. As the possibilities of international action seemed to have been exhausted, Burma would have to work out by itself a solution of the remaining difficulties. While giving credit to the authorities in Formosa for their efforts, Burma considered that the Nationalist Government would remain responsible so long as there were any Kuomintang troops on Burmese soil. Expressing gratitude to the United Nations for its strong moral support, Burma hoped that it would continue to exercise its moral influence to bring about the disarming and internment of the remaining foreign forces, declare itself against any outside assistance to those forces, call upon Members to enforce that prohibition, and keep the matter on the agenda of the General Assembly.

The representative of China stated that the forces in Burma were composed of irregulars, which included persons of other than Chinese nationality, who had entered Burma against the express orders of the Chinese Government. It would neither maintain relations with the remnant irregulars nor furnish them with any form of assistance or support. It could not be held responsible for their continued presence or any of their activities in Burma or elsewhere.

The representative of Thailand, referring to the charge that irregulars had crossed the Thai-Burmese frontier into Burma, emphasized that that frontier had been closed since 1952, and that any movement across it was subject to control and supervision.

On October 29, 1954, the General Assembly, with China not participating in the vote, adopted a resolution which: (1) noted with satisfaction that nearly 7,000 persons had been evacuated from Burma; (2) expressed its appreciation of the efforts of the United States and Thailand in achieving evacuation; (3) deplored the fact that considerable foreign forces with a significant quantity of arms still remained in Burma, and had failed to respond to the declarations of the General Assembly that they should either leave Burma or submit to internment; (4) called once more on those forces to submit to disarmament and internment; (5) assured Burma of its continuing sympathy with and support of the efforts of that Government to bring about a complete solution of the serious problem; (6) urged all states to take all necessary steps to prevent the furnishing of any assistance which might enable foreign forces to remain in Burma or to continue their hostile acts against that country; and (7) invited the Government of Burma to report on the situation to the Assembly as appropriate.

REQUEST OF THAILAND FOR THE DISPATCH OF OBSERVERS BY THE PEACE OBSERVATION COMMISSION

On May 29, 1954, Thailand brought to the attention of the Security Council the situation in Indo-China as a threat to the security of Thailand. On June 3, the representative of the U.S.S.R. opposed the inclusion of the item on the grounds that the restoration of peace in Indo-China was being considered by the Conference of Foreign Ministers at Geneva. Consideration of the matter submitted by Thailand might impede a successful solution at Geneva. The item was included in the agenda.

The representative of Thailand stated to the Council that a very real danger existed that fighting in neighboring territories might spread to Thailand and to other countries in the area. The Viet Minh forces which still remained in Laos and Cambodia were well organized; there was evidence that they had received support from outside Indo-China, and these forces intended to overthrow the legal Governments of Cambodia and Laos. He added that the propaganda of the Viet Minh and of the foreign governments with which it was associated had spread serious and false charges against Thailand, and within Thailand itself, alien elements obedient to the political philosophy of the Viet Minh had maintained disquieting activity.

The representative of Thailand submitted a draft resolution to request the Peace Observation Commission to establish a sub-commission with authority: (1) to dispatch observers to Thailand, (2) to visit Thailand if necessary, and (3) to make reports and recommendations to the Security Council. The majority of the members of the Council supported the draft resolution, and considered that the situation described by Thailand warranted United Nations observation. The U.S.S.R. opposed the draft resolution on the grounds that it represented a camouflaged attempt by the United States to deepen the conflict in Indo-China and to prepare for military intervention. On June 18, 1954, the draft resolution was put to the vote and received 9 votes in favor, 1 against (U.S.S.R.), and 1 abstention. The draft resolution was not adopted, since the vote against was that of a permanent member.

Questions Relating to the Middle East

THE PALESTINE QUESTION

PARTITION PLAN ADOPTED BY THE GENERAL ASSEMBLY IN 1947. On April 2, 1947, the United Kingdom asked that a special session of the General Assembly be called to examine the question of Palestine. The session, held between April 28 and May 15, 1947, established a Special Committee on Palestine, consisting of representatives of eleven Member States, which, after a visit of inspection in the Middle East, presented a report on the question. The document contained twelve general recommendations, a majority plan, and a minority plan. The majority plan called for the partition of Palestine into an Arab State, a Jewish State, and an international regime for Jerusalem, the three to be linked in an economic union. The minority plan proposed an independent federal State comprising an Arab State and a Jewish State with Jerusalem as its capital.

On November 29, 1947, the Assembly voted for the majority plan. The plan was accepted by the Jewish agency, but rejected by the Arab Higher Committee which advocated the establishment of an Arab State that would protect the rights of the Jewish minority.

The resolution provided that the British Mandate over Palestine was to terminate, and the British armed forces were to be withdrawn, as soon as possible, and not later than August 1, 1948. (The United Kingdom later announced its intention to terminate the Mandate on May 15, 1948.) The two independent States and the special international regime for Jerusalem were to come into existence two months after the withdrawal of the British armed forces. Boundaries were established for the Arab State, the Jewish State, and the City of Jerusalem. A Joint Economic Board was to be established. The Trusteeship Council was to prepare and approve a detailed Statute of the City of Jerusalem.

The Assembly established the United Nations Palestine Commission consisting of Bolivia, Czechoslovakia, Denmark, Panama and the Philippines to implement its recommendations, and requested the Security Council to take the necessary measures to implement the plan and, if necessary, to consider whether the situation in Palestine constituted a threat to peace, and determine as a threat to the peace under Article 39 of the Charter any attempt to alter by force the settlement envisaged by the Assembly's resolution.

The reports of the Palestine Commission having revealed a steady deterioration of the situation in Palestine, the Security Council, after studying suggestions presented by its permanent members for ending violence, adopted a proposal calling for a new special session of the Assembly, which met in New York from April 16 to May 14.

SECOND SPECIAL SESSION OF ASSEMBLY, AND SECURITY COUNCIL APPEALS FOR A TRUCE. On May 6, 1948, the Assembly approved recommendations which it had requested the Trusteeship Council to present for the protection of the City of Jerusalem and its inhabitants.

On May 14, it rejected a joint United States-French proposal for a temporary international regime for Jerusalem, based on Chapter XII of the Charter (Trusteeship). At the same time, it decided to appoint a United Nations Mediator for Palestine, and to relieve the Palestine Commission of its responsibilities. The Mediator was to use his good offices to assure the protection of the Holy Places and to promote a peaceful adjustment. He was also requested to cooperate with the Truce Commission for Palestine which had been appointed by the Security Council.

On May 20, 1948, the Assembly's Special Committee chose Count Folke Bernadotte, President of the Swedish Red Cross, as Mediator. (The second special session of the Assembly adjourned on May 14. On the same day, the Mandate of the United Kingdom over Palestine expired, and a Jewish State was proclaimed under the name of Israel.)

Meanwhile, on April 17, the Council adopted a resolution calling for a truce between the Arab and the Jewish communities in Palestine. On April 23, it established a Truce Commission for Palestine composed of representatives of those members of the Council which had career consular officers in Jerusalem—Belgium, France and the United States—(Syria, which also had a consular officer in Jerusalem, informed the Council that it would not appoint a representative on the Commission.) The Commission was to assist the Council in supervising the truce called for in the April 17 resolution.

INTERVENTION OF ARAB STATES IN PALESTINE. On May 15, 1948—the day after the United Kingdom relinquished its Mandate over Palestine, and the new State of Israel was proclaimed—the Arab States instituted armed action in Palestine.

The Security Council on May 22, called on all governments and authorities to abstain from any hostile military action in Palestine. It requested on May 29, the observation of a four-week truce which became effective on June 11, 1948. On July 7, the Security Council urgently appealed to the interested parties to accept the prolongation of the truce for such period as might be decided on in consultation with the Mediator. The Provisional Government of Israel agreed to extend the truce, but the Arab States refused. Hostilities broke out anew.

On July 15, the Council, invoking Chapter VII of the Charter, ordered all authorities and governments concerned to desist from further military action and to issue cease-fire orders. The Council's resolution declared that failure to comply with this order would be construed as a breach of the peace which would require immediate consideration of enforcement measures to be taken under the Charter.

On August 19, in response to an appeal from the Mediator, the Council warned that both Arab and Jewish authorities would be held responsible for any violation of the truce.

ASSASSINATION OF MEDIATOR. On September 17, the Mediator, Count Bernadotte, and the Chief of the French observers, Colonel André Serot, were shot and killed in the Israel sector of Jerusalem. The Mediator was succeeded in his functions by Ralph J. Bunche, with the title of Acting Mediator.

ACTION BY ASSEMBLY AT THIRD SESSION. On December 11, the Assembly, following the suggestions of a report which Count Bernadotte had prepared before his death, adopted a resolution which, among other things, provided for: (a) the establishment of a Conciliation Commission of three members (France, Turkey and the United States), which was instructed to take steps to assist the parties concerned to achieve a final settlement on all questions; (b) the protection of the Holy Places in Jerusalem, and free access to them through arrangements under United Nations supervision; and (c) further steps to be taken by the Security Council to insure Jerusalem's demilitarization, and instruction to the Conciliation Commission to present detailed proposals for a permanent international regime. It further provided that those of the Arab Refugees who had fled from Palestine who wished to return home and live at peace with their neighbors should be permitted to do so. Instructions were given to the Conciliation Commission to facilitate repatriation, resettlement, rehabilitation of refugees, and payment of compensation for damaged property. (For an account of United Nations assistance to Palestine refugees, *see pages 120-122*.)

FIGHT IN NEGEV AREA AND CALL FOR ARMISTICE. Meanwhile, large-scale fighting between Palestine Jews and Egyptians broke out in the Negev area of Palestine in October 1948, and hostilities were renewed again in November and December. The Security Council, in resolutions adopted on October 19, November 4, November 16, and December 29, called upon the parties to order a cease-fire, and to seek an agreement. The Egyptian and the Israeli Governments having signified their acceptance, the Acting Mediator set the deadline for the cease-fire on all fronts for January 7, 1949.

ARMISTICE AGREEMENTS. The Governments of Egypt and Israel signed a General Armistice Agreement at Rhodes on February 24, 1949; Lebanon and Israel, at Ras en Naqoura on March 23; the Hashemite Kingdom of Jordan (including former Trans-Jordan) and Israel, at Rhodes on April 3; and Syria and Israel, at Manhanayim on July 20. The armistice agreements instituted mixed armistice commissions to supervise the implementation of the agreements.

On August 11, 1949, the Security Council adopted a resolution which, among other things, urged the parties concerned to negotiate a final peace settlement, either directly or through the Palestine Conciliation Commission; relieved the Acting Mediator of any further responsibility under Security Council resolutions; and provided for the continued service of such United Nations observers as might be necessary to observe the cease-fire, and to help in the implementation of the armistice agreements.

ACTION OF THE ASSEMBLY, THE TRUSTEESHIP COUNCIL, AND THE CONCILIATION COMMISSION. At the end of 1951, the Conciliation Commission, in its tenth progress report to the General Assembly, expressed the opinion that during its existence it had been unable to make substantial progress in the task given to it by the General Assembly, although it had successively employed all the procedures at its disposal under the relevant Assembly resolutions. While recognizing that both sides had expressed their desire to cooperate with the United Nations towards the achievement of stability in Palestine, it believed that neither side was ready to seek that aim through full implementation of the Assembly resolutions.

At its sixth session, the General Assembly, after rejecting a U.S.S.R. draft resolution proposing abolition of the Commission in view of its failure to carry out the task entrusted to it, adopted a resolution noting with regret that the Commission had been unable to fulfil its mandate. The Assembly considered that the governments concerned had the primary responsibility for reaching a settlement of their outstanding differences in conformity with the Assembly resolutions. It urged them to make full use of United Nations facilities to that end. The Commission should continue its efforts to secure implementation of the Assembly's resolutions on Palestine, and should, therefore, be available to the parties to assist them in reaching agreement on outstanding questions.

Since adoption of the above Assembly resolution, the Conciliation Commission has remained at the disposal of the parties. Its work has been principally concerned with the release of refugee accounts blocked in Israel (a process approaching completion towards the end of 1955), and with a program of identification and evaluation of Arab Refugee property in connection with the question of compensation.

JERUSALEM. After considering reports of the Conciliation Commission, the General Assembly adopted on December 9, 1949, a resolution restating its intention that Jerusalem should be placed under a permanent international regime as a *corpus separatum* to be administered by the United Nations, and providing appropriate safeguards for the Holy Places. The Trusteeship Council was designated to discharge the responsibility of the Administering Authority.

The Trusteeship Council prepared a statute for the internationalization of Jerusalem, and asked its President to request Israel and Jordan to cooperate in its implementation. The President reported in June that the two Governments had in effect refused to cooperate in carrying out the projected statute. The Council reported this position to the Assembly which, at its fifth session (1950), failed to reach a definite decision.

ACTION OF THE SECURITY COUNCIL, THE UNITED NATIONS TRUCE SUPERVISION ORGANIZATION, AND THE MIXED ARMISTICE COMMISSIONS. Since 1949, the Security Council has been confronted with a number of complaints from one or another party to the Armistice Agreements. It has been assisted in its action by the United Nations Truce Supervision Organization (UNTSO), an organ composed of international observers and headed by a Chief of Staff (successively Major-Generals W. E. Riley, of the United States [until June 23, 1953], Vagn Bennike, of Denmark [until August 11, 1954] and E. L. M. Burns, of Canada). The Chief of Staff supervises, as Chairman of the four Mixed Armistice Commissions, the implementation of the Armistice Agreements, and reports to the Security Council.

The great majority of the complaints has been dealt with by the Mixed Armistice Commissions. The intervention of the Security Council has been limited to the cases in which one of the interested parties or any other Member State has requested its action. Among the most important of these were the complaints related to the Jordan River (1951-1953), the Suez Canal (1951, 1954, 1955), Qibya, Nahhalin, Gaza, Patish, Nahal Oz, and Lake Tiberias incidents.

Jordan River

A number of incidents considered by the Security Council resulted from disputes between the parties on the extent of their respective rights in the Demilitarized Zones and in the Defensive Areas. The Armistice Agreements, which totally (in the Demilitarized Zones) or partially (in the Defensive Areas) exclude the presence of armed forces of both parties, do not refer to the question of territorial sovereignty in these regions.

(a) *Drainage of Huleh Marshes.* A dispute between Syria and Israel arising from Israel's drainage project in the Huleh marshes area was considered by the Security Council in May 1951. The Council instructed Israel to suspend its operations until an agreement for their continuation had been arranged by the Chairman of the Syrian-Israeli Mixed Armistice Commission. Israel maintained that it had the right to continue work on land in the area not owned by the Arabs, while Syria argued that the Council's resolution called for a complete halt to the drainage operations irrespective of the question of land ownership. Subsequently, in a report in June 1951, the Chief of Staff announced the failure to implement the decisions of the Security Council calling on Israel: (a) to return Arab civilians (removed to Israeli territory) to the Demilitarized Zone, and (b) to withdraw Israel's police unit from the Zone. In July, the Chief of Staff reported that a group of Arab civilians had been returned to the Demilitarized Zone. In October 1952, he further stated that the Israeli police exercised control over practically the entire area, and that the works of drainage had resulted in a considerable loss of the water available for irrigation in Syria.

(b) *Works on the West Bank of the River Jordan.* In October 1953, the Security Council was informed by Syria that Israel had started, in the Demilitarized Zone between Syria and Israel, works to divert the River Jordan in order to make it flow into Israeli territory.

The Chief of Staff reported to the Council that he had given instructions to stop the work until an agreement was reached. Israel stated that the project which was of vital economic importance for the development of the region was perfectly legitimate; Syria had no lawful right to prevent any development project in the Demilitarized Zone. Nevertheless, Israel was willing to arrange a temporary suspension of the works without prejudice to the merits of the case itself.

After adopting unanimously a resolution taking note with satisfaction of the statement of Israel, the Council failed, owing to the negative vote of the U.S.S.R., to adopt another resolution, among other things, requesting the Chief of Staff to take such steps as he might deem appropriate to effect a reconciliation of the views of the parties. The representative of the Soviet Union stated that he had opposed the resolution because it would delegate too much authority to the Chief of Staff in solving the dispute.

Suez Canal

(a) *Restrictions on the Passage of Ships through the Suez Canal.* In July 1951, Israel complained to the Security Council concerning the restrictions imposed by Egypt on the passage of ships through the Suez Canal. The right of ships to traverse the high seas and international highways was a corner stone of the law of nations. Moreover, in view of the signature of the Egyptian-Israeli Armistice Agreement, Egypt could not exercise unilateral belligerent rights.

Egypt replied that according to international law, Armistice Agreements did not terminate the state of war existing between the parties which retained rights of belligerency such as, in the present case, the rights of blockade, the right to capture neutral vessels attempting to break the blockade, and the right to seize contraband of war.

On September 1, 1951, the Council adopted a resolution which, after stating that the Egyptian interference with the passage through the Suez Canal of goods destined for Israel was inconsistent with the objectives of a peaceful settlement between the parties and the establishment of a permanent peace in Palestine set forth in the Armistice Agreement, and could not be justified on the grounds that it was necessary for self-defence, called upon Egypt to terminate the restrictions on passage of international commercial shipping and goods through the Canal, and to cease all interference with such shipping beyond that essential to the safety of shipping in the Canal itself and to the observance of the international conventions in force.

(b) *New Israeli Complaint on Restrictions imposed on Shipping through the Suez Canal.* On January 28, 1954, Israel complained to the Security Council that Egypt had maintained regulations and practices ruled illegitimate by the resolution of September 1, 1951, and had extended them to shipping to Israel through the Gulf of Aqaba.

A resolution, which would have the Council call upon Egypt to comply with its resolution of September 1, 1951, was put to the vote on March 29, 1954, but was not adopted, owing to the negative vote of the U.S.S.R. The representative of the Soviet Union explained that he had opposed the resolution because it disregarded the impossibility of settling international problems by imposing upon one of the parties a decision which it considered absolutely unacceptable.

(c) *Bat Galim.* In September 1954, Israel protested to the Security Council against the seizure by Egypt at the southern entrance of the Suez Canal of an Israeli vessel, the *Bat Galim,* bound for Haifa, and demanded the immediate release of the ship, its cargo, and its crew.

Egypt contended that the shipping agreement concluded between Egypt and Israel of July 23, 1953, prevented any ship of either party from entering the territorial waters of the other party unless compelled to do so. Israel replied that the passage of the *Bat Galim* through the Suez Canal, an international waterway, was completely legal, and in conformity with the resolution of the Security Council of September 1, 1951.

During the debate, the question of the status of the Suez Canal under the 1888 Constantinople Convention, and the extent of the rights of Egypt to interfere for security reasons in the free passage of ships through the Canal, as well as the rights of the Security Council to enforce execution of the Constantinople Convention, were discussed at some length.

After Egypt announced in January 1955, the release of the crew and its willingness to free the ship and the cargo under certain conditions, no new resolution was adopted by the Council, but its President observed that the majority of the members of the Council regarded the resolution of September 1, 1951, as having continued validity, and expressed the hope that an agreement between the parties for the release of the ship and the cargo would be speedily worked out.

Qibya. In October 1953, Jordan informed the Council of an attack launched by Israeli regular troops on the village of Qibya in Jordan, resulting in the killing of 42 civilians. The Mixed Armistice Commission had clearly condemned Israel for that aggression.

Israel expressed its unreserved regret for the loss of innocent life at Qibya, but stressed that this incident was but the consequence and the result of the state of tension prevailing on the Israeli-Jordan border, which was in turn caused mainly by marauding and infiltration from Jordan into Israeli territory, and by the refusal of Jordan to negotiate the establishment of peaceful relations between the two countries.

In November, the Security Council, after hearing the report of the Chief of Staff, adopted a resolution expressing the strongest censure of the Israeli retaliatory action at Qibya, and requesting Jordan to strengthen the measures it had already taken to prevent unauthorized crossing of the demarcation line.

Nahhalin. On March 30, 1954, Jordan charged that large Israeli military armed forces had attacked the Jordan village of Nahhalin, resulting in the killing of nine persons and the wounding of eighteen. The Jordan-Israeli Mixed Armistice Commission had condemned Israel in the strongest terms for that aggression. On April 5, Israel complained of numerous violations of the Israeli-Jordan Armistice Agreement, and of a Jordanian attack on a bus near Scorpion Pass on March 17, 1954. The Chief of Staff reported that investigation made by United Nations observers on the Scorpion Pass incident had proved inconclusive; concerning the Nahhalin attack, evidence found had established without question the responsibility of the Israeli attackers. No resolution was adopted by the Security Council on the incident.

Gaza. On March 1, 1955, Egypt reported to the Security Council that an Israeli armed force had penetrated into Egyptian territory, east of Gaza, and after blowing up buildings of military camps and a water pump-house, had ambushed Egyptian reinforcement troops, killing 39 Egyptians and wounding 32 others.

On March 3, 1955, Israel submitted a complaint against Egypt charging continuous violations of the armistice and the resolutions of the Council.

The report of the Chief of Staff stressed the responsibility of Israel for the attack at Gaza, but noted at the same time that infiltration was one of the main causes of the prevailing border tension; it suggested, in order to decrease that tension, concrete measures such as the institution of joint patrols along the demarcation line, negotiation of a local commanders' agreement, erection of a barbed wire obstacle, and manning of all outposts and patrols by regular Egyptian and Israeli troops.

On March 29 and 30, the Council unanimously adopted two resolutions, the first one condemning Israel for the attack committed at Gaza, the second calling upon the parties to cooperate with the Chief of Staff in implementing his proposals. In August and September 1955, Israel and Egypt informed the Council of a renewal of hostilities in the same region. The Security Council adopted unanimously a resolution endorsing suggestions of the Chief of Staff concerning the separation of armed forces of both parties, and calling upon the parties to cooperate with the Chief of Staff.

Patish and Nahal Oz. On April 4, 1955, Israel charged Egypt with repeated attacks against Israel with special reference to: (1) an armed assault at Patish on March 24; (2) repeated attacks on patrols and units patrolling the Israeli-Egyptian border at the Gaza strip between March 28 and April 3, 1955; and (3) an attack on an Israeli army patrol, and on the village of Nahal Oz on April 3, 1955.

The Chief of Staff reported that the most important factor contributing to the increased tension in the area had been the mining of tracks used by Israeli army vehicles. The most urgent step to be taken to improve the situation in the Gaza area was to institute joint patrols. Following a brief discussion, the President of the Council observed that there was no need for any new action by the Council, inasmuch as the facts brought to the Council's notice and the possible measures to avert frontier incidents had been fully covered in the resolutions adopted by the Council on March 29 and 30. He appealed to the parties to give full effect to these resolutions.

Lake Tiberias. On December 13, 1955, Syria informed the Council of a large-scale attack launched on December 11-12, by Israeli armed forces in the eastern part of Lake Tiberias. It requested the Council to recommend the expulsion of Israel from the United Nations, and pressed for the adoption of sanctions against Israel.

Israel replied that this particular incident was the consequence of the policy of harassment initiated, in violation of the fishing rights of Israel in this region, by Syrian army posts against Israeli fishing boats on Lake Tiberias. Evidence had been found of standing orders given to the Syrian outposts to fire on Israeli boats approaching within a limit of 250 to 400 metres of the shore, in violation of the Israeli-Syrian Armistice Agreement.

The report of the Chief of Staff stressed the striking disparity between the scale of the retaliation and the provocation cited by Israel.[4]

UNITED NATIONS RELIEF FOR PALESTINE REFUGEES

Relief for Palestine refugees first began in November 1948, when the General Assembly authorized the advance of $5,000,000 for the purpose of relief; urged all countries to contribute to a special fund; and appealed to WHO, IRO, FAO, UNICEF and UNESCO to accord their full cooperation in the field of relief.

The United Nations Relief for Palestine Refugees (UNRPR) was established on December 1, 1948, and received voluntary contributions of $35,000,000 from 33 Governments. It signed agreements with voluntary organizations which assumed the responsibility of direct relief. After 1948, the number of refugees receiving daily rations increased to 900,000.

On December 8, 1949, at its fourth session, the Assembly established the United Nations Relief and Works Agency for Palestine Refugees in the Near East (UNRWAPRNE or UNRWA) to carry out relief and works projects in collaboration with the local governments. The same resolution also established an Advisory Commission to advise and assist the Director of the Agency. The Commission was composed of representatives of France, Turkey, the United Kingdom and the United States and was empowered to coopt not more than three additional members from contributing governments. On May 1, 1950, the assets and liabilities of UNRPR were transferred to UNRWA, which officially assumed responsibility and established its headquarters in Beirut, Lebanon.

At its fifth session, the Assembly extended the mandate of UNRWA until June 1952, and directed it to establish a reintegration fund for projects for permanent reestablishment requested by host countries and approved by the Agency. The cost for direct relief was estimated at $20,000,000 and for reintegration at $30,000,000, and was to be met by governmental contributions channeled through a Negotiating Committee set up for this purpose. Meanwhile the Secretary-General was authorized to advance funds not exceeding $5,000,000 from the United Nations Working Capital Fund.

At its sixth session, the Assembly, in response to proposals submitted by the Director and the Advisory Commission, endorsed a program envisaging the expenditure, over a three year period starting July 1, 1951, of $50,000,000 for relief and $200,000,000 for integration.

A resolution adopted by the Assembly at its seventh session recognized that immediate realization of the goals of this program had not proved possible, and that increased relief expenditures were required. The resolution authorized $23,000,000 for the fiscal year ending June 30, 1953, and $18,000,000 until June 30, 1954, and empowered the Agency to draw additional amounts for relief from the reintegration funds estimated at $100,000,000.

---

[4] On January 19, 1956, the Council adopted unanimously a resolution which, after noting that there had been interference by the Syrian authorities with Israeli activities on Lake Tiberias but that this interference in no way justified the Israeli action, condemned the attack of December 11, as a flagrant violation of the provisions of the Syrian-Israeli Armistice Agreement and called on both parties to cooperate with the Chief of Staff to carry out these provisions in good faith.

At its eighth session, the Assembly decided, without prejudice to the rights of the refugees to repatriation and compensation, that the mandate of UNRWA should be extended until June 30, 1955. It authorized the Agency to adopt a budget for relief amounting to $24,800,000 for the fiscal year ending June 30, 1954, and to adopt a provisional budget of $18,000,000 for the fiscal year ending June 30, 1955. It considered that the projects' fund should be maintained at $200,000,000 until June 30, 1955, and urged UNRWA and the governments of the area to continue to seek acceptable projects to enable the fund to be utilized for its original purposes. The Advisory Commission was authorized to increase its membership by not more than two additional members. Belgium and Lebanon were subsequently added to the membership of the Advisory Commission.

On December 4, 1954, the General Assembly decided, at its ninth session, without prejudice to the rights of the refugees to repatriation or compensation, to extend the mandate of UNRWA for five years ending June 30, 1960. It requested the Agency to continue its consultation with the Conciliation Commission for Palestine in the best interests of their respective tasks, with particular reference to paragraph 11 of resolution 194 (III) on repatriation and compensation, and requested the governments of the area to continue to cooperate with the Director in carrying out projects capable of supporting substantial numbers of refugees. The General Assembly further decided to maintain the rehabilitation fund of $200,000,000, and approved a relief budget of $25,100,000 and a rehabilitation budget of $36,200,000 for the fiscal year ending June 30, 1955.

The report of the Director to the tenth session recalled that the Assembly had assigned the Agency the tasks of both relief and rehabilitation. Rehabilitation, which was a most controversial task, had been rendered difficult by human, political and economic factors deriving basically from the unhealthy situation prevailing in the Near East since the conflict of 1948. Both the refugees and the host governments held the United Nations largely responsible for the plight of the refugees. Although the relations between the Agency, on the one hand, and the host governments and the refugees, on the other, had improved somewhat, new difficulties had recently arisen which might seriously hamper the Agency in its relief work.

Indeed, unless the refugees were given the opportunity to make the choice between repatriation and compensation provided for in paragraph 11 of resolution 194 (III), or some other political solution to the Palestine problem were found, it would not prove feasible to carry out fully the resolutions concerning the reintegration of the refugees into the economic life of the Near East. UNRWA would be unable to complete its task of reintegration until the consent and cooperation of the refugees and the host governments were fully forthcoming.

On December 3, 1955, the General Assembly adopted a resolution which directed the Agency to pursue its programs for relief and rehabilitation within the limits of the contributions, appealed to Member and non-member States to make the necessary contributions, and requested the governments of the area, without prejudice to paragraph 11 of resolution 194 (III) on repatriation and compensation, to facilitate the work of the Agency and to ensure the protection of its personnel and property. It welcomed the substantial progress made by the Government of Jordan and the Agency toward resolving the difficulties which had impeded the granting of rations to refugee children in Jordan, and appealed to private organizations to provide increased assistance to the additional claimants not receiving aid.

During the discussion of UNRWA's report in the *Ad Hoc* Political Committee, the representatives of the Arab States asserted that failure to settle the refugee problem was mainly caused by Israel's refusal to comply with United Nations resolutions on the subject. The only realistic solution lay in giving the refugees the opportunity to choose between repatriation and compensation. Only then would implementation of other resolutions concerning the reintegration of the refugees into the economic life of the Near East become feasible.

The representative of Israel said that the military action taken by the Arab States against his country had been responsible for the creation of the refugee problem. But instead of devoting their resources to meet that responsibility, those States perpetuated the existence of the problem by holding in suspension all the major rehabilitation projects. Resettlement of the refugees in Arab States was in the interest of those countries and of the refugees, while their repatriation would constitute a danger to Israel. Reiterating his Government's willingness to discuss the question of compensation, he welcomed the proposed international loan to pay compensation for the land abandoned by the refugees.

THE IRANIAN QUESTION

On January 19, 1946, Iran informed the Security Council that U.S.S.R. interference in its internal affairs might result in "international friction".

Eleven days later, after discussion, the Council took note of the readiness of the parties to negotiate and asked them to inform it of the result of their negotiations.

On May 6, Iran reported the withdrawal of Soviet troops except from the province of Azerbaijan, and, fifteen days later, apparent evacuation from there as well. Thereupon, the Council adjourned discussion.

THE SYRIAN AND LEBANESE QUESTION

On February 4, 1946, Lebanon and Syria brought to the attention of the Security Council the continued presence there of British and French troops. A resolution expressing confidence that the troops would be withdrawn as soon as practicable was not adopted because of the negative vote of the U.S.S.R., but France and the United Kingdom nevertheless stated that they would give effect to the majority view.

The withdrawal of French and British troops from Syria was completed during the first two weeks of April. On May 9, Lebanon expressed satisfaction with the outcome of negotiations in which France agreed to withdraw all but a small group of its troops by August 31, and the United Kingdom its troops, except a small liquidation party, by June 30.

THE ANGLO-IRANIAN OIL QUESTION

On September 28, 1951, the United Kingdom asked Security Council consideration of its dispute with Iran: the failure by the Iranian Government to comply with provisional measures indicated by the International Court of Justice in the Anglo-Iranian Oil Company case (*see page 300*).

On October 1, the Council decided to place the item on its agenda. The U.S.S.R. and Yugoslavia voted against, on the ground mainly that the actions taken by Iran were entirely within its domestic jurisdiction.

The basic United Kingdom case was that Iran was flouting a decision of the International Court of Justice, causing grave economic loss not only to the United Kingdom but to the entire free world, and creating an inflammatory situation which might involve a threat to peace.

Iran contended that the United Kingdom's complaint was baseless and that the Security Council was without jurisdiction in the case. Iran's oil resources were the property of its people and had been nationalized through the exercise of the right of domestic jurisdiction, with provision for indemnification and the payment of compensation to those whose operations were affected. Apart from the fact that the indication of the Court was not a decision and, therefore, even if valid, was not binding, it was not Iran but the United Kingdom which had flouted the principles and abused the processes of law and justice.

After six meetings, the Council adjourned debate on October 19, until the International Court of Justice ruled on its own competence in the matter (*see page 301*).

At adjournment, the Council had before it two draft resolutions, one submitted by the United Kingdom, the other presented by Ecuador.

The United Kingdom draft called for the early resumption of negotiations in an effort to resolve the differences, and for the avoidance of any action which would further aggravate the situation or prejudice the positions of the parties. The Ecuadorian proposal, without taking a stand on the Council's competence, advised the parties to reopen negotiations as soon as possible in a fresh attempt to settle their differences.

THE QUESTION OF CYPRUS

At the request of Greece, the General Assembly considered at the ninth session, the question entitled "Application, under the auspices of the United Nations, of the principle of equal rights and self-determination of peoples in the case of the population of the Island of Cyprus".

The Assembly decided on December 17, 1954, that for the time being it did not appear appropriate to adopt a resolution on the question of Cyprus, and decided not to consider the item further.

Following a request from Greece that the Cyprus question be considered by the General Assembly at its tenth session, the General Committee discussed the question of the inclusion of the item.

The representative of the United Kingdom reiterated the position of his Government, that the United Nations was not competent to deal with the matter which was essentially one of domestic jurisdiction. No agreement had been reached at the Conference in London concerning Cyprus, but the United Kingdom was convinced that a solution could be worked out if negotiations were pursued in an atmosphere free of political activity. Greece was seeking to establish its own sovereignty over Cyprus through a campaign of incitement to violence and subversion. The United Nations, he contended, would be taking a dangerous course if it supported such ambitions.

The representative of Greece stated that Greece was repeating its action at the ninth session of the Assembly in sponsoring a petition put forward by a distinct national entity which was entitled under the Charter of the United Nations to claim the application of the principles of the Charter relating to equal rights and self-determination of peoples. Greece had tried in vain every expedient to obtain a settlement outside the United Nations. He contended that the British claim of domestic jurisdiction in regard to Cyprus was irrelevant. Since the ninth session, the situation in Cyprus had deteriorated considerably. It was the duty of the United Nations to take up the question. Greece, for its part, would continue to approach the question in a constructive spirit.

The representative of Turkey opposed the inclusion of the item in the agenda as it involved a question of domestic jurisdiction. Moreover, the proposed item was not based on the principle of self-determination, but was aimed at annexation. The item also envisaged the unilateral revision of an international treaty.

The General Committee decided to recommend to the Assembly not to include the question in its agenda.

On September 23, 1955, the Assembly adopted the recommendation of the General Committee.

Questions Relating to Africa

TREATMENT OF PEOPLE OF INDIAN ORIGIN IN THE UNION OF SOUTH AFRICA

At the request of India, the General Assembly considered the treatment of people of Indian origin in the Union of South Africa at the second part of the first session in 1946. India had complained that the Union Government had enacted certain discriminatory legislation against Indians—notably the Asiatic Land Tenure and Representation Act of 1946. This segregated Indians both commercially and residentially, India stated, and violated the Charter's human rights provisions and the 1927 "Cape Town Agreement" between India and South Africa (renewed in 1932) which defined the status of South African Indians.

A situation had therefore arisen, India maintained, which was likely to impair friendly relations between the two countries. India called on the Assembly to recommend "that the Union Government revise its general policy as well as legislative and administrative measures affecting Asiatics in South Africa, to bring them into conformity with the principles and purposes of the Charter". Further, the Assembly should request South Africa to report to the next session on the measures taken.

South Africa took the view that a state was not subject to outside control or interference in its domestic affairs. The legislation referred to, it said, concerned matters within its domestic jurisdiction and did not fall within the competence of the Assembly. South Africa denied that the Cape Town Agreement was an instrument giving rise to treaty obligations.

South Africa proposed that the International Court of Justice should be asked for an advisory opinion on whether the matter before the Assembly was essentially within South Africa's domestic jurisdiction. Rejecting this proposal, the Assembly on December 8, 1946, stated that, because of the treatment of Indians in the Union of South Africa, friendly relations between two Member States had been impaired, and were likely to be further impaired unless a satisfactory settlement were reached. The Assembly therefore expressed the opinion that the treatment of Indians in the Union should be in conformity with the international obligations under the agreements concluded between the two Governments and the relevant provisions of the Charter. It asked the two Governments to report to the next session.

The reports by India and South Africa to the Assembly's second session showed that efforts to arrange discussions had failed. India had insisted that South Africa should accept the Assembly's resolution as a basis of discussion. South Africa was unwilling to do this on the ground that acceptance would imply an admission that the Union Government had broken the agreements and violated the principles of the Charter.

Two proposals were put before the second session of the Assembly, but neither received the necessary two-thirds majority. At the request of India, however, the Assembly took up the question again at its third session, and on May 14, 1949, invited India, Pakistan and South Africa to hold a round-table discussion, taking into consideration the purposes and principles of the Charter and the Universal Declaration of Human Rights.

At preliminary talks in Cape Town in February 1950, agreement was reached on an agenda for a round-table conference to explore ways and means of settling the question, but India declined to go ahead with the conference on the ground that the Union Government had resorted to new discriminatory legislation. South Africa contended that this was a matter of domestic jurisdiction.

The Assembly, on December 2, 1950, recommended that the three Governments proceed to hold a round-table conference on the basis of their agreed agenda, "bearing in mind the provisions of the Charter . . . and of the Universal Declaration of Human Rights". The resolution stated that a policy of racial segregation (*apartheid*) was necessarily based on doctrines of racial discrimination. In the event of failure to hold the conference before April 1, 1951, or to reach agreement within a reasonable time, a commission of three members was to be established to assist the parties in carrying through appropriate negotiations.

The Assembly called on the three Governments, pending the conclusion of the negotiations, to refrain from taking any steps which would prejudice success, particularly implementation or enforcement of the provisions of the Group Areas Act, which the South African Parliament enacted in 1950.

In separate communications to the Secretary-General in March 1951, South Africa and India explained their positions. The Union was unable to accept the Assembly's resolution as the basis for a round-table conference on the ground that the terms of the resolution constituted intervention in a matter essentially within the Union's domestic jurisdiction. However, South Africa adhered to the policy agreed on at Cape Town in 1950.

India, on the other hand, considered that the resolution was best designed to secure discussion of the subject in an atmosphere free from prejudice. Since South Africa had declined a conference on the basis of that resolution, India felt that it had no option but to bring the matter to the notice of the United Nations for action.

Thus, at its sixth session, the Assembly provided for the establishment of a special commission to assist India, Pakistan and the Union in carrying through negotiations for solving the long-standing issue. Considering that a policy of racial segregation (*apartheid*) was based on doctrines of racial discrimination, it called on the Union Government to suspend its implementation or enforcement of the provisions of the Group Areas Act, pending the conclusion of the proposed negotiations.

One member of the three-member commission was to be nominated by South Africa, one by India and Pakistan, and the third by the other two members, or, in default of agreement between those two within a reasonable time, by the Secretary-General. However, these provisions were not implemented, for the parties adhered to their previously stated positions.

At the seventh session, then, the Assembly noted that the Union had expressed its inability to accept the previous resolution in respect of the resumption of negotiations, and had continued to enforce the Group Areas Act. It established a United Nations Good Offices Commission—with Cuba, Syria and Yugoslavia appointed members—to arrange and assist in negotiations between the Union and India and Pakistan for achieving a satisfactory solution in accordance with the principles and purposes of the Charter and the Universal Declaration of Human Rights. Pending the conclusion of those negotiations, it called on the Union to suspend the implementation or enforcement of the provisions of the Group Areas Act. It also asked the Good Offices Commission to report to the eighth regular session.

The Good Offices Commission reported to the Assembly on September 14, 1953, that the Government of the Union having considered the Assembly's resolution of the previous year as unconstitutional and having refused to recognize the Commission, the Commission, despite its efforts, had been unable to carry out its task.

The General Assembly decided at its eighth session to continue the Good Offices Commission, which was requested to report to the ninth session the extent of progress achieved, together with its own views on the problem and any proposals which, in its opinion, might lead to a settlement.

The Good Offices Commission reported in September 1954 that it had been unable to discover any new procedure whereby it could arrange negotiations between the parties, nor could it submit any proposal likely to lead to a peaceful settlement of the problem, since the Union continued to maintain that the General Assembly resolution was unconstitutional and that, consequently, it could grant no recognition to the Commission.

The General Assembly at its ninth session, suggested that the Governments of India, Pakistan and the Union of South Africa seek a solution of the question by direct negotiations, and designate a government, agency or person to assist them in settling the dispute, and decided that, if within six months the parties had not reached an agreement on these suggestions, the Secretary-General should designate a person to assist them in settling the dispute.

As attempts by the three Governments concerned to initiate new direct negotiations were unsuccessful, the Secretary-General, in accordance with the terms of the Assembly resolution, designated Ambassador Luis de Faro, Jr., (Brazil) in June 1955, to discharge the functions called for in the General Assembly resolution. India and Pakistan stated that they would extend full cooperation, but the Union Government informed the Secretary-General that it was obliged, regretfully, to decline to collaborate with the Ambassador in order not to prejudice its juridical position. On September 15, the Ambassador had concluded that in view of the attitude of the Union Government there was nothing further he could do to facilitate negotiations between the parties.

At the tenth session, in the General Committee, the Union of South Africa reiterated its view that inclusion of the item would be contrary to the Charter as the question fell within the domestic jurisdiction of the Union, and that its legal position could not be affected by the fact that the item had been irregularly included in the agenda of other sessions.

The General Assembly included the item in its agenda and referred it to the *Ad Hoc* Political Committee. A month prior to the consideration of this question by the Committee, the Government of the Union of South Africa had recalled its delegation from the General Assembly after the voting in the same Committee on its recommendations on the question of race conflict in South Africa resulting from the policies of *apartheid* of the Union Government (*see page 128*).

On December 14, 1955, the General Assembly adopted a resolution urging the parties concerned to pursue negotiations with a view to bringing about a settlement of the question, and requesting them to report as appropriate, jointly or separately, to the General Assembly at its next session.

RACE CONFLICT IN SOUTH AFRICA RESULTING FROM *APARTHEID*

A related question, that of race conflict in South Africa resulting from the policy of *apartheid* of the Government of the Union of South Africa was dealt with in 1952, at the seventh session of the Assembly at the request of thirteen States—Afghanistan, Burma, Egypt, India, Indonesia, Iran, Iraq, Lebanon, Pakistan, the Philippines, Saudi Arabia, Syria and Yemen. The sponsors contended that the race conflict was creating "a dangerous and explosive situation, which constitutes both a threat to international peace and a flagrant violation of the basic principles of human rights and fundamental freedoms which are enshrined in the Charter of the United Nations."

The Assembly's decisions were embodied in two resolutions. The first established a three-man commission to study the racial situation in the Union, and invited the Union to extend its full cooperation. The commission was asked to report its conclusions to the eighth session.

The second resolution declared that in a multi-racial society, harmony and respect for human rights and freedoms, and the peaceful development of a unified community are best assured when patterns of legislation and practice are directed towards insuring equality before the law of all persons regardless of race, creed or color, and when economic, social, cultural and political participation of all racial groups is on a basis of equality. It also affirmed that governmental policies of Member States which are not directed toward those goals, but are designed to perpetuate or increase discrimination, are inconsistent with the pledges of the Members under Article 56 of the Charter. The Assembly solemnly called on all Member States to bring their policies into conformity with their obligation under the Charter to promote the observance of human rights and fundamental freedoms.

South Africa made it clear that it regarded these resolutions as contrary to the guarantee in Article 2, paragraph 7, of the Charter, which precludes the United Nations from intervening "in matters which are essentially within the domestic jurisdiction of any state".

The Commission, in its first report submitted to the General Assembly on October 3, 1953, noted that the Union of South Africa had maintained the position expressed in the Assembly and, consequently, had not recognized the Commission. In the absence of cooperation from the Union Government, the Commission had been obliged to base its report essentially on an analysis of the legislative and administrative provisions in force in the Union, on a study of books and documents, on statements by witnesses, and on information communicated by certain Member States.

It was maintained in the report that the right of the General Assembly to undertake any study and make any recommendation which it might deem necessary in connection with the implementation of the principles to which the Member States had subscribed by signing the Charter was incontestable and that the exercise of its functions under that right did not constitute an intervention prohibited by Article 2, paragraph 7, of the Charter. After reviewing the nature and extent of the Union Government's policies, the report stated that there could be no doubt that the position in the Union was likely to impair the general welfare or friendly relations among the nations, in the sense of Article 14 of the Charter. The doctrine of racial superiority on which the policy of *apartheid* was based was scientifically false, dangerous to internal peace and international relations, and contrary to "the dignity and worth of the human person".

On December 8, 1953, an amended seventeen-Power draft resolution was adopted by the General Assembly, by which the Assembly: noting with concern the Commission's conclusion that the racial policies of the Government of the Union of South Africa were contrary to the Charter and the Universal Declaration of Human Rights, reaffirmed a resolution of November 19, 1946, calling upon governments to put an immediate end to religious and so-called racial persecution; reaffirmed its resolution of the previous year; requested the Commission to continue its study of the development of the racial situation in South Africa and to suggest measures which would help to alleviate the situation and promote a peaceful settlement; invited the Union Government to extend its full cooperation to the Commission; and requested the Commission to report to the General Assembly at its ninth session.

The report of the Commission to the ninth session of the General Assembly, analyzed the new laws and regulations providing for differential treatment of various sections of the population in the Union, and described the recent developments in the racial situation in that country. In conformity with the Commission's terms of reference, the report detailed a number of measures which might help to alleviate the situation. After stressing that the new laws which it had reviewed were incompatible with the provisions of the Charter and the Universal Declaration of Human Rights and that the policy of *apartheid* constituted a grave threat to the internal situation and foreign relations of the Union of South Africa, the Commission concluded that the road of gradual integration was the only one that seemed likely to lead to a peaceful future.

On December 14, 1954, the Assembly adopted a revised twenty-Power draft resolution, by which the Assembly, recalling its resolution of November 19, 1946, invited the Government of the Union to reconsider its position in the light of the principles of the Charter, taking into account the pledge of all Member States to respect human rights and fundamental freedoms without distinction as to race, as well as the valuable experience of other multi-racial societies; invited it also to take into consideration the suggestions of the Commission for a peaceful settlement; and requested the Commission to keep under review the problem of race conflict in the Union, and to report to the Assembly at its tenth session.

In the third report of the Commission covering the period between August 1954 and July 1955, it was stated that the general aims of the policy of *apartheid* had not changed, and that it was consistent neither with the obligations assumed by the Union of South Africa under the Charter nor with certain provisions of the Universal Declaration of Human Rights. However, in the implementation of the *apartheid* policy, a certain flexibility and gradualism already noted in the first report had become more marked, and the Commission was of the view that the process of *apartheid* had slowed down and become cautious. The Commission considered that a solution should be sought in frequent inter-racial, round-table discussions and other such contacts.

At the outset of the discussion in the *Ad Hoc* Political Committee, the representative of the Union of South Africa, recalling that his Government had always challenged the right of the General Assembly to deal with this matter which was essentially within the domestic jurisdiction of the Union, stated that his delegation would not participate in or be present during any discussion of the item. However, he reserved his right to take part in the vote on any draft resolution which might be submitted on the question.

On November 9, the *Ad Hoc* Political Committee adopted a seventeen-Power draft resolution. After the voting, the South African representative, who had returned to the Committee to participate in the voting, stated that once again the provisions of Article 2, paragraph 7, had been contravened. His Government had always stood firm on what it sincerely believed to be the meaning of Article 2, paragraph 7, and it had been with that particular understanding of the meaning and scope of the Article that his Government had signed the Charter. The object of the *apartheid* policy was to help the Bantu to have pride in themselves as a people, and to maintain their own way of life, with a sense of responsibility towards themselves and towards the larger community of which they formed a part. Every state had internal conflicts and policies about which it could not subordinate its own decisions to that of an international organization. The inquiry initiated by previous resolutions, which was now to continue, was a flagrant violation of Article 2, paragraph 7, such as no sovereign state could tolerate. In view of what had happened, his Government, after serious consideration, had decided to recall its delegation to the United Nations from the present session of the General Assembly.

On December 6, 1955, the General Assembly adopted the draft resolution recommended by the *Ad Hoc* Political Committee, subject to a major change. The provision of the draft resolution providing for continuance of the Commission failed of adoption by the Assembly. The resolution as adopted, after recalling previous resolutions, commended the Commission on the Racial Situation in the Union of South Africa for its constructive work; noted with regret that the Government of the Union again refused to cooperate with the Commission; recommended that the Government of the Union take note of the Commission's report; expressed its concern at the fact that the Government of the Union continued to give effect to the policies of *apartheid*, notwithstanding the request made to it by the Assembly to reconsider its position in the light of the high principles contained in the Charter, and taking into account the pledge of all Member States to promote respect for human rights and fundamental freedoms without distinction as to race; reminded the Government of the Union of the faith it had reaffirmed, in signing the Charter, in fundamental human rights, and in the dignity and worth of the human person; and called on the Government of the Union to observe the obligations contained in Article 56 of the Charter. By this Article, Members pledge themselves to take joint and separate action in cooperation with the United Nations for the achievement of solutions of international economic, social, health and related problems, and for the promotion of universal respect for, and observance of, human rights and fundamental freedoms.

THE EGYPTIAN QUESTION

Contending that Britain was maintaining troops in Egyptian territory against the will of the people, Egypt requested the Security Council on July 8, 1947, to direct the total and immediate evacuation of such troops and the termination of the administrative regime in the Sudan. The United Kingdom replied that the troops were being maintained in accordance with the 20-year treaty of 1936, that Egypt had rejected a new treaty on the Sudan in 1946, and that therefore the earlier treaties remained effective.

Between August 5 and September 10, 1947, the Security Council considered the complaint. None of the three draft resolutions submitted were adopted.

THE FORMER ITALIAN COLONIES

As a result of the Second World War, the colonies of Libya, Eritrea and Italian Somaliland were detached from Italy and, with the exception of the Fezzan region of Libya, placed under temporary British administration. The Fezzan was placed under French administration. At the Paris Peace Conference in 1947, Italy renounced all claims to its former colonies and, under Article 23 of the Italian Peace Treaty, their final disposition was to be determined by France, the United Kingdom, the United States and the U.S.S.R., within one year of the enactment of the Treaty, that is, by September 15, 1948. If those Powers were unable to reach agreement by that time, the question was to be referred to the United Nations General Assembly.

On the failure of the four Powers to reach agreement, the issue was referred to the Assembly, which took it up at the second part of its third session in April 1949. A decision was postponed to the fourth session, except for a minor resolution which asked the Economic and Social Council, in its plans and activities regarding underdeveloped regions, to take into consideration the economic and social advancement of the former Italian colonies.

At the fourth session, after several weeks of debate, the Assembly adopted a resolution dealing with all three territories.

The Assembly decided that Libya, comprising Cyrenaica, Tripolitania and the Fezzan, should become an independent and sovereign state not later than January 1, 1952, and that Libya should then be admitted to the United Nations. To assist the Libyans in drawing up a constitution and establishing an independent government, Adrian Pelt, an Assistant Secretary-General of the United Nations, was appointed United Nations Commissioner. He was to be aided and advised by a Council of Ten, consisting of representatives nominated by Egypt, France, Italy, Pakistan, the United Kingdom and the United States, in addition to one representative from each of the three Libyan provinces, and a representative of the Libyan minorities.

Somaliland, the Assembly decided, should become an independent sovereign state ten years from the date of Assembly approval of a Trusteeship Agreement for the territory, with Italy as the Administering Authority in the interim period. An Advisory Council, comprising representatives of Colombia, Egypt and the Philippines, would aid and advise Italy.

The Assembly instructed the Trusteeship Council to complete a draft Trusteeship Agreement for the territory (see page 269), to be approved finally by the Assembly at its fifth session.

The Assembly's resolution, dealing with Eritrea, stated that a Commission of investigation, consisting of the representatives of Burma, Guatemala, Norway, Pakistan and the Union of South Africa, should be dispatched to the territory. After examining the situation on the spot and consulting the Governments interested in the question (Ethiopia, Egypt, Italy, France and the United Kingdom), the Commission was to report not later than June 15, 1950.

LIBYA. After consultations in Libya and with various governments, the United Nations Commissioner in Libya convened the first formal meeting of the United Nations Council at Tripoli on April 25, 1950.

A Preparatory Committee of Twenty-One to establish the National Assembly was set up in July 1950. It agreed that the National Assembly should be composed of 60 representatives, on the basis of equal representation for each of the territories of Libya, and that its first meeting should be held on November 25, 1950.

Meanwhile, on November 17, 1950, the General Assembly adopted a resolution calling on the authorities concerned to insure the early, full and effective implementation of that resolution and, particularly, the realization of the unity of Libya, and the transfer of power to an independent Libyan Government by January 1, 1952; recommended that a National Assembly, to be convened before January 1, 1951, should establish a provisional government and that the Commissioner, aided by the Council, should draw up a program for the transfer of power in cooperation with the Administering Powers; and urged the Economic and Social Council, the specialized agencies, and the Secretary-General to extend to Libya such technical and financial assistance as it might request.

Later, on December 15, the Assembly adopted resolutions relating to the economic and financial provisions to be applied under the Peace Treaty with Italy. The main resolution contained ten articles governing matters relating to Italian assets in Libya, and provided for the establishment of a United Nations Tribunal to assist in implementing the resolution.

In the meantime, on December 2, 1950, the Libyan National Assembly declared that Libya should be a federal state, with the Emir of Cyrenaica as King. On March 29, 1951, the National Assembly unanimously established a "provisional federal

Government" for Libya, which was to contact the Commissioner concerning the transfer of power.

A program for the transfer of powers to the provisional Government was approved by the United Nations Council for Libya on October 2, 1951, and, five days later, a Constitution establishing a United Kingdom of Libya, was approved unanimously by the National Assembly.

On December 24, 1951—more than a week before the deadline set by the General Assembly—Libya was proclaimed an independent and sovereign State by King Idris I, and the Administering Powers transferred all authority to the Libyan Government. On January 3, 1952, Libya applied for membership in the United Nations.

At its sixth session in Paris, the General Assembly, on February 1, 1952, congratulated the people and Government of Libya upon the attainment of independence. It considered that Libya, as an independent and sovereign State, should now be admitted to the United Nations. The Assembly also asked the Economic and Social Council to study ways and means by which the United Nations could furnish additional assistance to Libya. Before adopting this resolution, the Assembly rejected a U.S.S.R. proposal for the withdrawal of foreign troops from Libya within three months, and the closure of foreign military bases in the country.

In another resolution, the Assembly considered that the problem of war damages in Libya should be examined within the general framework of that country's overall economic development. It recommended that sympathetic consideration be given by United Nations agencies to the Libyan Government's requests for assistance for economic development programs, including the repair or reconstruction of war-damaged property and installations, public and private.

At the tenth session, on December 6, 1955, the Assembly decided to terminate the United Nations Tribunal in Libya at the end of the year, upon the establishment of an Italian-Libyan Mixed Arbitration Commission.

(For admission of Libya to membership in the United Nations, *see page 79.*)

ITALIAN SOMALILAND (*See page 269.*)

ERITREA. On June 10, 1950, the United Nations Commission for Eritrea completed its report which contained three sets of proposals. The delegations of the Union of South Africa and Burma recommended that Eritrea should be constituted as a self-governing unit in a federation with Ethiopia, under the sovereignty of the Ethiopian Crown, after a transitional period not exceeding three years. The delegation of Norway recommended the reintegration of Eritrea into Ethiopia. The delegations of Guatemala and Pakistan recommended that Eritrea should become an independent sovereign state after a ten-year trusteeship with the United Nations itself as the Administering Authority.

The General Assembly's Interim Committee considered the Commission's report and reported that, while informal discussions among the delegations to the Committee had resulted in a compromise formula, time did not permit consideration of that formula by the Committee itself.

At its fifth session, the Assembly on December 2, 1950, adopted a resolution which included a detailed plan whereby Eritrea was to constitute an autonomous unit federated with Ethiopia under the sovereignty of the Ethiopian Crown. An Eritrean Government was to be organized, and a Constitution prepared and put into effect during a transitional period not to extend beyond September 15, 1952. The appointment of a United Nations Commissioner, to be assisted by experts appointed by the Secretary-General, was also called for. By secret ballot, Eduardo

Anze Matienzo, permanent representative of Bolivia to the United Nations, was elected.

The Commissioner arrived in Asmara on February 9, 1951. After nine months of consultations with representatives of Eritrean parties and organizations, with the British administration and the Ethiopian Government, he held a series of round-table discussions with a panel of legal consultants in Geneva, and prepared a draft Constitution.

The first democratic elections held in Eritrea took place on March 25-26, 1952, and, on April 28, the Representative Assembly of 68 members was officially opened. The Commissioner tabled the draft Constitution (in Tigrinya, Arabic and English) on May 3, and explained briefly its contents.

On May 14, the Assembly unanimously adopted and ratified the Federal Act and, on July 10, 1952, the Constitution, as a whole, was unanimously adopted.

The United Nations Commissioner officially approved the draft Constitution on August 6, 1952. It was formally ratified by the Emperor of Ethiopia, on August 11, 1952, and entered into effect on September 11, 1952, following the ratification of the Federal Act by the Emperor.

The establishment of the Federation of Eritrea with Ethiopia was formally welcomed by the General Assembly, by unanimous vote, on December 17, 1952.

Meanwhile, in accordance with a General Assembly resolution of January 29, 1952, a United Nations Tribunal in Eritrea was formally installed at Asmara on September 4, 1952, with executive jurisdiction on the disposal of the properties of the former Italian administration. The three judges of the Tribunal were: Hugo G. L. Wickstrom, of Sweden; Vicente Sánchez Gavito, of Mexico; and Faiz Yörükoglu, of Turkey.

PROCEDURE FOR DELIMITING THE BOUNDARIES OF THE FORMER ITALIAN COLONIES. The question of delimiting the boundaries of the former Italian colonies was considered by the General Assembly and the Interim Committee during 1949-50. On December 15, 1950, the Assembly recommended, with respect to Libya, that the part of its boundary with French territory not already delimited by international agreement should be delimited, on Libya's achievement of independence, by negotiation between the French and Libyan Governments, assisted on the request of either party by a third person to be selected by them or, failing their agreement, to be appointed by the Secretary-General.

The boundaries of Somaliland with British Somaliland and Ethiopia should be delimited by bilateral negotiations between the United Kingdom or the Ethiopian Government respectively, and the Administering Power. In the event of disagreement, a United Nations Mediator, to be appointed by the Secretary-General, was to assist the parties. In the event of further disagreement, resort was to be had to a procedure of arbitration.

With respect to any other boundaries not delimited by international agreement, the Assembly recommended that the parties concerned should seek to reach agreement by negotiation or arbitration.

THE QUESTION OF MOROCCO

At the sixth session of the General Assembly in 1951, six Members—Egypt, Iraq, Lebanon, Saudi Arabia, Syria and Yemen—complained of violation by France in Morocco of the principles of the Charter and the Declaration of Human Rights and asked the Assembly to consider the matter.

France contended that inclusion of the item in the agenda and discussion in the Assembly would worsen rather than clarify the situation. Those supporting consideration of the item argued that Morocco was entitled to immediate independence and that the situation required discussion, since all other means of influencing France had been exhausted. The question was, they contended, clearly within the scope of the Charter. Nevertheless, the Assembly postponed consideration of the question "for the time being".

In 1952, the same six States, together with seven others—the same thirteen Asian-African Members which had sponsored consideration of the Tunisian question—asked the Assembly to take up the question of Morocco. This time the Assembly agreed to do so, over the objection of France, which indicated, as in the case of Tunisia, that its delegation would be unable to participate in the discussion.

During the general debate, the Minister for Foreign Affairs of France said that the United Nations was precluded from discussing the Moroccan question by the Treaty of Fez of 1912 between France and Morocco, which provided that the foreign relations of Morocco could be conducted only through France, and by Article 2, paragraph 7, of the Charter, which prohibited the United Nations from intervening in matters essentially within the domestic jurisdiction of a Member State.

In the Committee, the sponsoring States cited the Act of Algeciras, an international treaty still in force signed by thirteen Powers, whereby the sovereignty of the Sultan had been guaranteed. Although it was clear, they said, that Morocco was *de jure* a sovereign State, the *de facto* situation was that the protecting Power, France, had been infringing on the rights of Morocco, and had attempted to gain a hold on that country's sovereignty in exchange for minor concessions.

On December 19, 1952, the Assembly adopted a resolution sponsored by eleven Latin American States, expressing confidence that France, in pursuance of its proclaimed policies, would "endeavor to further the fundamental liberties of the people of Morocco, in conformity with the purposes and principles of the Charter", and expressing the hope that the parties would "continue negotiations towards developing the free political institutions of the people of Morocco, with due regard to legitimate rights and interests under the established norms and practices of the law of nations". It also appealed to the parties "to conduct their relations in an atmosphere of good will, mutual confidence and respect and to settle their disputes in accordance with the spirit of the Charter, thus refraining from any acts or measures likely to aggravate the present tension".

The thirteen Asian and African Members had desired the Assembly to request France and the Sultan to enter into negotiations for an early peaceful settlement in accord with the sovereignty of Morocco, the aspirations of its people and the United Nations Charter. When their own draft resolution was rejected, they supported the Latin American proposal.

On July 9, 1953, the same thirteen Asian and African States, together with Liberia and Thailand, requested that the General Assembly consider the question of Morocco at the eighth session, stating that the policies pursued by France, in spite of the Assembly's recommendation, had caused an aggravation of the situation.

On August 21, the same countries requested an urgent meeting of the Security Council to investigate the international friction and danger to international peace and security which had arisen by the unlawful intervention of France in Morocco and the overthrow of its legitimate Sovereign, and to take appropriate action under the Charter.

The Security Council, after debating the question of including the item in its agenda at six meetings between August 26 and September 3, decided not to include the item in the agenda.

The General Assembly, on September 17, included the question of Morocco in its agenda.

France did not participate in the discussion on the question on the ground that it considered such discussion an outright intervention by the United Nations in matters essentially within the domestic jurisdiction of France, in contravention of Article 2, paragraph 7.

Thirteen of the sponsoring Asian and African States proposed that the Assembly recommend that democratic representative institutions for the people of Morocco be established through free elections on the basis of universal suffrage, and that all necessary steps be taken to insure within five years the complete realization by the people of Morocco of their right to full sovereignty and independence.

In the view of those supporting the joint draft resolution, the French Government, far from justifying the confidence expressed in the General Assembly's resolution of the previous year, had replied by deposing the Sultan and by declaring the Istiqlal party illegal in order to eliminate all opposition to the so-called reforms prepared at the request of the French settlers. The General Assembly had confirmed its competence in the matter by deciding at two sessions to discuss the question, and by adopting a resolution. Moreover, that competence was based on various factors such as the violation by the French Government of the Act of Algeciras and the Treaty of Fez, the infringement of the obligations of the French Government under Chapter XI of the Charter, and the violation of human rights and of the rules of international law.

A number of representatives opposing the joint draft resolution questioned the competence of the United Nations in the matter. The Treaty of Fez, which had been expressly accepted by all the signatories of the Act of Algeciras, provided that the conduct of Morocco's external affairs was the sole responsibility of France. Moreover, international security was not at stake. Other representatives considered that the United Nations was competent, but would not support the draft resolution because they feared discussion of the question would lead to a stiffening of attitude on the part of the parties concerned.

A draft resolution submitted by Bolivia provided that the General Assembly should renew its appeal for the reduction of tension in Morocco, and again express its confidence and hope that the free political institutions of the people of Morocco would be developed in conformity with the spirit of the Charter.

The First Committee rejected the Asian-African draft resolution and adopted the Bolivian draft resolution, as amended by India, Indonesia and Burma, that the Assembly recognize the right of the people of Morocco to complete self-determination in conformity with the Charter, and urge that the right of the people of Morocco to free democratic political institutions should be insured.

On November 3, 1953, the draft resolution recommended by the First Committee failed to obtain a two-thirds majority, and was not adopted.

The General Assembly again considered the question of Morocco at the ninth session at the request of fourteen Asian and African States, which recalled that no resolution had been adopted at the previous session, and that France had not taken any effective steps to further fundamental liberties and to develop the free political institutions of the people of Morocco.

In the general debate in the Assembly, the representative of France emphasized that France intended to call upon the Moroccan people gradually, but as quickly as possible, to manage their own affairs within the framework of Moroccan sovereignty. France would not share with anyone its responsibilities in that regard, but would carry them out in conformity with its traditions and in loyalty to the spirit of the Charter. As at previous sessions, the representative of France did not attend the meetings at which the question was considered.

On December 17, 1954, the General Assembly adopted a resolution originating with twelve of the sponsoring Asian-African States whereby, noting that some delegations had declared that negotiations between France and Morocco would be initiated regarding the Morocco question, the Assembly postponed the consideration of the item for the time being, and expressed confidence that the negotiations would bring about a satisfactory solution.

The question of Morocco was considered by the General Assembly at the tenth session at the request of the same fourteen Asian and African States. They contended that France had not taken any steps to negotiate the issue with the true representatives of the Moroccan people, and that the situation had been aggravated by further repressive measures.

During the general debate in the General Assembly, it was declared that the restoration of the exiled Sultan and the recognition of the right of the Moroccan people to independence and self-determination were prerequisites for a settlement of the issue. It was also stated that the Arab countries had nothing against the cooperation of Morocco with France, provided the arrangement was made on a basis of freedom and equality after Morocco had achieved independence.

The representative of France declared that his Government, alert to the realities of the day, would carry out its own decisions to make of Morocco a modern, democratic and sovereign State, united with France by the ties of freely accepted inter-dependence, and that it had prepared the way for the constitution of a representative Moroccan Government capable of introducing reforms.

After the General Assembly had decided on September 30, 1955, to include the Algerian question in its agenda, the representatives of France ceased to attend the meetings of the General Assembly and of standing Committees until after the General Assembly decided, on November 25, that it was no longer seized of the Algerian question.

On December 3, 1955, the General Assembly adopted a resolution submitted by 31 states, whereby the Assembly, noting that negotiations[5] between France and Morocco would be initiated regarding the question, decided to postpone further consideration of the item.

THE TUNISIAN QUESTION

DISCUSSION IN THE SECURITY COUNCIL. Eleven Asian and African Members of the United Nations asked the Security Council on April 2, 1952, urgently to consider "the present grave situation in Tunisia". They believed that suitable action by the Council would help toward a better understanding between the Tunisian and French peoples and fulfilment of Tunisian national aspirations. Certain earlier communications from the Tunisian Government had been circulated as Security Council documents at the request of Pakistan, in one of which, dated January 12, 1952, the Prime Minister of Tunisia stated that the domestic sovereignty of the Bey had been maintained intact under the Treaty of Bardo of 1881, by which France had established a protectorate over the territory. The subsequent establishment of a system of direct administration had led to constant unrest in Tunisia. To remedy that state of affairs, France had undertaken to abandon direct administration and to permit development towards internal autonomy. Negotiations between French and Tunisian representatives, however, had proved impossible since France insisted on conditions contrary to the Treaty of Bardo, such as the participation of French settlers in Tunisia's political institutions.

---

[5] On March 2, 1956, a joint declaration on the status of Morocco was signed by representatives of France and Morocco by which France recognized the independence of Morocco.

The Security Council debated inclusion of the item in its agenda at three meetings on April 4, 10 and 14. France argued that the application of January 12 was not receivable under the Charter, and was invalid because the Bey's seal had not been attached. Several weeks previously, it might have been argued that there was a domestic dispute, not between France and Tunisia, but between the Residency-General and certain Ministers. However, since the agreement between the Bey and the Resident-General, the Council could only note that any situation or dispute had disappeared.

In their letters of April 2, the eleven States—Afghanistan, Burma, Egypt, India, Indonesia, Iran, Iraq, Pakistan, the Philippines, Saudi Arabia and Yemen—said that, since the Tunisian application of January 12, the Prime Minister and other Ministers of the Tunisian Government had been arrested and the situation had continued to deteriorate. France explained that the Resident-General's decision concerning the former Ministers had been based primarily on the need to insure, in his conversations with the Bey, an atmosphere in which he could freely express his views.

After considerable discussion, the proposal to include the question in the agenda was defeated on April 14.

CONSIDERATION BY THE GENERAL ASSEMBLY. After the Security Council had rejected their request to consider the Tunisian situation, the eleven States, together with two others—Lebanon and Syria—asked on June 20, that a special session of the General Assembly be summoned. A special session was not convened, owing to lack of a majority in favor. Therefore, on July 30, the same thirteen States asked that the Tunisian question be included in the provisional agenda of the seventh regular session. The Assembly approved this request on October 16, and the First Committee considered the question.

In the General Committee and in the Assembly itself, France declared its relations with Tunisia essentially a matter of domestic jurisdiction, and declined to participate in the discussion. Discussion on the wisdom of proposals submitted was consequently linked with discussion on competence.

A draft resolution, submitted by the thirteen sponsoring States, to recommend that negotiations between France and Tunisia be resumed to implement the right of self-determination and providing for the appointment of a commission of good offices to assist in the negotiations, was rejected in the First Committee.

A draft resolution, based on a proposal submitted by eleven Latin American States, was adopted by the General Assembly on December 17, 1952. It expressed confidence that France would endeavor to further the development of free institutions; it expressed the hope that the parties would continue negotiations with a view to bringing about self-government for the Tunisians; and it appealed to the parties concerned to settle their disputes in accordance with the spirit of the Charter.

The General Assembly included the Tunisian question in its agenda for the eighth session at the request of fourteen Asian and African countries. France again declined to participate in the discussion, and again the question of competence was extensively debated.

A draft resolution submitted by thirteen of the sponsoring States was adopted in modified form by the First Committee. It provided that the General Assembly should recommend that all necessary steps be taken to insure the realization by the people of Tunisia of their right to full sovereignty and independence. Despite amendment in plenary session, the draft resolution was not adopted, having failed to obtain a two-thirds majority.

The Tunisian question was again included in the agenda of the ninth session of the General Assembly at the request of the fourteen Asian and African countries.

On October 4, 1954, in the course of the general debate, the representative of France reiterated that France intended to fulfil the promises made to the peoples for which it was responsible, that they would be enabled to manage their own affairs. France would not share with anyone the responsibilities which it had assumed and which it proposed to discharge. It had assumed those responsibilities because they derived from its Constitution, from treaties it had concluded, from its traditions, and from loyalty to the spirit of the Charter.

During the consideration of the question by the First Committee, the representative of France was absent.

A draft resolution proposed by the fourteen Asian-African States was approved in revised form by the First Committee on December 16 and adopted by the General Assembly on December 17, 1954. By the terms of this resolution, the Assembly, noting with satisfaction that the parties concerned had entered into negotiations[6] which were still in progress, expressed confidence that the negotiations would bring about a satisfactory solution and decided to postpone for the time being further consideration of the question.

THE QUESTION OF ALGERIA

On January 5, 1955, Saudi Arabia brought to the attention of the Security Council the "grave situation in Algeria". The Saudi Arabian Government reserved its right to request a meeting of the Council to consider the matter. An explanatory note on the question was circulated to the members of the Council at the request of Saudi Arabia.

On July 29, 1955, fourteen Asian and African States requested that the question of Algeria be included in the agenda of the tenth session of the General Assembly.

Three of the sponsoring States, India, Iraq, and Pakistan, were invited, at their request, to participate in the discussion in the General Committee as to whether to include the item.

The representative of France, opposing inclusion of the item, stated that Algerian affairs were essentially within his Government's domestic jurisdiction. Algeria was an integral part of metropolitan France and had been so since 1834. Any Algerian, whether a Moslem or a Christian, was a French citizen and, from the age of 21, an elector. The United Nations, therefore, was prohibited by the Charter from intervening in this matter. The fact that Algeria had been conquered was immaterial, since that had been true also of other provinces of France. The right of self-determination of peoples was referred to in Article 1 of the Charter only as a purpose; no special method for attaining it was laid down.

The representatives of Egypt, Iraq, Pakistan, Thailand, India and the U.S.S.R. supported inclusion of the item, contending that the situation in Algeria had worsened, and the severe repressive measures had aggravated the difficulties between France and the Algerian nationalists. Since November 1, 1954, war had, in fact, broken out in Algeria. International concern regarding the situation in Algeria had been demonstrated by the fact that it had been brought to the notice of the Security Council by the Saudi Arabian delegation, and by the stand taken by the Bandung Conference urging the French Government to seek a peaceful solution. Regarding the contention that Article 2, paragraph 7, of the Charter precluded intervention, it was noted that until 1830 Algeria had been independent, maintaining diplomatic and treaty relations with numerous states. Only thirty years later was Algeria completely conquered. Its current status was defined in 1870 by the French Government without the Algerian people being consulted. Despite theoreti-

---

[6] Negotiations between France and Tunisia resulted in a protocol of agreement signed on March 20, 1956.

cal equality, in practice the Algerians did not enjoy the same rights as Frenchmen. Moreover, the General Assembly had always claimed competence in questions involving human rights, especially the right of self-determination.

The representatives of the United Kingdom, the United States and New Zealand were of the opinion that, under Article 2, paragraph 7, the United Nations was precluded from intervening in the Algerian question. The case of Algeria, an integral part of France, was different from that of Morocco or Tunisia, which were French protectorates.

The General Committee decided not to recommend inclusion of the item in the agenda.

The report of the General Committee on this item was examined by the Assembly at six meetings, during which considerable further debate took place on the question of competence. The recommendation of the General Committee not to include the Algerian question in the agenda was rejected on September 30.

After the vote, the representative of France declared that, in a matter which was essentially within the domestic jurisdiction of his country, his Government refused to accept any intervention of the United Nations which would be in defiance of the provisions of the Charter, and would consider as null and void any recommendation which the General Assembly might make on the matter. Having stated that the vote which had been taken might influence the relations between France and the United Nations, the French delegation ceased to attend the meetings of the General Assembly and its standing Committees.

On November 23, the Chairman of the First Committee drew attention to the proposal submitted that day by Chile, Colombia, Cuba and Ecuador that the General Assembly decide to delete the item, "The Question of Algeria", from its agenda. The First Committee decided to adjourn until November 25, to enable Members to consult among themselves in order to bring about harmony among the Members of the Organization on the Algerian item. On November 25, the First Committee adopted a procedural motion submitted by India that the Assembly decide not to consider further the question of Algeria at the tenth session.

On the same day, the General Assembly decided without debate or objection to adopt the proposal recommended to it by the First Committee on the question of Algeria.

Thereupon, numerous representatives expressed regret at the absence of France from the Assembly's debates, and also expressed their hope that France would soon resume its place and that the Algerian problem would be solved in a peaceful manner. Several representatives, while expressing their agreement with the decision just taken, reiterated that the United Nations was competent to deal with the Algerian question and that the decision adopted by the Assembly did not imply that the United Nations would not at a later stage deal once more with the question if France failed in its efforts to solve it. The representative of the United States pointed out that the crisis which had been solved by the General Assembly's decision showed the grave implications which might be entailed for the United Nations by taking up questions on which the action sought would conflict with the provisions of Article 2, paragraph 7.

Questions Relating to Europe

THE SPANISH QUESTION

The General Assembly's first resolution on Spain, February 9, 1946, recommended that Member States should act in accordance with a resolution of the San Francisco

Conference and a three-Power statement at the Potsdam Conference. The San Francisco Conference had resolved that Charter provisions for membership could not apply to states whose regimes had been installed with the help of the armed forces of ex-enemy countries so long as those regimes were in power; and, at the Potsdam Conference, the United Kingdom, the United States and the U.S.S.R. had stated that they would not support the Franco Government for admission.

In April 1946, Poland asked the Security Council to declare the existence of the Franco regime a threat to international peace and security, and to call on all Members of the United Nations to sever diplomatic relations with it. This proposal, however, was not carried.

On June 6, the majority of a sub-committee of five appointed by the Council reported that the activities of the Franco regime constituted not an existing threat, but a "potential" menace to international peace. It suggested that its findings should be transmitted to the Assembly with a recommendation that, unless the Franco regime were withdrawn and other conditions of political freedom satisfied, the Assembly should recommend the severance of diplomatic relations. A resolution embodying these recommendations, however, was not carried because of the negative vote of one of the permanent members, the U.S.S.R., which held that the findings had incorrectly labeled the Franco regime a "potential" rather than an "existing" threat to peace. The U.S.S.R. also considered that the Council, rather than the Assembly, was the appropriate organ to call for the severance of diplomatic relations.

On December 12, the Assembly recommended that the Franco Government should be barred from membership in international agencies established by or brought into relationship with the United Nations. It further suggested that the Security Council should consider adequate measures to remedy the Spanish situation if a democratic Spanish Government were not established within a reasonable time. Finally, it recommended that Members should immediately recall their ambassadors and ministers plenipotentiary accredited to Madrid and report to the Secretary-General.

The Secretary-General reported to the second session of the Assembly on the implementation of this resolution.

At its second session, the Assembly "expressed confidence" that the Security Council would take steps with regard to Spain whenever the situation there warranted it.

The Spanish question was again considered by the Assembly at the second part of its third session, but no action was taken.

In 1950, the Assembly renewed consideration of the question and, on November 4, revoked its recommendation for the withdrawal of ambassadors and ministers and its recommendation designed to debar Spain from membership in the agencies. It considered that the establishment of diplomatic relations and the exchange of ambassadors and ministers with a government did not imply any judgment on the domestic policy of that government. Moreover, because the specialized agencies were technical and largely non-political in character and had been established to benefit the peoples of all nations, they should be free to decide for themselves whether the participation of Spain was desirable.

(*See also sections on Admission of New Members, page 79, and Members of the United Nations and Specialized Agencies, appendix.*)

THE GREEK QUESTION

Several issues arising from the situation in Greece have been considered by the United Nations.

U.S.S.R. APPLICATION. The question was first taken up when, on January 21, 1946, the U.S.S.R. submitted to the Security Council that the continued presence of British troops in Greece constituted interference in Greek internal affairs likely to endanger peace and security. The United Kingdom stated that British troops were in Greece by agreement with the Greek Government, and Greece denied interference. After discussion, the Council accepted its President's suggestion to take note of the declarations and consider the matter closed.

UKRAINIAN APPLICATION. On August 24, 1946, the Ukrainian S.S.R. complained to the Council that the policies of the Greek Government constituted a threat to peace.

Greece denied the charges and referred to frontier incidents allegedly provoked by Albania. On September 11, 1946, Albania itself asked the Council to take up the situation on the Greco-Albanian frontier allegedly resulting from continued violations by Greek soldiers. Four draft resolutions were proposed, but all were rejected, and the Council regarded the case as closed.

GREEK APPLICATION. On December 3, 1946, Greece asked Council consideration of the situation in northern Greece resulting from aid allegedly provided to Greek guerrillas by the country's northern neighbors. These charges were denied by Albania, Bulgaria and Yugoslavia.

On December 19, the Council established a commission of investigation composed of one representative of each member of the Council for 1947 (Australia, Belgium, Brazil, China, Colombia, France, Poland, Syria, the U.S.S.R., the United Kingdom and the United States) to ascertain the causes and nature of the alleged border violations and to make proposals for averting a repetition

The Committee of Investigation, after investigations conducted in northern Greece, submitted a report which contained recommendations accepted by nine members of the Commission. A draft resolution providing for the appointment of a Commission, as envisaged in these recommendations, failed of adoption. In August, Greece requested consideration of the question as a threat to the peace under Chapter VII of the Charter, but draft resolutions submitted by Australia and the United States to deal with the question under Chapter VII also failed of adoption. On September 15, 1947, the Council removed the question from its agenda.

Meanwhile, in March 1947, when the United States explained to the Council its policy in giving aid to Greece and Turkey, the U.S.S.R. criticized it as unilateral action and said such aid should be given through the United Nations. A U.S.S.R. proposal to establish a special commission, composed of representatives of the members of the Council, to insure that aid received by Greece from outside was used only in the interests of the Greek people, was rejected by the Council on April 18.

ASSEMBLY DECISIONS IN 1947. The Council was unable to adopt any resolution in July and August 1947, and the Assembly took up the question in September. The Assembly called on Albania, Bulgaria and Yugoslavia to do nothing to aid the Greek guerrillas. It asked those three countries and Greece to cooperate in settling their disputes through the establishment of normal diplomatic relations, frontier conventions, and cooperation in solving refugee and minority problems. The Assembly established a United Nations Special Committee on the Balkans (UNSCOB), consisting of the representatives of Australia, Brazil, China, France, Mexico, the Netherlands, Pakistan, Poland, the U.S.S.R., the United Kingdom and the United States, to assist the four Governments in complying with its recommendations and to observe how far they did so.

Poland and the U.S.S.R. declared that they would not participate in the work of the Committee because they considered that its functions violated the sovereignty of Albania, Bulgaria and Yugoslavia.

In its first report, covering the period to June 16, 1948, UNSCOB said that only the Greek Government had complied with its request to station observation groups along the frontiers. The Committee had consistently endeavored to assist Albania, Bulgaria and Yugoslavia, on the one hand, and Greece, on the other, to establish normal diplomatic and good neighborly relations. Greece had cooperated with it, but Albania, Bulgaria and Yugoslavia had refused to do so, and had not recognized it as a duly constituted body of the United Nations. For these reasons, the Committee had been unable to aid the four Governments substantially in implementing the Assembly's recommendations.

ASSEMBLY DECISIONS IN 1948. On November 27, 1948, the Assembly again called on Albania, Bulgaria and Yugoslavia to stop supporting Greek guerrillas. Member States were asked to refrain from direct or indirect help to any armed group fighting against the Greek Government.

The Assembly decided to continue the Special Committee with the same terms of reference, and it authorized UNSCOB to consult the Interim Committee at its discretion.

In another resolution embodying certain paragraphs of a U.S.S.R. proposal, the Assembly called on Greece, on the one hand, and Albania and Bulgaria, on the other, to establish diplomatic relations; and recommended that Greece, Albania, Bulgaria and Yugoslavia renew the conventions for the settlement of frontier questions or conclude new ones, and settle the refugee question in a spirit of mutual understanding.

During the Assembly session, a Conciliation Committee was established in November 1948, to devise methods and procedures for resolving the differences between Greece, Albania, Bulgaria and Yugoslavia. It consisted of the President of the Assembly, the Secretary-General, and the Chairman and the Rapporteur of the Assembly's First Committee. Some progress toward agreement appeared to be made but, with the close of the session, the Conciliation Committee ended its work, and a copy of a statement by the Chairman was sent to UNSCOB.

UNSCOB meanwhile was continuing its work of mediation and observation. In its report to the fourth session of the Assembly, it stated that Albania and Bulgaria had assisted the Greek guerrilla movement, and had also encouraged the Greek guerrillas in their attempts to overthrow the Greek Government. Yugoslavia had aided the guerrillas, but this aid had diminished and might even have ceased. The report stated that the continuance of the existing situation in Greece was a threat to that country's independence and a threat to peace in the Balkans.

ASSEMBLY DECISIONS IN 1949. At the Assembly's fourth session, the U.S.S.R. proposed that the Assembly should appeal to the parties to cease military operations and should recommend measures including a general amnesty, supervised elections, a joint commission for frontier supervision, cessation of military assistance to the Greek Government, fixing of a time limit for withdrawal of foreign troops from Greece, and dissolution of the Special Committee on the Balkans. The Assembly rejected this draft resolution.

On November 18, 1949, the Assembly adopted a resolution stating that active assistance given to the Greek guerrillas by Albania in particular, by Bulgaria, and by certain other states, including Romania, was contrary to the Charter and endangered peace in the Balkans. It declared that further foreign assistance to the guerillas would seriously increase the danger to peace, and would justify a special session of the Assembly to consider steps necessary to remove this danger.

Albania, Bulgaria and the other States concerned, were again called on to cease rendering support to the guerrillas, and all Members of the United Nations and other states were asked to refrain from assisting them, and from providing arms or other war materials to Albania and Bulgaria until those countries stopped assisting them.

The Assembly decided that the work of the United Nations Special Committee on the Balkans should be continued.

ASSEMBLY DECISIONS IN 1950. On December 1, 1950, at its fifth session, the Assembly took note of the Special Committee's conclusion that there remained a threat to Greece's political independence and territorial integrity. The Assembly continued the Special Committee with its previous mandate until the sixth session, but provided that, even before then, the Committee could recommend its own dissolution to the Interim Committee.

Concerning those members of the Greek armed forces who had been captured by the Greek guerrillas and taken into countries north of Greece, the Assembly noted the Special Committee's observations that, with the exception of Yugoslavia, the other states concerned were detaining these persons and called for repatriation of those who wished it.

In its report to the sixth session, the Special Committee stated that the threat to Greece continued, although changed in character since the retreat of the guerrilla forces in 1949. The guerrillas were receiving external aid from Albania, Bulgaria, Czechoslovakia, Hungary, Poland and Romania. The Committee recommended considering "the advisability of maintaining United Nations vigilance over the Balkans in the light of the present nature of the threat to peace in that area".

ASSEMBLY DECISIONS IN 1951. The Assembly endorsed this report, expressed appreciation to the Special Committee and its observers, and discontinued the Committee. It then provided for the establishment of a Balkan Sub-Commission by the Peace Observation Commission. To the Sub-Commission it gave authority: (a) to dispatch observers to any area of international tension in the Balkans on the request of any state or states concerned, but only to the territory of states consenting thereto; (b) to visit any area in which such observation is being conducted; and (c) to consider such data as may be submitted to it by its members or observers, and to report to the Peace Observation Commission and to the Secretary-General for the information of Member States. (See page 71.)

REPATRIATION OF GREEK CHILDREN. UNSCOB had reported that during 1948, some 25,000 Greek children had been removed from Greece and retained in the territories of the northern neighbors of Greece and other countries. In November 1948, the Assembly asked for the return to Greece of all Greek children who asked to be returned, or whose parents or close relatives requested it.

A year later, the Assembly instructed the Secretary-General to ask the International Committee of the Red Cross and the League of Red Cross Societies to continue their efforts, and urged all United Nations Members and other states harboring Greek children to cooperate.

Another year later, the Assembly noted "with grave concern" that not a single child had been returned to his native land and, with the exception of Yugoslavia, no country harboring those children had complied definitely with the previous resolutions. In a new effort to bring about repatriation, the Assembly set up a Standing Committee composed of the representatives of Peru, the Philippines and Sweden, and asked the International Red Cross organizations to continue their efforts.

At its sixth session, in February 1952, the Assembly recognized that the United

Nations must continue its efforts to enable the Greek children to return to their homes. Once again it urged all countries harboring them to facilitate their early return. It continued the Standing Committee and asked the International Red Cross organizations to continue their work.

The Assembly noted "with satisfaction" that Greek children had been repatriated from Yugoslavia, and expressed the hope that rapid progress would be possible with the repatriation of those in Czechoslovakia.

At its seventh session in 1952, the Assembly decided that work for the repatriation of Greek children, except in Yugoslavia, should be suspended until conditions were established which would make such action practical and useful, and that the Standing Committee should be discontinued.

The Assembly noted with satisfaction that further groups of children had been repatriated from Yugoslavia, and it requested the Red Cross to continue its work there until all Greek children had been repatriated.

THE CORFU CHANNEL QUESTION

On January 10, 1947, the United Kingdom brought to the Security Council's attention a dispute with Albania concerning damage to British warships and injury to British naval personnel by mines in the Corfu Channel during October 1946. Britain alleged that Albania was responsible. Albania denied the charge and accused Britain of violating its sovereignty in territorial waters. A proposal to find that an unnotified minefield was laid by Albania or with its connivance failed of adoption.

On the United Kingdom's proposal, the Council then recommended that Britain and Albania refer their dispute to the International Court of Justice. (*For subsequent developments, see Legal Questions, page 293.*)

FREE TERRITORY OF TRIESTE

The responsibility of insuring the independence and integrity of the Free Territory of Trieste—including the appointment of a Governor—was accepted by the Security Council on January 10, 1947. This acceptance was implicit in the Council's approval of certain articles and annexes to the proposed peace treaty with Italy relating to the establishment of the Free Territory and a Free Port, under the Council's supervision.

On the question of the appointment of a Governor, the Council decided on July 10, 1947, to establish a sub-committee to collect additional information about candidates. Subsequently, the Council asked its permanent members to hold an informal consultation on the subject, and later also requested Yugoslavia and Italy to consult with each other in an effort to agree on a candidate. However, no agreement was reached, and a U.S.S.R. proposal to appoint Colonel Hermann Fluckiger, of Switzerland, as Governor was rejected by the Council on May 10, 1949.

Meanwhile, on July 28, 1948, Yugoslavia charged that certain financial agreements between Italy and the Allied Military Command of the British-United States zone of occupation in Trieste were in contradiction to obligations contained in the Italian Peace Treaty, and were aimed at the economic incorporation of Trieste into Italy. Yugoslavia asked the Council to declare the financial agreements in violation of the Peace Treaty, and to assure the respect by the United States and the United Kingdom of their international obligations. The United States, the United Kingdom and France termed Yugoslavia's charges unfounded. While advocating revisions in the Trieste provisions of the Treaty, they would, pending a new solution, continue to regard the Treaty as binding. The Three-Power Declaration of March 20, 1948 (concerning such revision and advocating transfer of Trieste to Italian sovereignty) had been made, they stated, partly because of the delay in appointing a Governor, and partly because of unsatisfactory conditions in the Yugoslav zone, which had been virtually incorporated into Yugoslavia.

Yugoslavia proposed that the Council declare the agreements between the Allied Military Command and Italy null and void. The Ukrainian S.S.R. proposed that the Council consider it urgently necessary to settle the question of the appointment of a Governor. Both draft resolutions were rejected by the Council.

On October 12, 1953, the U.S.S.R. submitted a draft resolution providing that the Council should appoint Colonel Fluckiger as Governor, and should implement the terms of the Treaty of Peace with Italy concerning the Free Territory of Trieste. On December 14, the United States moved that further consideration of the question be postponed pending the outcome of current efforts to find a solution. This motion was approved. On October 5, 1954, Italy, the United Kingdom, the United States and Yugoslavia transmitted to the President of the Security Council one copy of a Memorandum of Understanding signed by them on the same date in London concerning the Free Territory of Trieste. The Memorandum, it was stated, had resulted from consultations between the four Governments following the failure to implement the terms of the Italian Peace Treaty concerning the Free Territory. The Memorandum provided for certain boundary adjustments between Yugoslavia and the Free Territory, on the completion of which the United Kingdom, the United States and Yugoslavia would withdraw their military forces from the area north of the new boundary, and relinquish the administration of that area to Italy. The Governments of Italy and Yugoslavia would then extend their civil administration over the areas allotted to them.

On October 12, the U.S.S.R. informed the President of the Security Council that his Government had noted the agreement between the four Powers and, in view of the fact that it would promote the establishment of normal relations between Italy and Yugoslavia, had taken cognizance of it.

THE CZECHOSLOVAKIAN SITUATION

At the request of Chile, the Security Council in March 1948, considered a request from Jan Papanek, permanent representative of Czechoslovakia, for an investigation of events preceding and succeeding the change of government in Czechoslovakia on February 22, 1948. Dr. Papanek charged that his country's independence had been violated by threat of force by the U.S.S.R., and that the coup had been carried out with the direct and indirect participation of the U.S.S.R.

The representative of the Soviet Union denounced the allegations as false. Czechoslovakia declined an invitation to participate in the discussion on grounds of domestic jurisdiction.

A proposal to appoint a sub-committee to receive evidence was rejected by the negative vote of the U.S.S.R.

THE BERLIN QUESTION

On September 29, 1948, France, the United States and the United Kingdom drew attention to the serious situation which had arisen "as the result of the unilateral imposition by the Government of the U.S.S.R. of restrictions on transport and communications between the Western Zones of Occupation in Germany and Berlin", action which they said was contrary to the obligations under Article 2 of the Charter and caused a threat to the peace.

The Security Council considered this question at several meetings beginning October 4. The U.S.S.R. questioned the Council's competence, contended that the measures taken by the U.S.S.R. had been necessitated by currency reforms in the Western Zones which threatened the Soviet Zone with economic collapse, and that separation of the Berlin question from the entire problem of Germany was artificial and would lead to erroneous decisions.

On the other hand, the United States contended that the question before the Council was not the entire problem of Germany, but the threat to international peace and security caused by the imposition and maintenance of the Soviet blockade of Berlin and other measures of duress against the three other occupying powers. By a vote of 9 to 2, the question was placed on the Council's agenda, whereupon the U.S.S.R. and the Ukrainian S.S.R. announced that they would not take part in the discussion.

From the time the Berlin question was first taken up, a number of Council members informally considered ways of solving the problem, and later submitted a draft resolution which was approved by nine members but vetoed by the U.S.S.R.

In another effort, the President of the Security Council addressed five questions relating to currency problems to the four occupying Powers and invited Belgium, Canada, China, Colombia, Syria and the Secretary-General each to nominate a financial or economic expert who, together with an expert from his own country (Argentina), were to meet in Paris as a Technical Committee on Currency and Trade in Berlin to consider and make recommendations. After several weeks of discussions, however, this Committee was unable to work out an acceptable solution.

United Nations representatives of the four occupying Powers held informal conversations on the Berlin question during the second part of the third session of the General Assembly and, on May 4, 1949, the Secretary-General was requested to notify the Council of the agreement reached.

HUMAN RIGHTS AND FUNDAMENTAL FREEDOMS: BULGARIA, HUNGARY AND ROMANIA

On March 16, 1949, Bolivia requested the General Assembly to study the legal proceedings against Josef Cardinal Mindszenty, Roman Catholic Primate of Hungary, in relation to Charter obligations concerning human rights and fundamental freedoms. The People's Court in Budapest on February 8, 1949, had convicted Cardinal Mindszenty of treason, attempting to overthrow the Republic, and speculating in foreign currency. It had sentenced him to life imprisonment. Three days after the Bolivian request, Australia asked the Assembly to deal with the "observance of fundamental freedoms and human rights in Bulgaria and Hungary, including the question of religious and civil liberty in special relation to recent trials of church leaders". A Sofia court had sentenced four leading members of the Supreme Council of United Protestant Churches of Bulgaria on March 8, 1949, to life imprisonment, and eleven other Protestant ministers to shorter terms.

On April 30, 1949, the Assembly adopted a resolution which expressed deep concern at the grave accusations made against the Governments of Bulgaria and Hungary. The Assembly noted that steps had been taken by several states signatories to the peace treaties with Bulgaria and Hungary regarding these accusations, and expressed the hope that measures would be diligently applied, in accordance with the treaties, to insure respect for human rights and fundamental freedoms. It decided to retain the question on the agenda of its fourth regular session.

At the fourth session, Australia raised a similar question with regard to Romania. On October 22, 1949, the Assembly recorded its opinion that the refusal of Bulgaria, Hungary and Romania to cooperate in efforts to examine the grave charges had justified the Assembly's concern.

The Assembly then asked the International Court of Justice for an advisory opinion on four questions relating to the peace treaties.

On the basis of the Court's opinions (*see page 309*), the Assembly at its fifth session adopted a further resolution on November 3, 1950, condemning the three Governments for "wilful refusal" to fulfil their obligation to appoint representatives to treaty commissions. The resolution noted the continuance of serious accusations against those Governments of violation of human rights. It invited Member States, particularly parties to the treaties of peace with Bulgaria, Hungary and Romania, to submit evidence in relation to the question to the Secretary-General for transmittal to Members.

COMPLAINT OF AGGRESSIVE ACTS OF THE UNITED STATES AND ITS INTERFERENCE IN THE DOMESTIC AFFAIRS OF OTHER COUNTRIES

At the request of the U.S.S.R., an item was placed on the agenda of the sixth session of the General Assembly entitled "Complaint of aggressive acts of the United States of America and its interference in the domestic affairs of other countries, as instanced by the appropriation of $100,000,000 to finance the recruitment of persons and the organization of armed groups in the Soviet Union, Poland, Czechoslovakia, Hungary, Romania, Bulgaria, Albania, and a number of other democratic countries, as well as outside the territory of those countries".

After discussion at four meetings, the First Committee on December 21, 1951, rejected a U.S.S.R. draft resolution condemning the United States Mutual Security Act of 1951. The proposal was reintroduced, however, when the Committee's report was taken up by the Assembly on January 11, 1952.

The U.S.S.R. complained that the appropriation of $100,000,000 by that Act to finance the recruitment of persons and the organization of armed groups in and outside the seven States named constituted aggressive activity by the United States and interference in the domestic affairs of other countries.

The United States, on the other hand, argued that the intention of its Congress was that the funds should be used to allow refugees from Eastern Europe to take part in the defence of the North Atlantic community if they chose to do so.

As in the First Committee, the Assembly rejected the U.S.S.R. draft resolution. A similar complaint that the United States was interfering in the internal affairs of other states by organizing subversive and espionage activities against the U.S.S.R., the People's Republic of China, the Czechoslovak Republic, and other peoples' democracies was submitted to the seventh session of the Assembly in October 1952 by Czechoslovakia.

A draft resolution was submitted by Czechoslovakia providing that the Assembly should: (1) condemn as acts of aggression and as interference in the internal affairs of other states in contravention of the Charter and of international law, the subversive activities organized by the United States Government against a number of states in application of the Mutual Security Act of 1951 and the Act of June 20, 1952, developing and supplementing the aforesaid Act; and (2) recommended that the United States repeal the parts of those Acts related to the appropriation of funds for the organization of subversive activities and espionage.

In opposition to the Czechoslovak draft resolution, it was stated that no additional funds had been voted in 1952 to supplement the Mutual Security Act of 1951. Of the funds voted in 1951, over 95 per cent was for regular military and economic assistance, forming a part of the larger sums the United States was spending under the Mutual Security Act and had previously spent under the Marshall Plan. The remaining 4 per cent was to help escapees who had no new citizenship, and was used to help the host countries provide reception and living quarters, food, clothing, medical care, vocational training and employment, and emigration advice. It was further maintained that a sovereign country had the right to furnish military and economic aid to those countries it wished to see developed. Assistance to refugees from Eastern Europe was not an interference in the domestic affairs of those countries, as such assistance was often given, for example, the U.S.S.R. had given refuge to many escapees from Spain.

Following rejection of the Czechoslovak draft resolution by the First Committee, it was reintroduced in the General Assembly where it was again rejected.

INVESTIGATION OF CONDITIONS FOR FREE ELECTIONS IN GERMANY

France, the United Kingdom and the United States, acting on a proposal by the German Federal Chancellor, brought to the General Assembly's sixth session a request for the appointment of an impartial international commission under United Nations supervision to carry out a simultaneous investigation in the Federal Republic of Germany, in Berlin, and in the Soviet Zone of Germany to determine whether existing conditions there made it possible to hold genuinely free elections throughout those areas, which would be a decisive step toward reunification. Such elections could not take place unless all the inhabitants of Germany had the opportunity freely to make known their views. The representatives of the German Democratic Republic and of the eastern sector of Berlin stated that the task of determining whether conditions in Germany would enable truly free elections to be held should devolve upon the Germans themselves, through a commission composed of representatives of East and West Germany, under the supervision of the four occupying Powers. Establishment of a commission of investigation, they contended, would constitute intervention in the domestic affairs of the German people.

In a resolution adopted on December 20, 1951, the Assembly considered it desirable to give effect to the request for appointment of a commission, having regard to the purposes and principles of the United Nations, taking due account of the responsibilities of the four Powers regarding Germany, and desiring to help achieve the unity of Germany in the interests of world peace.

The resolution established a commission composed of representatives of Brazil, Iceland, the Netherlands, Pakistan and Poland. Poland, however, declined to accept membership on the ground that the resolution was illegal and contrary to the Charter, particularly Article 107 and Article 2, paragraph 7.

In carrying out immediately the simultaneous investigation to ascertain and report whether conditions made "genuinely free and secret elections" throughout those areas possible, the Commission was to investigate the following matters so far as they affected the holding of free elections: (1) the constitutional provisions in force and their application as regards the various aspects of individual freedom; (2) freedom of political parties to organize and carry out their activities; and (3) the organization and activities of the judiciary, police and other administrative organs. The Assembly directed the Commission to report as soon as possible on the results of its efforts to arrange with all the parties concerned for undertaking its work. The Commission was to report by September 1, 1952, on the results of its activities.

On April 30, 1952, the Commission submitted a unanimous report covering the period from February 11 to that date. It had decided that its first task was to make the necessary arrangements with all the parties concerned to enable it to undertake its work.

During a visit to Germany from March 16 to 23, the Commission concluded satisfactory arrangements concerning the required arrangements with the Allied

High Commission for Germany, the Government of the Federal Republic of Germany, the Inter-Allied *Kommandatura* in Berlin (in so far as the authority of that body extended over those areas of Berlin over which the French, United Kingdom and United States commanders in Berlin exercised authority), and the Government of the western sector of Berlin.

However, the Commission was not able to establish contact with the authorities in the Soviet Zone of Germany and in the eastern sector of Berlin, and was thus unable to make the necessary arrangements with them. The Commission regretfully concluded that at that time there was little prospect of its being able to pursue its task.

However, the Commission reported it would remain at the disposal of the United Nations and the parties concerned, and would make a further attempt to implement its mandate whenever it seemed likely that new steps might lead to positive results.

COMPLAINT OF HOSTILE ACTIVITIES AGAINST YUGOSLAVIA

Yugoslavia complained on November 9, 1951, that for more than three years the U.S.S.R. had been organizing pressure against it in order to threaten its territorial integrity and national independence. That pressure had been applied both directly and through the Governments of Hungary, Bulgaria, Romania, Albania, Czechoslovakia and Poland in actions which violated the generally accepted principles regarding relations among nations.

Accordingly, having exhausted all normal diplomatic means for eliminating the situation, Yugoslavia asked the General Assembly to take action. Specifically, it proposed that the Assembly recommend that Yugoslavia and the seven other States conduct their relations and settle their disputes in accordance with the spirit of the Charter, conform in their diplomatic intercourse with the rules and practices customary in international relations, and settle frontier disputes by means of mixed frontier commissions or other peaceful means of their choice. Yugoslavia submitted a draft resolution to this effect.

The U.S.S.R. and other delegations maintained that the groundless Yugoslav complaint had been intended to mislead public opinion, and to divert the attention of the Yugoslav people from the efforts of their leaders to make Yugoslavia a docile instrument of the aggressive policy of the United States.

The Assembly, on December 14, adopted the Yugoslav draft resolution.

AUSTRIAN STATE TREATY

The question of an appeal to the signatories to the Moscow Declaration of November 1, 1943, for an early fulfilment of their pledges toward Austria was taken up by the General Assembly at its seventh session at the request of Brazil; and Brazil, together with Lebanon, Mexico and the Netherlands, submitted the draft resolution which the Assembly adopted on December 20, 1952.

In this, the Assembly earnestly appealed to the U.S.S.R., the United Kingdom, the United States and France—the Governments concerned—to make a renewed and urgent effort to reach agreement on the terms of an Austrian treaty so that the occupation might soon be terminated, and Austria might fully exercise the powers inherent in its sovereignty.

However, on the contention that the Assembly was not legally entitled even to consider the subject, the Byelorussian S.S.R., Czechoslovakia, Poland, the Ukrainian S.S.R. and the U.S.S.R. did not participate in the consideration of the item, did not take part in the vote, and stated that they would not recognize the validity of any resolution which might emerge. They based their contention on Article 107 of the

Charter. This states that "Nothing in the present Charter shall invalidate or preclude action, in relation to any state which, during the Second World War, has been an enemy of any signatory to the present Charter, taken or authorized as a result of that war by the Governments having responsibility for such action."

Questions Relating to the Western Hemisphere

THE QUESTION OF THE COMPLAINT OF GUATEMALA

On June 19, 1954, the Minister for External Relations of Guatemala requested the President of the Security Council to convene a meeting urgently in order that, in accordance with Articles 34, 35 (concerning peaceful settlement of disputes) and 39 (concerning, *inter alia,* acts of aggression) of the Charter, the Council might take the measures necessary to prevent the disruption of peace and international security in Central America, and also to put a stop to the aggression in progress against Guatemala.

The Security Council met on Sunday, June 20. After the adoption of the agenda, the President invited the representatives of Guatemala, Honduras and Nicaragua to participate in the discussion.

The representative of Guatemala stated that Guatemala had been invaded by expeditionary forces forming part of an unlawful international aggression which was the outcome of a vast international conspiracy and was masked as a rising of exiles. The Guatemalan Government had two requests to make. In the first place, the Security Council should send a warning to the Governments of Honduras and Nicaragua, calling upon them to apprehend the exiles and the mercenaries who were invading Guatemala, and whose bases were in Nicaragua and Honduras. Secondly, the Guatemalan Government requested that an observation commission of the Security Council should be constituted in Guatemala, and in other countries if necessary, to verify the fact that the countries accused by Guatemala had connived at the invasion.

The representatives of Honduras and Nicaragua both stated their opinion that the matter should be dealt with by the Organization of American States, when their Governments would be heard and could defend themselves.

The representative of Brazil, calling attention to Chapter VIII of the Charter (concerning regional arrangements), and particularly to Article 52, paragraph 3, introduced a joint draft resolution sponsored by Brazil and Colombia, which provided that the Security Council should refer the complaint of the Government of Guatemala to the Organization of American States for urgent consideration, and should request the latter to inform the Council as soon as possible, as appropriate, on the measures it had been able to take on the matter.

The representative of France proposed that a final paragraph should be added to the draft resolution whereby the Council, without prejudice to such measures as the Organization of American States might take, would call for the immediate termination of any action likely to cause further bloodshed, and would request all Members of the United Nations to abstain, in the spirit of the Charter, from giving assistance to any such action. The amendment was accepted by the sponsors of the joint draft resolution.

The representative of Guatemala declared that Articles 33 and 52 were inapplicable since the case did not constitute a dispute but was one of aggression. The Guatemalan request was based on Articles 34, 35 and 39, which gave his country an unchallenged right to appeal to the Security Council.

The joint draft resolution was supported by the majority of the members of the

Council. The representative of the U.S.S.R. opposed the draft resolution, stating that the Council had before it a clear and obvious case of aggression committed by neighboring states. The Council should take immediate steps to end that aggression.

The joint draft resolution, as modified, received 10 votes in favor and 1 against. Since the negative vote was that of a permanent member (U.S.S.R.), the draft resolution was not adopted.

The representative of France then reintroduced his amendment to the joint draft resolution as a separate draft resolution, which was unanimously adopted.

At the request of the representatives of Guatemala and of the U.S.S.R., the Council met again on June 25, 1954. The provisional agenda read "Cablegram dated June 19, 1954, from the Minister for External Relations of Guatemala addressed to the President of the Security Council and letter dated June 22, 1954, from the representative of Guatemala addressed to the Secretary-General". During the discussion on the adoption of the agenda, the President ruled, on a point of order raised by the representative of the U.S.S.R., that the representative of Guatemala should not be invited to participate in the meeting until the agenda was adopted. The representative of the U.S.S.R. challenged the President's ruling. The challenge was put to the vote, and rejected. After further discussion, the question of the adoption of the agenda was put to the vote. The agenda, however, was not adopted because of a lack of a majority.

During the discussion which preceded the vote, several representatives expressed the view that any decision which the Security Council might take on the question of the adoption of the agenda should not be interpreted as meaning that the Council was divesting itself of its responsibility in the case of the Guatemalan complaint. Certain representatives felt that in any event the question should be placed on the agenda; the discussion could then be deferred.

On June 27, the Chairman of the Inter-American Peace Committee informed the Secretary-General that the Committee had established itself as a fact-finding committee and was proceeding to Guatemala, Honduras and Nicaragua. On July 5, another communication stated that the three countries concerned had informed the Peace Committee that the dispute between them had ceased to exist.

On July 9, the Minister for External Relations of Guatemala, in a cablegram to the President of the Security Council, stated that "the occurrences that prompted the previous Government to appeal to the Security Council in the communication of June 19 and subsequent correspondence" had ceased and that peace and order had been restored.

ECONOMIC QUESTIONS

World Economic Conditions and Trends

The world economic situation is reviewed every year by the Economic and Social Council, in accordance with a General Assembly recommendation of October 1947. Background information for these discussions is provided by the Secretariat in the form of factual analyses of world economic conditions and trends. Reports published by the end of 1955 have included the following:

Salient Features of the World Economic Situation, 1945-47.
Survey of Current Inflationary and Deflationary Tendencies.
Economic Report: Salient Features of the World Economic Situation, 1945-47.
This was supplemented by *Selected World Economic Indices.*

Major Economic Changes in 1948.

Recent Developments in the World Economic Situation.

Major Economic Changes in 1949.

World Economic Report, 1949-50 supplemented by *Review of Economic Conditions in the Middle East,* and *Review of Economic Conditions in Africa.*

World Economic Report, 1950-51, with the following three supplements: *Recent Changes in Production, Summary of Recent Economic Developments in Africa,* and *Summary of Recent Economic Developments in the Middle East.*

World Economic Report, 1951-52, supplemented by *Review of Economic Conditions in the Middle East.*

World Economic Report, 1952-53, supplemented by *Summary of Recent Economic Developments in Africa; Enlargement of the Exchange Economy in Tropical Africa;* and *Summary of Recent Economic Developments in the Middle East.*

International Flow of Private Capital, 1946-52.

World Economic Report, 1953-54, supplemented by *Economic Developments in the Middle East, 1945-54; Review of Economic Activity in Africa, 1950-54; The Scope and Structure of Money Economies in Tropical Africa;* and *The Quest for Freer Trade.*

Discussions in the General Assembly and the Economic and Social Council on the world economy have led, on several occasions, to recommendations for appropriate measures by Member Governments and the specialized agencies.

Thus, in March 1951, after examining the world economic situation in the light of rearmament measures arising from the fighting in Korea, the Council recommended that United Nations Member Governments: (1) take special measures during the period of shortages to achieve adequate production and an equitable international distribution of capital goods, essential consumer goods and raw materials "especially needed for the maintenance of international peace and security, the preservation of standard of living and the furthering of economic development"; (2) take measures to regulate world market prices of essential goods at equitable levels and relationships; and (3) do everything possible to forestall inflationary measures.

Such measures were again advocated by the Council in August 1951, when it also recommended that industrialized countries, in the light of the over-riding needs of defence, should try to insure that supply difficulties did not interfere with the development plans of the less developed economies.

On January 26, 1952, the General Assembly recommended a number of measures aimed at combating inflation, and at maintaining and raising the living standards of the working population of Member States threatened by the possible adverse effects of recent world economic developments and declines in real wages. Economic and commercial relations, between all countries, the Assembly also considered in this regard, were most important for raising living standards in both exporting and importing countries.

The question of inflation was again taken up by the Council in August 1953, when examining inflationary problems engendered by the maintenance of high levels of economic activity or by the process of economic development. Member States which had dealt with such problems were asked to give the Council the benefit of their experience. The following year, after receiving such information, the Council recommended at its eighteenth session that Member States follow economic trends closely, and that they be prepared to take prompt action to safeguard high and expanding production and employment levels. It drew the attention of Member States to the need to give due regard to the effect of any action upon the levels of employment, stability and economic development of other Member States, including the under-developed countries. It invited the International Labor Organization to continue its important work in the field of employment problems. At the same time, the Council recommended that national and international efforts should be intensified to reduce instability in the prices of primary commodities and to facilitate the flow of capital to under-developed countries. (*See sections below on* International Commodity Trade *and* Financing of Economic Developments.)

Commercial Policies and World Trade

The economic welfare of most countries, as the General Assembly pointed out on November 20, 1950, depends on their imports and exports, which, in turn, are directly affected by prevailing international commercial policies. This subject should therefore be thoroughly and continuously studied by the United Nations and its specialized agencies, the Assembly recommended, reaffirming a resolution of the previous year calling on the Economic and Social Council to give further consideration to the question.

Since 1952, both the Assembly and the Council have given considerable attention to international trade questions and particularly to the possibility of expanding world trade. The topics considered included: the removal of existing trade obstacles, the development of inter-regional trade, arrangements for international consideration of trade questions, and restrictive business practices affecting international trade. (*See section on* "Restrictive Business Practices" *below.*)

In mid-1953 at its sixteenth session, the Council drew attention to the stimulating effect on business activity and employment which the removal of obstacles to international trade would have on business activity and employment.

Special attention was devoted in the following year to questions related to the removal of these obstacles and to the means of developing international economic relations. Council members were generally agreed that an expansion of international trade was desirable, and attention was drawn to the desirability of expanding inter-regional trade, and in particular East-West trade.

In mid-1954, at its eighteenth session, the Council reaffirmed a previous recommendation that governments should take all practicable steps to facilitate the further expansion of mutually beneficial international trade. It also requested the Secretary-General to report on factors tending to limit international trade, including a study of the problems involved in promoting trade within and between all the various geographical and currency areas. In another Council resolution adopted at the eighteenth session, the Secretary-General was asked to prepare a technical report on the practical conditions under which inter-regional trade relations might be strengthened through the organization, within the framework of the United Nations, of consultations among experts from interested countries on trade between the various regions of the world.

In mid-1955, the Council resumed consideration of the possible expansion of world trade in the light of the special reports prepared by the Secretary-General. It urged governments: (1) to continue their efforts to promote the expansion of world trade and, in particular, to support established international institutions working in that field; (2) to reduce or remove—as soon as conditions permitted and having regard to special problems arising from the needs of under-developed countries—barriers to trade which had been imposed for balance-of-payments reasons; (3) to conduct their international trade relations and policies with due regard to the harmful effects they might have on other countries, particularly on those dependent on exports of relatively few commodities; (4) to follow policies which would promote a high level of production, employment and investment; (5) to take measures to facilitate trade, including the expansion of their trade promotion services; (6) to bear in mind the possible use of technical assistance in fields related to trade; and (7) to continue to avail themselves of the services offered in the field of trade by the United Nations and its three regional commissions, as well as by the specialized agencies concerned.

In another resolution adopted at its mid-1955 session, the Council indicated certain steps that might be taken both by the regional commissions and the Secretary-General to facilitate the organization of inter-regional trade consultations. A third resolution asked the Secretary-General for a report on international procedures and bodies concerned with the development of trade cooperation. This was to be considered in connection with the discussion on the expansion of international trade due to take place at the Council's 22nd session in mid-1956.

Restrictive Business Practices

Restrictive business practices by private or public commercial enterprises may restrain competition, and limit access to markets and to the means of production necessary for economic development. This was recognized by the Economic and Social Council in a resolution adopted in September 1951. They may also foster monopolistic control and harm the expansion of production and trade. The Council accordingly recommended that whenever such practices have that effect, Member States should take measures and cooperate with each other to prevent such practices by public and private enterprises.

The Council established an *Ad Hoc* Committee on Restrictive Business Practices composed of representatives from ten Member Governments, to submit studies and also reports to implement its recommendations. The Committee submitted a report to the Council on *Restrictive Business Practices,* and an analysis (prepared by the Secretariat) of governmental measures dealing with such practices. The Secretariat also prepared a study for the Council containing the *Texts of National Legislation and other Governmental Measures relating to Restrictive Business Practices.* In 1953, the Council examined the studies and requested the Secretary-General to transmit them, for examination and comment, to United Nations Member States, to the specialized agencies concerned, and to interested governmental and non-governmental organizations.

In May 1955, the Council resumed consideration of the *Ad Hoc* Committee's report on *Restrictive Business Practices* and comments received through the Secretary-General, from Members of the United Nations and interested agencies.

The Secretary-General also submitted a report to the Council on *Current Legal Developments,* and a study of ten industries with respect to *Restrictive Business Practices in International Trade.*

The Council decided to resume consideration of the matter at a later session. At the same time, it asked the Secretary-General: (1) to circulate to Members any further information on laws, measures and policies adopted by Member States; (2) to circulate the views of appropriate inter-governmental bodies and agencies on restrictive business practices; (3) to assist in making appropriate arrangements to enable Member States to avail themselves of any opportunities to share the experience gained in countries with an established body of laws and practices on restrictive business practices; and (4), in order to help the Council in further consideration of the matter, to continue to summarize information about restrictive practices in international trade, and to prepare a bibliography on the nature of such practices and of their effect on economic development, employment and international trade.

Food Shortages and Famine

The immediate postwar period was marked by critical food shortages, and both the United Nations and the Food and Agriculture Organization (FAO) concerned themselves with ways of overcoming the shortages. Thus, in February 1946, the General Assembly of the United Nations urged all governments and peoples to take immediate and drastic action to conserve food supplies and to insure the maximum output of grains. The following May, FAO called a special meeting in Washington on urgent food problems, at which a number of short-term and long-term recommendations to meet the situation were made.

By December 1946, the General Assembly was in a position to note that millions of lives had been saved by the common efforts of United Nations Members. Nevertheless, in view of the likelihood that food shortages would continue into 1947, it urged governments and the international agencies concerned to adopt measures, or carry on with existing measures, to overcome the expected shortages, and to achieve an equitable allocation and prompt distribution of available supplies.

The shortages, however, persisted. So in March 1948, the Economic and Social Council, acting on FAO's initiative asked the specialized agencies concerned and the regional economic commissions, in consultation with FAO, to study further measures to increase food production.

The next important step came in December 1948, in the General Assembly. It invited Member States to give high priority to measures needed: (1) to raise productivity, avoid food losses through wastage, and improve marketing and distribution, especially in under-developed and war-devastated areas; (2) to reduce appreciably burdensome taxes hampering the sale and consumption of foodstuffs; and (3) to eliminate profiteering in the marketing of essential foodstuffs. The Assembly also called on the Council, in consultation with FAO and other specialized agencies, to continue efforts to improve world food production and trade, and to study the problems of providing the production facilities necessary to enable underdeveloped and war-devastated countries to increase food supplies; and measures for improving storage, marketing and distribution facilities, for reducing taxes, and for insuring stability of prices, with a view to raising the nutrition level of undernourished populations.

Early in 1949, the Council recommended continued promotion of measures to increase food production and decrease food wastage, and asked FAO for further studies. Later that year in July, the Council affirmed the urgency of international and national action to increase the availability of food, and to assist in the disposal of local surpluses on terms acceptable to exporting and importing countries.

Problems of food shortages and famine were again considered by the Council in August 1951. FAO, it recommended, should keep existing or emerging food shortages in individual countries under continuous surveillance, and maintain its periodic studies of such problems. Also, in cases of pending critical food shortages or famine, FAO should submit emergency reports to the FAO Council and Conference, and also to the Secretary-General for transmission to the Economic and Social Council.

Hunger and famine problems also came up before the General Assembly in January 1952, when it urged all governments to cooperate in attacking these problems along the following lines: (1) they should give a high priority to food production, and continue their efforts to carry out the measures advocated by the Assembly in December 1948; (2) they should place adequate emphasis on food production in their national economic development plans; (3) they should facilitate the transport of food to potential or actual emergency famine areas by the most expeditious means; and (4) they should intensify their cooperation with FAO in its efforts to increase food production.

The Assembly further urged all governments: (1) to promote and facilitate the work of the voluntary non-governmental agencies organized to meet famine conditions and promote agricultural development; (2) to further public awareness and participation in such work; (3) to correlate and integrate the resources and programs of such organizations with their own relief resources and programs; and (4) to furnish current listings of the functions, programs and potential resources of agencies of this kind within their countries. People in all countries were called upon to give increasing support to the work of voluntary non-governmental agencies.

All Members of the United Nations were asked to cooperate fully on the study made by the FAO Council on ways and means of establishing an emergency food reserve to be made promptly available to Member States threatened or affected by serious food shortages or famine.

Assistance to regions suffering food shortages and famine, the Assembly also recommended, should not be made subject to demands for political, economic or military privileges for the countries giving such aid.

In June 1952, the Economic and Social Council unanimously approved a system of alerting the world in the event of famine resulting from natural disasters. By this, FAO would continue and develop its arrangements for detecting famine emergencies, and appraise the Secretary-General promptly on the scope and duration of any emergency developing in any country. The Secretary-General would thereupon coordinate all measures for relief, non-governmental, governmental and intergovernmental. Governments of countries vulnerable to famine were also asked to set up advance arrangements for coordinating all national efforts and for the speedy receipt and distribution of aid.

Endorsing the FAO Council's opinion that food production must be at least 1 or 2 per cent ahead of the rate of population increase, in order to achieve some improvement in nutritional standards, a second Council resolution called on all Member States to help achieve this general objective by "preparing and executing agricultural development programs adapted to conditions in their respective countries". It also asked FAO to continue to give special attention to requests from under-developed countries for technical assistance in preparing and executing such programs.

The need for coordinated joint action by FAO and other international bodies to raise food output, it was recognized by the General Assembly on December 22, 1952, was essential both to foster the economic development of under-developed countries—many of which face serious food problems—and to relieve hardships, particularly where there was an immediate threat of food shortages.

It therefore called the attention of the Economic and Social Council, the specialized agencies concerned, and the Technical Assistance Board to the need for action to this end. The Council was also asked to report annually to the Assembly on United Nations and specialized agency action to cope with "the problem of the continuing lack of an adequate production of foodstuffs".

Considerable attention was given by the Council to food production problems at its mid-1953 session, when it noted with approval the continued emphasis given by FAO to operational activities in this sphere.

The following year, the question of establishing a world food reserve came up for discussion by the General Assembly. An Assembly resolution adopted on December 14, 1954, stated the need for continued national action and international co-operation to raise food production levels and standards of food consumption in many areas of the world, where famine or chronic malnutrition was a major problem, and also to prevent unduly large short-term fluctuations in agricultural prices and, to this end, to promote the rational disposal of intermittent agricultural surpluses. Expressing appreciation of the valuable work done by FAO, the Assembly asked the Secretary-General to invite FAO to prepare a factual and comprehensive report on what had been and was being done in connection with setting up a world food reserve to help relieve emergency situations and to counteract excessive price swings. The study was to go to the Economic and Social Council, which was asked to report its conclusions to the Assembly. The Council was scheduled to discuss the matter at its first session in 1956.

International Commodity Arrangements

To facilitate inter-governmental consultation or action on commodity problems, the Economic and Social Council established an Interim Coordinating Committee for International Commodity Arrangements in March 1947. As of December 31, 1955, this body consisted of a Chairman, nominated by the Contracting Parties to the General Agreement on Tariffs and Trade; a member chosen by the Food and Agriculture Organization (FAO), who was concerned particularly with agricultural primary commodities; a member specializing in non-agricultural primary commodities; and a member of wide experience in the problems confronting countries undergoing development whose economies are primarily dependent on the production and international marketing of primary commodities. The two latter members were nominated by the Secretary-General.

To minimize duplication in the work of various international bodies concerned with commodities, the Committee had, by the end of 1955, prepared the *Review of International Commodity Arrangements 1947*, and a *Review of International Commodity Problems* for each of the years from 1948 to 1954. These studies dealt with current commodity problems and their relation to general economic conditions. They also contained the Committee's observations and recommendations on inter-governmental consultation and action. The *Reviews* from 1949 to 1953 also gave production, trade and price data for some 20 primary commodities.

Action to facilitate the calling of inter-governmental conferences on specific commodity problems was taken by the Economic and Social Council in August 1950. On that occasion, it unanimously authorized the Secretary-General to convene such conferences to discuss measures to meet special difficulties which might arise in connection with a particular primary commodity. This he does on the advice of the Interim Coordinating Committee for International Commodity Arrangements, acting on the request of an appropriate inter-governmental study group and in keeping with the principles of Chapter VI (Inter-Governmental Commodity Agreements) of the Havana Charter. (*See section on* International Trade Organization.)

In August 1954, the Council reaffirmed that the Interim Coordinating Committee should continue to exercise the functions of convening inter-governmental study groups, of making recommendations to the Secretary-General on convening commodity conferences, and of coordinating the activities of individual commodity study groups and councils.

The Council at the same time decided to rest the other responsibilities previously discharged by the Committee in a new body, a subsidiary organ of the Council called the Commission on International Commodity Trade. Consisting of eighteen members, its terms of reference are: to examine measures designed to avoid excessive fluctuations in prices of the volume of trade in primary commodities, and to keep the movement of world primary commodity markets under constant review.

The International Wheat Agreement of 1953, in force between four exporting and 41 importing countries, was due to expire on July 31, 1956. To consider the renewal or replacement of this agreement a United Nations Wheat Conference was convened in October 1955, and it was due to hold its second session in February 1956.

The existing International Sugar Agreement, ratified or acceded to by 23 countries, became effective at the beginning of 1954, and was subject to review in 1956.

An International Tin Agreement was agreed to after two sessions of a United Nations Tin Conference held in 1950 and 1953, but had not yet been ratified by the end of 1955.

An agreement on olive oil was adopted in October 1955, by a United Nations conference on olive oil, for submission to governments.

Studies on rubber, cotton, wool and tea were being undertaken by inter-governmental study groups. The work of these organizations has been related to the economic program of the United Nations through the Interim Coordinating Committee for International Commodity Arrangements.

Economic Development of Under-Developed Countries

The United Nations has always been concerned with ways and means of aiding under-developed countries, at their request, to develop their economies. Technical assistance has been provided by both the United Nations and the specialized agencies to help meet their need for the technical knowledge and skills required to plan and execute economic development programs and projects. Much attention also has been devoted to the financing of economic development. Other relevant questions on which United Nations organs have acted include: the influence of international economic and commercial policies on economic development, measures for increasing productivity, industrialization, balanced economic growth, land and agrarian reform measures, the development of arid zones, and the conservation and utilization of resources. (*See below.*)

TECHNICAL ASSISTANCE

Action by the Economic and Social Council to provide technical assistance for the economic development of under-developed countries was taken as early as March 1947. In accordance with a General Assembly decision of the previous December, the Council instructed the Secretary-General to establish the necessary machinery within the Secretariat for giving such aid to under-developed Member nations. This he was to do in close cooperation with the specialized agencies.

In August 1948, on the recommendation of the Economic and Employment Commission, the Council informed Member States requiring expert assistance that they might call on the Secretary-General to organize international teams of experts provided by or through the United Nations and the specialized agencies.

The following December, the Assembly voted $288,000 for the following forms of technical assistance for the economic development of under-developed countries: (a) the organization, through the United Nations, of international teams of experts; (b) fellowships for the training abroad of experts from under-developed countries; (c) the training of technicians within the under-developed countries through visits by experts to instruct local personnel, and to aid in organizing technical institutes; and (d) the provision of facilities to aid governments to obtain technical personnel, equipment, supplies and other services required, including the organization of seminars and the exchange of current technical information on development problems. These services were to be provided by the Secretary-General in cooperation with the specialized agencies.

The Assembly also set forth the principles under which technical assistance was to be given so as to further the political and economic independence of the countries requesting such aid. These principles governed all technical assistance operations by the United Nations and specialized agencies. (*For further details, see* Guiding Principles *below.*)

In November 1949, the Assembly placed this program, financed from its regular annual budget, on a continuing basis instead of the previous year-to-year basis. In recent years, the sum set aside for the program has amounted to $479,000 annually.

EXPANDED PROGRAM OF TECHNICAL ASSISTANCE

Early in 1949, the Economic and Social Council began to study a possible framework for an expanded program of technical assistance, in which the United Nations, and several of its related specialized agencies, would participate jointly.

A comprehensive plan for an "Expanded Program of Technical Assistance" was accordingly worked out by the Council in the summer of 1949, and was unanimously approved by the General Assembly on November 16, 1949. This program was to be financed from voluntary contributions by Members of the United Nations and/or the specialized agencies, to be paid into a Special Account kept by the Secretary-General.

GUIDING PRINCIPLES. The primary objective of the expanded program, as set forth in the *Observations and Guiding Principles* governing its operation, is to help underdeveloped countries "to strengthen their national economies through the development of their industries and agriculture, with a view to promoting their economic and political independence in the spirit of the Charter of the United Nations, and to insure the attainment of higher levels of economic and social welfare for their entire populations."

Technical assistance under the program, the Guiding Principles laid down, was to be rendered by the participating organizations at the request of governments and in agreement with them. It was for them, too, to decide on the kind of assistance given.

Further, the countries desiring assistance should perform, in advance, as much of the work as possible in order to define the nature and scope of the problem involved.

The technical assistance furnished was not to be a means of foreign economic and political interference in the internal affairs of the country concerned. Nor was it to be accompanied by any political considerations. It was to be given only to or through governments. It was to be designed to meet the needs of the country concerned and provided as far as possible in the form which that country desires.

The Guiding Principles laid down, too, that the participating organizations should "avoid distinctions arising from the political structure of the country requesting assistance, or from the race or religion of its population."

Rules were further set out in the list of "Observations" to govern: the selection of competent experts to act in accordance with the program's aims; and the selection of technical assistance projects not only to meet the purposes of the program but also so that due regard might be paid to the urgency of the needs of the various applicants for such aid and to their geographical distribution.

Three major forms of technical aid are provided under the expanded program, as follows: (1) technically-qualified experts, sent out at the request of underdeveloped countries, to advise governments and train local staff in a wide variety of economic development fields; (2) fellowships or scholarships, granted to enable nationals of under-developed countries to study modern methods in similar fields abroad, often in conjunction with the sending of an expert; and (3) the organization of training centers and seminars on a regional basis to enable experts of several countries to exchange ideas and experience in particular technical fields. In addition, a limited amount of equipment is provided for demonstration and teaching purposes in support of development projects.

PARTICIPATING ORGANIZATIONS. Taking part in the expanded program and sharing in its funds are the United Nations, ILO, FAO, UNESCO, ICAO, WHO, ITU and WMO. Some of these Organizations have continued to operate additional technical assistance projects financed from their own regular annual budgets (the "regular programs"), apart from activities undertaken under the Expanded Program. In the field, there is only an administrative distinction between the missions financed from expanded program funds, and those provided for under "regular" programs. The Organizations, under the direction of the Economic and Social Council, have given careful attention to coordination between the two programs.

OBLIGATIONS OF AIDED COUNTRIES. When a government asks for technical assistance under the Expanded Program, it is expected to give all necessary and directly relevant information about the problems on which it seeks help. It should give information on what other technical assistance it receives or has requested in the same field from sources other than the United Nations and specialized agencies. It is also expected: to give "full and prompt consideration" to the technical advice given, to set up its own coordination machinery, to assume a substantial part of the local currency costs of the services provided, to publish information or provide material for study and analysis of the results achieved, and to give publicity to the program within its own territory.

ADMINISTRATIVE, POLICY-REVIEW ARRANGEMENTS. Machinery for the operation of the Expanded Program includes a Technical Assistance Board (TAB) and a Technical Assistance Committee (TAC).

TAB consists of the executive heads of the participating Organizations or their representatives, under an Executive Chairman, appointed by the Secretary-General of the United Nations, after consulting the executive heads of the other participating Organizations. The International Bank and the International Monetary Fund also cooperate in the work of the Board, to coordinate their technical assistance activities with those under the Expanded Program, but they do not receive any allotments from the Special Account for this program.

The function of the Technical Assistance Board is to coordinate and supervise operations under the Expanded Program, to submit reports on activities already undertaken and on funds received, and to consolidate the yearly requests from each recipient country into an overall program for submission to the Technical Assistance Committee.

By the end of 1951, TAB had found it necessary to appoint its own "Resident Representatives" or Liaison Officers in those countries where the volume of assistance given required direct liaison between the Board, the participating Organizations and the government. The number of Resident Representatives and Liaison Officers has steadily increased, 28 Offices being planned for 1956, to cover 48 countries and territories. Their major role is to assist governments in drawing up requests for yearly programs; in addition, they help in planning the fellowship scheme; coordinate Expanded Program activities with those of other technical assistance programs in their area—such as the United States bilateral and British Commonwealth Colombo Plans; render administrative services to the experts of all the Organizations participating in the Program; and report quarterly to the Executive Chairman of TAB on the progress of the program in their country or countries of assignment.

The Technical Assistance Committee consists of all eighteen Economic and Social Council members. It examines each year's program presented to it by TAB, makes recommendations to the Council, and reviews the working relationships between the participating Organizations with a view to the best possible coordination.

FINANCING OF EXPANDED PROGRAM. Operations under the Expanded Technical Assistance Program, as explained above, are financed from voluntary contributions by governments which are Members of the United Nations and/or the specialized agencies. Contribution pledges are announced at a conference of government representatives called for the purpose, after negotiations with governments conducted through the General Assembly's Negotiating Committee on Extra-Budgetary Funds. The Pledging Conference is usually held at United Nations Headquarters in New York, during the regular annual session of the General Assembly in the last quarter of each year. Contributions made in fulfilment of the pledges are used to help meet the cost of technical aid provided in the financial period after the conference.

The following is the record of contribution pledges by governments. To pay for operations during the eighteen months ending December 31, 1951, 54 governments promised the equivalent of $20,035,578. For 1952, 65 governments pledged the equivalent of $18,797,232. For 1953, 69 governments pledged the equivalent of $22,405,633. For 1954, 74 governments pledged the equivalent of $25,342,462. For 1955, 70 governments pledged the equivalent of $27,966,017. For the following year, pledges, as of the end of 1955, totalled the equivalent of about $28,000,000 offered by over 65 governments. Not all the pledges for 1956, however, had been made at that time.

Operating on a system whereby funds are pledged at yearly intervals, the Program has been faced, during its first five years of operation, with financial instability. The Technical Assistance Board has had to plan its program in advance of each operational year, with little assurance as to the amount of funds which would be available to carry it out. In addition, pledges by all governments are subject to parliamentary approval, and such approval, appropriation and payment of the sums into the Special Account were sometimes delayed far into the period for which the funds were intended. For this reason, the Economic and Social Council in 1954, recommended that a Working Capital and Reserve Fund be built up for the Program. Under the terms of the Council's 1949 resolution on setting up the Expanded Program, a permanent reserve of $3,000,000 had been maintained. Its 1954 resolution made provision for adding a further $3,000,000 to this reserve during 1954, 1955 and 1956, therefore building it into a total fund of $12,000,000 to be used as a means of insuring financial stability, and assuring funds with which to carry over projects from year to year should governments' payments be delayed.

As a further step towards stabilizing the financial basis for the Program, the General Assembly asked, as early as December 1952, that the Negotiating Committee on Extra-Budgetary Funds begin to explore the possibility of governments making long-term rather than yearly pledges. Although the Program is still on an annual basis, several governments have responded to this request with indications of financial support over a period of years.

COUNTRY PROGRAMMING. From the inception of the Expanded Program until the end of 1954, the funds contributed yearly into the Special Account were allocated among the participating Organizations on the basis of fixed percentages. As the Program progressed, however, it was felt that a somewhat more flexible system and one more adequately responsive to the needs of the under-developed countries would be preferable. To meet this need, the Economic and Social Council drew up a new programming system in July 1954, which was endorsed by the General Assembly on November 26, 1954. Under the terms of the Assembly's resolution, funds for the 1956 program and subsequent years would no longer be distributed on a fixed percentage basis, but on the basis of requests and priorities submitted by the individual governments which request technical assistance. During the course of 1955, therefore, officials of recipient governments met with representatives of the participating Organizations and the Technical Assistance Board to draw up lists of project-requests for 1956. Governments were asked, for the first time, to indicate their own priority preferences.

TECHNICAL ASSISTANCE ADMINISTRATION

A Technical Assistance Administration was established within the United Nations Secretariat on July 31, 1950, to provide for the efficient operation of the United Nations technical assistance activities under the regular and expanded programs, including the United Nations advisory social welfare services and the program for training in public administration (see sections on Advisory Social Welfare Services and Training in Public Administration). This Administration, headed by a Director-General, also coordinates the United Nations technical assistance activities with those of Member Governments and the specialized agencies.

TRAINING IN PUBLIC ADMINISTRATION

Training in public administration is provided by the United Nations as an integral part of its technical assistance activities.

In December 1948, the General Assembly decided that an International Center for Training in Public Administration should be established.

In December 1949, the General Assembly appropriated funds to finance a program of action in 1950. The sum of $145,000 was voted in 1950, to pay for operations in the following year, and budget allocations were stabilized at this figure in January 1952, when the Assembly placed the program of technical assistance in public administration on a continuing basis.

Activities under the program include the granting of fellowships and scholarships in public administration, the holding of seminars, conferences, meetings of experts and training centers.

Under its agreement with the Secretary-General, the International Institute of Administrative Sciences in Brussels provides for the use of United Nations Member States documentary material on specific aspects of public administration.

ADVISORY SOCIAL WELFARE SERVICES

The United Nations advisory social welfare services were first set up by the General Assembly in December 1946. In November 1949, the operation was put on a continuing, instead of the previous year-to-year, basis. For some years, the amount of $768,500 was voted annually for the provision of services, but in 1955, the appropriation was increased to $1,000,000 for operation in 1956. Administration of the program came under the Technical Assistance Administration when this Administration was set up in 1950. (For further details, see section on "Advisory Social Services" below.)

TRAINING OF APPRENTICES AND SKILLED WORKERS

Special consideration has also been given by the Economic and Social Council to the training of apprentices and skilled workers, a matter also occupying the attention of the International Labor Organization. ILO, the Council recommended at its eleventh session (July-August 1950), should actively pursue and develop its extended program of facilitating the training of such personnel. This was to be done in cooperation with the United Nations and the other specialized agencies. It also recommended that Member States give full cooperation and support to ILO's efforts to extend the possibilities of training apprentices and technical workers abroad.

Organizations taking part in the Expanded Program, the Assembly recommended in January 1952, should give sympathetic consideration to requests for placing teams of workers, foremen and technicians from under-developed countries in appropriate enterprises abroad. This is to enable them: to acquire the technical proficiency needed in their home countries, to train other workers, or to adapt the techniques acquired to conditions in their own countries.

RECORD OF TECHNICAL ASSISTANCE

During the period July 1, 1950 to July 1, 1955, technical assistance was given to more than 110 countries and territories under the Expanded Program, and the regular United Nations program. They received the services of experts, fellowship awards for their nations, or both. Among these countries and territories were the following:

Aden, Afghanistan, Alaska, Argentina, Australia, Austria, Bahama Islands, Barbados, Bechuanaland, Belgian Congo, Bolivia, Borneo (North), Brazil, British East Africa, British Guiana, British Honduras, British Somaliland, Brunei, Burma, Cambodia, Cameroons (French-administered), Ceylon, Chile, China (Taiwan), Colombia, Costa Rica, Cuba, Curacao, Cyprus, Dominican Republic, Ecuador, Egypt, El Salvador, Ethiopia, Fiji Islands, Finland, French Equatorial Africa, French Morocco, Gambia, Gold Coast, Greece, Guadeloupe, Guatemala, Haiti, Hawaii, Honduras, Hong Kong, Iceland, India, Indonesia, Iran, Iraq, Israel, Italy, Ivory Coast, Jamaica, Japan, Jordan, Kenya, Korea (Republic of), Laos, Lebanon, Leeward Islands, Liberia, Libya, Luxembourg, Macao, Madagascar, Malaya, Malta, Martinique, Mauritius, Mexico, Netherlands Antilles, Nepal, New Caledonia, New Hebrides, New Zealand, Nicaragua, Nigeria, Pacific Islands Trust Territory, Pakistan, Panama, Papua and New Guinea, Paraguay, Peru, Philippines, Portugal, Portuguese Guinea, Puerto Rico, Federation of Rhodesia and Nyasaland, St. Lucia, Samoa, Sao Thome, Sarawak, Saudi Arabia, Seychelles, Sierra Leone, Singapore, Somaliland (Italian-administered), Spain, Spanish Guinea, Spanish Morocco, Spanish West Africa, Sudan, Surinam, Syria, Tanganyika, Thailand, Togoland, Trieste, Trinidad and Tobago, Tunisia, Turkey, Uganda, Uruguay, Venezuela, Vietnam (Republic of), Virgin Islands, West New Guinea (Irian), Windward Islands, Yemen, Yugoslavia and Zanzibar.

More than 6,000 experts have been sent out to more than 85 of these countries and territories, and were recruited from as many as 77 different countries. More than 100 governments were enabled, through Expanded Program fellowship and scholarship grants, to send over 7,000 of their nationals abroad to study modern techniques in some 98 countries and territories. Numerous training centres and seminars were organized in all the regions of the world.

When the Expanded Program first went into operations, many of the experts provided through it were sent out in teams on overall survey missions, as governments explored the general economic context in which their development plans would be undertaken. After the first two years, the emphasis of assistance shifted more towards specific training and advisory projects, mostly in conjunction with government development schemes, and often in active collaboration with the technicians supplied under other technical assistance schemes. The major fields in which technical aid has been extended under the Expanded Program are: basic surveys of resources and building up administrative services; power, transport and communications; industrial production and mining; agricultural production; auxiliary services to industry and agriculture; health services; education; community development; and other social services.

FINANCING OF ECONOMIC DEVELOPMENT

Financing the economic development of under-developed countries has been the subject of many years' discussion and study in the General Assembly, the Economic and Social Council, and other United Nations bodies dealing with economic questions.

Deliberations in the earlier years of the United Nations were concerned mostly with general issues such as: the inadequacy of funds available in under-developed countries for economic development; the role of financing in the process of economic growth; the methods to be used in mobilizing domestic, foreign and international capital for economic development; and the role of the International Bank for Reconstruction and Development in helping to speed the advancement of under-developed economies. Studies and reports prepared in this connection both by the United Nations Secretariat and independent groups of experts appointed by the Secretary-General, included one on *Measures for Economic Development of Under-developed Countries,* and one on *Domestic Financing of Economic Development.*

Emerging from this work was general agreement, to cite a General Assembly resolution of November 1950, that speedier economic development required technical and financial assistance from abroad, and also that it depended primarily on the development efforts of the under-developed countries themselves.

After agreement was reached on questions of general principle, the various United Nations organs concerned themselves increasingly with specific aspects of the problems of financing economic development. Prominent among these problems was that of accelerating the flow of both private and public capital to under-developed areas for development purposes. Four possible methods of meeting this problem were considered, as follows: (a) the establishment of an international finance corporation to facilitate the financing of productive private enterprise especially in under-developed countries; (b) the establishment of a Special United Nations fund originally conceived as a means to provide grants-in-aid and low-interest, long-term loans; (c) the stimulation of the international flow of private capital; and (d) the improvement, stabilization and better utilization of the exports proceeds of under-developed countries.

Discussions on providing capital for productive private ventures have led to the International Bank preparing a statute governing the operations, role and membership of an International Finance Corporation to be set up as an affiliate of the International Bank *(see section below on* "International Finance Corporation" *for details).* Concern about making more public capital from abroad available to the less developed countries has resulted in a number of resolutions both in the Economic and Social Council and General Assembly on proposals for setting up a Special United Nations Fund for Economic Development *(For details, see below).* Deliberations on the movement of private investment capital have centered mainly on the question of the best institutional arrangements and measures to be adopted both by capital-importing and capital-exporting countries to encourage the international flow of private capital (*For details, see below*). The problem of stabilizing the export earnings of under-developed countries and of establishing an equitable relationship between the world market prices of the primary commodities they sell abroad and the manufactured goods which they import were subjects for study by the Commission on International Commodity Trade (*For details, see* "Raw Material Prices" *below, and also section above on* "International Commodity Arrangements").

A number of studies dealing with these specific aspects of financing economic development have been prepared, at the request of the Economic and Social Council and the General Assembly, by the Secretariat of the United Nations, the International Bank, and by committees or individual experts appointed for the purpose.

PLANS FOR SPECIAL FUND. An international system of grants-in-aid, the General Assembly recognized in a resolution of January 12, 1952, is one of the means required to meet the need for new sources of international financing necessary to speed up the economic development of under-developed countries. Such a system should not be a permanent one, but it should be correlated with the efforts of under-developed countries themselves.

Believing further that plans should be initiated without delay for increasing the flow of international public funds for economic development, the Assembly accordingly asked the Economic and Social Council for detailed plans for establishing, as soon as circumstances permit, a special fund for grants-in-aid and long-term, low-interest loans. The purpose of such a fund was to help under-developed countries, at their request, accelerate their economic development and finance basic non-self-liquidating development projects, such as the construction of roads, irrigation schemes, and educational and health services.

A nine-member committee was set up by the Secretary-General to prepare a detailed report on a Special United Nations Fund for Economic Development (SUNFED). Their report was examined by the Council and the Assembly in 1953. Various governments also gave their comments on the plan for such a Fund.

In December 1954, the Assembly asked for a further study of the proposal, to be made by an *ad hoc* group with the help of the Secretary-General, in order to provide a full and precise picture of the form or forms, functions and responsibilities which such a Special United Nations Fund for Economic Development might have. The report was also to deal with the relations between the Fund and the Technical Assistance Board, and with the International Bank and other specialized agencies.

The report was examined by the Council and the Assembly in 1955. On December 9 that year, the Assembly, pointing out the need of under-developed countries for additional means to speed the development of economic and social schemes basic for economic progress (the "infra-structure"), invited Members of the United Nations and specialized agencies concerned with economic and social matters to submit their precise views on the establishment, role, structure and operations of a Special United Nations Fund for Economic Development. They were to do so through the Secretary-General by March 31, 1956. At the same time, the Assembly set up a sixteen member *ad hoc* committee to analyze the replies and comments of governments with a view to submitting an interim report to the Economic and Social Council for its mid-1956 session, to the General Assembly at its 1956 session and its final report to the Council's session due to be held in the first half of 1957. The committee was to consist of representatives of the following governments: Canada, Chile, Colombia, Cuba, Egypt, France, India, Indonesia, Norway, the Netherlands,

Pakistan, Poland, the United Kingdom, the United States, the U.S.S.R. and Yugoslavia.

As to the time for the eventual establishment of the Special Fund, the General Assembly unanimously adopted a resolution on December 7, 1953, whereby the governments of United Nations Member States declared themselves ready to ask their peoples, when sufficient progress had been made with internationally-supervised worldwide disarmament, to devote a portion of the savings from such disarmament to an international fund, within the framework of the United Nations, to help in the reconstruction and development of under-developed countries.

On December 11, 1954, the Assembly called for further studies on the establishment of SUNFED, which it hoped would take place as soon as possible, and urged governments to review their respective stands on giving material support to the Fund, in accordance with changes in the international situation and other relevant factors, both national and international. It renewed this appeal to governments on December 9, the following year, and arranged for further reports on the matter by a committee of government representatives, as described above.

Several countries, mostly those which are economically less developed but also some of the more advanced countries, have expressed the view in the Assembly and in the Economic and Social Council that creation of the Fund should not be made contingent upon the achievement of internationally-supervised worldwide disarmament. Others have made the point, however, they are not yet in a position to contribute to such a Fund, partly because of continuing defence needs and partly because of other commitments. They have also argued that it would be unwise to set up the Fund before those countries likely to be the biggest contributors do contribute to the Fund's resources.

In December 1954, the Assembly noted that there was a growth of support for the establishment of SUNFED, and expressed the hope that conditions more favorable to the creation of an international fund would be created in the near future and that savings from internationally-supervised worldwide disarmament would provide additional means for financing the economic development of under-developed countries and would further the aims and objectives of such a fund.

INTERNATIONAL FINANCE CORPORATION. The proposal for an International Finance Corporation has been under discussion since 1951, in the Economic and Social Council and in the General Assembly. In response to a request made by the General Assembly on December 11, 1954, the International Bank, in consultation with governments that are members of the Bank, drafted Articles of Agreement for the proposed corporation. The Corporation, which is to have an authorized capital of $100,000,000, is designed to supplement the Bank's lending activities and, while legally distinct, is to be administered by the latter. The Corporation would be empowered to provide capital to private enterprises in countries that are members of the Bank without requiring governmental guarantee. The Corporation is authorized to share in the profits of such enterprises, but would not take part in their direction. In April 1955, the Articles of Agreement of the International Finance Corporation were transmitted by the International Bank to governments. The Corporation will commence operations when the agreement has been ratified by 30 governments with a total capital subscription of $75,000,000. By January 1956, nine governments with capital subscriptions totalling $56,761,000 had completed legislative action authorizing them to become members of the organization, and a number of others had initiated such action. (Note. The International Finance Corporation was formed on July 25, 1956.)

PRIVATE CAPITAL. The question of stimulating the international flow of private capital to under-developed countries has been under consideration by the General Assembly and the Economic and Social Council over a period of some years. Specific recommendations, designed to stimulate the flow of private capital both to countries seeking to attract private capital as well as to those that are able to make private investments abroad, were made by the General Assembly on December 11, 1954. It was recommended, for instance, that the governments concerned reexamine their policies, legislation and administrative practices with a view to making adjustments that might facilitate international investment. Both groups of countries were also encouraged to negotiate treaties that would stimulate private investment by various methods, including prevention of double taxation and insurance of certain non-business risks of foreign investment. The Secretary-General, who, in accordance with earlier resolutions, had issued several reports on the international flow of private capital, was requested to report periodically on the nature and economic significance of private international capital movements, and on measures adopted by governments affecting them.

In another resolution adopted on December 11, 1954, the Assembly addressed itself more particularly to the effect which tax measures in capital-exporting and capital-importing countries might have in stimulating the flow of private capital to under-developed countries. It requested the Secretary-General to continue his studies of this question for submission to the Economic and Social Council, which in turn would report the results of its deliberations to the Assembly.

RAW MATERIAL PRICES AND FINANCING. Action to help finance economic development through the establishment of fair and equitable world prices for primary commodities and through national integrated economic development programs was envisaged by the General Assembly in a resolution of December 22, 1952.

It recommended that, when adopting measures affecting world raw material prices, Member Governments should consider the effect of such measures on the terms of trade of countries in the process of development—to insure an adequate, just and equitable relationship between prices of primary commodities and those of capital and other manufactured goods. The object was to enable these countries to accumulate more domestic savings, establish fair wage levels for their working populations, and thus help reduce the present disparity between their living standards and those of highly industrialized countries. Governments should also consider other aspects of the problem of undue fluctuations in the terms of trade, but without prejudice to the recommendation of price relationships. And they should intensify their efforts to reduce restriction on primary commodity imports.

To insure stable primary commodity prices in keeping with adequate, just and equitable parity prices, and to safeguard the continuity of economic and social progress in all countries, whether producers or consumers of raw materials, the Assembly further recommended that governments conclude multilateral and bilateral agreements or arrangements for individual primary commodities as well as for groups of such commodities and manufactured goods.

Recommended, too, was the execution of integrated development programs to enable countries in the process of development to make rational use of proceeds from primary production, absorb their "surplus active population" and improve living standards. (*See section below on* "Integrated Economic Development.")

Three studies were also called for by this resolution. One, by a group of experts, appointed by the Secretary-General, dealt with practical measures to implement the recommendations on price relationships and undue fluctuations in terms of trade and on integrated development measures. A second study, undertaken by the Secretary-General, dealt with financial repercussions which changes in the terms of trade between primary commodities and capital and other manufactured goods have on the national incomes of countries in the process of development. The third study, also undertaken by the Secretary-General, dealt with the impact of important synthetic products on international demand for natural primary products.

All these reports, the Economic and Social Council noted on April 30, 1954, emphasized the need to devise effective measures of international cooperation to solve the grave problems of the inadequacy and instability of earnings from primary commodity exports which affect most countries in the process of development. To facilitate the adoption of measures to solve these problems justly and equitably, it also considered it was necessary to have specialized machinery within the United Nations framework permanently concerned with examining proposals that could provide satisfactory solutions for the problems. It was accordingly decided to set up an advisory body to the Council, to be known as the Commission on International Commodity Trade. (*For further details, see section above on* "International Commodity Trade.")

ROLE OF AGRARIAN REFORM IN ECONOMIC DEVELOPMENT

Considerable attention has been paid by the United Nations and its specialized agencies in recent years to the role of agrarian reform in economic development. A study prepared in accordance with the General Assembly resolution of November 20, 1950, and published in 1951, dealt with the repercussions of unsatisfactory forms of land tenure systems and other features of agrarian structure on the development of under-developed countries. This report, entitled *Land Reform: Defects in Agrarian Structure as Obstacles to Economic Development* was considered by the Council in 1951, when it adopted a number of detailed recommendations on the agrarian reform question. The following year, the General Assembly urged all governments to carry out the recommendations of the Economic and Social Council on matters of agrarian reform.

In April 1954, the Council considered two reports prepared, in response to an earlier request by the Secretary-General in cooperation with FAO and ILO. One of these reports was entitled *Progress in Land Reform,* and the other *Rural Progress Through Cooperatives.* The former was based on replies of governments to questionnaires regarding progress in land reform. The second report assessed the contribution which cooperatives could make to technical, economic and social progress.

The Council's resolution noted that although a number of countries had made considerable progress in land reform there was still a pressing need for further opportunities for improvement along the lines recommended earlier by the Council and the Assembly.

The Council therefore urged governments to continue their efforts in that direction; it recommended that the International Bank give sympathetic consideration to applications for loans involving development projects designed to implement agrarian reform programs and that FAO in consultation with the Secretary-General, take steps to set up working parties for on-the-spot studies of special problems, and arrange regional conferences for the exchange of information. The Council also asked that the Secretary-General prepare a further report, in collaboration with FAO and ILO, on the impact of land reform measures already undertaken on agricultural employment and production, on standards of living of the rural population, and on economic development in general.

In addition, the Council invited governments to extend all appropriate assistance in the formation and development of cooperatives. It asked the Secretary-General also to prepare a report, in collaboration with FAO and ILO, on the various forms of help that governments and other bodies could provide for achieving the full potentialities of cooperatives, and on the demarcation of sectors in which cooperative organization might be considered suitable.

On December 11, 1954, the General Assembly reiterated its earlier recommendations to Member States to institute, whenever appropriate, land reform measures designed to encourage land ownership and to pursue fiscal investment policies which would contribute to the expansion and improvement of agriculture.

The Assembly also recommended that Member States, in implementing land policy programs should observe the principle of equitable treatment in the economic, political and social field with a view to improving the condition of rural peoples, and that they respect the free establishment of agricultural associations, and also such institutions of the indigenous population as might be compatible with economic and social progress and modern techniques. It was further recommended that they promote the general welfare, including measures aimed at providing agricultural workers with the possibility of earning adequate pay.

The Assembly endorsed the Council's recommendation that the International Bank give sympathetic consideration to applications for loans from under-developed countries for projects intended to implement agrarian reform programs. Also endorsed was the Council's recommendation that the International Bank consider making such loans on terms which would place the smallest feasible burden on borrowing countries.

Expressing support for Member States carrying out land reform programs in conformity with its resolutions, the Assembly hoped, too, that high priority would be given on requests for United Nations technical aid for studying or executing land reform programs.

INTEGRATED ECONOMIC DEVELOPMENT, INDUSTRIALIZATION AND PRODUCTIVITY

The need for a continuing, comprehensive and methodical study of economic development in achieving a better direction of effort and resources for the economic advancement of under-developed countries was recognized by the General Assembly in a resolution of January 12, 1952, which made two requests of the Economic and Social Council:

First, it should promote studies of a program for the rapid industrialization of under-developed countries. These should include studies on the economic, social, fiscal, technical and organizational problems involved, and on the roles which both industrially advanced and under-developed countries must play. Second, it should, as soon as practicable, submit concrete proposals to the Assembly for measures that might aid such countries in connection with these problems.

The need for coordinated policies for industrial diversification in harmony with the development of agricultural production was stressed by the Council in a resolution of July 11, 1952. It asked the Secretary-General for a study on the problems singled out by the Assembly the previous January. He was also asked to give special attention to these problems in continuing his general and specific studies on economic development.

In addition, the Council drew the attention of governments to the technical assistance services available through the United Nations and specialized agencies for preparing and executing integrated development programs.

Further recommendations on integrated development programs were made by the Assembly in connection with the role of raw material prices in financing development (see above).

To insure more rapid world economic progress, a General Assembly resolution of

January 12, 1952, pointed out, closer international cooperation was needed to facilitate the best use of the world's manpower resources, natural resources and productive equipment. The Assembly accordingly asked the Economic and Social Council to study the varying ways in which the productivity of people everywhere could be increased by the application of existing scientific and technical knowledge. The Council was also asked to recommend, as soon as practicable, methods of making the results of these studies available to under-developed countries at their request.

Governments of under-developed countries, the Council recommended on July 10, 1952, should consider the problems of raising productivity as an integral part of economic development. They should also consider establishing national productivity centers, to stimulate research and disseminate information on improved practices and techniques.

Full advantage should be taken of the expanded technical assistance program to improve existing productive apparatus. Counties in the same region might cooperate in raising productivity by joint studies of common problems, and, wherever possible, by joint action.

Another recommendation was that governments should promote the economic integration of international markets by expanding foreign trade on a stable and equitable basis so as to help increase world productivity.

In addition, Secretariat studies on problems of raising productivity in under-developed countries were to be continued, particularly in the spheres of agriculture, manufacturing, mining, transport, construction industries, and distributive trades. Also requested was a Secretariat study on labor's role in: (a) framing, developing and implementing programs to increase productivity; (b) devising methods to insure a fair reward for the human effort applied to increasing productivity; and (c) extending purchasing power so as to make productivity increases permanent. The question of increasing productivity was again discussed by the General Assembly at its seventh session. (See also section on "Food Shortages.")

In 1953, the Secretary-General submitted a paper to the Council reviewing the action taken on integrated economic development by the United Nations and specialized agencies and proposing further consideration of certain topics in this field not yet taken up by the Council. The discussion in the latter body elicited substantial agreement on the role of industrialization as a means of achieving integrated economic development, bearing in mind, however, the need for promoting the balanced development of the various sectors of the economy, and especially of agriculture and industry. In the light of this debate, the Council requested the Secretary-General on April 23, 1953, to prepare a study of the processes and problems of industrialization, which might assist the under-developed countries in preparing programs of rapid industrialization, and dealing with the role which the industrially-advanced countries could play in this connection. The Council at the same time asked that a bibliography be prepared of the studies undertaken by the various organs of the United Nations and of other important books and documents on the subject of industrialization, and a report of the organization and functioning of development corporations.

With regard to productivity, the Council considered two working papers in mid-1953, prepared by the International Labor Office and the Food and Agriculture Organization, respectively, dealing with particular aspects of productivity.

The close relationship between the problems of integrated economic development and productivity and their links to the broader problems of development were further reaffirmed by the Council in 1954, in connection with a progress report submitted by the Secretary-General on the progress of the several studies on industrialization. A full debate on the two questions took place in the Council in April

1955, when it had before it a number of documents submitted by the Secretary-General in response to its earlier requests. The major part of these studies, issued in 1955 under the title *Processes and Problems of Industrialization in Under-developed Countries* dealt with the earlier stages of industrialization, and emphasized the measures which the governments concerned, and international organizations, too, might take in order to speed up the pace of industrialization. The documents also analyzed some of the economic and social implications of such processes.

Together with this document the Council also considered: a working paper on the nature and results of efforts to increase industrial productivity in under-developed countries, an analysis of the evolution and functioning of development corporations, a bibliography of the processes and problems of industrialization, and a list of the subjects relating to industrialization not yet dealt with by the United Nations and the specialized agencies.

In its resolution, the Council restated its belief that industrialization integrated with other forms of development was essential to the economic advancement of under-developed countries, and recognized the need both for vigorous international cooperation in order to accelerate progress, and for further study of particular aspects of these questions. The Council further asked that the bibliography be kept up to date by the issuance of periodic supplements, and amplified to include information on research in progress, and that a survey be made of the work projects in progress on matters related to industrialization and productivity, to be undertaken by the United Nations and the specialized agencies. The Council also requested the Secretary-General to prepare and submit a program of work planned with particular reference to the questions of accelerating industrialization and raising productivity in under-developed countries, and of utilizing available forms of international assistance as fully and efficiently as possible for this end. These documents were to be completed in the early part of 1956.

MIGRATION AND ECONOMIC DEVELOPMENT

Many countries are grappling with over-population problems—reflected in unemployment, under-employment, poverty and under-consumption due to lack of suitable land and employment opportunities. Others, however, have vast areas of cultivable land but lack population as well as capital. To help meet this situation, the General Assembly, on December 22, 1952, recommended that, as part of their general economic development, countries of emigration and immigration conclude bilateral and multilateral agreements to equip, transfer and resettle emigrant groups, without racial or religious discrimination.

The Assembly also requested the continued active cooperation of the Secretary-General, the specialized agencies (particularly the International Bank) and other interested international organizations in economic, financial and administrative aid for the equipment, transfer and training of emigrant groups.

RIGHT TO EXPLOIT NATURAL RESOURCES FREELY

One of the essentials for economic development is to encourage under-developed countries in the further use of their resources. Peoples, as an Assembly resolution of December 22, 1952, pointed out, have an inherent sovereign right, which accords with the United Nations Charter, to use and exploit their natural wealth and resources freely.

In exercising this right wherever they deem it desirable for their own progress and economic development, all Members, it was recommended, should pay due regard, consistent with their sovereignty, to the need for maintaining the flow of capital in conditions of security, mutual confidence and economic cooperation among nations. They should also refrain from acts, both direct and indirect, designed to impede any state in exercising its sovereignty over its natural resources.

The question of sovereignty over natural wealth and resources was frequently raised in subsequent years in connection with discussions in the Commission on Human Rights, the Economic and Social Council, and in the General Assembly. In 1954, for instance, the Commission proposed that a special commission be set up by the Assembly to conduct a full survey of the status of the rights of peoples and nations to "permanent sovereignty over their natural wealth and resources, and to make recommendations, where necessary, for strengthening that right."

Later, in completing its work on the two draft Covenants on Human Rights (*see section below on* "Human Rights"), the Commission affirmed that the right of peoples and nations to self-determination as affirmed in these drafts included the right to "permanent sovereignty over their natural wealth and resources." Subsequently, in July 1955, the Economic and Social Council also recommended the creation of a commission to survey the status of this right and, in this connection, to pay due regard to the rights and duties of states under international law, and to the importance of encouraging international cooperation in the development of under-developed countries. The matter was further debated during discussion on the draft human rights covenants at the Assembly's tenth session in the last quarter of 1955, but no final decision on the matter was reached.

Conservation and Utilization of Resources

UNITED NATIONS SCIENTIFIC CONFERENCE

A United Nations Scientific Conference on the Conservation and Utilization of Resources (UNSCCUR), attended by experts from over 50 countries, was held at Lake Success from August 17 to September 6, 1949, in accordance with an Economic and Social Council decision of March 1947. Its purposes were to discuss techniques and exchange experience rather than to formulate policies. No recommendations were therefore made to governments or organizations, and each of the contributors and participants functioned in an individual capacity.

The work of the Conference showed that a new era of prosperity awaited mankind if modern techniques were universally applied and scientific knowledge used to discover and create new resources and make better use of existing resources.

The proceedings of the Conference have been made available in published form. Other ways of using and spreading the information pooled made available at the Conference have also been considered by the Council.

CONSERVATION AND UTILIZATION OF NON-AGRICULTURAL RESOURCES

In March 1951, the Council decided on an international program of action for conserving and utilizing non-agricultural resources. The Secretary-General, it decided, should initiate a systematic survey and inventory of non-agricultural resources. The Council also asked the Secretary-General: to give consideration to requests for technical assistance in the organization and planning of national surveys and inventories of such resources; and to give further and detailed consideration to any general international action that might be taken, particularly in promoting an integrated approach to, and a systematic analysis of, problems involved in the conservation and use of any particular resources. Member States, specialized agencies, and interested non-governmental organizations, the Council also recommended, should cooperate with the Secretary-General in these matters.

Progress in promoting the effective and sustained use of the world's natural resources as a means of further economic development, the Council further recognized by this resolution, could also be made through exchanging information at regional conferences on particular types of resources or particular resource problems common to a group of countries. It therefore asked the Secretary-General to explore the scope of holding such conferences, at the request of the Member States concerned and in consultation with the appropriate regional economic commissions and specialized agencies.

The present program of the United Nations in the sphere of the conservation and utilization of non-agricultural resources arises out of this Council decision of March 1951, to initiate a systematic survey and inventory of non-agricultural resources. Three fields of activity have been developed in this respect, concerning mineral resources, energy resources and water resources. How this has come about and what has been done are briefly outlined below.

MINERAL RESOURCES

The Secretary-General had been authorized under the above-mentioned resolution to "establish, as necessary, small ad hoc committees of experts to consider specific resource surveys and inventory problems". Because of the importance of iron ore for economic, and more especially industrial, development, the Secretary-General selected iron ore resources as the first subject of study under the program. In 1952, he appointed a group of experts to study and prepare recommendations on standard concepts and terminology for use in surveys and inventories of iron ore resources. A preliminary meeting of the experts was held in New York in June 1953, to consider questions concerning the scope of the technical papers assigned to them, points of terminology, and the general structure of the joint report. A second and final meeting was held in March 1954, at Geneva, at which the individual papers were reviewed. The outcome of this collaboration was the publication in October 1954, of *Survey of World Iron Ore Resources: Occurrence, Appraisal and Use*. This report (which came before the Council in 1954) contains a series of recommendations for the systematic and uniform appraisal by countries of their iron-ore resources, and a tentative world appraisal of such resources to show how these recommendations should be applied.

The principal recommendation of the experts was that each country should in the near future see that an appraisal is made of its iron-ore resources. The national appraisal should be established, they said, on the basis of already existing data. After a certain period, to be fixed by the Economic and Social Council, the national appraisals could be collated by the Secretary-General and published as a world appraisal.

The experts also submitted a number of technical and economic suggestions for the drawing up of these first national appraisals. They pointed out that the preliminary world appraisal which they had made suffered from many unavoidable limitations because of incomplete knowledge at this stage. If reliable appraisals were to be made in the future, they observed, these must be done on a national basis, and with the aid of an internationally adopted standard terminology.

The experts' report also contained a study of the problems involved in the production of iron from iron ore and, to a lesser extent, in the production of steel.

At the same time that this experts' report on iron-ore resources was being prepared, a preparatory study by the Secretariat was in progress on the non-ferrous metals industry. This study, published in October 1955 under the title of *Non-*

Ferrous Metals in Under-Developed Countries, assessed the position of the under-developed countries as producers and consumers of the major non-ferrous metals. It reviewed trends in the use of these metals and short-term fluctuations in demand and prices. It also sought to provide an up-to-date picture of the distribution of smelting and refining capacity, and it discussed at some length the problems involved in maximizing the development potential of the various activities directly based on the exploitation of non-ferrous ore resources.

Attention was being given to the possibility of setting up an *ad hoc* committee of experts on copper, lead and zinc to survey the resources in these metals and their long-term problems.

ENERGY RESOURCES

The work of the United Nations on conservation and utilization of non-agricultural resources includes a continuous review of the economics of energy development and utilization. In addition, the Secretariat prepared three papers for presentation to the International Conference on the Peaceful Uses of Atomic Energy held in Geneva in August 1955. These dealt with "World Requirements of Energy, 1975-2000", "Contribution of Nuclear Energy to Future World Power Needs", and "Some Economic Implications of Nuclear Power for Under-Developed Countries".

WATER RESOURCES

In June 1952, the Council asked the Secretary-General to promote and coordinate international activities concerning water resource development, and to report periodically to the Council on the activities of international organizations in this field. He presented an interim report to the Council's eighteenth session in mid-1954 entitled, "Development and Utilization of Water Resources". The report was prepared in the light of preliminary consultations with the specialized agencies most immediately concerned, and in the light of exploratory discussions with specialists attached to other organizations concerned with water resources.

The report noted that in many areas water supplies were currently inadequate to meet the growing demand, and that the trend towards an increasingly acute shortage of water in many regions was slowing down economic development. There was therefore a need for full knowledge of all water resources, both surface and underground, as well as for knowledge of how water resources should be managed in order to get the most benefit from available supplies. The report selected three areas as being the most feasible and vital in which international action to help governments should be taken as soon as possible: (1) the gathering and coordination of hydrological data, (2) the extension of knowledge of the techniques of watershed management, and (3) the study of industrial needs in any over-all plans for water development. The report also examined ways and means of integrating and co-ordinating activities at the national, regional and international levels.

As a result of the Council's discussion of this report, a unanimous resolution was adopted on August 2, 1954, recommending, among other things, that particular attention should be given by governments and the United Nations organizations concerned to: (1) the assembly of hydrological data; (2) the technique of water-shed management; and (3) domestic, urban, agricultural and industrial use of water. The Secretary-General, the regional economic commissions, and the specialized agencies concerned were invited to take all practical steps, in cooperation with governments, that would help strengthen international technical cooperation in the development and utilization of water resources. The Technical Assistance

Board and the Council's Technical Assistance Committee were also invited to give special attention to requests for technical assistance for that purpose.

Finally, the resolution asked the Secretary-General: to continue along the lines suggested in his report the efforts for strengthening international technical cooperation on water matters and improving the coordination of related activities; to consult on these matters with governments, inter-governmental bodies and non-governmental organizations; and to report to the Council not later than 1956, on these consultations with suggestions for possible further action.

Upon the adoption of this decision of the Council, there was convened in Geneva what was called the First Inter-Agency Meeting on International Cooperation with respect to the Development and Utilization of Water Resources. The participants were the Secretariat members directly concerned with water problems in the United Nations Department of Economic and Social Affairs; the Technical Assistance Administration; the Economic Commission for Europe; the Economic Commission for Asia and the Far East; the Food and Agriculture Organization; the International Bank for Reconstruction and Development; the United Nations Educational, Scientific and Cultural Organization; the World Health Organization; and the World Meteorological Organization.

Unanimous agreement was reached on arrangements for improving the exchange of information on water resource projects and activities. It was decided that a central repository of such information be established by the Secretariat at United Nations Headquarters. Agreement was also reached on: arrangements for inter-agency cooperation in the study of matters bearing on the development and utilization of water resources, and in the preparation of handbooks; arrangements for the assembly and study of data on water problems in substantive fields, and in geographic areas not covered or only partially covered so far by United Nations organizations; and on steps to promote cooperation in water questions with international scientific and technical organizations outside the "United Nations family". It was decided that an inter-agency meeting on water questions should be held at least once a year to review past activities and consider action programs and plans.

A Second Inter-Agency Meeting was held at the beginning of August 1955, again in Geneva. A review was made of the work initiated during the previous year in such domains as hydrology, preparation of handbooks, and consultation with governments and international scientific and technical organizations interested in the field of water resources. Problems dealt with concerned further possible action in respect of legal questions, the question of providing training facilities in integrated water resource development, and the utilization of saline water.

Among the projects which were completed or in progress as a result of inter-agency decisions were: (1) a handbook on watershed management, by FAO; (2) a preliminary study on the industrial uses of water, by the United Nations Secretariat; and (3) a preliminary study on national water boards, by the United Nations Secretariat.

DEVELOPMENT OF WATER RESOURCES AND ARID LANDS

One basic reason for the low living standards of certain under-developed countries, according to a General Assembly resolution of November 20, 1950, is the inadequacy of cultivated acreage. Their continual population increases require urgent measures to develop their resources, it pointed out. To raise living standards and to promote equitable distribution of land, it is therefore necessary to develop arid zones, and thus increase the areas now being cultivated.

Accordingly, the Assembly called on the Economic and Social Council to consider such measures for the development of arid land as: (1) devoting sufficient technical and financial means to the study of the relevant scientific and practical problems, (2) promoting and coordinating the activities of the United Nations and the specialized agencies to that end, and (3) furnishing appropriate technical assistance to the governments concerned.

The development of arid lands was considered by the Council in March 1951, in connection with problems of water control and utilization. Believing it desirable that international measures in the general field of water control and utilization should be coordinated within the United Nations system, it asked the Secretary-General, to consider the entire field of water control and utilization as related to the problems of the arid zones.

At the Council's fourteenth session, on June 2, 1952, a new emphasis was given to the great importance of the better use and control of water resources for economic development, and for solving the problems of arid land development. Considered at this session was a report prepared by the Secretary-General on *Development of Arid Land* in response to an Assembly request of December 1950. Described in this study were the main activities of the United Nations and the specialized agencies on the development of arid land, the technical and financial measures, and the coordination of these measures. It was considered in conjunction with another report by the Secretary-General on *International Cooperation on Water Control and Utilization*.

The Council asked the Secretary-General to assume responsibility for promoting and coordinating international activities for more effective use of water resources and for cooperative action among international and national organizations to this end.

Members of the United Nations, specialized agencies and other interested organizations, the Council recommended, should cooperate with the Secretary-General in executing this program, which also includes collaboration with UNESCO, FAO and other specialized agencies in studies on the development of arid zones. In addition, the Council decided, among other things, to continue giving careful attention to the work of specialized agencies on arid lands.

In subsequent years, the Council has considered the question of arid land development as an integral part of the more general subject of the development and utilization of water resources.

Research on arid zone problems is encouraged by the United Nations Educational, Scientific and Cultural Organization (UNESCO), which has set up an Advisory Committee on Arid Zone Research. (*See chapter on* UNESCO.)

Technical assistance to aid various countries in meeting some arid zone problems has also been provided—for instance, by the United Nations Technical Assistance Administration, UNESCO, the Food and Agriculture Organization, and the World Meteorological Organization.

Full Employment and Economic Stability

Measures to maintain full employment and economic stability were first discussed by the Economic and Social Council at its fourth session (1947), and are now discussed there every year.

Many governments, the Council noted with satisfaction in August 1949, were ready, if conditions warranted, to put into effect measures for increasing purchasing power and for promoting full employment. All governments considering such measures, it urged, should, as far as possible, avoid those likely to result in restricting international trade. And it invited the Secretary-General to appoint a small group of experts to prepare, in the light of the current world economic situation, a report on national and international measures required to achieve full employment, as a basis for eventual Council action. (The experts' report, entitled *National and International Measures for Full Employment*, was considered in detail at the Council's eleventh session.) The Secretary-General was further asked to publish brief up-to-date reports on full employment measures taken in various countries (which he has since done).

Stressing the need for immediate action, especially in countries having an important share in world trade, the General Assembly recommended in November 1949, that each government consider, as a matter of urgency, its international responsibility under Articles 55 and 56 of the Charter to take action to promote and maintain full and productive employment. The Assembly also asked the Council, in considering full employment, to give attention to unemployment and under-employment questions, especially in under-developed countries and particularly in such critical fields as agriculture.

The difficulty of comparing employment and labor statistics on an international plane was examined at the Council's tenth session. Considering that comparative data would be useful for a detailed study of full employment problems and would facilitate the drafting of specific recommendations, the Council called the attention of United Nations Members to a resolution concerning employment, unemployment and labor statistics adopted by the Sixth International Conference of Labor Statisticians.

A unanimous resolution on measures to maintain full employment and to meet the problems of unemployment and under-employment in under-developed countries was adopted at the Council's eleventh session (July-August 1950), when it decided to discuss full employment once every year.

Governments, it declared, could achieve and maintain full employment in an expanding world economy under conditions insuring fundamental political and economic freedoms to the individual. Each government, it recommended, should each year publish a statement of its economic objectives for the ensuing year or for an appropriately longer period.

Wherever practicable, such statements should be accompanied by a statement of quantitative goals or forecasts for employment, production, consumption investment, and other pertinent measurable economic factors indicating significant economic trends.

It was also recommended that governments should formulate, announce and periodically review, in the light of current and forseeable economic trends, the policies, programs and techniques which it intended to pursue in the interests of full employment and general economic progress.

Other recommendations to governments included the following: (1) They should intensify their efforts, while pursuing employment and other domestic goals, to achieve and maintain equilibrium in their payments balances; this equilibrium should be at the highest level of mutually beneficial trade. (2) They should achieve and maintain, to the extent feasible, a high level and regular flow of international investment capital for development purposes. (3) They should strive to prevent lapses in this flow which resulted from or which were associated with economic recessions. (4) They should continue to cooperate in efforts to achieve these results by both national and international measures. (5) In their economic policies and programs, they should seek to avoid measures likely to affect adversely the balance of payments or employment levels of other countries; in the event of a domestic recession, they should act, to the extent feasible, to offset such adverse effects. (6) They should cooperate in investigating ways to prevent domestic recessions spreading to other countries.

Governments were also asked to forward appropriate information to the Secretary-General for necessary studies, reports and analyses on both national and international measures for full employment.

The Council, in addition, urged the International Bank for Reconstruction and Development to use all practicable opportunities in the event of a recession to increase its resources for expanding the volume of its loans. At the same time, the International Monetary Fund was urged to make its resources available to its members to meet needs arising from economic recessions. It should do so as fully and as readily as its Articles of Agreement allowed.

The Secretary-General, further, was asked to appoint a group of three to five technical experts to formulate and analyze alternative practical ways for reducing the impacts of possible national recessions. (Their report, entitled *Measures for International Economic Stability*, was considered by the Council in the summer of 1952.)

The Secretary-General was also asked to appoint and assist a small group of experts to report on and propose national and international measures to reduce unemployment and under-employment in under-developed countries. (*See section on* Financing Economic Development.)

Governments, the specialized agencies, and the Secretary-General, it was further recommended, should pursue action already undertaken in the field of migration. In doing so, they should take into consideration the importance of facilitating the international mobility of labor to solve full employment problems.

Finally, the Council asked the Secretary-General and the appropriate specialized agencies to provide technical assistance, upon requests, to help governments carry out the objects of its resolution.

In noting this resolution with satisfaction on December 12, 1950, the General Assembly asked governments to cooperate with the Secretary-General in making the studies which the Council had requested of him.

Another Assembly resolution of December 12, 1950, concerned the possible aggravation of unemployment and under-employment in under-developed countries following mechanization of certain branches of agriculture and industry. This problem, the Assembly therefore emphasized, should be studied by the expert group set up to study measures to reduce unemployment and under-employment in under-developed countries.

The report of these experts appeared in May 1951, under the title *Measures for the Economic Development of Under-Developed Countries* (*see section on* Financing Economic Development). Their analysis of unemployment and under-employment problems led them to the conclusion that it was necessary to create new employment rapidly, which was the task of economic development. "And this," they stated, "is the reason why the emphasis of our report is upon economic development rather than upon unemployment."

Problems of maintaining full employment in developed countries and ways of solving the unemployment problems of under-developed countries were again discussed by the Council in August 1951.

Despite the current improvement in their foreign trade balances, the Council recognized, under-developed countries might find it difficult to increase productivity at a desirable rate without continued growth in capital equipment and without more technical assistance. It agreed, too, that while the reduction of unemployment and under-employment in these countries depended primarily on their efforts to achieve balanced economic development, it also required a high level of economic activity in the industrially advanced countries. The Council therefore decided to discuss the problems of reducing structural unemployment and under-employment in under-developed countries once every year, beginning in 1952.

The Council also asked the Secretary-General: to amend his questionnaire to governments on employment matters so as to take into account the special problems of under-developed countries; and to give special attention to requests for technical assistance to improve the economic and statistical services of governments in this connection.

To secure world economic stability and full employment, international action must supplement national efforts, the Council recognized on July 10, 1952, after considering recommendations in the experts' report, *Measures for International Economic Stability*, requested by previous Council resolutions.

One of the experts' recommendations was for international commodity arrange-ments (including buffer stocks financed perhaps by the International Bank) to reduce the impact of short-run swings in the demand and supply of primary products.

No specific reference in favor of international commodity agreements appeared in the final Council resolution, but the Council did ask the Secretary-General for a study of the relative price movements of various types of goods on the world market.

Governments of developed countries, it also recommended, should bear in mind: (1) the possible effects of their domestic economic policies not only on their own economies and payments balances but also on those of others, and (2) the gen-eral advantages of greater stability for the international flow of capital and trade.

On August 4, 1953, after a discussion on the relationship between full employ-ment and inflation, the Council asked Member States which had experience in dealing with inflationary pressures associated with high levels of economic activity or with the process of economic development, to submit written statements on the subject to the Secretary-General, who would summarize and circulate them to the Council.

At the same time, the Council asked the Secretary-General to invite Member Governments to state their views on measures they might consider necessary to prevent adverse effects on their respective economies resulting from reduced de-fence expenditures. The Council also called upon all governments to reduce obstacles to international trade as a means of increasing employment and of at-taining other economic aims. Recognizing that the level of monetary reserves available to Member States was an important factor influencing the feasibility of maintaining international economic stability at optimum levels of output, con-sumption, trade and employment, the Council further requested the International Monetary Fund to continue to keep the adequacy of such reserves under review for the purpose of helping countries to meet temporary disequilibria in their inter-national payments.

In 1954, the Council drew the attention of Member States to the documents surveying the experience of governments in dealing with inflationary tendencies at high levels of economic activity. It recommended, in a resolution of August 4, 1954, that Member States be prepared at any time to take action to maintain high and expanding levels of production and employment in the face of reductions in demand, but to avoid action that would have adverse effects upon employment and economic development in other states. The Council also recommended that national and international efforts should be intensified to reduce instability in the prices of primary commodities and to facilitate the flow of capital to under-developed countries. (*See section on* Financing Economic Development.)

No substantive resolutions on the full employment question were taken by the Council in 1955.

Development of International Travel

International travel, as the Economic and Social Council recognized in a resolution of March 31, 1955, is important in promoting international understanding and cultural relationships, in fostering international trade, in furthering economic development and in helping to improve balances of payments. The Council accordingly invited Members of the United Nations and the specialized agencies to examine the beneficial effect of an increase in tourist traffic on their internal economies; to survey their tourist facilities to determine existing deficiencies; and to encourage the development of transport, hotel and other necessary facilities, amenities and attractions.

They were also invited: to simplify, wherever possible, exit and entry procedures for tourists, and cooperate in developing travel arrangements to facilitate tourism; to encourage the exchange of technical advice between countries with well-developed tourist programs and facilities and those with less experience; and to give adequate support to official organizations engaged in developing tourism and to encourage their cooperation with private agencies. Non-governmental organizations in the tourist field were invited to increase their efforts to promote international travel.

In addition, the Council asked organs of the United Nations and appropriate specialized agencies to give favorable consideration to constructive projects designed to increase tourist facilities and promote travel.

Also envisaged by the resolution was a study by the Secretary-General of available travel statistics to be made with a view to the establishment of uniform definitions, standards and methods. Requested, too, was a report by the Secretary-General on the measures taken in response to the resolution.

Statistical Questions

The statistical activities of the United Nations are carried out under the guidance of the Statistical Commission, a functional commission of the Economic and Social Council which advises the Council and the Secretary-General. The Commission first met in 1946 and has held eight sessions; its ninth session was scheduled for April 1956, in New York.

The central agency for the collection, analysis, publication, standardization and improvement of statistics serving the general purposes of international organizations is the United Nations Statistical Office, which functions in cooperation with the secretariats of the regional economic commissions and the specialized agencies, each of the specialized agencies being responsible for the collection of special statistics relevant to its activities.

COLLECTION AND PUBLICATION OF STATISTICS

One of the functions of the statistical services of the United Nations is the collection and publication of data from many countries in periodic as well as in *ad hoc* reports. The data published are obtained from official governmental sources, and cover the most significant economic and social subjects. Three basic reference works are published every year: the *Statistical Yearbook,* which contains a comprehensive collection of international statistics, most of which cover a twenty-year period; the *Demographic Yearbook,* designed as a central source of demographic data; and the *Yearbook of International Trade Statistics,* which contains detailed statistics for 100 countries covering approximately 98 per cent of world trade. *Statistics of National Income and Expenditure,* which appears semi-annually, gives estimates of national income and its components. The need for more current information is met by more frequent publications, among which is the *Monthly Bulletin of Statistics* containing monthly or quarterly data for approximately 3000 series. Periodically, a *Supplement* is issued to complement the *Bulletin* by providing more detailed definitions and explanatory notes about the scope, coverage, methods of compilation, and other factors affecting the international comparability of statistics. Current figures are also given in the following current publications: *Population and Vital Statistics Reports, Commodity Trade Statistics,* and the *Direction of International Trade* (published jointly with the International Monetary Fund and the International Bank for Reconstruction and Development).

In addition, special reports on various subjects appear from time to time, such as *World Energy Supplies in Selected Years, 1929-1950; Survey of Social Statistics; World Weights and Measures* (published in collaboration with the Food and Agriculture Organization); *Retail Price Comparisons for International Salary Determination; List of Statistical Series Collected by International Organizations; Directory of International Standards for Statistics.* Reports on *Sample Surveys of Current Interest* are issued annually to draw attention to sampling methods and techniques which are being used in various countries. Some of the information collected by the Statistical Office is not published, but is used internally and is available on request to interested agencies and inquirers.

DEVELOPMENT OF INTERNATIONAL STANDARDS

To promote the development of national statistics and the improvement of their comparability is the first task assigned to the Statistical Commission in its terms of reference. Good international statistics must have good national statistics as their basis, and it is therefore essential that international agencies and national statistical offices collaborate in the formulation of uniform guiding principles, definitions, concepts and methods. They are drawn up in consultation with national governments taking account of current statistical practices. Thus, the *International Standard Industrial Classification* was approved by the Statistical Commission in 1948, and a *Standard International Trade Classification* was approved in 1950. In adopting these standard classifications, the Economic and Social Council has recommended that governments adopt the systems of classification for their national statistical systems, or rearrange their data in accordance with these classifications for purposes of international comparison. Countries accounting for about 81 per cent of world trade are now reporting their trade according to the Standard International Trade Classification. Other fields for which standards have been approved by the Statistical Commission include population censuses, vital statistics, migration statistics, transport statistics, basic industrial statistics, index numbers of industrial production, and national income statistics.

IMPROVEMENT OF NATIONAL STATISTICS

In addition, the Statistical Office prepares guides and manuals in its *Studies in Methods Series* to assist governments in implementing recommended statistical practices. The manuals are intended to cover each major aspect of statistics. Manuals have already been issued on population census methods, methods of national income estimation, concepts and definitions of capital formation, industrial censuses and related inquiries, statistical organizations, and on vital statistics methods.

TECHNICAL ASSISTANCE IN STATISTICS

United Nations technical assistance in the field of statistics to less developed countries has increased considerably with the growth of the Expanded Technical Assistance Program. The Statistical Office cooperates with the United Nations Technical Assistance Administration and the specialized agencies concerned in arranging for international seminars, conferences and training centres, at which statisticians from under-developed countries meet for consultation among themselves and with experts from statistically more developed countries. Activities of this type have included seminars and training centres in the various fields of statistics held in Mexico, France, Egypt, India, Panama, Lebanon, Chile, Costa Rica, Brazil, Finland, Ceylon, Ecuador, Japan, the Philippines and Afghanistan. Over 920 participants have attended these centres. This figure does not include the participants at permanent training centres in Chile and the Philippines.

Facilities to enable statisticians from under-developed countries to study more advanced statistical techniques in the more developed countries are also provided, through fellowships and scholarships. Thus, 137 fellowships in statistics have been granted by the United Nations Technical Assistance Administration.

An important aspect of United Nations aid in improving national statistics is the provision of expert consultants, on requests, to countries seeking such assistance. The United Nations has provided 100 statistical experts to 36 countries. (Technical aid in statistics is also provided by the specialized agencies in the particular fields of activities falling within their specialized spheres.)

Fiscal Questions

Fiscal problems have for many years been a matter for consideration by the Economic and Social Council and other United Nations organs.

In the tax field, the Council has concentrated its attention on international tax relations. Thus, the Council has examined the question of obstacles to the flow of international trade and investment which may result from uncoordinated actions of governments in the field of taxation. On this, the Council has urged Member Governments to pursue a policy of concluding bilateral agreements aimed at avoiding double taxation. In addition, the Council, and the General Assembly, too, have asked the Secretary-General to study the possibility of stimulating the flow of capital to under-developed countries through tax incentives, particularly by allowing the comparatively low tax rates and special exemptions offered by those countries to become more fully effective in attracting foreign investors. (See "Financing Economic Development" above.)

The Council's actions in the budget field have dealt with problems of government financial reporting, the development of sound principles of budgeting and accounting, the improvement of budgetary practices and international public finance statistics.

Until 1954, the Council was advised on fiscal problems by its Fiscal Commission. The activities of this commission, however, were discontinued in 1954 as, at that time, the fiscal work of the United Nations had become well established, and the Secretariat had received adequate guidance from the Fiscal Commission and the Council.

The work program of the Secretariat in the fiscal field includes the preparation of studies and reports on the subjects considered by the Council; the maintenance of a fiscal information service; and the provision of technical advice, information and assistance, on request, to governments, as well as to organs of the United Nations and the specialized agencies.

TECHNICAL ASSISTANCE

In accordance with Council resolutions, highest priority among the fiscal activities of the United Nations has been given to rendering technical assistance to governments at their requests. Such aid has been provided through expert missions working in the recipient countries as well as through the training of a number of their budget and tax officials in other countries, including training within the Fiscal and Financial Branch of the Secretariat. In 1955, nine countries received expert assistance in the fiscal field, and close to 30 fellowships and scholarships were granted for study abroad. Besides organizing training facilities for budget and tax officials in government offices and universities outside their home countries, the United Nations has helped to establish training courses in fiscal subjects in the assisted countries themselves.

In addition to giving aid to individual countries, the United Nations has sought to further the improvement of fiscal practices through more general projects. Thus, regional workshops on problems of budget reclassification and management were held, in response to the interest expressed by Member Governments, in Mexico City, during September 1953, and in Bangkok, during September 1955. Preliminary drafts of *A Manual for the Classification of Government Accounts* served as the basic working documents in these workshops. Published in 1954 was a report on budget management, containing a summary of discussions and major conclusions of the Mexico Workshop, participants in which included budget officials from the republics of Central America, the Caribbean area, Mexico and the United States. *A Report on Budget Reclassification in the ECAFE Region* was to be issued early in 1956.

A report on tax matters was published by the United Nations in 1954 under the title *Taxes and Fiscal Policy in Under-developed Countries;* this drew upon the experience gained in the operation of the United Nations and other technical assistance programs. A *Manual on Income Tax Administration,* prepared in collaboration with Harvard University, was scheduled for publication in 1956.

PUBLIC FINANCE INFORMATION

As part of its fiscal information service, the Secretariat of the United Nations has published *Public Finance Information Papers* on Colombia, Egypt, Iran, Iraq, Italy and Peru, and two *Public Finance Surveys* dealing more comprehensively with the public finances of India and Venezuela.

Another study, *Public Debt, 1914-1946* presents tabular data for 52 countries from 1914 to 1946, and up to 1947 for some 20 countries.

A public finance questionnaire has been prepared jointly by the United Nations and the International Monetary Fund, to obtain public finance data from governments. This information gives a comprehensive picture of the cash transactions of governments and their inter-relationship with changes in government cash holdings and in outstanding public debt. Information based on such data is currently published in the Fund's monthly bulletin *International Financial Statistics* and in the *Statistical Yearbook* of the United Nations. The *Statistical Yearbook* also gives sub-classifications of categories, expenditures and receipts in its public finance chapter.

TAX STUDIES

United Nations Publications on international tax problems include: *International Tax Agreements.* Volumes I, II, IV and VI of this contain the texts of agreements for the avoidance of double taxation and the prevention of fiscal evasion;

Volume V, *World Guide to International Tax Agreements,* superseding Volume III, gives information on the status of all known tax agreements, and was to be brought up to date by a supplement (Volume VII), still in preparation at the end of 1955.

Tax Treatment of Foreign Nationals, Assets and Transactions. A series covering the practices of 34 countries.

Corporate Tax Problems. A comparative approach to techniques for the avoidance of international double taxation of corporate profits and dividends. Studies on the relevant tax rules of selected countries have also been issued.

In the course of its work on the role of tax measures in stimulating the flow of investment capital to under-developed countries, the Secretariat has published a study on *The Effects of Taxation on Foreign Trade and Investment,* and a volume on *United States Income Taxation of Private United States Investment in Latin America.* Other studies to follow were to deal with the tax treatment which private foreign capital invested in under-developed countries is accorded both in the country of origin and the country where it is invested.

In response to an invitation by the Economic and Social Council to universities to cooperate with the Secretary-General, Harvard University, in the United States, has launched a research and training program in tax law and fiscal policy through the International Program in Taxation of the Law School, which is closely coordinated with the Secretariat's work in these fields. Contemplated under the program was the publication of a World Tax Series, which would give comprehensive and up-to-date information on national tax systems. Harvard University further cooperates with the Secretary-General in the study on tax problems of agriculture. Work on this subject was initiated by the Secretariat at the request of, and in cooperation with, the Food and Agriculture Organization. Harvard University published much of the findings of this study to date, in the *Papers and Proceedings of the Conference on Agricultural Taxation and Economic Development* held at Harvard University early in 1954.

BUDGET STUDIES

Among the budget studies of the United Nations are:

Budgetary Structure and Classification of Government Accounts. Published early in 1951, this is the first part of a major analytical project on the improvement of public finance reporting for international comparability, and on basic principles for budget formulation, budget execution, managerial use of accounting, and control. It includes an analysis of the main features of the budget systems of Italy, Sweden, the United States and the U.S.S.R.

Government Accounting and Budget Execution. Published in 1952, this study sets forth procedures in government accounting; it also analyzes the accounting systems followed in France, the Netherlands, Sweden and the United States.

A Manual for the Classification of Government Accounts. This study was scheduled for publication in 1956.

Transport and Communications

SPECIALIZED AGENCIES IN THE FIELD OF TRANSPORT AND COMMUNICATIONS

Established inter-governmental agencies in the fields of aviation, posts, telecommunications and meteorology, the Economic and Social Council decided in 1946, should be brought into relationship with the United Nations as specialized agencies. This was subsequently done by agreements with the International Civil Aviation Organization, the International Telecommunication Union, the Universal

Postal Union, and the World Meteorological Organization. (*See section on* Specialized Agencies.)

To deal with shipping matters, it was agreed at a United Nations Maritime Conference (held in Geneva, February 19 to March 6, 1948) to establish the Inter-Governmental Maritime Consultative Organization. This organization has not yet started functioning. (*See also section on* Specialized Agencies.)

A report is submitted to each session of the Transport and Communications Commission reviewing the progress of the work of specialized agencies whose activities are wholly or partly concerned with transport and communications, with particular reference to the coordination of those activities.

INLAND TRANSPORT

As for inland transport questions, many are dealt with on a regional basis, in accordance with a Council decision of March 1947. Those of a worldwide character—such as international road transport matters and long-term aspects of coordinating inland transport—are reviewed by the Transport and Communications Commission, as decided by various Council resolutions.

ROAD AND MOTOR TRANSPORT

Convention. A United Nations Conference on Road and Motor Transport was convened by the Secretary-General in August-September 1949, in accordance with a decision by the Economic and Social Council. Its object was to conclude a new worldwide Convention on Road and Motor Transport, since the two 1926 Conventions and the 1931 Convention on the Unification of Road Signals were obsolete. It adopted a new Convention on Road Traffic, and also drew up a protocol on road signs and signals.

The Convention on Road Traffic came into force on March 26, 1952. The States which were parties to the Convention at the end of 1955 were: Australia, Austria, Belgium, Cuba, Czechoslovakia, France, Greece, Israel, Italy, Luxembourg, Monaco, Netherlands, the Philippines, Sweden, Syria, the Union of South Africa, the United States, the Vatican City and Vietnam.

Road Signs and Signals. The United Nations Conference on Road and Motor Transport also prepared an optional Protocol on Road Signs and Signals. In view of the general desire to arrive at a later stage at the establishment of a common worldwide system, based on a reconciliation between the "international" or "European" system and the "American" system, the Conference recommended that the necessary study of the problem of reaching worldwide agreement on a uniform system be undertaken within the United Nations by the Transport and Communications Commission with the assistance of experts.

A group of experts on road signs and signals was set up in 1950, to devise a worldwide system of road signs and signals. In the course of 1950-1952, the Group prepared a draft instrument (which became known as the 1953 draft Protocol on a Uniform System of Road Signs and Signals) incorporating the proposed uniform system.

In 1953-1954, at the request of the Economic and Social Council, the Secretary-General conducted an inquiry among governments to obtain their views on the contents of the draft Protocol.

A report, prepared for the Transport and Communications Commission, and submitted in February 1955, stated that the replies and comments received from a large number of countries seemed on the one hand to raise serious obstacles to an early acceptance of a worldwide uniform system, while, on the other, indicating a sufficient interest in the principle of eventual unification. In the light of this situation, the Council on the Commission's recommendation, decided to recommend that governments consider the provisions of the draft Protocol on a uniform system of road signs and signals as recommended practices when revising their systems of road signs and signals, either unilaterally or bilaterally, or in regional agreements, in order to further the progressive achievement of uniformity in the field.

In the meantime, the Protocol on Road Signs and Signals, prepared at the 1949 Conference, came into force on December 20, 1953. The countries which had ratified or acceded to the Protocol by the end of 1955 were: Austria, Belgium, Cuba, Czechoslovakia, France, Greece, Italy, Luxembourg, Monaco, the Netherlands and Sweden.

Licensing of Drivers. Uniform, minimum regulations for the licensing of motor vehicle drivers were drafted in 1952, by a group of experts from different regions of the world, appointed by the Secretary-General in accordance with a Council decision of August 1951. Their task was to consider problems of driver licensing regulations and practices, and to advise the Transport and Communications Commission on the desirability of establishing a uniform set of minimum licensing regulations.

The Economic and Social Council in April 1953 decided that governments should be requested to consider the recommendations of the Committee of Experts in connection with their domestic laws and regulations. In May 1955, the Council reviewed the question and, in accordance with the recommendations of the Transport and Communications Commission, decided that the inquiry with governments should be continued so as to receive their observations and indications as to steps taken, or contemplated with respect to implementing the recommendations of the Committee of Experts.

At the same time, the World Health Organization (WHO) was invited to provide assistance in the preparation of detailed recommendations on requirements and methods determining mental and physical fitness of applicants for driving permits. In August 1955, a meeting was held under the auspices of WHO to prepare a handbook relative to mental and physical standards for drivers. When completed, the handbook was to be circulated by the Secretary-General to governments—as a supplement to the report and recommendations of the Committee of Experts—for consideration in connection with their domestic driver licensing laws and regulations.

DEVELOPMENT OF INTERNATIONAL TRAVEL

Questions relating to international travel were included in the agenda of the Transport and Communications Commission in accordance with a Council resolution of March 1947, under which the Commission was entrusted with the task of advising the Council on travel matters, and of reporting to it from time to time as appropriate.

Under this continuous assignment, the Secretary-General submitted a report to the Commission in February 1955, on developments in the field of travel, including the activities of the specialized agencies and other international organizations. The Commission took further note of the fact, stated in the Secretary-General's report, that the United States Government had proposed the inclusion in the provisional agenda of the Council's nineteenth session of an item on the development of international travel, its present increasing volume and future prospects. (*See section above on* Development of International Travel *for details of Council's action.*)

PASSPORT AND FRONTIER FORMALITIES

To prepare the ground for a world conference on ways of easing passport and frontier formalities, a meeting of experts was held at Geneva in April 1947, on the initiative of the Economic and Social Council. The meeting made a number of recommendations to help ease the existing difficulties with respect to passports and frontier formalities, by reducing the number of documents required and simplifying those that remained. It recommended use of a universally accepted type of passport, and suggested reduction of fees. It further suggested the simplification of visa requirements and of frontier formalities in such matters as police controls, customs inspection of luggage, facilities for exchanging money, currency control, and public health inspection.

These recommendations were then analyzed by the Secretariat, at the Council's request, in the light of the practices of Member States and their willingness to change these practices. After discussion of this study in the Transport and Communications Commission, the Council in August 1948 pointed out to Member States the desirability of reducing, simplifying and unifying passport and frontier formalities to the extent consistent with national security.

Another Secretariat study, surveying postwar progress, difficulties, and facilities granted to particular groups of travellers, was discussed by the Commission in March 1951, when it asked for further progress reports in this field.

In February 1953, the Commission requested the Secretary-General to circulate to governments of Member States the standard visa format recommended by the International Civil Aviation Organization (ICAO) to facilitate the movement of persons in international air transport, and to request their views on the question of its application to international travel by all means of transport.

The Transport and Communications Commission, at its seventh session held in February 1955, recommended that a new inquiry be addressed to governments, requesting information on progress in the implementation of recommendations by the 1947 meeting of experts. The Commission also proposed recommending to governments that, as a recommended practice, they consider using the ICAO standard visa format for international travel by all means of transport. In May 1955, the Council endorsed the Commission's recommendations. A new inquiry was subsequently addressed by the Secretary-General to governments in July 1955.

CUSTOMS FORMALITIES

In accordance with a Council resolution of August 1951, the Secretary-General ascertained the views of governments on the desirability of concluding two worldwide conventions relating to customs formalities: (1) for the temporary importation of private vehicles and their equipment, and (2) for tourism. A report was submitted to the session of the Transport and Communications Commission in February 1953. Subsequently, on the recommendation of the Commission, the Council instructed the Secretary-General to convene a conference of governments.

The United Nations Conference on Customs Formalities for the Temporary Importation of Private Road Motor Vehicles and for Tourism was held in New York in May-June 1954. Three instruments were prepared and opened for signature at the Conference, which was attended by representatives of 47 governments, observers from eight other states, and observers from twelve interested international organizations. These instruments were: the Convention concerning Customs Facilities for Touring, an Additional Protocol to the Convention relative to the Importation of Tourist Publicity Documents and Material, and the Customs Convention on the Temporary Importation of Private Road Vehicles. Either of the Conventions was to enter into force when ratified or acceded to by fifteen states. The Additional Protocol would come into force after five ratifications or accessions. The countries which had ratified these instruments by the end of 1955 were: Belgium, Cambodia (only the Touring Convention), Canada (except for the Additional Protocol), Ceylon (except for the Additional Protocol), Denmark and Japan (except for the Customs Convention on the Temporary Importation of Private Road Vehicles).

TRANSPORT OF DANGEROUS GOODS

In 1950, the Transport and Communications Commission suggested an examination of the problem of the transport of dangerous goods by various means of transport. A study was carried out, in consultation with competent international and national bodies, with a view to determining which aspects of the problem were appropriate for uniform or approximately uniform regulation. At the Commission's suggestion, the Economic and Social Council requested the Secretary-General to appoint a Committee of Experts which met in Geneva in August and September 1954, and prepared a report. The report included detailed recommendations concerning the classification, listing and labelling of dangerous goods, the shipping papers for such goods, and also recommendations about the procedure to be followed in working out uniform regulations for the packing of dangerous goods. In 1955, the Council invited the Secretary-General to circulate the report to governments and interested international organizations for comments, and to reconvene the Committee of Experts in order to examine those replies and establish final recommendations, to recommend a procedure for keeping the list of principal dangerous goods up to date, and to consider further the problem of packaging.

POLLUTION OF SEA WATER

Problems arising from the pollution of sea water were considered at the eleventh session of the Economic and Social Council, when it instructed the Secretary-General to ask Member Governments for their views on a number of specific points.

Noting that some governments had already undertaken studies on the problem, the Council in August 1951 invited other governments, with the technical facilities to do so, to undertake similar studies and communicate the results to the Secretary-General, who was to transmit them to the Inter-Governmental Maritime Consultative Organization (IMCO) when it started functioning.

In the course of his consultations with governments, the Secretary-General was informed by the United Kingdom Government that it intended to issue invitations to the major maritime powers to attend an *ad hoc* diplomatic conference in London in April-May 1954. The Secretary-General later informed the Council that the London Conference, which was attended by the representatives of 42 governments and at which the United Nations was represented, had adopted the International Convention for the Prevention of Pollution of the Sea by Oil, 1954, as well as several resolutions. In one resolution of the conference, the United Nations was asked to undertake the collection, analysis and dissemination of technical information about oil pollution. In June 1954, the Council instructed the Secretary-General to give effect to this resolution, and to keep the Transport and Communications Commission informed of the performance of this task during the period that the Inter-Governmental Maritime Consultative Organization was not established.

DISCRIMINATION IN TRANSPORT INSURANCE

The question of discrimination in transport insurance was first considered in March 1951 by the Commission. As a result of its recommendations, the Economic and Social Council in August 1951, asked Member Governments to adopt as far as possible a policy of non-discrimination in transport insurance, and to permit the placing of transport insurance on the most economical basis. The Commission requested the Secretary-General to study the matter further. He submitted a report to the Commission's sixth session, in February, 1953, summarizing available information on this problem. In April 1953, the Council, on the Commission's recommendation, decided to bring the Secretary-General's study to the attention of governments. It also instructed him to bring the relevant resolutions of the Council and the Commission and the study by the Secretary-General to the notice of: (1) the Contracting Parties to the General Agreement on Tariffs and Trade (GATT), for possible action; and (2) to the International Monetary Fund, with a view to examination by the Fund of the possibility of achieving relaxation of exchange controls as applied to transport insurance.

The Secretary-General has been requested to keep the Council and the Commission informed of developments in this field. At its seventh session (February 1955), the Commission was informed by the Secretary-General that GATT had consulted governments, and that the matter had been retained on the agenda for consideration by the Contracting Parties at their tenth session at the end of the year. It was further informed that the Fund would continue to promote and encourage the lessening of restrictions on all current international payments and the relaxation of exchange restrictions, including those affecting transport insurance.

UNIFICATION OF MARITIME TONNAGE MEASUREMENT

This problem is kept under review by the Transport and Communications Commission, pending the coming into being of the Inter-Governmental Maritime Consultative Organization (IMCO) which will ultimately deal with it.

Regional Economic Commissions

The three regional economic commissions of the Economic and Social Council are: the Economic Commission for Europe (ECE), established March 28, 1947; the Economic Commission for Asia and the Far East (ECAFE), established March 28, 1947; and the Economic Commission for Latin America (ECLA), established February 25, 1948. The Council has postponed final action on the proposal for a Commission for the Middle East.

ECONOMIC COMMISSION FOR EUROPE (ECE)

The United Nations Economic Commission for Europe (ECE) is charged with facilitating concerted action to raise the level of European economic activity, and to maintain and strengthen the economic relations of European countries, both among themselves and with other countries.

The members of ECE are the European Members of the United Nations, and the United States. Non-European Members of the United Nations may be invited to participate in ECE work in which they have a special interest, as they may in ECAFE and ECLA. Since 1953, the Soviet Union and eastern European countries have taken an increasingly active part in the day-to-day work of ECE, thus extending the scope and range of its activities and making it the all-European organ for economic cooperation.

ECE's headquarters are in Geneva. Ten sessions of the Commission had been held by the end of 1955, the first two in 1947, and the rest annually in each of the succeeding years, all in Geneva.

ECE has committees on agriculture, coal, electric power, housing, industry and materials, inland transport, steel, timber, and trade, which in turn have assigned many problems to sub-committees and working parties. *Ad hoc* meetings and consultations are convened from time to time to work on special problems. The standing subsidiary bodies meet in private at regular intervals throughout the year, bringing together experts in their fields from all parts of Europe to define problems and negotiate concrete agreements for concerted government action to solve them.

The meetings are serviced by a secretariat which collects essential information and performs research work both on the specific marketing, production and supply difficulties which are the concern of the individual committees, and on important general developments in the European economy and its world setting. The secretariat publishes, besides its statistical periodicals, an annual *Economic Survey of Europe*, quarterly *Economic Bulletins for Europe*, and comprehensive economic and technical reports on specific industries or sectors of economic activity. These facts and analyses often serve to focus attention on trouble spots in the region's economy, and so help governments to decide on appropriate remedial action.

Public sessions of the Commission are devoted mainly to examining the overall European economic situation, to reviewing progress in the various spheres of ECE work, and to establishing new fields of activity in which inter-governmental cooperation can be effective.

Besides the public and private meetings of ECE, a considerable number of study trips to eastern and western European countries have been held under its auspices to permit experts to share, on the spot, experience and knowledge in such fields as housing, agriculture, coal and timber.

ECE organs and their secretariat maintain close collaboration with other international economic bodies, both within and outside the United Nations family, as well as with appropriate non-governmental business and professional organizations. They also cooperate with the United Nations Technical Assistance Program.

AGRICULTURE. The Committee on Agricultural Problems resumed its meetings in 1954 after an interruption of four years, and all European countries and the United States have been represented at its recent sessions. Its basic object is to develop inter-European trade in agricultural products, in particular, trade between eastern and western European countries.

To this end, it reviews the current situation in a number of important agricultural products; considers long-term trends in production, consumption and trade; examines existing obstacles to trade; and studies the principle on which long-term bilateral trade arrangements can be set up.

Through its Working Party on Standardization of Perishable Foodstuffs, it has drawn up an international protocol for the standardization and quality control of fruit and vegetables, which has already been accepted by fourteen European countries; work is proceeding on establishing more detailed standards for certain vegetables, poultry, eggs and fish.

Other working parties are considering the standardization of conditions of sale for selected agricultural products (such as cereals, potatoes and citrus fruit) by drawing up model contract clauses. The Working Party on the Mechanization of Agriculture was continuing studies of methods of harvesting and green fodder conservation, and the mechanization of dairy farming.

The Food and Agriculture Organization (FAO) cooperates closely with ECE in this work and supplies the senior members of the staff concerned. Among published studies are annual reports on "Prices of Agricultural Products and Fertilizers", and on "Output and Expenses of Agriculture".

COAL. Europe has been afflicted with many coal problems since the Second World War. ECE's Coal Committee and its subsidiary bodies have attacked these problems on a number of fronts. Earlier efforts included the allocation of scarce supplies of coal and coke. The Committee now seeks to insure that Europe's fuel needs are satisfied as economically as possible, to contribute to stability in the coal market, and to promote the rational use of solid fuels. It also serves as a forum for the exchange of information on stocking policies and of technical knowledge, for example, on new processes for making coke and ways of avoiding fuel waste.

After a two-year trial period, an international classification system for hard coals by type, and a system of statistical grouping of hard coal were amended and adopted to facilitate coal trade. An international classification of hard coal by size was also adopted, and a proposal for an international classification system for high-temperature, hard-coal coke was formulated. Work is proceeding on an international system for classifying brown coals and lignites.

An *ad hoc* group of experts was studying the usefulness and feasibility of drawing up conditions of sale for solid fuels.

As part of its study of coal in relation to other forms of energy, the Committee has examined developments in the European gas economy and their impact on coal. A secretariat report on this matter was published as part of a series which included "The Price of Oil in Western Europe". Attention is also being given to implications arising from prospects of producing nuclear power.

New matters under study included district heating, underground gasification of solid fuels, and the use of low-grade fuels in power stations.

ELECTRIC POWER. The ECE Committee on Electric Power assists Europe to meet its rapidly growing requirements for electric energy. Its meetings, attended by leading experts from all parts of Europe, analyze the power situation during the previous year (consumption, production, international exchanges of electricity, investments, etc.) and examine the trends for the future. These periodic reviews produce much information of general use and single out problems requiring international action. The question of producing electric power from nuclear reactors is on the agenda.

The Committee studies closely the legal and administrative difficulties hampering international transfers of power, and the development of hydro-electric resources of interest to two or more countries; it then makes recommendations to governments, for example, to reduce formalities impeding the flow of electricity across frontiers. Negotiations are held under the auspices of the secretariat to facilitate the conclusion of agreements on power. Thus in 1955, a treaty was signed between Austria and Yugoslavia regulating the operation of power stations on the Drava river.

An inter-governmental body known as "Yougelexport", set up under the Committee's auspices, has elaborated detailed proposals for the construction of large hydro-electric power plants and transmission lines on Yugoslav territory to produce power for Austria, the Federal Republic of Germany and Italy. The Committee has also studied possibilities for exports from other countries, notably Austria, Luxembourg and Turkey.

A special working party studies problems connected with the production, transmission, distribution and use of electric power in rural areas, as well as related economic, administrative and financial questions. Ten of 36 reports on these questions have already been published. Among other technical studies was one on lowering construction costs of hydro-electric power stations.

HOUSING COMMITTEE. The Housing Committee analyzes housing policies, building plans and programs, and financing methods in the European countries. As background, the Committee collects extensive facts and figures with an agreed terminology. Thanks to its efforts, comparable statistics are now published covering almost every European country. Also published is a qualitative and quantitative analysis of the housing situation in Europe. Among problems selected for urgent study were housing management, slum clearance and methods of financing private and cooperative building.

Another group of problems studied by the Housing Committee includes technical matters such as trends in mechanization of building operations, prefabrication, and other factors which could reduce building costs. The Committee is assisted in respect of certain of these matters by the International Council for Building Research, which was set up under its auspices. In its work to promote the sharing of experience and technical cooperation between member countries, the Committee has gone beyond simple exchanges of information and documentation to organizing visits, meetings of experts and study tours, producing thereby a vast increase in mutual contacts on technical and economic questions. An example is the study tour in Poland.

Another type of assistance is the Committee's sending of a mission of experts from seven countries to Yugoslavia and Turkey. Their report analyzes the housing situation and building industry in those two countries, and makes specific recommendations, including proposals for assistance by the more highly industrialized countries.

INLAND TRANSPORT. The ECE Inland Transport Committee is the main inter-governmental instrument used to formulate a general transport policy for Europe. The object of that policy is essentially to organize transport at the European level so as to provide the required services as economically, efficiently and uniformly as possible; to facilitate trade; and to reduce the cost of the goods carried. Successes have already been scored in the step-by-step solution of questions affecting rail, road and waterway transport.

Some of the formal conventions, protocols and other agreements signed in ECE concern simplified customs procedures for tourists, touring and commercial vehicles and containers, international transport of goods by road, maximum weights and dimensions for vehicles, road signs and signals, the construction of main international highways, facilities for passengers and goods crossing frontiers by rail, standardization of wooden packaging for fruit and vegetables, automatic signalling at unguarded level crossings, the elimination of double taxation of automobiles, the contract for international carriage of goods by road, and customs-free temporary importation of private aircraft and pleasure boats.

Work was under way on European agreements concerning other problems, for example, the transport of perishable foodstuffs and of dangerous goods, as well as the unification of rules on collisions in inland navigation. Studies were continuing on the renewal, standardization and utilization of railway rolling stock, and also on the improvement of rail transport equipment.

In the field of traffic safety, the Committee's efforts to reduce road accidents cover the fitness of drivers; the behavior of road users and road building; the improvement of signs and signals; and vehicle construction, equipment and maintenance.

ENGINEERING INDUSTRY. To facilitate international trade in engineering products, a special group of experts has produced progress toward unified contract practices. A set of general conditions for the export of plant and machinery has been agreed upon, and is being used on an ever increasing scale in international commerce. Work was proceeding on the drafting of model contract clauses specifying general conditions for the erection of plants abroad.

Another group of experts is concerned with improving agricultural machinery. It promotes the exchange of technical information on the subject, examines difficulties impeding trade in agricultural machinery, and studies problems of the production and use of this machinery, particularly cereal harvesting and soil preparing machinery and agricultural tractors.

STEEL INDUSTRY. The Steel Committee is less an "action" body than many other ECE committees, but it is influential in contributing facts and opinion which lead to action in and outside of the industry. Its work program is considered reasonable and practical by the high level representatives of governments and industry who participate. Without making recommendations for action, they nevertheless discuss the action implications arising, for example, from their periodic review of the short-term trends and problems of the European steel industry. The reviews take place on the basis of an annual market survey prepared by the Secretariat. This discusses major trends in production, consumption and trade in steel and steel-making raw materials, and includes a more detailed treatment of key questions arising during the year. The main emphasis is at present on: (a) the development of steel consumption and demand, assessed in relation to the growth of steel-making capacity; (b) investment programs in the light of probable requirements and raw material availabilities; and (c) developments overseas affecting possibilities for direct and indirect exports of European steel.

Long-term trends and problems are also studied. The main long-term problems of the steel industry are closely connected with demand, which may be influenced by substitution or by developments within steel consuming industries. A series of inquiries was nearing completion on substitution between steel and aluminium, plastics, asbestos-cement, timber and concrete. At the same time, a number of inquiries have been made on the growth of production capacity in relation to consumption trends in principal industries. Reports have been published on flat steel and tubes, whose trends are being kept under review. A report on railway material was in preparation, and other sectors to be tackled were wire and wire products, heavy and light sections, castings and forgings, and special steels.

The Committee further keeps under review prospects of expanding trade in steel within Europe and between Europe and overseas, particularly the less developed countries. The Committee facilitates exchanges of information on technical questions by the publication of an annual report on technological developments, and by the exchange of visits between experts. Like other ECE committees, the Steel Committee promotes the collection and improvement of statistics in its field, and advises the secretariat on the preparation of a quarterly bulletin providing detailed European statistics on a comparable basis.

The Committee has already prepared and recommended to governments a general definition of iron and steel-making capacity, and was considering the possibility of establishing definitions of rolling-mill capacity. It was also considering the possibility of standardizing conditions of sale of steel products, and of iron, chrome and manganese ores. A directory of international and national organizations in Europe and the United States concerned with iron and steel was being published.

TIMBER TRADE. Essentially, the ECE Timber Committee represents wood-using industries and timber traders. It collaborates closely, even holds joint meetings, with the FAO European Forestry Commission which represents foresters. This collaboration has enhanced mutual understanding of the problems of both sides, and has led to a variety of joint action (stimulated by the ECE/FAO secretariat study *European Timber Trends and Prospects*) on matters of common concern, notably: (a) raising wood supplies to sustain the expanding European economy, while paying full regard to principles of sound forest policy; (b) facilitating a smooth expansion of trade in forest products; and (c) raising productivity in the forest and in forest industries.

An instance of this collaboration is the FAO/ECE Joint Committee on Forest Working Techniques and the Training of Forest Workers. Its working groups deal with matters as diverse as work performance, forest workers' training (in which ILO cooperates), tractor testing, logging in mountainous regions, glossaries, etc. Their field work provides an example of effective all-European collaboration at the technical level.

While there has been a steady expansion in recent years in the number of technical projects carried out under the auspices of the Timber Committee, the economic side of the Committee's work has by no means been neglected. Thus, the Committee reviews periodically the situation in the sawn softwood, pitprops and pulpwood markets. This has contributed to greater stability in the market. In connection with sessions of the Committee, opportunity is provided to interested countries to discuss special problems affecting exports and imports of timber and timber products. Work in hand on the standardization of general conditions of scale for timber was likely to facilitate intra-European trade in timber. Meanwhile, the joint FAO/ECE secretariat was studying trends in the use of wood and its products; this study, which combines the economic and technical approaches, aimed to clarify the role of forest products in the European economy in the longer term.

As a regular service, the secretariat publishes a quarterly, *Timber Bulletin for Europe*, which includes market reviews, and production, trade and price statistics.

DEVELOPMENT OF TRADE. Many of the Commission's efforts are directed to the important matter of increasing trade both within Europe itself, and between Europe and other regions. Nearly all ECE's committees have worked on developing trade in specific commodities, and many of the Commission's statistical and analytical studies have served as market guides for those wishing to purchase or sell various kinds of goods.

Overall trade matters are the special concern of the Committee on the Development of Trade, which reviews developments in intra-European, especially East-West trade, including obstacles to this trade, as well as possibilities for further expanding it. Long-term trading arrangements were under study, as well as possibilities of expanding trade between Europe and other parts of the world.

During the third annual Consultation of Experts on East-West Trade, held in the autumn of 1955, 118 sets of bilateral talks took place between experts from 24 European countries, and eastern and western Germany. According to government testimony, these Consultations have contributed significantly to a welcome expansion of trade in Europe.

A system for voluntary non-automatic multilateral payments compensation has been presented to governments as a way of approaching a greater multilateralism in East-West trade and payments. Work was continuing on problems of arbitral settlement of commercial disputes, and on improving the organization and trade-promotion effectiveness of international trade fairs and exhibitions.

DEVELOPMENT OF SOUTHERN EUROPE. In its *Economic Survey of Europe in 1953*, the secretariat called particular attention to the problems of the economic development of southern Europe, pointing out that the gap between rural pauperism there and industrial progress and higher living standards in north-western Europe continued to widen in recent years, and stressing that the development of industrially and agriculturally retarded countries is in the long run in the interest of Europe as a whole. This study led the Commission to call upon a group of experts from Greece, Italy, Turkey and Yugoslavia to examine further, in cooperation with the secretariat, the problems of the area, and draw up recommendations to raise living standards in their countries and to promote the expansion of the European economy in general.

In their final report, prepared also with the help of specialists provided by the Technical Assistance Administration and published in March 1956, the experts of the four countries, whose population comprises 68,000,000 inhabitants (not counting those of northern Italy), stressed that a major benefit of the project had been the influence which this novel type of cooperation had upon actual planning and programming of economic development in the four countries.

The report gave a detailed description and comparison of the development problems and prospects of the four countries, with a special chapter devoted to the problem of external financing. Against this background, the report described the experts' exploration of specific possibilities for joint action by their countries in a number of fields, and concluded with specific recommendations to increase the degree of utilization of available production resources and to reduce substantially the under-utilization of labor. The importance of outside assistance to the balanced agricultural and industrial development of the region was underlined, including the role which could be played by more liberal imports of their products and a greater inflow of capital from abroad. The experts initiated action in a number of fields, but singled out three as of crucial importance for the economic development of their countries and deserving a high priority as objects for foreign financing: land melioration, afforestation and highway development, the latter including a 3,700-mile circular tourist route through the four countries.

While the group of experts had completed its work, much remained to be done, and each of the ECE committees had been asked to give all possible assistance in its particular field.

ECONOMIC COMMISSION FOR ASIA AND THE FAR EAST (ECAFE)

The main tasks of the Economic Commission for Asia and the Far East (ECAFE) are to: initiate and participate in measures designed to facilitate concerted action for the economic reconstruction and development of Asia and the Far East; make or sponsor investigations and studies of economic and technological problems and developments within Asia and the Far East; and undertake or sponsor the collection, evaluation and dissemination of economic, technological and statistical information. ECAFE provides certain technical advisory services to governments at their request; and it assists its parent body, the United Nations Economic and Social Council, in dealing with economic problems in the region (including, in particular, technical assistance). In all these activities, ECAFE's aim is to assist in raising the level of economic activity in Asia and the Far East, and to maintain and strengthen the economic relations of these areas both among themselves and with other countries of the world.

To enable it to fulfil these functions satisfactorily, ECAFE is empowered to make recommendations on any matters within its competence directly to governments of members or associate members, governments admitted in a consultative capacity, and specialized agencies. The Commission is required to submit for the Council's prior consideration any of its proposals for activities that have important effects on the economy of the world as a whole. It is clearly understood that regional cooperation can be achieved only on a strictly voluntary and agreed basis, and that the Commission is to take no action in respect of any country without the agreement of that country.

Through its subsidiary bodies, ECAFE deals with practically all important branches of Asian economic life. The main spheres of ECAFE's activities are economic development, research and planning, trade, finance, inland transport, flood control and the development of water resources, housing and certain social welfare activities. Work in these fields is carried out through convening meetings and seminars, through research and studies, the organization of training centres and study tours, and through advisory services.

The Commission's headquarters are at Sala Santithan (Peace Hall), Bangkok, Thailand. It had 22 members by the end of 1955—Afghanistan, Australia, Burma, Cambodia, Ceylon, China, France, India, Indonesia, Japan, Laos, Nepal, the Netherlands, New Zealand, Pakistan, the Philippines, the Republic of Korea, Thailand, the U.S.S.R., the United Kingdom, the United States and Vietnam. It also had two associate members at that date—Hong Kong, and Malaya and British Borneo. The number of associate members has dwindled in the last few years with a corresponding increase in the number of members. In response to the Commission's express desire that associate members responsible for their own international affairs be enabled to become full members, the Economic and Social Council resolved in 1954, that Cambodia, Ceylon, the Republic of Korea, Japan, Laos, Nepal and Vietnam be admitted to full membership, provided they apply for it and make an annual financial contribution. These particular countries have done so, and all of them except Japan and the Republic of Korea were admitted to United Nations membership in December 1955. Associate members thus have all the privileges of full members except the right to vote in plenary meetings of the Commission. Their representatives can also be elected to the office of Chairman or Vice-Chairman of the Commission. The so-called ECAFE region, that is the area covered by the Commission's activities, now extends to: Afghanistan, Brunei, Burma, Cambodia, Ceylon, China, the Federation of Malaya, Hong Kong, India, Indonesia, Japan, Korea, Laos, Nepal, North Borneo, Pakistan, the Philippines, Sarawak, Singapore, Thailand and Vietnam.

One of ECAFE's most important functions is to provide a forum for Asian (and non-Asian) representatives to meet, to establish personal contacts, to review existing economic conditions and problems, to exchange ideas and experiences, and to reach conclusions helpful to national and international action.

The Commission's sessions, sometimes described as a "Parliament of Asia", are a representative gathering of cabinet ministers, diplomats, high-ranking government officials, representatives, and other experts of the governments. Attendance at these sessions (and at other ECAFE meetings) includes, in addition to the Commission's members and associate members, observers from the specialized agencies, non-governmental organizations, and sometimes also observers from United Nations Member States not represented in ECAFE, as well as distinguished guests from non-United Nations members.

The Commission's first session was held in Shanghai in 1947. Since then sessions have been held every year (in the beginning twice a year) in a different country: in Baguio (Philippines), Octacamund (India), Lapstone (Australia), Singapore, Bangkok (Thailand), Lahore (Pakistan), Rangoon (Burma), Bandung (Indonesia), Kandy (Ceylon), and Tokyo (Japan). Twelve sessions had been held by the end of 1955.

ECAFE's activities have developed along three main lines: first, fact-finding, fact-recording and analysis; next, recommendations for governmental and inter-governmental action; and finally, the rendering of advisory services. ECAFE organizes and provides facilities for seminars, training centres, and group visits of Asian experts to foreign countries. Basically, ECAFE's activities are directed towards helping governments to help themselves. They have developed more and more from study and research—though these continue to be an important part of its activities—to concrete action.

At its Tokyo session in 1955, the Commission resolved that ECAFE had reached a stage when it could undertake an extensive survey and an analytical appraisal of factors and problems of economic growth and development in the region, and offer governments, if requested, its services for the examination of economic development programs in a regional context. The secretariat, through its newly set up economic development section, was given certain definite tasks: to survey economic development in agreement and cooperation with the governments concerned; to develop a body of techniques of programming economic development suitable for the ECAFE region; to study basic economic development problems and to analyze basic development policies; and to study methods of projecting economic trends, with a view to assisting governments in the preparation of future development programs or the revision of existing ones. It was also decided at the Tokyo session that a team of senior staff members of the ECAFE secretariat, headed by the executive secretary, might pay visits to the countries of interested governments in 1955 and 1956, to render further technical advisory services, especially in connection with the formulation and implementation of economic development programs.

ECAFE can only make recommendations. Decisions and the execution of proposals rest with governments. The bulk of ECAFE's recommendations, however, have been accepted by governments and put into effect. The Commission has thus contributed to the economic development in Asia in many significant ways. It has helped the countries of the region by identifying specific economic problems and selecting them, either because they are urgent or because they lend themselves to regional treatment, or by directing regional action by way of achieving cooperation among the members of the Commission. ECAFE has produced some 600 documents, many of which contain important studies which have been made available to all Members of the United Nations, as well as to the public. These studies have had a considerable influence in assisting policy-making. ECAFE's annual *Economic Survey* and its quarterly *Economic Bulletin* carry a wealth of analyzed information and data covering important aspects of the economic conditions in the region.

The organizational structure of the Commission evolved gradually, subsidiary bodies coming formally into being only after recognition of a clear need and considered debate by the Commission. The first significant advance in the organization of the Commission's work was the setting up of a Committee on Industry and Trade, to be followed later by a Committee on Inland Transport. A Bureau of Flood Control and Water Resources Development is also a part of the ECAFE secretariat. Under the Committee on Industry and Trade at present are sub-committees for electric power, iron and steel, mineral resources development, and trade. Under the Inland Transport Committee come sub-committees for highways, railways and waterways. These subsidiary bodies meet either once a year or, in some cases, every other year. In addition, *ad hoc* conferences, working parties and seminars are convened. Thus, ECAFE has held two trade promotion conferences, three regional statistical conferences, regional technical conferences on flood control as well as on water resources development, and a regional mineral resources conference. It has also held meetings of working parties on the mobilization of domestic capital, small-scale and cottage industries and handicraft marketing, financing of economic development, intra-regional trade and payments problems, standard international trade classification, budgetary reclassification, preparation of a regional geological map, housing and building materials, trained personnel for economic development, economic development planning, and a draft convention for the measurement of inland navigation craft. Seminars have been held on the use of power alcohol, and public industrial enterprises. Altogether, ECAFE, since its inception in 1947, has convened some 80 meetings up to December 1955, either under its own auspices, or in some cases in cooperation with other United Nations agencies, especially the United Nations Technical Assistance Administration (TAA), and some of the United Nations specialized agencies.

With the help of TAA, and the support of a number of governments, ECAFE has organized study tours, some of them global, thereby enabling Asian technicians and other experts to observe modern developments in foreign countries. Such group visits have been organized for: inland waterway experts and senior railway officials to Europe, the United States and Japan; for lignite experts to Australia; for cottage industry directors to Japan; for mining engineers and geologists to the U.S.S.R.; and for iron and steel experts to Japan.

In partnership with TAA, and with the support of the host Government—Pakistan —and other governments, ECAFE organized the first regional railway training centre in Asia, which was opened in 1954 at Lahore, Pakistan, for training courses in railway operations and signalling. ECAFE also gave the impetus to regional research centres for housing and building materials set up in Bandung (Indonesia) and in New Delhi (India), and, with ILO, to a regional training centre for diesel marine mechanics in Rangoon (Burma).

Following a review of the Commission's activities and work since its beginning, the Economic and Social Council decided in mid-1951, that the Commission be continued on a permanent basis (as had been proposed by the Commission at an earlier session).

INDUSTRY AND TRADE. Great emphasis is given in ECAFE's activities and deliberations to questions connected with industrial development. This is partly because industrialization promises fuller utilization of manpower—which is considered most important for the region—and partly because industrialization appears to promise quicker returns in increased productivity and higher standards of living. Among the early activities of the ECAFE secretariat in this regard, was the preparation of a report on industrial development in the region, and of detailed studies of Asia's main industries. Work on industrial development planning continues to be one of the secretariat's high-priority projects, now carried out in coordination with the general survey of economic development in the region. ECAFE's activities have been closely connected with short-term and long-term problems of industrial development and implementation facing the governments. Among the specific problems dealt with, are methods designed to augment supplies of key materials and commodities, development of special management, production, and marketing techniques for small-scale industries, etc. Particular attention has been given to the problem of training of personnel for economic development. In view of the vast human resources of the region, the Commission stressed the need for labor-intensive techniques, and the importance of traditional methods of self-help and cooperation among the people. ECAFE's work has developed in particular in the following branches of Asian industry and trade: cottage and small-scale industries, electric power, housing and building materials, iron and steel industries, mineral resources, and trade promotion.

COTTAGE AND SMALL-SCALE INDUSTRIES. Improved production and marketing techniques have been recommended by ECAFE on the basis of studies, meetings of working parties, and study tours. Activities have been concentrated on such selected subjects as ceramics, hand-woven textiles, bamboo and basket ware, and hand-made paper. Exhibitions of Asian handicraft products have been organized in connection with working party meetings, as well as "market clinics" at which ECAFE experts advised on production and marketing. A five-week study tour to Japan was organized in 1954, together with TAA, for a group of Asian cottage and small-scale industry experts. ECAFE's studies and recommendations have drawn attention to the need for standardization of cottage products, introduction of common facility services, role of governments in stimulating demand for small industries' products, etc. ECAFE proposals for the construction of ceramics pilot plants have been adopted by the Thai Government for a ceramics plant in Bangkok.

ELECTRIC POWER. Aid in developing the production and utilization of electricity in the region has been rendered through studies dealing in particular with the generation, transmission and utilization of electricity in various industries; techniques of estimating future power demands; the requirements and availabilities of power plant and equipment; coordinated development of hydro and thermal power; rural electrification; standardization; etc. Progress in Asian electric power development is kept under continuous review, and ECAFE's findings are published annually in the Commission's Electric Power Bulletin for Asia and the Far East. Following an ECAFE sub-committee meeting in Tokyo in 1954, a study tour was organized for delegates to observe important electric power installations and manufacturing establishments in Japan.

ATOMIC POWER. The keen interest of Asian countries in the use of atomic energy for industrial and other peaceful purposes was noted at the ECAFE session held in Tokyo in 1955, when the secretariat was instructed to keep in touch with further developments and to disseminate information on the subject.

HOUSING AND BUILDING MATERIALS. ECAFE has taken an increasing interest in housing and building problems. An expert in this field was attached to its secretariat and a comprehensive report on housing and building materials in Asia was issued with many recommendations for increased use of indigenous building materials. ECAFE participated in the United Nations seminar on housing and community improvement, the south-east Asia regional conference of the International Federation of Housing and Town Planning, and the Government of India's International Exhibition of Low-Cost Housing, as well as in an inter-secretariat working party on housing and building materials. Proposals made at ECAFE's meeting have led to the establishment of a regional research centre in Indonesia on humid climate building problems and a similar centre in India on building problems in hot climates. Advisory services have been rendered, too, for self-help projects, and on a number of other problems in various countries.

IRON AND STEEL. ECAFE has participated, actively through studies, study tours, working parties, and the dissemination of information, in the creation and expansion of Asia's iron and steel industry. Existing iron and steel industries and plans for expansion have been surveyed. Technical studies and discussions have dealt in particular with various processes for making iron without coking coal, re-rolling mill practices, scrap classification, and manufacture of steel in oxygen converters recently developed in Austria. A directory of research and laboratory facilities has been prepared, as well as a list of main technical libraries and a selected bibliography of relevant iron and steel publications (in cooperation with UNESCO). Advisory services have been provided for Burma, Ceylon and Thailand, and a study tour to Japan has been organized.

MINERAL RESOURCES. There is an urgent need in Asian countries for geological surveys, exploration and development of mineral resources, and the proper processing and utilization of these resources. In all fields, ECAFE has made its contribution. Preparations for drawing up an Asian regional geological map were taken in hand at a working party meeting of senior geologists held in Bangkok, in cooperation with the International Geological Congress and the Cartographic Office of the United Nations. The secretariat publishes an annual report on mining development in Asia and the Far East. Other studies include reports: on problems and prospects of the metal mining industry in the ECAFE region, Australian lignite industry in relation to the development of low-grade coal deposits in Asia, and on kaolin, etc. Study tours have been organized in cooperation with the United Nations Technical Assistance Administration to Japan and to Europe, including the U.S.S.R. Advisory services have been rendered to the Governments of Afghanistan, Burma, Ceylon, the Republic of Korea and Thailand. Laboratory testing facilities have been arranged for several countries of the region. Six countries in Europe and America, and seven countries of Asia have joined the scheme for ECE–ECAFE inter-regional exchange and laboratory investigations of low-grade coals, as worked out by the two secretariats. Advice on methods of locating underground water at a self-help settlement north of Bangkok has been given to the Government of Thailand. In cooperation with the Economic Commission for Europe, the ECAFE secretariat is promoting the exchange of coal samples for laboratory investigations from countries of the region with countries in Europe and America. Samples of Thailand lignite were sent to four countries in Europe and the United States for scientific determinations.

TRADE PROMOTION. Two large trade promotion conferences have been held, under ECAFE auspices in Singapore in 1951 and in Manila in 1953, and numerous studies have been prepared by the secretariat on intra-regional and inter-regional trade. ECAFE helps national trade promotion agencies by supplying them with information, advice on such problems as training in trade promotion techniques, arrangement of international trade fairs, simplification of customs formalities, providing facilities for transit trade of landlocked countries, licensing and remittance procedures, improved commercial intelligence, and marketing research facilities. ECAFE acts as a clearing house for collection and dissemination of commercial information and publishes some of the material collected in its *Trade Promotion News;* its *Trade Promotion Series;* and its *Calendar of Regional Conferences, Seminars, Fairs and Exhibitions.* A study on trade between Europe and Asia was published in cooperation with ECE and FAO. ECAFE has assisted governments on such matters as improving their trade promotion machinery, the marketing of goods, arbitration facilities, use of commodity boards, etc. A Glossary of Commodity Terms has also been published.

INLAND TRANSPORT. It would be far beyond ECAFE's resources to try to cope with all the questions arising out of the transport deficiencies of the region, but the Commission has made an energetic effort to tackle at least some of the outstanding problems, partly through research and technical studies, and it has been able to render advisory services to governments in this regard. General transport problems dealt with include the coordination of the different forms of transport, the collection of transport statistics, an analytical comparison of data showing the performance of various transport systems, refrigeration in transport, etc. Information and technical literature has been distributed and a library of technical books and films has been built up. In addition, ECAFE issues a quarterly *Transport Bulletin.*

In the field of road transport, the Commission has prepared standard forms for a highway register, a highway bridge register, a register for recording data on cement concrete road pavement, and yet another register for the preparation and presentation of highway project schemes. These are intended to insure uniformity, efficiency and economy in establishing useful inventories of highway assets and their requirements; and to form a good basis for planning, programming, and implementing highway maintenance, improvement and expansion. Other important studies have dealt with improved types of road construction, maintenance and repair of vehicles, and the training of mechanics. At an ECAFE conference in Manila, questions of low-cost roads, soil stabilization, and highway safety were discussed at an international forum in Asia for the first time.

One of the most important and significant steps taken by ECAFE to facilitate concerted regional action was in the field of inland navigation. A uniform system of measurement of vessels was proposed and a draft convention worked out. This convention when accepted will facilitate considerably international movement of vessels, reduce time of detention on borders, and thereby increase carrying capacities. A round-the-world study trip was organized in cooperation with TAA, as well as a number of smaller-scale study tours. These helped to create a nucleus of high-level personnel familiar with the most modern inland water transport craft, and techniques for the introduction of many administrative, technical and operational reforms in various Asian countries. ECAFE has assisted the International Labor Organization in setting up a regional training centre for inland water transport personnel in Rangoon, Burma, especially for training diesel marine engineers.

In the field of railways, studies have been prepared on a variety of technical subjects, such as track construction and maintenance, track sleepers, diesel locomotives, railcars, locomotive boiler water treatment, prevention and speedy disposal of railway claims, turn round of wagons, and prevention of accidents. ECAFE's activities in cooperation with TAA have led to the creation of the first regional Asian trairning centre for railway operating and signalling officials in Lahore, Pakistan, set up with the support of the Government of Pakistan and other countries. The curriculum for the centre was drawn up according to the recommendations of a group of railway officials from the region who had made a study tour to Europe, America and Japan to observe modern practices and techniques; this trip was organized by ECAFE jointly with TAA. Tours have also been arranged for delegates to meetings of ECAFE's railway sub-committee to inspect railway installations, and to observe at first hand modern developments and techniques; such tours were arranged in Europe and Japan.

RESEARCH AND PLANNING. Pioneering work has been done by the ECAFE secretariat in collecting, assessing and promoting the development of statistics; and in reporting, through ECAFE, publications on economic developments and problems in the region. The Commission's annual *Economic Survey of Asia and the Far East,* published by the secretariat, has been found useful by governments not only for purposes of analyzing economic trends but also for policy formulation. For the world at large it is a unique source of information and reference. Between issues of the *Survey,* up-to-date information is published in the quarterly *Economic Bulletins for Asia and the Far East,* which include a mid-annual survey and quarterly statistical supplements as well as special articles on particular aspects of the region's economy. ECAFE's statistical files are kept up-to-date in cooperation with governments, the United Nations Statistical Office at United Nations Headquarters in New York, and the specialized agencies. A comprehensive classified index has been compiled. Statistical development was helped by three regional statistical conferences organized by ECAFE, together with the United Nations Statistical Office.

ECONOMIC DEVELOPMENT AND PLANNING. Increasing attention is being given in ECAFE's work to problems of economic development and planning. Thus, a working party of experts on economic development and planning has met to discuss programming techniques, after a series of meetings held in the course of three or four years, on the mobilization of domestic capital, taxation and deficit financing. Working groups of experts have also met to examine the problems of budgetary reclassification and payments.

FLOOD CONTROL AND WATER RESOURCES DEVELOPMENT. The need for effective measures to check the large-scale problems of flood control peculiar to Asia led to the establishment of an ECAFE Bureau of Flood Control in 1949; later, the Bureau's terms of reference were extended to cover the wider field of water resources development and the Bureau was renamed the Bureau of Flood Control and Water Resources Development. These changes reflected a widening of the scope of the Bureau's activities from flood control to multiple-purpose river basin development. The Bureau has published a Manual describing the principles for planning multiple-purpose development projects, and incorporating various suggestions by experts who attended an ECAFE regional conference on water resources development. In addition, surveys of the development of water resources in various countries were being prepared.

In its *Flood Control Series*, the Bureau regularly publishes original contributions to technical problems, such as sedimentation, flood control methods, hydrologic problems, silting and river-bank protection. Uniform standards for methods and records of hydrologic measurements have been prepared and published in the *Flood Control Series*. The Bureau has also published a Glossary of Hydrologic Terms.

The Bureau distributes technical reports and publications, and its *Flood Control Journal* serves to spread up-to-date information about the development of water resources in various countries.

The Bureau undertakes field investigations of flood control methods on major rivers of the region, and publishes its findings in its *Flood Control Series*. It also initiates and promotes international cooperation in the development of rivers which involve the boundaries of more than one country. Thus, field investigations and studies have been carried out in the lower Mekong River since 1949, and preparations for another study in the same area were in hand in December 1955, to ascertain the possible use of the potential resources of the river for irrigation, water power and navigation for the five countries bordering on it.

Studies in the field of flood control have been carried out in earthwork construction, silting, and scouring of rivers and canals.

Technical assistance has been given to a number of countries: this aid has been given to the Ganga and Brahmaputra River Commissions on flood control problems, and studies carried out by the Bureau were extensively used by the Indian Government in the preparation of a scheme to control the flood flow of the River Kosi (also called the "River of Sorrow"). The Bureau advised in the revision of the water laws of the Republic of China, and assisted in making a general review of the development of water resources in Taiwan. It also gave advice on a proposed flood control scheme in the Brantas river basin in East Java, in Indonesia. Assistance has been given to the new water resources training centre established by the Indian Government at the University of Roorkee, in India, the centre serving national as well as regional purposes. In Thailand, the Bureau helped the Royal Irrigation Department in setting up hydraulic model tests of the Chao Phya Barrage, the first of their kind ever to be carried out in Thailand. The results of these investigations helped to shape the final design and led to saving no less than 10 million Baht equivalent to about $500,000 (U.S.). The Yan-Hee multiple-purpose scheme, in Thailand, was also reviewed.

AGRICULTURE. ECAFE has devoted considerable efforts to the economic aspects of agricultural development problems. Cooperation with FAO led to a joint ECAFE/FAO agriculture division being set up at ECAFE's secretariat in Bangkok, staffed partly by ECAFE and partly by FAO. This division reviews agriculture and flood developments in the region, price policies, credit and marketing for the use of both ECAFE and FAO. It prepared a report on agricultural development of Thailand, and a study on rice and rice price policies in the Far Eastern countries. ECAFE participated in FAO's Center on Land Problems in Asia and the Far East held in Bangkok, and various special technical FAO meetings on rice.

SOCIAL DEVELOPMENT PROGRAMS. United Nations efforts to achieve closer integration of the secretariat's economic and social activities led to the establishment within ECAFE of a social affairs unit to deal with questions of social policy, population, community development, social defence, regional town and country planning, family and child welfare, and training of welfare personnel.

COOPERATION WITH OTHER UNITED NATIONS AGENCIES. Close cooperation is maintained with the United Nations Technical Assistance Administration. ECAFE is able to bring to the notice of TAA many regional needs for technical assistance. TAA has sought ECAFE's advice in preparing its own operational program, and in dealing with country requests. ECAFE assists experts and missions in their respective fields. TAA collaborated with ECAFE in some important regional projects, as indicated above, and has made the services of its experts available for certain ECAFE meetings and seminars.

ECAFE cooperates actively with specialized agencies, especially FAO, ILO, UNESCO, WHO and WMO, through the machinery of working parties, special projects, and missions.

ECONOMIC COMMISSION FOR LATIN AMERICA (ECLA)

The principal tasks of the Economic Commission for Latin America (ECLA) consist of the initiation of measures: for promoting concerted action to deal with postwar economic problems, for raising the economic level of Latin American countries and for maintaining and strengthening the economic relations of these countries, both between themselves and with other countries of the world. Among its further functions are the following: to carry out or sponsor research or studies on economic and technological problems; to provide for the collection and distribution of economic, technological and statistical information; to coordinate its activities with those of other organs of the United Nations, of the specialized agencies and of the appropriate organs of the inter-American system, with a view to avoiding duplication; to assist in formulating and implementing coordinated policies for economic development in the region; and to aid the Economic and Social Council and its Technical Assistance Committee in carrying out the United Nations technical assistance programs, especially in the appraisal of activities under these programs in Latin America.

ECLA's headquarters are at Santiago, Chile. The Commission also has an office in Mexico City.

MEMBERSHIP. The members of the Commission are: Argentina, Bolivia, Brazil, Chile,

Colombia, Costa Rica, Cuba, the Dominican Republic, Ecuador, El Salvador, France, Guatemala, Haiti, Honduras, Mexico, the Netherlands, Nicaragua, Panama, Paraguay, Peru, the United Kingdom, the United States, Uruguay and Venezuela. Provision has also been made for the admission of associate members, and, as in the case of the other regional commissions, for inviting any non-member of ECLA which is a Member of the United Nations to participate in a consultative capacity in discussions on any matter of particular concern to it.

SESSIONS. By the end of 1955, the Commission had held six sessions—in Santiago, Chile, June 1948; in Havana, May-June 1949; in Montevideo, June 1950; in Mexico City, June 1951; in Rio de Janeiro, April 1953; and in Bogota, August-September 1955. The Committee of the Whole met in Santiago, Chile, during February of the years 1952 and 1954, and in May 1955. It also held an extraordinary meeting in July 1954, to discuss ECLA's participation in the conference of Ministers of Finance or Economy at Rio de Janeiro.

ECONOMIC SURVEYS. An annual *Economic Survey of Latin America*, reviewing economic trends and conditions in the region, is prepared by the ECLA secretariat. Surveys have been published for the years 1948, 1949, 1950, 1951-1952, 1953, and 1954.

Complementary to the annual *Economic Survey* is the secretariat's *Economic Bulletin for Latin America*. The first regular issue was to appear in February 1956, and it was intended to publish the *Bulletin* twice yearly.

ECONOMIC DEVELOPMENT. The need for systematic studies of long-term economic trends and development problems in Latin America has been stressed by the Commission from the time of its first session. The lack of comprehensive analytical studies meant that the main task of the Commission and its secretariat, in the early years of their work, was necessarily that of examining and evaluating these and related questions.

The problems of economic development have been the object of particularly thorough discussion. In 1951, for instance, ECLA recommended that member governments should adopt specific and coordinated measures to promote the economic development of their countries, with full and productive employment of their natural resources and domestic savings, supplemented by foreign investment. They were also to take into account the need for expanding foreign trade in order to increase their supplies of goods essential for economic development.

Another recommendation made by ECLA in the same year, was that the Latin American Governments should formulate periodic economic development programs. The Executive Secretary was asked to assist them when they so requested, both in this task and in the preparation of applications for technical assistance to be submitted to the Technical Assistance Administration. Recommendations on the financing of economic development were also adopted.

The Commission further invited the Central American Governments to establish an inter-governmental economic cooperation committee, to coordinate activities designed to promote the economic integration of the countries concerned. (*See below.*)

In addition, the secretariat was requested to prepare: studies on economic development in each individual Latin American country, a survey of the various aspects of the process of economic development, a comparative analysis of economic development problems, and an examination of development plans and programs and their results.

At the end of 1955, work in the economic development field covered such matters as techniques of programming, the financing of economic development, economic development within individual countries, the establishment or expansion of particular industries, the economic integration of Central America, surveys of technical research and training, the training of economists, technical assistance in Latin America, and social aspects of economic development.

PROGRAMMING OF ECONOMIC DEVELOPMENT. This is an aspect of research and practical action on which ECLA is intensively engaged. The governments have displayed great interest in such questions. A preliminary study on the technique of programming economic development, which was presented by the secretariat at the Commission's fifth session, was published in 1955, under the title of *An Introduction to the Technique of Programming*, as the first volume in a general series on *Analyses and Projections of Economic Development*.

The secretariat has made a beginning on the country studies with two special analytical surveys, one on Brazil and the other on Colombia, which were presented at the sixth ECLA session, and in the preparation of which the secretariat received the full support and cooperation of the governments concerned. These serve as a basis for measuring the rate of economic growth over the last 30 years. After the sixth ECLA session, work was begun on the studies of the economic development of Argentina and Bolivia.

Among other studies initiated by the secretariat towards the close of 1955, were the following: a *preliminary statement on monetary and fiscal policies* for programming economic development, and a *study of administrative organization and procedures for the planning and execution of economic development programs*.

MANPOWER AND SOCIAL ASPECTS OF ECONOMIC DEVELOPMENT. As an integral part of its work on economic development, the secretariat has compiled information on the availability and utilization of manpower in various sectors of economic activity. The constitution of a Division of Social Affairs in the ECLA secretariat in 1955, was designed to give additional impetus to the study of the social aspects of economic development, a topic on which a progress report was presented at the sixth session of the Commission.

TRAINING PROGRAM FOR ECONOMISTS. As a step towards supplying the lack of economists specializing in questions of economic development, the ECLA secretariat, in collaboration with the United Nations Technical Assistance Administration, has organized as from 1952, a training program at ECLA Headquarters in Santiago. Some fifteen Latin American economists participate in this program, which usually begins in April and lasts until September. In 1955, a double program was organized, comprising the regular Santiago course and, as an innovation, another in Colombia, of an intensive and experimental nature.

FINANCING ECONOMIC DEVELOPMENT. Considerable attention has been devoted by the Commission to methods of making more capital available for economic development, by increasing domestic saving and by expanding the flow of foreign capital; by loans from international lending agencies and by direct private investments. A number of studies have been prepared on these matters.

At its third session, the Commission expressed the view that the International Bank for Reconstruction and Development should intensify the implementation of its loans policy for under-developed areas. At the last ECLA session, the secretariat was asked to submit proposals on the most appropriate means for governments: (1) to raise the rate of domestic capital formation, through the provision of facilities and incentives for increased saving; and (2) to direct such saving into productive channels. The Commission further asked the secretariat to prepare studies and reports on the following subjects: inflationary pressures, the monetary and other related policies best adapted to the economic development needs of Latin American countries, the organization and structure of capital markets in Latin America, and the influence which the fiscal system of the capital-exporting countries may exert on the decisions of private investors to place their capital abroad.

In addition, the Executive Secretary was asked to cooperate with the governments of member countries, at their own request, in the formulation of currency, credit and taxation policies; and to advise them on appropriate measures for increasing saving and channelling it towards purposes consistent with economic development.

International financing institutions, the Commission recommended, should note the expansion of demand created by economic development in under-developed countries. They should also adjust their lending to the economic development programs of Latin American countries, so that resources allocated to financing would be available throughout the period covered by the programs in question.

It was further recommended that cooperation between the secretariat and the International Bank should be continued and strengthened. Note was taken with satisfaction of an offer by the International Monetary Fund to collaborate with the secretariat in making an analysis of monetary and exchange problems relating to economic development.

Another study, on the effect of tax measures on foreign private investment in Latin America, was prepared in 1952, by the ECLA secretariat and the Fiscal Division of the United Nations.

In later studies, ECLA has stressed constantly the fact that the collaboration of international capital for financing purposes is essential if the rate of growth of the Latin American countries is to be accelerated. In a *Report on International Cooperation in a Latin American Development Policy* presented by ECLA to the meeting of Ministers of Finance or Economy, held at Rio de Janeiro from November 22 to December 2, 1954, the need for long-term productive loans at rates of interest as low as the financial markets would permit was pointed out. Three types of international financing were examined: (1) direct private investment; (2) loans by the international credit institutions to the public sector of the economy, granted for basic investment; and (3) loans to Latin American entrepreneurs. The creation of a special investment fund was suggested.

At the sixth session, the Commission discussed in detail the study of the legal, economic and financial system governing the investment of foreign capital in Latin America (*Foreign Investment in Latin America*), prepared by the Department of Economic and Social Affairs of the United Nations. The Commission advocated that studies on this subject should be brought up to date and continued.

ECONOMIC INTEGRATION OF CENTRAL AMERICA. In 1950, the Commission recommended that Latin American Governments, when drawing up economic development programs, should take into account the possibilities of expanding markets for their goods through reciprocal trade agreements.

In compliance with the wishes of the governments concerned, the Commission requested its secretariat in 1951, to prepare studies on ways and means of integrating the economies of the Central American Republics, namely Costa Rica, El Salvador, Guatemala, Honduras and Nicaragua.

The Ministers of Economy of these Republics met in August 1952, at Tegucigalpa, Honduras, in accordance with the Commission's suggestion, to discuss the economic integration of their countries. As background material, they had before them preliminary studies prepared by the ECLA secretariat. The Ministers decided to establish their committee (Central American Economic Cooperation Committee) on a permanent basis, and to make a beginning on the gradual integration of their economies. Several recommendations at this meeting were aimed at encouraging the governments concerned to submit requests to the United Nations and its specialized agencies for technical assistance in developing their industrial and agricultural resources, transport systems, and technical training facilities.

The Committee, which is a subsidiary organ of ECLA, gets support from the United Nations Technical Assistance Administration. A Joint Working Group, under the chairmanship of a member of the ECLA staff, and including representatives of FAO, TAA, ILO and UNESCO, advises the Economic Cooperation Committee on the formulation of applications for technical assistance, and on the studies that must be carried out on the basis of a coordinated program. In addition, the International Civil Aviation Organization collaborates in the preparation of specific projects.

The second regular meeting of the Economic Cooperation Committee was held at San José, Costa Rica, in October 1953, and was followed by an extraordinary meeting at San Salvador, in May 1955. The third regular meeting was to take place in Managua, Nicaragua, in January 1956.

The steps taken so far towards the economic integration of Central America have included research and special studies on specific aspects of the Central American economy as a whole. Transport problems (relating to railways, shipping and air and road transport) have been studied, and were examined, *inter alia*, at a seminar held in San José, Costa Rica, in June 1953, at which 23 technical experts from the Central American countries and Panama were present.

Among the achievements of the Economic Cooperation Committee are the following: the establishment of a standard customs classification for the five Republics, which is being applied by their governments; the creation in San José of an Advanced School of Public Administration to serve the whole of Central America; the setting-up of two Sub-Committees, one on Central American Trade, and the other, on Statistical Coordination, to be responsible for standardizing the statistical methods of the five republics; the founding of a Central American Institute for Industrial Research in the city of Guatemala; and a project for the installation of a Central American pulp and paper mill in Honduras.

At the San Salvador meeting, it was recommended that governments intensify their efforts to conclude bilateral free trade treaties, and a proposal for drawing up a multilateral Central American free trade agreement was put forward.

Several technical missions are also making field studies on agriculture and forest industries, and on the problem of electric energy, as well as on the possibility of setting up a technical and administrative training institution in Central America.

TECHNICAL ASSISTANCE. The Commission has given considerable thought to the technical assistance needs of the Latin American countries. At its second session, it asked the Executive Secretary to establish secretariat facilities to aid member governments in appraising their most urgent technical assistance needs. The Secretary-General was invited, in the course of the Commission's third session, to make as full and active use as possible of the ECLA secretariat wherever its help might be of value to member governments, not only in making such appraisals and formulating requests for technical assistance, but also in the practical application of the aid needed. The Commission also requested progress reports on technical assistance in Latin America to be submitted to each of its sessions.

Since 1949, the ECLA secretariat provided advisory services on a number of occasions, mainly in the form of collaboration in certain operational aspects of the United Nations technical assistance program, or of expert advice on various economic development problems, at the direct request of member governments.

The question of technical assistance for Latin America was examined in detail in the ECLA study on *International Cooperation in a Latin American Development Policy*, to which reference has already been made. This survey pointed out that in the granting of such assistance, priority should be given to the needs of the Latin American entrepreneur operating on a medium or small scale.

At ECLA's fifth and sixth sessions, stress was laid on the close relationship between economic development and technical assistance. Secretariat studies by ECLA on the technique of programming economic development were felt to be a useful instrument for determining the technical assistance requirements of the various countries. Attention was drawn to the fact that if technical assistance is to achieve its full effect, it must be integrated with over-all development programs.

AGRICULTURE AND LIVESTOCK PRODUCTION. Work on agricultural and stock-breeding problems has been carried out in close cooperation with FAO. Thus, on the basis of a report by a joint ECLA/FAO working party, set up in October 1948, the Commission at its second session recommended a series of measures which Latin American governments might consider with a view to: insuring the better supply and use of agricultural machinery, fertilizers and pesticides; improving transport and storage facilities; providing credit for farmers; and expanding facilities for research, and for the education and training of agricultural personnel. A joint ECLA/FAO program was instituted to help implement ECLA's recommendations, and to carry out activities of common interest to both Organizations. Studies of the agricultural problems of Brazil, Chile and Ecuador have been made under this program and a section in the special studies on the economic development of Brazil and Colombia has been devoted to agriculture.

In addition, an ECLA/FAO Cooperative Unit made a number of recommendations, and gave advice to several Central American Governments on the development of agricultural credit institutions. At its third session, ECLA arranged for studies of this subject to be carried out in other Latin American countries. It also authorized in cooperation with FAO and interested governments, the undertaking of preparatory work for an expert meeting on agricultural credit. A Seminar on Central American Agricultural Credit, attended by technical experts from twelve Latin American countries, was held in Guatemala City from September 15 to October 15, 1952. Every aspect of agricultural credit was discussed and analyzed, with emphasis being laid on the expansion of such credit in connection with over-all economic development programs.

ECLA at its fourth session again recommended that the governments concerned should take measures to solve the agrarian problems of the Latin American countries.

It was at its fifth session, however, that the Commission devoted special attention to agrarian structure in Latin America, from the standpoint of land tenure, size of farms, and other institutional factors. It also discussed the problem of investment in agriculture, agricultural development programs and activities in individual countries, and the cultivation and marketing of coffee as an important element in the economic development of the producer countries. Resolutions were adopted on sampling techniques and their utilization for the study of economic problems in agriculture, on country studies of agricultural development, on studies of the coffee industry in relation to economic development, on agricultural statistics, on agricultural credit, on agrarian reform, on the banana industry, and on hard fibres.

In addition to the problems of agriculture dealt with in the studies of the economic development of various Latin American countries and in the annual *Economic Survey*, a study of coffee production in selected countries of the region and of its effect on economic development was a task on which ECLA was engaged at the end of 1955, under the joint ECLA/FAO program.

The situation of agriculture in Latin America was discussed in detail at the Commission's sixth session, on the basis of a study on *The Selective Expansion of Agricultural Production in Latin America and its relationship to Economic Development*, presented jointly by the ECLA secretariat and FAO.

Particular interest was shown in the problem of agricultural surpluses, and it was resolved, *inter alia*, to request FAO to afford the countries concerned fuller opportunities of participating in the deliberations of the Washington consultative subcommittee; and to recommend to countries holding surpluses, that in formulating and adapting their agricultural production policies, they take into special consideration the possible repercussions of such policies on the trade of the countries of this hemisphere. With regard to coffee, the Commission expressed the hope that producer and consumer countries would make a united effort to prevent exaggerated price fluctuations. Other resolutions referred to the study of the livestock situation in Latin America, to the industrial transformation of agricultural products, and to research in the Amazon area to be undertaken by the ECLA secretariat and FAO.

STUDIES OF INDUSTRIES AND MEETINGS OF EXPERTS. The problems of industry and mining in the Latin American countries have been the object of continuous study by the ECLA secretariat. Preliminary analyses of industrial and mining production appear in its *Economic Surveys*, in the *Economic Bulletin of Latin America*, and in studies on economic development problems. The following are the principal studies on specific industries:

(1) *Productivity of Labor in the Cotton Textile Industries of Five Latin American Countries*. Presented at ECLA's fourth session, this study indicated the extent to which improved organization and the modernization of equipment would help in increasing production in the textile industries.

(2) *A Study of the Iron and Steel Industry in Latin America*. Such a study was presented at the fifth session of the Commission. This is a study of the existing iron and steel industries or those in the process of organization in seven Latin American countries, with a view to their further development. A Meeting of Experts on the Latin America iron and steel industry was held in Bogotá, at the invitation of the Government of Colombia, from October 13 to 31, 1952. The participants—117 experts—and the authors of the 82 background papers contributed were chosen from nineteen different countries. The agenda covered problems relating to fuel, iron reduction, steel-making and economic aspects.

(3) *Iron and Steel Transforming Industries*. A general paper on this subject was presented at the sixth ECLA session. It deals with the industry's main technical and economic problems, based on an investigation of individual plants taken as representative samples. These studies on the iron and steel transforming industries in Latin America were to be the object of discussion at a meeting of experts similar to that which examined siderurgical problems at Bogotá. The meeting of technical specialists on the mechanical industries was to be held in 1956 at Sao Paulo, Brazil, under the auspices of ECLA, the United Nations Technical Assistance Administration, the Brazilian Government, and the *Asociaçao Brasileira de Metais*.

(4) *Possibilities of the Development of the Pulp and Paper Industry in Latin America*. This joint ECLA/FAO study demonstrates that it would be possible for Latin America not only to meet the whole of its domestic demand as forecast for 1965, but also to be in a position to manufacture an exportable surplus of approximately 1,500,000 tons annually, that is, to produce almost 3,000,000 tons of newsprint a year.

To follow up the preliminary study of the pulp and paper industry, the secretariat, in collaboration with FAO, the United Nations Technical Assistance Administration, and the Government of Argentina, arranged a Latin American Meeting of Experts, held at Buenos Aires from October 19 to November 2, 1954. Major questions relating to the industry, including demand; traditional and potential resources; the efficacy of technical processes; equipment; production costs; financing and marketing; as well as economic, political and social aspects; were the subject of nine secretariat documents and 75 technical papers presented by outside experts. The meeting was attended by 186 experts from many parts of the world, and definite conclusions were reached regarding the expansion of the pulp and paper industry in Latin America.

(5) *Chemical Industries.* After a certain amount of preliminary work, including the collection of data on the relationship between income and the consumption of chemical products for industry, a study of the chemical industries in Latin America was begun in 1955.

ENERGY. A preliminary study of existing and potential energy resources, its production and consumption was begun early in 1954, and was presented to the Commission's sixth session. The energy situation in Latin America as a whole has been reviewed, and its comparison with that of the rest of the world showed that substantial investment was necessary for energy production to be increased to meet the needs of an expanding economy.

TRADE PROBLEMS. At ECLA's first session, requests were made for several secretariat studies on the terms of trade and on various aspects of commercial policy. One of these studies, *Prospects for Trade Expansion,* advocated special trade and payments agreements to secure a high level of trade with Europe, and the development of trade within the Latin American region. The reports were considered at the second session, in the course of which further studies on the expansion of foreign trade and its relation to economic development were requested.

A secretariat study, *Trade Trends and Policies of Latin American Countries,* was accordingly prepared for the third session. This dealt mainly with the failure of Latin America's trade with Europe to return to prewar levels. The Commission, considering that a coordinated investigation of the problem on broader lines was needed, instructed its Executive Secretary to undertake, in consultation with the Executive Secretary of the Economic Commission for Europe, a joint study on the possibilities of expanding trade between Latin America and Europe. ECLA's Executive Secretary was also asked to prepare studies on the expansion of trade within the Latin American region itself.

At its fourth session, the Commission considered the following studies: a joint ECLA/ECE/FAO report on *Trade between Europe and Latin America* (a revised version of which was published at the beginning of 1953); secretariat studies on the capacity of the United States to absorb Latin American products, and on the effects of the United States defence program on trade with Latin America; and a progress report on intra-regional trade.

The comprehensive study on *Trade between Europe and Latin America* marked an important step in the consideration of the subject. It contains a full analysis of Latin America's structure of payments and trade with Europe during the last fifty years.

The Commission, agreeing to widen the scope of the studies on inter-Latin-American trade then in progress, asked for an interim report on the possibilities of expanding trade within the region itself.

At the Commission's fifth session, the secretariat presented a study on trade between the countries of the southern zone of Latin America, which constitutes about 80 per cent of Latin America's total intra-regional trade.

A complementary study was presented at the sixth session. This analyzed the flow of trade between: (1) the countries of Greater Colombia (Colombia, Ecuador, Panama, and Venezuela), and between (2) Mexico, Central America and the West Indies. It also surveyed recent trends in reciprocal trade between the seven countries of the southern zone, in a revised and amplified version of the report submitted to the fifth ECLA session. It also dealt with problems relating to trade and payments policy, the characteristics and prospects of commodity trade among the Latin American countries, and maritime transport.

Towards the end of 1955, the ECLA secretariat was working on two other studies connected with world trade, one on the terms of trade and the role of international trade in economic development, and the other on the possibilities of expanding exports from the region.

At its sixth session, the Commission voiced its conviction that the time had come for the theoretical examination of the problems of inter-Latin American trade to give place to the search for practical solutions. It resolved that a Trade Committee composed of representatives of member countries should be set up within the Commission, to formulate specific procedures in harmony with the bilateral or multilateral commitments of the countries concerned, but in no way precluding the continued expansion of trade with other regions of the world.

BALANCE-OF-PAYMENTS PROBLEMS. Deeply concerned with postwar balance-of-payments and trade disequilibrium problems, the Commission at its first session, asked the International Monetary Fund for a report on the possibilities of establishing a system of multilateral compensation of international payments for Latin America.

After examining at its second session the Fund's report (*Multilateral Compensation of International Payments*) and various secretariat studies, the Commission came to the conclusion that conditions were not favorable to the establishment of a multilateral compensation arrangement for the region. It felt, however, that there were possibilities of partial multilateral compensation of payments among the countries of Latin America and the rest of the world, and requested the International Monetary Fund, with the secretariat's assistance, to make further studies along these lines.

The international payments problem was again discussed at the third session, in connection with payments agreements concluded between Western European countries.

In response to a request from ECLA's Committee of the Whole, a study on the possibilities of effecting multilateral compensation settlements between Latin American and European countries through the European Payments Union was prepared in 1952 for ECLA's fifth session. This question had been discussed at that session, using as a basis for discussion the preliminary report on *Implications of the European Payments Union,* which the ECLA secretariat had asked a consultant familiar with the operation of the European Payments Union to prepare. The Commission discussed the problem in detail, and resolved to recommend to interested governments that they provide the secretariat with the background information needed for the continuance of the studies on this subject.

PROPOSAL TO ESTABLISH AN ECONOMIC COMMISSION FOR THE MIDDLE EAST

Recognizing that cooperative measures among all Middle Eastern countries could be of practical assistance in raising the region's level of economic activity and standard of living, and in strengthening the economic relations of those countries among themselves and with other parts of the world, the General Assembly on October 31, 1947, invited the Economic and Social Council to study the question of establishing an Economic Commission for the Middle East.

In the summer of 1948, an *ad hoc* Committee set up by the Council to consider this matter, recommended that the structure of the proposed commission be similar to that of other regional economic commissions. It should consist of the following Member Sates: Afghanistan, Egypt, Ethiopia, Greece, Iran, Iraq, Lebanon, Saudi Arabia, Syria, Turkey and Yemen. Other countries should be admitted to membership by the Council after consultation with the Commission.

In July-August 1948, the Council decided to defer consideration of the question. But the General Assembly on December 4, 1948, recommended expeditious consideration.

In view of the unsettled situation in the Middle East, the Council, however, postponed further action at its eighth, ninth and tenth sessions, and again at its thirteenth session in August-September 1951.

SOCIAL, HUMANITARIAN AND CULTURAL QUESTIONS

Human Rights

UNIVERSAL DECLARATION OF HUMAN RIGHTS

The achievement of international cooperation in promoting and encouraging respect for human rights and fundamental freedoms is one of the purposes of the United Nations defined in the Charter.

In fulfilment of this objective, the General Assembly on December 10, 1948, adopted, without a dissenting vote, the Universal Declaration of Human Rights. Its 30 articles set forth man's inalienable personal, civil, political, economic, social and cultural rights, and provide for their enjoyment without discrimination and subject only to such limitations as are determined by law solely for the purpose of securing due recognition and respect for the rights and freedoms of others and of meeting the just requirements of morality, public order and the general welfare in a democratic society. The Declaration includes the right to life, liberty, and security of person; to freedom from arbitrary arrest; to a fair trial by an independent and impartial tribunal; to be presumed innocent until proved guilty according to the law and with non-retroactivity of the law; to freedom from interference with privacy, home or correspondence; to freedom of movement and residence; to asylum; to a nationality; to own property; to freedom of thought, conscience and religion; to freedom of opinion and expression; to association and peaceful assembly; to elections and participation in government; to social security; to work; to rest and leisure; to a standard of living adequate for health and well being; to education; and to participate in the social life of the community.

The Assembly proclaimed these rights and freedoms as "a common standard of achievements for all peoples and all nations," and called upon all Member States, the Secretary-General, and the specialized agencies to help spread awareness of them throughout the world.

The Declaration is becoming widely known. Through the efforts of the United Nations, Member and non-member governments, the specialized agencies and interested non-governmental organizations, the Declaration has been translated into some 50 languages and disseminated among large sections of the world's population.

Since its proclamation, the influence of the Declaration has been reflected in the work of the United Nations and the specialized agencies; in inter-governmental organizations such as the Organization of American States and the Council of

Europe; in treaties and agreements such as the peace treaty with Japan of September 8, 1951; and in national constitutions, legislations and court decisions. Italy and Yugoslavia, for example, under the "Special Statute" annexed to the "Memorandum of understanding between the Governments of Italy, the United Kingdom, the United States and Yugoslavia regarding the Free Territory of Trieste, London, October 5, 1954," are called upon to insure that in their respective areas all inhabitants, without discrimination, shall fully enjoy the fundamental rights and freedoms laid down in the Declaration; all the rights set forth in the Declaration are guaranteed and detailed provisions relating to their application are laid down.

HUMAN RIGHTS DAY

December 10, the date on which the General Assembly adopted the Universal Declaration of Human Rights, was proclaimed as Human Rights Day by the Assembly in 1950. The Assembly invited all states and interested organizations to observe this day each year to celebrate the proclamation of the Declaration. Every year an increasing number of programs, utilizing all media of information and sponsored by both governments and private organizations, have been organized in both Member and non-member states in observance of Human Rights Day.

DRAFT COVENANTS ON HUMAN RIGHTS

The Commission on Human Rights has been engaged ever since its establishment in 1947 in preparing an international bill of rights. The international bill was initially conceived in three parts: a declaration, a covenant, and measures of implementation. The Declaration was proclaimed by the General Assembly on December 10, 1948. The General Assembly in 1955 was considering two draft covenants with measures of implementation, which were completed at the tenth session of the Commission in 1954, relating, respectively, to civil and political rights and economic, social and cultural rights.

In formulating its drafts, the Commission has been guided by observations of governments, instructions of the General Assembly and the Economic and Social Council, the cooperation and suggestions of the specialized agencies, and comments of non-governmental organizations.

The principal questions which have arisen in the course of the preparation of the drafts were the following: whether there should be one or two covenants dealing with civil and political and economic, social and cultural rights; whether the limitations to the rights should be set forth in general terms in an article or specified in detail under each of the rights concerned; whether there should be an article on the right of self-determination; whether there should be an explicit recognition of the equal rights of men and women; whether the covenants should include international measures of implementation; whether the covenants should apply to all territories of a federation and metropolitan and other territories of a state; and whether reservations should be permitted or not.

As early as 1950, the Commission submitted a draft covenant to the Council which was called the first draft international covenant and related to civil and political rights. At that time, the Commission suggested and the Council approved the preparation of further covenants dealing with other categories of rights. The General Assembly in 1950, however, requested the drafting of a single covenant to include both civil and political rights, and economic, social and cultural rights. Subsequently, the General Assembly revised its opinion and requested the preparation of two draft covenants on the different categories of rights, both to be submitted simultaneously and to contain as many similar provisions as possible.

The economic, social and cultural rights are set forth in general terms subject to an over-all limitations clause. Articles relating to civil and political rights are drafted more elaborately and include limitations within themselves, either in some detail or in general terms; there is also an article permitting derogations from some of these rights in times of emergency.

Both covenants include an article on the right of self-determination. They also include an article on equal rights of men and women as well as an article on non-discrimination in the enjoyment of the rights.

Both covenants contain articles stating that their provisions extend and are equally applicable to a metropolitan state and to all its territories, whether they are non-self-governing, trust or colonial territories. Although the General Assembly had asked the Commission to study a federal state article aimed at securing the maximum extension of the covenant to the constituent units of federal states and at meeting the constitutional problems of such states, the covenants contain articles which automatically extend their provisions to all parts of federal states without any limitations or exceptions.

Both covenants contain international measures of implementation. Objection against such provisions, particularly on the grounds that they would infringe on the sovereignty of states, were rejected. While the Commission considered provisions relating to the receipt and the examination of petitions from individuals and organizations with respect to alleged violations of the covenants, it decided not to include them.

No decision was reached on the admissibility or non-admissibility of reservations, particularly as regards the covenant on civil and political rights, but proposals concerning reservations were forwarded to the General Assembly.

The draft covenant on economic, social and cultural rights contains articles on: the right to work; just and favorable conditions of work; trade union rights; social security; rights relating to motherhood and childhood and to marriage and the family; right to adequate food, clothing and housing; right to an adequate standard of living; right to health; right to education; a plan for implementing compulsory primary education; rights relating to culture and science; and right to property. The states parties are to undertake to achieve progressively the full realization of these rights. The implementation of these rights is based on a system of periodic reports to be determined by the Economic and Social Council after consultation with states parties and the specialized agencies concerned. The reports will deal with the progress made in achieving the rights, and may indicate factors and difficulties affecting the degree of fulfilment of the obligations undertaken. The Council may submit reports to the General Assembly and bring to the attention of international organs matters arising out of reports which may assist such organs in deciding on the advisability of international measures likely to contribute to the progressive implementation of the rights. International action includes such methods as conventions, recommendations, technical assistance and studies with governments.

The draft covenant on civil and political rights contains articles on: the right to life; inhuman or degrading treatment; prohibition of slavery; servitude and forced labor; liberty and security of person; treatment of persons deprived of their liberty; contractual obligations; freedom of movement; expulsion of aliens; fair trial; prohibition of retroactive application of criminal law; recognition as a person before the law; privacy; home; correspondence; honor and reputation; freedom of thought, conscience and religion; freedom of opinion and information; right of peaceful assembly; right of association; rights relating to marriage; political rights; equality before the law; rights of minorities; prohibition of advocacy of nations; racial or religious hostility; and right of property. Each state party is to undertake to respect and to insure to all individuals within its territory and subject to its jurisdiction, the rights in the covenant without distinction of any kind such as race, color, sex, language, religion, political or other opinions, national or social origin, property, birth or other status. Each state further undertakes to take the necessary steps to adopt such legislative measures which are required to give effect to the rights in the covenants. The states parties are also to undertake to insure that any person whose rights are violated shall have an effective remedy and to insure that such a remedy shall be enforced when granted. A Human Rights Committee, elected by the International Court of Justice, is to be established to consider any alleged violation of the covenant submitted to it by a state party after failure of direct negotiations between the states concerned. The Committee's functions are to be those of fact finding and conciliation. It may request advisory opinions from the International Court of Justice through the Economic and Social Council. It shall not deal with a case which is before the International Court of Justice. After the Committee has submitted its report on a matter, any state concerned may have recourse to the International Court of Justice. There is a special provision on implementation of the article on self-determination. The Committee is to submit an annual report on its work to the General Assembly. The states parties are also to report periodically on the measures which they have taken to put the provisions of the covenant into effect.

Both covenants include provisions concerning relations between the United Nations and the specialized agencies, and an article relating to the destruction or limitations of the rights and freedoms recognized in the covenants and the safeguarding of rights recognized independently of the covenants.

The draft covenants have been under consideration by the Third Committee of the General Assembly since 1954. The Committee has so far approved the texts for both covenants of a preamble and an article on the right of self-determination, and deferred further consideration of Article 2 of the draft covenant on economic, social and cultural rights relating to general obligations of states, until it has considered the provisions setting forth those rights.

SELF-DETERMINATION

In response to requests of the General Assembly, the Commission on Human Rights at its eighth session adopted, and forwarded through the Economic and Social Council, two recommendations on the right of self-determination, which were approved with some revision by the Assembly in 1952. The first resolution recommends that Member States uphold the principle of self-determination of all peoples and nations, facilitate the right of self-determination in territories under their administration—through plebiscites or other recognized democratic means—preferably under the auspices of the United Nations—and insure direct participation of the indigenous populations in the legislative and executive organs of the territories. The second recommends that states administering non-self-governing territories voluntarily include in the information transmitted by them under Article 73e of the Charter details regarding the extent to which the right of peoples and nations to self-determination is exercised by the people of those territories, and "in particular regarding their political progress and the measures taken to develop their capacity for self-determination, to satisfy their political aspirations and to promote the progressive development of their free political institutions." This resolution was also placed on the 1953 agenda of the Committee on Information from Non-Self-Governing Territories.

In a third resolution, the Assembly asked the Commission to continue preparing recommendations concerning international respect for the right of peoples to self-determination, particularly as regards the possible steps which might be taken by various organs of the United Nations and specialized agencies to develop international respect for the right. Subsequently, the Assembly, considering that the Commission at its ninth session had been unable, due to lack of time, to prepare such recommendations, requested the Commission to give due priority at its tenth session to the formulation of recommendations. The Commission adopted two draft resolutions at its tenth session, and asked the Economic and Social Council to transmit them to the General Assembly. The Council felt it more desirable to return the recommendations to the Commission for further consideration. The General Assembly in 1953 again requested the Commission to complete its recommendations. Upon the recommendation of the Commission, the Council decided to transmit to the General Assembly for its consideration two draft resolutions proposed by the Commission at its eleventh session. These drafts were similar to those formulated by the Commission at its tenth session. The Council also decided, on its own initiative, to transmit a third draft resolution.

The first draft resolution proposes that the General Assembly establish a commission to conduct a full survey of the status of the right of peoples and nations to permanent sovereignty over their natural wealth and resources—having due regard to the rights and duties of states under international law and to the importance of encouraging international cooperation in the economic development of under-developed countries—and to make recommendations where necessary for strengthening that right. The second draft resolution contemplates the establishment by the General Assembly of a commission which would examine any situation resulting from alleged denial or inadequate realization of the right to self-determination; provide its good offices for the peaceful rectification of any such situation; and, if within six months no adjustment of the situation could be effected, report the facts with appropriate recommendations to the General Assembly. The third draft proposes that the Assembly establish an *ad hoc* commission on self-determination, consisting of five persons to be appointed by the Secretary-General, to conduct a thorough study of the concept of self-determination. The terms of reference of the Commission would include examination of: (a) the concept of peoples and nations; (b) the essential attributes and the applicability of the principle of equal rights and of self-determination, including the rights and duties of States under international law; (c) the relationship between the principle of self-determination and other Charter principles; and (d) the economic, social and cultural conditions under which the application of the principles is facilitated.

The General Assembly postponed consideration of these drafts to 1956.

HUMAN RIGHTS YEARBOOK

The United Nations *Yearbook on Human Rights* for 1952, the seventh volume to appear, contains human rights provisions of constitutions newly adopted or amended during the year 1952, texts or summaries of laws relating to human rights and summaries of important judicial decisions, in more than seventy states. The volume also includes texts applicable to trust and non-self-governing territories, and reproduces human rights provisions in international treaties and agreements. A survey of the activities of the United Nations during the year in the field of human rights, with the indication of all sources, is also provided. The *Yearbook* for 1953 was to include material of the same kind as that for 1952 and would appear in 1956.

COMMUNICATIONS CONCERNING HUMAN RIGHTS

At its fifth session in 1947, the Economic and Social Council approved a statement made by the Commission on Human Rights that "it has no power to take any action in regard to any complaints concerning human rights". A resolution adopted by the Council at this session, and subsequently amended, lays down a procedure whereby communications concerning human rights are brought to the attention of the Commission on Human Rights. The Secretary-General compiles two lists of communications: (1) a non-confidential list with a brief indication of the substance of each communication dealing with the principles involved in the promotion of universal respect for and observance of human rights; and (2) a confidential list containing a brief indication of the substance of other communications concerning human rights. In the non-confidential list, the identity of the authors of communications is revealed, unless they express a wish to the contrary. In the confidential list, their identity is not divulged, except in cases where they state that they have already divulged their names or have no objection to this being done.

The Secretary-General acknowledges receipt of the communications and furnishes each State Member with copies of the communications which refer to that State or to territories under its jurisdiction.

The confidential list, together with replies by governments, is presented to the members of the Commission on Human Rights in private meetings. Between December 31, 1953, and January 15, 1955, for example, 5,982 communications have been received and included in the confidential list by the Secretary-General.

At each session, the Commission on Human Rights takes note of the distribution of the lists of communications. At its last four sessions, the Commission decided to make public the summary record of its private meeting.

The same procedure is applied in the Commission on the Status of Women and in the Sub-Commission on Prevention of Discrimination and Protection of Minorities with regard to communications concerning these matters.

HUMAN RIGHTS AND PEACE TREATIES

On June 21, 1946, the Economic and Social Council recommended that "pending the adoption of an International Bill of Rights the general principle shall be accepted that international treaties involving basic human rights, including to the fullest extent practicable treaties of peace, shall conform to the fundamental standards relative to such rights set forth in the Charter." Obligations to guarantee the enjoyment of human rights and fundamental freedoms were undertaken in the 1947 Peace Treaties by Italy (Article 15 of the Peace Treaty), Romania (Article 3), Bulgaria (Article 2), Hungary (Article 2) and Finland (Article 6). The State Treaty with Austria of May 15, 1955, contains human rights provisions based on the 1947 precedents and also provisions concerning the protection of certain ethnical minorities. The Peace Treaty with Japan, San Francisco, September 8, 1951, refers in the preamble to the Universal Declaration of Human Rights and the intention of Japan to strive to realize the objective of the Declaration. The agreements relating to the Free Territory of Trieste of 1954, provide for the guarantee of the rights and freedoms set forth in the Universal Declaration and the application thereof.

FREEDOM OF INFORMATION

"Freedom of information", the General Assembly resolved on December 14, 1946, "is a fundamental human right, and the touchstone of all the freedoms to which the United Nations is consecrated".

This has since been the keynote of a wide-ranging investigation into various aspects of freedom of information, including study both of the rights, obligations and practices which should be included in the concept of this freedom, and of professional and technical problems involved in the flow of international news.

The United Nations Conference on Freedom of Information, held at Geneva in 1948, adopted and referred to the Economic and Social Council three draft conventions and 43 resolutions concerning such matters as war-mongering and false and distorted reports, the shortage of newsprint, the economic security of journalists, drafting of an international code of ethics for journalists, establishment of an International Court of Honor, elimination of discriminatory taxes affecting the work of foreign information agencies and news personnel, and the free reception and exhibition of news-reels.

The draft convention on the gathering and international transmission of news sought an undertaking by contracting states that they would give correspondents of other countries access to sources of news on an equal basis with their own nationals; would facilitate the entry, travel and residence of foreign correspondents; and would censor outgoing dispatches in peacetime only on exceptional grounds, and then in accordance with previously established regulations. The articles of this convention have been approved by the General Assembly, but not opened for signature.

The draft convention concerning the institution of an international right of correction, also proposed by the Conference, aims at giving states which are directly affected by what they consider to be a false news dispatch disseminated abroad by overseas information media the possibility of securing commensurate publicity for a correction. After examining and redrafting some parts of the Conference draft, the General Assembly on December 16, 1952, approved and opened for signature a Convention on the International Right of Correction. As of the end of 1955, the Convention had been signed by seven countries and ratified or acceded to by two. Six ratifications or accessions are required to bring it into force.

The draft convention on freedom of information which the Conference proposed, spelled out certain guarantees of freedom of information which signatory states would give to their own nationals and to nationals of other signatories lawfully within their territories. These guarantees would be subject to permissible, clearly-defined restrictions. After experiencing considerable difficulty in reaching agreement on the draft convention, particularly as regards the article which enumerates permissible restrictions, the General Assembly, in 1950, set up a special fifteen-country committee to reexamine the draft. The committee produced a new draft, but differences of opinion later became evident, in the Economic and Social Council and the General Assembly, on how to proceed further. In 1954, the Assembly decided to consider the draft convention again not later than at its eleventh session (1956).

From 1947 to 1952, work in freedom of information was also carried on by the Sub-Commission on Freedom of Information, a subsidiary body of the Commission on Human Rights, consisting of twelve experts serving in their personal capacity with the consent of their governments. The Sub-Commission spent its first session (1947) planning the Geneva Conference on Freedom of Information; its second session (1948) mainly in formulating a statement of the rights, obligations and practices which should be included in the concept of freedom of information; its third session (1949) mainly in drawing up a program of work for future sessions; and its fourth (1950) and fifth (1952) sessions in drafting and redrafting an international code of ethics for information personnel. In addition, the Sub-Commission passed on to its superior bodies in the United Nations a number of recommendations on such matters as the newsprint shortage, the jamming of radio broadcasts, the closing down of the Argentine newspaper *La Prensa*, and the encouragement and development of independent domestic information enterprises.

The Economic and Social Council in 1952 decided not to continue the Sub-Commission, appointing instead, a Special Rapporteur for an experimental period of one year. The Council selected Salvador P. López, of the Philippines, a former newspaper editor and also a former Chairman of the Sub-Commission, and requested him, in his personal capacity, to prepare "a substantive report concerning major contemporary problems and developments," together with recommendations for practical action.

Mr. López's report, which was eventually considered by the Council in 1954, evaluated the work of the United Nations and specialized agencies in freedom of information, examined in detail the "present situation and practical problems," and made a series of recommendations to the Council concerning the direction future work should take.

After considering the report, the Council decided to request the Secretary-General, in conjunction with the specialized agencies concerned, to study a number of separate aspects of freedom of information, with the result that in 1955 the Secretary-General submitted to the Council the following reports and studies:

Program to promote among news personnel a wider knowledge of the United Nations, of foreign countries and of international affairs;

Current principles and practices involved in the censorship of outgoing news dispatches;

Legal aspects of the rights and responsibilities of media of information;

The problem of protecting sources of information of news personnel; and

Public and private monopolies and their effects on freedom of information.

In addition, UNESCO and the International Telecommunication Union submitted a joint study of the problem of transmitting press messages, and the ITU reported on the response of governments to a recommendation adopted at its Buenos Aires Plenipotentiary Conference (1952) concerning the unrestricted transmission of news by telecommunication services.

After examination of these reports and studies, the Council in May 1955 urged all states to cease peace-time censorship of outgoing news dispatches, and to facilitate the unrestricted transmission of news by telecommunication services. The Secretary-General was asked to forward certain recommendations made by UNESCO concerning the transmission of press messages to the ITU for study, and to transmit the survey of legal aspects of the rights and obligations of information media to information enterprises and professional associations. In addition, the Council requested the Secretary-General, in consultation with UNESCO, to make a further study of information media in under-developed countries; and also requested him to take steps, again in collaboration with UNESCO, to put into operation a program to promote freedom of information by providing such services as experts, fellowships and seminars, taking account, in the latter instance, of suggestions which the Secretary-General himself had made in his "Program to promote among news personnel a wider knowledge of the United Nations."

Assistance which might be given on the international level to under-developed countries in building up, by various methods, their information media, has been the subject of decisions and recommendations by the Sub-Commission on Freedom of Information, the Economic and Social Council, and the General Assembly. In 1954, at its ninth session, the Assembly authorized the Secretary-General to render, at the request of Member States, services which do not fall within existing technical assistance programs, in order to assist such states in promoting freedom of information. The next year, following recommendations by the Commission on Human Rights and the Economic and Social Council, the Assembly's decision was included in a consolidated authorization to the Secretary-General to proceed with a broad program of advisory services in the field of human rights.

TRADE-UNION RIGHTS

ESTABLISHMENT OF AN INTERNATIONAL PROCEDURE FOR SAFEGUARDING TRADE-UNION RIGHTS. Progress in the promotion of trade-union rights has been based largely on close collaboration between the United Nations and the International Labor Organization. ILO in 1948 adopted the Convention on Freedom of Association and Protection of the Right to Organize, and early in 1949, the Economic and Social Council considered the question of enforcing trade-union rights (freedom of association).

The Governing Body of ILO established a Fact-Finding and Conciliation Commission in January 1950, and the Council, in its resolution 277(X) of February 17, 1950, accepted its services on behalf of the United Nations.

In accordance with this resolution, communications from governments, trade unions, or employers' associations which allege infringements of trade-union rights are brought to the attention of the Economic and Social Council.

Allegations against member states of ILO are forwarded to the Governing Body of ILO "for consideration as to referral to the Commission." Allegations against Members of the United Nations not members of ILO are forwarded to the Fact-Finding and Conciliation Commission only with the consent of the government concerned. If such consent is not forthcoming, the Council considers such refusal with a view to taking any appropriate alternative action designed to safeguard the freedom of association rights involved in the case.

The Council's resolution asked ILO to arrange that the Fact-Finding and Conciliation Commission would transmit to the Council any reports on cases regarding non-members of ILO. ILO was also asked to include in its annual reports to the Council an account of the Commission's work.

ACTION TAKEN BY THE ECONOMIC AND SOCIAL COUNCIL. Up to its fifteenth session, the Council decided, at each session, to transmit to the Governing Body of the ILO allegations relating to states members of this Organization, which had been brought to its attention by the Secretary-General. Since one allegation charging violations of trade-union rights in the Cameroons under French Administration was already before the Trusteeship Council, the Economic and Social Council at its twelfth session asked the Secretary-General to report to it the action taken by the Trusteeship Council. At the thirteenth session of the Economic and Social Council, the Secretary-General reported that the Trusteeship Council had considered that "none of the cases cited could be regarded as obstructing trade-union rights". At the Council's fifteenth session, the Secretary-General was requested to transmit directly to the Governing Body of the ILO, without any prior examination by the Council, all allegations against states members of this Organization which would be received in the future. This decision does not concern allegations against states non-members of the ILO which are still submitted to the Economic and Social Council.

Since the U.S.S.R., a Member of the United Nations, was not, up to April 1954, a member of the ILO, the Secretary-General asked this Government whether it consented to have various allegations relating to it forwarded to the Governing Body of the ILO. No reply was ever received. When the U.S.S.R. became a member of the ILO, the Council at its eighteenth session, decided to forward all allegations relating to this country, and all the documents relating thereto, to the Governing

Body of the ILO. Another allegation relating to a State Member of the United Nations but not a member of the ILO, namely Saudi Arabia, had been submitted to the seventeenth session of the Council. The Government of that country had not replied to the Secretary-General's request that it consent to the forwarding of this allegation to the ILO. At its resumed nineteenth session, the Council asked the Secretary-General again to make such a request to the Government of Saudi Arabia.

Several complaints relating to states or territories which, at one time or another, were not members either of the United Nations or of the ILO, have been brought to the attention of the Economic and Social Council. They concerned Japan, Romania, the Saar, Spain and the Free Territory of Trieste. At various sessions, the Council requested the Secretary-General to forward the complaints to the governments or authorities concerned, and to invite them to present their observations on these complaints, bringing to their attention the provisions of Council resolution 277 (X).

At the Council's thirteenth session, the allegation relating to Japan, together with a reply from the competent authorities concerned, were forwarded to the Governing Body of the ILO after Japan had become a member of this Organization.

The competent authorities of the Free Territory of Trieste have sent their observations on the complaint relating to this Territory. The Council at its fifteenth session considered that no question of trade-union rights was involved, and dismissed the allegation as not meriting further consideration.

No further action was taken by the Council on the complaint relating to the Saar, with regard to which the Government concerned had sent its observations.

The Governments of Romania and Spain have not sent any observations on the substance of the allegations relating to them. The Council at its seventeenth session invited these Governments to reconsider their attitude, and indicate their willingness to cooperate with the United Nations in its efforts to safeguard trade-union rights. At its resumed nineteenth session, the Council took note with regret of the fact that neither Government had responded to these invitations.

Allegations relating to the Democratic People's Republic of Germany were brought to the attention of the Council at its resumed nineteenth session. The Council decided to refer these allegations to the ILO "for its consideration".

FORCED LABOR

The United Nations in cooperation with the International Labor Organization, for some years, has been engaged in a survey of the problem of forced labor and measures for its abolition.

At its Santiago, Chile, session early in 1951, the Economic and Social Council decided to establish an *ad hoc* committee on forced labor composed of not more than five independent members, to be appointed jointly by the Secretary-General and the Director-General of the International Labor Office. The International Labor Organization had previously expressed its willingness to cooperate with the Council in the establishment of such a committee.

The *ad hoc* Committee's terms of reference were to study the nature and extent of the problem raised by the existence in any part of the world of "systems of forced or 'corrective' labor which are employed as a means of political coercion or punishment for holding or expressing political views." This it was to do by examining the texts of laws and regulations, and their application in the light of the principles of the Charter, and those of the Universal Declaration of Human Rights. The Committee was to report on the progress and results of its studies both to the Council and to ILO.

On June 27, 1951, the Secretary-General and the Director-General of ILO announced establishment of the *ad hoc* Committee, consisting of Sir Ramaswami Mudaliar, former President of the Economic and Social Council, and head of the Indian Delegation at the San Francisco Conference of 1945; Paal Berg, former Chief Justice of the Norwegian Supreme Court; and Felix Fulgencio Palavicini, of Mexico, former Ambassador to Great Britain, France and Italy. Mr. Palavicini, who died in February 1952, was replaced by Enrique García Sayán, a statesman and jurist of Peru, former Minister of Foreign Affairs and Professor of the Faculty of Law, University of San Marcos, Lima.

The Committee held four sessions, three of them in Geneva and one in New York. At its first session, it defined its terms of reference and decided "to discharge its task, within the limits of its terms of reference, without prejudice of any kind and with complete impartiality and objectivity, on a universal basis, with the sole aim of safeguarding human rights and improving the situation of workers." It also addressed a questionnaire to governments and invited non-governmental organizations to submit information and documentation on the problem of forced labor.

The second and third sessions of the Committee were devoted mainly to a study of the relevant information and documentation, and to the hearing of a number of non-governmental organizations and private individuals. It prepared summaries of the allegations and documentary material relating to different countries and territories, and sent these to the governments concerned for comment.

At its fourth and last session in April-May 1953, the *ad hoc* Committee completed its study of the allegations and documentary material, including comments of several governments, and drew up its findings and conclusions concerning the existence of forced labor. In its final report, the Committee set forth these findings and conclusions relating to specific countries and territories, and also its general observations on the problem. It stated, in general, that its inquiry had revealed the existence in the world of two principal systems of forced labor, the first being employed as a means of political coercion or punishment for holding or expressing political views, and the second being employed for important economic purposes. It considered such systems as a violation of the fundamental rights of the human person as guaranteed by the Charter of the United Nations and proclaimed in the Universal Declaration of Human Rights, and urged that such systems of forced labor should be abolished.

The report of the *ad hoc* Committee was considered by the General Assembly at its eighth and ninth sessions, and by the Economic and Social Council at its seventeenth session. Both the General Assembly and the Council condemned the existence of systems of forced labor and appealed to all governments to reexamine their laws and administrative practices in the light of present conditions and the increasing desire of the peoples of the world to reaffirm faith in fundamental human rights and in the dignity and worth of the human person. This appeal was supported by ILO. In addition, the Assembly requested the Council and ILO to continue their efforts towards the abolition of systems of forced labor.

Following the completion of this work, the Council asked the Secretary-General in cooperation with the Director-General of ILO to prepare a further report which would contain any new information on systems of forced labor submitted by Member Governments, specialized agencies, and non-governmental organizations, together with the comments of governments concerned. A report containing such information and comments was submitted to the Council, which was to consider it at its twenty-first session to be held early in 1956.

Genocide

Genocide — the killing of a group of human beings — the General Assembly unanimously affirmed on December 11, 1946, is a crime under international law which the civilized world condemns.

On December 9, 1948, the General Assembly unanimously adopted the Convention on Genocide. The Convention declares genocide a crime under international law whether committed in time of peace or of war. Five kinds of acts, aimed at destroying "a national, ethnical, racial, or religious group as such," are punishable as genocide: killing members of a group, causing them serious bodily or mental harm, deliberately inflicting conditions on the group to bring about its physical destruction, imposing measures to prevent births within the group, and forcibly transferring children from it to another group. Not only genocide itself but also conspiracy or incitement to commit it, as well as attempts to commit genocide and complicity in the crime, are punishable under the Convention.

Whether they are constitutionally responsible rulers, public officials, or private individuals, those guilty of genocide shall be punished, according to the Convention.

States adhering to the Convention are required to pass the necessary laws to give effect to it, and to grant extradition in cases of genocide. Those guilty of genocide are to be tried in the country where the crime was committed, or by such international tribunals as may have jurisdiction.

Subsequently, the General Assembly asked the Secretary-General to invite non-member states of the United Nations which were, or which later became, active members of a specialized agency or parties to the Statute of the International Court of Justice to become parties to the Convention on Genocide.

The Convention came into force on January 12, 1951. It will remain effective for ten years, and thereafter for five-year periods in countries which continue to adhere to it. Should the number of adhering countries be less than sixteen, it will cease to be in force.

Through December 31, 1955, instruments of ratification or accession to the Convention have been deposited by the following 50 states: Albania (with reservations regarding Articles IX and XII), Australia, Belgium, Brazil, Bulgaria (with reservations regarding Articles IX and XII), the Byelorussian S.S.R. (with reservations regarding Articles IX and XII), Cambodia, Canada, Ceylon, Chile, China, Costa Rica, Cuba, Czechoslovakia (with reservations regarding Articles IX and XII), Denmark, Ecuador, Egypt, El Salvador, Ethiopia, France, the German Federal Republic, Greece, Guatemala, Haiti, Honduras, Hungary (with reservations regarding Articles IX and XII), Iceland, Israel, Italy, Jordan, the Republic of Korea, Laos, Lebanon, Liberia, Mexico, Monaco, Nicaragua, Norway, Panama, the Philippines (with reservations regarding Articles IV, VI, VII and IX), Poland (with reservations regarding Articles IX and XII), Romania (with reservations regarding Articles IX and XII), Saudi Arabia, Sweden, Syria, Turkey, the Ukrainian S.S.R. (with reservations regarding Articles IX and XII), the U.S.S.R. (with reservations regarding Articles IX and XII), Vietnam and Yugoslavia.

(*For reservations to the Convention made by some adhering states, and the advisory opinion of the International Court, see the chapter on* LEGAL QUESTIONS.)

Status of Women

The United Nations organ primarily concerned with the promotion of women's rights is the Commission on the Status of Women, established in 1946 to prepare studies and recommendations in economic, social, political, and educational fields.

For the most part, recommendations are made in the form of draft resolutions for adoption by the Economic and Social Council. Studies requested by the Commission are made by the Secretary-General, and the International Labor Office and UNESCO collaborate on reports within their respective competence. Non-governmental organizations are frequently requested to supply information on their activities and methods.

The Commission has dealt with a variety of questions relating to women's rights; among those occupying its continued attention are political rights, economic rights and opportunities, access to education, property rights, and legal status under family law and under nationality law. The Commission has also regularly considered the United Nations technical assistance programs and advisory services in relation to the status of women, and has also reviewed the status of women in trust and non-self-governing territories.

POLITICAL RIGHTS

At its first session in 1946, the General Assembly recommended that all Member States grant women political rights equal to those of men. Existing discrimination against women in public services and functions has been studied by the Commission.

The Convention on the Political Rights of Women was adopted on December 20, 1952, at the seventh session of the General Assembly. Parties to the Convention agree to accord to women the right to vote, to be elected to public bodies, and to hold public office and perform public functions on equal terms with men. As of December 31, 1955, 40 states have signed the Convention and 22 have become parties. States Members of the United Nations or of the specialized agencies or parties to the Statute of the International Court of Justice have been invited to sign and ratify or accede to the Convention.

Each year the General Assembly and the Commission on the Status of Women consider the progress of women's political rights under national laws as reported annually by the Secretary-General.

Political and civic education of women has occupied the attention of the Commission, and in this field the role of the non-governmental organizations has been stressed particularly. The Secretary-General submits reports to the Commission on information concerning the methods used by these organizations and their activities in the educational sphere. Emphasis is placed on civic and political education in countries where women either do not yet have political rights or have only recently acquired them.

Pamphlets on political education and on the Convention on the Political Rights of Women have been published by the United Nations.

ECONOMIC RIGHTS

The Economic and Social Council in a resolution adopted at its twentieth session, in 1955, explicitly recognized the importance of granting women equal rights with men in all branches of economic life. It recommended that governments adopt legislation and other measures, and encourage action to remove economic discrimination against women and to provide them with equal rights to employment, pay, rest and material security in case of old age, illness, or loss of capacity to work.

The question of equal pay for equal work has figured importantly in the work of the Commission on the Status of Women. Collaboration between the International Labor Organization and the United Nations resulted in the ILO Convention (No. 100) and Recommendation (No. 90) on Equal Remuneration for

Work of Equal Value for Men and Women Workers which were adopted in 1951. The Commission and the Economic and Social Council have repeatedly urged the acceptance by governments of the principle of equal pay, and encouraged non-governmental organizations to inform public opinion on the subject and to report on their activities and techniques for the benefit of other non-governmental organizations and of the Commission itself. The International Labor Office has reported annually to the Commission on action taken by governments in various countries to achieve equal pay for equal work, and the Secretary-General has prepared reports based on information from non-governmental organizations on their activities directed to having the principle of equal pay accepted by public opinion and actually applied.

The Council has also concerned itself with vocational and technical training opportunities, vocational guidance, and employment services for women, and has urged governments to avail themselves of services provided in technical assistance programs in order to improve the opportunities for women in these fields. A joint report on vocational and technical training for women has been prepared by the ILO and UNESCO for the tenth session of the Commission on the Status of Women to be held in 1956.

Employment opportunities for women, including part-time work and work for older women, have been considered by the Commission on the basis of reports by the Secretary-General and by the ILO. In this connection, the development of cottage industries and handicrafts has been discussed. The Council, at its 20th session, took note of a report by the ILO on development of opportunities for women in such industries and recommended its use by governments. The ILO is continuing its studies on the subject and informs the Commission on the Status of Women of progress achieved.

EDUCATIONAL OPPORTUNITIES

The provision of equal educational opportunities for men and women at all levels has been urged by the Economic and Social Council. The Council has recommended that no distinction be made on the basis of sex with respect to access to education, the basic curriculum and elective subjects; on the distribution of scholarships for education in all fields; and in preparation for all careers. The introduction of free and compulsory education has been recognized by the Council as particularly important to increased school attendance by girls in areas where comparatively few girls attend primary schools. UNESCO has presented to the Commission on the Status of Women reports on educational opportunities for women, including studies on access to primary and secondary education.

PRIVATE LAW

The status of women under laws on the family and on women's property rights has been extensively studied by the Commission on the Status of Women. Much of the information on the subject was received from governments in reply to questionnaires prepared by the Secretary-General. After considering various reports by the Secretary-General, the Commission recommended that governments insure the equality of rights and duties of spouses in conformity with the principle enunciated in the Universal Declaration of Human Rights. This recommendation has been adopted by the Council, as were also specific recommendations made by the Commission for equality of parental rights and duties; for the right of a married woman to have a legal domicile independently of that of her husband; for the right of a married woman to engage in work without her husband's authorization; and for statutory matrimonial property regimes affording women equal rights with respect to separate or family property during marriage, and equitable sharing of property at dissolution. The Commission receives annual reports from the Secretary-General which bring up-to-date information on the legal status of women in private law.

Certain ancient laws and customs relating to marriage and the family have been viewed by the Commission as basic impediments to the attainment of women's basic rights as contemplated in the United Nations Charter and in the Universal Declaration of Human Rights. The Economic and Social Council at its eighteenth session in 1954, acted favorably on a recommendation by the Commission requesting action by the General Assembly along the lines suggested by the Commission. The General Assembly at its ninth session in the same year complied with the request of the Council and urged all states, including those administering trust and non-self-governing territories, to take measures to abolish the practices of bride price and child marriage, to guarantee widows custody of their children, to insure the right freely to choose a spouse, and to establish civil registers for marriages and divorces.

NATIONALITY OF MARRIED WOMEN

The Commission on the Status of Women has taken a position against laws providing for automatic loss or acquisition of nationality by a woman because of marriage to a man of a different nationality. Pursuant to the request of the Commission, the Economic and Social Council has recommended that governments accord to women the same right as men to retain their nationality on marriage. An international convention on nationality rights of married women has also been proposed by the Commission. Such a convention was drafted by the Commission and transmitted by the Council to the General Assembly. Under this draft convention, each contracting state would agree that neither the celebration nor dissolution of a marriage between one of its nationals and an alien should have any automatic effect on the wife's nationality; provision is also made for facilitating the voluntary acquisition by an alien woman of her husband's nationality. The General Assembly at its tenth session in 1955 considered and approved the substantive articles of the convention, but postponed consideration of the final clauses until its eleventh session.

A publication on nationality of married women containing legal provisions in force in 79 states was prepared in 1954, and changes in legal provisions on the subject are reported annually to the Commission by the Secretary-General.

TECHNICAL ASSISTANCE AND ADVISORY SERVICES

Many of the United Nations activities under the technical assistance programs directly or indirectly relate to the status of women. The Commission on the Status of Women considers annual progress reports by the Secretary-General on activities under the technical assistance programs which bear particularly on the advancement of women. The Economic and Social Council has recommended that governments consider appointment of qualified women to positions in which they could share in formulating and planning requests for technical assistance, and that they encourage increased participation by women in seminars and conferences organized under the technical assistance programs. The international organizations participating in the technical assistance programs have been requested by the Council to give sympathetic consideration to requests by governments for technical assistance in promoting the economic and social advancement of women.

The General Assembly at its eighth session in 1953 approved the decision of the Economic and Social Council to render, at the request of Member States, services outside the scope of the existing technical assistance programs in order to assist these states in promoting and safeguarding the rights of women. Subsequently, at its tenth session in 1955, the General Assembly established a broad program of advisory services in the field of human rights which embraced previous separate programs including one relating to the rights of women. The Secretary-General reports to the Commission on the Status of Women, *inter alia,* on the progress of the program.

STATUS OF WOMEN IN TRUST AND NON-SELF-GOVERNING TERRITORIES

The Commission on the Status of Women receives annual reports on the status of women in trust and non-self-governing territories which are based on the information supplied by the Administering Authorities to the Trusteeship Council and to the Committee on Information from Non-Self-Governing Territories. These reports are considered in connection with each of the subjects relating to women's rights. Recommendations by the Commission and the Council, however, rarely apply only to trust and non-self-governing territories, since for the most part the problems relating to the status of women in dependent areas also exist in some sovereign states.

Missing Persons

Of all the problems caused by the Second World War, one of the saddest is the disappearance, without any evidence of death, of millions of human beings. These disappearances have resulted mostly from deportations, incarceration in concentration camps, and other methods of extermination practiced by the Nazis and some of their allies.

This has given rise, in many instances, to legal difficulties. Thus, heirs cannot establish title and so inherit the property of missing persons; a surviving spouse cannot remarry; and the guardianship of orphan children cannot be definitely established. In view of such circumstances, the Economic and Social Council in August 1948 asked the Secretary-General to prepare a convention in collaboration with IRO and other competent organizations to deal with the problem.

The Council at its session in March 1949, set up an *ad hoc* committee to study the draft convention, and to prepare either a further draft or other proposals. The *ad hoc* committee's draft was submitted to the General Assembly, to be opened for signature during the latter's fourth session. The Assembly, however, decided on December 3, 1949, to call an international conference of governments, not later than April 1, 1950, to conclude a multilateral convention on the matter.

The Conference met at Lake Success from March 15 to April 6, 1950, and established and opened for accession a Convention on the Declaration of Death of Missing Persons.

The Convention provides for the establishment, within the framework of the United Nations, of an International Bureau for the Declaration of Death. The Secretary-General was to determine its seat, composition, organization and methods of operation. The Convention came into force on January 24, 1952.

The Assembly approved the establishment of the International Bureau, expenses of which should be assessed upon non-members which may become parties to the Convention. It opened in Geneva on October 1, 1952, as a separate unit within the European Office of the United Nations.

Commission on Prisoners of War

An item—Failure of the U.S.S.R. to repatriate or otherwise account for prisoners of war detained in Soviet territory—was placed on the agenda of the 1950 General Assembly at the request of Australia, the United Kingdom and the United States. In a joint memorandum, the three countries declared that, at the end of hostilities in Europe and in the Far East in 1945, large numbers of military personnel of the various nationalities were in the hands of the allied Powers whose prompt repatriation "was demanded by accepted international practice and no less by the elementary principles of humanity." The memorandum recalled the agreements entered into by the allied Powers to repatriate prisoners of war, and stated that: "The Soviet Union has not complied fully with these agreements." Evidence existed, the memorandum continued, to show that statements of the U.S.S.R. that it had completed repatriation of all Japanese and German prisoners of war, except for persons detained in connection with war crimes or on account of illness, were "not true." In submitting the matter to the General Assembly, the three Governments hoped that it would consider means to obtain full information on all these persons and to secure their repatriation.

The Assembly expressed concern at the fact that large numbers of prisoners taken in the Second World War had neither been repatriated nor otherwise accounted for, according to information presented to it. It recalled that both by recognized standards of international conduct and the 1949 Geneva Convention, and by specific agreements between the allies, this problem should already have been solved. Upon the cessation of hostilities, all prisoners with the least possible delay, should have been given unrestricted opportunity for repatriation. The Assembly therefore called on all governments concerned to conform to these requirements, to publish full information, and transmit it to the Secretary-General by April 30, 1951.

With a view to settling the question in a purely humanitarian spirit and on terms equitable to all governments concerned, the Assembly requested the Secretary-General to establish an *ad hoc* Commission composed of three qualified and impartial persons chosen by the International Red Cross or by the Secretary-General himself.

The *ad hoc* Commission would determine whether the information furnished was adequate or whether there was "reasonable ground" for believing that prisoners had not been repatriated or otherwise accounted for. In such case the Commission was to ask the governments concerned for full information and was authorized to use the good office of any qualified or impartial person or organization. All governments concerned were also urged to cooperate with the Commission and to grant it access to their respective countries.

The U.S.S.R. objected to the Assembly's handling of this question since, it contended, Article 107 of the Charter excluded this matter from the competence of the United Nations. The Soviet delegation also stated that the repatriation of prisoners of war had been completed a long time ago. The Polish delegation insisted that the question had not been brought forward for humanitarian reasons only, but as a propaganda weapon against the Soviet Union.

On June 26, 1951, the Secretary-General announced the establishment of the *ad hoc* Commission. The members of this Commission are: Countess Bernadotte, the widow of the late United Nations Mediator in Palestine, Count Folke Bernadotte; Judge José Gustavo Guerrero, of the International Court of Justice; and Judge Aung Khine, Judge of the High Court, Rangoon, Burma.

As directed by the Assembly, the Secretary-General requested all governments to transmit the names of prisoners of war still held by them, the reasons for which they were still detained, and the places in which they were detained. He also asked for the names of prisoners who had died while under their control, and the date and cause of death, and the manner and place of burial in each case.

The Commission held its first series of meetings at United Nations Headquarters from July 2 to August 15, 1951. Emphasizing the non-political role of its mission, the Commission stated that it was considering the problem purely on a humanitarian basis, and requested the governments concerned to cooperate with it in this task.

At its second session, held in Geneva in January and February 1952, the Commission consulted with the representatives of ten governments closely concerned with the problem of prisoners of war. Most of the sessions were held in private. The Commission considered new information presented and examined replies from governments from which information had been requested under the terms of the Assembly's resolution. Certain governments were asked for supplementary information and for information which had not been supplied in response to the Secretary-General's original request.

The Commission held its third session in Geneva in August and September 1952. Again a number of governments were represented by delegates who consulted with the Commission in private session and supplied it with new information. At this session, the Commission prepared a special report for the Secretary-General. This stated that, owing to the lack of cooperation of the Soviet Union, its work had been paralyzed and the difficulty increased of verifying the large amount of information furnished by other governments directly concerned in the repatriation of prisoners who had not yet returned to their homes.

The Commission requested the Secretary-General to transmit this report to Member States and hoped that a fresh appeal for international cooperation among the Members of the United Nations and to their spirit of humanity might give more promising direction to the work that had so far been carried on with only limited success.

At its fourth session in August and September 1953, the Commission prepared a progress report to the Secretary-General in which it surveyed the developments that had taken place since its establishment in 1950, concerning repatriation and clarification of the fate of prisoners of war. In summing up the situation, the Commission indicated that in sectors where the full cooperation of governments had been given, the problem of prisoners of war no longer existed, while in sectors where that cooperation had been withheld the problem remained in its entirety. The Commission emphasized therefore the importance which it attached to the questions addressed to governments concerning prisoners who had died in captivity and those who were still detained in connection with war crimes.

The Commission's progress report was considered by the General Assembly at its eighth session in December 1953. The Assembly noted with satisfaction that some progress had taken place in the repatriation of prisoners of war since 1950, but at the same time it reiterated its grave and continuing concern at the evidence that large numbers of prisoners of the Second World War were still unrepatriated or otherwise unaccounted for. It appealed to all governments which were still holding such prisoners to grant them, with the least possible delay, the unrestricted opportunity of repatriation, as required by recognized standards of international conduct and by the relevant international agreements. While noting that a large amount of valuable information had been made available to the Commission, the Assembly expressed concern over the fact that the refusal of certain governments and authorities to cooperate with the Commission frustrated its efforts to solve the problem. The Assembly asked the Commission to continue its work, and addressed an appeal to all governments and authorities, which had not already done so, to give their full cooperation to the Commission, to supply the information it requested, and to grant it access to areas in which prisoners of the Second World War were detained.

The Commission held its fifth session from March 29 to April 2, and its sixth session from September 6 to 18, 1954. Both sessions were held in private.

At the end of the fifth session, the Commission issued a declaration in which, among other things, it expressed the view that the problem of prisoners of war, if treated in a non-political way, was not intrinsically insoluble; reaffirmed its intention to pursue its efforts in a humanitarian way until the question was finally settled; noted that further progress had been accomplished in repatriation of prisoners and clarification of the fate of those previously listed as missing; emphasized that the problem would not be completely solved until full accounting had been made of all prisoners who were or had been detained in the custody of a foreign Power; and, believing that the residual problem of prisoners of war could be readily solved if the will to solve it was there, stressed the importance it attached to the appeal by the General Assembly to all governments concerned to put forward their best efforts to effect its solution.

At its sixth session, the Commission examined the progress achieved since its last report and prepared a further report for transmission to the General Assembly. It reported that altogether some 40,000 former prisoners of war were repatriated in 1953-54, a situation which it described as progress and confirmation of its opinion that the problem was not insoluble. From its review it concluded that "there is no single solution but rather that several forms of cooperation will lead to the repatriation of the remaining prisoners and bring about the clarification of the fate of many of those who are still missing. The cooperation of governments with the Commission, of government with government, of national Red Cross Society with national Red Cross Society, and the intensive investigative efforts of the governments whose nationals are involved have all contributed to reduce the magnitude of the problem."

The Commission did not hold any session in 1955, but submitted an interim report to the General Assembly in which it gave an account of the further progress that had been made in the repatriation of prisoners of war and detained civilians, as well as the clarification of the fate of hitherto missing persons, largely through negotiations conducted directly between the governments concerned or indirectly through the cooperative efforts of Red Cross Societies. The Commission noted with particular interest the negotiations that were taking place with a view to the release of all German and Japanese prisoners from the Soviet Union and all Japanese prisoners from China.

Plight of Survivors of Nazi Concentration Camps

The plight of survivors of concentration camps who, under the Nazi regime, were victims of the so-called scientific experiments was considered by the Economic and Social Council at its eleventh session. The Council asked the Secretary-General to consider, in consultation with the competent authorities and institutions, the means of alleviating their plight.

The Secretary-General communicated with the Allied High Commission in Germany, the Federal Government of Germany, the German Democratic Republic, IRO, WHO, the International Tracing Service, and the International Committee of the Red Cross, and reported to the Council at its spring session in 1951.

The Council appealed to the competent German authorities to consider making the fullest possible reparation for the injuries suffered by such persons; invited IRO and any authority succeeding it in the administration of the reparation funds, and voluntary agencies distributing these funds, to alleviate the plight of victims as far as possible; and invited WHO to assist in the health aspects of the problem. The Council also requested the Secretary-General to study the possibility of securing voluntary contributions to supplement reparation measures if the latter proved inadequate.

The Secretary-General reported to the Council's thirteenth session in the summer of 1951, the result of his further discussions with the appropriate authorities.

On July 26, 1951, the Government of the Federal Republic of Germany had taken the decision to afford practical assistance in special cases of need to such surviving victims of experiments on human beings living abroad and persecuted on grounds of race, religion, opinions or political convictions, as were for various reasons ineligible for reparation under the compensation laws in force.

The Council welcomed the decision of the Federal Republic of Germany to assume responsibility for this problem, and appealed to it to assist as generously as possible. Member States and non-members, the specialized agencies concerned, and voluntary agencies were requested to assist the Federal Republic in investigating cases of victims not residing in its territory.

The occupying authorities were invited to give sympathetic consideration to applications for remittance of funds to victims in Germany. The Soviet Control Commission for Germany was requested to reply to the Secretary-General's inquiries concerning this problem. Agencies responsible for administering and distributing reparations funds were requested to continue their efforts to alleviate the plight of victims.

The Council requested the Secretary-General to make available to the Federal Republic the information which he had collected or might collect in the future and to inform it of the Council view that the investigation and certification of individual claims against that Government was a matter of its own primary responsibility. Finally, the Council reiterated the need for prompt action and positive measures.

In accordance with the Council's request, the Secretary-General began immediately to transmit to the Federal Government information concerning the victims. As of the end of 1955, he had supplied information concerning 528 requests for assistance.

Two further progress reports have been presented to the Council on the implementation of its decisions, and in particular on the action taken by the Government of the Federal Republic of Germany. This Government reported that, as of September 1, 1952, 156 cases had been dealt with: a total of DM 351,673.20 had been paid as compensation to 108 applicants, while 48 requests had been rejected. An arrangement has been made for the granting of assistance to victims living outside Germany in the currency of the country they now live in.

Social Services

FAMILY, YOUTH AND CHILD WELFARE

Out of the dual heritage of the League of Nations and the United Nations Relief and Rehabilitation Administration (UNRRA), an extensive social welfare program and practical assistance to governments has been developed during the last decade.

In the first years, the most pressing calls were for emergency action to meet the needs of children and families in areas devastated by war. Since then the General

Assembly and the Economic and Social Council recognized that international action in family and child welfare should be the primary responsibility of the Social Commission and the United Nations Secretariat.

The Secretary-General gave priorities for comprehensive long-range programs in the social field, the main objectives being assistance to governments in raising the levels of living of their peoples, with the promotion of economic and social development in the less developed countries given primary consideration.

Implementation of this policy has led to new developments towards a gradual reorientation of all aspects of the United Nations social welfare programs, including family and child welfare.

The United Nations is carrying on an extensive study program in the field of family and child welfare. The first introductory report on *Children Deprived of a Normal Home Life*, published in 1952, has since been followed by a series of other technical studies such as *Adoption of Children, Economic Measures in Favor of the Family*, and a study on *Methods of Administration to the Needy*. These studies provide a useful basis for governments interested in assessing their own measures for family security, and suggest lines of future action at both national and international levels. The *International Directory of Nationwide Organizations Concerned with Family and Youth and Child Welfare* provides information on organizations both governmental and voluntary which are directly concerned with family and child welfare.

Legislations and administrative measures for protection of children adopted in various countries is contained in *The Legislative and Administrative Series on Child, Youth and Family Welfare*, periodically published from 1949 to 1951. Summaries of data collected from various governments on their existing child welfare programs and new developments have been published in two volumes entitled *The Biennial Report on Community, Family and Child Welfare* in 1952 and 1955.

The International Social Service Review, a new publication, in the future will be a medium for the dissemination of information in the field of social services. It will be devoted to the United Nations technical studies, reports of major technical activities and similar information. The first issue published in 1955 includes an account on *United Nations Activities in the Field of Family and Child Welfare*, a report on *Home Help Services*, and a study on *Day Care Services for Children*.

Direct assistance to governments in strengthening family and child welfare programs is normally provided through social welfare advisers, experts, fellowships, and technical seminars.

Several expert missions on family and child welfare have been made available upon the requests of governments to Bolivia, Burma, Costa Rica, Ecuador, Israel, Iran, Pakistan, Thailand and Yugoslavia. Greater opportunities also have been made available to all countries for their personnel to observe and study abroad through fellowships. The regional interchange of study and observations within Europe have likewise contributed toward improving of existing social services of the countries participating in such programs.

The exchange of information on common problems, and the pooling of experience and sharing of techniques have been made possible on an increasingly large scale through seminars and working groups to promote child welfare and training of personnel. Such seminars were held in the Arab states of the Middle East in Beirut in 1949, in Cairo in 1950, in Damascus in 1952, and in Baghdad in 1954. In Europe, seminars on foster home care for children were held in Norway in 1952, in Sweden in 1953, and in France in 1954. A seminar on Children in Incomplete Families was also held in Frankfurt, Germany, in 1955; it was attended by 50 officials engaged in child welfare.

The Secretary-General is responsible for continuing development of an integrated international program for child welfare. A Working Group of Long Range Activities for Children, composed of technical officers of the United Nations, representatives of UNICEF, and the specialized agencies concerned, assists the Secretary-General in planning and implementation of this program. The Working Group has initiated major types of action for promotion of a comprehensive inter-agency program, such as assistance to governments in the assessment of children services. These assessments were undertaken at the request of the governments of Burma, El Salvador and Syria. The assessments include a comprehensive account of the status of children in relationship with the family and the community in each of their three countries, and of health, education, employment, and social and economic security services.

In Latin and Central America, the Middle East, and Asia the regional social welfare advisors closely collaborate with UNICEF in the training of personnel, and maternity and child welfare programs.

WELFARE OF THE AGED

A declaration of the rights of another vulnerable age group—old people—was first considered by the General Assembly in 1948. A preliminary survey summarizing documentation on measures for the benefit of aged persons, and the effect of such measures on their standard of living was prepared in 1950. A further study on the problems of aging populations was being undertaken at the request of the Population Commission. The study would include chapters on the welfare of the aged and would be submitted for consideration to both the Population and Social Commissions in 1957.

Maintenance of Family Levels of Living. A report on *Economic Measures in Favor of the Family,* issued in 1952, contains summaries of laws and administrative regulations in force on June 30, 1949, in 24 countries, and surveys the principal forms of economic advantages available to the family as they emerge from these laws and regulations. At the recommendation of the Social Commission at its tenth session in May 1955, the International Labor Organization and other specialized agencies concerned will cooperate with the United Nations in a joint study of policies designed to maintain and improve family levels of living. A group of experts would meet in 1956 to assist in the examination of the technical problems involved.

A report on *Methods of Social Welfare Administration,* issued in 1950, deals with the assistance aspects of social security. A subsequent report dealing with *Methods of Administering Assistance to the Needy* was completed and published in 1952.

An additional report on assistance to the needy in less developed areas was to be published early in 1956. This report contains information on existing conditions and schemes of public assistance in operation in nine countries in the Middle East, the Far East and Latin America, and discusses the most satisfactory methods of administering such assistance in these areas.

REHABILITATION OF THE HANDICAPPED

The General Assembly, in adopting in December 1946 resolution 58 (I) concerning the establishment of the Program of Advisory Social Welfare Services, included rehabilitation of the handicapped as an area in which technical assistance should be made available to governments. The provision of assistance in the form of experts, fellowships and technical equipment began in 1947.

To strengthen international cooperation in this field, the Social Commission, at its December 1949 session, requested the Secretary-General to draft a comprehensive program to be carried out by the United Nations and the appropriate specialized agencies in cooperation with interested non-governmental organizations. This program was approved in its final form by the Economic and Social Council in 1952.

The purpose of the coordinated international program is to assist governments at their request to develop adequate services for the prevention of disability and the rehabilitation of handicapped persons. In recent years, emphasis has been on technical assistance to under-developed countries in Asia, the Middle East and Latin America. Under the Technical Assistance Program, the following main categories of activities have developed: (1) survey and advisory missions, (2) demonstration and training projects, (3) fellowships and scholarships, (4) special equipment, and (5) seminars and study groups.

During the years 1947-1955, the United Nations has employed 44 experts to work in 39 countries. Demonstration and training projects have been established in Egypt (welfare of the blind), Guatemala, India, Indonesia, Venezuela and Yugoslavia. A research and pilot project concerned with the problems of the blind in rural areas in under-developed countries was being established in Uganda. Five training courses and seminars have been organized in Europe and two regional courses in the welfare of the blind have been held at the demonstration center in Egypt. A regional conference was held in India in 1950. Special equipment has been provided to several countries, primarily under the UNICEF program.

The following publications have been issued: *Report of the United Nations Conference of Experts on Physically Handicapped Children for Countries of Southeast Asia, Modern Methods of Rehabilitation of the Adult Disabled, Rehabilitation of the Handicapped*, a special issue of the Social Welfare Information Series, *Services for the Physically Handicapped*, and *United Nations European Seminar on the Rehabilitation of the Adult Disabled* (published by the Government of Yugoslavia in cooperation with the United Nations). The second issue of the *International Social Service Review*, to be published early in 1956, would be devoted to rehabilitation.

A close working relationship exists between the United Nations, the specialized agencies and several international non-governmental organizations. These non-governmental organizations established in 1953 the Conference of World Organizations Interested in the Handicapped, which acts as a coordinating body among 26 international non-governmental organizations and maintains liaison with the United Nations and the specialized agencies.

REFERENCE SERVICES IN THE SOCIAL FIELD

In 1955, renewed emphasis was placed on the need for collecting and disseminating current information on developments in the social field. Thus the social reference center which had been established in 1947, primarily to carry on technical information services in child welfare transferred from the League of Nations and which had been expanded in 1952 to include information on activities in family and child welfare, was reorganized as a unit collecting basic information and reference material on all aspects of United Nations work in the social field, namely, social policy and development, population, social services, community development, housing and community planning, and the prevention of crime and the treatment of offenders.

As a means of disseminating information, the *Social Welfare Information Series*, which included information submitted by governments on current literature published and national conferences held in their respective countries on social welfare matters, particularly those covered by the program of the Social Commission, was published since 1946. With the publication of an international issue containing a bibliography of publications of the United Nations and specialized agencies in the social field covering the period 1946-1952, the *Series* was discontinued in 1955; material of the nature contained in the *Series* is included in the new publication, *International Social Service Review.*

The compilation and publication of directories has been undertaken with the collaboration of governments, voluntary organizations, and schools of social work. Thus in 1950, a list of schools of social work was included as an annex to the study on *Training for Social Work;* this list was revised and brought up to date and published in 1955 as an *International Directory of Schools of Social Work.* An *International Directory of Nation-Wide Organizations Concerned with Family, Youth and Child Welfare,* covering 48 countries and about 1,800 organizations, was issued in 1953.

TRAINING OF SOCIAL WELFARE PERSONNEL

A study entitled *Training for Social Work—an International Survey* provides a detailed description and analysis of the methods of training in educational institutions of various countries for the professional preparation of social workers. The second study in the series completed in 1954 is directed more particularly to the training of social workers in organized schools of social work at the graduate and undergraduate levels. It showed a marked increase in the number of schools established during the period 1950-1954 and indicated at the same time the shortage of trained social workers in many countries. The report is further supplemented by an *International Directory of Schools of Social Work* which gives information on a total of 422 schools in 53 countries.

The Economic and Social Council recommended that social work, in principle, should be a professional function performed by men and women who have received professional training, and that the training, whether provided at universities or special schools of social work, should be of the highest quality to do justice to both the variety and the unity of social work.

As part of a survey of methods of increasing the supply of qualified personnel, and in view of the insufficient number of professional workers, as well as the particular needs of under-developed areas, the Social Commission and the Council recognized the importance of training auxiliary and community workers. An introductory report on this subject entitled *In-Service Training for Social Welfare* disseminated information in 49 countries on the training methods, and suggested lines for training of people who lacked the necessary advanced preparation, and to keep trained staff up to date.

To initiate training programs for auxiliary and community workers, a series of technical meetings of experts were held; the first took place in Gandhigram, India, in December 1952, and was attended by experts from India, Burma, Ceylon, the Philippines and Thailand, and the representatives of the United Nations, FAO, ILO, UNESCO and WHO. The second was held in Beirut, Lebanon, with experts from Egypt, Iran, Iraq, Jordan, Palestine and Syria participating. The third was held in Bogotá, Colombia, in December 1954, and brought together experts from Colombia, Costa Rica, Cuba, Guatemala, Haiti, Jamaica and Mexico.

On the basis of the findings and proposals of the three expert meetings contained in a report on the *Training of Auxiliary and Community Workers,* the tenth session of the Social Commission in May 1955 recommended extending the training programs for professional and auxiliary social workers through direct assistance to governments.

Direct assistance continued to be given to various governments in providing experts to advise nationals of various countries in the training of social welfare in their countries, in organization and administration of social welfare services, in social welfare services, in social welfare training, and in case work and group work methods. Future activities of the United Nations Social Welfare training program will concentrate on giving assistance to governments in developing their training programs, will prepare studies with special reference to regional requirements in social work training, and will continue to organize regional seminars and conferences for the development and content and techniques of social work at all levels.

Social Policy and Development

ANALYSIS OF SOCIAL CONDITIONS AND SOCIAL DEVELOPMENT

Action in this field has consisted mainly of studies of methods of measuring and comparing living conditions, surveys of actual living conditions, and reporting of measures used to improve living conditions.

DEFINITION AND INTERNATIONAL COMPARABILITY OF STANDARDS OF LIVING

The lack of generally accepted definitions of standards and levels of living, and of yardsticks by which these can be internationally compared and changes measured, has been a serious difficulty in the preparation of international surveys of social conditions (see below), as well as in efforts to assess the effects of technical assistance programs.

The Economic and Social Council was requested by the General Assembly to provide adequate statistical methods for publication by the Secretary-General of annual reports showing changes in absolute levels of living conditions in all countries. The Council requested the Secretary-General, in cooperation with the International Labor Organization and other appropriate specialized agencies, to convene a small group of experts to prepare a report on the most satisfactory methods of defining and measuring standards of living and changes therein in the various countries, having regard to the possibility of international comparisons. The meeting took place in June 1953.

The experts concluded, in their Report on International Definition and Measurement of Standards and Levels of Living, that there is no single index of the level of living as a whole that can be applied internationally. They recommended that the problem be approached by analysis of various "components" representing internationally accepted values (health, nutrition, education, etc.) and by the use of various statistical "indicators" for these components. They also concluded that an annual report on levels of living would not be feasible at present, and felt that the most satisfactory procedure would be to survey levels of living in the reports on the World Social Situation (see below) at four-year intervals. The experts' recommendations, in general, have been endorsed by the Social Commission and the Economic and Social Council. One of their recommendations—for a considerable expansion of studies at the level of family living—has since been discussed and supported by a meeting of experts convened by the International Labor Office.

REPORTS ON THE WORLD SOCIAL SITUATION AND PROGRAMS OF SOCIAL DEVELOPMENT

The General Assembly invited the Economic and Social Council to consider drafting a general report on the world social and cultural situation. The Council, after examining a memorandum on the subject submitted by the Secretary-General to the Social Commission, requested the preparation of a report limited to the social situation. *A Preliminary Report on the World Social Situation,* compiled by the Secretary-General in cooperation with the specialized agencies concerned—ILO, FAO, UNESCO, and WHO—was submitted in 1952 to the eighth session of the Social Commission and the fourteenth session of the Council. This report brought together descriptions and analyses of world conditions in regard to population, health, nutrition, education, conditions of work and employment, income and welfare, and special conditions of need. It included also separate chapters on social conditions in Latin America, the Middle East, and South and Southeast Asia. It did not attempt to cover the entire field embraced by the word "social," but concentrated particularly on standards of living, with special reference to the less developed areas.

The Council considered that the Preliminary Report, which was limited to existing social conditions, should be supplemented by a survey of measures taken to improve social conditions. Such a report, the *International Survey of Programs of Social Development,* prepared by the Secretary-General in cooperation with the four specialized agencies named above and the appropriate non-governmental organizations, was issued in 1955. It describes the main trends in social programs since 1945, with examples drawn from countries throughout the world. The Council, in view of the Survey's practical value for governmental, inter-governmental and non-governmental agencies concerned with social problems, recommended that governments take appropriate measures to bring it to the attention of interested agencies in their countries.

The Council has also requested a second report on the World Social Situation for publication in 1956. This second report is to emphasize changes that have taken place since the Preliminary Report and to give particular attention to the problems of peoples undergoing rapid transition, especially through urbanization. It is to be followed at a two-year interval by another survey of programs, emphasizing changes since the first survey.

COMMUNITY ORGANIZATION AND DEVELOPMENT

In the operation of the United Nations and the specialized agencies' technical assistance programs, an increasing role has been assigned to approaches and techniques relying on local communities as units of action and seeking to stimulate local initiative and leadership. Governmental agencies make special efforts to provide technical services, such as child and family welfare, health and education, locally, in a coordinated and integrated manner combining outside assistance with organized local self-determination and effort. Such methods and techniques are often identified under the broad term "community organization and development." On August 9, 1951, the Economic and Social Council requested the Secretary-General of the United Nations to undertake a thorough study of community welfare centers and, in association with the Technical Assistance Board and the specialized agencies concerned, to promote the development of such centers.

The research work being carried on by the United Nations is based in large measure on material supplied by Member and non-member governments and non-governmental organizations, as well as on the findings of special survey missions conducted in Mexico and the Caribbean area, the Middle East, South and Southeast Asia, and certain countries of Africa south of the Sahara. Together with other material assembled by the United Nations, this material has been utilized in the preparation of a series of country monographs showing the progress already made in community organization in individual countries. Monographs on community centers in Australia, the Belgian Congo, Ceylon, Egypt, France, Israel, Italy, New Zealand, Switzerland, the United Kingdom and the United States have been published or are in the process of publication. Finally, a study-kit designed to assist in the training of auxiliary and community workers for national programs of community improvement, and a bibliography of important literature available in this field have also been prepared.

Experts in community organization and development are provided through the technical assistance program on request to assist governments in formulating national programs of community improvement, in establishing demonstration pilot projects, and in organizing training facilities for community workers.

ANDEAN INDIAN SURVEY

To give effect to a recommendation of the General Assembly, the Economic and Social Council at its summer session in 1950 stressed the importance of raising the living standards of the aboriginal populations of the American continent.

Following discussions among representatives of the United Nations and specialized agencies, the governments concerned, and experts on Andean Indian problems, the ILO Committee of Experts on Indigenous Labor recommended at its first session in January 1951, that a joint inter-agency field working party should develop programs for the integration of indigenous populations into the social and economic life of certain Latin American countries. It was decided to limit the activities of the working party initially to Bolivia, Ecuador and Peru, countries with large indigenous populations.

Requests for technical assistance were subsequently received from the governments of these three countries, and the Technical Assistance Board approved the establishment of a joint field mission to the Andean highlands.

The team was composed of representatives of the United Nations, ILO, FAO, UNESCO and WHO, working under the leadership of the expert appointed by ILO. Several projects were under way in Bolivia, Ecuador and Peru with regional direction from an office in Lima, Peru.

MIGRATION

It has long been recognized that migration constitutes a problem requiring international action. While bilateral arrangements on migration for the purpose of employment and land settlement have played an important role, more and more frequently governments have called for the help of international organizations in the field of migration. The international program in this field is directed towards promoting such migratory movements as are necessary for the social (including demographic) and economic development of emigration and immigration countries, and for assuring adequate standards of living, both to the migrants and the local populations of countries of resettlement; establishing standards of treatment for immigrants in order to protect their legitimate interests; and promoting social and cultural integration and adjustment of immigrants to their new environment.

In the implementation of this program, the United Nations deals with the social, economic and demographic aspects of migration; the ILO with migratory movements in connection with its manpower program; the FAO with land settlement as an important aspect of migration; and the WHO and UNESCO with those aspects falling within their respective competences. The United Nations High Commissioner for Refugees has an interest in the question inasmuch at it is closely connected with his mandate of protection of refugees and the solution of their problems.

SOCIAL ASPECTS OF MIGRATION

The Economic and Social Council very early recognized the need to avoid duplication between the work of the different organs of the United Nations and the specialized agencies in the field of migration. Thus, in March 1947, it invited the Population and Social Commissions, after appropriate consultations, to report to the Council on a practical plan for allocating functions among the various organs concerned in the field of migration. The recommendations of the Commissions were considered by the Council in 1948, and resulted in a resolution allocating responsibilities in the field. The plan included a working arrangement between the Secretariat of the United Nations and the International Labor Office which allocated their respective responsibilities; it also provided the basis for achieving the coordination of these responsibilities through a Technical Working Group on Migration established under the auspices of the Administrative Committee on Coordination. This Group is now convened and serviced by the ILO which assumes, under the Administrative Committee on Coordination, the responsibility at the inter-secretariat level for promoting cooperation and good coordination in this field.

The Secretary-General at the request of the Council undertook a study on the administrative practices of governments with respect to assistance to indigent aliens. It revealed frequent discrimination against aliens in need of public assistance and the fact that in some countries legislation and/or practices require expulsion or deportation of aliens who have become indigent or public charges. As a result of the study, the Council made recommendations aimed at improving the situation of indigent aliens.

A study on *Simplification of Formalities and Reduction of Costs for Migrants* included a survey of administrative procedures applied to migrants by governments and suggestions on the objectives to be achieved. The Economic and Social Council adopted a resolution drawing the attention of governments to the recommendations contained in the study and invited them to consider the possibilities of adjusting their existing practices and procedures accordingly — in particular by means of bilateral agreements. The resolution also requested the Secretary-General, in cooperation with the interested specialized agencies and non-governmental organizations, to promote the best practical means for simplifying formalities and reducing their costs.

In another study, the situation and the need for national and international action which exist in connection with expulsion (also called, in some countries, deportation) of foreign immigrants, were analyzed and conclusions as to the necessary improvements of the existing situation outlined.

One of the aims of international action for the protection of migrants is to avoid separation of family groups or to limit such separation to the shortest possible period. It is recognized, however, that this is not always possible, and action has therefore been taken by the United Nations to insure the protection of families which have remained in the country of emigration. In this connection, attention has been devoted to facilitating the prosecution of claims and enforcement of judgments for the maintenance of destitute families of emigrants. In following up the pre-war endeavors of the League of Nations and of the International Institute for the Unification of Private Law, towards the solution of this problem, and as a result of a study prepared for the Economic and Social Council, the texts of two international conventions have been drawn up with a view to insuring that destitute families receive support from the head of the family who lives in another country, without delay and with minimum of formalities and free of costs. One of these conventions (Convention on Enforcement Abroad of Maintenance Orders) to be applied in countries whose laws permit the execution of foreign judgments, has been approved by the Council in 1954 with the recommendation to governments that they use it as a guide for the preparation of bilateral treaties or uniform legislation to be enacted by individual orders. The other instrument (Convention on the Recovery Abroad of Claims for Maintenance), the objective of which is to facilitate a support order in the country where the person responsible for the family's support lives, was to be the subject of a conference of plenipotentiaries to be held at the United Nations Headquarters in May-June 1956.

A compilation of laws relating to the legal situation of immigrants in some principal countries of immigration was completed for the United Nations by the International Institute for the Unification of Private Law in 1953. It included such subjects as residence conditions, property rights and naturalization. Another compilation completed in 1954 covered the international instruments related to the same question.

A *Handbook of International Measures for the Protection of Migrants and General Conditions to be Observed in their Settlement* was published in 1953. Prepared with the cooperation of the interested specialized agencies, it serves as a valuable tool to government officials and voluntary agencies in developing migration opportunities and negotiating arrangements for the care and protection of immigrants.

In implementing its program in the field of migration, the United Nations and the interested specialized agencies maintain a close cooperation with non-governmental organizations which are active in this field and which provide services to migrants that often go beyond the possibilities of governmental agencies. In this respect, the Economic and Social Council in 1948 requested the Secretary-General to consult with such organizations and to seek their advice in order to ascertain whether they can make arrangements for coordinating their respective services. The United Nations, together with the International Labor Organization, have sponsored the sessions of a Conference of Non-Governmental Organizations Interested in Migration. Between 1950 and 1955, five sessions of this Conference were held in Geneva or New York. They considered the most important migration questions such as general principles of the protection to migrants, information to be given to emigrants before their departure, assistance to indigent aliens, simplification of administrative procedures for migrants, integration of migrants in the countries of settlement, legal assistance to migrants, problems of migrants belonging to professional categories, etc. The next session of the Conference was scheduled for 1957.

Social Defence

THE PREVENTION OF CRIME AND THE TREATMENT OF OFFENDERS

In June 1946, the Economic and Social Council instructed the Social Commission to consider the development of effective international machinery to study the prevention of crime and the treatment of offenders on a broad international basis, and to consult with the International Penal and Penitentiary Commission (IPPC) in this connection.

The Economic and Social Council in August 1948 adopted a resolution to the effect that the United Nations should assume leadership in the promotion of work in this field, making the fullest use of the knowledge and experience of competent international organizations. Negotiations between the United Nations and the IPPC led to an agreement providing for the dissolution of the latter body and for the transfer of its functions to the United Nations. This agreement was approved by the General Assembly in 1950, and in 1951 the IPPC was dissolved and integrated into the United Nations. In the plan of integration, provision was made for the creation of extensive international machinery for work in prevention of crime and the treatment of offenders.

INDIVIDUAL CORRESPONDENTS. In March 1951, the Economic and Social Council invited all Member States and all former members of the IPPC which were not Members of the United Nations to appoint one or more persons of expert professional or scientific qualifications and experience in the field to act as individual correspondents of the Department of Social Affairs. Individual correspondents under this plan have the responsibility of keeping the Secretariat informed of current developments relating to the prevention of crime and the treatment of offenders in their respective countries, to collect information requested for the purpose of studies and research carried out by the United Nations, and otherwise to assist the Secretariat in carrying out the program of the Organization in the field. Up to the end of 1955, 41 countries had appointed 85 individual correspondents.

REGIONAL CONFERENCES. Periodic technical conferences have been organized in different regions of the world in the form either of meetings of national correspondents of the region or of technical assistance seminars. These conferences are designed to study questions in the field of social defence on a regional basis. The following conferences have been held so far: United Nations Conferences of the European Consultative Group, Geneva, 1952 and 1954; Latin American Seminar, Rio de Janeiro, 1953; Middle East Seminar, Cairo, 1953; and Asia and the Far East Seminar, Rangoon, 1954.

WORLD CONGRESS. The first United Nations Congress on the Prevention of Crime and the Treatment of Offenders, following those organized by the IPPC from 1872 to 1950, was held in Geneva, from August 22 to September 3, 1955. It adopted a set of Standard Minimum Rules for the Treatment of Prisoners and recommendations on the selection and training of personnel for penal and correctional institutions, on open institutions, and on prison labor, expressing the hope that technical assistance to governments would be provided with a view to the implementation of the various recommendations. The Congress also discussed extensively the prevention of juvenile delinquency, making suggestions for further studies of the problem. The report of the Congress was to be published in 1956.

INTERNATIONAL ADVISORY COMMITTEES OF EXPERTS. In 1949, 1950, 1953 and 1955 the Secretary-General convened international committees of experts to advise him and the Social Commission on the formulation of policies and programs for study and international action. The next meeting was to be convened in 1957.

INTERNATIONAL REVIEW OF CRIMINAL POLICY. Since 1952, the United Nations Secretariat has issued the *International Review of Criminal Policy*, a bi-annual publication. The *Review* is designed to serve as an authoritative international channel for the dissemination and exchange of technical information in the field of social defence, and contains articles, notes and a topical bibliography of current technical literature. Since 1954, the *Review* has been published in a tri-lingual edition (English, French and Spanish).

COORDINATION OF ACTIVITIES OF INTERNATIONAL ORGANIZATIONS. In 1948, the United Nations established under its auspices a committee consisting of representatives of the interested specialized agencies and the principal international non-governmental organizations concerned with the prevention of crime and the treatment of offenders. This committee held meetings in 1949, 1950, 1952 and 1954. Meetings have been devoted to coordination and to the mutual exchange of information on the activities of participating organizations. The next meeting was to take place in 1956.

JUVENILE DELINQUENCY. A comprehensive questionnaire on this subject was sent to governments in 1949, and the replies received were used by the Secretariat for the preparation of national monographs. On the basis of these and of supplementary information, regional comparative surveys of juvenile delinquency were prepared. The surveys dealing with Europe, Latin America and North America were published in 1952. Those dealing with Asia and the Far East and the Middle East were published in 1953. Number nine of the *International Review of Criminal Policy* contains a survey of the treatment of juvenile delinquents in Australia and New Zealand. The problem of juvenile delinquency has also appeared as a subject for discussion on the agenda of the regional conferences as well as on the agenda of the first United Nations Congress on the Prevention of Crime and the Treatment of Offenders. A study entitled "The prevention of juvenile delinquency", prepared by the Secretariat for the Congress, was published in numbers seven and eight of the *International Review of Criminal Policy*. Another study for the Congress, entitled "The prevention of juvenile delinquency in selected European countries", was undertaken by the Institute for the Study and Treatment of Delinquency, London, at the request of the Secretariat and was published in 1955.

From 1947 to 1954, 95 fellowships and scholarships were awarded in the field of juvenile delinquency under the Technical Assistance Program.

PROBATION. A comprehensive international survey and comparative analysis of adult probation and related measures was prepared by the Secretariat and published in 1951. A complementary study on the practical results and financial aspects of adult probation in selected countries was published in 1954. Another supplementary study relating to the methods applied by social workers and the courts for the recommendation of probation and the decision to make a probation order in individual cases was to be undertaken in 1956-57.

Upon the recommendation of the Social Commission, the Economic and Social Council in August 1951 adopted a resolution urging governments to give favorable consideration to the adoption and development of probation as a major instrument of policy in crime prevention and the treatment of offenders.

A European Seminar on Probation, under the Technical Assistance Program, was held in London in October 1952, and was attended by representatives of seventeen countries. The work of the seminar dealt primarily with the problems connected with the introduction of the probation system and the practical use of probation as a method of treatment. The report of this seminar was published in 1954.

MEDICO-PSYCHOLOGICAL AND SOCIAL EXAMINATION OF OFFENDERS. A European seminar on this subject, organized in collaboration with the World Health Organization, and attended by teams of experts appointed by eighteen governments, was held under the Technical Assistance Program in Brussels in December 1951. The subject was dealt with from the scientific, judicial and administrative points of view. The papers prepared for the seminar, together with the conclusions of the seminar, were published in a special issue of the *International Review of Criminal Policy*, number three.

OTHER STUDIES. Besides those already mentioned, the Secretariat has also published studies on *The Indeterminate Sentence, Parole and After-Care*, as well as a report on *Jail Administration in India*. A study on various aspects of *Prison Labor* was carried out in connection with the United Nations Congress on the Prevention of Crime and the Treatment of Offenders.

Projects being carried out by the United Nations included criminal statistics, the prevention of types of criminality resulting from social changes and accompanying economic development in less-developed countries, short term imprisonment, and the treatment of types of offenders against whom society needs particular protection.

STANDARD MINIMUM RULES FOR THE TREATMENT OF PRISONERS. An original set of rules had been prepared by the International Penal and Penitentiary Commission and endorsed by the League of Nations in 1934. A revision was made by the IPPC before its dissolution, and the revised draft was discussed in 1952-1954 at the regional conferences. The Secretariat prepared a consolidated draft which was submitted to the first United Nations Congress on the Prevention of Crime and the Treatment of Offenders, held in 1955. A final text of the Standard Minimum Rules was adopted unanimously by this conference. It was to be submitted to the Social Commission and to the Economic and Social Council for further action. In this connection, it is envisaged to ask governments to report every three years on the application of the Rules in the administration of penal institutions and the progress made, and to publish such information in the *International Review of Criminal Policy*.

TRAFFIC IN PERSONS AND EXPLOITATION OF THE PROSTITUTION OF OTHERS

The Convention for the Suppression of the Traffic in Persons and of the Exploitation of the Prostitution of Others, which was approved by the General Assembly in December 1949, has been signed by thirteen governments, five of which have deposited with the Secretary-General instruments of ratification. In addition, eleven governments have deposited instruments of accession.

As a consequence of the adoption by the General Assembly of the above-mentioned Convention, a new questionnaire was prepared and approved by the Social Commission and the Economic and Social Council in 1951. The new text forms the basis of the reports of governments in this field. Following a decision adopted by the Social Commission at its tenth session and approved later by the Economic and Social Council, the Secretariat has discontinued separate publications summarizing these reports and is presenting instead selected information from these reports in the *International Review of Criminal Policy*.

The Social Commission, at its tenth session held in 1955, has given high priority to two studies in the field of prostitution, one on a program of action to combat the traffic in persons and the exploitation of the prostitution of others, and the other on measures prerequisite to and in conjunction with the suppression of the regulation of prostitution and particularly the abolition of licensed houses. Reports on these studies were to be presented to the Social Commission at its twelfth session.

Housing and Planning

Problems of housing and physical planning, including building, are an integral part of United Nations activities. At its first session in 1946, the General Assembly noted the magnitude and gravity of housing problems in various parts of the world, and recommended that the Economic and Social Council expedite the study of these problems on the international level, and that it consider holding a meeting of experts to advise on the establishment of an international mechanism which would encourage and coordinate research and the exchange of information among nations and define standards and levels of housing capable of general application.

The Council in 1949 requested the Secretary-General to formulate a long-range integrated program in housing, physical planning and building, covering social, economic, technological and administrative aspects. This program, prepared by a technical working group of the Administrative Committee on Coordination in consultation with the specialized agencies and the inter-governmental and non-governmental organizations concerned, emphasized that primary responsibility for its implementation and for the coordination of international activities in these fields should rest with the United Nations. The program was approved by the Council at its tenth and eleventh sessions in 1950.

In agreement with the Bureau of Economic Affairs, the responsibility for United Nations activities in housing, physical planning and building is centralized in the Bureau of Social Affairs, in the Housing and Planning Section of the Housing and Community Development Branch. The Bureau works in close cooperation with the regional economic commissions, the specialized agencies, and the interested inter-governmental and non-governmental organizations. The Bureau is also responsible for dealing with the substantive aspects of operational projects in these fields undertaken within the framework of the United Nations program of technical assistance.

The continuing housing shortage throughout the world and the serious social consequences resulting from it led both the General Assembly and the Economic and Social Council in 1952 to reiterate the urgent need for international action and practical measures to assist governments in increasing the supply of housing for lower-income groups, with special emphasis on developing practical methods of financing housing and community improvement programs from domestic or external sources. Special attention was also drawn to the need for further development of regional activities, as well as national technical assistance operations in these fields. At its ninth and tenth sessions in 1953 and 1955, the Social Commission again emphasized the importance of financing of housing and community improvement programs, and of regional (physical) planning as a requisite to the balanced development of economic, social and technological resources within the national framework. The Economic and Social Council approved these recommendations and also suggested the holding of regional meetings of experts in the financing of housing and community improvement.

These recent trends have led to a reorientation of the integrated program to effect an even closer relationship between the elements of the various study aspects and the technical assistance program. The resulting program may be briefly outlined as follows:

(a) study of housing conditions and promotion of national programs and policies of housing and community improvement;

(b) study of methods of financing housing and community improvement programs and assistance to governments in solving their problems in this respect;

(c) extension of housing for low-income groups through the promotion of research in low-cost housing techniques and its practical application;

(d) study of trends in regional (physical) planning as an integral part of overall development plans and direct assistance to governments in the establishment of planning programs and policies, including the training of planning personnel.

Studies undertaken on the basis of this program are published in reports and in special issues of the United Nations publication *Housing and Community Development*, the first eight issues of which were published under the title *Housing and Town and Country Planning*.

Reports published to date cover such subjects as minimum standards of occupancy and fitness for habitation of urban dwellings enforceable under penalty low-cost housing in the Caribbean area and in South and Southeast Asia, housing conditions and programs as part of the *Preliminary Report on the World Social Situation* and the *International Survey of Programs of Social Development*, urban land policies, housing aspects pertaining to definition and measurement of living standards in the

Report on International Definition and Measurement of Standards and Levels of Living, and financing of housing and community improvement programs. Special issues of *Housing and Town and Country Planning* were devoted to stabilized earth construction, community services and facilities for large-scale housing developments, housing in the t opics, urban land problems and policies, and building research. The first issue under the new title of *Housing and Community Development* dealt with international action in Asia and the Far East in housing, building and planning, and forthcoming issues were to be devoted to the United Nations Seminar on Housing through Non-Profit Organizations, Copenhagen 1954; technical assistance in the fields of housing, building and planning; world housing conditions and programs; financing of housing and community improvement programs; and regional (physical) planning. Also in preparation were a report on current methods and practices of mobilizing self-help and housing cooperatives; an international catalogue of films and film strips in housing, building and planning; and a manual on stabilized earth construction techniques.

The new trend in te hnical assistance activities has been to consider individual projects based on government requests as part of a long-range plan of assistance to an entire region. Thus, experience gained in a particular country may be extended to neighboring countries facing similar problems. The increasing number of requests for advice by government agencies on policies and programs of housing, planning and the development of the building and building materials industries has contributed in large measure to this trend.

Seventy-four fellowships and scholarships for study abroad have been awarded during 1953-1955. Assistance was being given to three regional housing research and training centers, one in Latin America and one each in hot-dry and hot-humid Asia and the Far East. Experts in rural housing and village planning have also been provided to assist the UNESCO Fundamental Education Centers in Latin America and the Middle East.

Seminars held included one in New Delhi in 1954 on housing and community improvement in Asia and the Far East, and one later in the year in Copenhagen, for Latin American participants, on financing housing through non-profit organizations. In the planning stage were a seminar workshop on rural planning in Latin America, another seminar on non-profit housing for participants from Asia and the Far East, a regional meeting of experts on financing of housing and community improvement in Latin America, and study tours on winter construction in the U.S.S.R. for participants from northern European countries and from Asia and the Far East.

The services of individual experts have been made available to governments in the following fields: formulation of national housing and building programs, preparation of surveys as bases for regional and city development plans, drafting of master plans for several capital cities [Amman (Jordan), Asunción (Paraguay), Djakarta (Indonesia), Cairo (Egypt), Karachi (Pakistan), and Kuala Lumpur (Federation of Malaya)], organization of national housing and planning agencies, teaching of housing and planning, rammed earth construction, financing of housing, emergency housing, housing design, improvement of housing and community facilities, development of building and building materials industries, and the establishment and equipment of national building research institutes.

Office of the United Nations High Commissioner for Refugees

The General Assembly on December 14, 1950, during its fifth session, adopted the Statute of the United Nations High Commissioner for Refugees, and elected

G. J. van Heuven Goedhart of the Netherlands as High Commissioner. The Office, which opened on January 1, 1951, was originally established for three years, but the mandate was subsequently extended until the end of 1958, and Dr. van Heuven Goedhart was reappointed High Commissioner for the same period. (Note. Dr. van Heuven Goedhart died in Geneva on July 8, 1956.)

The High Commissioner's mandate extends to all persons who have fled from their native lands for fear of persecution; for political, racial or religious reasons; and who are unwilling or unable to claim the protection of their own governments. However, refugees who have been given full rights of citizenship by their countries of residence, such as those in India and Pakistan and the German refugees, are outside the mandate. The Arab refugees from Palestine are being looked after by the United Nations Relief and Works Agency for Palestine Refugees in the Near East (UNRWA) (see page 120).

Of the more than two million refugees presumed to come within the High Commissioner's mandate, approximately one million live in Europe. Groups of refugees not within the competence of UNRWA are living in the various states in the Middle East and Turkey. Approximately 14,000 refugees of European origin are in China. By the end of 1955, over 70,000 refugees under the High Commissioner's mandate were still living in some 200 official camps in Austria, Germany, Greece and Italy (including Trieste). Thirty to fifty thousand others were in unofficial camps.

The three main functions of the Office are international protection, promoting permanent solutions to the problems of refugees, and administering emergency aid. These activities can be supplemented by decisions taken by the General Assembly to which the High Commissioner reports through the Economic and Social Council. On October 21, 1954, the General Assembly decided that the High Commissioner should carry out a four-year program designed to promote the integration and resettlement of some 300,000 refugees who had not yet become established. The program aims at solving the problems of these refugees on a permanent basis, and is focussed on clearing the camps.

As the budget of the High Commissioner's Office is an integral part of the United Nations Budget, and only administrative expenses may be financed out of the yearly allotment, which usually amounts to between $650,000 and $700,000, the carrying out of the four-year program is dependent upon voluntary contributions. The General Assembly, therefore, established a United Nations Refugee Fund (UNREF) to finance the four-year program and requested the Negotiating Committee for Extra Budgetary Funds, in cooperation with the High Commissioner, to negotiate with the governments of Member and non-member states for voluntary contributions towards the fund.

Although the target of $16,000,000 subsequently set for the four-year period (1955-58) was for governmental contributions, donations from private sources have been and were continuing to be encouraged.

The Economic and Social Council during its nineteenth session in 1955, at the request of the General Assembly, established an UNREF Executive Committee which is responsible for giving directives to the High Commissioner in the planning and carrying out of his program, and for controlling disbursements from UNREF.

The 20 members appointed to this committee, fifteen of whom were members of the High Commissioner's Advisory Committee which held its last session at the end of 1954, are as follows: Australia, Austria, Belgium, Brazil, Colombia, Denmark, the Federal Republic of Germany, France, Greece, the Holy See, Iran, Israel, Italy, the Netherlands, Norway, Switzerland, Turkey, the United Kingdom, the United States and Venezuela.

The Executive Committee, at its first session, appointed a Standing Program Sub-Committee of twelve members to examine programs and projects before sessions of the main committee, and to authorize the carrying out of approved projects subject to funds being available.

The Executive Committee, which is scheduled to meet twice a year, also carries on the advisory functions of the High Commissioner's Advisory Committee which it has replaced.

The Headquarters of the High Commissioner's office are at the *Palais des Nations,* Geneva, Switzerland, and branch offices or sub-offices are in the following areas: Europe (Athens, Bonn, Brussels, The Hague, London, Luxembourg, Munich, Nürnberg, Paris, Rome, Vienna); the Middle East (Cairo); Latin America (Bogotá); and North America (New York). An office is also maintained in Hong Kong jointly with the Inter-governmental Committee for European Migration.

The following is a description of the activities of the Office and its relations with other organizations.

INTERNATIONAL PROTECTION

Through diplomatic negotiations, the High Commissioner promotes international agreements on the legal status of refugees with particular regard to their documentation (for example, travel documents and birth certificates), and he seeks to protect the interests of refugees in relation to general international agreements. Through his branch offices, the High Commissioner keeps in touch with the authorities in the various countries with a view to safeguarding and improving the legal, social and economic position of the refugees. The most important international agreement concerning refugees is the Convention Relating to the Status of Refugees, of July 28, 1951, which was drawn up in Geneva and, by the end of 1955, had been ratified by the following sixteen States: Australia, Austria, Belgium, Denmark, Ecuador, France, the Federal Republic of Germany, Iceland, Israel, Italy, Luxembourg, Monaco, Norway, Sweden, Switzerland and the United Kingdom. This Convention codifies in 44 articles the rights and legal status of refugees and guarantees to them, *inter alia,* the same treatment as nationals in such matters as access to courts, elementary education, public relief, and social security. According to the terms of the Convention, the High Commissioner is called upon to supervise its application.

For the purposes of the Convention, a "refugee" is a person who has been considered as such under the prewar conventions and agreements, and under the Constitution of IRO. In addition, the term includes any person who has become a refugee as a result of events occurring before January 1, 1951. At the time of signature, ratification or accession, each contracting state makes a declaration whether the words "events occurring before January 1, 1951," should be understood to mean events in Europe, or in Europe and elsewhere.

Other recently adopted international instruments which provide for the protection of refugees are: a protocol to the convention providing for the assimilation of stateless persons, extending its provisions to refugees who have their habitual residence in a state party; protocols adopted by the committees of the Council of Europe, the provisions of which enable refugees to benefit from social security and medical assistance schemes; the Convention on Declaration of Death of Missing Persons; and a protocol to the Universal Copyright Convention, extending some of its provisions to refugees.

An agreement on refugees seafarers drafted at a conference of maritime countries, it was hoped, would be open for accession before long.

PROMOTING PERMANENT SOLUTIONS

The problems of the refugees may be solved permanently through repatriation, emigration or integration. Although the High Commissioner does not carry out repatriation or migration operations under his Statute, he is called upon to coordinate governmental and private efforts to promote voluntary repatriation or assimilation within new national communities, and to promote the admission of refugees to the territories of states. Although the possibilities for repatriation or emigration to overseas countries are limited and the emphasis, therefore, was being placed on integration into the countries of Europe where the refugees were living, there were still many refugees eligible for migration, and the High Commissioner had recently invited the governments of certain overseas immigration countries also to consider admitting limited numbers of refugees who normally could not qualify for resettlement overseas because of ill health, age, lack of a skill, or family composition. Some European countries have already accepted refugees in these categories.

FOUR-YEAR PROGRAM—PLAN OF OPERATIONS

UNREF projects cover a wide range of activities and involve countries with widely differing conditions. They fall into three main categories: emergency aid, "difficult cases" (the old, the ill and the disabled), and permanent solutions, and are being carried out in Austria, Belgium, China, Egypt, Germany, Greece, Iran, Italy, Jordan, Lebanon, Syria and Turkey. For at least 1955 and 1956, special attention was to be given to solving the problems of refugees in camps. The projects include housing settlement, vocational training, credit facilities for setting up small businesses, establishment in rural or urban occupations, aid to university students, employment counselling, and placement. Plans were also under way for the "difficult cases" to be settled in local institutions or to be given annuities. Projects for emergency aid, begun before the new program was launched and financed out of the refugee emergency fund established in February 1952, and absorbed by the new Fund, were being continued and would be extended as more money became available, to help other refugees requiring medical care and supplementary feeding. Provision was also made for the settlement of "difficult cases" from China, the Middle East and elsewhere. It was planned to support the voluntary agencies' efforts to find sponsors in Australia and Latin America for individuals then in camps. These efforts were continuing.

At the end of 1955, it was estimated that nearly 23,000 refugees were being assisted, or would soon be, under the UNREF plan of operations for that year. Sixty projects were in various stages of implementation covering aspects of the permanent solutions, "difficult cases", and emergency aid programs in twelve countries. Delays in the receipt of contributions to UNREF affected to some extent the implementation of projects envisaged for the year as only approximately three-fourths of the target of $4,200,000 for governmental contributions had been received in spite of the generosity of thirteen European countries, and Australia, Canada, Colombia, New Zealand and the United States. The proceeds from private and public campaigns, notably in the Netherlands where nearly a million dollars were collected, helped, however, to increase the fund.

Approximately 135 projects, involving the expenditure of $4,400,000, were envisaged for 1956. The target for the year had to be increased as government contributions up to the end of 1955 fell short of the amount required. The plan of operations would be considered by the Planning Sub-Committee and by the UNREF Executive Committee during its second session in January 1956.

RELATIONS WITH VOLUNTARY AGENCIES

The voluntary agencies concerned with refugee work have always played an important role in carrying out the operational part of the High Commissioner's program. These agencies have been and are consulted both at field and headquarters level in the planning phases of the program for permanent solutions and emergency assistance. Advisory boards consisting of representatives of the voluntary agencies and government officials have been established by the High Commissioner's branch offices in countries where the new Program is being carried out. These boards assist the office of the High Commissioner in drawing up projects for submission to the UNREF Executive Committee. At headquarters, close contact with the agencies is maintained by regular meetings between representatives of the Standing Conference of Voluntary Agencies Working for Refugees and representatives of the Office of the High Commissioner.

RELATIONS WITH INTER-GOVERNMENTAL AND GOVERNMENTAL ORGANIZATIONS

Close cooperation is maintained with certain specialized agencies of the United Nations, particularly the ILO, UNESCO and WHO, and with other inter-governmental organizations such as the Council of Europe and the Organization for European Economic Cooperation, and with the Inter-governmental Committee for European Migration, particularly in maintaining the joint operation of the Inter-governmental Committee for European Migration and the Office of the High Commissioner for the settlement of European refugees stranded in China. The office of the High Commissioner also maintains close relations with the United States Escapee Program in exchanging information and in coordinating the work for refugees registered with the latter, all of whom come under the High Commissioner's mandate.

NOBEL PEACE PRIZE

The Nobel Peace Prize for 1954 was awarded to the Office of the High Commissioner for Refugees, and it was subsequently decided to use the money (approximately $35,000), to finance the closure of the Tinos Refuge Centre in Greece.

United Nations Children's Fund (UNICEF)

The United Nations Children's Fund (UNICEF) was created by the General Assembly on December 11, 1946, to assist children of war-devastated countries, and to raise the general level of child health. In December 1950, the General Assembly revised the Fund's terms of reference, shifting the emphasis from emergency relief to aid for continuing child care programs, particularly in under-developed countries. Emergency aid is provided children in such catastrophes as earthquakes, floods, droughts, typhoons and dislocations caused by war. At the end of 1953, the Assembly decided that the Fund should continue indefinitely.

UNICEF has brought the United Nations directly into the lives of many millions of persons in remote parts of the world.

Its purpose is to make a permanent contribution to the welfare of large numbers of children through programs which countries will be able to carry on by themselves after initial UNICEF stimulus. UNICEF furnishes supplies and equipment which assisted governments are unable to provide. Related technical assistance and advice are provided by other United Nations departments and specialized agencies, including the Bureau of Social Affairs, the Technical Assistance Administration, the World Health Organization, and the Food and Agriculture Organization. UNICEF aid, provided only at the request of governments, is given without regard to race, creed, nationality status or political belief.

UNICEF is financed not through the regular United Nations budget, but by voluntary contributions from governments and individuals. Some seventy governments contributed to UNICEF in 1955.

During 1955, UNICEF aid reached over 32 million children in some 90 countries and territories. The 1956 target of allocations, as in several preceding years, was set at $20 million.

UNICEF aid is predicated on the understanding that primary responsibility for the care of children rests on individual countries, with UNICEF supplementing and stimulating the use of local resources. Aided countries are responsible for the actual carrying out of UNICEF-assisted programs. To do this they assume the additional budgetary and administrative commitments called for. This results in UNICEF aid for projects in which local interest is strong. Establishing an administrative and budgetary pattern on national, provincial and local levels facilitates continuation of the programs after UNICEF aid ends. Thus the value of UNICEF assistance is more than doubled and the principle of self-help is fostered.

UNICEF is governed by a 26-member Executive Board, which meets twice a year to make allocations for programs and to review progress and policies. The Board is responsible through the Economic and Social Council to the General Assembly. UNICEF is an integral part of the United Nations; its personnel are members of the Secretariat and the Executive Director is appointed by the Secretary-General.

The principal types of projects assisted by UNICEF are:

1. *Maternal and Child Welfare Services and Training.* UNICEF provides equipment and supplies for maternal and child welfare centers, children's hospitals or wards, school health services, clinics and laboratories. Products supplied are wifery kits; scales, thermometers, needles and syringes; transport; hospital equipment; drugs; sera, vaccines, common medicines, soap and disinfectants; powdered milk, fish-liver oil capsules and other diet supplements; and health education materials. Because of the great need for trained personnel, particularly in rural areas, these maternal and child welfare services provide training facilities for local personnel, as well as direct services to children and mothers. UNICEF sends supplies and equipment, for midwifery training centers, schools of nursing, teaching, hospitals, and pediatric wards, and under certain conditions pay stipends in local currency for midwife and supervisory trainees.

2. *Mass Health Programs.* UNICEF provides supplies and equipment for the control or eradication of diseases widely affecting children, such as malaria, yaws, tuberculosis, trachoma, leprosy, and diphtheria and whooping cough. Such assistance includes providing DDT, sprayers, penicillin and other antibiotics; providing transport; providing needles, syringes, laboratory and clinic supplies; providing vaccines, field equipment and health education materials; and providing equipment for the local production of insecticides, antibiotics and vaccines.

3. *Child Nutrition.* UNICEF provides dried skim and whole milk and fish-liver oil capsules for supplementary feeding carried out through school lunches and at maternal and child welfare centers. UNICEF also provides equipment for drying and pasteurizing milk and for other methods of milk conservation in order to insure that more locally-produced, safe milk will be available for children. In many countries, UNICEF-aided milk conservation projects permit the continuation, through the use of local milk supplies, of child nutrition programs formerly assisted with UNICEF-imported dried milk. UNICEF is also working with FAO to encourage the better use and development of other local high protein foods for children,

particularly in areas where there is little immediate prospect for developing an adequate local milk supply. UNICEF has already provided equipment for one plant in Chile, which processes edible fish flour to be used to enrich bread and various dishes. Another plant in Indonesia manufactures a soybean and peanut powder fortified with vitamins and minerals which, when reliquified, makes a vegetable "milk". Development of other products of high protein which are locally available, economical and acceptable is being actively explored.

4. *Programs Benefitting more than one Region.* UNICEF provides assistance for the International Children's Center in Paris, which trains persons from several geographical regions and agencies in various aspects of child care.

5. *Emergency Situations.* UNICEF provides food, drugs to control epidemics, and other supplies for children and mothers suffering from such catastrophes as floods, earthquakes, famines, droughts, volcanic eruptions, and the aftermath of war and civil strife.

Following is a list of the 92 countries and territories receiving UNICEF aid at the end of 1955:

AFRICA (20)

Basutoland	Kenya	Southern Rhodesia
Bechuanaland	Liberia	Tanganyika
Cameroons	Mauritius	(British Trusteeship)
(French Trusteeship)	Morocco	Togoland
French Equatorial Africa	Nigeria, Federation of	(French Trusteeship)
French West Africa	Northern Rhodesia	Tunisia
Gambia	Nyasaland	Uganda
Gold Coast	Sierra Leone	

ASIA (22)

Afghanistan	Indonesia	Sarawak
Burma	Japan	Singapore
Cambodia	Korea	Solomon Islands
Ceylon	Malaya, Federation of	Thailand
China (in Taiwan)	Netherlands New Guinea	Vietnam
Fiji	North Borneo	Western Samoa
Hong Kong	Pakistan	(New Zealand
India	Philippines	Trusteeship)

EASTERN MEDITERRANEAN (13)

British Somaliland	Israel	Somaliland
Egypt	Jordan	(Italian Trusteeship)
Ethiopia	Lebanon	Sudan
Iran	Libya	Syria
Iraq		Turkey

EUROPE (7)

Austria	Italy	Spain
Finland	Portugal	Yugoslavia
Greece		

THE AMERICAS (30)

Antigua	Dominican Republic	Nicaragua
Barbados	Ecuador	Panama

THE AMERICAS (cont'd.)

Bolivia	El Salvador	Paraguay
Brazil	Grenada	Peru
British Guiana	Guatemala	St. Kitts
British Virgin Islands	Haiti	St. Lucia
Chile	Honduras	St. Vincent
Colombia	Jamaica	Surinam
Costa Rica	Mexico	Trinidad and Tobago
Dominica	Montserrat	Uruguay

National UNICEF committees are encouraged to assist individual citizens to greater awareness of children's needs in their own and other countries, and to broaden citizen participation in UNICEF. Their functions vary in different countries, but in general, they aim to promote governmental, organizational and individual interest in the worldwide needs of children and the international assistance available through UNICEF. Committees established in countries receiving UNICEF aid help by assessing local conditions and advising governments on specific needs, and by planning for participation by non-governmental agencies and interested individuals. National committees, wherever appropriate, sometimes also assist in fund-raising efforts for the benefit of UNICEF.

Narcotic Drugs

In February 1946, the United Nations assumed the functions and powers relating to the international control of narcotic drugs formerly entrusted to the League of Nations. During the past decade, the Organization has sought to restore this control to its pre-war status, and, if possible, to increase its effectiveness by securing the more widespread adherence of states to the existing treaties on narcotics, and by concluding new instruments to close the remaining gaps. It has also provided expert assistance to countries needing it, and sponsored research on relevant scientific and administrative problems.

Five international organs play principal roles in international narcotics control: The Economic and Social Council and the Commission on Narcotic Drugs are the chief policy-making bodies; the Permanent Central Opium Board, the Drug Supervisory Body, and the Expert Committee on Drugs Liable to Produce Addiction of WHO carry out administrative, semi-judicial and technical functions.

The Commission on Narcotic Drugs is one of the functional commissions of the Economic and Social Council and successor to the Advisory Committee of the League of Nations on the Traffic in Opium and Other Dangerous Drugs. It is composed of fifteen governments chosen by the Council, because they are the principal manufacturers of narcotic drugs, or are producers of opium or coca leaf, or are primary targets of the international illicit traffic. The present members (December 1955) are Canada, China, Egypt, France, Greece, India, Iran, Mexico, Peru, Poland, Turkey, the U.S.S.R., the United Kingdom, the United States and Yugoslavia.

The Commission reviews annually the drug situation and the status of narcotics control in all countries, considers what improvements are necessary in the international control system, and prepares new measures for this purpose.

Its influence derives largely from its power to appeal to public opinion. It affords an international forum where any government whose control of narcotic drugs is inadequate or, in particular, whose territory has been used as a base for the illicit traffic, may be publicly called to account.

The Permanent Central Opium Board consists of eight private persons elected by the Economic and Social Council on the basis of their technical competence and impartiality, and the Drug Supervisory Body of four private persons, two of whom are chosen by WHO, one by the Permanent Central Opium Board and one by the Commission. Both organs usually meet in spring and autumn. The Drug Supervisory Body examines governmental estimates of medical and scientific needs for narcotics and, if necessary, may propose their amendment to the government concerned; while the Permanent Central Opium Board reviews statistical data on many phases of the licit trade in narcotics, and is empowered by the treaties to take certain measures to insure their proper observance by all Contracting Parties.

The WHO Expert Committee is composed of specialists chosen by the Executive Board who meet annually, *inter alia*, to determine whether newly-developed drugs notified by governments are addiction-producing or capable of being converted into addiction-producing drugs.

LEGISLATIVE DEVELOPMENTS

The United Nations has the task of adapting the treaty machinery to changing conditions, and under its auspices three new protocols dealing with special aspects of narcotics control have been adopted.

Most of the organs referred to above replaced others, now defunct, to which the treaties assigned specific functions. It was necessary to transfer these powers legally, and a Protocol accomplishing this was concluded at Lake Success on December 11, 1946. At the end of 1955, there were 56 parties to the Protocol.

The Limitation Convention of 1931 only provided for the control of drugs made from certain alkaloids of opium and the coca leaf. Beginning in 1939, however, pharmacologists began to develop synthetic narcotics, that is, narcotics made from inorganic materials, which now constitute the more numerous category. This situation likewise required international action which took the form of a Protocol adopted at Paris on November 19, 1948, to which 47 states have adhered by the end of 1955. In effect, this Protocol enlarged the scope of the 1931 Convention so that its more comprehensive controls could be applied to all addiction-producing drugs. Approximately 30 new drugs have been placed under international control under this treaty.

Over-production of such narcotic raw materials as opium and coca leaf is endemic, and surpluses of licitly-produced opium and coca leaf tend to find their way into the illicit traffic unless stringent national controls are strictly enforced. This situation has long worried the Commission, especially as regards opium, the source of illicit morphine and heroin.

In 1950-1951, the Commission studied a comprehensive plan to reorganize the opium trade as an international monopoly, to apportion production among producing countries on the basis of set quotas, and to set a price at which the opium would be sold. The opium-producing and drug-manufacturing countries, however, could not reach agreement on a treaty of this kind.

Accordingly, the Commission turned to an alternative plan proposed by France, which was more acceptable to governments and which formed the basis of a third protocol adopted by the United Nations Opium Conference held in New York during May-June 1953. This Protocol limits the use of, and international trade in, opium to medical and scientific needs, and seeks to control production through the indirect method of limiting the opium stocks which each state may keep. It provides that producing states must license farmers producing opium and specify the areas to be sown; producing states must also set up an agency to which all the opium thus produced has to be delivered as soon as possible after harvesting. Only opium produced in one of seven named countries may be exported, and estimates and statistics similar to those furnished for manufactured drugs under the earlier treaties are required for opium. The Protocol also empowers the Permanent Central Opium Board to utilize, when required, such supervisory or enforcement measures as requests for information, proposal of remedial measures, local inquiries, or the imposition of an opium embargo. Fifteen states by the end of 1955, adhered to this Protocol, and ten more adherences, including two from states authorized to export opium were needed before it would enter into force.

In 1955, the Commission considered and approved, with amendments, a guide or code to assist parties in applying the provisions of the Protocol, which had been prepared by C. Vaille (France).

Another legislative task of the policy-making organs has been the codification of the nine existing narcotics treaties into a "Single Convention". As early as 1946, it had been proposed that measures be taken to remedy the great complexity of the provisions contained in the instruments which had accumulated over 34 years. In 1948, the Economic and Social Council invited the Secretary-General to prepare a draft convention to replace them. This was done, and at several sessions the Commission has considered the draft and made certain substantive modifications. At its tenth session (May 1955), the Commission requested the Secretariat to prepare a new text, incorporating its decisions and to examine the revised text before submitting it to governments for observations. This new text is now in preparation and may be ready for the Commission's eleventh session.

Besides uniting in one instrument the existing provisions, the Single Convention, as revised by the Commission, would contain the following new measures: (1) application of controls similar to those applied to opium, to poppy straw and the coca leaf, and prohibition of the production and use of cannabis, except for scientific purposes; (2) amalgamation of the Permanent Central Opium Board and Drug Supervisory Body; (3) provision that Parties "undertake to use their best endeavors" to provide medical treatment, care and rehabilitation of drug addicts "on a planned and compulsory basis", where the seriousness of the problem and their economic resources warrant it; and (4) recommendation that Parties prohibit, even for medical use, certain specifically dangerous drugs.

IMPLEMENTATION OF TREATIES

In its annual review of the functioning of the control system, the Commission on Narcotic Drugs relies heavily on information furnished by the Parties to the Secretary-General and to the Permanent Central Opium Board and Drug Supervisory Body. These data include: (a) *estimates of narcotics* needed for medical and scientific purposes forwarded to the Permanent Central Opium Board and published annually in the December of the year preceding that to which they relate (*Estimated World Requirements of Drugs);* (b) *statistics* on production and manufacture of, international trade in, and consumption of, narcotics forwarded to the Permanent Central Opium Board and published annually in the December of the year following that to which they relate (*Report to the Economic and Social Council on the Work of the Board);* (c) *annual reports* prepared in accordance with a form drafted by the Commission and forwarded to the Secretary-General in two instalments in March (data on illicit traffic) and in June (other data) of the year following that to which they relate; the data on illicit traffic being published in full and most data appearing in an annual summary prepared by the Secretariat (*Summary of Annual Reports);* (d) *reports on important cases of illicit traffic* having international significance, forwarded to the Secretary-General and summarized and published by the Secretariat on a bi-monthly basis (*Summary of Illicit Transactions and Seizures*); (e) *texts of laws and regulations* relating to the control of narcotic drugs forwarded to the Secretary-General and published in full and which are also summarized by the Secretariat once a year (*Annual Summary of Laws and Regulations Relating to the Control of Narcotic Drugs);* (f) lists of names and addresses of *persons or firms authorized to manufacture narcotic drugs* and of the drugs to be manufactured forwarded to the Secretary-General and published at irregular intervals; (g) *information on national authorities* empowered to issue certificates and authorizations for the import or export of narcotics requested and published at irregular intervals by the Secretary-General.

SUPPRESSION OF THE ILLICIT TRAFFIC IN NARCOTIC DRUGS

In the Commission, members seek to uncover the channels utilized for illicit traffic and to devise and strengthen methods of combating it. During its last two sessions the Commission set up a Committee on Seizures composed of representatives especially concerned in this problem, and in 1955 decided that the Committee should meet every year for three days in advance of the Commission's annual session.

The importance of the illicit traffic has risen in proportion to the growing effectiveness of controls over the licit channels along which narcotics move for medical and scientific purposes. The Commission and its Committee review the situation on the basis of the data in the annual reports and seizure reports of governments, the information made available by the International Criminal Police Commission, and the statements on national situations made by representatives and observers. Decisions such as the following were taken in 1955: to bring to the attention of the Portuguese Government the traffic in heroin from Macao to Hong Kong, to notify the Governments of Bolivia and Ecuador of the possibility that the illicit manufacture of crude cocaine has been increasing, to record concern at the situation in Lebanon, to draw the attention of governments to the increasing use of airlines by traffickers travelling as passengers, and to stress the importance of providing adequate penalties for traffickers.

THE PROBLEM OF THE COCA LEAF

In 1949, at the request of the Governments of Bolivia and Peru, a special Commission of Inquiry visited those countries to study the effects of the chewing of the coca leaf on the inhabitants and to investigate the possibility of limiting production. The Commission found that the chewing of the leaves was harmful and proposed that it be gradually suppressed. This approach having been accepted by the South American Governments most directly concerned, the Economic and Social Council recommended in 1954 that the technical assistance services should give due consideration to any requests from these countries for assistance in developing appropriate administrative or social measures for the gradual suppression of the habit and urged these Governments to limit as quickly as practicable the cultivation and export of the coca leaf to legitimate purposes and to abolish progressively the coca-chewing habit.

RESEARCH

The policy-making organs have established research programs as the most practical way of tackling various other problems.

These include a program to determine the geographical origin of opium by scientific means and thereby to throw further light on the channels utilized by traffickers and on the short-comings of present control measures. The Economic and Social Council established this program in 1948 and 1949, inviting governments to nominate participating scientists (there were 39 by the end of 1955) and to furnish opium samples (24 governments have done so). The Secretariat participates in this work as a coordinating agency for the distribution of samples and for the dissemination of findings; it also conducts its own laboratory research (for seven years in facilities made available by the United States Government in New York and soon in a new Laboratory being constructed in the *Palais des Nations*, Geneva). For several years, the question of utilizing the methods for practical purposes has been under consideration, and in 1955 the Commission decided to request governments to send important current seizures of opium in the international illicit traffic to the Secretariat for "investigation of origin", and to authorize the Secretary-General to arrange for such investigations and to report on determinations of origin reached to the governments concerned.

In 1953, a research program was undertaken jointly by WHO and the United Nations to deal with fundamental control problems arising from the development of the synthetic narcotics. Two reports on this work have already appeared under the title of "Synthetic Substances with Morphine-Like Effects". The first dealt with "chemical aspects", while the second was entitled " Relationship between Chemical Structure and Analgesic Action". Two further reports on the relationship between analgesic action and addiction liability, with a discussion of the chemical structure of addiction-producing substances and on clinical experiences with morphine-like analgesics were planned. This work would facilitate the identification of new drugs as addiction-producing and thereby their prompt submission to national and international control measures.

Special attention has been directed to two other basic problems—cannabis (Indian hemp) and remedial aspects of drug addiction—since 1953 and 1954 respectively.

Cannabis, known under a variety of names and forms such as marihuana, hashish, takrouri, etc., has been less rigidly controlled on the international level than other narcotics. Its illicit consumption has been steadily increasing and widening. In order to learn what measures would best fit this situation, the Commission asked the Secretariat to study the following aspects of the problem in representative countries and territories: the licit and illicit cultivation of the cannabis plant and its wild growth; the production of hemp fibre and hempseed from the cannabis plant; the legal production of cannabis, cannabis resin, etc., and the purposes for which they are used; the international trade in these substances; the manufacture of medicines from cannabis and their role in present-day medicine; the legal nonmedical consumption of cannabis in countries where this is still authorized; the illicit traffic in cannabis; and the legal aspects of controlling cannabis. A number of surveys along these lines have been prepared (for Brazil, Union of South Africa, Basutoland, Bechuanaland, Northern and Southern Rhodesia and Swaziland) and surveys for other countries were in preparation. In 1954, the Economic and Social Council requested FAO to study with the United Nations Secretariat the possibility of replacing the cannabis plant, as a source of fibre and oilbearing seeds, by a narcotic-free plant serving the same industrial purposes. This joint study drew attention to the possibility either of breeding a narcotic-free variety of the cannabis plant or of replacing it, where circumstances were favorable, by other fibrous plants. Experimental breeding work was being conducted in the Federal Republic of Germany and the United States, and the joint study would be reviewed by the Commission at its next session.

The elimination or reduction of drug addiction is, of course, the *raison d'etre* of narcotics control. In addition to the many indirect methods of attacking it already mentioned, a program to discover its causes and to study the methods of treating addicts and of restoring them to society was being pursued. The Commission requested the Secretariat to study such questions as: the classification and reporting of addicts; the treatment of addicts (compulsory or non-compulsory, insitutional or non-institutional); after-care and rehabilitation; financial aspects of curing addiction; treatment of addicts in penal law; and the role of education and propaganda in deterring addiction.

Population Questions

DETERMINANTS AND CONSEQUENCES OF POPULATION TRENDS

The English edition of the report on the inter-relationships of demographic, economic and social factors entitled "The Determinants and Consequences of Population Trends," was printed early in 1954. Translation into French has been completed, and a Spanish translation was also planned. A short, non-technical summary of certain aspects of the report was issued in 1954 under the title "Population Growth and Standards of Living in Under-developed Countries". A committee of experts appointed by the Secretary-General met during 1953 and prepared a report on gaps in the present knowledge of the inter-relationships of demographic, economic and social factors.

POPULATION PROBLEMS OF UNDER-DEVELOPED COUNTRIES

The majority of findings of existing studies relate to more or less industrialized countries. To help overcome the difficulty arising from the lack of adequate data and research relating to less developed countries a pilot field study was carried out jointly with the Government of India in Mysore State, on the relationships between population changes and economic and social factors. Tabulation and analysis of the data have been completed and a draft report prepared. It consists of two main parts, one relating to an analysis of the survey results and the other to the methodological aspects. The draft report has been distributed among Indian Government officials and other qualified experts for their comments and criticism. After revising the various chapters on the basis of the observations and suggestions received, the final report was expected to be ready for printing early in 1956.

For the historical study of population trends and social and economic factors in India as a whole, considerable data relating to irrigation, famines, rail and road communications, industrial development and urbanization have been collected, as well as information on limitation of the data owing to changes of definitions or methods of collection or to differences in geographic coverage. An analytical report on this study was to be published at a later date.

MORTALITY, FERTILITY AND MIGRATION STUDIES

In an effort to throw more light on the problem of studying mortality in relation to economic and social factors, particularly as regard infant mortality, the Secretary-General has prepared in cooperation with WHO a monograph entitled "Foetal, Infant and Early Childhood Mortality". The two volumes of this report, one dealing with "Statistics" and the other with "Biological, Social and Economic Factors", have been published in English and in French in 1954. The methodological aspects in measuring infant mortality are discussed in a report entitled "The Measurement of Infant Mortality" which together with two accompanying commentaries were published in "Population Bulletin of the United Nations" No. 3.

Because large segments of the world's populations are not as yet covered with adequate mortality statistics, the Secretary-General has undertaken an analysis of the existing life table mortality rates by sex and age groups in an effort to determine whether a pattern of mortality can be found which will be generally applicable to the populations for which adequate mortality data are lacking. A report entitled "Age and Sex Patterns of Mortality—Model Life Tables for Under-developed Countries" which gives patterns of transition from high to low mortality levels has been prepared and was to be published shortly in English and in French.

In the field of fertility the Secretary-General is carrying out an extensive study on recent birth rate trends with the aim to determine the extent to which the recent increases in the birth rate in most countries of Europe, North America and Oceania, reflect actual changes in fertility patterns. Some of the findings in this study were briefly outlined in a paper "Recent Fertility Trends in Countries with Low Fertility" presented to the World Population Conference. The full report was scheduled for publication during the first part of 1956. Another study dealing with a survey and evaluation of vital statistics and census data that are available for analysis of fertility patterns in British West Indies was under preparation and it was expected to be made ready for publication in the near future.

In the field of migration the Secretary-General has prepared reports on "Sex and Age of international migrants. Statistics for 1918-1947", "International Research on Migration", and "Elements of Immigration Policy". One report on "Bibliography of Sources of Migration Statistics" was to be available soon for circulation. Two other papers on migration prepared by the Secretariat for the World Population Conference are "A Survey of Inter-Continental Migration in the Post-War Period" and "Effects of recent and possible future migration on the population of Argentina, Brazil, Italy and India".

AGE STRUCTURE, LABOR-SUPPLY AND THE AGING OF POPULATION

The changing levels in fertility and mortality produce different patterns of age and sex composition of the various populations with considerable bearing upon the problems of labor supply, employment and unemployment and the aging of populations. Using the data from the 1950-51 censuses of population, the Secretary-General in collaboration with the ILO has undertaken a study of age-structure and potential labor supply, the relative size of the active and dependent groups in the population and the patterns of labor force participation by age groups in countries at different levels of economic development. This analysis is expected to provide a basis for preparing estimates of labor supply for countries in the process of economic development. Preliminary results of this study have been presented to the World Population Conference under the titles: "A Comparison of Recent Census Statistics on the Economically Active Population", and "Age Structure and Labor Supply". A more comprehensive report was expected to be completed in 1956.

The report on the aging of populations and its economic and social implications has been completed and would shortly be published. Topics included in this study were: definitions of aging, its demographic causes, economic aspects and social implications, and future trends of aging in both economically developed and under-developed areas of the world. Preliminary results of this study have been given in a paper of the World Population Conference: "Aging of Population; future trends" and in an article "The Cause of the Aging of Populations: declining mortality or declining fertility?" published in the Population Bulletin No. 4.

POPULATION ESTIMATES AND FORECASTS

The work on population estimates, projection and forecasts continues in the Population Branch of the United Nations. Four relevant papers were prepared by the Secretariat for the World Population Conference under the titles: "Some attempts to measure the accuracy of international population statistics", "Past and Future Population of the World and its Continents", "Framework for Future Population Estimates 1950-1980", and "Towards a General Methodology of Population Projections, by Sex and Age, for Countries with Only a Moderate Amount of Statistics". Future population estimates by sex and age for two geographic regions were published under the titles: "The Population of Central America (including Mexico), 1950-1980" and "The Population of South America 1950-1980".

In the series of manuals on methods of population estimates the first report entitled "Methods of Estimating Total Population of a Country for Current Dates" appeared in 1952. A second manual dealing with methods of appraising the accuracy of basic data for population estimates would shortly be published.

A handbook was under preparation which would present the methods developed by the United Nations for the purpose of estimating future populations in sufficient detail to enable the governments and other agencies in countries having only moderate amounts of statistical information to apply the same, or similar, methods. The handbook was to be published early in 1956.

OTHER PROSPECTS

A preliminary edition of a "Multilingual Demographic Dictionary" has been prepared with the cooperation of the International Union for the Scientific Study of Population in three languages, English, French and Spanish, and distributed to various experts for comments and observations. A revised final edition of the dictionary was to be published at a later date.

Considerable progress has been made in the plans for training programs in demographic techniques on an international level. A report under the title "Training in Techniques of Demographic Analysis" has been published, and two regional Demographic Seminars, one for the population of Asia and the Far East and the other for the Latin American countries, were to be held in Bandung, Indonesia, and in Rio de Janeiro, Brazil, respectively, during the months of November and December 1956. This might well lead to the establishment of a few permanent centers for demographic training and research, situated in strategic regional locations where the needs for such establishment are the greatest.

WORLD POPULATION CONFERENCE

The World Population Conference, which was held in Rome from August 31 to September 10, 1954, was a major scientific meeting attended by more than 450 experts from all parts of the world. Practically all the foremost students of population problems in every major country were present, and they were joined by a large number of leading experts in such fields as economics, sociology, anthropology, genetics, medicine and public health, social welfare statistics, and the physical sciences relevant to the conservation and development of natural resources.

The purpose of the Conference, as stated in the resolution of the Economic and Social Council, was solely an exchange of views and experience among experts and, consequently, the Conference adopted no resolutions or recommendations for action of any kind. The papers presented for the occasion and the discussions during the Conference, however, did much to clarify the scientific basis for policy decisions and actions concerning population trends on the part of public bodies both at the national and the international level.

International Cooperation on Cartography

The Economic and Social Council at its sixth session in 1948 recognized that the application of cartography to many problems that confront governments, the United Nations and the specialized agencies can speed economic and social development, reduce its cost and increase its effectiveness. In many instances, information necessary to the planning and prosecution of development programs can be supplied most accurately by reliable maps. Adequate information is lacking for approximately three quarters of the world's land area.

To assist the governments in developing their cartographic work, the Council studied the question of calling regional conferences dealing with cartographic questions and, as a first step, convened a United Nations Regional Cartographic Conference for Asia and the Far East, which was held at Mussoorie, India, from February 15 to 25, 1955, and was attended by representatives of eighteen countries and by observers from two specialized agencies and three international organizations. The consideration of the various items, both general and technical, together with the resolutions adopted, are contained in the report of the Conference. One of the most significant recommendations was that, in view of the value of the Conference deliberations to the countries of the region, a second such Conference for the region was to be held not later than 1958.

Furthermore, under the Council's instruction, the Secretary-General has set up a Cartographic Office to serve as a Center for the international exchange of technical information, including the publication of a periodical cartographic bulletin entitled *World Cartography*. Four volumes of this bulletin have been issued since 1951, and Volume V, covering the year 1955, was in preparation. Under further Council instructions, the Office took over the functions of the Central Bureau, International Map of the World on the Millionth Scale, which consists mainly of assistance to interested governments in coordinating the publication of the sheets of the Map, and in exchanging information relating to the Map. Working relationships with the national cartographic agencies in charge of this project have been strengthened and consultations were held with them regarding the preparation of the amendments to the existing specifications of the Map.

At the request of the Council, the Secretary-General consulted with governments on the question of the adoption of a standard method of writing geographical names on maps, and an interim report, containing the comments and proposals received from 22 governments and three specialized agencies, was submitted to the above-mentioned United Nations Regional Cartographic Conference which recommended the United Nations to set up a Committee of Experts to draw up the general framework of a program looking toward maximum uniformity in this field.

QUESTIONS CONCERNING NON-SELF-GOVERNING TERRITORIES

Committee on Information from Non-Self-Governing Territories

Under Article 73e of the Charter, Administering Members of the United Nations undertook to transmit regularly to the Secretary-General "statistical and other information of a technical nature relating to economic, social and educational conditions in the territories for which they are respectively responsible. . . ." Such information, after being summarized and analyzed by the Secretariat, is studied by a committee appointed by the General Assembly. This committee, known as the Committee on Information from Non-Self-Governing Territories, may make specific recommendations to the General Assembly, designed to speed the progress of dependent peoples toward self-government and independence.

The composition of the Committee on Information from Non-Self-Governing Territories in January 1956 was as follows: Australia, Belgium, France, the Netherlands, New Zealand, the United Kingdom and the United States (administering members); and Burma, China, Guatemala, India, Iraq, Peru and Venezuela (non-administering members). In 1955, information on 58 territories was submitted to the Secretary-General.

The first committee set up by the General Assembly to deal with this question was an *ad hoc* body for 1947. This *ad hoc* body was subsequently replaced by a Special Committee on Information from Non-Self-Governing Terrritories which first met in 1948. The Assembly asked this organ to examine the information transmitted on economic, social and educational conditions in the Non-Self-Governing Territories, and to report back to the Assembly. This Special Committee met again in 1949, at which time the Assembly decided to appoint a new committee for a further three-year term. This organ, with somewhat broader terms of reference, met in 1950, 1951 and 1952. It was, for example, charged with examining the relevant factors in deciding at what stage dependency ends and self-government begins. In addition to examining the information submitted and any relevant studies made by the specialized agencies, the committee was to consider data concerning measures taken to carry out previous Assembly recommendations on economic, social and educational conditions in the territories.

From 1949 onwards, the committees have been constituted so as to include an equal number of members transmitting information under Article 73e, and of non-administering members elected by the Assembly on as wide a geographical basis as possible.

Scope of Information Transmitted

In cases where administrative practices would permit, the Assembly in November 1948 asked Members to supply the required information six months after the end of the administrative year in each territory.

The information received during 1947 was analyzed, summarized and classified by the Secretariat under the headings of labor, public health and agriculture. Although agreeing with the methods followed by the Secretariat, the Committee urged that the analyses be expanded to cover general economic conditions; living standards of the local, European and other groups; birth and death rates; and information on the part played by the indigenous population in local government. The Assembly accordingly asked that the information transmitted be as complete as possible, and approved a Standard Form to guide the administering powers.

This form contains an optional section on geography, history, government, population statistics and civil rights in non-self-governing territories, and mandatory sections on social, educational and economic conditions. Some Members voluntarily transmitted information under the optional section in 1946 and 1947, including information on the government of the territories they administer.

When in 1949, the Committee on Information was first established on a three-year basis, the General Assembly resolved that each year it should devote particular attention to one of the three major subjects within its terms of reference. Following this plan, a report was first adopted by the Committee on educational conditions in the dependent areas. This was followed the next year by a report on economic conditions and, in the third year, one on social conditions. Further reports on each of these subjects were compiled for the Assembly's consideration in 1953, 1954 and 1955. Thus, by May 1955, the Committee on Information had completed its second cycle of discussions of economic, social and educational conditions in the dependent territories. (*See below for various recommendations.*)

Constitutional Changes in Territories

The question of constitutional changes and political developments in the territories, and the competence of the United Nations to consider such developments, has arisen on a number of occasions in both the Committee on Information's debates and in the General Assembly. The latter in November 1948 endorsed a recommendation which welcomed any development towards self-government in a territory, but at the same time considered it essential that the United Nations be informed of any changes as a result of which an Administering Member thought it unnecessary to transmit further information. The Members concerned were asked to send the Secretary-General full information on such changes, including the constitution, legislative act or executive order establishing the government of the territory, and the constitutional relationship of the territorial government to the metropolitan country.

Explanatory statements received from France, the United Kingdom and the United States were considered by the 1949 Committee, which decided that under its terms of reference, it was not competent to consider questions of definition. It later referred the question to the General Assembly, where certain of the Administering Members maintained that they alone were competent to decide whether or not the peoples of a territory had attained full autonomy. The Assembly declared that it could express its opinion on the principles which should guide Members in determining the territories on which they were obliged to transmit information. In 1949, the Committee's recommendations and the resolutions of the General Assembly on Non-Self-Governing Territories took a more concrete form. Thus, the Assembly invited Administering Members to give equal treatment in education to all inhabitants, and, if separate educational facilities were provided for different communities, to give full data on their costs and methods of financing.

The Assembly also invited the Administering Members to promote the use of the indigenous languages and suggested that, wherever possible, teaching in the elementary, primary and secondary schools should be in these languages. The Members concerned were asked to inform the Secretary-General on the action taken and the results achieved.

The Assembly emphasized the importance of promoting the technical training of the inhabitants of Non-Self-Governing Territories and asked Administering States to cooperate with specialized international bodies to see if it were possible to provide adequate training facilities in economic development, agriculture, education, labor, public health and social welfare. It also asked the appropriate specialized agencies to take account of conditions in the territories in their work in such specific fields as economic development, study of soil erosion, training of public health personnel, study of nutrition problems, application of international labor conventions, migrant labor in Africa, development of social welfare services, and the question of improving tropical housing.

In any activities affecting Non-Self-Governing Territories, the specialized agencies concerned were asked to take account of the relevant experiences of various states. The Secretary-General was asked to collaborate with the agencies, bringing

to their attention comments made in the Committee regarding agriculture, education, labor, public health and social welfare.

Assembly's 1950-51 Recommendations

In 1950 and 1951, the General Assembly endorsed a series of recommendations
concerning Non-Self-Governing Territories, touching on such issues as increased
technical aid for the dependent areas, closer participation of the territories in the
work of the Committee on Information, and the factors to be taken into account
when deciding whether a territory has or has not reached a full measure of self-
government.

At its fifth session in 1950, the Assembly invited the governments of the Administering States to submit, on behalf of the territories, requests for technical assistance
under the United Nations Expanded Program. It recommended that Administering
Governments transmit as full a report as possible on such applications, including
information on the manner in which assistance granted was integrated into long-
range plans for development. Referring to the equal applicability of the Declaration
of Human Rights and the proposed Covenant on Human Rights to Non-Self-Governing Territories and sovereign states alike, the Assembly requested Administering
Governments to report on the extent to which the Declaration was implemented in
their respective territories. With the consent of the Member concerned, the Secretary-General was authorized to make use of comparable statistical information on a
regional basis, taking into account all elements necessary for scientific and objective
comparison. The Assembly noted the cessation of information by the Netherlands
concerning Indonesia, which became an independent, sovereign State in 1950.

At its sixth session in 1951, the Assembly endorsed the past work of the Committee and its work program for 1952. A proposal on the Committee's title also was
adopted unanimously. This considered the Committee's original title too long and
"not conducive to the broadest dissemination of knowledge of the important work
being done by the Committee." The Assembly therefore decided that the Committee would henceforth be known as "Committee on Information from Non-Self-
Governing Territories."

The Assembly also endorsed the Committee's report on economic conditions and
problems of economic development in Non-Self-Governing Areas. The Secretary-
General was asked to transmit the report, for their consideration, to Administering
Members, the Economic and Social Council, the Trusteeship Council, and the
specialized agencies concerned.

Another resolution invited the Committee to examine the possibility of associating the territories "more closely in its work", and to report on its findings to
the Assembly.

Measures for studying the factors to be taken into account in deciding whether a
territory is one whose people have or have not yet attained a full measure of self-
government was the subject of another proposal. This invited Member States to
transmit to the Secretary-General a statement of their governments' views on the
factors to be considered in this connection. The Assembly also appointed a ten-
member committee to carry out a further study of the factors, taking into account
all available information. A resolution noting the cessation of the transmission of
information on the Netherlands Antilles and Surinam took into account steps taken
by the Netherlands for the establishment of "a new constitutional order to replace
the present interim arrangement" regarding the Netherlands Antilles and Surinam.
(*See page 267.*) The Assembly reaffirmed a statement contained in its resolution

222 (III) welcoming any development of self-government which might have taken place in territories previously styled as non-self-governing.

Finally, the Assembly adopted a proposal concerning the revision of the Standard Form for the guidance of Members, in connection with information from Non-Self-Governing Territories.

Committee Renewed in 1952

In 1952, the General Assembly again considered the question of the future of the Committee on Information, whose three-year term was then due to expire. The Committee itself recommended its renewal for another three years. Assembly debate found a majority of Members favoring the continuance of the Committee, but divergent views arose regarding the period for which the organ should be prolonged. Several representatives contended that the Committee, having proved its value to the Assembly, should henceforward function on a permanent basis. All proposals of permanence were opposed by the Administering Members. The Fourth Committee subsequently recommended that the Committee on Information, after a further three-year term, should continue for as long as there exist territories whose people have not yet reached full self-government. The Assembly, in plenary action, failed to endorse this proposal and adopted a modified resolution. This recognized the valuable work done so far by the Committee on Information, and resolved to continue the organ for another three years until 1955 (see 1955 proposals).

Another Assembly resolution expressed the view that participation of qualified indigenous representatives in the work of the Committee on Information was desirable. Accordingly, the Assembly invited the Administering Members to make such participation possible. The Administering Members argued that the proposal implied dual representation of states on the Assembly's committees which, they maintained, should remain associations of sovereign and responsible governments. The Administering Members also opposed a provision which invited the Administering States to furnish executive and legislative organs in the territories with the special reports prepared annually by the Committee on Information, together with all relevant resolutions of the General Assembly. A third provision was that, after further study of the question, the Committee on Information should recommend ways for the direct participation in its discussions by local representatives from those territories which have attained a wide measure of responsibility for economic, social and educational policies, and report on its findings to the eighth Assembly session.

Another 1952 Assembly resolution called for the abolition of all laws and practices of racial discrimination in the Non-Self-Governing Territories. The Administering Members were asked to examine all such laws with the aim of abolishing discriminatory practices, or provisions of a racial or religious character. The proposal recommended that all public facilities should be open to all inhabitants of the territories, without discrimination of race, and that laws should be examined frequently to ascertain whether their protective aspect was still predominant, and whether provision should be made for special exemptions. The Assembly commended all measures designed to improve community understanding among students of the needs and problems of the community as a whole, and called the attention of the Commission on Human Rights to its resolution.

Factors for Deciding Measures of Autonomy

The General Assembly has expressed concern that when information on a territory is discontinued by the Administering Member State the people of that territory should have attained the goals set forth in Chapter XI of the Charter, and particularly a "full measure of self-government". The Assembly consequently adopted certain criteria to be used as a guide in deciding in each individual case whether such a stage has actually been reached. These criteria, endorsed by the Assembly in November 1953, after a two years' study by special committees, are known as "the factors which should be taken into account in deciding whether a territory is, or is not, a territory whose people have not yet attained a full measure of self-government." The Assembly's resolution on factors reasserted that each concrete case should be considered and decided upon in the light of its particular circumstances, taking into account the right of self-determination of peoples. The Committee on Information from Non-Self-Governing Territories was asked to take the initiative in proposing modifications as might seem necessary in the light of circumstances, at any time to the list of factors.

Assembly's 1953 Recommendations

At its eighth session in 1953, the Assembly endorsed a report surveying educational conditions in the dependent territories. In a resolution on educational problems in the territories, the Assembly recommended that the Administering Members should seek the technical advice of the United Nations Technical Assistance Administration, and make the greatest possible use of the facilities of the specialized agencies. The Assembly recommended also that the Administering Members make the greatest possible use of offers by other Members for furthering educational advancement in the Non-Self-Governing Territories through fellowships, scholarships and internships to qualified students from the territories, and invited the Secretary-General to communicate the report on education, as well as the resolution, to the Administering Members, the Economic and Social Council, the Trusteeship Council, and to the specialized agencies concerned.

In another 1953 recommendation, the Assembly again referred to the question of indigenous participation in United Nations work concerning dependent territories. On this subject, the Assembly invited the Administering Members with territories whose inhabitants have attained a larger measure of responsibility for economic, social and educational policies to attach to their delegations indigenous representatives specially qualified to speak on these matters as they relate to the territories. The Assembly also requested the Committee on Information from Non-Self-Governing Territories to continue to study means of securing a progressive increase in the participation of duly qualified representatives of peoples of the Non-Self-Governing Territories in its work.

In a companion resolution, the Assembly expressed hope that those Members, who have not hitherto found it possible to do so, would find it appropriate to associate with their delegations persons specially qualified in the functional fields within the Committee's purview.

The Assembly also recommended that the Secretary-General consider the desirability of continuing and increasing the recruitment of suitably qualified inhabitants of Non-Self-Governing and Trust Territories for the United Nations Secretariat, and invited the Secretary-General to draw the attention of the specialized agencies to this resolution with a view to a similar policy being followed as far as possible by those agencies.

The Assembly at its eighth session also took action on the changed status of Puerto Rico. It recognized that the people of Puerto Rico had attained a new constitutional status by democratic means, that the association between the Commonwealth of Puerto Rico and the United States had been established as a mutually agreed association, that the Puerto Ricans effectively exercised their right to self-determination, and that the territory had clearly become an autonomous political entity. The Assembly considered that "due to these circumstances the declaration regarding Non-Self-Governing Territories and the provisions established under it in Chapter XI of the Charter can no longer be applied to the Commonwealth of Puerto Rico."

Assembly's 1954 Recommendations

The voluntary transmission of information concerning political developments in the Non-Self-Governing Territories was the subject of a recommendation endorsed by the General Assembly in 1954. Under Article 73e of Chapter XI of the Charter, the Administering States agreed to transmit regularly to the United Nations "statistical and other information of a technical nature relating to economic, social and educational conditions in the territories for which they are respectively responsible. . . ." The interpretation of this Chapter has proved to be a controversial issue at several sessions of the General Assembly. The issue was again considered by the Assembly at its ninth session, when it endorsed two proposals on the subject.

One of these appealed to the Administering Members to submit information voluntarily on political developments in the territories for which they are responsible.

The resolution recalled earlier proposals adopted by the Assembly on this question and noted, with satisfaction, that some Administering Members had already voluntarily transmitted information on the development of self-governing institutions in the dependent territories. The Assembly noted, however, that other Administering Members had not yet transmitted such information. The resolution also invited the Administering Members to give the United Nations "their utmost cooperation" in this matter.

A closely allied resolution proposed that United Nations visiting missions should, with the agreement of the Administering Member concerned, tour dependent territories before any change in their political status took place, in order to ascertain the aspirations of the indigenous peoples.

The Assembly considered that the Committee on Information from Non-Self-Governing Territories might study means by which it could, at the appropriate time, draw the Assembly's attention to forthcoming changes in the status of the territory concerned. The Committee on Information was invited to include in its annual report to the Assembly any proposals which it deemed desirable concerning the implementation of this resolution.

GREENLAND'S CHANGED STATUS

A noteworthy feature of the 1954 Assembly's review of issues concerning dependent peoples was formal recognition that one of the oldest of all dependent territories had become fully self-governing and need no longer be the subject of information to the United Nations. This was Greenland—a Nordic dominion since early Viking days—whose people had, as the Assembly agreed, freely exercised the right of self-determination and decided upon integration with Denmark, under whose administration they had been.

Denmark had previously informed the United Nations of the constitutional change in Greenland's position. Denmark stated that Greenland had become an integral part of the Danish Realm on June 5, 1953, with rights corresponding to those of other parts of Denmark. Accordingly, Denmark considered it was no longer obliged to submit, under Article 73e of the Charter, further information on the territory.

The territory's new status was brought to the Assembly's attention by Hermod Lannung, of Denmark, who attributed the maturity of the territory to the fact that Denmark had spent much more on each individual Greenlander—man, woman and child—than on each person in Denmark.

Three other 1954 Assembly proposals on Non-Self-Governing Territories concerned educational advancement in such territories, the work of the Committee on Information and the submission of information common to regional groups of dependent territories. On the latter question, the Assembly recognized that conditions in the various regions, and in particular territories, might present special problems. It therefore asked the Committee on Information to study, at its 1955 session, the manner in which its future reports to the Assembly might "most appropriately" be directed to the consideration of data or recommendations concerning the special problems of regional groups of territories.

Assembly's 1955 Recommendations

At its tenth session in 1955, the General Assembly resolved that a comprehensive review of the progress achieved in the Non-Self-Governing Territories since the establishment of the United Nations was "highly desirable", and that such a survey should make it possible to ascertain the extent to which the peoples of the dependent territories were advancing towards the attainment of the goals set in Chapter XI of the Charter. A resolution to this effect considered that such an examination would require careful preparation with the assistance of the specialized agencies concerned. It invited the Secretary-General, after consultation with the specialized agencies concerned, to submit to the General Assembly, for consideration at its eleventh session, in 1956, a report on the main points that might be useful in such an examination.

RENEWAL OF COMMITTEE ON SAME BASIS

Action concerning the continuation of the Committee on Information from Non-Self-Governing Territories was taken by the Assembly at its 1955 session. The Assembly recommended that the Committee should be renewed on the same basis for a further term of three years. It also recommended that the Committee should comprise the Members transmitting information under Article 73e of the Charter, and an equal number of non-administering Members elected by the Fourth Committee on behalf of the General Assembly.

The Assembly further instructed the Commitee to examine the summaries and analyses of the information transmitted, and to submit regularly to the Assembly a report with such substantive recommendations as it might consider desirable, relating to functional fields generally, but not with respect to individual territories. It was recommended that the Committee should, without prejudice to the annual consideration of all the functional fields enumerated in Article 73e of the Charter, give special attention to educational, economic and social conditions, in turn, and should consider the information transmitted in respect of these questions in the light of the reports approved by the General Assembly on such conditions in the territories.

The resolution asked the General Assembly at its regular session in 1958 to reconsider the question of continuing the Committee on Information from Non-Self-Governing Territories, together with the questions of the composition and terms of reference of this or any such future committee. Administering Members were again invited to attach to their delegations indigenous persons specially qualified to speak on economic, social and educational policies in the territories.

The Fourth Committee, on behalf of the Assembly, elected India, Iraq, Venezuela and China to fill the vacancies on the Committee on Information. As a result, the composition of the Committee beginning January 1, 1956, was: Australia, Belgium, France, the Netherlands, New Zealand, the United Kingdom and the United States (administering members); and Burma, China, Guatemala, India, Iraq, Peru and Venezuela (non-administering members).

REPORT ON SOCIAL CONDITIONS

The 1955 report of the Committee on Information was primarily concerned with social conditions in the Non-Self-Governing Territories. A survey of community development and similar movements designed to promote better living standards by stimulating the active participation of the whole community, figured among the report's important passages. A second major section dealt with race relations in the territories. While confirming general condemnations of racial discrimination, the report emphasized the development of positive programs for collaboration in public affairs among all groups. Public health, nutrition and labor issues were among other topics. The Assembly endorsed this report on special conditions.

As adopted, the Assembly's recommendation invited the Secretary-General to communicate the report, for their consideration, to the Administering Member States, the Economic and Social Council, the Trusteeship Council, and the specialized agencies concerned. The resolution expressed satisfaction at the increased cooperation between the Administering Members and the international bodies concerned, and requested the latter in the work undertaken by them to take full account of the views expressed in the report on social conditions in Non-Self-Governing Territories.

The attention of the specialized agencies concerned was drawn to the sections of the report dealing with labor, race relations, nutrition and public health.

It was also hoped that the collaboration between the Secretary-General and the specialized agencies, and between the Administering Members and the international bodies concerned, would be maintained and extended in the interest of the co-ordinated development of the Non-Self-Governing Territories in all fields.

Two other Assembly resolutions concerned information on community development in the dependent territories, and educational advancement in those areas. On the first question, the Assembly invited the Administering Member States to render as complete and up-to-date information as possible on programs and progress in community development in the territories. For this purpose, the Members were asked to take into account a modification in the Standard Form which serves as a guide to Members in the transmission of information. The resolution on educational advancement noted a progress report submitted by the Secretary-General on the offers of scholarships and training facilities made by Members for students of Non-Self-Governing Territories under Assembly resolution 845 (IX) of November 22, 1954. It invited the Secretary-General to continue to furnish an annual report on such offers, and the extent to which they had been made use of.

SURINAM AND THE NETHERLANDS ANTILLES

The attainment of autonomy by two former dependent territories in the Western Hemisphere—Surinam and the Netherlands Antilles—was the subject of another 1955 Assembly resolution. In a proposal relating to the cessation of the transmission of information under Article 73e, the Assembly resolved that it was no longer necessary for the Netherlands, as the Administering Member nation involved, to transmit information under Article 73e on these two territories. In April 1955, the

Netherlands informed the Committee on Information that, under a new consitutional status of the Kingdom of the Netherlands, resulting from a Round-Table Conference at The Hague in 1954, its former colonies, Surinam and the Netherlands Antilles, had become equal partners with the Netherlands itself.

In its preamble, the resolution recalled a 1948 resolution whereby the Assembly, while welcoming any development of self-government in Non-Self-Governing Territories, considered it essential that the United Nations be informed of changes in the constitutional status of any such territory as a result of which the responsible government concerned considered it unnecessary to transmit information under Article 73e.

The resolution also noted the communication by which the Government of the Netherlands transmitted to the Secretary-General the constitutional provisions embodied in the Charter for the Kingdom of the Netherlands, promulgated on December 29, 1954, together with an explanatory memorandum.

The resolution further noted the documentation submitted and the explanations provided that the peoples of Surinam and the Netherlands Antilles "have expressed, through their freely elected representative bodies, their approval of the new constitutional order, and also of the opinion of the Government of the Netherlands." Finally, the Assembly expressed the view that, "without prejudice to the position of the United Nations, as affirmed in General Assembly resolution 742 (VIII) adopted on November 27, 1953, and such provisions of the Charter of the United Nations as might be relevant, on the basis of the information before it, as presented by the Government of the Netherlands, and as desired by the Government of the Netherlands, the cessation of the transmission of information under Article 73e of the Charter in respect of Surinam and the Netherlands Antilles, is appropriate."

Territories on which Information has been Submitted

The Non-Self-Governing Territories on which Information was transmitted to the United Nations in 1955 were as follows, by geographical location: Central African Territories: Belgian Congo, French Equatorial Africa, Northern Rhodesia, Nyasaland; East African Territories: British Somaliland, French Somaliland, Kenya, Uganda, Zanzibar; South African Territories: Basutoland, Bechuanaland, Swaziland; Indian Ocean Territories: Comoro Archipelago, Madagascar, Mauritius, Seychelles; West African Territories: French West Africa, Gambia, Gold Coast, Nigeria, Sierra Leone; Mediterranean Territories: Cyprus, Gibraltar, Morocco, Tunisia; Caribbean Territories: Bahamas, Barbados, Bermuda, British Guiana, British Honduras, Jamaica, Leeward Islands, Trinidad and Tobago, Virgin Islands, Windward Islands; Asian Territories: Brunei, Federation of Malaya, Hong Kong, North Borneo, Sarawak, Singapore; Pacific Territories: American Samoa, Fiji, Gilbert and Ellice Islands, Guam, Hawaii, New Hebrides, Pitcairn Island, Solomon Islands, Netherlands New Guinea, Papua, Cook Islands, Niue Islands, Tokelau Islands; Other Territories: Aden, Alaska, Falkland Islands, St. Helena.

TRUSTEESHIP QUESTIONS

The Trust Territories

A basic objective of the International Trusteeship System, as defined in Chapter XII of the Charter, is to prepare the people of the territories for self-government or independence. Chapter XIII of the Charter defines the functions, powers and procedures of the Trusteeship Council, a principal organ of the United Nations, which supervises the administration of the eleven territories placed under Trusteeship, by considering reports, examining petitions and making periodic visits of inspection. Prior to the Second World War, these territories were administered as League of Nations Mandates. They are:

Cameroons, under British administration; Cameroons, under French administration; New Guinea, under Australian administration; Nauru, under Australian administration; Ruanda-Urundi, under Belgian administration; Tanganyika, under British administration; Togoland, under British administration; Togoland, under French administration; Western Samoa, under New Zealand administration; the Trust Territory of the Pacific Islands (Marianas, Marshalls, and Carolinas), under United States administration; and the Trust Territory of Somaliland, under Italian administration.

The former Italian colony of Somaliland was added to the list of territories placed under Trusteeship by a decision of the General Assembly in November 1949. It was placed under Trusteeship for a period of ten years, pending independence as a sovereign state. Italy was designated as the Administering Authority during this period, assisted by an Advisory Council comprising the representatives of Colombia, Egypt and the Philippines. At its sixth session in 1950, the Trusteeship Council compiled and approved a draft Trusteeship Agreement for Somaliland, and Italy assumed provisional administration of the territory on April 1, 1950. Seven months later the Assembly approved the draft Trusteeship Agreement and Somaliland formally came under Trusteeship until 1960.

Prior to 1955, Italy was not a member of the United Nations, but as the Administering Authority in Somaliland, it participated in the Trusteeship Council's work without the right to vote. At the Assembly's tenth session in 1955, Italy was admitted to United Nations membership, and consequently became a full member of the Trusteeship Council.

Composition of the Trusteeship Council

The Trusteeship Council regularly meets twice a year to examine the annual reports submitted on the territories by the Administering Authorities, and to carry out its other supervisory functions. The Council's composition was arranged by the authors of the Charter as a means of achieving a balance between the general responsibilities of all United Nations Members for the implementation of the Charter, and the particular and additional responsibilities which the Administering Authorities bear for the actual administration of the Trust Territories.

The Council is evenly divided between Administering Members on the one hand, and non-administering members on the other—at present seven of the former and seven of the latter. The membership of the Council changes partly from time to time. Each Administering Authority is entitled to a continuing seat; so are China and the U.S.S.R., because they are permanent members of the Security Council. The other five members are elected for three-year terms by the General Assembly. In January, 1956, the membership of the Council was as follows:

Administering members: Australia, Belgium, France, Italy, New Zealand, the United Kingdom and the United States.

Non-administering members: Burma, China, Guatemala, Haiti, India, Syria and the U.S.S.R.

Trusteeship Agreements

A Trusteeship Agreement contains the precise terms under which Trust Territories are to be administered, and must be agreed upon by the states directly concerned. Although the terms of the Agreements vary, they include most of the following provisions:

1. Definition of the territory to which the Agreement applies.

2. Designation of the Administering Authority.

3. Obligations of the Administering Authority: to so administer the territory as to achieve the basic principles of Trusteeship as contained in the Charter;

to be responsible for the peace, order, and good government of the territory and to insure that it plays its part in the maintenance of international peace and security;

to develop free political institutions and to give the inhabitants an increasing share in the government;

to protect native rights over land, and not to allow native land or natural resources to be transferred except with the previous consent of the competent public authority.

to insure equal treatment in social, economic, industrial and commercial matters for all United Nations Members and their nationals, provided that the interests of the territory's inhabitants come first;

to develop education;

subject only to requirements of public order, to guarantee to the inhabitants freedom of religion, worship, speech, press, assembly and petition.

4. Rights of the Administering Authority:

It is to have full powers of legislation, administration and jurisdiction in the territory. (Certain Agreements specify that it may administer the territory as an integral part of its own territory, subject to the provisions of the Charter and the Agreement.)

It may constitute the territory into a customs, fiscal or administrative union, or federation with adjacent territories under its control.

It may establish naval, military and air bases, erect fortifications, and take other measures necessary for defense, and may also use volunteer forces, facilities and assistance from the territory in carrying out obligations to the Security Council, and for local defense.

It may organize public services and works on conditions it thinks just.

It may create fiscal monopolies, if they serve the interests of the inhabitants, and other monopolies under conditions of proper control, provided that, in the case of monopolies granted to non-governmental agencies, there is no discrimination on the grounds of nationality.

It may arrange for the cooperation of the territory in regional organizations.

5. Amendments of the Agreements are to be in accordance with the terms of the Charter.

6. Any dispute between the Administering Authority and another United Nations Member on the interpretation or application of an Agreement, which cannot be settled otherwise, is to be submitted to the International Court of Justice.

Most of these provisions are included in the Strategic Area Agreement for the Trust Territory of the Pacific Islands, though in less detail than in the others. This Agreement also differs in certain other respects. The "most-favored-nation" treatment is reserved for the Administering Authority, and the extent to which the Trusteeship Council's powers and functions apply is made dependent on security requirements. The question of air-traffic rights is specifically reserved for separate agreements. The United States, as the Administering Authority, may from time to time close certain areas for security reasons. (The United States, for example, informed the Security Council on December 2, 1947, that Eniwetok Atoll, one of the islands in the territory, had been closed so that the United States might conduct nuclear fission experiments there.)

The Charter provides that the Trusteeship Council formulate a questionnaire, on the basis of which the Administering Authority for each Trust Territory is to submit an annual report to the Council. The Council provisionally adopted a draft questionnaire on April 25, 1947.

The Provisional Questionnaire contains detailed questions concerning the government of a Trust Territory, and the political, economic, social and educational advancement of its inhabitants. It was sent to each Administering Authority as the basis for the first annual report on each Trust Territory. The Administering Authorities have been invited to make suggestions for the improvement of the questionnaire, which will be adapted as necessary to each Trust Territory.

Examination of Annual Reports

One of the Trusteeship Council's main functions is to examine the annual reports submitted by the Administering Authorities presenting a comprehensive picture of the political, economic, social and educational progress in the Trust Territories. The procedure for examining these reports covers a number of distinct stages: (1) an opening statement by the Special Representative of the Administering Authority; (2) questions by Council members to the Special Representative for further explanation of points in the reports; (3) replies of the Special Representative; (4) general debate on the report, with expression of views and conclusions on the administration; (5) formulation of these views, conclusions and recommendations by a drafting committee of the Council; and (6) consideration and approval by the Council of the drafting committee's report. The Council then submits its own recommendations in its annual report to the General Assembly.

After examining administrative reports on the various territories, the Council has, in the course of its sixteen sessions, made a series of recommendations to the Administering Authorities. In general, it has proposed that the people of each territory should take an increasing share in the political, economic and social life of the territory and, in speeding its development, has urged that educational facilities should be further expanded. Its more specific recommendations have included: improved living standards and higher wages, more hospital and health services, better roads and industrial development, the abolition of corporal punishment and improvements in penal systems, greater participation of the indigenous inhabitants in economic and social spheres, and increased representation in local governments. In some cases, the Council has urged that more widespread measures be taken against racial discrimination, and has recommended increased technical and agricultural guidance.

Visiting Missions to Trust Territories

Another clause in the Charter's provisions concerning Trusteeship provides for the dispatch of periodic Visiting Missions to the territories—a step forward since the days of the Mandates System. As requested by the Council in 1947, the Assembly has appropriated the necessary funds for one annual Visiting Mission.

By January 1956, all the Trust Territories had been visited at least three times by missions sent out by the Trusteeship Council. A new series of visits were to commence in February 1956, with the dispatch of a mission to the Pacific Trust Territories (*see below*).

ORGANIZATION OF VISITING MISSIONS

The General Assembly in December 1950 pointed out that a second series of visits to Trust Territories, commencing in 1951, presented an opportunity of again reviewing possibilities of improving the organization and methods of functioning of the Missions. The Assembly asked the Trusteeship Council to take into account, among other matters, the advisability of: arranging for Visiting Missions to remain long enough in each territory to be able to fulfil their task adequately, reducing the number of territories to be visited by a single Mission, extending the duration of visits without diminishing their frequency, and selecting members for each Mission as much as possible from among representatives actually serving on the Council. At its eighth session, the Council established a committee to study the whole question.

After considering the Committee's report, the Council, at its ninth session decided that, in arranging for all future Visiting Missions, it would be guided by the principles set forth in the General Assembly's resolution 434(V), and would take into account the various observations made in the Committee's report. The Council also amended a draft statement to be used by the Missions in explaining the purpose of their visit to the territory's inhabitants.

MISSIONS TO EAST AFRICAN TRUST TERRITORIES

The first Visiting Mission was sent to East Africa in the summer of 1948, and visited Tanganyika and Ruanda-Urundi. This Mission was composed of four members—Henri Laurentie, of France, Chairman; E. W. P. Chinnery, of Australia; Lin Mousheng, of China; and E. Woodbridge, of Costa Rica. The Mission made observations and recommendations on political development, on the question of interterritorial organization, on economic and social conditions, and on education and health matters.

The Council considered the Visiting Mission's reports during its fourth and fifth sessions, together with the observations of the Belgian Government on the report on Ruanda-Urundi, and of the United Kingdom with respect to Tanganyika.

The second Visiting Mission to tour the East African Trust Territories was dispatched in July 1951. The Mission consisted of Enrique de Marchena, of the Dominican Republic, Chairman; G. R. Laking, of New Zealand; Mom Chao Dilokrit Kridakon, of Thailand; and William I. Cargo, of the United States. In a tour of about three months, the Mission visited Ruanda-Urundi, Tanganyika and Somaliland, the latter territory being visited for the first time by a Trusteeship Mission. Reports on the respective territories were considered by the Trusteeship Council at its eleventh session in the summer of 1952, in conjunction with the annual administrative reports on these territories.

The third Visiting Mission to the East African Trust Territories went out in July 1954. The Mission was composed of the following representatives: John Stanhope Reid, of New Zealand, Chairman; Rafael Eguizábal, of El Salvador; Rikhi Jaipal, of India; and Mason Sears, of the United States. The Mission's reports on Ruanda-Urundi, Tanganyika and Italian-administered Somaliland were examined by the Trusteeship Council at its fifteenth session, in January-March 1955.

MISSION'S RECOMMENDATIONS ON TANGANYIKA AND RUANDA-URUNDI

In its reports on Tanganyika and Ruanda-Urundi, the Mission expressed particular concern over the rate of political advancement in the two territories. A majority of the Mission found that at its present rate of development, Tanganyika's eight million Africans could attain self-government within the present generation on the basis of a political time-table. In its report, the Mission stated: "The promise of self-government to the present generation as the goal of a generation of effort should prove to be a necessary cohesive and inspirational force. The Mission believes that it should also be possible, within the main target, to set intermediate targets and target dates for phases of development."

The conception of a timed advance was not accepted by the Administering Authority, however, which issued a statement on the subject. In this the United Kingdom delegation stated: "Declared policy in Tanganyika is one of development by stages, the ground being consolidated and the future reviewed in the light of experience before each important step. The rigidity imposed by a time-table would be inimical to the harmonious development of political institutions responding to consecutive stages of economic and social evolution. This does not mean that progress must be slow."

In appraising conditions in Ruanda-Urundi, the Mission believed it was possible to prepare the people of that country for self-government within 20 to 25 years' time. This and other major recommendations were opposed by Pierre Ryckmans, of Belgium, when he introduced the Administering Authority's annual report to the Trusteeship Council. Mr. Ryckmans stated that the Mission had based its report on preconceived ideas and historical examples "foreign to Ruanda-Urundi."

The Mission's conclusions regarding a political time-table, in the case of both Tanganyika and Ruanda-Urundi, were not accepted by the Chairman, John S. Reid, of New Zealand, who felt they were ambiguous. The obligation to bring the people to self-government or independence as soon as possible was contained in the Trusteeship Agreement, and no doubt was expressed to the Mission in respect of the determination of the Administration to achieve that aim. Mr. Reid did not consider that it was either possible on the evidence available, or helpful to the people, to attempt at that time to set a limit to this process in terms of years.

MISSIONS TO WEST AFRICA

The first Visiting Mission to the West African Trust Territories was dispatched in November 1949 to the two Togolands under British and French administration and the two Cameroons under British and French administration, respectively. The Mission, which spent about six weeks in the region, was composed of Awni Khalidy, of Iraq, Chairman; Alfred Claeys-Bouuart, of Belgium; Benjamin Gerig, of the United States; and Antonio R. Pedrueza of Mexico. The Mission's reports on the four territories were considered by the Council at its Geneva session in January-April 1950, in conjunction with the annual administrative reports on the territories.

A second Visiting Mission to the four Trust Territories in West Africa left New York in August 1952. The members of this Mission were: R. A. Peachey, of Australia, Chairman; Robert Scheyven, of Belgium; H. E. Yang, of China; and Roberto E. Quiros, of El Salvador. In addition to making a special study of the Ewe and Togoland unification problem, the Mission made the customary investigation of conditions in the two Togolands and the two Cameroons. Its reports on each of the territories were examined by the Trusteeship Council at its June session in 1953.

A special report dealing with the Togoland problem was considered by the Council at the second part of its eleventh session, in November 1952, and subsequently by the General Assembly.

In August-September 1955, a third Visiting Mission went out to the two Trust Territories of British and French Togoland, while in the Autumn of 1955, a further mission toured the two Cameroons, under British and French administration.

The Mission to the Togolands was charged with making a special investigation of the Togoland Unification Question. The Mission, appointed by the Trusteeship Council at its fifteenth session, was composed of the following members: S. K. Banerji, of India, Chairman; J. M. McMillan, of Australia; Salah Eddine Tarazi, of Syria; and Robert R. Robbins, of the United States. Its report on the Togoland question was considered by the General Assembly at its tenth session, in 1955 (*see section on Togoland and Ewe petitions, page 276*).

The 1955 Mission to the two Cameroons was composed of Max H. Dorsinville, of Haiti, Chairman; Robert Scheyven, of Belgium; Hsi-Kun Yang, of China and Edward W. Mulcahy, of the United States. This Mission toured the French Cameroons from October 18 to November 18, 1955, and the British-administered Cameroons from November 18 to December 4, 1955. Its reports on conditions in these two territories were to be examined by the Trusteeship Council at its seventeenth session in February 1956.

MISSIONS TO PACIFIC TRUST TERRITORIES

The first Visiting Mission to tour the Trust Territories in the Pacific area left Lake Success in April 1950, to visit New Guinea, Nauru, Western Samoa, and the Marshalls, Marianas and Carolines, the Pacific Islands Trust Territory. The Mission was composed of Sir Alan Burns of the United Kingdom, Chairman; T. K. Chang, of China; Jacques Tallec, of France; and Victorio D. Carpio, of the Philippines. As in the previous cases, a small Secretariat staff accompanied the Mission, which spent 110 days touring the widely scattered territories. The Mission's reports were submitted to the Council's eighth session during January-March 1951, and considered in conjunction with the annual reports submitted by the Administering Authorities of the four Pacific Territories.

The Pacific Trust Territories were visited for the second time by a Trusteeship Council Mission in the spring of 1953. This Mission was composed of Enrique de Marchena, of the Dominican Republic, Chairman; Léon Pignon, of France; N. Rifai, of Syria; and W. A. C. Mathieson, of the United Kingdom. The Mission reported to the Trusteeship Council in June 1953.

A third Visiting Mission to the Pacific Trust Territories was sent out in February 1956. It was composed of the following members: Sir John Macpherson, of the United Kingdom, Chairman; José Rolz Bennett, of Guatemala; Daniel Massonet, of Belgium; and E. Chacko, of India. This Mission was due to report to the Trusteeship Council's eighteenth session in June 1956.

Petitions

Another of the Trusteeship Council's important tasks is to examine petitions submitted by the people of the Trust Territories, and any others which might concern the affairs of one or more of the territories, or the operation of the Trusteeship System. By the end of its sixteenth session in 1955, the Council had considered about eight thousand petitions and communications from, or concerning the Trust Territories. In addition, numerous petitions had also been received by the Visiting Missions while touring the territories.

The petitions have ranged over a wide field, from individual complaints against alleged injustices, to group protests concerning conditions in the territories. Thus, a Cameroonian has wanted a wooden leg, the women of a small Pacific island asked the Council to persuade their menfolk to consume less strong drink, and the donkey-cart drivers in Mogadiscio have complained about their taxes. Each petition has been sympathetically examined by the Council which, in some instances, has heard the petitioners themselves present their cases orally.

The following examples illustrate the importance of the petitions procedure in the Trusteeship System.

WESTERN SAMOANS' PLEA FOR SELF-GOVERNMENT

In November 1946, the Administrator of Western Samoa invited all Samoans to a public gathering to discuss the proposed Trusteeship Agreement for Western Samoa which the New Zealand Government, as the Mandatory Power, had submitted to the General Assembly. The Samoan representatives, while agreeing that the Trusteeship Agreement was an advance over the League of Nations Mandate, felt its acceptance would bring them no nearer self-government. Therefore, they petitioned that Western Samoa be granted self-government, and that New Zealand thereafter act as protector and adviser.

On April 24, 1947, at the suggestion of New Zealand, the Council decided to send a Mission to Western Samoa. Its members were Francis B. Sayre, of the United States, Chairman; Pierre Ryckmans, of Belgium; and Senator Eduardo Cruz-Coke, of Chile. The Mission interviewed officials of the Administration, Samoan leaders, members of the non-indigenous community, spokesmen for the religious missions, and other representative groups and individuals, and inspected schools, hospitals, religious missions and other institutions.

While the mission was in Western Samoa, the Government of New Zealand carried on independent consultations with representatives of both the Samoan and the non-indigenous populations regarding the transfer to them of a greater measure of responsibility in the government, and kept the Mission informed of progress. On its part, the Mission, before leaving Western Samoa, informally notified the New Zealand Government of the broad conclusions of its report. It agreed that New Zealand's plans for the reorganization of the Government of Western Samoa were closely in line with its own recommendations. New Zealand adopted these plans on November 25, 1947, in the Samoan Amendment Act, 1947.

As the first of a series of progressive steps toward eventual full self-government for the people of Western Samoa, the Act provided for:

(a) appointment of a High Commissioner and Deputy High Commissioner in place of an Administrator and a Deputy Administrator;

(b) establishment of a Council of State with advisory functions, comprising the High Commissioner and the Fautua (High Chiefs and Advisers);

(c) establishment of a Legislative Assembly with an absolute majority of Samoan members to take the place of the Legislative Council; and

(d) granting of power to the proposed Legislative Assembly to make laws for the peace, order and good government of Western Samoa, and to dispose of the revenues of the territory.

On December 5, 1947, the Trusteeship Council noted with satisfaction the policy of the New Zealand Government, and resolved that the people of Western Samoa should be encouraged and assisted to assume increasing responsibilities in self-government, and should be accorded full self-government as soon as they were capable of assuming the responsibilities involved.

In the last few years, Western Samoa has advanced rapidly along the road to self-government. Early in 1953, the New Zealand Prime Minister announced that the Samoans would have a chance to work out their own political destiny at a constitutional convention, which was held in November-December 1954. Among other measures, the Convention adopted a resolution on the question of the relationship with New Zealand. According to this, the special relationship between the territory and New Zealand should be maintained indefinitely, although its form might change with changing circumstances and constitutional developments. It was expected that this relationship would eventually be based on an alliance or agreement somewhat similar to the present arrangement between the United Kingdom and the Kingdom of Tonga.

In April 1954, elections in Western Samoa returned three Samoans to executive office, while three others were nominated by their districts and confirmed by the Fono of Faipule, an advisory legislative body composed entirely of Samoans. Eleven Samoan legislators represented the territory's eleven political districts at the end of 1955.

TOGOLAND UNIFICATION QUESTION

Of the many hundreds of petitions which have been received by the Trusteeship Council since the inception of the Trusteeship System, a large number have emanated from the two West African Trust Territories of British and French-administered Togoland. These petitions, both written and oral, have been almost exclusively concerned with what has become known as the Togoland Unification Question, an issue originating in demands, first made in 1947, by the large Ewe tribe for the unification of the Togolands under a single administration.

The first of the Ewe petitions were examined by the Trusteeship Council at its second session, at which time France and the United Kingdom, as the two Administering Authorities concerned, submitted a joint memorandum on the question. This detailed various proposals for meeting the Ewe grievances, including the following measures: (1) instructions to local authorities to remove, as far as possible, obstacles which impede the movement of individuals, the transport of their personal property, and commerce in local goods; (2) establishment of a zone designed to remove all disabilities resulting from the customs frontier, while retaining the present system of exchange control; (3) measures to remove double taxation and equalize the tax burden; (4) the teaching of both English and French in the secondary schools of the respective territories to the maximum extent which staff and equipment allowed, and the establishment of a university fund to permit exchange of especially qualified students; and (5) establishment by the French and British Governments of a Standing Consultative Commission for Togoland Affairs to insure the implementation of the above measures.

The British and French Governments considered that these measures would reduce and eventually remove the frontier difficulties.

The Council acknowledged that the frontiers dividing the Ewe people had been a cause of real difficulty to them. It welcomed the proposed measures as an earnest and constructive initial effort to meet the immediate difficulties. The Council recommended that the Administering Authorities assist and encourage the Ewes to develop their capacity for self-government, and report on measures adopted to fulfil the wishes of the Ewe people. The Council then decided that the Visiting Missions to West Africa should devote special attention to the problem.

After investigating the question in November-December 1949, the Visiting Mission presented a special report to the Council in which it agreed unanimously that the problem had been created by inevitable economic and other material inconveniences caused by the multiple frontiers and had assumed proportions which made it essentially political. The problem was again the subject of lengthy debates at the Council's sixth and seventh sessions. At the latter in July 1950, the Council noted a plan by the two Administering Authorities to establish an enlarged Consultative Commission for ascertaining the real wishes and aspirations of the inhabitants of all parts of the two Trust Territories.

FURTHER CONSIDERATION. The question was next considered by the General Assembly during its fifth session, when complaints were received from political parties in French Togoland regarding the elections held there in connection with the Consultative Commission, and allegation of false arrests during the elections. The Assembly adopted a resolution recommending that the Administering Authority concerned (France) inquire into those complaints. Results of this inquiry were presented to the Trusteeship Council at its eighth session in 1951, when further efforts were made to find a solution. In a report to the Council, Professor Paulin Baptiste, who had been appointed by France to conduct the inquiry, reached the following conclusions: (1) at the tribal stage of development, which was that of the majority of Togolanders, only a "two-stage electoral system" would enable everyone to express his opinion, and in that respect it was therefore "absolutely democratic"; and (2) the elections held according to that system, and as they were actually conducted, "insure in fact and in law the equitable representation of all sections of the population, and comply with the resolution adopted by the Trusteeship Council on July 14, 1950."

The Council then adopted a resolution which asked the two Administering Authorities to formulate, as soon as possible, "substantive proposals for a practicable solution" to the Ewe problem. It also urged the Ewe groups to cooperate in the present efforts of the Authorities, who were asked to report on their further efforts to the Council at its ninth session in July 1951.

At the Council's various hearings, spokesmen of the tribal groups submitted their views. Thus, Sylvanus Olympio, President of the All-Ewe Conference, told the Council that as a first step toward a solution, there should be increased harmonization of the two administrations, increased participation by Africans in those administrations, and the introduction of measures for the creation of an autonomous territory within five years. Conflicting views were forthcoming from other Togoland spokesmen.

At the Council's ninth session, France and the United Kingdom submitted a joint memorandum which proposed the establishment of a joint council, composed of representatives from each of the Togolands, to advise the Administering Authorities on matters of common concern to the peoples of the Territories. The Council approved this proposal, and recommended that the two Administering Authorities proceed with their plans to establish the proposed joint council which should be given sufficiently broad responsibilities to enable it to function with respect to "all questions of common concern, including questions of political, economic, social, educational and cultural development."

ASSEMBLY'S 1952 ACTION. Further action on the Togoland issue was taken at the Assembly's 1952 session, following consideration of a special report submitted by the Visiting Mission which toured the Togolands in the autumn of 1952. The Mission reported that the unification demands had now become "a live political issue" finding wide support in both British and French Togoland. Despite the widespread desire among the people for unification, the Mission found, however, that no single form of unification was accepted by a majority of the population, and that no administrative change was at present warranted in the two territories.

The Assembly also heard indigenous representatives from the territories, and the statements of the two Administering Authorities. In a comprehensive resolution, the Assembly recalled the statements of the Administering Authorities that their policy was to develop representative political institutions and democratic political activity, and that when the period of Trusteeship ended, the indigenous people would have full freedom of choice on their political future. The Assembly then resolved that the Administering Authorities should exert every effort to achieve a "prompt, constructive and equitable settlement," taking into account the fully expressed wishes of the Ewes, and the basic objectives of the Trusteeship System.

The Togoland problem was considered at subsequent sessions of the Trusteeship Council and the General Assembly in 1953-55. A solution was constantly sought through efforts to arrange means whereby the peoples of the two territories, with their close economic, social and cultural ties, might clarify their own aspirations. The rapid advance during the last few years of the neighboring Gold Coast towards autonomy has had a large influence on the problem, since British Togoland has been administered as an integral part of the Gold Coast.

This new influence became clearly apparent in July 1954, when the Trusteeship Council considered a special memorandum from the United Kingdom concerning the future status of British Togoland. The United Kingdom stated that when the Gold Coast achieved its self-government within the very near future it would no longer be able to administer British Togoland in the present way, that is, as a Trust Territory. The United Kingdom was satisfied that to administer it separately would be neither practicable politically nor desirable in the interests of the inhabitants of the Territory itself, particularly at a time when they would naturally expect to join in the consummation of the processes of developing self-government in which they had marched shoulder to shoulder with the people of the Gold Coast.

During the Trusteeship Council's consideration the United Kingdom also explained that the people of British Togoland had now progressed to a point where, if they chose to join the Gold Coast, this would amount to fulfilment of the objectives of the Trusteeship System, and the Trusteeship Agreement should therefore be terminated. The United Kingdom believed that, after forty years of administration as a dependent people, the British Togolanders would soon be in a position to achieve full self-government.

This new situation was noted by the General Assembly at its ninth session in December 1954. The Assembly then noted that, as the Gold Coast assumed full responsibility for its own affairs, the people of British Togoland would have reached a stage of development at which the objectives of the Trusteeship System would have been substantially achieved, and the Trusteeship Agreement should therefore be terminated.

The Assembly subsequently decided on steps to ascertain the wishes of the inhabitants as to their future "without prejudice to the eventual solution they may choose, whether it be independence, unification of an independent Togoland under British administration with an independent Togoland under French administration, unification with an independent Gold Coast, or some other self-governing or independent status." The Assembly then recommended that a mission should visit the Togolands to conduct a special survey of the problem, and report back to the Trusteeship Council in time for the Council to report to the Assembly.

After touring the Togolands in August-September 1955, the Mission—headed by S. K. Banerji of India—issued a special report on the Togoland question. In brief, the Mission proposed that a plebiscite be held at an early date in British Togoland to determine its political future. The plebiscite, to be supervised by a United Nations commissioner and observers, would ask the population whether they wanted the Trust Territory integrated with the neighboring Gold Coast, on the threshold of independence, or wanted to continue to be administered under the Trusteeship System, pending the ultimate determination of the territory's political future.

As to French Togoland, the Mission noted that there were distinct differences of opinion on the political future of this Territory, and considered that "only a freely conducted consultation of the wishes of the people of the territory would disclose the real strength of the two opposing views."

The Mission, in making its proposals, underlined the importance of reaching an early settlement of the problem, declaring: "The Mission sincerely hopes that with the assistance of such enlightened and democratic Administering Authorities as the United Kingdom and France, the suggestions made would provide a democratic and practicable solution, at an early date, for the future of Togoland under British administration and Togoland under French administration, and would give to the world a practical demonstration of the attainment by two Trust Territories of the objectives of Trusteeship, and the decision by their own people of the political future of their Territories."

ASSEMBLY ENDORSES PLEBISCITE PROPOSAL. Opening yet another chapter in the eight-year old Togoland problem, the Assembly on December 15, 1955, endorsed the recommendation for a plebiscite to be held in British Togoland. In a comprehensive resolution, adopted after long debate on the Mission's report, the statements of Togoland spokesmen, and various draft proposals introduced by representatives, the Assembly recommended that the Administering Authority of British Togoland organize and conduct "without delay," under United Nations supervision, a plebiscite in the territory, in order to ascertain the wishes of the majority of its inhabitants as to their political future.

The Assembly noted the statement of the United Kingdom Government that the Gold Coast would attain its independence in the near future and that, consequently, it would be impossible thereafter to administer British Togoland in the present way. The Assembly also accepted the recommendations submitted by the Visiting Mission to the effect that the wishes of the people of British Togoland as to their future should be ascertained by plebiscite.

Eduardo Espinosa y Prieto, of Mexico, was appointed to serve as the United Nations Plebiscite Commissioner in British Togoland, and he was requested to exercise, on behalf of the General Assembly, the powers and functions of supervision defined by the Visiting Mission in its special report.

The resolution provided for observers and staff to be appointed by the Secretary-General in consultation with the Plebiscite Commissioner. It further requested the Commissioner to submit a report on the organization, conduct and results of the plebiscite to the Trusteeship Council for its consideration, and for transmission to the Assembly at its eleventh session in order that the "latter may, in consultation with the Administering Authority, assess the results and determine the further action to be taken on the attainment of independence by the Gold Coast and in the light of all the circumstances and in accordance with the Charter of the United Nations and the Trusteeship Agreement."

Finally, the Assembly requested the Trusteeship Council "in virtue of the provisions of the Trusteeship Agreement and the Charter to continue to exercise its functions, either at its regular or special sessions as may be necessary, and to take into consideration any matter that may arise, or be referred to it, in respect of the Trust Territory."

In regard to French-administered Togoland, the Assembly endorsed the conclusion of the Visiting Mission that the implementation of the political reforms contemplated by the Administering Authority would help in ascertaining the wishes of the inhabitants as to their future at an early date by direct and democratic methods.

The Assembly, in this resolution, recommended that the consultation with the population be conducted, as in the case of British Togoland, under the supervision of the United Nations. The Trusteeship Council was asked to undertake a special study of the question, in consultation with the Administering Authority at its seventeenth regular session in 1956, and if possible to report to the eleventh session of the General Assembly.

The Assembly's resolution was adopted exactly eight years after the first petition was received from the Ewe people, first bringing the Togoland question onto the international stage. The Plebiscite Commissioner, together with United Nations observers, was scheduled to arrive in British Togoland early in 1956, and the plebiscite was due to take place on May 9, 1956.

Progressive Development of Trust Territories and Attainment of Objective of Autonomy

A number of recommendations designed to hasten the pace of overall development of the Trust Territories towards the Charter's goal of autonomy have been endorsed by the General Assembly and the Trusteeship Council in recent years. In 1949, the Assembly, in supporting several Council proposals on this question, asked the Council to include in its annual reports a special section outlining the measures taken by the Administering Authorities to expedite advancement in the territories. The Assembly also recommended the abolition of any existing discriminatory laws and practices in all Trust Territories.

Following the Assembly's recommendations on over-all advancement, the Council in 1950 adopted a single resolution which took into account all proopsals. This noted that some steps were already being taken by the Administering Authorities to implement the provisions contained in the recommendations. It further recommended the complete abolition of corporal punishment in all Trust Territories where it still exists, and requested expert advice from the International Labor Organization on problems of migrant labor and penal sanctions for breach of labor contracts by indigenous inhabitants. The resolution further urged the Administering Authorities to insure that no discriminatory laws or practices contrary to the principles of the Charter and of the various Trusteeship Agreements should exist in any Trust Territory. The Council decided to include special sections in its annual reports to the Assembly with measures taken to implement these recommendations.

At its tenth session in 1955, the General Assembly endorsed another resolution on the question of the attainment by the Trust Territories of the objective of self-government or independence. The Assembly recalled its earlier resolutions by which it invited the Administering Authority of each Trust Territory, other than Somaliland under Italian administration, to include in each annual report information concerning measures taken or contemplated towards self-government or independence, and estimates of the time required for such measures, and requested the Trusteeship Council to include in each of its reports to the Assembly, a separate section dealing with the subject, and stating, in each case, its conclusions and recommendations. The Assembly noted that the Council in July 1955, had instructed each of its drafting committees on the annual reports—beginning with the Council's seventeenth session in 1956—to prepare appropriate draft conclusions and recommendations concerning the question of the attainment of autonomy by the territory concerned.

The Assembly then renewed its request to the Council to include in its future reports its conclusions and recommendations on the measures taken or contemplated in the Trust Territories towards the attainment of self-government or independence.

The Assembly also drew the attention of the Council to the importance it continued to attach to this question.

Administrative Unions Affecting Trust Territories

Certain Trusteeship Agreements authorize the Administering Authority to form customs, fiscal or administrative unions between a Trust Territory and adjacent colonies, and to establish common services between these territories. The Assembly, at its third session, endorsed the Council's view that an administrative union "must remain strictly administrative in its nature and its scope," and that its operation must not result in any conditions which will obstruct the separate political, economic, social and educational development of the Trust Territory as a distinct entity.

The Assembly then asked the Council to report on all aspects of the matter to the Assembly's fourth session, recommending safeguards to preserve the distinct political status of Trust Territories, and to enable the Council to exercise its supervisory functions effectively. Where appropriate, the Council was to seek an opinion from the International Court of Justice on whether such unions came within the scope of the Charter and the Trusteeship Agreements, and were compatible with them.

In January 1949, the Trusteeship Council established a Committee on Administrative Unions to outline the various aspects of the problem and to collect all available information.

The Committee's report contained studies on the arrangements affecting Tanganyika, the Cameroons under British administration, New Guinea, and the Cameroons and Togoland under French administration. Information later made available by Belgium on Ruanda-Urundi, and by the United Kingdom on Togoland under British administration, was also transmitted to the Council. In each instance, the Council was assured by the Administering Authority concerned that the existing administrative arrangements were not inconsistent with either the objectives of the Trusteeship System or with the terms of the Trusteeship Agreements.

The Council concluded that it could make no final decision on the question, but would have to continue to examine the operation of existing or future administrative unions. It transmitted to the General Assembly the Committee's report and other documentation. The Administering Authorities concerned were asked to furnish separate information on each Trust Territory in their annual reports.

The question was again considered by the General Assembly at its fourth session, when it asked the Council to give special attention to the desirability of the following measures:

the Administering Authorities should inform the Council in advance before they created new administrative unions or extended the scope of existing unions;

that, if an administrative union made it impossible to provide clear and precise separate data for a Trust Territory, the Administering Authority concerned should accept such Council supervision over the unified administration as the Council might deem necessary for effectively discharging its responsibilities under the Charter;

that separate judicial organizations and legislatures be set up in each Trust Territory; and that any type of legislative action originating in any other legislative body with headquarters in a neighboring colony should be eliminated; and

that account should be taken of the freely expressed wishes of the inhabitants before forming or extending any administrative, customs or fiscal union.

In July 1950, the Council decided to establish a Standing Committee on Administrative Unions, charged with making regular examinations of administrative unions. This Committee was asked to report to each Council session on any union in which a Trust Territory under review participated. The question was again considered by the Assembly at its seventh session. The Trusteeship Council, in a special report, gave a detailed analysis of administrative unions then affecting six Trust Territories in Africa and one in the Pacific.

After considering this report, and observations thereon by the Special Committee on Administrative Unions, the Assembly asked the Administering Authorities to continue the prompt transmission of complete information on the operation of all administrative unions to the Council, indicating the benefits and advantages derived by the indigenous inhabitants from such unions. The Assembly expressed the hope that the Administering Authorities would consider the freely expressed wishes of the inhabitants before establishing, or extending, the scope of the unions, and consult the Council on any changes in existing unions, or any proposal to establish new ones. Finally, the Assembly asked the Council to continue its regular examination of all administrative unions affecting Trust Territories, with special regard to the interests of the inhabitants of the territory concerned, the terms of the Charter, and the Trusteeship Agreements.

A Trusteeship Council resolution in 1953 authorized the Standing Committee to continue its regular examination of each administrative union affecting a Trust Territory, to study the administrative unions not only with regard to certain safeguards outlined by the Council, but also with regard to the interests of the inhabitants of the Territory, and the terms of the Charter and the Trusteeship Agreements.

In its report to the sixteenth session of the Trusteeship Council in June 1955, the Standing Committee noted that the conclusions of its regular reports to the Council had been based primarily on the specified safeguards. In reviewing this approach, however, it had come to the conclusion that these safeguards had lost some of their importance in view of developments. The Committee therefore stated that while it would continue to pay attention to application of the safeguards, and would continue to request the Secretariat to submit relevant information on them, it would include such information in its reports to the Council only if deemed necessary. Instead, the Standing Committee agreed that it would continue to examine the operation of the existing administrative unions affecting the different Trust Territories.

The Trusteeship Council took note of the Standing Committee's decision regarding the procedure to be followed, and adopted draft conclusions and recommendations offered by the Standing Committee in regard to the Cameroons under British Administration, Tanganyika and New Guinea. Two draft resolutions presented by the U.S.S.R. that would have recommended localization of legislative and administrative organs in the Trust Territory of New Guinea and the Cameroons under British Administration were rejected by the Council.

Educational Advancement in Trust Territories

The importance of speeding educational progress in the Trust Territories has been a matter of constant concern to the Trusteeship Council. After reviewing the Council's report, the General Assembly, at its third session in 1948, observed that "the creation of a system of universal education for the inhabitants without exception or discrimination" was required for their development toward self-government, as envisaged in the Charter. Accordingly, the Assembly made several recommendations. As requested, the Council on February 9, 1949, asked the Administering Authorities to intensify their efforts to increase educational facilities, even if this meant increasing budgetary expenditures. It proposed that primary education should be free and that access to higher education should not depend on ability to pay. It suggested that facilities for training indigenous teachers should be improved and expanded. The Administering Authorities were asked to report annually on educational progress in each Trust Territory.

The Assembly had requested the Council to study the financial and technical implications of expanding the facilities for higher education in Trust Territories in Africa, and to examine the possibility of establishing in 1952, and maintaining, a university for the indigenous inhabitants of these territories. The Council was to consult with Administering Authorities which already provided facilities for higher education in Africa and, if it wished, with UNESCO. On March 1, 1949, the Council established a committee to make a preliminary study of the whole question.

This committee reviewed the existing and planned facilities for higher education in the African Trust Territories. It heard statements by experts, including representatives of UNESCO, and by representatives of Belgium, France and the United Kingdom, the Administering Authorities concerned. The latter considered the proposal to establish a single university for all the Trust Territories in Africa impracticable primarily because of linguistic and financial difficulties, and the shortage of teachers and pupils.

The Council at its fifth session recommended, among other things, that: (1) Belgium carry out as soon as possible its plan to establish a university centre in Ruanda-Urundi, and consider establishing by 1952 preparatory schools of higher education; (2) France consider establishing institutions of higher education for Togoland and the Cameroons, but especially for the latter, if possible by 1952, as well as technical or professional university institutes and colleges; and (3) the United Kingdom consider establishing facilities for higher education, including vocational and technical education, in Tanganyika, and increase the number of scholarships for students in Togoland and the Cameroons.

The Council also recommended that the number of scholarships for higher education both in Africa and overseas be progressively increased. It urged that fellowships, scholarships and internships set up by the United Nations and the specialized agencies be made available to qualified students from Trust Territories.

On November 15, 1949, the General Assembly endorsed the Council's action. It also declared that racial discrimination in regard to educational facilities available to different communities in the Trust Territories was not in accordance with the principles of the Charter, the Trusteeship Agreements and the Universal Declaration of Human Rights. It asked the Council to include specific information on the question in its annual reports, and proposed that the Council continue to devote particular attention, in consultation with the Administering Authorities and the specialized agencies, to long-range programs of educational expansion in Trust Territories.

In further action on educational advancement, the Assembly in 1951 invited Member States to make available to qualified students from the territories fellowships, scholarships and internships. Since that time, several countries have responded. At its thirteenth session, in 1954, the Trusteeship Council adopted revised procedures for administering the scholarship program. These permitted applications to be made either through government authorities in the territories or through the Secretary-General.

At its sixteenth session in 1955, the Trusteeship Council considered a fourth progress report on the fellowship, scholarship and internship program. The report, covering June 1954 to June 1955, showed that altogether 45 scholarships or fellowships, in comparison with 38 in the previous period, had been offered by seven Member States to students from the Trust Territories. Four Member States had continued offers previously made (Indonesia, six fellowships; the Philippines, eleven scholarships; Turkey, two scholarships; and Yugoslavia, ten fellowships or scholar-ships), two Member States previously offering scholarships had made new offers for the year 1955-1956 (India, two scholarships as compared with four scholarships in the previous period; and the United States, four scholarships as compared with five in the previous period), and an additional Member State had made offers of scholarships (the U.S.S.R., ten scholarships). In addition, one Member State (Syria) had offered to assign three instructors to teach the Arabic language in Somaliland under Italian administration.

Of the scholarships and fellowships offered, ten were awarded. Of the successful candidates, one was from the British Cameroons, one from the French Cameroons, two from Italian Somaliland, one from Tanganyika, four from British Togoland, and one from Western Samoa.

The Secretary-General also stated in his report that he had included in the United Nations information material prepared for dissemination in the Trust Territories, details of the offers of facilities, and the procedure to be followed in submitting applications, and that this information had also been included in the UNESCO handbook "Study Abroad".

Participation of Indigenous Inhabitants of Trust Territories in Work of Trusteeship Council

The General Assembly in 1951 asked the Trusteeship Council to study possi-bilities of associating the indigenous people of the territories more closely in its work, considering that such participation would provide an effective means of promoting progress towards equality with the populations of Member States. The Council at its eleventh session in 1952 expressed hope that all the Administering Authorities would "find it appropriate" to associate suitably qualified indigenous persons in the Council's work, as part of their delegations, or in any other manner which they considered desirable. At its seventh session, the Assembly endorsed a proposal which went a little further than the steps proposed a year earlier. This stated that the object of the Trusteeship Council's recommendation on this subject would "be better achieved" through the active participation of indigenous persons in the governments of the various territories, as well as in the Council's work. Further, the Assembly considered it "both desirable and necessary that the in-digenous inhabitants of the Trust Territories should have every opportunity of developing their ability to take charge in due course of the public affairs of their territories."

Further action on this question was taken by the General Assembly in 1954, when it made the following recommendations to the Trusteeship Council: that, in order to develop further the participation of the indigenous inhabitants in its work through the medium of Visiting Missions, the Council instruct each Mission: (a) not only to consider such expressions of public opinion as might be spontaneously brought before it by all sections of the population, but also to take the initiative in seeking out public opinion on all important problems, and to undertake popular consultations in whatever form it might deem appropriate; and (b) to report fully on the development of the free expression of the wishes of the people and on the main trends of their opinions, and to make recommendations concerning the further development of a free public opinion.

The Assembly also recommended that, in order to develop further the partici-pation of indigenous inhabitants in its work through the medium of their right of petition, the Council should: (a) examine and propose concrete action upon peti-tions which might reflect public opinion on questions of general concern to the development of the territory; (b) request the Administering Authorities to make copies of their annual reports promptly available to the peoples of the territories; and (c) instruct each Visiting Mission to encourage in the territories public discussion on the annual reports, and to report on the extent to which facilities had been made available to the population for the purpose.

The Assembly further recommended that, as a means of insuring, in cases which it deemed urgent, that a given situation in a Trust Territory met with the freely expressed wishes of the people, the Council should immediately grant a hearing to those qualified representatives of public opinion who applied for one, or in the case of representatives who were unable to travel, the Council should examine all communications, letters or telegrams expressing their points of view. The Assembly finally reiterated the views and recommendations of its earlier resolutions on the subject. The Council noted these recommendations at its sixteenth session.

Rural Economic Development of Trust Territories

At its fifth session, the General Assembly paid special attention to the importance of rural economic development in Trust Territories. Recognizing that the equitable distribution and proper use of the land are essential to economic and social progress in all the territories, the Assembly made two recommendations. First, the Trusteeship Council should study prevailing laws, policies and practices in the territories relating to the utilization and alienation of land, taking into account the present and future needs of the indigenous inhabitants, the future economic needs of the territories, and the economic effects of transferring land to non-indigenous persons. Secondly, in the light of this study, the Council should make recommendations to the Administering Authorities with a view to the economic and social development of the indigenous populations.

Closely allied to this question was an Assembly resolution dealing with technical assistance for Trust Territories. This asked the Administering Authorities to make full use of the facilities available under the United Nations Expanded Technical Assistance Program, and the regular technical aid programs of the United Nations and its specialized agencies for economic expansion, social welfare services and training in public administration.

The Council at its eighth session established a special committee to study prevailing policies, laws and practices relating to land utilization and alienation in Trust Territories. Several progress reports on the Committee's work have subsequently been submitted to the Council. At its sixteenth session in 1955, the Council was informed that certain new measures of importance to the questions under study had been taken in a number of territories. Accordingly, the Committee asked the Council to agree to postponement of a final report on the study of rural economic development. The Council acceded to this request.

Dissemination of Information on the United Nations in the Trust Territories

The dissemination of information on the United Nations to the inhabitants of Trust Territories was discussed by the Trusteeship Council in 1948. The Council then invited the Administering Authorities to furnish lists of officials in the territories to whom its records and other documents might be sent, and also to suggest appropriate channels through which information media on the United Nations might be sent to the general public in the territories. The Assembly in 1952 emphasized that the peoples of the Trust Territories should receive adequate information concerning the purposes and operation of the United Nations and of the Trusteeship

System in particular. It was recommended that the Administering Authorities should take all appropriate steps to disseminate such information among the population and schools, and report details of such steps to the Secretary-General.

Periodic reports on this question have been submitted by the Secretary-General and considered by the Trusteeship Council. At its sixteenth session in 1955, the Council was informed of the latest arrangements for the provision of United Nations information in Trust Territories. There had been some increase in the distribution of the United Nations official records to the Trust Territories, the development of good operational contacts with the authorities in the administrations or with media of information, teachers and non-governmental organizations, and a definite increase in the flow of United Nations information to the public in several Trust Territories. The production of special material suitable for the varying readership levels of the territories, however, called for further effort on the part of the United Nations Secretariat and further cooperation by the Administrations. The Council noted this report.

Financing Economic Development in Italian-Administered Somaliland

The question of the financing of economic development plans in Somaliland under Italian administration was considered by the General Assembly at its ninth session in 1954. The Assembly endorsed a resolution in which it requested the Secretary-General to consider, in agreement with the Italian Government, the advisability of asking the International Bank for Reconstruction and Development to send a mission of experts to study the situation and the possibilities of economic development in the territory. The Assembly also requested the Trusteeship Council to continue its study of the question and on the basis of the conclusions of the 1954 Visiting Mission and the report of the Bank, if the plan for the proposed mission were carried out, to decide on practical measures for financing the economic development plans for Italian Somaliland and to report to the next General Assembly.

At its sixteenth session in 1955, the Trusteeship Council considered a report from the Secretary-General on the question. In this, he stated that the Italian Government had endorsed the General Assembly proposal to ask the International Bank to send a mission of experts to study the situation and the possibilities of economic development in the Trust Territory, and that, consequently, a meeting of the representatives of the Italian Government, the International Bank and the Secretary-General was held to discuss questions relating to the implementation of the resolution. However, the President of the International Bank later informed the Secretary-General of his reluctance to accede to the request for a mission, in view of the heavy schedule of operational activities to which the Bank was committed, and the availability of alternative means for carrying out such a study through a mission of experts organized by the Secretary-General. The representative of Italy subsequently informed the Trusteeship Council that the Italian Government considered it desirable that the International Bank should consider the matter again, and agree to dispatch a mission. To this end, the Italian Government would be glad to address a direct invitation to the Bank requesting also that the final report should be presented concurrently to the Trusteeship Council. The representative of Italy further stated that such a report would enable his Government to submit to the Trusteeship Council a plan on the problems which required immediate examination, and those relating to the economy of the territory after 1960, when it would become independent. The Council subsequently adopted a resolution noting these statements and recommending the Administering Authority to make a formal request as proposed by the International Bank. The Council hoped that the International Bank would reconsider its position in view of the general consensus of opinion in favor of a Bank mission, and agree to send a mission to the territory as early as possible.

Somaliland-Ethiopian Frontier Question

The question of the delimitation of the frontier between Somaliland under Italian administration and the neighboring country of Ethiopia was considered by the General Assembly in 1950. The Assembly then recommended that the portion of the boundary which was not already delimited by international agreement should be delimited by bilateral negotiations between the Ethiopian Government and the Administering Authority of the Trust Territory. The frontier question arose again at the Assembly's 1954 session, when a resolution was endorsed urging the Governments of Italy and Ethiopia to exert their "utmost efforts" to achieve a final settlement of the frontier issue by direct negotiations.

Further consideration of the question followed at the Assembly's tenth session, which noted the progress made in discussion of the matter between the two Governments concerned during 1955. The Assembly then recommended the Governments of Italy and Ethiopia should expedite their current direct negotiations in order that the frontier issue might be settled as soon as possible. The resolution also asked the two Governments concerned to report on the progress of their negotiations to the eleventh session of the Assembly.

Use of United Nations Flag in Trust Territories

A proposal that the United Nations flag be flown in all Trust Territories, as a symbol of United Nations interest in promoting the welfare and progress of the indigenous peoples, was endorsed by the General Assembly in 1949. During the Trusteeship Council's consideration of the proposal, the representatives of the Administering Authorities explained certain difficulties which, they maintained, made implementation of the Assembly's resolution either impractical or undesirable. When the subject was reintroduced at the Council's seventh session in 1950, it was recommended that the United Nations flag be flown over all Trust Territories, side by side with that of the Administration, and with the territorial flag if there should be one. The resolution stated that the Administering Authorities had "latitude to handle any practical difficulties of administration which this recommendation might create."

The Question of South West Africa

With one exception, all the territories which had been under League of Nations Mandate have either become independent states or been placed under the International Trusteeship System. The exception is the former German colony of South West Africa, over which the Union of South Africa was awarded a Mandate after the First World War.

A South African representative told the General Assembly in 1946, that South West Africa was sparsely populated and unable to support itself, and that a majority of the territory's inhabitants desired its incorporation in the Union. The Assembly recommended instead that South West Africa be placed under the International Trusteeship System, and it invited the South African Government to propose a Trusteeship Agreement.

In 1947, the South African Government informed the United Nations that it had decided not to proceed with the incorporation of South West Africa into the Union, but would maintain the *status quo* and administer the territory in the spirit of the

Mandate. It undertook to submit reports on its administration for the information of the United Nations. The first of these reports was submitted to the second Assembly session, which referred it to the Trusteeship Council.

In 1947, and again in 1948, the Assembly reaffirmed its recommendation that South West Africa be placed under the Trusteeship System, and that a Trusteeship Agreement be submitted. It recommended that the Union continue reporting annually on its administration of South West Africa until it had reached agreement with the United Nations on the future status of the territory.

In 1949, the Council notified the General Assembly that the Union Government had decided not to submit any further reports on its administration of South West Africa. The Council also noted that the arrangement for closer association between South West Africa and the Union had been put into effect under the terms of the South West Africa Affairs Amendment Act, 1949.

In November 1949, the Reverend Michael Scott, representing certain sections of the indigenous population of South West Africa, asked that no decision regarding the disposal of South West Africa be reached until the Herero and Berg-Damara tribes were permitted to express their views before the United Nations. He also charged that the South West Africa Affairs Amendment Act passed by the Union Government was tantamount to annexation.

COURT'S OPINION IN 1950

The Assembly in 1949 asked the International Court of Justice for an advisory opinion on South West Africa. Handing down its advisory opinion on July 11, 1950, the International Court unanimously found that South West Africa is a territory under the international Mandate assumed by the Union of South Africa on December 17, 1920. The Court further found that the Union "continues to have international obligations" under the League of Nations Covenant and Mandate, including the obligation to transmit petitions from the territory, and that the provisions of Chapter XII of the Charter apply to it in the sense that they provide a means whereby the territory might be brought under the Trusteeship System. However, the Court found that the Charter does not impose a legal obligation on the Union Government to place the territory under Trusteeship. Nevertheless, it held that the Union, acting alone, was not competent to modify the territory's international status. Such competence rested with the Union acting with the consent of the United Nations.

At its 1950 session, the Assembly again resolved that the normal way of modifying the territory's international status would be by means of a Trusteeship Agreement, in accordance with the provisions of Chapter XII of the Charter. The Assembly also established a committee to confer with the Union Government on procedural matters in connection with the Court's advisory opinion concerning the territory's international status. The committee, consisting of Denmark, Syria, Thailand, the United States and Uruguay, was authorized, "as an interim measure," to examine any report which might be submitted by the Union on the administration of the territory, as well as petitions and any other questions which might be submitted to the Secretary-General. The committee was asked to report to the Assembly's sixth session.

Following a series of meetings with representatives of the Union Government, the committee on October 17, 1951, reported that South Africa was prepared to reassume its international obligations under the League Mandate by negotiating a new international instrument with France, the United Kingdom and the United States—the three remaining members of the Principal Allied and Associated Powers of the First World War. In this way, South Africa would have a direct legal obligation to those three Powers, but not to the United Nations. The Union Government was prepared to agree to final confirmation of the proposed instrument by the United Nations. In a counter-proposal the *ad hoc* Committee suggested the setting up of United Nations machinery as analogous as possible to the League machinery. This body could then formulate terms for international supervision of the territory "no more extensive or onerous than those existing before." No agreement was reached on these proposals, but the Committee reported its willingness and that of the Union Government to consult further on the basis of the two proposals.

With regard to its other task, the Committee reported that it was unable to comply with the Assembly's instructions since no report on the territory had been forthcoming.

"A SOLEMN APPEAL"

Pursuing the question at its 1951 session, the General Assembly made a "solemn appeal" to the Union Government to reconsider its position on South West Africa, and urged it to resume negotiations with the special committee for an agreement providing for the full implementation of the advisory opinion handed down by the International Court. The Assembly also urged the Union to submit reports on its administration of the territory and to transmit petitions to the United Nations from communities or sections of the territory's population. Another part of the eighteen-point resolution declared that, since the Union Government cannot avoid its international obligations by unilateral action, the United Nations cannot recognize as valid any measures which might be taken by that Government which would modify the international status of South West Africa. Finally, the Assembly reconstituted an *ad hoc* Committee to confer with the Union concerning means of implementing the Court's advisory opinion.

A second resolution reiterated the view that the normal way of modifying South West Africa's international status would be to place it under the Trusteeship System, in accordance with the provisions of Chapter XII of the Charter.

1952 CONSULTATIONS

Further consultations between the *ad hoc* Committee on South West Africa and the Union Government's representatives took place during 1952. In its report to the seventh session of the General Assembly, the *ad hoc* Committee stated that further efforts to solve the issue had proved "inconclusive." The Committee reported that the chief points of difference in these consultations were: a fundamental disagreement on how supervision of the Union's administration of the territory was to be carried out; and the failure to agree on who should be the "second party" with whom the Union would conclude a new instrument for the administration of the territory.

The Assembly, at its seventh session, postponed further consideration of the South West Africa question until its eighth session, but asked its *ad hoc* Committee to continue talks with the Union during 1953 toward a settlement of the issue. Letters submitted to the Assembly's Fourth Committee by the Rev. Michael Scott, spokesman for tribal groups in the territory, were referred to the *ad hoc* Committee for its examination.

1953 ACTION

During the eighth session of the General Assembly, the representative of the Union of South Africa repeated his Government's view that the 1950 opinion of the International Court of Justice was purely advisory, and did not have the same status as a verdict in a court of law. He said that the Union was still prepared to negotiate an agreement with the former Allied Powers, but not with the United Nations, which, he contended, had not been a party to the original mandate agreement. In the course of debate, the majority of representatives claimed that the South African Government's disagreement with the opinion of the International Court was unjustifiable, and many maintained that the Union had virtually incorporated the territory as a fifth province.

Following Fourth Committee discussion, the General Assembly again made a "solemn appeal" to the Union of South Africa to reconsider its position on the status of the territory, and to place it under the United Nations Trusteeship System. It set up a new seven-member Committee on South West Africa to examine reports in accordance with the procedure of the former Mandates System; to report to the Assembly on conditions in the territory; and to prepare procedures for examining reports and petitions. Finally, the Committee was authorized to continue negotiations with the Union Government in order to fully implement the International Court's 1950 advisory opinion. A second resolution reiterated earlier resolutions adopted by the Assembly to the effect that South West Africa should be placed under the Trusteeship System, in accordance with Chapter XII of the Charter.

COMMITTEE'S RENEWED EFFORTS FOR NEGOTIATION

The new Committee on South West Africa held 39 meetings by September 1954, and in its report to the ninth session of the General Assembly reviewed its efforts: (1) to resume negotiations with the Union of South Africa toward solution of the territory's status on the basis of the International Court's opinion; (2) to have the Union Government submit annual reports on the mandated territory and cooperate with the Committee in the examination of the reports; and (3) to have the Union forward petitions from inhabitants living in South West Africa, and cooperate with the Committee in its examination. All of these efforts were unsuccessful, the Committee reported. The South African Government had informed the Committee of its doubts that new negotiations within the scope of the Committee's terms of reference would lead to any positive results, and had declined to submit reports and petitions.

Accordingly, the Committee examined, as directed by the General Assembly, such information and documentation as was available—a 900-page document prepared by the Secretary-General, and press reports from the territory—and presented its own report to the General Assembly. As requested by the Assembly, the Committee also drafted special rules of procedure for the Assembly's examination of reports and petitions relating to the mandated territory. These rules provided for an annual report on South West Africa, whether from the Union Government or the Committee itself, and for Assembly decisions on South West African matters, to be arrived at by a two-thirds vote.

The South African representative announced his Government's rejection of the Committee's procedural proposals and reiterated the view that since the League of Nations Mandate had lapsed, South Africa had no legal obligation to negotiate with the United Nations on the territory. He noted that under the League of Nations Covenant, a unanimous vote was required, while the procedure in the General Assembly would require only a two-thirds majority. This, he held, would deprive the Union of the right to prevent a decision with which it did not agree. However, the Assembly adopted the procedural rules essentially as proposed by the Committee.

Another Assembly resolution specifically asked the International Court of Justice whether the voting procedure adopted by the Assembly for consideration of the South West African question was a correct interpretation of the Court's 1950 advisory opinion. The Assembly also expressed concern that the administration of South West Africa was "in several respects not in conformity with the obligations of the Government of the Union of South Africa under the Mandate". It invited the Union Government to cooperate with the Committee on South West Africa, and to submit reports on its administration of the mandated territory and assist the Committee in the examination of such reports. Action on two proposals concerning petitions was deferred until the International Court had rendered an advisory opinion on voting procedure.

COURT'S OPINION IN 1955

In June 1955, the International Court unanimously handed down its opinion that the rule adopted by the ninth session of the Assembly in regard to voting procedure on the South West Africa question was a correct interpretation of the 1950 advisory opinion.

At its tenth session, the General Assembly considered a second report from its Committee on South West Africa, in which it was stated that there had been little improvement in the welfare of the indigenous population; that racial discrimination was prevalent; and that the main efforts of the administration were directed almost exclusively in favor of the European inhabitants. The Assembly adopted the report from its Committee, with South Africa casting the lone dissenting vote. The Assembly also endorsed the advisory opinion of the International Court on the question of voting procedure; confirmed that the Committee on South West Africa could grant oral hearings to petitioners; invited the Secretary-General to use his good offices with the Union Government to permit an indigenous school principal in South West Africa to obtain a passport and take up a scholarship at Oxford; agreed to transmit to a petitioner the observations contained in the report of the Committee on South West Africa on education in the territory and the proposed transfer of control over Native affairs from the Administrator of South West Africa to the Union's Minister of Native Affairs.

Three other recommendations regarding petitions were approved. The last of the Assembly's resolutions on South West Africa took note of a hearing granted by the Fourth Committee to the Reverend Michael Scott on behalf of indigenous people of the territory, and transmitted his statements to the Committee on South West Africa for its study and consideration.

LEGAL QUESTIONS

International Court of Justice

(For the provisions of the Charter and the Statute governing the composition, competence, decisions and advisory opinions of the International Court of Justice, see pages 35-37.)

PARTIES TO THE COURT'S STATUTE

MEMBERSHIP IN THE UNITED NATIONS. Since the inception of the United Nations up to December 31, 1955, the following States, in addition to the original Members of the United Nations, have been admitted to membership, and in accordance with

Article 93, paragraph 1, of the Charter, have become parties to the Statute of the International Court of Justice:

1946. Afghanistan, Iceland, Sweden, Thailand (formerly Siam).

1947. Pakistan, Yemen.

1948. Burma.

1949. Israel.

1950. Indonesia.

1955. Albania, Austria, Bulgaria, Cambodia, Ceylon, Finland, Hungary, Ireland, Italy, Jordan, Laos, Libya, Nepal, Portugal, Romania, Spain.

APPLICATION OF NON-MEMBER STATES. The following States have become parties to the Statute of the International Court of Justice in accordance with Article 35, paragraph 2, of the Statute:

Switzerland. On November 15, 1946, the Security Council, at the request of Switzerland, recommended that that country become a party to the Statute on the following terms:

1. acceptance of the Statute;

2. acceptance of the obligations under Article 94 of the Charter (in which each Member of the United Nations undertakes to comply with the decision of the Court in any case to which it is a party; and which further provides that if one party fails to comply with the Court's decision, the other party may have recourse to the Security Council); and

3. an undertaking to contribute to the expenses of the Court an equitable amount assessed by the General Assembly from time to time after consultation with the Swiss Government.

These recommendations were adopted by the Assembly. On July 28, 1948, Switzerland made a declaration accepting those conditions, and became a party to the Statute.

Liechtenstein. On December 1, 1949, the General Assembly on the recommendation of the Security Council decided that Liechtenstein be admitted on the same conditions as those laid down in the case of Switzerland. On March 29, 1950, Liechtenstein made a declaration accepting those conditions, and became a party to the Statute.

San Marino. On December 9, 1953, the General Assembly on the recommendation of the Security Council decided that San Marino be admitted on the same conditions as those laid down in the case of Switzerland and Liechtenstein. On January 18, 1954, San Marino made a declaration accepting those conditions, and became a party to the Statute.

Japan. On December 9, 1953, the General Assembly on the recommendation of the Security Council decided that Japan be admitted on the same conditions as those laid down in the case of Switzerland and Liechtenstein. On March 25, 1954, Japan made a declaration accepting those conditions, and became a party to the Statute.

PARTICIPATION IN ELECTING MEMBERS OF THE COURT

On October 8, 1948, the General Assembly, on the recommendation of the Security Council, decided the conditions on which a state which is party to the Statute of the Court but not a Member of the United Nations might participate in electing the members of the Court. These are:

(1) It shall be on an equal footing with the United Nations Members in respect to those provisions of the Statute which regulate the nominations of candidates for election by the Assembly.

(2) It shall participate in the Assembly elections of members of the Court in the same manner as United Nations Members.

(3) If in arrears in the payment of its contribution to the expenses of the Court, it shall not participate in electing the members of the Court in the Assembly, if the amount of its arrears equals or exceeds the amount of the contribution due from it for the preceding two full years. The Assembly may, nevertheless, permit such a state to participate in the elections if it is satisfied that the failure to pay is due to conditions beyond the state's control.

NEED FOR GREATER USE OF THE COURT

The General Assembly on November 14, 1947, recommended that United Nations organs and the specialized agencies should, from time to time, review the difficult and important points of law which have arisen in the course of their work and which involve questions of principle, including points of law relating to the interpretation of the United Nations Charter or the constitutions of the specialized agencies. Such points of law should be referred to the International Court of Justice for an advisory opinion, provided the organ or agency was duly authorized by the Assembly to approach the Court.

The Assembly also drew the attention of the states which had not yet accepted the compulsory jurisdiction of the Court to the desirability of the greatest possible number of states accepting this jurisdiction with as few reservations as possible. It further drew the attention of the Members to the advantage of inserting in conventions and treaties arbitration clauses providing for the submission to the Court of disputes concerning the interpretation or application of such conventions or treaties.

As a general rule, the Assembly recommended, states should submit their legal disputes to the Court.

ACCEPTANCE OF COMPULSORY JURISDICTION OF THE COURT

The following 32 States have, by declarations made in accordance with Article 36, paragraphs 2 to 5, of the Statute of the Court, accepted or renewed the acceptance of the compulsory jurisdiction of the Court:

Australia	Haiti	Netherlands	Sweden
Canada	Honduras	New Zealand	Switzerland
China	India	Nicaragua	Thailand
Colombia	Israel	Norway	Turkey
Denmark	Liberia	Pakistan	Union of South Africa
Dominican Republic	Liechtenstein	Panama	United Kingdom
El Salvador	Luxembourg	Paraguay	United States
France	Mexico	Philippines	Uruguay

IRAN WITHDRAWS ACCEPTANCE OF JURISDICTION. On July 9, 1951, the Foreign Minister of Iran cabled the Secretary-General withdrawing Iran's acceptance of compulsory jurisdiction. By ordering interim measures in the Anglo-Iranian Oil Case, Iran stated, the Court had acted outside its jurisdiction, and "shaken the confidence" of the Government and people of Iran. (*For details of the Anglo-Iranian Oil Case, see page 300.*)

CASES BEFORE THE COURT

CORFU CHANNEL CASE. The first case considered by the Court was that involving certain incidents in the Corfu Channel (*see page 143*). On May 22, 1947, the

United Kingdom addressed an application to the International Court of Justice asking that the Court decide that the Albanian Government was internationally responsible for the loss and injury, and was under an obligation to make reparation or pay compensation to the Government of the United Kingdom; and that the Court should determine the reparation or compensation.

Albania agreed by letter to appear before the Court. However, it expressed the opinion that the United Kingdom application was not in conformity with the Security Council's recommendation, because instituting proceedings by unilateral application was justified neither by the Charter nor by the Court's Statute.

In December 1947, Albania filed with the Court a preliminary objection to the application on the ground of inadmissibility. In March 1948, the Court rejected the Albanian objection on the ground, among others, that the Albanian Government's letter constituted a voluntary and indisputable acceptance of the Court's jurisdiction, and that the reservations stated in the letter were intended only to maintain a principle and prevent the establishment of a precedent.

Immediately after the delivery of judgment, the Albanian and United Kingdom Governments concluded a special agreement. According to this, they submitted the following two questions to the Court:

"(1) Is Albania responsible under international law for the explosions which occurred on October 22, 1946, in Albanian waters and for the damage and loss of human life which resulted from them and is there any duty to pay compensation?

"(2) Has the United Kingdom under international law violated the sovereignty of the Albanian People's Republic by reason of the acts of the Royal Navy in Albanian waters on October 22 and on November 12 and 13, 1946, and is there any duty to give satisfaction?"

On the first question, the Court gave judgment that "the People's Republic of Albania is responsible under international law for the explosions which occurred on October 22, 1946, in Albanian waters and for the damage and loss of human life that resulted therefrom." The Court reserved for further consideration the assessment of the amount of compensation.

On the second question, the Court gave judgment that the United Kingdom did not violate the sovereignty of Albania by reason of the acts of the British Navy on October 22, 1946. It unanimously gave judgment that by reason of the British Navy acts in Albanian waters in the course of the operations of November 12 and 13, 1946, the United Kingdom had violated the sovereignty of Albania, and that this declaration of the Court constituted in itself appropriate satisfaction.

Albania held that the Court had no jurisdiction to assess the amount of compensation, and took no part in the hearings on this question. The Court appointed two experts to assess the value of the damage. On December 15, 1949, it fixed the amount of compensation to be paid by Albania to the United Kingdom at £843,947 (approximately $2,400,000).

(Albania, to date, has not paid the compensation due the United Kingdom, and the latter Government has not sought recourse of the Security Council, according to Article 94 of the Charter. This Article states, *inter alia,* that if a party to a case fails to perform the obligations incumbent upon it under a judgment rendered by the Court, the other party may have recourse to the Security Council, which may, if it deems necessary, make recommendations or decide upon measures to be taken to give effect to the judgment.

(The United Kingdom, however, in the case of the monetary gold removed from Rome in 1943—brought before the Court by Italy (*see page 304*)—asked the Court to rule that the gold be delivered to the United Kingdom in partial satisfaction of the Court's judgment of December 15, 1949.)

COLOMBIAN—PERUVIAN ASYLUM CASE. Following a military rebellion in Peru on October 3, 1948, a decree of the Peruvian Government charged a political party—the American People's Revolutionary Party—with having prepared and directed the rebellion, and denounced its leader, Victor Raul Haya de la Torre, a Peruvian citizen, as responsible. Summonses were published, ordering him to appear before the Examining Magistrate. On January 3, 1949, Mr. Haya de la Torre sought asylum in the Colombian Embassy in Lima. Asylum having been granted, the Colombian Ambassador informed the Peruvian Government, and asked for guarantees of safe-conduct to enable Mr. Haya de la Torre to leave the country. Subsequently, the Colombian Ambassador stated that Mr. Haya de la Torre had been "qualified" as a political refugee. The Peruvian Government disputed Colombia's right of unilateral and definitive "qualification", and refused to grant a safe-conduct. By agreement of the two Governments, the case was submitted to the International Court of Justice by the Government of the Republic of Colombia on October 15, 1949.

In its judgment, delivered on November 20, 1950, the Court decided that Colombia, as the State granting asylum, was not competent to qualify the offence by a unilateral and definitive decision binding on Peru.

On Colombia's second submission that Peru was under obligation to issue a safe-conduct to enable the refugee to leave the country in safety, the Court's finding was that the guarantees provided for refugees in the Havana Convention were applicable solely to a case where a territorial state, in this case Peru, demanded the departure of the refugee from its territory, which was not the position in this case. The Court decided that the Colombian Government was therefore, "not entitled to claim that the Peruvian Government should give the guarantees necessary for the departure of Mr. Haya de la Torre from the country with due regard to the inviolability of his person."

In a counter-claim, Peru had asked the Court to declare that the asylum granted by the Colombian Embassy violated the Havana Convention, first, because Mr. Haya de la Torre was accused of a common crime, and, secondly, because the urgency that was required under that Convention in order to justify asylum was absent in that case.

The Court rejected the first point of the counter-claim. The only charge against Mr. Haya de la Torre, the Court declared, was that of military rebellion which was not a common crime. On the second point regarding "urgency", the Court declared that at the time the asylum was granted, there was no case of urgency within the meaning of the Havana Convention, since three months had elapsed between the military rebellion and the grant of asylum. The Court came to the conclusion that the grant of asylum was not in conformity with the Havana Convention.

Immediately after the judgment, Colombia asked for an interpretation, and put three questions to the Court. Was the judgment, it asked, to be construed as meaning: (a) that the qualification made by the Colombian Ambassador of the offence imputed to Mr. Haya de la Torre was correct, and legal effect should be given to it; (b) that Peru was not entitled to demand surrender of the refugee, and that Colombia was not bound to surrender him; or (c) that Colombia was bound to surrender the refugee?

On the first question, the Court found that the point had not been submitted to it by the parties. On the other two points, the Court declared that the question of surrender had not been included in the submissions of the parties, and the Court could not decide on it. Finally, said the Court, the necessary condition for a request for interpretation—that there should be a dispute as to the meaning and scope of the judgment—was not satisfied, since no such dispute between the parties had been brought to the attention of the Court. Colombia's request for interpretation was, therefore, inadmissible, the Court declared.

HAYA DE LA TORRE CASE. On November 28, 1950, the day after the delivery of the Court's judgment on Colombia's request for interpretation, the Government of Peru requested the Colombian Government to deliver Mr. Haya de la Torre, on the basis of the Court's judgment. After informing Peru that it did not feel itself bound to deliver him, Colombia, on December 13, filed an application with the Court instituting new proceedings. Was Colombia bound to deliver the refugee to Peru in terms of the Court's judgment of November 20, 1950, Colombia asked the Court? If this claim was dismissed, then as an alternative claim Colombia requested the Court to adjudge if it was or was not bound to deliver Mr. Haya de la Torre to Peru "in accordance with the law in force between the parties and particularly American international law."

Peru had also requested the Court to state in what manner the judgment should be executed by Colombia, and had further invited the Court to dismiss the Colombian submission by which the Court had been asked to state, solely, that Colombia was not bound to deliver Mr. Haya de la Torre, and at the same time to declare that the asylum ought to have ceased immediately after the judgment of November 20, 1950, and must in any case cease forthwith, in order that Peruvian justice might resume its normal course, which had been suspended.

In its judgment, the Court examined, in the first place, the admissibility of the intervention of the Cuban Government. That Government, having availed itself of the right conferred by the Court's Statute, had filed a declaration of intervention stating its views on the interpretation of the Havana Convention. The Court stated that the subject matter of the present case related to a new question—the delivery of Mr. Haya de la Torre to the Peruvian authorities—which had not been decided by the judgment of November 20. Accordingly, the Court decided to admit the Cuban intervention.

On the merits of the case, the Court observed that both parties desired that the Court make a choice among the various courses for terminating the asylum. Such a choice could not be based on legal considerations, but only on grounds of practicability or of political expediency. It was not part of the Court's judicial function to make such a choice.

The surrender of the refugee was a new question which had only been brought before the Court by the application of December 13, 1950. The Court noted that, according to the Havana Convention, diplomatic asylum had to be terminated as soon as possible; however, the Convention did not give a complete answer to the question of the manner in which it should be terminated. Nor did it provide for cases in which the asylum had not been regularly granted and where the territorial state had not requested the departure of the refugee.

While, in principle, asylum could not be opposed to the operation of national justice, an obligation to surrender a person accused of a political offence because the asylum was irregularly granted would amount to rendering positive assistance to the local authorities in their prosecution of a political refugee, and such assistance could not be admitted without an express provision to that effect in the Convention.

As regards Mr. Haya de la Torre, the Court had declared in its judgment of November 20, that it had not been proved that the acts of which he had been accused before asylum was granted constituted common crimes. Consequently, the Court decided, Colombia was under no obligation to surrender him to the Peruvian authorities.

As regards the Peruvian submissions concerning the termination of the asylum, the Court declared that Peru was legally entitled to claim that the asylum which had been irregularly granted should cease; however, the addition "in order that Peruvian justice may resume its normal course, which has been suspended"—which appeared to involve, indirectly, a claim for the surrender of the refugee—could not be accepted by the Court.

The Court thus concluded that the asylum must cease, but that Colombia was under no obligation to bring this about by surrendering the refugee. There was no contradiction between these two findings, since surrender was not the only way of terminating asylum.

The Court accordingly declared unanimously that it was not part of the Court's judicial function to make a choice among the different ways in which asylum might be brought to an end; it declared that Colombia was under no obligation to surrender Mr. Haya de la Torre to the Peruvian authorities; it declared unanimously that the asylum ought to have ceased after the delivery of the judgment of November 20, 1950, and should terminate.

(Note—At the tenth International Conference of American States, held at Caracas, Venezuela, in March 1954, it was announced that an agreement between Colombia and Peru had been signed at Bogotá by which Mr. Haya de la Torre would be given safe-conduct out of Peru. Mr. Haya de la Torre left Lima, Peru, on April 16, 1954, and arrived in Mexico City, Mexico, the next day.)

ANGLO-NORWEGIAN FISHERIES CASE. On September 28, 1949, the United Kingdom submitted an application claiming that a Norwegian decree of 1935 closed considerable areas off the Norwegian coast which, under international law, were high seas, open to the fishing vessels of all nations. The United Kingdom asked the Court to lay down the principles of international law to be applied in defining and, in so far as was necessary, to define the limits within which Norway was entitled to reserve a fisheries zone. It also asked for damages for all interference with United Kingdom shipping vessels by Norway outside these limits. Oral proceedings before the Court, which had begun on September 25, were concluded on October 29, 1951. The President of the Court then declared the oral proceedings closed, reserving, however, the Court's right to reopen them if it considered such a course desirable for the purpose of calling for further information.

On December 18, 1951, the Court, by a vote of 10 to 2, found that the method used by Norway in the decree for the delimitation of the zones was not contrary to international law, and by 8 to 4, decided that the base lines which had been fixed were fixed by a method not contrary to international law.

THE FRANCO-EGYPTIAN CASE. This case arose from France's complaint that the Egyptian Government had taken certain measures against the persons, property, rights and interests of French nationals and French-protected persons in Egypt. France invoked the Montreux Convention regarding the abrogation of capitulations in Egypt. The case was filed on October 13, 1949. On February 21, 1950, however, the French Government informed the Court that the measures taken by Egypt had since been withdrawn, and that the case was virtually settled. No objection being made to this by Egypt, the case was ordered removed from the Court's list on March 29, 1950.

CASE CONCERNING THE RIGHTS OF NATIONALS OF THE UNITED STATES IN MOROCCO. On October 28, 1950, the Government of the French Republic instituted proceedings before the International Court of Justice against the Government of the United States concerning the rights of nationals of the United States in Morocco.

The French Government asked the Court to declare that American nationals in Morocco were not entitled to preferential treatment, and should be subject to the laws and regulations in force within the Shereefian Empire, in particular those relating to imports not involving an official allocation of currency.

By order dated November 22, 1950, the Court specified the time limits for the filing of further pleadings.

On June 21, 1951, the Government of the United States made a preliminary objection. The United States argued that discrimination in favor of French imports was a direct violation of the treaty rights of the United States granting its nationals immunity from local laws and forbidding prohibitions on American imports. By applying the decree to United States citizens, the United States contended, France was guilty of a violation of international law.

The arguments on both sides found common ground in the Act of Algeciras of 1906, proclaiming in French Morocco respect for "economic liberty without any inequality," a legal document unaffected by the establishment of the French Protectorate over Morocco by the Treaty of March 30, 1912. In the Protectorate Treaty, France was accorded no privileged economic position in Morocco.

The Court, in the judgment which it handed down on August 27, held unanimously that the provisions of the Residential decree of December 30, 1948, contravened the rights which the United States had acquired under the Act of Algeciras, because they exempted France from control of imports without allocation of currency, while subjecting the United States to such control.

Also at issue in the case was the right of United States nationals to have cases to which they are parties heard in the United States Consular Courts in the French zone of Morocco. Governing this point was the treaty between the United States and Morocco dated September 16, 1836. France, in the exercise of her protective functions, was bound by all treaty obligations to which Morocco had been subject before the Protectorate and which have not been terminated or suspended by arrangement with the interested states. Under the 1836 treaty, it was provided that "if any of the citizens of the United States or any persons under their protection, shall have any dispute with each other, the Consul shall decide between the parties."

France contended that the word "dispute" meant only civil disputes. But the Court held unanimously that "dispute" referred to both civil and criminal disputes, insofar as they related to breaches of the law committed by a United States citizen (or protégé) upon another.

The United States further asserted that consular jurisdiction was acquired in all cases in which a United States citizen or protégé was a defendant, through the effect of the most-favored-nation clause. The most extensive privileges of consular jurisdiction were granted by Morocco in treaties with Great Britain in 1856 and Spain in 1861, which insured the right of nationals of those countries, even when defendants, to be judged by their own consular courts. The intention of the most-favored-nation clauses, the Court said, was to maintain fundamental equality without discrimination among all countries concerned. Since both Spain and Great Britain had relinquished this particular right of consular jurisdiction, the Court decided by a vote of 6 to 5, that the United States no longer might claim it, not being entitled to rely on clauses of treaties no longer in force.

Another United States argument for extending consular jurisdiction to all cases in which its citizens were involved was that the Act of Algeciras granted this right. The Court pointed out that certain provisions of the Act did recognize a limited consular jurisdiction for the purpose of judicial proceedings specifically described therein. By a vote of 10 to 1, the Court held the consular jurisdiction of the United States continued to exist to the extent that might be necessary to render effective those provisions of the Act which depended on the existence of consular jurisdiction. "But the Court cannot, by way of interpretation, derive from the Act a general rule as to full consular jurisdiction which it does not contain. On the other hand the Court cannot disregard particular provisions involving a limited resort to consular jurisdiction which are, in fact, contained in the Act and which are still in force as far as relations between the United States and Morocco are concerned." Thus the Court held that citizens of the United States might invoke consular jurisdiction insofar as the subject matter came within certain categories of the Act of Algeciras.

The Court unanimously rejected a further argument of the United States for consular jurisdiction based on the claim that United States nationals were not subject, in principle, to the application of Moroccan laws unless those laws had received the prior assent of the United States. This claim, the Court said, was linked with the regime of capitulations—the most-favored-nation claim—and fell within them. There was nothing "in any of the treaties under consideration in the case conferring upon the United States any such right."

AMBATIELOS CASE. The Hellenic Government, having taken up the case of one of its nationals, the ship owner N. E. Ambatielos, on April 9, 1951, instituted proceedings asking the Court to declare that the claim made by Mr. Ambatielos against the Government of the United Kingdom must, in accordance with the terms of the treaties concluded in 1886 and 1926 between Greece and the United Kingdom, be submitted to arbitration. The Government of the United Kingdom, on the other hand, contended that the Court had no jurisdiction to decide on that question.

Three Anglo-Greek agreements were involved in this case. First, an 1886 treaty containing an arbitration clause which specified that disputes between the two parties which arose out of that treaty and could not be settled by negotiation should be submitted to an *ad hoc* arbitration tribunal. Second, a 1926 treaty which superseded the 1886 treaty provided that any dispute as to the interpretation or the application of its provisions should be submitted to the Permanent Court of International Justice. Third, a 1926 declaration between the two States stated that disputes concerning the validity of claims on behalf of private persons based on the 1886 treaty should be settled according to the arbitration clause of that treaty.

In its preliminary objection, the United Kingdom asserted that the 1926 declaration was independent of the 1926 treaty and, therefore, the Ambatielos dispute was not within the Court's jurisdiction. Greece, on the other hand, contended that the declaration was part of the 1926 treaty, and that the International Court was competent to decide the case on its merits.

On July 1, 1952, the Court, by 13 votes to 2, found that it was without jurisdiction to decide on the merits of the Ambatielos claim; and, by 10 votes to 5, that it had jurisdiction to decide whether the United Kingdom was under an obligation to submit to arbitration, in accordance with the declaration of 1926, the difference as to the validity of the Ambatielos claim, insofar as this claim was based on the treaty of 1886.

On July 18, 1952, the Court made an order prescribing time-limits for filing the reply and the rejoinder on the merits. It then heard and examined the contentions of both parties, as well as the text of the agreements in question.

The Court delivered its judgment on May 19, 1953. The Declaration of 1926, said the Court, related to a limited category of differences which the treaty of 1886 provided should be settled by arbitration, namely, differences as to the validity of claims on behalf of private persons based on the treaty of 1886. The Court concluded that the claim presented by the Hellenic Government was within the meaning of the 1926 Declaration. Consequently, by 10 votes to 4, the Court held that the United Kingdom was under an obligation to submit to arbitration.

The United Kingdom, in the hearings before the Court in 1952, declared that it was willing to have the Court act as the arbitral tribunal if the Judges ruled in favor of arbitration.

ANGLO-IRANIAN OIL COMPANY CASE. On May 26, 1951, the United Kingdom filed an application with the Court instituting proceedings on the differences between the Government of Iran and the Anglo-Iranian Oil Company. These arose from the Iranian Oil Nationalization Act of May 1, 1951.

The United Kingdom asked the Court to declare that the Iranian Government was bound to submit the dispute to arbitration under the terms of the 1933 Convention between Persia (as Iran was then called) and the Anglo-Persian Oil Company, and to accept and carry out the arbitral award.

Alternatively, the United Kingdom asked the Court to declare that implementing the Oil Nationalization Act would be contrary to international law, insofar as it unilaterally annulled or altered the terms of the Convention. Moreover, the application asked the Court to declare:

that the Convention continued to be legally binding on Iran, and that by denying the Anglo-Iranian Oil Company the exclusive legal remedy provided in the Convention, Iran had committed a denial of justice contrary to international law;

that the Convention could not lawfully be annulled, or its terms altered, by Iran except by agreement with the Oil Company, or under the conditions of the Convention; and

to adjudge that the Government of Iran should give full satisfaction and indemnity for all acts committed in relation to the Anglo-Iranian Oil Company which were contrary to the agreement, and to determine the manner of such satisfaction and indemnity.

The application was immediately communicated to the Iranian Government.

On June 22, the United Kingdom made a request for indication of provisional measures of protection under Article 41 of the Statute of the Court. Hearings began on this request on June 30.

Interim Measures Ordered. The Court ruled on July 5 that the Anglo-Iranian Oil Company should continue under the direction of its management as it was constituted prior to May 1, 1951—the date when Iran adopted the Oil Nationalization Act. This was, however, subject to modification brought about by agreement with a Board of Supervision which, the Court decided, should be established by agreement between the Governments of Iran and the United Kingdom.

In opening the proceedings on June 30, the President noted the procedure instituted by the Court in this case. He then announced that the Iranian Foreign Minister had cabled the Court, stating reasons for which, in the view of the Iranian Government, the Court should reject the United Kingdom request to indicate interim measures.

In delivering its order, the Court adopted the following operative clauses:

1. The Iranian Government and the United Kingdom Government should each insure that no action was taken which might prejudice the rights of the other party in respect of carrying out any decision on merits which the Court might subsequently render;

2. The two Governments should insure that no action of any kind was taken which might aggravate or extend the dispute submitted to the court;

3. The two Governments should each insure that no measure of any kind should be taken designed to hinder the carrying on of the industrial and commercial

operations of the Anglo-Iranian Oil Company, Ltd., as they were carried on prior to May 1, 1951;

4. The Company's operations in Iran should continue under the direction of its management as it was constituted prior to May 1, 1951, subject to modification as might be brought about by agreement with the Board of Supervision referred to in Paragraph 5;

5. In order to insure the full effect of the preceding provisions, which in any case retained their own authority, there should be established by agreement between the Iranian Government and the United Kingdom Government a board to be known as the Board of Supervision, composed of two members appointed by each of the said Governments and a fifth member who should be a national of a third state and should be chosen by agreement between these Governments, or, in default of such agreement and upon the joint request of the parties, by the President of the Court. The Board would have the duty of insuring that the Company's operations would be carried on in accordance with the provisions of the above. It would, among its duties, have the duty of auditing revenue and expenses and insuring that all revenue in excess of the sums required to be paid in the course of the normal operations and other normal expenses incurred by the Anglo-Iranian Oil Company, Ltd., were paid into accounts at banks to be selected by the Board on the under-taking of such banks not to dispose of such funds except in accordance with the decisions of the Court or the agreement of the parties.

On July 9, 1951, Iran withdrew its acceptance of the compulsory jurisdiction of the Court (*see page 293*).

However, in June 1952, the case was called before the Court and Iran appeared, one of her counsel being the Prime Minister, Mohammed Mossadegh. Iran con-tended that the Court lacked jurisdiction in the matter, because no dispute between two governments existed on which the Court had power to make a ruling. The Iranian Declaration of 1932 (accepting the jurisdiction of the Court), it was con-tended, limited that jurisdiction to disputes arising after the ratification of the Declaration with regard to the application of treaties or conventions accepted by Iran subsequent to the ratification of the Declaration.

The United Kingdom claimed that the Declaration was to apply to all treaties; and, furthermore, that the United Kingdom, as a nation entitled, under an agree-ment, to be treated equally with the most favored nation, was entitled to rely on treaties which Iran had concluded with Denmark, Switzerland and Turkey after the date of the Iranian Declaration.

On July 22, 1952, the Court ruled that it lacked jurisdiction in the dispute and declared that the interim order, indicating measures of protection pending a final decision, ceased to be operative and the measures lapsed.

Basis of Jurisdiction. The judgment referred to the principle that the will of the parties was the basis of the Court's jurisdiction and noted that in the present case juris-diction depended on declarations accepting the Court's compulsory jurisdiction made by Iran and the United Kindom under Article 36, paragraph 2, of the Statute.

These declarations contained the conditions of reciprocity, and as Iran's decla-ration was more limited, it was on that declaration that the Court must base itself.

According to this declaration, the Court had jurisdiction only when the dispute related to the application of a treaty or convention accepted by Iran. Iran main-tained that, according to the actual wording, jurisdiction was limited to treaties subsequent to the declaration. The United Kingdom maintained that earlier treaties might also come into consideration.

In the view of the Court, both contentions might, strictly speaking, be compatible with the text but the Court could not base itself on a purely grammatical interpretation. It must seek an interpretation which was in harmony with a natural and reasonable reading of the text, having regard to the intention of Iran when it formulated its declaration. A natural and reasonable way of reading the text led to the conclusion that only treaties subsequent to ratification came into consideration. To reach an opposite conclusion, special and clearly established reasons would be required, but the United Kingdom was not able to produce them.

IRANIAN DECLARATION. On the contrary, it might be admitted that Iran had special reasons for drafting its declaration very restrictively and for excluding earlier treaties. For at that time Iran denounced all treaties relating to the regime of capitulations. Iran was uncertain about the legal effect of unilateral denunciation. In the circumstances, it was unlikely that Iran would be willing on its own initiative to agree to submit to the International Court disputes relating to all these treaties.

Moreover, the Iranian law by which the Majlis approved and adopted the declaration before it was ratified provided decisive confirmation of the Iranian intention, for it stated that the treaties and conventions were those which "the Government will have acccepted after ratification."

Earlier treaties were thus excluded by the declaration so that the United Kingdom could not rely on them. It invoked some subsequent treaties—those of 1934 with Denmark and Switzerland and of 1937 with Turkey—by which Iran undertook to treat the nationals of those powers in accordance with the principles and practice of ordinary international law.

The United Kingdom claimed that the Anglo-Iranian Oil Company was not treated in accordance with those principles and practices, and to rely on the above treaties, though concluded with third parties, found itself on the most favored nation clause in the two instruments it concluded with Iran, namely the treaty of 1857 and the commercial convention of 1903. But the two latter treaties which were the sole legal connection with the treaties of 1934 and 1937 were anterior to the declaration. The United Kingdom could not therefore rely on them; consequently it could not invoke subsequent treaties by Iran with third states.

1933 Agreement. Did the settlement of disputes between Iran and the United Kingdom effected in 1933 through the League of Nations result in an agreement between the two Governments which they regarded as a treaty or convention?

The United Kingdom maintained it did. It claimed that the agreement of 1933 between Iran and the Company had a double character, being a concessionary contract and a treaty between two states. In the view of the Court, that was not the case. The United Kingdom was not a party to the contract. The contract did not constitute a link between the two Governments and did not regulate relations between them. Under the contract Iran could not claim from the United Kingdom any rights which it might claim from the Company, nor could it be called upon to perform toward the United Kingdom any obligation which it was bound to perform toward the Company. This juridical situation was unaltered by the fact that the concessionary contract was negotiated through the good offices of the Council of the League of Nations through its rapporteur. The United Kingdom, in submitting its dispute with Iran to the League Council, was only exercising the right of diplomatic protection in favor of its national. Thus the Court arrived at the conclusion that it lacked jurisdiction.

NOTTEBOHM CASE. This case was submitted on December 10, 1951, by an application filed by Liechtenstein against Guatemala, claiming damages in respect of various measures which Guatemala had taken against the person and property of Friedrich

Nottebohm, alleged to be a citizen of Liechtenstein. The application referred to the declarations by which both parties had accepted the compulsory jurisdiction of the Court.

Guatemala submitted a preliminary objection to jurisdiction, based on the fact that the declaration by which it had accepted the compulsory jurisdiction of the Court had been made on January 27, 1947, for a period of five years and had, therefore, expired on January 26, 1952. Liechtenstein, on the other hand, relied on Article 36, paragraph 6, of the Statute, which provides that "in the event of a dispute as to whether the Court has jurisdiction, the matter shall be settled by the decision of the Court."

In its judgment delivered on November 18, 1953, the Court said that in the absence of any agreement to the contrary, an international tribunal had the right to decide as to its own jurisdiction and had the power to interpret for this purpose the instruments which governed its jurisdiction. Although the Guatemalan declaration expired on January 26, 1952, the Court had previously been seized of the case. Since neither in its declaration nor in any other way had Guatemala indicated that the time limit provided for in its declaration meant that the expiry of the period would deprive the Court of jurisdiction to deal with the cases of which it had been previously seized, the Court must exercise its powers as they were defined in the Statute. Accordingly, the Court came to the conclusion that it had jurisdiction to deal with the claim of Liechtenstein. It unanimously rejected the preliminary objection and resumed the proceedings on the merits, fixing time limits for the filing of further pleadings.

On April 6, 1955, the Court delivered its judgment on the merits of the case. Since Liechtenstein contended that Mr. Nottebohm was its national by virtue of the naturalization conferred upon him, the Court examined the necessary conditions for the naturalization of foreigners in Liechtenstein, as well as the practice of states concerning nationality. The Court pointed out that Mr. Nottebohm had always retained his family and business connections with Germany, and that there was nothing to indicate that his application for naturalization in Liechtenstein was motivated by any desire to disassociate himself from the Government of his country. On the other hand, he had been settled for 34 years in Guatemala, which was the center of his interests and his business activities. There was thus the absence of any bond of attachment with Liechtenstein, but there was a long-standing and close connection between him and Guatemala, a link which his naturalization in no way weakened.

For these reasons the Court, by 11 votes to 3, held the claim of Liechtenstein to be inadmissible.

MINQUIERS AND ECREHOS CASE. On December 6, 1951, the Government of the United Kingdom filed with the Court the text of a special agreement concluded between that Government and the French Government, requesting the Court to determine whether the sovereignty over the islets and rocks of the Minquiers and Ecrehos groups belonged to the United Kingdom or to the French Republic.

The two groups of islets in question lie between the British Channel Island of Jersey and the coast of France. The Ecrehos lie 3.9 sea miles from the former, and 6.6 sea miles from the latter. The Minquiers lie 9.8 sea miles from Jersey, and 16.2 sea miles from the French mainland, and 8 miles from the Chausey Islands, which belong to France.

The United Kingdom and France each submitted relevant documents in support of its claim of sovereignty over those islets.

With regard to the Ecrehos in particular, and on the basis of various medieval documents, the Court held the view that the King of England exercised his justice and levied his rights in those islets. The documents also showed that there was at that time time a close relationship between the Ecrehos and Jersey. From the beginning of the nineteenth century, the connection became closer again because of the growing importance of oyster fishery.

With regard to Minquiers, the Court noted that in 1615, 1616, 1617 and 1692, the manorial court of the fief of Noirmant in Jersey exercised its jurisdiction in the case of wrecks found at the Minquiers because of the territorial character of that jurisdiction. At the end of the eighteenth century and during the nineteenth and twentieth centuries, there were also facts which showed that Jersey authorities had in several ways exercised ordinary local administration in respect of the Minquiers during a long period of time. For a considerable part of the nineteenth century and the twentieth century, British authorities had exercised State functions in respect of the islets. The Court further found that the facts invoked by the French Government could not be considered as sufficient evidence of the intention of that Government to act as sovereign over the islets.

In its judgment delivered on November 17, 1953, the Court unanimously found that the sovereignty over the islets and rocks of the Ecrehos and Minquiers groups, insofar as these islets and rocks are capable of appropriation, belongs to the United Kingdom.

MONETARY GOLD CASE. By an application dated May 19, 1953, the Government of Italy instituted proceedings before the Court against France, the United Kingdom and the United States concerning the monetary gold removed from Rome in 1943.

The background for the Italian application was as follows: In 1943, the Germans seized a certain amount of monetary gold in Rome, which was the property of the National Bank of Albania, and transferred it to Germany. The Final Act of the Paris Convention on Reparation, signed in 1946 by eighteen states, including the United States, France, the United Kingdom and Albania, and to which Italy subsequently adhered, provided that monetary gold found in Germany should be pooled for distribution among the countries entitled to participate in the pool in proportion to their respective losses of gold as a result of looting by Germany. France, the United Kingdom and the United States were responsible for that distribution.

In respect of the gold removed from Rome in 1943, the three Governments, confronted with competing claims by Albania and Italy, requested the opinion of an arbiter. At the same time they declared (Washington statement of April 25, 1951) that if the finding of the arbiter should be in favor of Albania, the gold would be delivered not to Albania, but to the United Kingdom in partial satisfaction of the judgment of the Court in 1949, in the Corfu Channel Case. (*See page 293.*) It was agreed, however, that Albania could, within 90 days of the communication of the arbiter's opinion, apply to the Court for determination of the question whether such delivery to the United Kingdom was proper; or that Italy could apply to the Court for the determination of the question whether the gold should not be delivered to Italy rather than to the United Kingdom. In accordance with the latter provision, and having accepted the jurisdiction of the Court, Italy filed with the Court its application which contained the following submissions:

1. that France, the United Kingdom and the United States should deliver to Italy, in partial satisfaction for the damage caused to Italy by the Albanian law of January 13, 1945, any share of the monetary gold that might be due to Albania; and

2. that Italy's right to receive the said share of monetary gold must have priority over the claim of the United Kingdom to receive the gold in partial satisfaction of the judgment in the Corfu Channel Case.

Time-limits for the filing of the pleadings were then fixed by the Court. However, instead of presenting its memorial on the merits, the Italian Government questioned the jurisdiction of the Court to adjudicate upon the first question relating to the validity of the Italian claim against Albania. The parties having been requested to submit their views on the problem thus raised, the Italian Government contended that the Court did not have sufficient basis for adjudication on the ground that the proceedings contemplated by the Washington statement and which subsequently became Italy's first submission to the Court were in reality directed against Albania and that Albania was not a party to the suit.

In its judgment delivered on November 18, 1953, the Court stated that it was unusual that an applicant state should challenge the jurisdiction of the Court, but this should be understood in the light of the circumstances of the case: it was the Washington statement, emanating from the three Governments, that had formulated the offer of jurisdiction accepted by Italy and had predetermined the subject matter of the suit; and it was after taking the initial step that Italy had felt some doubt and had filed a preliminary objection to the competence of the Court. By this objection, Italy's acceptance of the jurisdiction of the Court had not become less complete or less positive than was contemplated in the Washington statements. To request the Court to settle the problem of jurisdiction was not tantamount to asking the Court not to determine the questions set out in the application under any circumstances. The Court concluded that unless the application was withdrawn, the Court was validly seized of the case.

The Court proceeded to consider the Italian objection to the jurisdiction in order to decide whether or not it could adjudicate upon the merits of the question submitted to it by the application. In this connection, the Court noted that the first submission in the Italian application centered around a claim by Italy against Albania, a claim to indemnification for an alleged wrong. Italy believed that she possessed a right against Albania for the redress of an international wrong which, according to Italy, Albania had committed against her. In order, therefore, to determine whether Italy was entitled to receive the gold, it was necessary to determine whether Albania had committed any international wrong against Italy, and whether there was an obligation on the part of Albania to pay compensation to Italy. In order to decide such questions, it was necessary to determine whether the Albanian law of January 13, 1945, was contrary to international law. To go into the merits of such questions would be to decide a dispute between Italy and Albania, and the Court could not decide such a dispute without the consent of Albania.

The Court found unanimously that, although Italy and the three respondent States had conferred jurisdiction upon the Court, that jurisdiction did not authorize it to adjudicate in the absence of the consent of Albania on the first claim submitted by Italy. As for the second claim, which related to the priority between the claims of Italy and the United Kingdom, it would only arise when it had been decided that, as between Italy and Albania, the gold should go to Italy. That claim was consequently dependent upon the first claim in the application. The Court accordingly found, by 13 votes to 1, that inasmuch as it could not adjudicate on the first Italian claim, it should refrain from examining the second.

"ELECTRICITÉ DE BEYROUTH" COMPANY CASE. On January 24, 1948, France and Lebanon decided to modify an agreement which had previously been concluded concerning the monetary and financial relations of the two countries. The new agreement included an undertaking by the Lebanese Government relating to the concessions of the French companies and companies with French capital in Lebanon. Article 23 of the agreement provided for the granting of jurisdiction to the Court. After the Lebanese Government had taken measures which the Electricité de Beyrouth Company, a French Limited company, considered contrary to the undertakings subscribed to by that Government, the French Government submitted, on August 11, 1953, an application to the Court instituting proceedings against the Government of Lebanon.

Time-limits were then fixed for the submission by the parties of their memorial and counter-memorial, and the French Government submitted its memorial within the time-limit prescribed.

By a letter dated July 13, 1954, Lebanon informed the Court that the presentation of the counter-memorial, as well as the continuation of the proceedings, was not devoid of object, having regard to the settlement of the dispute by the parties which had been ratified by the Lebanese Parliament, and that the French Government had agreed to discontinue the proceedings before the Court as soon as the settlement had been made.

On July 23, 1954, the French Government informed the Court that in view of its ratification of the agreement with Lebanon to settle the dispute, the French Government was not pursuing the proceedings and requested that its case be removed from the Court's list.

TREATMENT IN HUNGARY OF AIRCRAFT AND CREW OF THE UNITED STATES OF AMERICA CASE. On March 3, 1954, the Government of the United States filed an application against Hungary and another one against the U.S.S.R. regarding an aircraft and crew of the United States which had been forced to land on Hungarian territory on November 19, 1951. The applications stated that the aircraft and its contents had been seized by the U.S.S.R. authorities stationed in Hungary; that the crew had been held under arrest and incommunicado by those authorities and surrendered by them to the Hungarian authorities on December 3, 1951; that, following that delivery the four airmen had been kept under arrest and incommunicado by the Hungarian Government; that on December 23 a trial had been held and the airmen had been sentenced for premeditated crossing of the Hungarian frontier and fined; and that the airmen had been released on December 28, 1951, on payment under protest by the United States Government of a sum of $123,605.15.

In its applications, the United States Government requested the Court to consider the two cases and to deal with them together, if the Court found it convenient and proper to do so. Noting that the Governments of Hungary and of the U.S.S.R. were qualified to accept the jurisdiction of the Court and that they might confirm that jurisdiction upon notification of the applications, the Government of the United States founded the jurisdiction of the Court on certain considerations stated in the applications and on Article 36, paragraph 1, of the Statute.

The Hungarian Government, by a letter dated June 14, 1954, informed the Court that it was unable to submit to the jurisdiction of the Court in this case. By a letter dated April 30, 1954, the U.S.S.R. Government also informed the Court that it regarded as unacceptable the submission by the United States of the case to the Court, and that there existed no subject for consideration by the Court.

On July 12, 1954, the Court, in view of those communications, issued separate orders that the cases be removed from its list.

AERIAL INCIDENT OF MARCH 10, 1953. On March 29, 1955, the United States filed an application with the Court against Czechoslovakia concerning an aerial incident within the United States zone of occupation in Germany. The application contained the following summary of facts: On March 10, 1953, the Government of Czechoslovakia willfully and unlawfully caused MIG-type military aircraft to cross the

Czechoslovakian-German frontier and, without any provocation, to pursue and attack a United States Air Force F.84-type aircraft engaged in peaceful routine patrol of the air space within the United States zone of Germany. As a result, the latter aircraft was destroyed. The damage thus caused also included personal injuries to the pilot, a United States national. The United States alleged that those acts constituted serious violations of international obligation on the part of Czechoslovakia, and claimed monetary and other reparation from the Czechoslovakian Government.

In accordance with the provisions of the Statute of the Court, the application was communicated by the Registrar of the Court to the Government of Czechoslovakia, and transmitted to all states entitled to appear before the Court. No further action was taken during 1955.

ANTARCTICA CASES. On May 14, 1955, the United Kingdom filed with the Court two applications, one against Argentina and the other against Chile, relative to certain Antarctica territories. The United Kingdom contended that the Government of Argentina, on the one hand, and the Government of Chile, on the other, had encroached upon certain territories which are under British sovereignty. It requested the Court to recognize the validity of its titles to sovereignty and to declare the pretensions of Argentina and Chile, as well as their encroachments in those territories, contrary to international law.

In accordance with the provision of the Statute of the Court, the applications were communicated to the two interested Governments, and transmitted to all other states entitled to appear before the Court. No further action was taken during 1955.

AERIAL INCIDENT OF OCTOBER 7, 1952 (United States—U.S.S.R.) On July 2, 1955, the United States filed with the Court an application against the U.S.S.R. relating to an aerial incident which occurred off the Island of Hokkaido (Japan). In its application, the United States alleged that on October 7, 1952, one of its aircraft was pursued over Japanese territory and then shot down into the sea by two aircraft of the U.S.S.R. It requested the Court to find that the U.S.S.R. was liable for the damages caused in the sum of $1,620,295.

In accordance with the provisions of the Statute of the Court, the application was communicated by the Registrar to the U.S.S.R. Government, and notified to all other states entitled to appear before the Court. No further action was taken during 1955.

CASE OF THE NORWEGIAN LOANS ISSUED IN FRANCE. By an application dated July 5, 1955, the Government of France instituted proceedings against the Government of Norway concerning certain Norwegian loans issued in France.

The facts as stated in the application were as follows: The Kingdom of Norway issued on the French market a certain number of international bonds, made payable in gold or including a gold clause, which were held by French nationals. Certain of the loans were floated by the Kingdom of Norway, others through the intermediary of state banks on various dates between 1885 and 1907. A Royal Decree dated September 27, 1931, suspended the convertibility of notes issued by the Bank of Norway and since that date the service of the loans referred to above had been effected on the basis of the nominal amount of the coupons or of the repaid bonds by payment of Norwegian kroner only. The French holders of the Norwegian gold bonds requested the resumption of the service of the loans on the basis of the nominal amount in gold. The war of 1939 interrupted the discussions which were subsequently resumed but without success. In 1953, the French Government, intervening on behalf of its nationals, entered into negotiations with the Government of Norway, but conversations between the experts appointed by the respective

Governments led to no result. The Government of France took up the question again in May 1954, in the course of commercial negotiations with the Norwegian Government, and proposed that the dispute should be settled by arbitration; the Norwegian Government did not accept this proposal.

In submitting the case to the Court, the Government of France requested the Court to adjudge and declare that the international loans issued by the Kingdom of Norway and by its state banks in the years indicated stipulate in gold the amount of the borrower's obligation for the service of the coupons and the redemption of bonds and that Norway could only discharge its obligation by the payment of the gold value of the coupons and the redeemed bonds.

By an order issued on September 19, 1955, the Court fixed the time-limits for the filing of pleadings as follows:

for the memorial of the Government of the French Republic: December 20, 1955;

for the counter-memorial of the Government of the Kingdom of Norway: April 20, 1956.

RIGHT OF PASSAGE THROUGH INDIAN TERRITORY CASE. On December 22, 1955, Portugal filed with the Court an application against India concerning the right of Portuguese officials and nationals, as well as foreigners authorized by Portugal, to cross India on their way between the Portuguese territory of Damão (littoral Damão) and the Portuguese enclaved territories of Dadrá and Nagar-Aveli, and between each of the two last-mentioned territories.

It was stated in the application that the territory of Portugal included certain areas in the Indian peninsula which are divided into three districts of Goa, Damão and Diu. The district of Damão comprised, in addition to its littoral territory, two parcels of territory which were completely surrounded by the territory of India and thus constituted two genuine enclaves: Dadrá and Nagar-Aveli. Portugal claimed that it undeniably possessed a right of passage to those enclaves. However, beginning July 1954, it was alleged, the Government of India had taken measures to prevent Portugal from exercising the right of passage. As a result, Portugal had been unable to come to the aid of the enclaves and their inhabitants when attacked and occupied by armed bands coming from Indian territory. Accordingly, Portugal asked the Court to recognize and declare that Portugal was the holder or beneficiary of a right of passage between the above-mentioned territories and that India, by preventing Portugal from exercising that right, committed an offense to the detriment of Portuguese sovereignty over the said enclaves and violated its international obligations. Portugal further requested the Court to adjudge that India should put an immediate end to this *de facto* situation by allowing Portugal to exercise the right of passage.

It was further stated in the application that the Court had jurisdiction to determine the dispute for the reason that both Portugal and India had accepted the compulsory jurisdiction of the Court. No further action was taken during 1955.

ADVISORY OPINIONS

CONDITIONS OF ADMISSION OF A STATE TO MEMBERSHIP IN THE UNITED NATIONS (Article 4 of the Charter). (*See page 76 for the question submitted to the Court by the General Assembly at its second session*). On May 28, 1948, the Court delivered its advisory opinion. Having examined the text of Article 4 of the Charter, the Court came to the conclusion that the conditions laid down in that Article for the admission of a state to membership in the United Nations were exhaustive. Moreover, to subject an affirmative vote for admission of an applicant state to the condition that other states be admitted with that state would prevent Members from exercising their judgment in each case with complete liberty, within the scope of the prescribed conditions. Such a demand, said the Court, was incompatible with the letter and spirit of Article 4. By 9 votes to 6, the Court was of the opinion that a Member was not juridically entitled to make its consent to the admission dependent on conditions not expressly provided by paragraph 1 of Article 4 and that, in particular, a Member could not subject its affirmative vote to the additional condition that other states be admitted at the same time.

REPARATION FOR INJURIES INCURRED IN THE SERVICE OF THE UNITED NATIONS. Following the assassination of Count Folke Bernadotte and of others serving the United Nations in Palestine, the Assembly on December 3, 1948, requested an advisory opinion of the International Court of Justice on the question of reparation for injury suffered in the service of the United Nations. Written statements were submitted to the Court by China, France, India, the United Kingdom and the United States. During public sittings held in March 1949, the Court heard oral statements on behalf of the Secretary-General and of Belgium, France and the United Kingdom. On April 11, 1949, the Court rendered the unanimous opinion that the United Nations is an international person—though not a state or a "super-state"—and has the capacity to maintain its rights by bringing international claims against Member as well as non-Member states to obtain reparation for damages caused to itself or to any of its agents. When the United Nations was bringing such a claim, it could do so only by basing it upon a breach of obligation due to itself. The Court declared that respect for this rule would usually prevent a conflict between the action of the United Nations and such rights as the agent's national state might possess. It further held that to insure the efficient and independent performance of its missions and to afford effective support to its agents, the Organization itself must be able to provide them with adequate protection.

COMPETENCE OF THE GENERAL ASSEMBLY FOR THE ADMISSION OF A STATE TO THE UNITED NATIONS. Can the General Assembly, by its own decision, admit a state to the United Nations when the Security Council fails to make a recommendation for such admission either because the applicant failed to obtain the requisite majority of seven votes, or because of the use of a veto by a permanent member of the Security Council?

A request for an advisory opinion on the question was submitted to the Court by the General Assembly at its 1949 session.

The Court gave its opinion on March 3, 1950. In such cases, the Court said, the Assembly cannot admit a new Member by its own decision, since the relevant article of the Charter lays down that the admission of any state to membership in the United Nations is to be effected by a decision of the General Assembly upon the recommendation of the Security Council.

INTERPRETATION OF PEACE TREATIES WITH BULGARIA, HUNGARY AND ROMANIA. At the second part of its third regular session in April 1949, the Assembly had expressed "deep concern at the grave accusations made against the Governments of Bulgaria, Hungary and Romania regarding the suppression of human rights and fundamental freedoms in those countries;" it drew the attention of these Governments to their obligations under the Peace Treaties, including the obligation to cooperate in the settlement of all these questions.

At its fourth session, in October 1949, the Assembly declared that the refusal of the three Governments to cooperate in its efforts to examine the charges brought against them justified its "concern". Confronted by the charges of Treaty violations made by certain Powers against the three Governments, particularly the charge that they had refused to designate their representatives to the Treaty Commissions for the settlement of disputes—a procedure prescribed in the Peace Treaties to deal with such disputes—the Assembly put four questions to the Court for an advisory opinion. Did a dispute exist between the three States and certain Allied and Associated Powers in accordance with the provisions of the Peace Treaties, the Court was asked. On March 30, 1950, the Court declared that a dispute did exist. To the further question whether, if a dispute did exist, the three States were obligated to nominate their representatives to the Treaty Commissions, the Court gave an affirmative answer. It then set a time limit of 30 days for the three countries to comply with its opinion. On their failure to nominate their representatives within this limit, the Court, on July 18, 1950, answered the remaining two questions. It decided that the fact that the three countries had not complied with the Court's opinion did not authorize the Secretary-General to appoint the third member of each commission. In view of this, the Court declared, the answer to the fourth question—will a commission of two members, one appointed by the Secretary-General, and the other by a party to the dispute be competent to make a definite and binding decision—was not necessary.

INTERNATIONAL STATUS OF SOUTH WEST AFRICA. With the exception of South West Africa, over which the Union of South Africa was granted a mandate after the First World War, all other territories under the League of Nations Mandates have either become independent, or have been placed under the United Nations Trusteeship System.

In 1946, 1947 and again in 1948, the Assembly reaffirmed its recommendation that South West Africa be placed under the Trusteeship System, and a Trusteeship Agreement submitted.

Owing to the refusal of the Union of South Africa to comply with the Assembly resolution, or to submit reports on this mandated territory to the Trusteeship Council, the Assembly in 1949, asked the advisory opinion of the Court on these points: (a) whether the Union Government still had international obligations under the League of Nations Mandate, and if so, what they were; (b) whether the provisions of the Trusteeship System applied to the Territory, and if so, in what manner; and (c) whether the Union Government had the right to modify the international status of the Territory, or, if not, what authority could determine and modify this status.

In its opinion given on July 11, 1950, the Court declared that the supervisory functions of the League with regard to mandated territories not placed under the new Trusteeship System were neither expressly transferred to nor assumed by the United Nations.

The Court ruled that the necessity for supervision continued to exist, despite the disappearance of the supervisory organ under the Mandates System.

The Court considered that the competence of the General Assembly to exercise such supervision and to receive and examine reports, as well as petitions, was derived from the provisions of the Charter, and that the Union was under an obligation to submit to the supervision and control of the Assembly and to render annual reports to it.

The Court was of the opinion that the Union of South Africa was under an obligation to accept the compulsory jurisdiction of the Court according to those provisions.

With regard to the question whether the provisions of the Trusteeship System applied to the Territory, the Court said that they were applicable in the sense that they provided a means by which the Territory might be brought under the Trusteeship System but that it was not compulsory under the Charter to place the Territory under the Trusteeship System by means of a Trusteeship Agreement.

The Court decided that the Union could not modify unilaterally the international status of the Territory, or any of the relevant international rules.

In the opinion of the Court, the General Assembly had the authority under the Charter to approve any modification of the international status of a territory under mandate which would not have for its purpose the placing of the territory under the Trusteeship System.

The Court was of the opinion that the Union of South Africa acting alone has not the competence to modify the international status of the Territory of South West Africa, and that the competence to determine and modify the international status of the Territory rests with the Union acting with the consent of the United Nations.

RESERVATIONS TO GENOCIDE CONVENTION. Responding to a request of the Assembly at its 1950 session, the Court gave its advisory opinion on the effect of reservations in ratifying or acceding to the Convention on Genocide. The Court's opinion, handed down on May 28, 1951, was:

First, "that a state which has made and maintained a reservation that is objected to by one or more of the parties to the Convention, but not by others, can be regarded as being a party to the Convention if the reservation is compatible with the object and purpose of the Convention; otherwise, that state cannot be regarded as being a party to the Convention."

Second, "(a) that if a party to the Convention objects to a reservation which it considers incompatible with the object and purpose of the Convention, it can in fact consider that the reserving state is not a party to the Convention;

"(b) that if, on the other hand, a party accepts the reservation as being compatible with the object and purpose of the Convention, it can in fact consider that the reserving state is a party to the Convention."

Third, "(a) that an objection to a reservation made by a signatory state which has not yet ratified the Convention can have the legal effect indicated in the reply to question I only upon ratification; until that moment such an objection merely serves as a notice to the other states of the eventual attitude of the signatory state;

"(b) that an objection to a reservation made by a state which is entitled to sign or accede, but has not yet done so, is without legal effect."

EFFECT OF AWARDS OF COMPENSATION MADE BY THE UNITED NATIONS ADMINISTRATIVE TRIBUNAL. On December 9, 1953, the General Assembly decided to request an advisory opinion from the Court on the question whether the Assembly had the right on any grounds to refuse to give effect to an award of compensation made by the Administrative Tribunal in favor of a staff member of the United Nations whose contract of service had been terminated without his assent; it further asked the Court, should its reply to that question be in the affirmative, to indicate the principal grounds on which it could lawfully exercise that right.

Written statements were presented to the Court on behalf of the International Labor Organization and on behalf of Chile, China, Ecuador, France, Greece, Guatemala, Iraq, Mexico, the Netherlands, the Philippines, Sweden, Turkey, the United Kingdom and the United States. In the course of hearings held for this purpose in June 1954, oral statements were submitted on behalf of France, Greece, the Netherlands, the United Kingdom and the United States.

In its opinion, delivered on July 13, 1954, the Court stated that the reply to be given to the first question depended on the Statute of the Tribunal, and on the Staff Regulations and Rules of the United Nations. After an examination of those texts, the Court found that the Tribunal was established as an independent and truly judicial body. The contracts of service were concluded between the staff member concerned and the United Nations represented by the Secretary-General. The judgment of the Tribunal, which was final and without appeal and not subject to any kind of review, had binding force upon the United Nations as the juridical person responsible for the proper observance of the contract of service. Since the Organization became legally bound to carry out the judgment and to pay the compensation awarded to the staff member, it followed that the General Assembly as an organ of the United Nations must likewise be bound. The General Assembly could always amend the Statute of the Tribunal and provide for the review of its awards; but, in the opinion of the Court, the Assembly itself, in view of its composition and functions, could hardly act as a judicial organ, all the more so as one party to the dispute was the Organization itself.

Having further refuted other arguments put forward in support of the view that the General Assembly might be justified in refusing to give effect to the awards of the Tribunal, the Court, by 9 votes to 3, answered in the negative the first question submitted by the General Assembly, and declared that it was unnecessary for the Court to consider the second question.

VOTING PROCEDURE ON QUESTIONS RELATING TO REPORTS AND PETITIONS CONCERNING THE TERRITORY OF SOUTH WEST AFRICA. In the advisory opinion given on July 11, 1950 (*see above*), the Court stated that the Union of South Africa continued to have international obligations binding upon it in respect of the territory of South West Africa and that the supervisory functions were to be exercised by the United Nations. That opinion was accepted by the General Assembly as a basis for supervision over the administration of the territory.

In 1954, a Committee of the General Assembly drafted sets of rules one of which, rule F, read as follows: "Decisions of the General Assembly on questions relating to reports and petitions concerning the territory of South West Africa shall be regarded as important questions within the meaning of Article 18, paragraph 2, of the Charter of the United Nations."

On November 23, 1954, the General Assembly decided to request an advisory opinion from the Court on the following questions:

1. whether the above-quoted rule F on the voting procedure to be followed by the General Assembly was a correct interpretation of the advisory opinion of the Court of July 11, 1950; and

2. if that interpretation was not correct, what voting procedure should be followed by the General Assembly in taking decisions on questions relating to reports and petitions concerning the territory of South West Africa?

In its opinion, delivered on June 7, 1955, the Court pointed out that the Assembly was primarily concerned with the question whether rule F corresponded to a correct interpretation of the following passage from the Court's opinion of 1950: "The degree of supervision to be exercised by the General Assembly should not, therefore, exceed that which applied under the Mandate System, and should conform as far as possible to the procedure followed in this respect by the Council of the League of Nations." The words "the degree of supervision", said the Court, related to the extent of the substantive supervision and not to procedural matters, such as the system of voting which was applicable in the time of the League of Nations. Consequently, rule F could not be regarded as relevant to the "degree of supervision". The word "procedure" used in the second part of the passage in question referred to those procedural steps whereby supervision was to be effected; but the voting system of the General Assembly was not in contemplation when the Court used those words. Moreover, in the opinion of 1950, the Court had said that the General Assembly derived its competence to exercise its supervisory functions from the Charter; it was, therefore, within the framework of the Charter that the Assembly must find the rules governing the making of its decisions in connection with those functions.

For those reasons, the Court was unanimously of the opinion that rule F corresponded to a correct interpretation of the opinion of 1950. The Court declared that since the first question had been answered in the affirmative, it was not necessary for the Court to consider the second question.

The International Law Commission

The International Law Commission is charged with promoting the progressive development of international law and its codification. Its fifteen members, elected by the General Assembly for a three-year[7] term, do not serve as representatives of governments but in their individual capacity as experts.

The Commission was established by General Assembly resolution 174 (II) of November 21, 1947; its activities are regulated by a statute annexed to the resolution. Since its adoption the statute has been modified by General Assembly resolutions 485 (V) of December 12, 1950 (amendment of article 13 regarding travel and subsistence allowances of the members), 984 (X) of December 3, 1955 (amendment to article 12 regarding the place of meeting of the Commission) and 985 (X) of December 3, 1955 (amendment to article 10 regarding the term of office of the members).

The first election of members took place at the third session of the General Assembly, in 1948.

The members as of the end of 1955, elected in 1953, were:

Gilberto Amado (Brazil); Douglas L. Edmonds (United States); Sir Gerald Fitzmaurice (United Kingdom); J. P. A. Francois (Netherlands); F. V. García-Amador (Cuba); Shuhsi Hsu (China); Faris Bey el-Khouri (Syria); S. B. Krylov (U.S.S.R.); L. Padilla Nervo (Mexico); Radhabinod Pal (India); Carlos Salamanca (Bolivia); A. E. F. Sandstrom (Sweden); Georges Scelle (France); Jean Spiropoulos (Greece); and Jaroslav Zourek (Czechoslovakia).

The term of the members was due to expire at the end of 1956, and a new election would be held during the eleventh session of the General Assembly.

Beginning in 1949, the Commission each year has held one session lasting from eight to eleven weeks.

Since it began its work, the Commission prepared a draft declaration on the rights and duties of states; formulated the principles of international penal law recognized in the Charter and judgment of the Nürnberg Tribunal; prepared a draft code of offences against the peace and security of mankind; studied the question of defining aggression; expressed an opinion regarding the desirability and possibility of establishing an international judicial organ for the trial of persons charged with genocide and certain other crimes; made recommendations on the problem of reservations to multilateral conventions; prepared draft conventions on the elimination or reduction of future statelessness; and submitted proposals concerning the ways and means for making the evidence of customary international law more readily available.

The Commission also prepared a draft convention on arbitral procedure which was referred back to the Commission by the General Assembly in December 1955, for continued study in the light of government comments and observations made

---

[7] By resolution 985 (X) adopted by the General Assembly at its tenth session in 1955, the term of office was, as from January 1, 1957, changed to five years. The members elected at the eleventh session of the General Assembly would consequently serve for a five-year term.

in the course of discussions held on the subject in the Assembly's Sixth (Legal) Committee.

In addition, the Commission was preparing drafts relating to the regime of the high seas and the regime of the territorial sea, subjects scheduled to be concluded at its 1956 session. Furthermore, the Commission was to continue the study of the law of treaties and of the question of diplomatic intercourse and immunities; and at its 1955 session, it also decided to begin the study of two other topics, consular intercourse and immunities and state responsibility.

DRAFT DECLARATION ON RIGHTS AND DUTIES OF STATES

Completed at the Commission's first session, the draft Declaration on Rights and Duties of States consists of fourteen articles. Four define basic rights of states: to independence, to the exercise of jurisdiction over state territory in accordance with international law, to equality in law, and to individual or collective self-defence against armed attack.

The basic duties of states are contained in ten of the articles. These are: to conduct international relations in accordance with international law and to observe legal obligations; to settle disputes by peaceful means, in accordance with law and justice; to refrain from intervention and from resorting to war or other illegal use of force; to refrain from assisting any state resorting to war or other illegal use of force, as well as any state against which the United Nations is taking preventive or enforcement action; to refrain from recognizing any territorial acquisition resulting from war or other illegal use of force; to refrain from fomenting civil strife in the territory of other states; to insure that conditions in its territory do not menace international peace and order; and to respect the human rights and fundamental freedoms of all persons within its jurisdiction without distinction of race, sex, language or religion.

At its 1949 session, the General Assembly commended the draft Declaration to the continuing attention of Member States and of jurists of all nations. It also invited the suggestions of Member States on: (1) whether any further action should be taken by the Assembly on the draft Declaration; and (2) if so, the exact nature of the document they wished drafted and the future procedure to be adopted in relation to it.

As the number of replies received from governments was considered too small to form the basis of a definite decision regarding the Declaration, the General Assembly, at its sixth session in 1951, decided to postpone further consideration of the matter, but in any case to undertake its consideration as soon as a majority of Member States had answered.

Eighteen Member States by October 18, 1952, had sent in their comments.

No comment has been received since that date, and no further development has taken place.

FORMULATION OF THE NURNBERG PRINCIPLES

At its 1946 session, the General Assembly unanimously affirmed the principles of international law recognized in the Charter and in the judgment of the International Military Tribunal for the prosecution and punishment of the major German war criminals (Nürnberg Tribunal). In the following year, it directed the International Law Commission to formulate those principles, and also to prepare a draft code of offences against the peace and security of mankind. At its second session (June-July 1950), the Commission completed a formulation of these principles.

The (seven) principles formulated state, *inter alia,* that the perpetrator of a crime under international law is personally responsible for the crime, and that he is not relieved from such responsibility, either because the act is not punishable under the law of any particular country, or because he acted as Head of State or responsible government official, or because he acted under superior orders, provided a moral choice was open to him. Another principle is that any person charged with a crime under international law has the right to a fair trial.

The Commission also defined crimes against peace, war crimes, and crimes against humanity, and laid down as a final principle that complicity in one of these crimes also constitutes a crime under international law.

At its 1950 session, the Assembly decided to send the Commission's formulations to Member Governments for comment. Further, the Assembly requested the Commission, in preparing a draft code of offences against the peace and security of mankind, to take account of observations on the Nürnberg principles made during the session or subsequently received from governments.

No further action was taken on the formulation of the Nürnberg principles.

DRAFT CODE OF OFFENCES AGAINST THE PEACE AND SECURITY OF MANKIND

The task of preparing a draft code of offences against the peace and security of mankind was entrusted to the Commission in 1947, by the same General Assembly resolution that requested it to formulate the Nürnberg principles. The Commission discussed the question of the code in a preliminary way at its first and second sessions, in 1949 and 1950. As mentioned above, the formulation of the Nürnberg principles was completed in 1950, and submitted to the Assembly which invited observations from Member Governments and asked the Commission to take account of the comments made on the formulation, when it prepared its final draft of the code.

At its third session in 1951, the Commission completed the draft of a code and submitted it to the General Assembly. The Commission decided to limit the code to offences containing a political element and endangering or disturbing the maintenance of international peace and security. It therefore omitted such matters as piracy, traffic in dangerous drugs, traffic in women and children, slavery, counterfeiting of currency, and damage to submarine cables. The Commission also decided that it would deal only with the criminal responsibility of individuals, and that no provisions should be included with respect to crimes by abstract entities. The offences enumerated in the code were characterized as "crimes under international law, for which the responsible individuals shall be punishable."

The following offences were included in the draft code: act of aggression (*for definition, see below*); threat of aggression; preparation, by the authorities of a state, for the employment of armed force against another state for any purpose other than national or collective self-defence or in pursuance of a decision or recommendation by a competent organ of the United Nations; incursion into the territory of a state from another state by armed bands acting for a political purpose; acts by state authorities connected with fomenting civil strife or terrorist activities in another state; violation by state authorities of treaty obligations concerning limitations of armaments, military training, fortifications, or other similar restrictions; annexation of a territory in violation of international law; genocide by authorities of a state or by private individuals; inhuman acts against the civilian population, when committed in connection with other offences under the code; acts in violation of the laws of war; and conspiracy, incitement or attempts to commit any of the offences defined in the code, as well as complicity in committing them. The fact that a person acted as Head of a state, or as a responsible government official, did not relieve him from responsibility. If a person acted pursuant to an order of his government or of a superior, he would be responsible only if a moral choice were in fact possible for him.

The Commission refrained from drafting an instrument for implementing the code; it thought that, pending the establishment of an international criminal court, the code might be applied by national courts. As the Commission deemed it impracticable to prescribe a definite penalty for each offence, it was left to the competent tribunal to determine the penalty for any offence under the code, taking into account the gravity of the particular offences.

At its 1951 session, the Assembly decided to postpone consideration of the draft code until the 1952 session, in view of the fact that the draft had only recently been communicated to governments. Consequently, the Secretary-General invited Member Governments to communicate to him, before June 1, 1952, any comments or observations which they might wish to make on the draft code. Replies were received from fourteen governments.

At the 1952 session of the Assembly, the item was omitted from the final agenda on the understanding that the matter would continue to be considered by the International Law Commission.

The Commission accordingly took up the matter again at its fifth session in 1953, and requested the special rapporteur to prepare a new report for submission at the sixth session. That report discussed the observations received from governments, and proposed certain changes in the text previously adopted by the Commission. The Commission decided to modify its previous text in certain respects, by, *inter alia*, adding a new offence to the list of crimes, namely the intervention by the authorities of a state in the internal or external affairs of another state by means of coercive measures. It also decided to omit the condition that inhuman acts against a civil population were crimes only when committed in connection with other offences defined in the code. The rule regarding crimes committed under order by a superior was reworded to say that the perpetrator of such a crime would be responsible if, under the circumstances at the time, it was possible for him not to comply with the order.

At its 1954 session, the General Assembly, considering that the draft code raised problems closely related to that of the definition of aggression, decided to postpone further consideration of the draft code until the new special committee on the question of defining aggression had submitted its report (*see directly below*).

DEFINITION OF AGGRESSION

In connection with the discussion of the item "Duties of states in the event of the outbreak of hostilities" in the First (Political and Security) Committee of the 1950 Assembly session, the U.S.S.R. proposed that the Assembly declare, among other things, that in an international conflict that state shall be declared the attacker which first commits one of the acts enumerated in the proposal.

The Assembly referred the U.S.S.R. proposal to the International Law Commission for formulation of its conclusions.

At its third session, held in Geneva from May 16 to July 27, 1951, the Commission first decided that it was undesirable to define aggression by a detailed enumeration of aggressive acts, since no enumeration would be exhaustive. It also thought it inadvisable unduly to limit the freedom of judgment of the competent organs of the United Nations by a rigid and necessarily incomplete list of acts constituting aggression. When an attempt was made to draw up a general definition in abstract terms, the majority of the Commission felt that this also would be unsatisfactory. On reconsideration, the Commission decided, however, to embody a general, although not exhaustive, definition of aggression in the draft code of offences against the peace and security of mankind (see above). It agreed to consider as one such offence "any act of aggression, including the employment, by the authorities of a state, of armed force against another state for any purpose other than national or collective self-defence or in pursuance of a decision or recommendation by a competent organ of the United Nations."

At its sixth session, the Assembly discussed the subject and came to the conclusion that it was possible and desirable to define aggression by reference to the elements which constitute the crime. At the Assembly's request, the Secretary-General submitted a detailed analysis which covered all aspects of the question.

The Assembly's discussion at the seventh session revealed the complexity of the question. Both the desirability of the attempt and the expediency of making it in the present world context were challenged by many Members and the practical value of a definition questioned. In particular, the Assembly recognized that detailed study was called for on the forms of aggression; the connection between a definition and the maintenance of peace; the question of the place of the definition on the Code of Offences against the peace and security of mankind; and the effect of a definition on the work of United Nations organs. Other problems were also raised or implied in the extensive committee debate. All these, the Assembly decided, should be studied by an expert group and continued and joint efforts made to formulate a generally acceptable definition with a view of promoting peace and security and developing international law.

The Assembly, in December 1952, decided to establish a fifteen-member Special Committee which was requested to submit to the Assembly at the ninth session draft definitions of aggression or draft statements of the notion of aggression. The Special Committee was to proceed on the assumption that the definition would be adopted by a resolution of the Assembly.

The Committee met at United Nations Headquarters from August 24 to September 21, 1953. It considered, inter alia, the questions raised by the Assembly at its seventh session, but did not take any decision of substance on any of these questions. The principal ideas put forward during its debates were summarized in the report submitted to the Assembly. Several texts were presented to the Committee which aimed at defining, in one form or another, aggression. The Committee, however, decided unanimously not to put the texts to a vote but to transmit them to the General Assembly and, for comments, to Member States.

Comments were received from eleven Member Governments.

At the 1954 session of the Assembly, the opinion was again divided as to the desirability of defining aggression; it was also divided with regard to the type of definition to be adopted. To coordinate the views expressed in the discussions, the General Assembly decided to establish another Special Committee consisting of nineteen members, and requested it to report to the eleventh session of the Assembly. This Committee was scheduled to meet in 1956.

INTERNATIONAL CRIMINAL JURISDICTION

At the request of the General Assembly, the International Law Commission during its second session studied the desirability and possibility of establishing an international judicial organ for the trial of genocide and certain other crimes. The Commission concluded that the establishment of an international criminal court was both possible and desirable. It recommended against such a court being set up as a chamber of the International Court of Justice.

The General Assembly at its fifth session set up a special committee to prepare one or more draft conventions and proposals relating to the establishment and statute of an international criminal court. The Committee, consisting of seventeen members, met in Geneva in August 1951, and completed a draft statute for an international criminal court.

The Committee's proposals included a court set up by means of a convention rather than by a General Assembly resolution. The convention, the Committee proposed, should be concluded under United Nations auspices by a conference called by the General Assembly.

The Court should have a permanent, rather than an *ad hoc,* structure. It would, however, function only when cases were submitted to it. It should be composed of nine judges representing as far as possible the main forms of civilization and the principal legal systems of the world. Its members would be elected for a nine-year term by the states parties to the court's statute, and the expenses of the court would be borne by those states rather than by the United Nations.

The Court's functions would be to judge crimes under international law, as might be provided in conventions or special agreements among states parties to the statute. Under the terms of the draft, the court would apply international law, including international criminal law, and, where appropriate, national law. The court should not deal with crimes under national law which are of international concern, such as counterfeiting, the traffic in persons, attacks on members of foreign governments, and so on.

The principal method of conferring jurisdiction on the court would be the conclusion among states parties to the statute of conventions to that effect, relating to cases which might arise with respect to one or more groups of crimes. In addition, jurisdiction with respect to any specific criminal act which had already been committed might be conferred by a special agreement between two or more states parties to the statute or by a unilateral renunciation of jurisdiction by a single such state in favor of the court. Any conferment of jurisdiction would require the approval of the General Assembly.

The Committee recommended that the General Assembly invite the conference of states convoked for establishing the court to draw up at the same time a protocol conferring jurisdiction on the court in respect of the crime of genocide.

The report of the Committee, together with the draft statute, was communicated to governments for their observations. Only a few governments had commented on the draft, however, by the Assembly's seventh session. The Assembly therefore urged Member States, especially those states who felt that further action should be taken, to furnish their comments and suggestions. The debate in the Sixth (Legal) Committee, to which the question had been referred, revealed a wide divergence of opinion, not only on some aspects of the draft statute, but also as to the fundamental question of principle, namely, whether the General Assembly should, at that juncture, proceed to take steps for the establishment of an international criminal court as a permanent body. The Assembly therefore decided to set up a new committee consisting of seventeen members, which met at United Nations Headquarters in the summer of 1953. The terms of reference of the committee were: (1) to explore the implications and consequences of establishing an international criminal court and of the various methods by which this might be done, (2) to study the relationship between such a court and the United Nations, and (3) to reexamine the draft statute.

In addition to the report and draft statute prepared by the 1951 Committee, the 1953 Committee had before it the comments submitted by governments.

The Committee decided that the best method of establishing an international criminal court would be by means of a convention prepared by an international diplomatic conference convened under the auspices of the United Nations; and that the court should not come into existence until jurisdiction had been conferred on it by a certain number of states and until a certain number of states had ratified the convention containing the statute of the court.

The Committee made a number of changes in the 1951 draft statute and in respect of several articles prepared alternative texts, one appropriate if the court were to operate separately from the United Nations and the other in case it were decided that the court should be closely linked with the United Nations.

It increased the number of methods by which jurisdiction might be generally conferred on the court by states, gave a fuller definition of the effect of conferment of jurisdiction, deleted a requirement that the General Assembly should approve the conferment of jurisdiction, and inserted a provision on the withdrawal of jurisdiction. The right to institute proceedings before the court was confined to states which had conferred jurisdiction over the offences involved, and a provision in the 1951 draft statute giving the right to the General Assembly or to any organization of states authorized by the Assembly was eliminated.

The report of the Committee was placed before the Assembly at its 1954 session. From the outset of the general debate, the suggestion was advanced that consideration of the question of international criminal jurisdiction should be postponed until a later session. The Assembly, considering the connection between the question of defining aggression, the draft code of offences against the peace and security of mankind and the question of an international criminal jurisdiction, decided to postpone consideration of the latter until it had taken up the report of the 1956 special committee on aggression, and until it had again taken up the draft code of offences.

RESERVATIONS TO MULTILATERAL CONVENTIONS

The Secretary-General asked the General Assembly at its 1950 session for directions on the procedure he should follow on reservations made by states as conditions to their adherence to or ratification of conventions adopted by the General Assembly, or multilateral treaties deposited with the Secretary-General.

The Assembly invited the International Law Commission to study the general problem of reservations to multilateral conventions.

The Commission proposed rules which it considered "the most convenient for states to adopt for the future." It considered that the criterion of compatibility of a reservation with the object and purpose of a multilateral convention, applied by the International Court of Justice to the Convention on Genocide, would not be suitable for application to multilateral conventions in general. (For the advisory opinion of the International Court of Justice on reservations to the Genocide Convention, see page 311.) The Commission believed that it might often be more important to maintain the integrity of a convention than to aim, at any price, at the widest possible acceptance of it.

While no single rule uniformly applied could be wholly satisfactory, the Commission felt that, subject to certain modifications, the rule suitable for application in the majority of cases might be found in the practice hitherto followed by the Secretary-General.

(The principle he had been following was that: "A state may make a reservation when signing, ratifying, or acceding to a convention, prior to its entry into force, only with the consent of all states which have ratified or acceded theretofore up to the date of entry into force; and may do so after the date of entry into force only with the consent of all states which have ratified or acceded.")

The Commission suggested that, in preparing future conventions, organs of the United Nations, specialized agencies, and states should insert provisions as to the admissibility or non-admissibility of reservations and as to the effect to be attributed to them.

The General Assembly on January 12, 1952, endorsed the Commission's recommendation that provisions regarding reservations should be inserted in future conventions. It also recommended to all states that they be guided by the advisory opinion of the International Court of Justice in regard to the Genocide Convention. It requested the Secretary-General:

(a) in relation to reservations to the Genocide Convention, to conform his practice to the advisory opinion of the Court; and (b) in respect of future conventions concluded under the auspices of the United Nations of which he is the depositary: (1) to continue to act as depositary in connection with the deposit of documents containing reservations or objections, without passing upon the legal effect of such documents; and (2) to communicate the text of such documents relating to reservations or objections to all states concerned, leaving it to each state to draw legal consequences from such communications.

NATIONALITY, INCLUDING STATELESSNESS

A topic selected for codification by the Commission at its first session was nationality, including statelessness. The Commission considered this subject primarily with respect to two problems: the nationality of married women and the elimination of statelessness.

At its second session in 1950, the Commission was asked by the Economic and Social Council to draft a convention regarding the nationality of married women, embodying certain principles which had been recommended by the Commission on the Status of Women. These principles were: (a) that there should be no distinction based on sex as regards nationality, and (b) that neither marriage nor its dissolution should affect the nationality of either spouse.

A draft of a convention on the nationality of married persons was submitted to the Commission at the fourth session in 1952, by its special rapporteur on nationality. The draft followed very closely the terms proposed by the Commission on the Status of Women and approved by the Economic and Social Council. The Commission, however, decided that the question of the nationality of married women could not suitably be considered by it separately but only in the context, and as an integral part, of the whole subject of nationality. The Commission therefore did not take further action with respect to the draft. On the other hand, the problem of the nationality of married women continued to be under consideration by other organs of the United Nations (*see page 225*).

At its third session in 1951, the Commission was notified of a request by the Economic and Social Council that it should prepare at the earliest possible date a draft international convention or conventions for the elimination of statelessness.

In pursuance of this request, the Commission at its fifth session in 1953, prepared two drafts, namely, a draft convention on the elimination of future statelessness, and a draft convention on the reduction of future statelessness which were transmitted to governments for comment.

At its sixth session, the Commission discussed the observations made by governments on the two draft conventions and redrafted some of the articles in the light of their comments. The most common observation made by governments was that some provisions of their legislation conflicted with certain articles of the draft conventions. Since statelessness is, however, attributable precisely to the presence of those provisions in municipal law, the Commission took the view that this was not a decisive objection for, if governments adopted the principle of the elimination, or at least the reduction, of statelessness in the future, they should be prepared to introduce the necessary amendments in their legislation. The draft conventions, each consisting of eighteen articles, on the one hand, aimed at facilitating the acquisition of the nationality of a country by birth within its borders, and on the other hand, at avoiding the loss of a nationality except when another nationality was acquired. The convention for the elimination of future statelessness would impose stricter obligations on the contracting parties than the one which had the more modest aim of merely reducing statelessness. The Commission stated in its report that it would be for the General Assembly to consider to which of the draft conventions preference should be given.

At the 1954 session of the Assembly, a majority of representatives expressed the opinion that the time was not ripe for immediate consideration of the substance of the draft conventions, and that the positions of Member States with respect to the drafts had not yet been sufficiently ascertained. On the other hand, the Assembly expressed its desire that an international conference of plenipotentiaries should be convened to conclude a convention for the reduction or elimination of future statelessness as soon as at least 20 states had communicated to the Secretary-General their willingness to cooperate in such a conference.

By the end of 1955, fourteen States had indicated their willingness to participate in the conference.

WAYS AND MEANS OF MAKING THE EVIDENCE OF CUSTOMARY INTERNATIONAL LAW MORE READILY AVAILABLE

In its report on its second session, the Commission had made these recommendations; that the widest possible distribution be made of publications relating to international law issued by organs of the United Nations; that the Assembly authorize the Secretariat to prepare and widely distribute eight groups of publications which would make the evidence of customary international law more readily available; and that the Assembly call to the attention of governments the desirability of their publishing digests of their diplomatic correspondence.

At its 1950 session, the General Assembly invited the Secretary-General to consider and report to the Assembly upon these recommendations.

On the basis of that report, the Assembly at its sixth session, noted with satisfaction that a *repertoire* relating to the interpretation of the Charter was already under way, and requested the Secretary-General to submit a report as to possible publication of a United Nations juridical yearbook, a consolidated index to the League of Nations *Treaty Series*, a supplementary list of treaty collections, and a *repertoire* of the practice of the Security Council. At its seventh session, the Assembly authorized the Secretary-General to undertake the publication: (a) of a list of treaty collections, and (b) of a *repertoire* of the practice of the Security Council. The resolution also requested the Secretary-General to prepare and circulate to Member Governments a comparative study of the extent to which development in customary international law and selected legal activities of the United Nations could usefully be covered by an expansion of existing United Nations publications, by new special publications of limited scope, and by a United Nations juridical yearbook.

A *repertoire* of the practice of the Security Council 1946-1951 was published in 1954, and a list of treaty collections was to appear in 1956.

The comparative study referred to above was circulated to the Member States during the tenth session of the General Assembly in 1955, in connection with its discussion of the question of printing the documents of the International Law Commission (*see below*).

ARBITRAL PROCEDURE

Among the topics selected for codification by the Commission at its first session in 1949, was Arbitral Procedure. On the basis of reports submitted by a special rapporteur the matter was discussed at the second, fourth and fifth sessions of the Commission.

Two currents of opinion were represented in the Commission. The first followed the conception of arbitration according to which the agreement of the parties is the essential condition not only of the original obligation to have recourse to arbitration, but also of the continuation and the effectiveness of arbitration proceedings at every stage. The second conception, which prevailed in the draft as adopted and which may be described as judicial arbitration, was based on the consideration that it was necessary to safeguard the efficacy of the obligation to arbitrate in all cases in which, after the conclusion of the arbitration agreement, the attitude of the parties threatens to render nugatory the original undertaking. A number of articles having that purpose were inserted in the draft.

At the fourth session, the Commission approved a Draft on Arbitral Procedure, consisting of 32 articles, with comments, which was submitted to governments for comment.

At its fifth session, in the light of replies made by governments the Commission introduced in the draft some alterations in order to simplify the procedure previously formulated. The General Assembly was asked to recommend the draft to Members with a view to the conclusion of a convention. The Assembly, at its 1953 session, decided to transmit the draft to Member States with the observations made in its Sixth (Legal) Committee, with a view to the submission by governments of whatever comments they deemed appropriate.

The Assembly took up the question again at its 1955 session. On the recommendation of its Sixth (Legal) Committee, the Assembly decided to refer the draft back to the International Law Commission, and to invite the Commission to consider the comments of governments and the discussion in the Sixth (Legal) Committee insofar as they might contribute further to the value of the draft. The Commission was asked to report on the matter at the 1958 session of the Assembly.

REGIME OF THE HIGH SEAS

The regime of the high seas was one of the topics which the Commission, at its first session in 1949, selected for codification and to which it gave priority. A questionnaire was sent to the governments of all Member States and a special rapporteur was appointed to study the question; he submitted reports at the second, third, fourth[8], fifth, sixth[8] and eighth[9] sessions.

At its second session, the Commission considered the topic, using as a basis of discussion the report of the special rapporteur, which outlined the various subjects which might, in his opinion, be studied with a view to the codification or the progressive development of international maritime law. The Commission then took the

---

[8] The report was not discussed until the following session.
[9] The report dealt also with the regime of the territorial sea.

view that it could not undertake a codification of maritime law in all its aspects, and that it would be necessary to select the subjects the study of which could be begun as a first phase of its work on the topic. The Commission thought that it could for the time being leave aside all those subjects which were being studied by other United Nations organs or by the specialized agencies, as well as those which, because of their technical nature, were not suitable for study by it. Lastly, it set aside a number of subjects, the limited importance of which did not appear to justify their consideration in the present phase of its work. The subjects selected for study by the Commission were: nationality of ships, collision, safety of life at sea, right of approach, slave trade, submarine telegraph cables, resources of the sea, right of pursuit, contiguous zones, sedentary fisheries, and the continental shelf.

The continental shelf is a term which geologists have long used to describe a particular formation of the bed of the sea off certain coasts where moderately shallow water extends for a considerable distance from the land, and then the seabed takes a plunge into great depths. The legal interest in the subject arises from recent engineering developments which make possible the exploiting of the natural resources of the seabed, in particular, oil. The legal problem is to reconcile such exploitation, which may be in the general interest, to the fact that the waters concerned are part of the high seas and therefore open to all for navigation and fishing.

At its third session, the Commission prepared a set of draft articles on the continental shelf and related subjects and invited governments to submit their comments on it.

The Commission at its fifth session, in the light of the comments received from governments, prepared final draft articles on the following questions: (1) continental shelf, (2) fishery resources of the high seas, and (3) contiguous zone. It recommended that the General Assembly adopt the draft articles by resolution. However, at its 1953 session, the Assembly decided not to deal with any aspect of the regime of the high seas until all the problems involved had been studied by the Commission and reported to the Assembly.

The Assembly, nevertheless, at the request of several delegations, took up the question again at its 1954 session. The question of substance, however, was not discussed and the Assembly merely requested the International Law Commission to devote the necessary time to the study of the regime of the high seas, the regime of the territorial sea, and all related problems in order to complete its work on these topics and submit its final report in time for the Assembly to consider them as a whole at its 1956 session.

At the fifth session, the Commission, besides preparing the draft on the continental shelf and related questions, had also requested the special rapporteur to prepare a new report covering subjects not dealt with in the earlier reports. While thereby reverting to the idea of codifying maritime law, the Commission decided not to include any detailed provisions on technical matters or to encroach on ground already covered in special studies by other United Nations organs or specialized agencies.

At its seventh session, the Commission considered the report submitted by the rapporteur in pursuance of this request, and adopted 38 provisional articles concerning the regime of the high seas. These articles were circulated to governments for comment.

After examining the comments by governments on the drafts previously prepared, the Commission at its eighth session proposed to group together systematically in a single report all the rules adopted by it in respect of the high seas, the territorial sea (*see below*), the continental shelf, contiguous zones, fisheries, and the protection of the living resources of the sea.

REGIME OF THE TERRITORIAL SEA

At the request of the General Assembly, the Commission in 1951 decided to initiate work on the regime of the territorial sea, and appointed its special rapporteur on the regime of the high seas as rapporteur also on this related subject.

At the fourth session, the special rapporteur submitted a report which contained, with annotations, a draft regulation divided into three chapters: general provisions (meaning of "territorial sea", and juridical status of the territorial sea and its bed and subsoil), limits of the territorial sea, and right of passage. The Commission discussed the report and expressed its views for the guidance of the rapporteur. It was also decided that the special rapporteur should be free to consult with experts with a view to elucidating some technical questions. Such a group met at The Hague in April 1953. Certain technical information was also sought from governments. In the light of the observations made by the Commission, by governments and by the group of experts, the rapporteur amended and supplemented his draft.

On the basis of this preparatory work, the Commission at its sixth session adopted a number of draft articles, with comments, which were submitted to governments.

At the seventh session, the Commission examined the comments received from governments and amended and supplemented its draft, which was again circulated to governments for comments, together with a number of articles concerning the regime of the high seas. As mentioned above, the Commission, in pursuance of the General Assembly's request, was to submit to the eleventh session of the Assembly in 1956 a final report on all the matters pertaining to the international law of the sea and being under consideration by the Commission.

LAW OF TREATIES

This topic was also selected for codification at the Commission's first session, and assigned to a rapporteur. Governments were requested to furnish the Commission with the texts of laws, decrees, judicial decisions, treaties, diplomatic correspondence, and other documents relevant to the subject. The Commission gave consideration to the topic from its second to fifth sessions; several preliminary drafts were prepared by successive rapporteurs, but no draft has yet been adopted by the Commission. The topic was still pending before the Commission.

DIPLOMATIC INTERCOURSE AND IMMUNITIES

By a resolution adopted at its 1952 session, the Assembly requested the Commission to undertake the codification of the topic "diplomatic intercourse and immunities."

A special rapporteur was appointed at the sixth session of the Commission; he prepared for the seventh session a report containing a draft for the codification of the law relating to diplomatic intercourse and immunities. The draft was divided into three parts: diplomatic intercourse in general (articles 1 to 11), diplomatic privileges and immunities (articles 12 to 26), and duties of a diplomatic agent (articles 27 and 28). A commentary followed the draft.

The Commission decided to postpone consideration of the subject until its eighth session.

CONSULAR INTERCOURSE AND IMMUNITIES

At its 1955 session, the Commission decided to initiate work on the codification of the topic "consular intercourse and immunities," and appointed a special rapporteur who was to present a report on the subject at the 1956 session.

STATE RESPONSIBILITY

At the 1955 session, the Commission also appointed a special rapporteur for the subject "state responsibility," and requested him to submit a report at the next session.

COOPERATION WITH INTER-AMERICAN BODIES

In accordance with article 26 of its Statute, which recognizes the advisability of consultation by the Commission with inter-governmental organizations whose task is the codification of international law, such as those of the Pan American Union, the Commission at its sixth session adopted a resolution whereby it asked the Secretary-General to take such steps as he might deem appropriate in order to establish a closer cooperation between the Commission and the inter-American bodies.

In accordance with that resolution and a further request made at the seventh session, the Secretary-General authorized the Secretary of the Commission to attend, in the capacity of an observer, the third meeting of the Inter-American Council of Jurists which was to be held in Mexico City in the beginning of 1956. The Secretary of the Commission was to report at the next session concerning such matters discussed by the Council as were also on the agenda of the Commission.

REVISION OF COMMISSION'S STATUTE

At its 1950 session, the General Assembly asked the Commission to review its Statute and suggest revisions desirable for promoting its work.

At its third session, the Commission recommended that, in the interest of promoting and expediting its work, it should be placed on a full-time basis after the new elections in 1953. Members should devote all their time to the work of the Commission, and should not exercise any political or administrative function or engage in any other occupation of a professional nature.

Taking note of this and other recommendations at its sixth session, the Assembly decided for the time being not to take any action on revision of the Statute until it had acquired further experience of the functioning of the Commission.

At its seventh session, the Commission recommended to the General Assembly an amendment to Article 12 of its Statute, to the effect that the Commission should sit at the European Office of the United Nations at Geneva (instead of New York), unless it decided otherwise after consultation with the Secretary-General.

The Commission also recommended to the General Assembly an amendment to Article 10 of the Statute, providing that members should be elected for a period of five years, instead of three.

These amendments were adopted by the General Assembly at its 1955 session.

The Assembly at the same session, invited the Commission to communicate its opinion concerning the amendment of Article 11 of its Statute, which concerns the filling of casual vacancies in its membership. Under the existing rule, such vacancies are filled by the Commission itself. In view of the extension of the term of office of the members from three to five years, the question was raised in the General Assembly as to whether in the future the casual vacancies should not be filled by the Assembly.

PRINTING OF THE DOCUMENTS OF THE INTERNATIONAL LAW COMMISSION

At its seventh session, the Commission adopted a resolution concerning the publication of its studies, special reports and summary records. This asked the Assembly to examine the possibilities of printing these documents. Documents of the Commission with few exceptions have been issued in mimeographed form.

The Assembly at its 1955 session adopted a resolution requesting the Secretary-General to arrange as soon as possible for the printing of the documents of the Commission. The studies, special reports, principal draft resolutions, and amendments of the first seven sessions were to be printed in their original languages; and the summary records of the first seven sessions were to be printed in English. The documents (including the summary records) of future sessions are to be printed in English, French and Spanish.

War Criminals

On October 31, 1947, the General Assembly reaffirmed its policy, laid down in 1946, that no action on refugees and displaced persons should interfere with the surrender and punishment of war criminals, quislings and traitors. It also reaffirmed its 1946 resolution which called for the arrest of war criminals and their return for trial in the countries where their crimes were committed.

The Assembly recommended that Member States continue to carry out their responsibilities concerning the apprehension of war criminals and their return for judgment. It was further recommended that states desiring the surrender of alleged war criminals by other Members support their requests with evidence that a reasonable *prima facie* case existed as to their identity and guilt. The Assembly reasserted that the trials of alleged war criminals should be governed by the principles of justice, law and evidence.

Privileges and Immunities

UNITED NATIONS

The General Assembly in February 1946 approved a Convention on the Privileges and Immunities of the United Nations. This was then submitted to every Member for accession. The main provisions of this Convention are as follows:

The United Nations shall possess juridical personality;

Its property and assets shall enjoy immunity from legal process except when that immunity is waived;

The premises and the archives of the United Nations shall be inviolable, and its property and assets shall be free from all direct taxes and customs duties;

In regard to its official communications, the United Nations shall enjoy treatment in the territory of each Member State which is no less favorable than that accorded by the government of that Member to any other government;

The representatives of Members, officials of the United Nations, and experts on missions of the United Nations shall enjoy such privileges and immunities as are necessary for the independent exercise of their functions; and

The United Nations may issue United Nations *laissez-passer* to its officials which shall be recognized and accepted as valid travel documents by the Member States.

On December 8, 1948, the Assembly urged all Member States to accede as soon as possible to the Convention on the Privileges and Immunities of the United Nations. It considered it essential for Members to approve the Convention's provisions if the United Nations were to perform its functions effectively. By the end of 1955, 45 Members had acceded.

The Assembly recommended in December 1946 that Member States grant diplomatic privileges and immunities to the judges and the Registrar of the International Court. Agents and counsel of parties before the Court, and assessors, witnesses, and experts should be granted such privileges and immunities as might be necessary for the independent exercise of their functions. The resolution also approved the agreement of June 1946, between the International Court and the Netherlands on the Court's privileges and immunities in the Netherlands.

On June 26, 1947, the United Nations concluded an agreement with the United States on all matters of privileges and immunities in regard to the Headquarters of the United Nations. This agreement entered into force on November 21, 1947. On December 18, 1947, an interim Headquarters Agreement was signed extending the appropriate provisions of the Headquarters Agreement to the interim Headquarters of the United Nations at Lake Success.

Agreements and arrangements relating to the privileges and immunities to be enjoyed by the United Nations, its organs, representatives of Member States, and officials of the United Nations attending United Nations conferences, commissions, and missions in the territories of Member and non-Member states are covered by special agreements between the United Nations and the states concerned.

SPECIALIZED AGENCIES

The Assembly, on November 21, 1947, approved a Convention on the Privileges and Immunities of the Specialized Agencies. By the end of 1955, 20 states had acceded to this Convention.

LAISSEZ-PASSER

The Secretary-General has concluded administrative arrangements with all the specialized agencies to enable them to use the United Nations *laissez-passer* in accordance with the authority conferred on them by the various agreements between the United Nations and the specialized agencies. The arrangements with some agencies are on a permanent basis, with some others they are on an annual renewal basis.

In June 1950, the International Court of Justice issued *laissez-passer* to the judges and to the Registrar and other officials of the Court, in accordance with the Assembly resolution of December 11, 1946, which recommended that Member States of the United Nations should recognize and accept such *laissez-passer*.

Permanent Missions to the United Nations

Since the creation of the United Nations, the practice has developed of establishing permanent missions of Member States at the seat of the Organization. Considering it necessary to regulate the submission of credentials of permanent representatives, the General Assembly on December 3, 1948, recommended that their credentials be issued either by the Head of the state or by the Head of the government or by the Minister of Foreign Affairs, and be transmitted to the Secretary-General. Changes of members of the permanent missions other than the permanent representatives should be communicated in writing to the Secretary-General by the Head of the mission. The Assembly further recommended that the permanent representative, in case of temporary absence, should notify the Secretary-General of the name of the member of the mission replacing him. Finally, Member States which wanted their permanent representatives to represent them on one or more of the organs of the United Nations should specify in their credentials the organs concerned.

In December 1955, 57 Members had permanent missions at the seat of the United Nations.

Registration and Publication of Treaties and International Agreements

Article 102 of the Charter provides that every treaty and international agreement entered into by any Member State after the coming into force of the Charter shall be registered and published by the Secretariat. (The Charter came into force on October 24, 1945). No party to a treaty or agreement not so registered may invoke it before any United Nations organ.

In order to close the gap between the League Treaty Series and the new United Nations Publications, the Assembly in February 1946 instructed the Secretary-General to invite Members to transmit treaties and agreements entered into before October 24, 1945, but which were not included in the League's Treaty Series. He was also to receive similar treaties and agreements from non-Member states for filing and publication.

Regulations to insure the orderly registration and publication of treaties and international agreements were adopted by the Assembly on December 14, 1946. Under these regulations, specialized agencies may also, subject to certain conditions, register or file and record a treaty with the Secretariat.

The Assembly on November 3, 1948, instructed the Secretary-General to insure that registered treaties or agreements be published with the least possible delay, and that the translations reach the highest possible level of accuracy and precision. Each Member was asked to take cognizance of the registration obligation under Article 102, and to take immediate steps to fulfil this obligation.

At its 1949 session, the Assembly asked the Secretary-General to publish all registered treaties and agreements as early as possible.

During 1955, a total of 526 treaties and agreements were registered with the Secretariat—eighteen *ex officio*, 439 by 26 Governments, and 69 by five specialized agencies. A total of 21 treaties and agreements were filed and recorded—nine by the Secretariat of the United Nations, one at the request of one government and eleven at the request of three specialized agencies. This brought up to 4,686 the total of treaties and agreements registered or filed and recorded by the end of 1955. In addition, during 1955, 220 certified statements relating to those treaties were registered and two certified statements were filed and recorded. This brought up to 874 the total of certified statements registered or filed and recorded by the end of 1955.

The texts of treaties and agreements registered or filed and recorded are published by the Secretariat in the *United Nations Treaty Series* in the original languages, followed by translations in English and French. Thirty-two volumes (110 to 141) of the *Treaty Series* were published in the course of 1955. The past years have shown a marked progress in the number of treaties registered.

Reparation for Injury Suffered in the Service of the United Nations

In 1949, the General Assembly authorized the Secretary-General to present claims against governments alleged to be responsible for the injury or death of United Nations agents in the performance of their duties. During 1950 to 1955, the Secretary-General determined in the following cases that the circumstances in which the United Nations agents concerned were killed in Palestine appeared to involve the responsibility of certain states. The action taken by the Secretary-General in each case is indicated below:

COUNT FOLKE BERNADOTTE

In April 1950, the Secretary-General made a claim against the Israeli Government for the sum of $54,628 as reparation for the monetary damage borne by the United Nations (*see page 115*). The claim by the United Nations was based upon three elements of responsibility: failure to exercise due diligence and to take all reasonable measures for the prevention of the murder; liability of the Government for actions committed by irregular forces in territory under the control of the Israeli authorities; and failure to take all the measures required by international law, and by the resolutions of the Security Council to bring the culprits to justice.

In the same year the Israeli Government paid the full amount of the claim presented by the United Nations without admitting the validity of all the legal contentions referred to above.

OLE HELGE BAKKE

The United Nations Guard was killed on July 13, 1948, while on service with the United Nations Mediator in Palestine. The Secretary-General, having determined that Mr. Bakke was killed in territory under the control of the Government of Jordan and by members of the Jordan armed forces, prepared a claim for the payment of $36,803.76 paid by the United Nations to Mrs. Marit Bakke, widow, and $3,800 for Mr. Bakke's mother. The Foreign Minister of Jordan replied that as the result of careful investigation it had been established to the satisfaction of the Jordan Government that Mr. Bakke had not been shot by a member of the Arab Legion. The suggestion of the Secretary-General for the establishment of a Fact-Finding Committee to ascertain the facts of the case, and to make recommendations both to the United Nations and the Jordan Government did not meet with the acceptance of the Jordan Government.

COLONEL ANDRE SEROT

In September 1952, the Secretary-General wrote to the Government of Israel requesting payment to the United Nations of the sum of $25,233 as reparation for the monetary damage borne by the Organization, as a consequence of the death of the United Nations military observer, Colonel André Sérot, who was assassinated will the United Nations Mediator, Count Bernadotte, in territory under the control of the Israeli Government. The Permanent Representative of Israel to the United Nations paid the amount demanded by the United Nations, and also a further sum of $575 (the equivalent of 200,000 French Francs) in payment for the claim for damage made by Colonel Sérot's father.

LT. COLONEL QUERU AND CAPTAIN PIERRE JEANNEL

In 1952, the Secretary-General addressed a letter to the Government of Egypt presenting a claim in the amount of $52,874.20 as reparation for the damage caused to the United Nations as the result of the deaths of these two observers. The Secretary-General determined that the two officers had been attacked and killed by Saudi Arabian troops under Egyptian Command after leaving their planes with the United Nations marking, which had landed at the Gaza airfield. In 1953, the Secretary-General wrote again to the Egyptian Government indicating that in addition to arbitration he would be prepared to consider any other means of settling the matter that might be suggested by the Egyptian Government. In reply, the Egyptian Government stated that the claim was being examined by the competent authorities. Since 1953, two further communications were addressed to the Egyptian Government on the question to which no reply had been received to date.

Proceedings in National Courts

The capacity of the United Nations to institute legal proceedings in national courts is governed by Article 104 of the Charter, and by Article 1 of the Convention of Privileges and Immunities of the United Nations. With respect to the United States, which has not yet acceded to the Convention, the International Organizations Immunities Act of 1945 provides that international organizations, including the United Nations, shall possess the capacity to institute legal proceedings.

The United Nations has brought legal actions in several countries on its own behalf and on behalf of the United Nations International Children's Emergency Fund (UNICEF) and the United Nations Relief and Works Agency for Palestine Refugees in the Near East, as for example, the taking of steps for the collection of certain maritime and other claims assigned by the United Nations Relief and Rehabilitation Administration to the United Nations for the benefit of UNICEF. Other actions included legal proceedings in New York courts regarding traffic accidents which involved United Nations vehicles, petitions brought in a California court in connection with the distribution of an estate, and an action in France involving the purchase of blankets from UNICEF.

In a case where a staff member employed by the Economic Commission for Latin America brought action against the Commission in the Arbitration Tribunal of Mexico City for the payment of termination indemnities and overtime, the Supreme Court of Mexico ruled that the Federal Employees Act of Mexico applied only to federal employees, and the Tribunal has no jurisdiction over controversies between an organ of the United Nations and its personnel. It further asserted that international commissions, as in the case in question, enjoyed immunities recognized by international law, and that the justice of the Mexican Union protected the Commission against the judgment of the Arbitration Tribunal.

Rules of Procedure of United Nations Organs

THE GENERAL ASSEMBLY

Following the work of a fifteen-member special committee, in October 1949, the General Assembly made several changes in its rules of procedure in order to expedite its work. One of the revised rules, for example, states that the Assembly may limit the time allowed each speaker and the number of times each representative may speak on any question.

Under a Charter provision, proposals relating to important questions require a two-thirds majority of Assembly Members present and voting. At its fourth session, the Assembly requested the Secretary General to present, at the fifth session, a thorough legal analysis of the question of the majority required for the adoption by the Assembly in plenary meeting of amendments to such proposals, and of the question of the majority required for the adoption of parts of such proposals when put to the vote separately.

The Secretary-General's report on the question was placed on the agenda of the fifth session of the General Assembly. The Assembly, on November 1, 1950, approved the Secretary-General's conclusion, and adopted a new rule of procedure—rule 84(a)—providing for a two-thirds majority for decisions on amendments to proposals relating to important questions, and on parts of such proposals when put to the vote separately.

A Special Committee studying the matter of legal and drafting questions in the Assembly had proposed that at some appropriate stage certain types of resolutions proposed for adoption by the General Assembly should be referred to the Sixth (Legal) Committee. The resolutions indicated were those calling for advisory opinions from the International Court of Justice, or reference to the International Law Commission, or contemplating an amendment to the Assembly's rules of procedure. As to other questions, the recommendation was that whenever a Committee felt that the legal aspect was important, it should consult the Legal Committee or a joint Committee of itself and the Legal Committee.

The Assembly decided that reference to the Legal Committee should be optional in all these categories except two. Recommendations to amend the rules of procedure are to be referred to the Sixth (Legal) Committee. Further, when the legal aspects are considered important, a Committee should refer it for legal advice to the Sixth (Legal) Committee or propose a Joint Committee.

On November 3, 1950, the Assembly adopted a resolution on "Uniting for Peace" which also provides for additions to certain rules and for a new rule. These amendments relate to the convening of emergency special sessions, and to their agenda and organization. By these amendments, emergency special sessions of the General Assembly in certain circumstances may be convened on 24 hours' notice on the vote of any seven members of the Security Council or a majority of the Members of the United Nations.

On October 23, 1953, the General Assembly, on the recommendation of the Sixth (Legal) Committee, took note of the report of the Special Committee which was appointed by the Assembly during the seventh session to consider measures to limit the duration of regular sessions of the Assembly, and amended Rule 38 to provide for the participation of the Chairman of the *Ad Hoc* Political Committee, whenever one was established, as a full member of the General Committee. Rule 39 was amended to provide that the Chairman of the *Ad Hoc* Political Committee might, in the same way as the Chairmen of the six main committees, designate the Vice-Chairman of the Committee to substitute for him in the meetings of the General Committee. An amendment to Rule 98 relating to priorities in each main committee, consequent upon the Assembly's decision at its seventh session to fix a closing, rather than a target, date for its sessions, was also adopted.

The General Assembly, on November 28, 1953, established a Committee on South West Africa which was requested, *inter alia*, to prepare for consideration by the Assembly a procedure for the examination of reports and petitions relating to that territory which should conform as far as possible to the procedure followed in that respect by the Assembly, the Council, and the Permanent Mandates Commission of the League of Nations. In the course of its ninth session, the General Assembly examined the report of the Committee on South West Africa and adopted, in a slightly amended form, six special rules proposed by that Committee. These rules relate to the procedure in regard to the consideration of reports submitted by the Union of South Africa on South West Africa, and of petitions submitted with respect to that territory to the Assembly. One of the rules provides that decisions of the Assembly on questions relating to reports and petitions concerning the territory of South West Africa should be considered as "important questions" within the meaning of Article 18, paragraph 2, of the Charter of the United Nations (for an advisory opinion of the International Court on this question, see under this chapter "International Court of Justice, Advisory Opinions").

THE SECURITY COUNCIL

The Security Council conducts its proceedings on the basis of provisional rules adopted at the Council's first meeting—with certain amendments made since.

THE ECONOMIC AND SOCIAL COUNCIL

The Council revised its rules of procedure in 1953, in order to adopt Spanish as a third working language of the Council and of its functional commissions.

The Eonomic and Social Council examined various questions relating to its organization and operations during the years 1954 and 1955. The Council stressed the importance of concentrating on the most important and pressing problems and the need for a more constructive discussion of important questions before it and for allowing adequate time for the preparation of relevant documents. It decided to hold two regular sessions each year and provided for a distribution of major topics between the two regular sessions. In addition, it invited the Secretary-General, with the assistance of appropriate officials of the Secretariat, to introduce both the discussion of the world economic situation and the discussion of the world social situation and to make it a practice to have questions relating to the world economic situation discussed in the Council with the participation of the Executive Secretaries of the regional economic commissions. The Council did not consider it necessary to amend any of its rules of procedure as a consequence of the above request to the Secretary-General.

THE TRUSTEESHIP COUNCIL

During its eleventh session, the Trusteeship Council adopted a number of amendments to its rules of procedure. One of the rules grants authority to the Visiting Missions of the Council to decide which of the communications they receive are intended for their own information, and which are to be transmitted to the Secretary-General for consideration by the Council. Another rule provides for the establishment of a Standing Committee on Petitions of six members to undertake a preliminary examination of all written petitions and of oral petitions which may be referred by the Council to it. During its fourteenth session, the Council adopted further amendments to its rules of procedure relating to the examination of petitions by the Standing Committee on Petitions. These amendments deal with the time-limit for the submission by the Administering Authority concerned of observations on petitions and also for holding meetings of the Standing Committee as often as necessary, depending on the volume of its work.

Official Seal, Emblem and Flag of the United Nations

The General Assembly on December 7, 1946, adopted an official seal and emblem of the United Nations, and recommended that Members prohibit the use of the emblem, name or initials of the United Nations without the authorization of the Secretary-General.

On October 20, 1947, the Assembly adopted a flag of the United Nations. Its design consists of the official emblem in white, centered on a light-blue background. The Secretary-General was directed to draw up regulations concerning its dimensions and proportions, and to adopt a code to regulate the use of the flag and protect its dignity.

THE FLAG CODE

The following is the text of the Flag Code, as amended by the Secretary-General on July 28, 1950:

1. *Design of Flag.* The flag of the United Nations shall be the official emblem of the United Nations, centered on a United Nations blue background. Such emblem shall appear in white on both sides of the flag except when otherwise

prescribed by regulations. The flag shall be made in such sizes as may from time to time be prescribed by regulation.

2. *Dignity of Flag.* The flag shall not be subjected to any indignity.

3. *Flag Protocol.* (1) The flag of United Nations shall not be subordinated to any other flag. (2) The manner in which the flag of the United Nations may be flown, in relation to any other flag, shall be prescribed by regulation.

4. *Use of Flag by the United Nations.* (1) The flag shall be flown (a) from all buildings, offices and other property occupied by the United Nations; (b) from any official residence when such residence has been so designated by regulation. (2) The flag shall be used by any unit acting on behalf of the United Nations, such as any Committee or Commission or other entity established by the United Nations, in such circumstances not covered in this Code as may become necessary in the interest of the United Nations.

5. *Use of Flag Generally.* The flag may be used in accordance with this Flag Code by Governments, organizations and individuals to demonstrate support of the United Nations and to further its principles and purposes. The manner and circumstances of display shall conform, insofar as appropriate, to the laws and customs applicable to the display of the national flag of the country in which the display is made.

6. *Use of Flag in Military Operations.* The flag may be used in military operations only upon express authorization to that effect by a competent organ of the United Nations.

7. *Prohibition.* The flag shall not be used in any manner inconsistent with this Code or with any regulations made pursuant thereto. On no account shall the flag or a replica thereof be used for commercial purposes or in direct association with an article of merchandise.

8. *Mourning.* The Secretary-General will prescribe by regulation or otherwise the cases in which the flag shall be flown at half-mast as a sign of mourning.

9. *Manufacture and Sale of Flag.* (1) The flag may be manufactured for sale only upon written consent of the Secretary-General. (2) Such consent shall be subject to the following conditions: (a) the flag shall be sold at a price to be agreed upon with the Secretary-General; (b) it shall be the responsibility of the manufacturer to insure that every purchaser of the flag is furnished with a copy of this Code as well as a copy of any regulations issued pursuant thereto, and that each purchaser is informed that his use of the flag is subject to the conditions contained in this Code and in the regulations made pursuant thereto.

10. *Violation.* Any violation of this Flag Code may be punished in accordance with the law of the country in which such violation takes place.

11. *Regulations.* (1) The Secretary-General may delegate his authority under the Code. (2) The Secretary-General or his duly authorized representative is the only person empowered to make regulations under this Code. Such regulations may be made for the purposes indicated in this Code and generally for the purpose of implementing or clarifying any provision of this Code whenever the Secretary-General or his duly authorized representative considers such implementation or clarification necessary.

REGULATIONS FOR DISPLAY

The flag regulations, prescribing the manner in which the United Nations flag is to be displayed and prohibiting its use for certain purposes, as drawn up by the Secretary-General and amended on October 30, 1950, may be summarized as follows:

The flag may be displayed or otherwise used, in accordance with the Flag Code, by governments, organizations and individuals to demonstrate support of the United Nations and to further its principles and purposes.

In such cases it may be displayed alone or with one or more other flags. When the United Nations flag is displayed with one or more other flags, the latter will on no account be displayed on a higher level than the United Nations flag, nor be larger than the United Nations flag.

The United Nations flag may be displayed on either side of any other flag without being deemed to be subordinated to any such flag within the meaning of article 3(1) of the United Nations Flag Code.

The United Nations flag should normally only be displayed on buildings and on stationary flagstaffs from sunrise to sunset. On special occasions, it may also be displayed at night. It should not be displayed on days when the weather is inclement. It should never be carried flat or horizontally but always aloft and free. It should never be used as drapery of any sort, never festooned, drawn back, nor up, in folds, but always allowed to fall free.

CLOSED CIRCLE OF FLAGS. In a closed circle of flags, flags other than the United Nations flag should be displayed in the English alphabetical order of the countries represented by the flags reading clockwise. The flagpole immediately opposite the main entrance of the main building determines the beginning of the circle. The United Nations flag should always be displayed on and not shifted from either the flagpole immediately opposite the main entrance of the main adjacent building or the flagpole in the centre of the circle of flags.

LINE, CLUSTER OR SEMI-CIRCLE OF FLAGS. In line, cluster, or semi-circle groupings, all flags other than the United Nations flag shall be displayed in the English alphabetical order of the countries represented by the flags starting from the left and reading clockwise. The United Nations flag should either be displayed in the centre of the line, cluster or semi-circle or, in cases where two United Nations flags are available, at either end of the line, cluster or semi-circle.

NATIONAL FLAG OF THE COUNTRY IN WHICH THE DISPLAY TAKES PLACE. The national flag of the country in which the display takes place should appear in its normal position according to the English alphabetical order.

When the country in which the display takes place wishes to make a special display of its national flag, such a special display can only be made where the arrangement of the flags takes the form of a line, cluster or semi-circle grouping, in which case the national flag of the country in which the display is taking place should be displayed at each end of the line of flags separated from the grouping by an interval of not less than one-fifth of the total length of the line.

USE OF FLAG GENERALLY. The United Nations flag may be used to demonstrate support of the United Nations and to further its principles and purposes. Its use is deemed especially appropriate on the following occasions: on all national and official holidays; on United Nations Day, October 24; on the occasion of any official event, particularly in honor of the United Nations; and on the occasion of any official event which might or is desired to be related in some way to the United Nations.

PROHIBITIONS. On no account is the United Nations flag or its replica to be used for commercial purposes or in direct association with an article of merchandise.

Neither the United Nations flag nor its replica shall be stamped, printed, engraved, or otherwise affixed on any stationery, books, magazines, periodicals, or other publications of any nature whatsoever in a manner which could imply that these were published by or on behalf of the United Nations, unless such is in fact the case, or in a manner which has the effect of advertising a commercial product.

Neither the United Nations flag nor its replica should be affixed in any manner on any article of any kind which is not strictly necessary to the display of the United Nations flag itself. In particular, the United Nations flag should not be reproduced on such articles as cushions, handkerchiefs and the like, nor printed or otherwise impressed on paper napkins or boxes, nor used as any portion of a costume or athletic uniform or other clothing of any kind, nor used on jewelry.

A replica of the United Nations flag may be manufactured in the form of a lapel button.

No mark, insignia, letter, word, figure, design, picture, or drawing of any nature shall ever be placed upon or attached to the United Nations flag or placed upon any replica thereof.

MOURNING. Whenever the Secretary-General of the United Nations proclaims that the United Nations is in official mourning, the United Nations flag, wherever displayed, shall be flown at half-mast during the period of official mourning.

The Chiefs of the United Nations missions, directors of information centres and specialized agencies away from the Permanent Headquarters are authorized by the Secretary-General to lower the United Nations flag to half-mast in cases where they wish to follow official mourning of the country in which they have their headquarters.

The United Nations flag when displayed at half-mast should first be hoisted to the peak for an instant and then lowered to the half-mast position. The flag should again be raised to the peak before it is lowered for the day. By "half-mast" is meant lowering the flag to one-half the distance between the top and bottom of the mast.

Crepe streamers may be affixed to flagstaffs flying the United Nations flag in a funeral procession only by order of the Secretary-General of the United Nations.

When the United Nations flag is used to cover a casket, it should not be lowered into the grave or allowed to touch the ground.

MANUFACTURE OF UNITED NATIONS FLAG. The Secretary-General has granted permission to sell the United Nations flag without reference to the Secretary-General as to the price to be charged.

Preparatory Work with regard to the Possible Holding of a General Conference of the Members of the United Nations in Accordance with Article 109 of the Charter

The question of the preparatory work with regard to the possible holding of a general conference in accordance with the provisions of the Charter was discussed by the General Assembly at its eighth session, during 1953. On the recommendation of the Sixth (Legal) Committee, the Assembly requested the Secretary-General to prepare, publish and circulate among the Member States during 1954 or shortly thereafter: (1) a substantive compilation of documents of the United Nations Conference on International Organization not yet published; (2) a complete index of the documents of that conference on the lines envisaged in the memorandum by the Secretary-General; and (3) a repertory of the practice of the United Nations organs appropriately indexed. In accordance with the above request, the documents of the Coordination Committee and of the Advisory Committee of Jurists of the San Francisco Conference on International Organization were published by the Secretary-General late in 1954. These documents were issued in four volumes, two containing texts in English and two containing texts in French. An index to the complete documentation of the conference consisting of two parts, namely, an index of the legislative history of each article of the Charter, and an alphabetical index to specific subjects were also published. With the publication of those documents all the official records of the San Francisco Conference have now appeared, the other documents having been issued in a fifteen volume publication, published shortly after the Conference. The Repertory of Practice of the United Nations organs has been issued in 1955 in five volumes, in English; the first two volumes were issued also in French. The Repertory of Practice constitutes a comprehensive summary of the decisions of the United Nations organs placed in the context of the relevant discussions; it is organized by Charter Articles and presented in such a way as to throw light on the questions of the application and interpretation of the Charter, which have arisen in practice. It covers the practice of the organs of the United Nations from the time when they began functioning until September 1, 1954.

United Nations Tribunals in Libya and Eritrea

In 1950, the General Assembly adopted certain economic and financial provisions relating to Libya and established a United Nations Tribunal in Libya consisting of three persons selected by the Secretary-General for their legal qualifications from the nationals of three different states not directly interested. The Tribunal was authorized to give instructions on their request to the Administering States in Libya and to the Libyan Government after its establishment, and the Italian Government for the purpose of giving effect to the economic and financial provisions mentioned above. It could also decide all disputes arising between the Italian and the Libyan Governments concerning the interpretation and application of the economic and financial provisions. The Secretary-General appointed as members of the Tribunal, V. Sanchez-Gavito, of Mexico; H. Wickström, of Sweden; and F. Yörükoglu, of Turkey.

Since the original decision to establish the Tribunal in 1950 did not specify the period of time for which it was established, the question of the continuation of the Tribunal was discussed by the Assembly in 1953 and 1955. With the full agreement of the Libyan and Italian Governments, the Assembly decided to terminate the Tribunal on December 31, 1955, and established in its place, with the same powers, functions and jurisdiction as that of the Tribunal, an Italian-Libyan Mixed Arbitration Commission consisting of three members, one of whom was to be appointed by the Italian Government, one by the Government of Libya, and the third by the Secretary-General of the United Nations.

In pursuance of Article 11 of General Assembly resolution 530(VI) concerning economic and financial provisions relating to Eritrea, a United Nations Tribunal was set up with a composition and functions similar to those of the United Nations Tribunal in Libya. The resolution establishing the Tribunal provided that as soon as the Tribunal's decisions had been announced on all the requests presented before December 31, 1953, the Tribunal would terminate. Having been informed by the President of the Tribunal that no request remained pending before the Tribunal as of December 31, 1953, the Secretary-General informed the Ethiopian and Italian Governments by a note dated April 26, 1954, that the functions of the Tribunal in Eritrea had come to an end on that date.

Recognition and Enforcement of Foreign Arbitral Awards

The Committee on the Enforcement of International Arbitral Awards, established by the Economic and Social Council in 1954, met at the Headquarters of the United Nations in 1955, and adopted a draft Convention on the Recognition and Enforcement of Foreign Arbitral Awards, and a report containing a commentary on each article of the draft Convention. During the same year, the Council adopted a resolution requesting the Secretary-General to transmit the draft Convention and the report of the Committee to governments and to prepare a report containing the comments of the governments and non-governmental organizations together with such observations as he might have for submission to the Council in 1956.

Maintenance Obligations

In accordance with a resolution of the Economic and Social Council, a Committee of Experts of seven members met in Geneva in 1952, to formulate the text of a model convention or model reciprocal law or both, on the subject of the recognition and enforcement abroad of maintenance obligations. The Committee prepared a "Draft Convention on the Recovery abroad of Claims for Maintenance" which would establish a system of judicial and administrative cooperation between states for the protection of dependents. It also formulated a "Draft of Model Convention on the Enforcement abroad of Maintenance Orders", which was recommended by the Economic and Social Council in 1954 to governments for use as a guide in preparing bilateral treaties or uniform legislation to be enacted by individual states. After consultations with governments, the Economic and Social Council decided, on May 17, 1955, to call a conference of plenipotentiaries to complete the drafting of and to sign the Convention on the Recovery Abroad of Claims for Maintenance. The Conference was scheduled to meet at the Headquarters of the United Nations during May and June 1956.

Other Legal Questions

UNITED NATIONS DAY

On October 31, 1947, the General Assembly decided that October 24, the anniversary of the entry into force of the Charter of the United Nations, should be officially called "United Nations Day", and be devoted to informing the peoples of the world of the aims and achievements of the United Nations and to obtaining support for its work. Member Governments were invited to cooperate in the observance of the anniversary.

UNIVERSAL CHILDREN'S DAY

On December 14, 1954, the General Assembly recommended that, with effect from 1956, a Universal Children's Day should be instituted by all countries, to be observed as a day of worldwide fraternity and understanding between children, and of activity devoted to the promotion of the ideals and objectives of the Charter and the welfare of the children of the world, and to the strengthening and broadening of the efforts made by the United Nations in favor and on behalf of all the children of the world. Governments of all states were invited to cooperate in the observance of the Universal Children's Day on the date and in the way which each considers appropriate.

INVITATION TO ORGANIZATION OF AMERICAN STATES AND TO ARAB LEAGUE TO ATTEND ASSEMBLY SESSIONS

The General Assembly on October 16, 1948, requested the Secretary-General to invite the Secretary-General of the Organization of the American States to be present as an observer at the sessions of the General Assembly.

A similar permanent invitation was extended to the Secretary-General of the League of Arab States by the General Assembly on November 1, 1950.

ADMINISTRATIVE AND BUDGETARY QUESTIONS

Budget of the United Nations

Budget appropriations through 1955 were:

Financial Year	Type of Appropriation	Date of Approval	Amount $
1946	Budget	Dec. 14, 1946	19,390,000
1947	Budget	Dec. 14, 1946	27,740,000
	Supplement	Nov. 20, 1947	876,568
1948	Budget	Nov. 20, 1947	34,825,195
	Supplement	Dec. 11, 1948	4,460,541
1949	Budget	Dec. 11, 1948	43,487,128
	Reduction	Dec. 9, 1949	283,048
1950	Budget	Dec. 10, 1949	49,641,773
	Reduction	Dec. 14, 1950	5,121,000
		(Reduction 8,000,000; increase 2,879,000)	
1951	Budget	Dec. 15, 1950	47,798,600
	Supplement	Dec. 20, 1951	1,126,900
1952	Budget	Dec. 21, 1951	48,096,780
	Supplement	Nov. 25, 1952	2,450,880
1953	Budget	Dec. 21, 1952	48,327,700
	Supplement	Dec. 9, 1953	1,541,750
1954	Budget	Dec. 9, 1953	47,827,110
	Supplement	Dec. 14, 1954	701,870
1955	Budget	Dec. 17, 1954	46,963,800
	Supplement	Dec. 16, 1955	3,264,200
1956	Budget	Dec. 16, 1955	48,566,350

During the first part of its first session, in February 1946, the General Assembly established a $25,000,000 reserve or contingency Fund called the Working Capital Fund. The amount was later reduced to $20,000,000 for the financial year 1947, and this figure was maintained at this level for 1948, 1949, 1950 and 1951. By a resolution of the sixth session of the Assembly, the Working Capital Fund for 1952 was increased to $21,239,203, by the application of the 1950 budget surplus. The General Assembly in December 1952, approved an increase to establish the Working Capital Fund for 1953 at $21,500,000, and this figure was maintained for 1954 and 1955. The Assembly in December 1955, reduced the Fund to $20,000,000 for 1956.

Member States contribute to the expenses of the budget and the Working Capital Fund on a scale determined by the General Assembly on the recommendation of its Committee on Contributions.

The scale for the 1956, 1957 and 1958 budgets ranged from 0.04 per cent (Costa Rica, Haiti, Honduras, Iceland, Liberia, Nicaragua, Paraguay and Yemen) to 33.33 per cent (United States).

The complete list of Member States and their rates of contribution for 1956, 1957 and 1958 shown as a percentage are given below (The assessment of the sixteen new Members admitted on December 14, 1955, was to be decided at the 1956 Assembly session.):

Member State	Per cent
Afghanistan	0.06
Argentina	1.28
Australia	1.80
Belgium	1.38
Bolivia	0.05
Brazil	1.20
Burma	0.11
Byelorussian Soviet Socialist Republic	0.53
Canada	3.63
Chile	0.33
China	5.62
Colombia	0.41
Costa Rica	0.04
Cuba	0.30
Czechoslovakia	0.92
Denmark	0.72
Dominican Republic	0.05
Ecuador	0.05
Egypt	0.40
El Salvador	0.06
Ethiopia	0.12
France	6.23
Greece	0.22
Guatemala	0.07
Haiti	0.04
Honduras	0.04
Iceland	0.04
India	3.25
Indonesia	0.56
Iran	0.30
Iraq	0.13
Israel	0.17
Lebanon	0.05
Liberia	0.04
Luxembourg	0.06
Mexico	0.77
Netherlands	1.25
New Zealand	0.48
Nicaragua	0.04
Norway	0.54
Pakistan	0.60
Panama	0.05
Paraguay	0.04
Peru	0.16
Philippines	0.45
Poland	1.70
Saudi Arabia	0.07
Sweden	1.59
Syria	0.08
Thailand	0.18
Turkey	0.69
Ukrainian Soviet Socialist Republic	2.02
Union of South Africa	0.78
Union of Soviet Socialist Republics	15.28

Member State	Per cent
United Kingdom of Great Britain and Northern Ireland........	8.55
United States of America	33.33
Uruguay	0.18
Venezuela	0.47
Yemen	0.04
Yugoslavia	0.40
TOTAL:	100.00

In November 1947, the Assembly empowered the Secretary-General to accept, at his discretion and after consultation with the Chairman of the Committee on Contributions, a portion of the contributions in currencies other than United States dollars. This authority has been renewed for every year since 1947.

Staff Regulations and Retirement

The General Assembly on February 13, 1946, adopted provisional staff regulations embodying the fundamental rights and obligations of the staff. At subsequent sessions, it amended these regulations in various details.

Permanent staff regulations were adopted on February 2, 1952, and amended at subsequent Assembly sessions.

On December 15, 1946, the Assembly adopted a provisional scheme for staff retirement, insurance and related benefits. On December 7, 1948, it adopted regulations for the United Nations Joint Staff Pension Fund; these became effective on January 23, 1949. Amendments to these regulations were adopted at subsequent Assembly sessions.

United Nations Administrative Tribunal

A United Nations Administrative Tribunal was established on November 24, 1949, to hear and pass judgment upon applications alleging non-observance of contracts of employment of staff members or of their terms of appointment. The Tribunal is composed of seven members, no two of whom may be nationals of the same state. Each case is heard by three members. The members of the Tribunal were appointed on December 9, 1949.

The General Assembly on November 8, 1955, amended the Tribunal's Statute in order to provide a procedure for review by the International Court of Justice of future Tribunal judgments if, in the opinion of a staff member, the Secretary-General or a Member State, the Tribunal has exceeded its competence or has erred on a question of law or procedure.

Tax Equalization

The General Assembly on November 20, 1947, requested Members which had not done so to take the necessary legislative action to exempt their nationals on the staff of the United Nations from national income taxation.

On November 18, 1948, the Assembly approved a Staff Assessment Plan—based on proposals submitted by the Secretary-General—under which all salaries paid by the United Nations would be subject to an assessment. It was provided that salary rates in effect on December 31, 1948, should be converted to gross rates on January 1, 1949. At the same time, the Assembly again urged Member States which had not done so, to exempt their nationals in the service of the United Nations from paying income tax on their earnings from the Organization. The Secretary-General's authority to reimburse staff members for national taxes paid on United Nations earnings has since been extended from year to year. The staff assessment plan was revised in certain details by the Assembly on November 10, 1949.

The General Assembly established a Tax Equalization Fund on January 1, 1956, to solve the problem of the United Nations having to reimburse staff members of United States nationality for income taxes paid the United States Government on their United Nations earnings. The Fund consists of revenue from the Staff Assessment Plan not otherwise disposed of by specific resolution of the Assembly, and the sum of $1,500,000 standing to the credit of Member States in the Working Capital Fund. Each Member State is granted a credit in the Fund corresponding to the percentage of its contribution to the regular budget; and, to the extent a staff member pays income taxes, his staff assessment, plus any amount by which the taxes exceed the staff assessment, will be refunded to him and charged against the account of the Member State levying the tax.

United Nations Telecommunications System

The General Assembly, on November 20, 1947, directed the Secretary-General to insure that the United Nations could proceed with negotiations then in progress to obtain the wave lengths (frequencies), call signs, and rights and privileges necessary for a United Nations telecommunications system, and to report to its third regular session. After considering the Secretary-General's report, the Assembly, on November 18, 1948, approved in principle the establishment of the system, and authorized the Secretary-General to present, to the Assembly's 1950 session, such recommendations for establishing it as he thought necessary. The General Assembly in December 1950 instructed the Secretary-General to proceed with a modified telecommunications system provided that the capital expenditure did not constitute a net addition to the United Nations budget. It also authorized him to accept appropriate voluntary contributions for this purpose.

At the sixth session of the General Assembly, the Secretary-General explained that it had been found possible to establish United Nations links between local telecommunication networks established in various areas, and the General Assembly noted his report on these developments.

The Headquarters Agreement between the United Nations and the United States provides that the United Nations may set up its own radio circuit between its Headquarters at New York and the European Office of the United Nations at Geneva; this has been done. The United Nations radio station at the European Office is in communication with United Nations radio stations at Jerusalem, Rawalpindi and Bangkok. Traffic from a United Nations radio station in Korea is relayed from Bangkok to Geneva. In its work of truce observation, the United Nations has found it necessary to establish local radio networks. United Nations Military Observer Groups in India, Pakistan and Kashmir have such a network, one station of which is at Rawalpindi. The United Nations Truce Supervision Organization at Jerusalem is connected by radio with United Nations Observer Groups in Israel, Lebanon, Syria and Jordan.

The arrangements for the operation of the United Nations radio stations have been made bilaterally between the Organization and the governments of states where the stations are situated, by a series of formal and informal agreements.

By Article 26 of the International Telecommunication Convention (Buenos Aires, 1952), the telecommunication operating services of the United Nations are entitled to the rights and bound by the obligations of the Convention and the

Regulations annexed thereto. In consequence, the United Nations is regarded as an Administration in connection with the operation of its telecommunication services. The International Plenipotentiary Telecommunication Conference at Buenos Aires in 1952 adopted Resolution 26 declaring that the United Nations network should never in normal circumstances compete with existing public channels of communications. Only United Nations traffic is therefore accepted for transmission over the network, and the traffic of the specialized agencies is carried, except in case of emergency, only when it is connected with and paid for by a United Nations program.

United Nations Radio

The functions of the Radio Division of the Department of Public Information are: to provide news and programs for rebroadcast by national radio and television networks, to provide facilities for radio and television correspondents at United Nations Headquarters or wherever the United Nations is at work, and to disseminate the news of the United Nations and its specialized agencies.

The operations are of many types: direct broadcasts of United Nations meetings, with a running commentary in English and French; daily news bulletins and magazine recordings made by delegates for rebroadcast in their own countries; transcriptions of feature programs and dramatic documentary presentations; and programs on the specialized agencies of the United Nations. During 1955, material was produced in 27 languages.

While most of the material is produced at Headquarters, an increasing amount in the form of records or tape recordings is received from the field by correspondents of the Radio Division or from the specialized agencies.

The shortwave operations of the Radio Division are conducted through the facilities leased from Member States or commercial stations. The Radio Division has nine studios in use for broadcasting, radio production and related radio and television activities. During 1955, an average of six hours of broadcasting per day was done. Shortwave operations increase during sessions of the General Assembly.

The Radio Division is divided into seven regional services: English Language, Latin American-Iberian, European, Chinese, Russian, Middle Eastern and South East Asian. In addition, Central Services is in charge of the Record Library and for making all technical arrangements for the broadcasts and for processing and dispatching transcriptions; in 1955 alone, over 33,000 transcriptions were shipped.

United Nations Postal Administration

As a result of a resolution of the General Assembly, adopted on November 16, 1950, the United Nations Postal Administration was established on January 1, 1951.

An agreement was signed on March 28, 1951, by Secretary-General Trygve Lie for the United Nations, and by Ambassador Warren Austin and Postmaster General Jesse Donaldson for the United States, which established the relationship between the two parties insofar as postal matters were concerned.

Under the terms of this agreement, the United States Post Office Department operates the United Nations Post Office Station on behalf of the United Nations. Services rendered at this Post Office are equal to those offered by any United States Post Office having comparable operations, except that only United Nations postage stamps and postal stationery are used, which are provided by the United Nations free of charge. The services offered by this Post Office Station, however, are not available to the general public, except on a first day of issue of a United Nations stamp.

The United Nations provides the United Nations Post Office Station with space, custodial services and utilities at Headquarters; the staff and equipment are provided by the United States Post Office Department.

The United States Post Office Department, in return for these services, retains all revenue from the sale of United Nations postage stamps and postal stationery at the United Nations Post Office Station. Furthermore, the United States Post Office Department is reimbursed by the United Nations for postage applied to all mail dispatched from United Nations Headquarters.

The United Nations, through its Postal Administration, engages in the sale of United Nations postage stamps and postal stationery for philatelic purposes. In addition to sales in response to orders received by mail, the United Nations Postal Administration operates a stamp counter in the Main Lobby of the General Assembly building at United Nations Headquarters, where visitors may purchase United Nations stamps for both philatelic and postage purposes, and where they may dispatch mail bearing United Nations stamps.

All orders for stamps and inquiries should be addressed to the United Nations Postal Administration, United Nations, New York.

The United Nations Postal Administration has so far issued the following stamps and stationery, on the dates stated:

October 24, 1951—1¢, 1½¢, 3¢, 5¢, 25¢, $1.00
November 16, 1951—2¢, 10¢, 15¢, 20¢, 50¢
December 14, 1951—6¢, 10¢, 15¢, 25¢ air post
July 18, 1952—2¢ postcard
August 29, 1952—10¢ air letter sheet
October 24, 1952—5¢ commemorative—United Nations Day, 1952
          (withdrawn March 1, 1955)
December 10, 1952—3¢ and 5¢ commemorative—Human Rights Day, 1952
          (withdrawn March 1, 1955)
April 24, 1953—3¢, 5¢ commemorative—Refugee
          (withdrawn June 11, 1955)
June 12, 1953—3¢, 5¢ commemorative—Universal Postal Union
          (withdrawn June 11, 1955)
September 15, 1953—3¢ embossed envelope (standard and legal)
October 24, 1953—3¢, 5¢ commemorative—United Nations Day, 1953
          (to be withdrawn May 9, 1956)
December 10, 1953—3¢, 5¢ commemorative—Human Rights Day, 1953
          (to be withdrawn May 9, 1956)
February 11, 1954—3¢, 8¢ commemorative—Food and Agriculture Organization
          (to be withdrawn May 9, 1956)
May 10, 1954—3¢, 8¢ commemorative—International Labor Organization
          (to be withdrawn May 9, 1956)
October 25, 1954—3¢, 8¢ commemorative—United Nations Day, 1954
December 10, 1954—3¢, 8¢ commemorative—Human Rights Day, 1954
February 9, 1955—3¢, 8¢ commemorative—International Civil Aviation Organization
May 11, 1955—3¢, 8¢ commemorative—United Nations Educational, Scientific and
          Cultural Organization
October 24, 1955—3¢, 4¢, 8¢, 15¢ United Nations Day souvenir sheet commemorative—
          United Nations Day, 1955
December 9, 1955—3¢, 8¢ commemorative—Human Rights Day, 1955

Stocks of the 3¢ Human Rights Day stamp of 1954, and the 15¢ souvenir sheet, issued on United Nations Day 1955, are exhausted, and these issues may no longer be obtained from the United Nations Postal Administration. The program for 1956 provided for four commemorative stamps, as follows:

February 17–3¢, 8¢ commemorative–International Telecommunication Union
April 6–3¢, 8¢ commemorative–World Health Organization
October 24–3¢, 8¢ commemorative–United Nations Day
December 10–3¢, 8¢ commemorative–Human Rights Day

The postal agreement provides for its termination by either party giving written notice twelve months in advance.

Gross revenue of the United Nations Postal Administration for 1955 amounted to $520,450.35.

United Nations postage stamps and postal stationery are sold for philatelic purposes at the European Office of the United Nations, Geneva, Switzerland.

During 1953, an office was opened in London, England, for philatelic sales to collectors in the sterling area. As of January 1, 1955, however, sales at this office were restricted to stamp dealers only.

United Nations stamps are sold, against payment in local currencies, through United Nations Information Centres in Copenhagen, Denmark; Sydney, Australia; and Karachi, Pakistan. It was hoped that in time more Information Centres would be included in this arrangement.

Approximately 5,200,000 pieces of mail from United Nations Secretariat members, from visitors, and as a result of the United Nations Postal Administration's activities, are dispatched annually from the United Nations Post Office Station at United Nations Headquarters.

United Nations Library

The United Nations Library occupies the seven-story building on the southwest corner of the Headquarters site. Before the move from Lake Success, this structure, built originally for the New York City Housing Authority, was the Manhattan office of the United Nations. Its present and permanent function is to provide information, research materials, and library services required by delegations and the Secretariat.

Holdings in books, periodicals and government documents number approximately 200,000 volumes, and form an active reference collection of material from many countries and in many languages. A selection of about 10,000 volumes constitutes the basic collection in the main reference room where the central card catalogue is located. Current issues of about 1,500 periodicals and back files of some 175 newspapers are available in the periodical room.

An entire floor is devoted to the Library's collection of the documents and publications of the United Nations and the specialized agencies, as well as books, periodicals and pamphlets concerning them. Another floor houses the Woodrow Wilson Memorial Library, a gift of the Woodrow Wilson Foundation. This includes sets of documents of the League of Nations, and the publications dealing with the League, the peace movements, and international relations between the two World Wars. A collection of about 50,000 maps and 2,000 geographical reference books (atlases, gazeteers, guides, etc.) is housed in a separate room. Other special collections of interest are those of microfilms, bibliographies, pamphlets, official gazettes and government documents.

The services of the main Library are supplemented in the Secretariat building by the archives, and by three branch collections for Economic and Social Affairs,

Legal and Security Council Affairs, and Trusteeship and Information from Non-Self-Governing Territories. An underground tunnel connects the Library and Secretariat buildings. A pneumatic tube rapidly delivers library materials to the Secretariat building, where a conveyor belt transports them to various floors.

HEADQUARTERS OF THE UNITED NATIONS

Site for Permanent Headquarters

The permanent Headquarters of the United Nations, the General Assembly decided in February 1946 should be located in the United States. Various sites were considered during that year in the northeastern United States, and in the area of San Francisco. On December 14, 1946, the Assembly accepted an offer of John D. Rockefeller, Jr., to give the United Nations $8,500,000 to acquire land in New York City for a permanent Headquarters site in the area bounded by First Avenue, East 48th Street, the East River, and East 42nd Street. Certain adjacent parcels of land which were not available to Mr. Rockefeller were to be given to the United Nations by the City of New York. The Assembly further requested the Secretary-General, with the assistance of an advisory committee, to take steps for the preparation of plans and estimates, and to submit them to the Assembly at its next regular session.

Agreement between the United Nations and the United States

Also on December 14, 1946, the Assembly authorized the Secretary-General to negotiate with United States authorities an agreement on the arrangements required as a result of establishing the permanent United Nations Headquarters in New York.

On June 26, 1947, the Secretary-General signed, with the Secretary of State, an Agreement between the United Nations and the United States. The Assembly approved this Agreement on October 31, 1947. At the same time, it authorized the Secretary-General to bring it into force, and to perform on behalf of the United Nations such acts or functions as might be required by the Agreement, which came into force on November 21, 1947.

According to this Agreement, the United Nations has the power to make necessary regulations for the Headquarters district (article III, section 8). When United States federal, state or local laws are inconsistent with such regulations, the latter will prevail. By Assembly resolution, the Secretary-General was empowered to formulate the regulations. He asked, however, that he be given more specific instructions.

By unanimous vote, therefore, the Assembly, at its fifth session, requested the Secretary-General to present any draft regulation for its approval. It also decided that when the Secretary-General considers it necessary to give immediate effect to any regulation, he should have the authority to make such a regulation, and should report his action to the Assembly as soon as possible.

United States Loan

On November 20, 1947, the General Assembly unanimously approved the permanent Headquarters plans, and authorized the Secretary-General to negotiate with the United States Government a $65,000,000 interest-free loan for the construction of the permanent Headquarters. The loan, it stated, should be for a term of not less than 30 years, repayable in annual instalments from the ordinary budget of the United Nations. The first payment was made from the 1951 budget.

The Secretary-General was further authorized to proceed with the construction and furnishing of the Headquarters as soon as the loan agreement was completed. He could modify the plans as necessary, provided he did not exceed the total authorized expenditure. An Advisory Committee was established to assist him in his task.

A loan agreement was approved by the Congress of the United States on August 5, and signed by the President on August 11, 1948. It provided for repaying the $65,000,000 loan without interest over a period from 1951 to 1982, in annual instalments ranging from $1,000,000 to $2,500,000. The Assembly, on November 18, 1948, noted with satisfaction the conclusion of the loan agreement. It also expressed its appreciation of the cooperation extended by the Government of the United States, the State of New York, and the City of New York.

History of Headquarters Construction

An April 13, 1947, the Secretary-General formally accepted the contributions of the City of New York. The City's gift included the transfer of several plots of land, and exclusive rights to the waterfront between 42nd and 48th Streets.

A Board of Design Consultants, composed of prominent architects and engineers from different parts of the world, drew up the basic design for the Headquarters. The plans provided, among other things, for a General Assembly hall, a Secretariat office building, a conference area for Council chambers and committee rooms, and underground garages, with appropriate landscaping of the entire site.

The cornerstone of the permanent Headquarters was laid on October 24, 1949— United Nations Day—by the Secretary-General at a special open-air plenary meeting of the General Assembly at the Headquarters site.

The entire Headquarters staff moved into the 39-story Secretariat building between August 1950 and June 1951.

There are three main elements in the group of buildings comprising the Headquarters—the General Assembly building, the Secretariat building, and the Conference building.

The Conference building, connecting the General Assembly building with the Secretariat building, contains three Council chambers, one each for the Security, the Economic and Social, and the Trusteeship Councils. Besides these chambers, there are meeting rooms for the Assembly's main committees, lounges for the delegates, several smaller conference rooms, a delegates' restaurant, and a cafeteria for the Secretariat. Three basement levels contain the printing and reproduction equipment, warehouse, maintenance workshops, and much of the mechanical equipment, including the plant controlling the air-conditioning throughout the whole group of buildings.

The General Assembly building houses the vast auditorium, measuring 165 feet by 115 feet, and 75 feet high. It contains sufficient seating for delegations, observers, and 234 seats for the press. Two tiers of booths around the sides of the hall are for information media, and there is accommodation for some 800 visitors. Underneath, in the two lower levels, are a large conference room, seven radio studios, four committee rooms, recording rooms, and a master control room for the communications system which serves the entire Headquarters. A two-level, underground garage for approximately 1,500 cars has been in use since June 1951.

PART III **THE SPECIALIZED AGENCIES**

INTRODUCTION

Much of the work toward achieving the United Nations aim of improved economic and social conditions for the people of the world is carried out by specialized inter-governmental agencies. The United Nations Charter provides that these agencies, "having wide international responsibilities . . . in economic, social, cultural, educational, health, and related fields," are to be brought into relationship with the United Nations.

The instruments defining this relationship are the individual agreements between the United Nations and the specialized agencies. These agreements are first negotiated by the Committee on Negotiations with Inter-Governmental Agencies established for this purpose by the Economic and Social Council; they are then submitted for approval to the Economic and Social Council, and by the Council to the General Assembly. Before coming into force, each agreement must also be approved by the appropriate organs of the specialized agency concerned.

Agreements with the following agencies came into force on the dates indicated:

International Labor Organization (ILO) ....December 14, 1946
Food and Agriculture Organization of the United
 Nations (FAO) ....December 14, 1946
United Nations Educational, Scientific, and Cultural
 Organization (UNESCO) ....December 14, 1946
International Civil Aviation Organization (ICAO) ....May 13, 1947
International Bank for Reconstruction and Development ....November 15, 1947
International Monetary Fund ....November 15, 1947
World Health Organization (WHO) ....July 10, 1948
Universal Postal Union (UPU) ....July 1, 1948
International Telecommunication Union (ITU) ....January 1, 1949
World Meterological Organization (WMO) ....December 20, 1951

An agreement with the proposed Inter-Governmental Maritime Consultative Organization (IMCO), approved by the United Nations General Assembly on November 18, 1948, will come into force when approved by the Assembly of IMCO, after that Organization is officially established.

The Havana Charter called for 20 acceptances to bring the International Trade Organization (ITO) into existence, but at the end of 1955 only two countries had accepted, one of them conditionally. Nevertheless, one of the main objectives of that Charter has been embodied in an international commercial treaty, known as the General Agreement on Tariffs and Trade (GATT). In the course of the ninth session of GATT (winter of 1954-1955), the Contracting Parties drew up an agreement providing for the establishment of an Organization for Trade Cooperation (OTC) to administer the General Agreement, and to come into being when it has been accepted by countries which account for a high proportion of world trade. The agreement establishing the OTC provides that the Organization may be brought into relationship with the United Nations as one of the specialized agencies.

The agreements in general follow a standard pattern. As a rule they provide for reciprocal representation at meetings, reciprocal inclusion of agenda items when requested, exchange of information and documents, uniformity of personnel arrangements, and coordination of statistical services as well as budgetary and financial arrangements. Each agency has agreed to consider any recommendation made to it by the United Nations, and to report to the United Nations on the action taken to give effect to any such recommendation. In the case of the agreements with the Bank and the Fund, the United Nations has agreed to consult with these agencies prior to making any recommendations.

Each agency has further agreed to assist the Security Council in carrying out its decisions for the maintenance or restoration of international peace and security, to assist the Trusteeship Council at the latter's request, and to cooperate with the United Nations in connection with the well-being and development of the peoples of the non-self-governing territories.

In pursuance of General Assembly resolution 377(V) of November 3, 1950, which provides that the General Assembly may make recommendations to Members for collective measures if the Security Council fails to act, and subsequent resolutions of the Economic and Social Council, ILO, FAO, UNESCO, WHO and ICAO have declared themselves willing to cooperate with the General Assembly in the maintenance of international peace and security. The International Bank and the International Monetary Fund have declared they would have due regard for recommendations of the General Assembly made pursuant to the resolution above. It was recognized by the Economic and Social Council that similar action was not required of ITU, UPU or WMO.

To implement the agreements, to avoid overlapping of activities, and, in general, to promote the coordination of efforts, an Administrative Committee on Coordination has been established by the Economic and Social Council. This Committee is composed of the Secretary-General of the United Nations and the executive heads of the specialized agencies brought into relationship with the United Nations.

A *Catalogue of Economic and Social Projects* is prepared annually for the Economic and Social Council by the United Nations Secretariat in collaboration with the specialized agencies. It indicates work planned or already undertaken by the United Nations and the specialized agencies, enabling the Economic and Social Council and the General Assembly to establish priorities by selecting programs on which joint action will be most effective and on which action is urgently required. Programs requiring coordinated action have, for example, been undertaken in the following fields: technical assistance for economic development, housing, fellowships, statistics, migration and manpower problems.

To improve administrative and budgetary coordination between the United Nations and the specialized agencies, consultations are constantly taking place. Arrangements have been made concerning, among other questions: a joint system of external audit; the common collection of contributions; mutual problems affecting the currency of contributions; common financial regulations; a Joint Staff Pension Fund; uniform recruitment policies, personnel regulations, salary, allowance and leave systems; the International Civil Service Advisory Board; and common administrative services.

The material on the following pages is intended to give in summary form an explanation of how each specialized agency came into being, of its functions and aims, and an indication of some of its main activities. (The membership of each agency is given in the tables on pages 412-413.)

INTERNATIONAL LABOR ORGANIZATION (ILO)

Functions

The International Labor Organization aims at contributing to the establishment of universal and lasting peace through the promotion of social justice.

Its tripartite structure is unique among the United Nations and the specialized agencies. Representatives of workers, employers and government join in determining ILO policies and supervising its activities. The aims and objectives of the ILO are indicated in its Constitution which was drawn up in 1919. Among the measures to which the ILO devotes itself are these: the regulation of hours of work, including the establishment of a maximum working day and week; the regulation of the labor supply and the prevention of unemployment; the provision of an adequate living wage; the protection of the worker against sickness, disease and injury arising out of his employment; the protection of the interests of workers when employed in countries other than their own; recognition of the principle of equal remuneration for work of equal value; recognition of the principle of freedom of association; and the organization of vocational and technical education.

The Declaration of Philadelphia, adopted by the International Labor Conference in 1944 and later annexed to the ILO Constitution, reaffirms the principles on which the Organization is based, and maintains that "all human beings, irrespective of race, creed, or sex, have the right to pursue both their material well-being and their spiritual development in conditions of freedom and dignity, of economic security, and equal opportunity."

Among the principles reaffirmed by the Declaration are the following:

(a) labor is not a commodity;

(b) freedom of expression and of association are essential to sustained progress;

(c) poverty anywhere constitutes a danger to prosperity everywhere; and

(d) the war against want requires to be carried on with unrelenting vigor within each nation, and by continuous and concerted international effort in which the representatives of workers and employers, enjoying equal status with those of governments, join with them in free discussion and democratic decision with a view to the promotion of the common welfare.

Origin

ILO was established in 1919 as an autonomous institution, associated with the League of Nations. Its original constitution formed part of the Treaty of Versailles and the other treaties of peace. In 1946, an agreement between the United Nations and ILO was signed which recognized the responsibility of ILO in the field of labor and of social conditions.

Organization

ILO works through the International Labor Conference, the Governing Body, and the International Labor Office headed by a Director-General.

The Conference is the policy-making body of the Organization and meets at least once a year. It is composed of national delegations comprising two government delegates and two delegates representing respectively employers and workers. Each delegate has one vote in the Conference.

The principal function of a conference is to establish international social standards in the form of international labor conventions and international labor recommendations. In addition, the Conference designates the members of the Governing Body, adopts the annual budget, examines the application of conventions and recommendations, and expresses itself on questions submitted to it by the Governing Body or raised by the delegates.

The Governing Body is the executive council of ILO. It is composed of 40 members: ten representing employers, ten representing labor, and 20 representing government. Each of the three groups represented at the Conference elects its own representatives to the Governing Body, with the exception of ten government representatives from the countries holding permanent seats as states of chief industrial importance, and which do not participate in the election of the other ten government representatives. Elections take place every three years.

The Governing Body elects the Director-General, and supervises the work of the International Labor Office and of the various committees and commissions of ILO. It determines policy and work programs, establishes the agenda for the Conference insofar as it is not fixed by the Conference itself, and prepares the annual budget. The Governing Body names its own committees to deal with particular problems.

The International Labor Office, located at Geneva, Switzerland, is the permanent secretariat of ILO. The Office provides the staff for the Conference, for the Governing Body, and for other meetings or conferences. It prepares the documents for these meetings; publishes periodicals, studies and reports of social and economic questions; and collects and distributes information on all subjects within the Organization's competence. It undertakes inquiries and programs of work as directed by the Governing Body or the Conference. Major programs in recent years have included labor-management relations, labor productivity and the investigation of forced labor.

The Office has branches at Bonn, London, New Delhi, Ottawa, Paris, Rio de Janeiro, Rome, Tokyo and Washington, as well as national correspondents in many countries. An office in New York maintains liaison with the United Nations.

The first Director of the ILO was Albert Thomas (France) (1919-32). His successors were Harold Butler (United Kingdom) (1932-38), John Winant (United States) (1939-41) and Edward Phelan (Ireland) (1941-48). The present Director-General is David A. Morse (United States), who has held the post since 1948.

Besides these three principal organs, the ILO acts through various specified subsidiary bodies such as regional conferences, industrial committees (also tripartite in structure) and various committees of experts.

ILO's activities are financed by a budget approved each year by the Conference, and raised each year from the governments of member States according to a scale of contributions approved by the Conference. The budget for the calendar year 1956 was $7,395,729.

ILO Membership

Orginally, membership in the Organization coincided with the membership of the League of Nations. Adherence to the League carried with it participation in ILO. Between 1919 and 1945, several countries not members of the League were admitted to ILO. Its Constitution now provides that any Member of the United Nations may become a member of ILO on accepting the obligations of members, and that countries not Members of the United Nations may be admitted to ILO by the Conference. As of December 31, 1955, 70 countries were members of ILO.

Activities

Since its establishment, ILO has played a leading role in raising living standards throughout the world. It works towards this goal, with the help of governments, employers and workers, in three basic ways: by setting international labor and social standards, by aiding countries to make their own social gains through technical assistance, and by gathering and distributing information of social and economic interest.

STANDARD-SETTING ACTIVITIES

The international principles are rules of conduct for nations seeking to solve their social problems, and to achieve objectives in a sound and orderly way. They are embodied in international conventions and recommendations adopted by the Conference by a two-thirds vote. Under ILO's Constitution, its members must submit each convention for consideration to the appropriate national authorities. If a convention is ratified, the government must report annually on the measures taken to give effect to it, and must transmit copies of its annual report to the most representative workers' and employers' organizations of the given country.

Special provisions are made for Federal states (for example, the United States, Canada and Switzerland) in cases where the subject matter of a given convention is normally dealt with through legislation by individual states, provinces or cantons. In these circumstances, direct action by the Federal government is not required.

Recommendations are not subject to ratification. Member States must periodically report on the state of legislation and national practice with regard to the standards established in the recommendations and in the conventions which they have not ratified.

In the 38 sessions of the International Labor Conference since 1919, a total of 104 conventions and 100 recommendations have been adopted. On January 1, 1956, 1,527 ratifications had been registered. Eighty-six of the conventions had received a sufficient number of ratifications to come into force. The conventions and recommendations taken together and designated as the "International Labor Code" cover such questions as these:

Employment and unemployment (employment services, national development schemes, provision for unemployment); general conditions of employment (wages, hours of work, weekly rest periods, annual holidays with pay); conditions of employment of children and young persons (minimum age, medical examinations, vocational training and apprenticeship, night work); women's employment (maternity protection, night work, employment in unhealthy work); industrial health, safety and welfare; social security; industrial relations; labor inspection; maritime labor; migration; statistics; and freedom of organization and protection of the right to organize.

The impact of this great body of principles cannot be statistically analyzed. The preliminary discussions and the act of adoption, as well as the periodic reports of governments, have made influential even those conventions that have not come into force. Certain provisions of the maritime conventions are now applied as a matter of course in the construction of new ocean-going vessels. Other conventions have been incorporated verbatim in national statutes.

TECHNICAL ASSISTANCE

From the beginning, ILO offered a form of technical assistance, known inside the ILO during the period between the First and Second World Wars as "advisory missions". These teams of experts might be called in by a country seeking to implement the provisions of a convention, or, on occasion, when no convention was involved and a country simply wished to use the collective experience of the Organization.

The reconstruction problems after the Second World War, and the need for economic development in many regions of the globe, caused a shift of emphasis in ILO's program of help to governments. The problem was no longer so clearly one of protecting standards as it was of creating higher standards of living and of productivity in an interdependent world. Since the inauguration of the Expanded Program of Technical Assistance of the United Nations and the specialized agencies in 1950, the ILO has worked within its framework. It has, in addition, worked with regional bodies such as the European Iron and Steel Community. In 1955 ILO's expenditure of United Nations technical assistance funds amounted to $2,624,553.

This sum provided technical assistance in several forms: expert advice, organization of training institutes and programs, exchange of technical information, grants for fellowships and worker-trainees, organization of seminars, and courses and equipment. In 1955, ILO had on assignment 238 experts. There were 306 worker-trainees, 114 fellowships, and 153 grants for attendance at seminars and training courses. Equipment authorizations amounted to $320,000.

The ILO has found that the creation of vocational training institutions is one of the most vital needs of under-developed countries. Such institutions fill an urgent need for countries seeking to develop their manpower resources, the results are relatively permanent, and the institutions themselves can be turned over to local authorities after a reasonable developmental period. Manpower organization, including vocational training, accounted for 50.9 per cent of ILO's technical assistance in 1955.

Training centers established and destined for eventual operation by the countries concerned include institutions for the following purposes: maintenance of diesel equipment used in inland water transport (Burma, but being expanded to a regional center on ECAFE's recommendation); maintenance of motor vehicles (centers in China, Indonesia and Thailand); maintenance of heavy earth moving equipment (Pakistan); national productivity and vocational training (Egypt); national productivity (India); vocational and technical training (jointly by ILO and UNESCO in Turkey); vocational training (Ecuador, Haiti, Indonesia and Libya); handicrafts and vocational training (Iran); and management training (Yugoslavia).

In addition, a Latin American regional training program through the *Senai* institute in Brazil, and labor administration training centers in Istanbul and Mexico City have been established.

Other projects include surveys, expert advice, and fellowships in the fields of productivity, cooperation and handicrafts, social security, and labor conditions and administration. The ILO bears the overall responsibility for the multi-agency regional Andean Indian Project in Bolivia, Peru and Ecuador.

The ILO maintains Field Offices at Lima, Istanbul, Bangalore and Mexico City in connection with the administration of this technical assistance program.

OTHER ACTIVITIES

In addition to the meetings of its principal organs, the ILO holds periodic regional meetings in America, Asia and Europe, and meetings of tripartite committees for eight principal world industries. Other committees consider work on such topics as plantations; salaried and professional employment; agriculture; cooperation; social security; accident prevention; industrial hygiene and safety; the employment of women, children and young persons; social policy in non-metropolitan territories; statistics; indigenous labor; and working conditions of seafarers.

From time to time, commissions of inquiry consider particular problems at the request of member States. In cooperation with the United Nations, committees investigate allegations of forced labor and violations of freedom of association.

ILO collects and analyzes information from all over the world, and makes it available in publications and in response to inquiries. The *International Labor Review, Industry and Labor,* the *Legislative Series* (a compilation of industrial legislation), the *Yearbook of Labor Statistics,* and *Industrial Safety and Health* are among the ILO's regular publications. In addition, there is a series of studies and reports and the free news monthly, *ILO News.*

FOOD AND AGRICULTURE ORGANIZATION OF THE UNITED NATIONS (FAO)

Functions

The founder nations of FAO, in the preamble to the Organization's Constitution, expressed their joint wish to raise levels of nutrition and standards of living; to secure improvements in the efficiency of production and distribution of all agricultural products; to better the condition of rural populations; and thus to contribute towards an expanding world economy.

To help its members in doing these things, FAO functions in three main ways:

(a) by providing an intelligence service, including not only facts and figures relating to nutrition, agriculture, forestry and fisheries, but also appraisals and forecasts of production, distribution and consumption in the industries concerned;

(b) by promoting national and international action towards the improvement of all aspects of the production, marketing, processing and distribution of the products of agriculture (here taken to include fisheries and forestry); conservation of natural resources; and of policies relating to such activities as the provision of credit and the formulation of commodity arrangements; and

(c) by furnishing, on request and largely through the United Nations Expanded Program of Technical Assistance, technical assistance to members in any of the above fields of operation.

Origin

The United Nations Conference on Food and Agriculture, which met in May 1943, at Hot Springs, Virginia, set up an Interim Commission to make plans for a permanent food and agriculture organization. The Commission drew up a draft Constitution for FAO and submitted it to governments. When the Constitution had been accepted by more than 20 governments, the first session of the FAO Conference was convened at Quebec, Canada. FAO came into being on October 16, 1945, with the signing of its Constitution at the opening of the Conference.

Organization

FAO works through a Conference, a Council, and a staff headed by a Director-General. The Conference is the policy-making body, in which each of the 72 member States has one vote. The Conference normally meets biennially. Between sessions of the Conference, the Council of FAO supervises the work of the Organization, reviews the world food and agricultural situation, and makes recommendations to member Governments and other international bodies on measures to improve the food and agricultural situation. The Council is composed of 24 member Governments elected by the Conference.

The secretariat is headed by a Director-General, chosen by the Conference. Philip V. Cardon (United States)[10] was elected in December 1953, for the next four years. Previous Directors-General had been Sir John (now Lord) Boyd Orr (United Kingdom, 1945-48) and Norris E. Dodd (United States, 1948-53). The staff is organized into five technical divisions—agriculture, economics, fisheries, forestry and nutrition—and the necessary administrative, informational and educational, and area liaison services.

Regional offices are maintained at Washington (for North America); Cairo (for the Near East); and Bangkok (for Asia and the Far East); and in Latin America, sub-regional offices, in Mexico City (for Northern Latin America and the Caribbean), in Rio de Janeiro (for Eastern South America), and in Santiago de Chile (for Western South America). Until 1951, temporary headquarters were set up in Washington, but in that year the Organization moved to its permanent home in Rome, which had been selected at a special conference session held in 1949. A small office is also maintained at Geneva, principally for work in cooperation with the Economic Commission for Europe.

National FAO Committees, by 1956, had been set up by 52 member States, to serve as points of contact between the Organization and governmental and non-governmental agencies.

FAO's annual budget was somewhat less than US $5,000,000 until 1951, after which it was increased, at the 1955 Conference, to $6,600,000 for 1956 and to $6,800,000 for 1957. In addition to its regular budget, FAO receives her share of the United Nations Special Fund which finances the United Nations Expanded Program of Technical Assistance; for 1955 and 1956, this amounted to approximately $8,000,000 annually. In its early years, FAO profited by a grant of $1,000,000 of residual funds from UNRRA; this was used in countries which had formerly received UNRRA aid, and included Austria, China, Czechoslovakia, Ethiopia, Greece, Hungary, Italy, Poland and Yugoslavia.

General Activities

In general, FAO's activities aim at providing increased supplies of food and other agricultural products, at prices which the ultimate consumer can afford. Parallel with this aim, is that of raising the standard of living of rural people everywhere. From the very nature of these aims, it is evident that the main part of FAO's work must consist always of long-term activities. In any given year, the program of work represents the continuation of certain services of widespread general interest, such as the provision of statistical information. The program also represents successive stages in the development of certain projects whose completion can reasonably be foreseen after some years, such as bringing a widespread livestock disease under control. Thirdly, the program includes short-term projects, such as the provision of advisory assistance to meet some specific request from a government; many problems in this group are now dealt with under the Expanded Program of Technical Assistance.

ECONOMICS

Almost before FAO had begun its work, the food shortages in many countries resulting from the Second World War led the Director-General to call a special meeting on urgent food problems at Washington, in May 1946. The International Emergency Food Council (IEFC) then formed was absorbed by FAO in 1948.

---

[10] For reasons of health, Philip V. Cardon, in March 1956, submitted his resignation as Director-General.

Certain of its work, however, has been continued by various committees of the FAO Council, especially by the Committee on Commodity Problems, which usually meets twice a year to examine the economic situation and prospects for each major agricultural commodity, and to consider related governmental policies and actions.

Between 1952 and 1955, agricultural production expanded to the point where world shortages of food had generally disappeared. Instead of having to allocate export food supplies so that countries which needed them could receive a proper share, as had been done earlier through the IEFC, the attention of governments began to be drawn more to finding adequate markets for the food they were producing. This situation was discussed at the FAO Conferences of 1953 and 1955. In 1955, FAO's annual publication, *The State of Food and Agriculture* gave a comprehensive review of the world's food and agricultural production in the ten years from 1945 to 1955. This showed that in the latter part of these years, food production had expanded much faster than had population growth; so that world food production had again caught up with population growth, and had brought *per capita* production for the world as a whole just about up to pre-war levels. The increase, however, had taken place largely in the best-fed countries, while in some regions, notably Latin America and the Far East, food production had not yet overtaken population growth, leaving *per capita* consumption below pre-war. Despite this, the recovery in the major importing countries, largely European, had expanded so much that markets for exports from other countries no longer kept up with their increased production. Large surpluses had piled up in North America and smaller surpluses were appearing in many other countries—even for rice in some parts of Asia.

This question of consumption not keeping up with expanding production occupied much of the time of the 1953 and 1955 sessions of the FAO Conference, and the Organization has given much attention since 1953 to both disposal and prevention of surpluses. Under the latter heading, efforts have been made both by member countries and in studies carried out at FAO to adjust production so as to center the expansion on the most needed products, and at the same time to increase food consumption through improved marketing; and to encourage better diets through direct measures to make more cheap food available to low income groups. A code of principles for the disposal of surpluses has also been worked out in FAO meetings and adopted by many of the major exporting and importing countries. This code of Principles and Guiding Lines of Surplus Disposal underlines the use of surpluses for: (a) increasing consumption of under-privileged groups, (b) meeting famines or other emergency conditions, and (c) aiding development of less developed countries. Pilot studies of practical measures for food surplus disposal have been conducted in several countries, including studies of distribution of dried skim milk, in Egypt and in Spain; and of the general use of surpluses to help finance economic development, in India. In addition, a governmental working party under FAO auspices has worked out proposals by which countries exporting dairy products can help less developed countries to improve their milk distribution arrangements, and can provide them both financial and surplus commodity help (largely through dry skim milk) in carrying out the plans. Teams of experts have already been sent to India and Pakistan to explore suggested projects in Calcutta and Karachi, and other proposals are pending.

Other recent developments include the drafting of an international olive oil commodity agreement under FAO auspices. This was put in final form at a Conference called by the United Nations, and is now open for adherence by both producing and consuming countries. It is directed toward improving the quality and market for olive oil, and to stabilizing both prices and distribution so as to eliminate the usual wide year-to-year fluctuations without changing the long-time trends. Discussions have also been held on possible measures to stabilize rice prices and marketing, and an international meeting to consider such measures was to be held in the Far East during 1956. A special study group for this purpose has been set up under the auspices of the FAO Committee on Commodity Problems.

In line with the need for more selective expansion of production and consumption, staff visits have been made to many under-developed countries, and regional consultations have been held in the Near East, the Far East and Latin America, to discuss regional cooperation in this field. These regional consultations will continue to be held from time to time. With the need for, and the emphasis on, the better adjustment of agricultural production to markets, there has been a steady growth in the national requests for technical assistance experts to be sent by FAO to assist individual countries in improving their agricultural statistics, their agricultural programs, and especially their marketing arrangements and methods.

Following up the first post-war world census of agriculture in 1950, publications have been issued summarizing the statistical results and the methods and procedures used in various countries. Much attention is being given to the development of plans for a wider and more comprehensive world census of agriculture for 1960. A number of meetings was to be held with national and statistical officials during 1956 and 1957, to develop concerted and uniform plans for the conduct of this census. It is expected that as a result of these efforts, the 1960 census would give a more accurate and comparable picture of the status of world agriculture than has ever been available at any time before.

AGRICULTURE

Although increased attention has been paid recently to the integration of the work of the various technical divisions of FAO, as well as to integration of the regular and technical assistance programs, certain activities remain tied essentially with the work of certain divisions. In the technical and institutional agricultural fields, FAO has continued to pay special attention to the development of basic natural resources, the application of improved methods of production and processing, the training of technicians at all levels, the improvement of the institutional framework of agriculture, and the establishment of basic governmental services.

General activities, involving several aspects of one subject are exemplified by the International Rice Commission, under which cooperative work is now being carried out in plant breeding; use of fertilizers; soil, plant and water relationships; mechanization; and processing. In Europe, the annual meeting of the European Committee on Agriculture provides for general coordination of activities in that region; this committee has recently paid special attention to methods of coordinating agricultural research.

LAND AND WATER RESOURCE DEVELOPMENT. In assisting governments to appraise and improve the use of their soil and water resources, FAO places great emphasis on the development of these resources in an integrated fashion. For instance, a team of experts in the fields of hydrology, engineering, soil survey and farm management, are preparing a plan for introducing irrigation in the densely populated area of the Ganges-Kobadak region in East Pakistan.

FAO is assisting Ceylon in its Gal Oya Development Scheme by training local personnel in the use of machinery, and helping the Gal Oya Development Board in the operation of a machinery maintenance and repair workshop.

In many parts of the world, FAO is conducting, with the cooperation of the respective governments, soil surveys and land classifications, and work on soil fertility improvements, the development of underground water resources, the use of farm machinery, and improvement of small farm implements.

Since the response of farmers to better production techniques often depends upon tenure conditions and their security on the land, FAO has conducted a series of regional conferences on land problems and tenure improvements for Latin America in 1953, the Far East in 1954, and the Near East in 1955. Many of the problems inherent in providing incentives to farmers have been clarified, so that governments can strengthen the efficiency of farming and also the security of farm families on the land. These problems include the levels of farm rents, conditions under which land is held, ways of adjusting the size of farms, and the consolidation of scattered holdings into more compact units.

PLANT PRODUCTION AND PROTECTION. Much attention is given to the promotion of national plant breeding programs, and to international cooperation on a regional basis, especially in regard to rice in the Far East, maize in Europe, and wheat and barley in the Near East. Extension of such activities into other regions and crops is under consideration. As a service to plant geneticists, FAO has published a "world list of plant breeders" indicating the crops on which each is working, and also world catalogues of genetic stocks of the two major food crops, rice and wheat.

FAO also assists governments in the development of seed production and distribution programs, including inspection and certification services, and also by distributing seed for experimental purposes and maintaining an index of information on new varieties of crop plants. Particular emphasis is given to the relatively neglected subjects of pasture and fodder production as a basis for improved systems of animal husbandry and crop rotation. Tropical crops will receive considerable attention in future years, and FAO is also widening its activities in the field of horticulture.

FAO has paid increasing attention to plant protection problems. In addition to operating the International Plant Protection Convention and serving as headquarters of the World Reporting Service on Plant Diseases and Pests, FAO has developed a number of regional projects for the study and control of some major pests. This includes playing a leading role in coordinating international action towards the prevention of locust plagues. Marked progress has been achieved in devising methods of controlling the olive fly, which seriously affects olive oil production in the Mediterranean area; and similar cooperative work is being initiated against the senn pest, which causes crippling losses to cereal crops in Near East countries.

ANIMAL PRODUCTION AND DISEASE CONTROL. Rinderpest, the most serious of livestock diseases from a worldwide point of view, is rapidly coming under control through large-scale vaccination. This is allowing more attention to be paid to a program of controlling the debilitating diseases, and especially parasitic diseases.

In Europe, the successful establishment, in conjunction with the International Office of Epizootics of the European Commission for the Control of Foot and Mouth Disease, with country members, is beginning to insure a rapid reporting of the incidence of this disease and of focusing attention for its control and possible eradication on a regional basis.

In Central America, the Central American Integration Organization (OIRSA) is being assisted both in the control of animal diseases and in the improvement of livestock production. Following the regional meetings held in 1955 on Livestock Production, in Buenos Aires (for South America) and Brisbane (for the Far East), greater attention is being given to the breeding of livestock for unfavorable environments, the improved nutrition of both livestock and poultry in undeveloped areas, and the conservation and improvement of range and natural grasslands.

At the same time, FAO, through collaboration with the European Association of Animal Production, is starting to disseminate the recent information on improved nutrition in livestock, as well as continuing to assist the work of the European Committee on Milk Butterfat Recording.

Close collaboration with UNICEF in many parts of the world is being undertaken to survey dairy potentialities in those countries, and to implement joint milk conservation programs for better dairy production, and hence national nutrition programs.

GOVERNMENT SERVICES TO AGRICULTURE. FAO recognizes that adequate facilities for agricultural research, institutions for the training of both farmers and technicians, and extension services to assist farmers in the application of the findings of research are basic to agricultural development. Assistance already given in the development of inter-country cooperation in agricultural research in Europe and Latin America will be extended to other regions as resources permit. A survey of agricultural education facilities in relation to need is now under way in Latin America, and experts have been assigned to countries for varying periods to assist in the strengthening of agricultural education programs. Agricultural extension development centers organized in five regions have emphasized the need for adequate extension services, and established guiding principles for their development. One result has been the formation and implementation of regional programs of training in improved methods of conducting extension work.

RURAL WELFARE. Agricultural credit facilities, farmers' cooperatives, rural industries, and rural welfare in general, are other subjects which get special attention in FAO. In Latin America, a system of supervised agricultural credits, designed particularly for small farmers, has been studied at meetings and seminars, and the results of these studies embodied in an FAO *Manual of Supervised Agricultural Credit in Latin America*. Likewise, cooperatives and the special techniques required for their development among illiterate and semi-literate farmers have been the concern of FAO through the medium of international meetings and publications. Rural industries so far given particular attention include the processing of dates, rubber (non-plantation), tea, and hides and skins. Two FAO publications—*Essentials of Rural Welfare* and *Fact Finding with Rural People*—are concerned with the problem of rural welfare.

NUTRITION

Since FAO activities have as a primary objective the obtaining of sufficient quantities of the right sort of food, nutritional principles underlie much of the Organization's work. In this field, FAO collaborates with WHO and UNICEF. A joint FAO/WHO Expert Committee on Nutrition, established in 1949, meets periodically to coordinate the work of the two Organizations, and to advise them on future plans. In 1955, there were expert committees on additives to foods and protein requirements. The nature and extent of nutrition problems in the Far East and Latin America have been studied at a series of regional conferences or committees; the fourth session of the Regional Nutrition Committee for South and East Asia was to take place in Japan in September 1956.

Special attention is given to dietary requirements, to education in nutrition, and to the application of food technology in developing protein-rich foods other than milk for use in feeding mothers and children. FAO, often in collaboration with UNICEF, helps governments to organize school feeding along sound lines.

In the field of home economics, which is associated with nutrition, efforts have been concentrated on improving home economics teaching in national institutions and on developing home economics extension programs. A Home Economics Information Exchange, established in 1953, disseminates material of value to home economics teachers in different parts of the world.

FISHERIES

Emphasis on the development of the world's fisheries by nations acting together rather than individually, governs FAO's fisheries work. Examples of this are seen in the studies aimed to achieve uniformity of methods and terminology, the collection and analysis of information on fisheries resources, and the world statistical summaries of information on fisheries production and trade.

FAO's Fisheries Division is also concerned with the development of comprehensive national and regional fisheries policies, as well as giving advice to member Governments on technical problems of catching, rearing and processing fish. Fish handling, marketing and distribution also occupy a good deal of attention, and FAO also helps to provide a liaison service between governments and those professional and commercial undertakings which design, manufacture and service fisheries equipment of all sorts. Similarly, the major problems impeding the development of important fisheries are brought to the attention of research bodies who may be able to help in their solution. In line with these policies are such meetings as those on fish-processing in 1950 and one to be held in 1956; the first International Fishing Boat Congress, organized by FAO in 1954, and its successor to be held in 1958; and the fishing gear and equipment congress scheduled for 1957.

As focal points for all this work, FAO founded the General Fisheries Council for the Mediterranean and the Indo-Pacific Fisheries Council. A third body for the Latin American region is shortly to come into being.

FORESTRY

Forests represent a renewable resource whose development is one of FAO's major assignments. In recent years, appreciation of the protective value of forests, and of the interdependence of forestry and agriculture has become much more widespread; so has cooperation between producers and users of timber, and between both these groups and research workers in all branches of forestry.

As in the case of fisheries, FAO, in forestry matters, uses the system of regional commissions to promote the interchange of technical and economic information between governments and between technicians. In forestry, however, the commissions are used also to advise on the formulation and implementation of national forest policies, and on their coordination at a regional level. At present, there are four such regional bodies, comprising the commissions for Europe, for Latin America, for Asia and the Pacific, and for the Near East. There is a sub-commission for the Mediterranean, as well as various technical committees, working parties and advisory panels of experts. FAO also provides the professional staff for the Timber Division of the Economic Commission for Europe. On an even wider scale, FAO helps to organize the World Forestry Congresses, the fourth of which was held in India in 1954, and the fifth, scheduled for 1960.

Continuing activities include the appraisal of the extent and nature of existing forests, and the scientific study and rational use of wood consumption and requirements. Proportionately more of the results of FAO's forestry work appears in the form of publications than is the case with the other divisions of FAO. For example, the results of a second world survey of forest resources was published under the title *World Forest Resources* in 1955. Read with the continuing series of *Yearbooks of Forest Products Statistics,* this report, while telling far more than was known before about the world's forests, is still only a progress report. Starting with a study entitled "European Timber Trends and Prospects," an analysis of world wood resources and requirements is being built up region by region; a section dealing with the Far East was expected to be completed in 1958.

An important continuing activity is to find ways and means of increasing the world's pulp and paper supplies. The industrial possibilities of unconventional materials were summarized in *Raw Materials for More Paper,* published in 1953. In 1954, the study *World Pulp and Paper Resources and Prospects* was issued. This was followed by the organization of a Latin-American meeting of pulp and paper experts at Buenos Aires. Later, in cooperation with the Economic Commission for Latin America, an advisory group was established to give an impartial assessment of alternative schemes for pulp and paper industries, and to suggest ideas for the initiation of new projects.

Other important lines of activity are the improvement of water-shed management and range management (forest grazing), the improvement of silviculture and forest management, and the improvement of planting practices and coordinated research. *Eucalypts for Planting, Poplars in Land Use,* and the publication in the "World Forest Planting Manual" series are designed to assist in extending the area and success of forest planting.

Technical assistance work in forestry is covered elsewhere. Mention should be made here, however, of the emphasis laid on improving productivity both in forest operation and in industries by the introduction of modern machinery and equipment. FAO collects and disseminates current information on new machines and equipment manufacturers throughout the world, and on the modernization of industries. A joint committee set up with the Economic Commission for Europe is concerned with the improvement of techniques and the training of forest workers; work of this nature is to be extended to other regions.

EXPANDED PROGRAM OF TECHNICAL ASSISTANCE

In its early days, FAO sent special missions to several countries requesting assistance in solving broad problems of development or rehabilitation. Such were the missions to Greece in 1946, to Poland in 1947, to Thailand in 1948, and to several Latin American countries. Although a similar mission was sent during 1955 to Yemen, this type of work, in general, ceased as a purely FAO activity since funds became available under the United Nations Expanded Program of Technical Assistance, from September 1950. Under this program, FAO continues to provide its component of joint missions sent to many countries and organized with other agencies, usually the International Bank. Most of the money spent under the Expanded Program of Technical Assistance falls under the first of three main headings: individual country projects, regional and similar projects, and training centers and fellowships.

From small beginnings in 1950, FAO's share of the Expanded Program funds increased rapidly, the sums available for 1955 and 1956 being, as noted above, in the neighborhood of $8,000,000 for each year, while the proportion of the total, around 28.5 per cent each year, is greater than that allotted to any other specialized agency. By December 31, 1955, the services of over 1,500 experts had been requested from FAO, and over 1,000 assignments had been completed. Under the fellowship program, which is an integral part of the Expanded Program and which is designed primarily to maintain the supply of government technicians to carry on at the end of assignments of the experts, 812 technicians had been sent abroad for study by December 31, 1955, 274 of these being sent out in 1955 alone.

Projects handled by FAO under the Expanded Program vary from the largest type of development scheme, calling for a large team of technicians, to those in which one expert is called upon to deal with a single, isolated problem. In the first category, it may be a matter of improving millions of acres of unproductive land, usually by irrigation or by some other system of water control, which in effect changes the whole face of vast areas of countryside, and creates new livelihoods for hundreds of thousands of human beings. At the other end of the scale, a single expert may be assigned to a problem of only immediate local interest even in the country making the request. Under this heading, for example, is the assignment of a silkworm expert to Afghanistan to study means of putting that country's silk industry on a modern footing. Another typical example is the sending of an expert to Chile to advise on the control of a type of wild bramble which was spreading so rapidly as to render thousands of valuable acres useless for any agricultural purpose.

Under the Expanded Program, every branch of FAO is able to do its share in helping under-developed countries. As more governments have come to realize what the program can mean to them, the scope of operations has steadily increased. In the agricultural field, many requests, especially in the Far East, have been connected with improved land and water use, which is fundamental to the large-scale development schemes taking place in that region.

Animal disease control, with wide national as well as international implications, is a subject which fits easily under the Expanded Program. Nevertheless, work being done in this field in some countries—as, for example, rinderpest in Ethiopia—is a legacy from the work started with UNRRA funds. Animal and plant breeding and crop improvement have been the subject of continual requests, and many member States have expressed their eagerness to improve their institutional and extension services. Recently, there has been an increase in requests for plant production and protection.

In economics, FAO experts at the end of 1955 were working on problems of statistics in sixteen countries; ten, on marketing problems; and fifteen, on agricultural programs, and other agricultural economic problems. Requests for this latter type of assistance show a marked upward trend. There are also requests for economists to advise on large development schemes for agriculture or forestry. Technical improvements have been the subject of many fisheries requests, especially where old-fashioned craft or primitive fishing techniques have been holding up development. There have also been inquiries into ways of improving the marketing of fish in the interior of many countries, as, for example, in Pakistan and Yugoslavia. In the former, a new fish harbor was designed for Karachi, while in the latter, the help of the educational authorities was enlisted to increase the awareness among all sections of the population of the value of fish as food. Important, too, have been the steps taken to increase fresh-water fisheries in such places as ponds, canals and flooded rice fields.

In forestry work under the Expanded Program, FAO aims to promote national forest policies, either through the sending of an advisory mission which is followed later by advice on specific technical projects, or by the introduction of efficient production techniques and the modernization of forest industries.

In Latin America, attention has been concentrated on the development of sound forest legislation, establishment or strengthening of national forest services, expansion of research, finding new uses and outlets for forest products, and in opening up forest resources. A forestry school has been established in Chile; a Latin-American forest research and training institute was started in Venezuela; missions have investigated pulp and paper production in a number of countries; and a mission is studying the possibility of developing Amazon forest resources.

In the Near East, technical assistance has been concerned mainly with the training of forestry personnel, research, afforestation programs, and forest range management. A regional research organization and training school are being started.

In the Far East, conditions vary widely, but as a whole forestry techniques are advanced. Emphasis has been placed on forest industries which are tied in with national plans for economic development, as in Pakistan, India, Burma and Indonesia. Regional training centers on mechanical logging, timber grading, and research methods have been held.

The technical assistance work of FAO's Nutrition Division includes assistance in various aspects of nutrition work, in particular, education and training in nutrition, the development of school feeding and related nutrition activities, the organization of national nutrition institutes, and services and food technology. The latter, which is rendered in cooperation with UNICEF, concerns, in particular, the processing of cheap protein-rich foods suitable for child feeding; it also deals with the broader aspects of food technology. Assistance in the field of home economics has been concerned, in particular, with the development in training institutes of a more adequate education in home economics, and in expanding extension programs to serve rural peoples.

Regional projects under the Expanded Program have covered a wide variety of subjects. In some cases, the Program is used to supplement projects already undertaken under the regular program, as, for example, the control of locusts in the Arabian Peninsula and in Central America, and the improvement of rice in the Far East. In projects under the Central American Integration Scheme, a number of experts are appointed for specific jobs covering special fields, as, for example, cotton production and slaughterhouse improvement. Many of the training courses conducted under the Expanded Program are also on a regional basis, such as, for example, tropical forestry or fish marketing; other courses are for national technicians only.

Finally, there is the fellowship program under the Expanded Program which permits technicians to be sent abroad to enable them to complete their studies. Wherever possible, the technician is returned to his home country before the expert, with whose assignment the technician's fellowship is connected, has completed his job. Thus, the returning fellow is able to take over where the expert leaves off, not only in carrying out actual operations but also in training other countrymen.

Publications

One of the first publications FAO produced was its *World Food Survey* (1946). In the years immediately after the Second World War, it was no easy task to measure the situation statistically, so almost at once the task of revising and improving this survey was begun. The second *World Food Survey* was published in 1952, and has been widely quoted in the press. From 1947 onwards, an annual report on *The State of Food and Agriculture* has appeared, together with the Director-General's report on *The Work of FAO*. With the two *World Food Surveys*, these two annual reports form a basic record of FAO's analysis of the situation and its practical attack on the problems of increasing the world's food production to meet the growing demands of an increasing world population. For the specialists, the *Yearbook of Food and Agriculture Statistics*, together with the *Yearbook of Forest Products Statistics* and *Yearbook of Fishery Statistics* fill in the statistical details of production, prices and trade. Some of the statistical series in these yearbooks are a continuation of the work of the former International Institute of Agriculture, which was absorbed into FAO in 1946, and the *Catalogue of FAO Publications, 1945-54* includes the available titles of the Institute. Copies of the catalogue in English, French or Spanish can be obtained from any sales agent, or direct from the Documents Service, Rome, Italy.

1. YEARBOOKS: *Yearbook of Food and Agriculture Statistics,* published annually since 1947 (Part I—Production, Part II—Trade); *Yearbook of Forest Products Statistics,* also published annually from 1947 (out of print); *Yearbook of Fishery Statistics,* 1947, 1948-49, 1950-51 (including an important supplement on nomenclature), 1952-53, (Part I—Production and Craft, Part II—International Trade). Food and agriculture statistics are kept up-to-date in the Monthly Bulletin of Agricultural Economics and Statistics, which also publishes commodity notes and one or two general articles each month. This bulletin now carries also the current fisheries statistics, which are sent separately to subscribers to the quarterly FAO *Fisheries Bulletin.* Forestry statistics are kept up-to-date by the quarterly publication of commodity reports in *Unasylva,* FAO's journal of forestry. A separate series of Commodity Bulletins and mimeographed Commodity Reports covering all the important agricultural products is also published. In 1952, FAO began its Commodity Policy Studies, a series of analytical studies of national and international policies for agricultural products, including nine titles by 1956, of which the most recent is *The Stabilization of the Olive Oil Market.*

2. Two FAO special studies have sold well and are in use as textbooks in all parts of the world. *The Efficient Use of Fertilizers* has been reprinted commercially by Messrs. Leonard Hill Ltd., of London; the second Spanish edition has been serialized in six Spanish language journals. The same British publisher published *Improving the World's Grasslands,* of which a second revised and enlarged edition was due for publication in 1956. Other works in ever-increasing demand are *Zebu Cattle of India and Pakistan, Soil Surveys for Land Development, Legumes in Agriculture, School Feeding; its Contribution to Child Nutrition,* and *Teaching Better Nutrition.*

3. Besides the regular series of agricultural studies (most of which, of course, are published by FAO itself), a first series of shorter booklets, the FAO Agricultural Development Papers, appeared in 1952, and now lists over 50 titles, including an important handbook on *Cereal Breeding Procedures,* and booklets on such topics as aspects of land reform, arid zones and use of small tools. To meet the demand, seven FAO monographs had to be reprinted in 1955, including the Spanish editions of *Training Rural Leaders* and *Breeding Livestock adapted to Unfavorable Environments.* Another publication, the *Multilingual Vocabulary of Soil Science,* first published in 1954, was exhausted within a few months and had to be reprinted in 1955. Other series of studies include many titles in Fisheries and Forestry.

4. Apart from the periodicals and bulletins already mentioned, FAO produces two important technical journals. The *World Fisheries Abstracts* appear in English, French and Spanish bi-monthly, and cover the whole field of fisheries technology, including boat design, equipment, food preservation, and fish detection methods. The FAO *Plant Protection Bulletin* reports monthly the incidence of all plant pests, the measures being adopted to control them, and such matters as changes in plant quarantine regulations; this is done under the provisions of the International Plant Protection Convention, whose purpose is to secure common and effective action to prevent the introduction and spread of pests and diseases of plant and plant products. Sample copies of any FAO periodical will be sent, on request to the Documents Service, FAO, Rome, Italy.

5. FAO Legislative Service reestablished as from January 1, 1952, the publication of an international collection of texts of food and agriculture legislation. Fundamental laws of considerable interest are translated into English, French and Spanish for immediate official distribution, and a completely comprehensive collection of *Food and Agricultural Legislation* is published quarterly, and is available on subscription. This continues a service begun by the former International Institute of Agriculture.

6. The Editorial Liaison Service arranges the serialization of FAO documentation in the technical press as a means of giving documents and publications a wider circulation than the relatively limited editions of the books themselves permit.

UNITED NATIONS EDUCATIONAL, SCIENTIFIC AND CULTURAL ORGANIZATION (UNESCO)

Functions

The purpose of the United Nations Educational, Scientific and Cultural Organization, as defined in its Constitution, is to "contribute to peace and security by promoting collaboration among the nations through education, science and culture in order to further universal respect for justice, for the rule of law, and for the human rights and fundamental freedoms for all," which are affirmed by the Charter of the United Nations.

To realize this purpose, UNESCO collaborates in the work of advancing mutual knowledge and understanding of peoples through all means of mass communication; gives fresh impulse to popular education and to the spread of culture; and maintains, increases and diffuses knowledge.

Origin

A Conference for the Establishment of an Educational, Scientific and Cultural Organization of the United Nations, meeting in London from November 1 to 16, 1945, drew up the Constitution of UNESCO. It also established a Preparatory Educational, Scientific and Cultural Commission to function until the Organization came into being on November 4, 1946, when its Constitution was formally accepted by 20 of its signatories, as required.

Organization

UNESCO works through a General Conference, an Executive Board, and a secretariat.

The General Conference, consisting of representatives from each member State, meets every two years to determine policies and programs. The 1956 session was to be held in New Delhi. UNESCO now has a total membership of 74.

The Executive Board, which meets at least twice a year, consists of 22 members responsible to their governments and elected by the General Conference. Under the authority of the General Conference, it is responsible for the execution of the program adopted by the Conference.

The secretariat is responsible for carrying out the program of action. It is headed by a Director-General nominated by the Executive Board and appointed by the Conference. The present Director-General is Luther H. Evans (United States).

National Commissions, composed chiefly of representatives of non-governmental organizations in each of the member States, link UNESCO with the educational, scientific and cultural life in each country, and assist in carrying out UNESCO's program.

A budget of $10,299,618 was approved for UNESCO's activities in 1955, and $11,318,212 for 1956.

It should be emphasized that, while UNESCO can make recommendations, no nation is required to follow those recommendations. Moreover, UNESCO's Constitution prohibits it from interfering in the domestic policies and practices of a country. UNESCO cannot even carry on a survey or establish a project in a country except on the explicit request and with the cooperation of the government of that country.

Activities

UNESCO's activities form part of the total United Nations and specialized agencies program designed to promote peace through collective security, and the economic and social progress without which no just and lasting peace is possible.

As in the case of other specialized agencies, UNESCO's activities fall largely into the area of economic and social progress, and they are all included in the list of priorities established by the Economic and Social Council for the program of the United Nations and specialized agencies.

UNESCO is concerned with the spread of knowledge: (1) to increase an understanding of ways of life, and thereby to encourage a greater sense of tolerance and brotherhood, and (2) to make people more efficient.

There are many ways of spreading knowledge, so the impression is easily gained that the program is diffuse and uncoordinated. When it is realized, however, that all items, large and small, contribute in some way to the spread of knowledge, the logic of the program becomes clearer, and its contribution to the total United Nations program can be more readily understood.

Knowledge is conveyed to others through educators, through men of science, and through a large body of people who may be called creative thinkers and doers—painters, philosophers, authors, musicians, and those who work on the stage, in museums or in libraries. It is also conveyed through documentation of all kinds, and through books, magazines, pamphlets, newspapers, radio, film, television, and even by the phonograph record. UNESCO therefore has to mobilize all these people and materials to enable it to carry out its task.

With a comparatively small budget of $11,000,000 yearly and a small staff (about 800 at the Headquarters in Paris to serve 74 member States), UNESCO cannot include on its payroll a vast number of creative people in all these fields; nor can it own a world-wide publishing business or operate an international radio network, film studios or a daily newspaper.

THE SPECIALISTS

Long before UNESCO existed, however, many of these people were already organized internationally in voluntary organizations, such as the International Council of Scientific Unions, the International PEN Club, and the International Federation of Secondary School Teachers. Such organizations play an important role in furthering the spread of knowledge by bringing together people in a particular profession for the exchange of experience and ideas. But since they function on a voluntary basis, their budgets are too small to enable specialists from distant lands to travel to their meetings, or to publish the results of their deliberations in an adequate manner. Although they are international in name, in fact they are often regional, and since money is more abundant in the industrialized countries, they tend to operate in Western regions and become limited to Western ideas.

UNESCO is therefore helping these organizations overcome their difficulties in various ways. It gives *financial aid* (in the form of subventions) to facilitate their meetings and publication programs. Such aid totalled more than $600,000 in 1955. In the natural sciences alone, over a period of four years, 1,500 scientists took part in meetings and discussion groups which they could not otherwise have attended.

In order to improve this network of living contacts, *new organizations* have been founded by UNESCO in fields where they did not exist, such as the International Theatre Institute, the International Music Council, the International Council of Philosophy and Humanistic Studies, the International Sociological Association, and the International Political Science Association.

The International Theatre Institute, for example, was organized in 1947, and now has 29 national theatre centres. International Theatre Week is celebrated in March every year to familiarize countries with representative foreign works. In the United States, this has extended to International Theatre Month. The International Theatre Institute also carries out studies on children's theatre, arranges for the exchange of young theatre people, and provides an exchange of information through a quarterly publication—*World Theatre*.

Thirdly, to compensate for the lack or inadequacy of national chapters of voluntary organizations in the under-developed regions, UNESCO has taken direct action (only in the scientific field, thus far) by operating *Science Cooperation Offices* in Montevideo (for Latin America), Cairo (for the Middle East), and New Delhi and Djakarta (for Asia). They serve as a link between the more highly developed and the under-developed countries in which there is a growing demand for detailed and current scientific information to aid economic development. They compile information on all scientific experimentation and publication in their areas, organize lecture tours by visiting scientists, and select candidates for scientific training abroad. Institutions apply to them for help in obtaining rare chemical products, microbial cultures and samples of seed; research workers are put in touch with specialists in their fields abroad; and a wide range of practical information is made available to support local campaigns in improved health, sanitation and agriculture.

Further assistance is given specialists through holding UNESCO-sponsored *seminars and meetings of experts* on specific problems. Numerous meetings of this kind have been held in various member States, including Belgium, Brazil, Burma, Canada, India and Sweden, on such subjects as teacher training, rural education, public library services, the philosophy of East and West, racial differences, and the exchange of television programs.

Specialists from member States are invited to these seminars and meetings to work out solutions and recommendations. Subsequently reports, in the form of pamphlets or handbooks, are published by UNESCO, so that the various professions may have the benefit of experience and ideas from all regions.

The expert meetings held in 1950 and 1951 on racial differences marked a significant advance in social science on this problem. As a result, two reports have been issued presenting evidence that there is no scientific basis for the contention that there is any "superior" race. In continuing its campaign for racial tolerance, UNESCO now stresses positive contributions made by different races and creeds.

DOCUMENTATION AND OTHER MATERIALS

The international collection and use of documentation constitute an increasingly complex problem because of the increased tempo of research and the number of languages in which such research is published. For example, in the natural sciences, the number of articles published each year in 50,000 periodicals is estimated at one million, not to mention books and pamphlets. To put this tremendous output at the disposal of research workers, teachers and students, or at least that part of it which interests them, is a formidable task.

UNESCO is therefore concentrating on the *standardization, collection and dissemination of specialized documentation* through the publication of bibliographies and abstracts. This work is largely carried out by voluntary organizations: national groups of specialists in bibliographical and documentation services have been established in over 40 countries, and an International Committee is coordinating their activities.

Under the technical assistance program, UNESCO is able to send experts to help governments set up national or regional *scientific and technical documentation centres* for the use of researchers and industries. Typical of these is the centre in Mexico City which was opened in 1951, and is now being operated by the Mexican Government. This centre is receiving more than 5,000 scientific and technical periodicals which are classified, summarized into abstracts, and translated into Spanish. These abstracts are published periodically in a bulletin, which represents a summary of one million printed pages, to enable scientists in Mexico and other Latin American countries to keep abreast of activities in their fields of work. The centre is equipped to provide, upon request, the full articles in Spanish, on paper or on micro-film. Similar centres have been set up with the aid of UNESCO experts in India, Turkey, Uruguay and Yugoslavia.

Additionally, services have been set up at Headquarters in Paris to aid the spread of knowledge on particular educational, scientific and cultural subjects. This operation is called the *clearing house* services, which distribute information from all member States on such subjects as fundamental education; the availability of fellowships and scholarships around the world; progress in the social sciences; copyright; library services; and new experiments and techniques in the sphere of radio, film, press and television. Several periodicals and publications are based on the information assembled in these clearing houses.

As for the role of books, press, film, radio and television—the media of mass communication—in furthering the spread of knowledge, UNESCO is operating in two ways.

Apart from the public information aspect (which is needed to gain support and understanding for its programs), an attempt is made to supply national outlets with a service of stories, articles and radio recordings on developments in education, science and culture which implement the purposes of UNESCO; as well as information about the economic and social work of the other specialized agencies as an aid to teaching about the United Nations.

More important, however, UNESCO can be of service to the media of mass communications by helping to reduce existing *barriers to the flow of materials* between countries, such as foreign currency, tariffs, quotas and copyright which prevent the purchase and use of books, films and other educational aids by people in different lands. This work is not only of assistance to book publishers, the film and radio industries, but also helps in the realization of one of the fundamental freedoms proclaimed by the United Nations—freedom of information.

As a first step, UNESCO tackled the currency problem by issuing coupons (UNESCO *Sales Coupons*) for the purchase of books, films and scientific materials. By this means, institutions and individuals in some 36 soft-currency countries have been enabled to buy these items available generally in hard-currency countries. At the end of 1955, $9,000,000 of coupons had been issued.

To overcome other barriers, UNESCO sponsored an *international agreement on the importation of many types of educational, scientific and cultural materials,* which eliminates customs duties on books, periodicals and newspapers, among other educational items. This agreement came into effect in May 1952, and, as a result, such items are easier to get and cheaper to buy in the 21 countries which have so far ratified it. Another agreement designed to speed the international flow of certain audio-visual materials is being applied by twelve nations.

Another barrier to the flow and freedom of information is of a less obvious nature. It concerns the *inadequacy of technical facilities* (printing presses, film studios, radio stations and receivers and news agencies) in many areas of the world, which have to rely on the output of the more industrialized countries, and are unable to make their own contribution to the flow of information and knowledge because of the lack of technical facilities.

To help remedy this situation, UNESCO has surveyed press, radio and film facilities throughout the world, covering 173 countries and territories. At present, funds available under UNESCO's aid to member States program are being used to send experts to help countries improve facilities.

In addition to its operation concerned with the creators and imparters of knowledge and with the materials produced by them, UNESCO also seeks to "put knowledge to work" by focusing on specific projects in education, science and culture. The justification for such projects lies in the fact that they have never been undertaken before or that, even though they have been started by individual countries, UNESCO (because of its international character) can promote them universally or within a group of countries.

EDUCATION

FUNDAMENTAL EDUCATION. More than half of mankind—1,200,000,000 men, women and children—can neither read nor write. These are the people who are also poor, ill-fed and have a life expectancy of under thirty years.

To meet this problem, a technique called "fundamental education" is employed—a term used by UNESCO to explain its approach to mass education (sometimes called community development), whereby the three "R's" primarily become tools by which people can learn to improve their health, diet, crops and standard of living. In other words, an alphabet of hygiene, nutrition, agriculture and home economics has to be taught to illiterates along with an alphabet of reading and writing.

A significant fact about fundamental education is that UNESCO seldom acts alone, but in collaboration with the World Health Organization, the Food and Agriculture Organization and the International Labor Organization, so that a four-fold attack is made simultaneously on ignorance, poverty, hunger and disease.

The development of fundamental education is hampered by a lack of teachers and a dearth of suitable teaching materials, not to mention the financial aspect. Since UNESCO does not have the means to carry out mass campaigns, it endeavors to assist various countries in this difficult task by a number of approaches.

A first example is the *Centre* set up in 1951 at *Patzcuaro, Mexico,* to train teachers for Latin America who will, in turn, go back to their own countries to train more teachers locally in this type of education. The 74 member States are agreed that such regional centres, training a nucleus of specialists and producing simple educational tools—posters, film-strips and readers designed for new literates and geared to the specific health and agricultural needs of the area—are the most important contributions UNESCO can make with the resources available. The Patzcuaro

Centre is a cooperative effort by UNESCO, the Mexican Government, and the Organization of American States. A similar centre was opened in 1953 at Sirs-el-Layyan, Egypt, for the Arab countries.

By the end of 1955, 228 students from sixteen Latin American countries had completed their training at Patzcuaro, and many of these graduates are now working in fundamental education projects in their home countries. The centre at Sirs-el-Layyan in Egypt has already graduated 92 students. One hundred and twenty trainees from eight countries and from among the Palestine refugees are now studying there.

Long before UNESCO came into being, *National Fundamental Education Projects* were being carried out by governments and voluntary organizations, from which valuable information and advice can be obtained for use elsewhere. UNESCO has therefore linked several of these projects into an information network for the exchange of experience and ideas; thus far the network consists of 56 projects in 20 countries and territories. UNESCO has provided expert missions to some of the projects and has made available educational tools through the Gift Coupon Plan.

Thirdly, extensive *surveys* have been conducted on the use of vernacular languages, methods of teaching reading and writing, and the use of audio-visual materials in the expansion of fundamental education. In the latter field, experiments have been carried out in Egypt, India and the Belgian Congo. A survey has been made of the Canadian Farm Forum (radio) project, covering a wide range of subjects including hygiene, domestic science, agriculture and civics as a guide to developing educational radio. Experts in educational broadcasting have been sent to Ceylon, Colombia and Pakistan.

Fourthly, since 1947, several governments have asked UNESCO to send *missions* to their countries to help plan the modernization of their educational systems. The results of these missions are now in evidence.

In Afghanistan, for example, which was visited in 1951, a fundamental education program has been launched; an educational film library was set up in the Ministry of Education; 60 rural schools were opened; a new institute for training secondary school teachers was established; and a teacher training and home economics course for women were begun. The agricultural college has been reorganized, and the engineering college has been considerably enlarged and equipped with modern tools.

After a UNESCO mission to Burma in 1951, the Burmese Government took steps to carry out its recommendations by increasing its budget for education from 25,000,000 to 55,000,000 rupees. It was planning to open 1,000 new primary schools, 200 junior secondary schools, 40 senior secondary schools, and a new teacher-training college.

In Thailand, where a UNESCO mission was sent in 1950, the Government has approved a ten-year plan for educational development. The plan was to start with an experiment in the Chachoengsao area, where authorities were attempting to reorganize all types and grades of educational activity, including pre-school, primary, secondary and vocational education and teacher training.

Realizing that the ability to read is no end in itself, and that a person may slip back into illiteracy within weeks unless he has something to read, UNESCO has given great attention to the development of *public libraries*. The first public library in India open to all castes and creeds has been set up by UNESCO and the Government of India. It is now in full operation, and is serving an average of 2,300 readers daily. An estimated 78 per cent of the visitors, including many children, who have their own reading room, had never visited a library before. This was developed as a pilot project for the entire continent. A similar model library has been opened at Medellin, Colombia, to serve as a demonstration centre for Latin America.

Finally, many countries request fundamental education experts under the United Nations *technical assistance* program for economic development. These experts initiate projects in local areas to train leaders of fundamental education campaigns. At the end of 1955, 41 experts were engaged in this work in eighteen countries including Afghanistan, Cambodia, Ceylon, Indonesia, Iraq and Liberia.

SCIENCE

RESEARCH: PROBLEM OF DESERTS. It is estimated that the arid and semi-arid regions of the world make up more than a quarter of the land surface. Because of the pressure of increasing populations, it is more than ever urgent that this unproductive land should be brought back to life.

Governments in many countries are giving this problem high priority, but unrelated local attempts to wrest production from the dry lands cannot be expected to achieve the required result.

UNESCO's work in this field is twofold: first, to make available the expert knowledge gained from the many experiments and projects carried out all over the world, and, second, to help in the development and expansion of desert research stations, encouraging them to devote time and study to certain major problems concerning deserts.

Under an advisory committee of nine scientists from Australia, Egypt, France, India, Israel, Mexico, Peru, the United Kingdom and the United States, UNESCO selects a particular field of research for study each year. In 1951 the study concerned underground water. Scientists know that there are vast seas of underground water in all areas of the world, including deserts, but much research is still required.

Eight scientists commissioned by UNESCO prepared a report on current research on this subject, which has thus provided research workers with the first comprehensive picture of what was being done all over the world on the problem of underground water, and the possibility of using it effectively in arid zones.

To combat the increasing encroachment of deserts on adjacent fertile lands, research in 1952 was concentrated on plant species which might be transplanted to halt the marching sands. A group of specialists, again commissioned by UNESCO, assembled world-wide data on promising species and strains which thrive under dry conditions in one area and might profitably be introduced into another.

Conferences on arid zone hydrology and on plant ecology were held in 1952 and 1953, while, in 1955, UNESCO cooperated with the American Association for the Advancement of Science in organizing a conference and a symposium in New Mexico on arid zone problems.

Research work in the arid regions and research stations was being strengthened in places as far distant as India and Chile, and Australia and the Sahara Desert. Eight of these stations have now been linked directly to UNESCO's program of research development. They are in Algeria, Egypt, French West Africa, India, Israel and the United States. In addition to coordinating their research with UNESCO, the centres would accept visiting scientists and fellowship holders, and would exchange their scientists and technicians with other institutions carying out similar work.

RESEARCH: SOCIAL SCIENCE. UNESCO is also endeavoring to encourage research and help focus social science studies on specific problems which contribute to tensions and misunderstanding between peoples and nations. One of these is a study of the effects of industrialization upon the lives of people, particularly in those countries where modern technical knowledge is now being introduced. It is hoped that a better understanding of this problem will minimize the misery caused by unsettled living conditions and disrupted family relationships which accompanied industrial movements in the nineteenth century. Studies have been undertaken on this subject in Africa and South Asia. A centre to study the effects of industrialization in Southern Asia was to be opened in Calcutta in January 1956, with the aid of the Indian Government.

In addition to studies such as these, UNESCO is able to assist member States requesting such help in the organization of research for diagnosing certain internal tensions. The Indian Government, for instance, asked for a UNESCO expert to help train teams of social science students for an analysis of religious tensions between different communities. The expert was dispatched, the teams trained, and the work was being carried out by the Indian Government.

RESEARCH: NUCLEAR PHYSICS. At UNESCO's instigation, a European Organization for Nuclear Research has been set up for basic research in the peaceful application of nuclear physics. The organization was established in July 1953, with twelve member States—Belgium, Denmark, France, the German Federal Republic, Greece, Italy, the Netherlands, Norway, Sweden, Switzerland, the United Kingdom and Yugoslavia. This marks the first time European states have set up a common body responsible for organizing scientific research. The laboratory for research in high energy particles was under construction at Meyrin, near Geneva.

SCIENCE TEACHING. Assistance to introduce the teaching of basic science into schools has been requested by several countries, particularly in South Asia, the Middle East and Latin America. In many of these areas, science teaching at the elementary level is unknown. There is a critical shortage of teachers in basic science, almost no laboratories, and little equipment.

To meet these vast needs, UNESCO has taken several steps: (1) ten simple *handbooks* have been prepared as aids to untrained teachers, the first four designed specifically for the elementary level; (2) catalogues of scientific equipment necessary for teaching science have been published, along with sample lessons and instruction in the preparation of simple equipment from local materials; (3) because many nations are unable financially to import the equipment they need, 150 *drawings and designs* have been prepared with detailed specifications on how to make basic scientific equipment; (4) through the *Sales Coupon,* schools in soft-currency countries have been enabled to pay in their local currency for scientific equipment from hard-currency countries; (5) through the *Gift Coupon* scheme, voluntary organizations in eight countries have made gifts of scientific materials to needy schools in the under-developed countries; (6) through funds available under the *technical assistance* scheme, it has been possible to send experts in the teaching of science to many of the under-developed countries which have requested them; and (7) five *scientific exhibits* were touring member States to popularize science. They covered astronomy and physics, new materials such as plastics and alloys, the physiology of the human senses, techniques of measuring distances in the universe, and energy and its transformations. Over six years, these exhibits have been seen by 2,000,000 persons in 32 countries.

CULTURE

An idea exists that culture is limited to intellectuals and the better educated, and consequently cannot be part of the daily life of the broad mass of people. Gradually over the years this idea is losing significance, but it is something against which UNESCO has had to fight.

The program of cultural activities, encompasses not only the various arts, such as the theatre, music, painting, sculpture, literature, museums and architecture, but also philosophy and the area of creative thought as a whole.

The various projects in the program are not being carried out merely to help the artist on his way (although this is an important by-product); rather an attempt is being made to relate the many fields of art to the broad area of education, both formal and fundamental. Thus it is hoped to make cultural subjects play a greater part in the daily lives of a greater number of people—with the consequent enrichment that this will bring. In other words, UNESCO desires to help people in different countries find out more about each other's thoughts, customs and ways of life by assisting in making this kind of knowledge available, and suggesting ways in which it can be integrated into educational programs.

Mention has already been made of UNESCO's financial aid to existing voluntary organizations in the cultural sphere, and the founding of new organizations to fill gaps in the present structure.

Some examples of projects to show the work now being carried out to relate cultural subjects to education follow.

In 1951, a seminar was held at Bristol University, England, on the role of *painting* and other visual arts in education, including methods, the training of teachers, and the materials employed. Thirty-five specialists from 20 countries took part. The conclusions and recommendations dealing with art education for children, young people and adults have been published, under the title "Art and Education". Several countries, in modernizing their educational systems, are introducing art classes for children for the first time.

In 1952, another seminar took place at the Brooklyn Museum, New York, at which educators and museum officials from 26 countries met to discuss the ways in which *museums* could become an integral part of education. Some 50 American museums joined in presenting examples of techniques used by museums in the United States in connection with education. The participants worked out plans of action for the use of museums in school programs and adult education classes in the developed countries, as well as the introduction of mobile museums as demonstration tools for health and agriculture in fundamental education.

Both of these seminars have helped to intensify the International Campaign for Museums which has been launched by the International Council of Museums, together with UNESCO.

In the same way, attention is being given to the place *music* should play in the education of young people; the desirability of giving children not only an appreciation of music, but also an opportunity to participate through bands, orchestras or choirs.

Additionally, as an aid to painting, UNESCO provides information about the best available *reproductions of works of art*. Three catalogues have been published covering color reproductions prior to 1860, and from 1860 to the present day. The most recent of these catalogues offers more than 600 black-and-white photographs of reproductions listed, together with exact information on size, cost and availability. They are useful tools for schools, colleges and even for individual buyers.

As regards *direct assistance for the artist*, perhaps UNESCO's most significant contribution to date is the adoption (after five years of preliminary work) of a Universal Copyright Convention, which provides protection throughout the world for the rights of authors and other copyright proprietors of literary, scientific and artistic works, including writing, musical and dramatic works, films, paintings and sculpture.

There are some multilateral copyright conventions now in effect, but none is worldwide in scope. The revised Berne Convention provides for protection of copyright in 43 countries, mostly European. Brazil and Canada are the only Western Hemisphere countries which adhere to this convention. There are several Pan-American conventions among the countries of the Western Hemisphere, the most important of which is the Buenos Aires Conventions (1910), with fifteen adherents. In some countries, foreign works enjoy little or no protection. Many countries do not adhere to any of these conventions.

The objective of the new convention was to include as many countries as possible which were not now signatories of existing conventions. At the same time, it sought to create more solid bonds between countries that had signed the Pan-American and Berne Conventions.

At an international conference held in Geneva in September 1952, the Universal Copyright Convention was signed by 35 countries. The Convention went into effect on September 16, 1955. By January 1, 1956, seventeen countries, including the United States, had joined it.

These examples of "putting knowledge to work" by no means cover the total program.

UNESCO also works for the extension of free and compulsory education, including women's education. A program for workers' education was initiated in 1952, and UNESCO-sponsored travel grants have enabled some 1,200 European workers to visit their counterparts in other countries. There are also various schemes for stimulating the exchange of persons for educational purposes. Emergency schools have been set up for Arab refugee children in the Middle East, and their enrolment has risen to over 100,000 boys and girls.

INTERNATIONAL CIVIL AVIATION ORGANIZATION (ICAO)

Functions

The aims and objectives of the International Civil Aviation Organization are to develop the principles and techniques of international air navigation, and to foster the planning and development of international air transport so as to:

ensure the safe and orderly growth of international civil aviation throughout the world;

encourage the arts of aircraft design and operation for peaceful purposes;

encourage the development of airways, airports and air navigation facilities for international civil aviation;

meet the needs of the peoples of the world for safe, regular, efficient and economical air transport;

prevent economic waste caused by unreasonable competition;

ensure that the rights of contracting states are fully respected and that every contracting state has a fair opportunity to operate international airlines;

avoid discrimination between contracting states;

promote safety of flight in international air navigation;

and promote generally the development of all aspects of international civil aeronautics.

Origin

The Convention providing for the establishment of the International Civil Aviation Organization was drawn up by the International Civil Aviation Conference held in Chicago from November 1 to December 7, 1944. ICAO came into being on April 4, 1947, 30 days after the Convention had been ratified by the required 26 states. A Provisional International Civil Aviation Organization (PICAO) operated under an agreement drawn up by the Chicago Conference, from June 6, 1945, until the formal establishment of ICAO.

The ICAO Convention superseded, as between contracting states, the provisions of two earlier agreements: the Paris Convention of 1919, which established the International Commission for Air Navigation (ICAN) to set up standards on technical matters, and the Pan-American Convention on Commercial Aviation drawn up at Havana in 1928.

Organization

ICAO works through an Assembly, a Council, a President of the Council, and a Secretary-General and their staff, and commissions and committees.

The Assembly consists of all 66 members of the Organization, each of which has one vote. It is convened by the Council annually. The Assembly decides the policy of the Organization, votes on the budget, and deals with any question not specifically referred to the Council.

The Council, composed of 21 states elected by the Assembly, meets in virtually continuous session. It carries out the directives of the Assembly. It elects its President, appoints the Secretary-General, and administers the finances of the Organization. It creates standards for international air navigation and collects, examines and publishes information concerning air navigation. It may also act, if requested by the countries concerned, as a tribunal for the settlement of any dispute arising among members relating to international civil aviation.

The Council is assisted in its work by an Air Navigation Commission and by four committees: air transport, legal, joint support of air navigation services, and finance.

The Secretary-General of ICAO appoints the staff of the Secretariat, and supervises and directs its activities.

ICAO maintains five field offices which serve as liaison between the Organization and its various member States: the North American Office, at ICAO headquarters in Montreal; the South American Office, at Lima; the European and African Office, at Paris; the Middle East Office, at Cairo; and the Far East and Pacific Office, at Bangkok.

The 1956 budget was $2,826,971 (Canadian).

Activities

Since August 1945, when the PICAO Interim Council met for the first time, ICAO and its provisional Organization have brought about concerted action by the nations of the world in the organization and maintenance of facilities and services necessary for international air transport. Patterns for meteorological services, traffic control, communications, radio beacons, and the other facilities required for safe international flight have been developed.

By 1956, regional air navigation meetings had been held covering all of the major international flying areas of the world as classified by ICAO. Meetings for the North Atlantic, European-Mediterranean, Caribbean, and Middle East regions were held during 1946; for the South Pacific, South American, and South Atlantic regions during 1947; for the European-Mediterranean, North Atlantic, North Pacific, and Southeast Asia regions during 1948; for the African-Indian Ocean region in 1949; for the Caribbean and Middle East regions in 1950; for the South American and South Atlantic regions in 1951; for the European and Mediterranean regions in 1952; for the Southeast Asia and South Pacific and Caribbean regions in 1953; for the North Atlantic region in 1954; and for the Pacific region in 1955. These meetings examined existing facilities for airports, navigational aids, communications, air traffic control, meteorology, operations, and search and rescue, and determined what additional facilities and operating procedures were needed to make flying in these regions safer, more economical and more regular.

The first regional air navigation meeting for the North Atlantic had proposed the establishment of weather stations in the North Atlantic Ocean to supply meteorological information for airlines flying that route. Subsequently, ten member States of ICAO, attending a special conference in September 1946, agreed to maintain thirteen ocean weather stations at specified points in the North Atlantic. In addition to meteorological information, these stations provide navigation aids, communications facilities, and search and rescue facilities throughout the region. Subsequent conferences have made certain changes in the ocean station network based upon experience in their operation. The present agreement, which would continue until 1958, involved nine stations manned by 21 ships and was participated in by thirteen nations.

ICAO arranged for the cooperative maintenance of other air transport, navigation and meteorological facilities required by aircraft flying over sparsely populated regions or regions of uncertain sovereignty. Two other sets of agreements, involving the maintenance and financing of air navigation services in Iceland and in Greenland and the Faeroe Islands, are now in effect. The Icelandic Agreement involves approximately $600,000 per year, and includes the financing of the Loran (Long Range Radio Aid to Navigation) station at Vik, Iceland, and of air traffic control, meteorology and communications services; eleven nations participate in this arrangement. The second arrangement involves the joint financing of ten meteorological stations and of the Loran station at Frederiksdal in Greenland, and of the Loran station at Skuvanes in the Faeroe Islands. Participating in this arrangement are ten of ICAO's member States.

To insure the highest practicable degree of uniformity in international civil aviation regulations, the ICAO Council has adopted fifteen sets of standards and recommended practices. The standards and recommended practices are constantly revised, and amendments are made when necessary. All fifteen sets of standards and recommended practices are in effect, as annexes to the ICAO Convention, in all territories of ICAO's member States. Standards were established for:

(1) personnel licensing—indicating the technical requirements and experience necessary for pilots and air crews flying on international routes;

(2) aeronautical maps and charts—providing specifications for the production of all maps and charts required in international flying;

(3) rules of the air—including general flight rules, instrument flight rules, and right-of-way rules;

(4) dimensional practices—providing for progressive measures to improve air-ground communications;

(5) meteorological codes—which specify the various systems used for the transmission of meteorological information;

(6) operation of aircraft in scheduled international air services—governing flight preparation, aircraft equipment and maintenance, and, in general, the manner in which aircraft must be operated to achieve the desired level of safety on any kind of route;

(7) aircraft nationality and registration marks;

(8) airworthiness of aircraft;

(9) facilitation of international air transport—to simplify customs, immigration and health inspection regulations at border airports;

(10) aeronautical telecommunications—dealing with the standardization of communications systems and radio air navigation aids;

(11) air traffic services—dealing with the establishment and operation of air traffic control, flight information and alerting services;

(12) search and rescue—dealing with the organization to be established by states for the integration of facilities and services necessary for search and rescue;

(13) aircraft accident inquiry—dealing with the promotion of uniformity in the notification, investigation of and reporting on aircraft accident

(14) aerodromes—dealing with the physical requirements, lighting and marking of international aerodromes; and

(15) aeronautical information services—dealing with the uniformity in methods of collection and dissemination of aeronautical information.

If a state is unable to put a standard into effect in its territory, it must notify ICAO of the differences between its own practices and those established by the international standard. The Council must in turn notify all other members of ICAO of these differences. Notification of non-compliance with recommended practices is, however, unnecessary.

The principal achievements of ICAO in the legal field are two international air law conventions, and a protocol of amendment to a third convention which has been in existence since 1929: the Convention on the International Recognition of Rights in Aircraft, adopted by the ICAO Assembly in June 1948; the Convention on Damage Caused by Foreign Aircraft to Third Parties on the Surface, adopted at a diplomatic conference in September 1952; and a protocol of amendment to the Warsaw Convention of 1929 concerning the liability of the air carrier to passengers and cargo, which was adopted by a diplomatic conference in September 1955 at The Hague. As of December 31, 1955, the first Convention had been signed by 27 countries and ratified by six without reservation, the second had been signed by 26; the Warsaw amendment had been signed by 26 states and would come into effect when ratified by 30 nations

Because of the relatively short period of time involved in international flight, the delays caused by customs, immigration and public health formalities at international airports have been more important to air transportation than to surface transport. For this reason, ICAO has conducted a campaign of facilitation designed to decrease the delays at airports and to limit the amount of paper work necessary for the transfer of passengers and goods between countries. This work has been aided by governmental facilitation committees set up in the Organization's various member States, and as a result, there has been a great decrease in the red tape involved in crossing international borders by air. ICAO international standards on the facilitation of international air transport lay down the maximum formalities and documentation requirements which any state may impose.

Agreements and contracts concluded by member States or by airlines in those states are registered with ICAO, and national aviation laws and regulations are filed by ICAO. By the end of 1955, some 1200 agreements and contracts had been registered. ICAO had also assembled an extensive collection of texts of national laws and regulations on aviation.

In the field of air transport, the Organization has studied the possibility of states imposing economic charges for the use of airports and air navigation facilities generally, having regard to the heavy costs of airports and air navigation facilities to municipal and national governments. As the Convention on International Civil

Aviation gives to non-scheduled flights a special status with the privilege of freedom of transit over the territories of all contracting states, ICAO approved, for the guidance of member States, a definition of a scheduled international air service. Other subjects studied by ICAO include transport costs and rates for international air mail, the problem of multiple, discriminatory and unfairly burdensome taxation, and the possibility of a multilateral agreement on the exchange of commercial rights for air service.

ICAO participates in the United Nations Expanded Program of Technical Assistance. Its budget for 1956 in this regard was more than one million dollars. ICAO's technical assistance activities are based upon the fact that under-developed countries very often are unable to build roads and railroads, and therefore have great need for the quick and easy transportation which the modern aircraft can bring. Most of the projects that ICAO has undertaken have had as their main object an increase in the safety or efficiency in air transport operations, and hence in the value of this form of transport and its utilization by the public. The Organization has placed primary emphasis on the development of the ground services required by civil aviation, but aid has also been given for such items as commercial pilot training and instruction in the repair and maintenance of aircraft. Advice has also been provided in such fields as the organization of government departments of civil aviation, the preparation of air laws and regulations, and airline organization and operation. ICAO missions have been sent to more than 20 countries, and fellowships for study abroad have been granted to nationals of some 25 states. In addition to aid devoted particularly to individual states, regional training projects in Mexico and in the Middle East were also in operation.

Under the terms of the Convention on International Civil Aviation, the ICAO Council may serve as an arbitral body in cases of disputes involving the terms of the Convention. To date, only one dispute had been brought to the attention of the Council. This concerned the complaint of the Government of India that the Government of Pakistan was discriminating against its air transportation services by refusing to allow direct transit of Indian aircraft from New Delhi across Pakistan territory to Kabul in Afghanistan. The dispute was brought before the ICAO Council in 1952, and the Council encouraged both parties to negotiate an amicable settlement. As a result of negotiations, the ICAO Council in January 1953 approved a plan which provided for the transit of Indian aircraft across the northwest territories of Pakistan in two corridors, and the supplying by the Pakistan Government of aviation fuel to Afghanistan in order that Indian aircraft could refuel in Kabul before returning to India. This settlement met with the approval of both the Indian and the Pakistan Governments.

ICAO continually collects, analyzes and publishes statistical information relating to international aviation services. It issues a wide range of technical publications, including operational standards, regional manuals, and multi-language glossaries, and it publishes the ICAO *Bulletin,* which contains a review of ICAO's current activities. A detailed report on the aims and work of ICAO is contained in the *Memorandum on ICAO;* this is free of charge in English, French and Spanish versions, and is obtained from the Public Information Office of ICAO, International Aviation Building, Montreal, Canada.

Two ten-minute documentary films, "Winged World" and "Decade in the Air", in English, French and Spanish sound versions, and in both 16-mm and 35-mm, and an Exhibition Picture Set designed for wall display are also available; queries concerning these should be addressed either to the ICAO Public Information Office, or the United Nations Information Centers.

INTERNATIONAL BANK FOR RECONSTRUCTION AND DEVELOPMENT

Functions

The principal purposes of the International Bank for Reconstruction and Development are as follows:

to assist in the reconstruction and development of its member States by facilitating the investment of capital for productive purposes, thereby promoting the long-range growth of international trade and the improvement of living standards;

to promote private foreign investment by guarantees of and participations in loans and other investments made by private investors; and

when private capital is not available on reasonable terms, to make loans for productive purposes out of its own resources or from funds borrowed by it.

Origin

The Articles of Agreement of the Bank were drawn up by the United Nations Monetary and Financial Conference, which met at Bretton Woods, New Hampshire (United States), from July 1 to 22, 1944. The conference, called by President Roosevelt, was attended by representatives of 44 nations.

The Articles of Agreement came into force on December 25, 1945, when they were signed by 29 governments.

The inaugural meeting of the Board of Governors of the Bank was held concurrently with that of the Board of Governors of the International Monetary Fund in Savannah, Georgia, from March 8 to 18, 1946. The meeting was devoted mainly to organization and administrative matters, and established the site of the Bank within the metropolitan area of Washington, D. C.

Organization

The Bank's administration is composed of a Board of Governors, Executive Directors, a President, other officers, and a staff.

All powers of the Bank are vested in the Board of Governors, which consists of one Governor and one alternate appointed by each member of the Bank. Each member State has 250 votes plus one vote for each share of capital stock held. Each Govenor exercises the voting power of the member he represents. The Board of Governors meets annually; additional meetings may be held if required.

The Board of Governors has delegated most of its powers to the Executive Directors, who normally meet once a month at the Bank's headquarters in Washington. There are sixteen Executive Directors. Five of them are appointed, one by each of the five members having the largest number of shares of capital stock, and the eleven others are elected by the Governors representing the remaining members. The Executive Directors function as a board, and each Executive Director is entitled to cast as a unit the number of votes of the member or members by whom he was appointed or elected.

The President is selected by the Executive Directors. He is *ex officio* chairman of the Executive Directors and chief executive officer of the Bank. Subject to the general direction of the Executive Directors on questions of policy, he is responsible for the conduct of the business of the Bank, and for the organization, appointment and dismissal of its officers and staff.

The President of the Bank is Eugene R. Black, of the United States.

Membership

The following 58 States were members of the Bank, as of December 31, 1955: Afghanistan, Australia, Austria, Belgium, Bolivia, Brazil, Burma, Canada, Ceylon, Chile, China, Colombia, Costa Rica, Cuba, Denmark, the Dominican Republic, Ecuador, Egypt, El Salvador, Ethiopia, Finland, France, the German Federal Republic, Greece, Guatemala, Haiti, Honduras, Iceland, India, Indonesia, Iran, Iraq, Israel, Italy, Japan, Jordan, Rep. of Korea, Lebanon, Luxembourg, Mexico, Netherlands, Nicaragua, Norway, Pakistan, Panama, Paraguay, Peru, the Philippines, Sweden, Syria, Thailand, Turkey, the Union of South Africa, the United Kingdom, the United States, Uruguay, Venezuela and Yugoslavia.

Capital of the Bank

The authorized capital of the Bank is $10,000,000,000. The capital stock is divided into shares of $100,000 each, available for subscription only to members and transferable only to the Bank. As of December 31, 1955, capital subscriptions of the Bank's 58 members totalled $9,050,500,000. The smallest subscription is for two shares of stock, and the largest, that of the United States, for 31,750 shares.

Only 20 per cent of the total subscribed capital is paid in, and this is the only part of the subscribed capital which may be used for loans. The remaining 80 per cent of the subscribed capital is subject to call by the Bank only when required to meet obligations of the Bank for funds borrowed or on loans guaranteed by it.

The 20 per cent paid-in capital is divided as follows: 2 per cent is in the form of gold or United States dollars and is immediately available for lending; 18 per cent is paid to the Bank in the various currencies of the member States, and can be used for loans only with the consent of the particular member whose currency is to be used. By December 31, 1955, funds available to the Bank for loans from its paid-in capital subscription had amounted to $983,280,000 consisting of: $178,280,000 from the 2 per cent paid-in portion of subscriptions of all members; $571,500,000 from the 18 per cent portion of the United States' subscription; and $233,500,000 from the 18 per cent portion of subscriptions made available by members other than the United States.

Activities

BORROWING OPERATIONS

Part of the money which the Bank lends is obtained by marketing its own obligations in the private capital market. By December 31, 1955, the Bank had sold 25 bond issues totaling the equivalent of $1,014,500,000: ten United States issues, three Canadian issues, two Netherlands issues, two United Kingdom issues, and eight Swiss issues.

At the same date the Bank had direct obligations outstanding, totaling the equivalent of $860,806,029 as follows:

$70,000,000 2% Serial Bonds of 1950, due 1956-62
$75,000,000 3% Three Year Bonds of 1953, due 1956
$50,000,000 2⅜% Five Year Bonds of 1954, due 1959
$100,000,000 3⅛% Fifteen Year Bonds of 1954, due 1969
$60,000,000 3⅛% Nineteen Year Bonds of 1952, due 1971
$150,000,000 3% Twenty-Five Year Bonds of 1947, due 1972
$50,000,000 3⅜% Twenty-Three Year Bonds of 1952, due 1975
$50,000,000 3% Twenty-Five Year Bonds of 1951, due 1976
$100,000,000 3¼% Thirty Year Bonds of 1951, due 1981

$22,727,273 3½% Fifteen Year Bonds of 1954, due 1969 (Can $25,000,000)
$13,636,363 3¼% Ten Year Bonds of 1955, due 1965 (Can $15,000,000)
$14,000,000 3½% Twenty Year Stock of 1951, due 1971 (£5,000,000)
$14,000,000 3½% Twenty Year Stock of 1954, due 1974 (£5,000,000)
$10,526,316 3½% Fifteen Year Bonds of 1954, due 1969 (f 40,000,000)
$10,526,316 3½% Twenty Year Bonds of 1955, due 1975 (f 40,000,000)
$581,733 2½% Serial Bonds of 1950, due 1956 (Sw fr 2,500,000)
$11,634,673 3½% Ten Year Bonds of 1952, due 1962 (Sw fr 50,000,000)
$11,634,671 3½% Twelve Year Bonds of 1951, due 1963 (Sw fr 50,000,000)
$11,634,671 3½% Fifteen Year Bonds of 1953, due 1968 (Sw fr 50,000,000)
$11,634,671 3½% Fifteen Year Bonds of 1953, November issue, due 1968
                                                        (Sw fr 50,000,000)
$11,634,671 3½% Eighteen Year Bonds of 1954, due 1972 (Sw fr 50,000,000)
$11,634,671 3½% Twenty Year Bonds of 1955, due 1976 (Sw fr 50,000,000)

In addition to its direct borrowing, the Bank has sold obligations of its borrowers received in connection with loans, both with and without its guarantee. By December 31, 1955, the bank had sold $58,919,844 of such obligations with its guarantee, and $165,699,575 without.

LENDING OPERATIONS

As of December 31, 1955, the Bank had made 139 loans, totaling $2,470,358,464 in the following 41 countries and territories: Algeria, Australia, Austria, the Belgian Congo, Belgium, Brazil, Ceylon, Chile, Colombia, Denmark, East Africa, Ecuador, El Salvador, Ethiopia, Finland, France, French West Africa, Guatemala, Honduras, Iceland, India, Iraq, Italy, Japan, Lebanon, Luxembourg, Mexico, the Netherlands, Nicaragua, Northern Rhodesia, Norway, Panama, Pakistan, Paraguay, Peru, Southern Rhodesia, Thailand, Turkey, the Union of South Africa, Uruguay and Yugoslavia.

Under its Articles of Agreement, the Bank is restricted to making loans for productive purposes which will assist in the reconstruction or development of its member States. Political conditions are examined only to the extent that they may affect economic conditions and prospects for repayment. Loans can be made only to member States, their political subdivisions, or to private enterprises located in the territories of members. Loans to private enterprises must be guaranteed by the government in whose territory the project is located, by the member's central bank, or by a comparable agency satisfactory to the International Bank. The Bank does not compete with private investment and does not make loans which can be obtained by the borrower in the private market on reasonable terms. The Bank may aid and encourage private investment by participating in or guaranteeing loans by private investors. The Bank may not make "tied loans" requiring its borrowers to spend the proceeds of their loans in a particular country.

In order to insure that its loans are sound and that they conform to the Articles of Agreement, the Bank applies businesslike banking practices to its investigations of loan applications. In addition, all loan agreements specify the purposes for which the loan was made, and the goods and services that may be purchased with the proceeds. Disbursements are made at the request of the borrower, who is required to furnish evidence that the money is to be used in payment or reimbursement for goods and services as agreed. The Bank further ascertains that the loans are used for the purposes agreed upon by maintaining supervision over the end-use of items purchased with its funds. This supervision is maintained through actual in-

spection of projects and installation of goods or machinery, and through periodic
reports from engineers and others concerned with the progress of a project.

Advisory Assistance

The Bank also provides advisory assistance to its member States in various ways.
Several states have requested the Bank to send missions to make comprehensive
surveys of their economies. Broadly, the objectives of these missions are to help the
state formulate a program of investment which will indicate priorities among the
important sectors of the economy and among types of undertakings within each
such sector, to suggest methods and measures to improve productive efficiency in
existing enterprises, and to recommend improvements in the government's economic
and financial policies and organization in order to facilitate and encourage further
development. Missions of this type have gone to British Guiana, Colombia, Cuba,
Guatemala, Iraq, Jamaica, Jordan, Malaya, Nigeria, Surinam, Syria and Turkey. The
reports of these missions, with the exception of Jordan which at the end of 1955 was
in preparation, have been submitted to the governments concerned and have been
published. Other international organizations have cooperated in furnishing personnel
for the missions. Thus, FAO has, jointly with the Bank, sponsored missions to
Uruguay and Chile to recommend measures for increasing and improving agricultural production.

There has been an increasing number of cases where member States have asked
the Bank for other types of assistance, such as advice on particular projects or
industries, or the services of financial or economic experts to serve as government
advisers. In some instances, the Bank has been able to fill these requests from its
own staff; in other cases, it has recommended outside consultants, often in collaboration with other international organizations.

Because the Bank has found that one of the greatest obstacles to economic
development is a lack of experience in planning, administration and management,
it has been giving increasing attention to means by which it can act as a focal point
for the study and discussion of development problems. For the past seven years,
training has been arranged within the Bank for officials from member States, both
in groups and individually.

As a further step in this direction, the Bank, with financial assistance from the
Rockefeller and Ford Foundations, has established an Economic Development
Institute in Washington, D. C. The Institute is a staff college at which senior officials
from the less developed countries can participate, together with Bank staff, in
an intensive study of development problems. The courses will be of six months
duration, and the first one was to begin in January 1956. There were to be fourteen
participants in the first course, all of whom were senior officials of the country or
territory of the member State, which nominated them. They were to come from
Belgium (African territories), Ceylon, Colombia, Egypt, Haiti, India, Japan,
Mexico, Nigeria, Pakistan, the Philippines, Thailand, Uganda and Yugoslavia.

The Institute has three full-time staff members, two of whom come from the
Bank's regular staff; other Bank staff contribute to the work of the Institute from
time to time. It also has visiting speakers who are authorities on various subjects
being studied at the Institute.

It is hoped that the Institute will increase the number of administrators skilled
in dealing with problems of economic policy and with the planning and administration of development programs. The Institute and the International Finance Corporation are the two new institutions of the Bank to be established in 1956.

INTERNATIONAL MONETARY FUND

Functions

The International Monetary Fund was established to promote international monetary cooperation through a permanent institution which provides the machinery for consultation and collaboration on international monetary problems. Its purposes are mainly:

to facilitate the expansion and balanced growth of international trade, and to contribute thereby to the promotion and maintenance of high levels of employment and real income, and to the development of the productive resources of all members as primary objectives of economic policy;

to promote exchange stability, to maintain orderly exchange arrangements among members, and to avoid competitive exchange depreciation; and

to give confidence to members by making the Fund's resources available to them under adequate safeguards.

Origin

The Articles of Agreement of the International Monetary Fund were drawn up by the United Nations Monetary and Financial Conference, which met at Bretton Woods, New Hampshire (United States), from July 1 to 22, 1944. The Conference, called by President Roosevelt, was attended by representatives of 44 nations.

After being submitted to the governments of the participating countries, the Articles of Agreement of the Fund came into force on December 27, 1945.

The inaugural meeting of the Board of Governors of the Fund was held in conjunction with that of the Board of Governors of the International Bank for Reconstruction and Development in Savannah, Georgia, from March 8 to 18, 1946.

It was mainly devoted to organizational and administrative matters. The Board established the site of the Fund within the metropolitan area of Washington, D. C., and elected the Board of Executive Directors of the Fund, to whom many of the powers of the Board of Governors were then delegated.

Organization

The Fund works through a Board of Governors, Executive Directors, a Managing Director, and a staff.

All powers of the Fund are vested in the Board of Governors, consisting of one Governor and one alternate appointed by each member. Voting power of the Governors is approximately in proportion to the size of the quota of the members which they represent.

The Executive Directors are responsible for the conduct of the general operations of the Fund, and exercise the powers delegated to them by the Board of Governors. Five of the Executive Directors are appointed by members having the largest quotas, and the nine others are elected by the Governors representing the remaining members. Each appointed Director casts all the votes of the country which appointed him, and each elected Director casts as a unit all the votes of the countries which elected him.

The Executive Directors elect a Managing Director, who must not be a Governor or an Executive Director. He is the chairman of the Executive Directors and chief of the operating staff. Under the direction of the Executive Directors, he conducts the ordinary business of the Fund.

The first Managing Director was Camille Gutt, of Belgium, who served a full five-year term ending May 5, 1951. He was succeeded by Ivar Rooth, of Sweden, who assumed his duties on August 3, 1951.

Membership

The Fund, as of December 31, 1955, had 58 members.

Resources of the Fund

As of December 31, 1955, assets of the Fund included, in round figures $1,807,900,000 in gold, $6,110,300,000 in various national currencies (including $1,705,800,000 in U. S. dollars), and $814,500,000 in currency balances not yet due from member countries whose initial par values have still to be agreed upon. Total assets were approximately $8,737,600,000. The subscriptions of those members of the Fund which attended the Bretton Woods Conference are equal to their quotas, which were fixed by the Articles of Agreement but may be revised by the Fund. The subscriptions and quotas of other members are fixed by the Fund at the time of their joining the agency. Each member must pay in gold 25 per cent of its quota or 10 per cent of its net official gold and dollar holdings, whichever is less. The balance is paid in the member's own currency. Non-negotiable, non-interest-bearing demand notes may be accepted from any member whose currency is not needed for the Fund's operations in place of that member's currency.

Activities

CONSULTATION

The Fund serves as a medium for consultation by its members on problems related to the international balance of payments, including currency par values, foreign exchange restrictions and discrimination, and use of the Fund's resources.

For the postwar period, the Fund agreement provided that members could maintain foreign exchange restrictions and adapt them to changing circumstances without the Fund's approval. Members were to withdraw exchange restrictions that were no longer necessary for balance-of-payments reasons. The Articles of Agreement provided further, however, that five years after the Fund began operations, and in each year thereafter, any member still retaining restrictions inconsistent with the Articles should consult the Fund about their further retention. The first series of these consultations began in March 1952, and became a major part of the Fund's activity through the end of the year.

The Fund made public a schedule of official par values for the currencies of 32 of its members on December 18, 1946, and listed 46 par values as of December 31, 1955. In announcing the initial parities, the Fund said they would probably require adjustments in the future, but this could be done in an orderly way through the Fund's consultative procedures. As postwar payments deficits persisted, the Fund in various statements emphasized the need for deflationary measures in deficit countries, noting indications that the exchange rates for some countries were becoming a restraining factor on exports. In the annual report published in September 1949, the Fund urged deficit countries to face "the risks and difficulties" of exchange rate adjustments. Devaluations in the fall and winter months of 1949-50 involved the currencies of 22 Fund members and eight other countries, and some further revisions have been made in consultation with the Fund.

EXCHANGE TRANSACTIONS

On March 1, 1947, the Fund began active exchange operations. These exchange transactions of the Fund are governed by the relevant provisions of the Articles of Agreement, as applied by the Executive Board. It was agreed in April 1948 that members receiving aid from the Economic Cooperation Administration should request a purchase of U. S. dollars only in exceptional and unforeseen circumstances.

Between March 1, 1947, and December 31, 1955, the Fund concluded exchange transactions with 27 of its members. These countries purchased U. S. dollars, pounds sterling, and Belgian francs aggregating $1,216,448,380, in exchange for an equivalent amount of their own currencies.

There are limits on the amount of currency any member may purchase from the Fund in exchange for its own currency, and members must, under specified circumstances, repurchase the amounts of their currencies that they have given to the Fund in exchange for other currencies. Total repurchases in gold and U. S. dollars on December 31, 1955, amounted to $62,495,754.15.

Sales to member countries through December 31, 1955 were as follows:

Country	U.S. Dollars	£ Sterling	Belgian Francs	Deutsche Mark
Australia	50,000,000			
Belgium	33,000,000			
Bolivia	2,500,000			
Brazil	112,500,000	20,000,000		
Chile	21,300,000			
Colombia	25,000,000			
Costa Rica	1,250,000			
Czechoslovakia	6,000,000			
Denmark	10,200,000			
Egypt	3,000,000			
Ethiopia	600,000			
Finland	9,500,000			
France	125,000,000			
India	99,980,000			
Indonesia	15,000,000			
Iran	26,250,000			
Japan		44,300,000		
Mexico	45,000,000			
Netherlands	62,500,000	1,500,000	300,000,000	
Nicaragua	500,000			
Norway	5,000,000		200,000,000	
Paraguay	875,000			
Philippines	10,000,000			
Turkey	25,000,000	2,000,000		18,480,000
Union of South Africa	10,000,000			
United Kingdom	300,000,000			
Yugoslavia	9,000,000			

In addition, the Fund, in November 1948, sold $6,135,544.24 to Norway in exchange for an equivalent amount in gold.

Repurchases by member countries as of December 31, 1955, follow:

Country	Gold	U.S. Dollars	Total
Australia	—	50,000,000.00	
Austria	192,292.46	7,307,449.33	
Belgium	9,460,423.29	12,125,283.46	
Burma	—	3,246,823.18	

Country	Gold	U.S. Dollars	Total
Brazil	19,733,192.47	83,266,807.53	
Ceylon	—	169,000.00	
Chile	1,884,318.19	10,594,990.09	
Costa Rica	77,000.00	2,046,269.64	
Denmark	—	10,963,500.00	
Egypt	829,766.03	7,678,163.64	
Ethiopia	416,405.41	1,617,736.77	
Finland	—	9,500,000.00	
France	57,000,002.35	22,999,997.65	
Germany	8,738,929.94	36,349,524.42	
India	—	87,402,000.00	
Iran	2,722,443.70	6,010,116.26	
Japan	—	124,037,897.17	
Lebanon	793,412.94	62,429.30	
Mexico	14,899,613.55	30,020,963.52	
Netherlands	27,351,584.75	48,028,947.37	
Nicaragua	—	498,676.07	
Norway	—	9,560,948.86	
Paraguay	—	375,000.00	
Peru	2,324,479.02	772,819.71	
Sweden	7,999,378.81	—	
Syria	914,988.98	539,134.53	
Turkey	9,999,628.40	9,998,100.67	
Union of South Africa	—	9,985,314.69	
United Kingdom	—	112,000,000.00	
TOTAL	**$165,337,860.29**	**$697,157,893.86**	**$862,495,754.15**

TECHNICAL ASSISTANCE

The Fund has maintained an extensive program of technical assistance through staff missions to many parts of the world, and provides studies, reports and publications on international subjects.

It has advised countries on changes in par values or exchange rates, modifications in multiple currency practices and exchange controls, and in questions of monetary, credit and fiscal policy that have an important bearing on international payments. Its technicians have assisted members in establishing and perfecting institutional machinery such as central banking systems and exchange control administration. With some countries, the Fund has conferred on techniques for improving their collection and presentation of financial statistics. It has discussed with members the monetary impact of development programs, levels of monetary reserves, use of Fund resources, gold transactions, and other questions important to economic development and harmonious international monetary relations.

Publications

The Fund publishes the following:

Annual Report: A record of Fund activities and commentary on current monetary developments. Free distribution. Published each September.

Annual Report on Exchange Restrictions: The sixth annual report on exchange restrictions, published in 1955, describes the procedure to be followed in the 1956 consultations between member countries and the Fund on the further retention of exchange restrictions. It also surveys recent developments in the field of restrictions and outlines the restrictive systems of individual countries. Free distribution.

International Financial Statistics: Monthly magazine, carrying individual sections for 58 countries, and showing price and production levels, exchange rates, money supply, volume and value of foreign trade, gold and foreign exchange holdings, money and capital market movements. Also includes comparative sections showing world trade, gold production, market exchange rates, and government bond quotations and yields, and other information. Subscription fee: $5.00 a year in the United States, or the equivalent in members' currencies.

International Financial News Survey: Digest of economic and financial news taken from periodicals of all countries.

Balance of Payments Yearbook: Six annual issues have been published. Balance of payments statements are presented on a comparable basis for more than 50 countries. An analysis of international deficits (or surpluses), and much additional balance of payments information is given in the accompanying text. Price U.S. $5.00.

Staff Papers: Currently published two or three times a year; makes available staff studies on international monetary and financial problems. Subscription for three issues is U.S. $3.50, single copies $1.50, or equivalent in other currencies.

Direction of International Trade: Compiled by the Fund and the International Bank for Reconstruction and Development, and published jointly by the Fund, the Bank and the United Nations. Trade-by-country statistics, expressed in U.S. dollars, are presented for 90 countries.

Publications given free distribution include addresses by Fund officials, explanatory booklets, reports of transactions, quarterly financial statements, and other public announcements.

WORLD HEALTH ORGANIZATION (WHO)

Functions

The Constitution of the World Health Organization defines health as "a state of complete physical, mental and social well-being and not merely the absence of disease or infirmity." The Organization's objective is "the attainment by all peoples of the highest possible level of health."

WHO, to attain this goal, embraces a wide range of functions, including the following:

(a) to act as the directing and coordinating authority on international health work;

(b) to assist governments in strengthening health services;

(c) to furnish appropriate technical assistance and, in emergencies, necessary aid upon the request of governments;

(d) to stimulate and advance work to eradicate epidemic, endemic and other diseases;

(e) to promote improved standards of teaching and training in the health, medical and related professions;

(f) to establish and stimulate establishment of international standards with respect to biological, pharmaceutical and similar products, and to standardize diagnostic procedures;

(g) to propose conventions, agreements and regulations with respect to international health matters;

(h) to foster activities in the field of mental health, especially those affecting the harmony of human relations;

(i) to promote cooperation among scientific and professional groups which contribute to the advancement of health;

(j) to contribute, in cooperation with other specialized agencies where necessary, to the improvement of nutrition, housing, sanitation, recreation, economic or working conditions, etc.; and

(k) to establish and maintain such administrative and technical services as may be required, including epidemiological and statistical services.

Origin

The founding of WHO goes back to a proposal made at the San Francisco Conference in 1945 envisaging the creation of a specialized instiution in the field of health.

In July 1946, an International Health Conference brought together in New York representatives of 61 countries, who drafted and signed the Constitution of WHO and established an Interim Commission composed of representatives of eighteen governments. This Commission, which was to continue to function until the ratification of the WHO Constitution by 26 Member States of the United Nations, carried on the most urgent work undertaken by such bodies as the League of Nations Health Organization, l'Office International d'Hygiène Publique, and UNRRA, and prepared for the establishment of WHO as a permanent organization.

The permanent World Health Organization came officially into being on September 1, 1948, after 26 Members of the United Nations, on April 7, 1948, had ratified its Constitution. April 7 has since been celebrated each year in all countries as World Health Day.

WHO at the end of 1955 numbered 81 Member States and four associate members.

Organization

The main organs of WHO are the World Health Assembly, the Executive Board, and the secretariat.

The World Health Assembly, the legislative organ, meets each year and is composed of representatives of all members. It determines the policies and programs of WHO, and votes on the budget.

The Executive Board, a technical and non-political organ, is composed of eighteen persons designated by as many member States elected by the Health Assembly. It meets at least twice a year to give effect to the decisions of the Assembly.

The secretariat, under the direction of Dr. M. G. Candau, Director-General, comprises the technical and administrative personnel of the organization; current work is entrusted to it.

Expert committees play an important part in most of the fields of WHO activity. Composed of specialists from all parts of the world, they advise the Organization on various technical aspects of its programs.

The activities of WHO have been progressively decentralized. Six regional organizations have been created, each having its office in one of the great geographic regions of the globe. These offices are located: in New Delhi, for South East Asia; in Alexandria, for the Eastern Mediterranean; in Manila, for the Western Pacific; in Washington, where the Pan American Sanitary Bureau acts as the regional office for the Americas; in Brazzaville, French Equatorial Africa, for Africa south of the Sahara; and in Geneva (which is to move to Copenhagen in 1957), for Europe.

The regular budget of WHO for 1956 was $10,203,084. To this figure should be added a part of the funds contributed by countries to the Technical Assistance

Program of the United Nations for the economic development of under-developed areas. In 1956, these funds amounted to some $6,500,000.

Activities

The activities of WHO may be divided as follows: (1) as a specialized agency of the United Nations, WHO is the one *directing* and *coordinating* authority on international health work; (2) to help countries strengthen and improve their own health services, *advisory services* are furnished by WHO through public health experts, demonstration teams for disease control, visiting specialists, consultants, etc.; and (3) WHO's *Central Technical Services:* epidemiology, standardization of drugs, a wide range of technical publications, administration of the international sanitary regulations, publication of the international pharmacopoeia, publication of health statistics, etc.

ADVISORY SERVICES

The programs originally given priority in WHO's work were the fight against malaria, tuberculosis and venereal diseases; improvement of maternal and infant health; sanitation; and nutrition. But this conception has gradually given way to a system allowing provision of all kinds of assistance needed by countries to improve the health of their populations.

The action of WHO is based on the principle that, although there exist techniques today which are effective in the fight against a great number of scourges which have afflicted humanity for a long time, many countries still possess neither the necessary knowledge nor the experienced personnel to apply these techniques. The advisory service of WHO attempts to remedy this situation.

On request of interested countries, WHO furnishes expert consultants and sends demonstration teams composed of specialists. These teams are matched by local personnel who are trained in modern methods of fighting disease and take over from the WHO teams after the latter's departure. Furthermore, the demonstration teams are often used as training centres for personnel from other parts of the same country, and even from other countries in the same region where similar health problems exist. In communicable disease control, the number of people who had been afforded a measure of protection as the result of control operations assisted by WHO against malaria, the treponemal diseases and TB, was well over 400 millions.

After constant expansion for the last seven years or more of WHO-assisted malaria control in many of the tropical areas of the world, it has become established that certain mosquitoes which carry malaria from man to man have become resistant against the residual insecticides—particularly DDT—the spraying of which has been the principal means of controlling this disease. As a result, the World Health Organization with support from UNICEF has launched a long-term program aimed at the total eradication of malaria. This was to be done by intensifying and generalizing spraying campaigns in large areas so that transmission of the disease could be effectively brought to an end. If member Governments cooperated by providing manpower and equipment, it was believed that a worldwide malaria eradication campaign might achieve its objective in most parts of the world within the next ten years.

The spirochaetes responsible for treponemal diseases, including syphilis, yaws, pinta and bejel, fortunately, have so far, shown no signs of developing a resistance against penicillin, now used in mass campaigns to control these diseases. In controlled campaigns against yaws, bejel and endemic syphilis, which have been assisted by WHO and supplied by UNICEF, and which have been in operation for a number of years, more than 56 million people have been examined, and 10 million treated. Constant improvement has been made in the penicillin preparations used for the purpose, and the cost has progressively diminished as a result of experience gained in controlled operations on a mass scale. Under the most favorable circumstances, the cost of examining persons for treponemal diseases was approximately 10 U.S. cents per person examined, and the cost of treatment of patients and contact was approximately 75 cents per person. These figures included all national and international expenditures involved. Mass campaigns against treponematoses have been and were being notably successful in the Caribbean area, in Fiji and Western Samoa, and in the Netherlands New Guinea, where they have been recently launched. They have also been successful in Haiti, Indonesia, Laos, Liberia, Malaya, Nigeria, the Philippines and Thailand, where they have been established for some time.

Many countries are being assisted by WHO in establishing TB control programs to cover the entire population. In conjunction with this, mass vaccination campaigns of children and young persons with BCG, which confers a measure of protection against infection, have been assisted by WHO over a number of years. These campaigns, which cover practically all of the less developed areas of the world, now involve the testing of about 43 million young people and the vaccinating of 15 million annually. In this work, as in other WHO activities, the United Nations Children's Fund (UNICEF) renders invaluable service by providing supplies and equipment.

Among zoonoses (diseases common to animals and man), WHO has been particularly active in combating brucellosis, an infection common to sheep and goats as well as man. Experiments to develop a vaccine for it are being carried out at the Brucellosis Centre of the Institute Pasteur, Tunis, with the assistance of the Food and Agriculture Organization of the United Nations and WHO. Other similar centres are aided in research, diagnosis and control of the disease. With respect to rabies, WHO has encouraged the development of a hyper-immune, anti-rabies serum. This serum is used in conjunction with the normal vaccine in cases where persons are bitten close to the central nervous system by dogs, wolves or other animals.

Among communicable diseases more prevalent in the economically advanced countries, WHO pays particular attention to influenza and poliomyelitis. A WHO chain of influenza centres has been set up throughout the world, at each of which the virus responsible for particular outbreaks is isolated. As regards poliomyelitis, WHO is actively encouraging research into and development of vaccines based on attenuated living strains of virus rather than on inactivated virus. In addition, WHO regional poliomyelitis laboratories have been designated, and national laboratories are being encouraged to cooperate in a coordinated program of investigation which is designed to supply epidemiological information needed for proper application of vaccines.

Bilharziasis, a disease communicated to man by water snails, prevalent in the Eastern Mediterranean, African, American and Western Pacific areas, is actively combated by snail destroying campaigns. WHO was assisting such efforts in Egypt, Syria and Iraq; it also maintains a demonstration project in the Philippines.

Trachoma, an eye disease which may lead to blindness, and which is prevalent in tropical and semi-tropical countries, is the subject of WHO-stimulated research on its etiology, epidemiology and therapy. Large-scale campaigns in Morocco, Tunisia and elsewhere were designed to prevent seasonal conjunctivitis, which is closely linked with the prevalence of trachoma. In Taiwan, mass treatment with good results against trachoma was given to school children. The battle against this disease, generally with WHO assistance, was being developed in the Eastern Mediterranean, Western Pacific and Southeast Asia regions.

PUBLIC HEALTH SERVICES

No country can fight disease successfully or promote the health of its people unless a well-organized health administration exists. In assisting countries to improve the general level of health of their populations, WHO has found, through experience, that every form of assistance it gives should help in the development of national health administrations. Hence WHO helps countries develop the following:

PUBLIC HEALTH ADMINISTRATION. WHO studies and advises countries on the planning of preventive and curative services, and on coordinating the various types of national health and medical services. Because public health facilities in many countries have not yet reached the masses of the population, particularly in the villages, this type of service in recent years has tended to concentrate more and more on rural health services. Assistance in rural health work is being given to many governments, particularly in the under-developed countries. This assistance takes the form of rural health demonstration and training centres, and providing plans for Rural Health Services. A Rural Health Conference was to be held towards the end of 1956 in South East Asia, so that the public health services of the countries concerned could interchange information on their respective problems and methods to solve them.

MATERNAL AND CHILD HEALTH. WHO deals with prenatal, maternal, infant and school health services, and with modern methods of obstetrics and pediatric care. A number of these programs are supported by UNICEF. Health services for mothers and children now have a high priority in most national health programs, and the present trend, particularly for rural areas, is towards developing health programs for mothers and children as part of a comprehensive public health service. A very important aspect of WHO assistance in maternal and child health programs is the training of personnel, including midwives, and the setting up of maternal and child health clinics. In European countries, WHO is active in giving assistance to the rehabilitation of handicapped children and the care of premature infants.

NURSING. Effective use of nursing personnel, increased recruiting and training schemes for nursing and midwives are features of the WHO program. Nearly all WHO demonstration teams include nurses. In addition, seminars, conferences and study groups to discuss nursing education and the administration of nursing and midwifery services are held in many parts of the world.

SOCIAL AND OCCUPATIONAL HEALTH. This deals with such topics as industrial hygiene, rehabiliation of the physically handicapped, medical aspects of social security and hospital administration, and the hygiene of seafarers.

HEALTH EDUCATION OF THE PUBLIC. The securing of public interest and the participation of the public in health activities are essential to the success of the health education of the public. Visual and other methods of achieving these objectives are adapted to local needs, and health educationalists are at work in a number of countries.

MENTAL HEALTH. WHO's aim is to make mental-hygiene practice an integral part of public-health programs. Particular attention is paid to the mental health problems of childhood, and meetings of a study group on the psycho-biological development of the child are regularly held. Alcoholism is another mental health problem on which WHO has convened conferences and gives advice to member Governments.

Consultants are also sent to countries requesting surveys and recommendations on how to deal with mental health problems.

NUTRITION. WHO is working with the United Nations Food and Agriculture Organization (FAO) on such problems as deficiency diseases, as, for example, endemic goitre, on infant feeding, on nutrition in relation to parasitic infection, and on other questions affecting large populations. Particular attention is paid to malnutrition and under-nutrition in infants and young children.

SANITATION. Sanitation, the bedrock of the preservation of health, receives top priority, and is a part of nearly every WHO program. It includes specifically: (1) urban and rural sanitation and hygiene; (2) housing and town and country planning; (3) food sanitation; and (4) flood control and waste disposal. WHO demonstrates efficient sanitation techniques and helps to train the necessary personnel.

DENTAL HEALTH. WHO has developed a dental health program, and is providing the services of consultants to governments to help them study dental problems and the resources available for organizing dental health services.

PALESTINE REFUGEES. WHO plans and directs the health program of the United Nations Relief and Works Agency for Palestine Refugees (UNRWA), which cares for more than 900,000 people. WHO recently reported that the general health of the refugees remained good, and that none of the quarantinable diseases had been reported during 1955. The main diseases were gastro-enteritis, dysentery, trachoma and conjunctivitis during the hot months, and upper respiratory infections in the rest of the year. There had been a marked decline in the reported cases of clinical malaria. The Gaza district (in which many refugees are living), the report went on to state, had been free from malaria-bearing mosquitoes since their eradication in 1949. Anti-larval work had been done since to control nuisance mosquitoes.

CENTRAL TECHNICAL SERVICES

These services include a great number of technical activities, several of which were begun by predecessors of WHO in the international field. One of these is the administration of International Sanitary Regulations adopted by the World Health Assembly, which represent, in fact, an international health legislation, since they come into force without subsequent ratification upon their adoption by the Assembly.

A new international health regulation, codifying the health measures applicable to ground, sea and air travel, was formulated in 1951, and replaced, as of October 1, 1952, all the health conventions previously in force. Another WHO health regulation is one which recommends to all countries that certain principles be followed in order to assure registration of diseases and deaths. To help countries in this task, WHO has published an international statistical classification manual of diseases and causes of death. In addition, WHO maintains an international centre for the compilation and analysis of medical and health statistics from all countries.

WHO also administers an information service on epidemic diseases. Daily radio-telegraphic broadcasts from Geneva and elsewhere inform governments of the appearance and spread of epidemics in whatever part of the world they occur, of the measures taken to contain them, and what precautions are necessary.

To protect the public health, WHO establishes international standards of strength and purity of medicines in current use. The first *International Pharmacopoeia*, containing several hundred prescriptions for preparations and medicines, was published in 1951; a second volume was published in 1955. International standards have been established by WHO for more than 70 biological products, such as penicillin, streptomycin, vitamins and vaccines, and experts are preparing standards for new substances.

WHO also takes part in the international control of drugs liable to produce addiction, and examines the properties of new drugs.

WHO, strictly speaking, does not engage in research, but gives its support to institutions, laboratories and research centres all over the world. In this manner, it participates in the research of numerous virus and parasitic diseases such as schistosomiasis, influenza and poliomyelitis, and stimulates demonstrations of new methods for the prevention and cure of these diseases.

WHO has a vast medical library in Geneva, and publishes several periodicals in order to inform national health administrations and scientists of progress in public health. Among WHO publications are the *Bulletin of the World Health Organization,* the *Chronicle of the World Health Organization,* the *Weekly Epidemiological Record,* the *Epidemiological and Vital Statistics Report,* and the *International Digest of Health Legislation.*

EDUCATION AND TRAINING

Shortages of health personnel—whether doctor, nurse, sanitary engineer, laboratory technician or other workers—plague every country. WHO helps develop training schools and teaching staffs for public-health work. In addition, WHO has awarded more than 5,000 fellowships to health workers for individual or group studies. The international character of the WHO fellowship program is exemplified by the fact that, during a one-year period, 1,100 fellows were received by 577 institutions in 42 countries. Among countries selected for study, 62 per cent were in Europe, and more than 2,000 fellowships have been awarded for study at European institutions since 1947.

WHO AND ATOMIC ENERGY

The World Health Organization has been interested in the health aspects of atomic energy since 1954, when it invited a group of consultants to discuss the general problem of atomic energy in relation to medicine and public health, and to assist its Director-General in deciding what part WHO should play in this rapidly-developing field. It was felt necessary that WHO should keep pace with current scientific development, particularly nuclear fission. In one of its resolutions, the World Health Assembly stated that the peaceful uses of atomic energy could "assist in lifting the burden of poverty, hunger and disease".

As a result of this meeting with the consultants, WHO outlined a preliminary program of work. Radioactive isotopes are coming into use in many countries, and a wide new field is opening. New discoveries affect laboratory procedures, diagnosis and treatment, and many of the older methods of research are being revised and refined. The total effect on the methods and possibilities of health work cannot be predicted, but enough is already known to justify WHO, in collaboration with the United Nations and the other specialized agencies, to include among its objectives a careful study of these new developments.

Another event which concerned the World Health Organization in the field of atomic energy was the International Conference on the Peaceful Uses of Atomic Energy, held at Geneva in August 1955. WHO presented two papers to this Conference, one on the general problem of protection against radiations from the point of view of public health, and the other on education and training in health and medical uses of atomic energy. WHO also placed at the disposal of the Conference a compendium of national legislative texts and regulations concerning protection against radiations which had recently been prepared.

The Conference emphasized the fact that there were two broad fields of interest to WHO: first, the establishment by research of the nature and incidence of atomic radiation as a hazard to health; and, second, the training of suitable personnel both in the uses of radioisotopes for diagnosis and treatment, and in the methods of protecting the public from atomic hazards.

Training, the first item on WHO's atomic energy program, is necessary to protect three distinct categories of workers from atomic radiation. These are: (1) specialists, physicians or physicists in atomic energy laboratories or plants; (2) public health administrators, particularly those interested in such questions as the disposal of radioactive waste; and (3) medical users of radioisotopes.

A second item on WHO's program is the collection and distribution of information on the health problems of atomic energy, and on the medical uses of radioisotopes.

The third item covers the health problems involved in the control of the location of reactors, and in the disposal of radioactive waste from factories, laboratories and hospitals.

The fourth item deals with the need for a greater standardization in the health aspects of atomic energy; this is comparable to work done by WHO in achieving agreement on international standards in other medical fields.

Finally, WHO's program in the atomic field involves the stimulation and coordination of research on the health aspects of radiation. This includes such problems as the study of the effects of radiation on human heredity, and research of diseases induced by radiation or the excessive absorption of radioisotopes in the human body.

WHO will collaborate in this work with other specialized agencies; with the International Labor Office, for example, on protection against radiation inside factories; with the Food and Agriculture Organization on the sterilization of food by radiation and the effect of radioactive effluents on food crops; and with the United Nations Educational, Scientific and Cultural Organization on the effect of radiation on animal genetics, and on regulations for the transport of isotopes.

WHO has already gone ahead with the first point of the program by helping to sponsor the first international training course for health physicists. This was undertaken in late 1955 in collaboration with the Government of Sweden and the Atomic Energy Commission of the United States. Physicists and physicians specializing in radiation work from ten countries in Europe attended the course. It covered such questions as health supervision at atomic reactors and radio-chemical laboratories, measurements of radiation required from the point of view of health, precautions in factories, and methods of radioactive waste disposal.

WHO in addition has made available fellowships for the medical study of radioisotopes.

UNIVERSAL POSTAL UNION (UPU)

Functions

The Universal Postal Union was founded to improve the exchange of international mails, a process formerly governed by numerous special agreements between countries or groups of countries. The old method involved great variety in postal rates, conditions of dispatching mails, methods of accounting, and other problems. For both the public and the administrations, difficulties grew as mail traffic increased.

UPU unites its member countries in a single postal territory for the reciprocal exchange of mail. Its aim is to insure the organization and improvement of postal services throughout the world through international collaboration. UPU fixes the international rates which may be charged by any postal administration in the world.

Origin

UPU was formally established on July 1, 1875, with the coming into force of the Universal Postal Convention adopted by the Postal Congress of Berne on October 9, 1874. It was first known as the General Postal Union, the name being changed at the Congress of Paris in 1878.

The first postal treaty introduced many changes and simplifications in prevailing conditions. For one, the practice of allotting a share of the proceeds from postal charges on letters, etc., to the dispatching country and the country of destination was abolished. Each administration kept the postage it collected and only paid, according to fixed scales, the intermediate administration providing transit of the mails. It guaranteed freedom of transit throughout the whole territory of the Union. It introduced arbitration to settle differences, and provided for setting up a central office, called the International Bureau, to be paid for by all the contracting states.

Various Postal Congresses since 1874 have extended and improved the original Convention. In a meeting in Paris in 1878, the Union became what is called an open union, which any country could join by a simple unilateral declaration of accession, requiring no preliminary consultation between members. From then on, applications for membership multiplied until they included practically the whole world, excepting only a few isolated areas. At the end of 1955, there were 95 members of the Union.

The conditions of easy accession remained in force until July 1, 1948. Countries now wishing admission must be approved by two-thirds of the member countries.

On October 8, 1948, the United Nations General Assembly asked assistance of UPU in the establishment of a United Nations Postal Administration. The Executive and Liaison Committee of UPU decided that the United Nations could, without being a member of UPU, set up a separate postal administration adhering to the Union, and represented by the United States postal administration. It was expected to observe the provisions of the Universal Postal Convention and its regulations. The United Nations Postal Administration is now in existence (*see page 342*).

Activities

The object of UPU was defined by the first article of the treaty of Berne. This, with amendments, reads:

"The countries between which the present Convention has been concluded form, under the designation of Universal Postal Union, a single territory for the reciprocal exchange of correspondence. The Postal Union has also for its object the organization and improvement of the various postal services, and to further within this sphere the growth of international collaborations."

The Union's activities are carried on within the bounds of these provisions. The founders wisely made provision from the beginning for plenipotentiaries to meet in congress periodically in order to perfect the Union's system, and to introduce the improvements thought necessary. In principle, these congresses take place at five-year intervals. Thus far, thirteen International Postal Congresses have met, including the one held at Brussels in 1952.

In addition, several conferences or committees, composed of delegates of postal administrations, also have been held to examine and discuss special technical questions, or to make preliminary preparations for some of these.

The instruments enacted by the congresses consist of a Universal Postal Convention, which contains the Statute of the Union and the provisions concerning the letterpost, and seven supplementary Agreements governing these services: insured letters and boxes, parcels, money orders, postal transfers, cash on delivery, collection of payments, and newspaper subscriptions.

The Congress of Paris in 1947 established a new organ of the Union, the Executive and Liaison Committee, entrusted with insuring the continuity of the work of the Postal Union during the interval between congresses. The Director of the International Bureau acts as Secretary-General of the Committee. The group meets in Berne, in principle, once a year.

Activities of the International Bureau

The International Bureau is the permanent, central organ of the Union. Its seat has been Berne since the Union was founded. It serves as a connecting link, a centre of information and consultation for the administrations of the Union's member countries. Its principal task is to collect and publish the vast amount of details and information which administrations have to communicate to each other. It carries out investigations, consultations and documentary and other work which members ask it to undertake. It publishes a monthly periodical in seven languages called *Union Postale.*

The International Bureau acts as a clearing house in settling accounts concerning international postal service, especially transit payments and reply-coupon accounts. This system allows the number of payments by administrations to be considerably reduced.

The Universal Postal Convention of Brussels, 1952, adopted the following provisions regulating the expenses of the Union and their division among the members of the Union:

1. Every congress fixes the maximum figure which the yearly ordinary expenses of the Union may reach. This expenditure, as also the special expenses due to the meeting of a congress, a conference, or a special committee, and any special work entrusted to the International Bureau, are borne in common by all the countries of the Union.

2. These are divided for this purpose into seven classes, each of which contributes to the payment of expenses in the following proportion:

1st class, 25 units
2nd class, 20 units
3rd class, 15 units
4th class, 10 units
5th class, 5 units
6th class, 3 units
7th class, 1 unit

3. When a new member is admitted, the Government of the Swiss Confederation decides, in agreement with the government of the country in question, the class in which the latter is to be placed for the purpose of sharing the costs.

The Congress of Brussels fixed at about 1,857,000 Swiss francs the maximum for the ordinary expenses of the Union.

The Executive Regulations of the Convention further provide that the Swiss authorities should supervise the expenditure of the International Bureau and advance to it the funds it requires.

INTERNATIONAL TELECOMMUNICATION UNION (ITU)

Functions

The International Telecommunication Union has three main purposes:

(1) to maintain and extend international cooperation for the improvement and rational use of telecommunication;

(2) to promote the development and most efficient operation of technical facilities in order to increase their usefulness, and, as far as possible, to make them generally available to the public; and

(3) to harmonize the actions of nations in the attainment of these common ends.

The term "telecommunication" is defined by international agreement as any transmission, emission or reception of signs, signals, writing, images and sounds, or intelligence of any nature by wire, radio visual or other electromagnetic systems; and the term "radiocommunication" as any telecommunication by means of electromagnetic waves (Hertzian waves) of frequencies between 10 kilocycles per second (kc/s) and 3,000,000 megacycles per second (Mc/s).

ITU has four main functions:

(1) It allocates to the several radiocommunication services, groups of radio-frequencies suitable for providing the channels of communications required by those services; and it registers the assignment of particular radio frequencies to stations. This function is directed towards achieving orderly use of the whole radio-frequency spectrum so as to avoid as far as possible harmful interference between the radio stations of different countries.

(2) It seeks to establish the lowest rates possible, consistent with efficient service and taking into account the necessity for keeping the independent financial administration of telecommunication on a sound basis.

(3) It promotes the adoption of measures for insuring the safety of life through telecommunication.

(4) It makes studies and recommendations, and collects and publishes information for the benefit of its members.

Origin

ITU came into being in 1865, when the International Telegraph Union was created in Paris. In 1932 in Madrid, the Telegraph Convention was combined with the Radiotelegraph Convention, and the International Telegraph Union became the International Telecommunication Union. In 1947 at international conferences held in Atlantic City, United States, the ITU readjusted its organizational structure, adopted measures designed to take account of certain advances that had been made in the techniques of telecommunication, and entered into an agreement with the United Nations whereby, among other provisions, the ITU is recognized as the specialized agency for telecommunications. A new convention was adopted containing provisions to give effect to the substantial changes that were made at that time.

The Union was governed from January 1949 until December 1953 by the International Telecommunication Convention adopted on October 2, 1947, by the Atlantic City Plenipotentiary Conference. A revised Convention adopted by the Plenipotentiary Conference of Buenos Aires (October 3 to December 22, 1952) entered into force on January 1, 1954. The Buenos Aires Conference made no substantial changes in the structure of the Union as adopted by the Conference of Atlantic City in 1947, but in the light of experience since 1947, a number of modifications designed to facilitate the working of the Union were made in the

Convention. It recommended that the Plenary Assemblies of the International Telegraph Consultative Committee and the International Telephone Consultative Committee should study the possibility of a fusion of those two bodies. It also authorized a higher maximum of ordinary expenditure for the years preceding the next plenipotentiary conference, which was due to be held in 1957.

Organization

The organization of the Union is, as follows: a Plenipotentiary Conference which is the supreme organ of the Union, Administrative Conferences, an Administrative Council, a General Secretariat, an International Frequency Registration Board, and three International Consultative Committees.

The Plenipotentiary Conference at which each member-country (90 members and 5 associate members) has the right to be represented, normally meets once every five years, at a place and date fixed by the preceding Conference. Each member has one vote in the Conference. It considers the report of the Administrative Council on the activities of the Union, approves the accounts and establishes the general basis for ITU's budget for the next five years, enters into and revises formal agreements with other international organizations, and deals with such other telecommunication questions as may be necessary. At its 1956 session, the Administrative Council was to examine the question of convening the next Plenipotentiary Conference, which should normally meet in 1957.

Administrative Conferences of all the members are, so far as practicable, held at the same time and place as the Plenipotentiary Conference. The Administrative Telegraph and Telephone Conference revises the International Telegraph Regulations and the International Telephone Regulations. The Administrative Radio Conference revises the Radio Regulations and the Additional Radio Regulations; this Conference also elects the members of the International Frequency Registration Board and reviews its activities. (The Regulations are annexed to the International Telecommunication Convention.) In addition to those so-called ordinary administrative conferences, there are regional administrative conferences which deal with questions concerning the countries of one region only, and other international administrative conferences which deal with special telecommunication questions of interest to all countries. With the agreement of almost all the members of the Union, the Administrative Council decided, at its 1955 session, that the Telegraph and Telephone Conference, already twice postponed, would not meet in 1956. Nor would the Radio Conference meet, the usefulness of which depends, to a great extent, on the progress made in introducing the order in the frequency spectrum recommended at the Atlantic City meeting. At the 1956 session of the Administrative Council, the question of whether these Conferences could usefully be convened would be considered.

The Administrative Council, which is composed of eighteen members of ITU elected by the Plenipotentiary Conference, supervises the Union's administrative functions between sessions of the Plenipotentiary Conference, reviews and approves the annual budget, appoints the Secretary-General and the two Assistant Secretaries-General, and coordinates the work of ITU with other international organizations. It meets annually at the seat of the Union. A new Council was elected at Buenos Aires in 1952.

The General Secretariat, headed by the Secretary-General, succeeds the Bureau of ITU, which had been located at Berne since 1868. The present Secretary-General is Marco Aurelio Andrada (Argentina).

In the field of radiocommunication, the International Frequency Registration Board (IFRB) technically examines and records the frequency assignments for all services notified by countries members of the ITU, and furnishes advice to those members to insure the operation of the maximum practicable number of radio channels in those portions of the spectrum where harmful interference may occur. The IFRB consists of eleven independent members, all nationals of different member-countries, elected at each ordinary Administrative Radio Conference. The members of the IFRB serve, not as representatives of any country or region, but as custodians of an international public trust. The creation of this Board was an innovation of the Atlantic City (1947) Conference, and is closely associated with the activities referred to later under the heading "Frequency Allocation".

The International Telegraph Consultative Committee (CCIT), the International Telephone Consultative Committee (CCIF), and the International Radio Consultative Committee (CCIR) study and make recommendations on technical, operating and tariff questions in their respective fields. Each Committee is composed of all members of ITU and any recognized private operating agencies interested in participating. Each Committee works through a Plenary Assembly, which normally meets every three years, study groups set up by the Plenary Assembly, and a Director appointed by the Plenary Assembly. In addition, each Consultative Committee is serviced by a specialized secretariat. The CCIF has a laboratory.

ITU had a budget of 5,990,130 Swiss francs to meet its ordinary expenses for the year 1956. Practically all the countries of the world are members of the ITU.

Activities

THE GENERAL SECRETARIAT

One of the most important duties of the General Secretariat is to collect, collate, publish and keep up-to-date the numerous documents essential for the day-to-day operation of telecommunication services. It is also responsible for the secretarial arrangements of conferences and meetings of the Union. It maintains relations both by correspondence and by meetings with the United Nations, the specialized agencies and other international organizations.

STUDIES OF THE INTERNATIONAL CONSULTATIVE COMMITTEES

The International Consultative Committees work continuously in their respective fields through study groups. These are composed of experts from governmental telecommunication administrations and recognized private operating agencies, etc., and they work by correspondence, by meetings in series of groups, or in plenary assemblies. In general, the studies of the consultative committees are made by the representatives of the more advanced administrations, but the results are placed at the disposal of all administrations. The next and last meeting of the Plenary Assembly of the CCIF would take place in Geneva in 1956, the next and last meeting of the Plenary Assembly of the CCIT would be held in Geneva in 1956, and the next Plenary Assembly of the CCIR would take place in Warsaw in 1956. The CCIF and the CCIT would be amalgamated in 1956 to form a new International Telegraph and Telephone Consultative Committee (CCIT), which was to come into force on January 1, 1957. The range of studies of the three consultative committees may be gathered from the following lists of study groups:

INTERNATIONAL TELEGRAPH CONSULTATIVE COMMITTEE (CCIT). CCIT study groups deal with the general technique of telegraphy; technical aspects of the establishment, operation and maintenance of telegraph channels; technical aspects of telegraph apparatus; phototelegraphy and facsimile; vocabulary, symbols and classification; technical aspects of switching in the service of start-stop apparatus; European telegraph network operated by start-stop apparatus; operational methods and quality of service; services offered to users and rates other than telex rates; and international service of telegraph subscribers and rates relating thereto. A joint study group CCIR-CCIT exists for phototelegraphy.

INTERNATIONAL TELEPHONE CONSULTATIVE COMMITTEE (CCIF). Study groups exist in the field of protection against interference, protection against corrosion, transmission (lines), transmission (apparatus), coordination line-radio (CCIF-CCIR), operating, tariffs, signalling and switching, and maintenance. There are also a Committee for the General Trunk Switching Plan, a Graphical and Letter Symbols Committee, a Committee on Telephone Vocabulary, and a Budget Committee.

INTERNATIONAL RADIO CONSULTATIVE COMMITTEE (CCIR). Study groups deal with transmitters, receivers, complete radio systems, ground wave propagation, tropospheric propagation, ionospheric propagation, standard frequency-time signals, monitoring, general technical problems, broadcasting, television, tropical broadcasting, operation questions, and vocabulary.

FREQUENCY ALLOCATION

Since the Cairo Conference in 1938, scientific and technological advances in the field of telecommunications, great increases in aeronautical and broadcasting activities, changes in traffic handling practices, and political rearrangements resulting from the Second World War, together rendered necessary an extensive revision of the Radio Regulations drawn up at Cairo and then in force. This revision was the main task undertaken by the Administrative Radio Conference held from May to October 1947 at Atlantic City, United States; it was held concurrently with the Plenipotentiary Conference.

One of the important acts of the Atlantic City Radio Conference was the preparation of a new worldwide allocation table embracing the allocation to specific services of all the radio frequencies extending from 10 kilocycles per second (kc/s) to 10,500,000 kc/s. This table was to replace the Cairo table which extended from 10 kc/s to 200,000 kc/s only.

It was the intention of the Atlantic City Radio Conference that the implementation of the new allocation table should be attained through a process involving a series of conferences between countries interested in each of several regions of the world, and in one or more of the radio services (maritime, aeronautical, broadcasting, etc.).

The Atlantic City Radio Conference appreciated the magnitude of the task, but difficulties rendered totally inadequate the time table set for the completion of the work.

The whole situation was reviewed at the Extraordinary Administrative Radio Conference (EARC) held in Geneva in 1951. This Conference adopted specific frequency assignments (allotment plans or lists) which would ultimately provide for some 80,000 frequency assignments to specific stations. Further, the Conference established procedures for transferring into their appropriate bands the fixed and high-frequency broadcasting stations, for which no specific assignment plans had been adopted, thus liberating those parts of the spectrum to which other services must be transferred. It is quite true that the difficulties inherent in the detailed assignment of frequencies have not been completely solved by the EARC Agreement, particularly since a number of countries have made substantial reservations. But the Agreement does provide members of the Union with methods of approach which should eventually lead to the achievement of the combined objective—the adoption of a new International Frequency List, the entry into force of the Atlantic City Table of Frequency Allocations, and the full application of the Radio Regulations—which, together with the associated parts of the Convention, are designed to secure the orderly use of radiocommunications.

TECHNICAL ASSISTANCE

ITU participates in the United Nations Expanded Program of Technical Assistance. Its role consists chiefly in preparing an annual program in the field of telecommunication, and in seeking and making recommendations on candidates for telecommunication posts under the technical assistance program. ITU supervises the activities of experts, and organizes the fellowship programs in the various recipient countries. In addition to technical assistance within this program, the work of the Consultative Committees which is put at the disposal of all members of the Union, represents in itself a form of technical assistance.

WORLD METEOROLOGICAL ORGANIZATION (WMO)

Functions

The World Meteorological Organization, as stated in the preamble to its Convention, is established "with a view to coordinating, standardizing, and improving world meteorological information between countries in the aid of human activities."

The purpose of WMO is:

to facilitate international cooperation in the establishment of networks of stations and centres to provide meteorological services and observations;

to promote the establishment and maintenance of systems for the rapid exchange of weather information;

to promote standardization of meteorological observations and insure the uniform publication of observations and statistics;

to further the application of meteorology to aviation, shipping, agriculture and other human activities; and

to encourage research and training in meteorology.

Origin

The Convention of the World Meteorological Organization was drawn up and adopted by the twelfth Conference of Directors of the International Meteorological Organization (IMO), held in Washington, D. C., in September-October 1947. The Convention, providing that members of the Organization would be states and territories maintaining their own meteorological services, was signed by the representatives of 42 states.

On March 23, 1950, that is, thirty days after the deposit with the Government of the United States of the thirtieth instrument of ratification of or accession to the Convention, the Convention came into force and WMO into being.

In order to insure the continuity of international collaboration by the various meteorological services, the pre-existing International Meteorological Organization (IMO) continued to function, and the United Nations recognized it as being the interim preparatory organ for WMO, until the formal establishment of WMO, which took place at the first Congress of the latter Organization, held in Paris in March-April 1951.

This Congress was preceded by an Extraordinary Conference of Directors of IMO, which, among other matters, decided to dissolve IMO after transfer of its activities, resources and obligations to WMO. The Congress accepted this transfer and IMO was dissolved on April 4, 1951, the date on which WMO entered into operation.

Organization

As provided by its Convention, WMO is headed by a President and two Vice-Presidents. It works through a World Meteorological Congress, an Executive Committee, regional meteorological associations and technical commissions set up by the Congress, and a permanent secretariat headed by a Secretary-General.

The Congress, composed of all members of WMO, meets at least once every four years. Each member designates as its principal delegate to the Congress the director of its meteorological service. The Congress is the policy-making body of the Organization. It adopts technical regulations covering meteorological practices and procedures, and determines the general policies for the fulfilment of the Organization's purposes.

The Executive Committee is composed, in addition to the President and Vice-Presidents of WMO, of the presidents of regional associations, and an equal number of directors of meteorological services of members. It meets at least once a year. As the executive body of the Organization, the Committee supervises the carrying out of Congress resolutions. Among other duties, it makes studies and recommendations, and provides members with technical information, counsel and assistance in the field of meteorology.

The regional meteorological associations, established by the Congress, are composed of those members of WMO with networks of meteorological stations lying in or extending into the respective regions. The Congress established six regional associations for the following regions, for which it defined their geographical limits: Africa, Asia, South America, North and Central America, South West Pacific, and Europe.

The regional associations meet as often as necessary. They promote the execution of the resolutions of the Congress and the Executive Committee in their respective regions, discuss matters of general meteorological interest, consider matters brought to their attention by the Executive Committee, coordinate meteorological and associated activities in their respective regions, and make recommendations to the Congress and the Executive Committee on matters within the purposes of the Organization.

The technical commissions established by the Congress are composed of experts. The technical commissions, each within its field of responsibility, keep abreast of and promote meteorological developments both in the scientific and practical fields; standardize methods, procedures and techniques in the application of meteorology; make recommendations to the Congress, including draft technical regulations; and collaborate with and advise other commissions of WMO and other international organizations. WMO established technical commissions for aerology, aeronautical meteorology, agricultural meteorology, bibliography and publications, climatology, instruments and methods of observation, maritime meteorology, and synoptic meteorology.

The secretariat of WMO carries out the duties allocated to it in the WMO Convention and the regulations of the Organization. Among its general functions are the following: to serve as the administrative, documentary and information centre of the Organization; to make technical studies as directed by the Congress and the Executive Committee; to organize and perform secretarial duties at sessions of the Congress and the Executive Committee; to prepare, edit, publish and distribute the publications of the Organization; to provide an appropriate public relations service for the Organization; to maintain liaison and collaborate with the secretariats of other international organizations; and to act as the channel for communications, notifications, invitations, etc. between the Organization, its members, the constituent bodies of WMO, and other international organizations.

The permanent location of the secretariat is Geneva. It has a budget of $1,700,000 to meet its ordinary expenses for 1956-1959. At the end of 1955, WMO had 92 members.

Activities

Details of some of the activities and projects of WMO, its Commissions and Regional Associations, are as follows:

WATER RESOURCE DEVELOPMENT

The help of the meteorologist and the hydrologist is needed to control the vast quantities of water flowing down the rivers into the sea, to prevent floods, and to harness the rivers so that electric energy and water may be provided for irrigation and industry.

WMO deals with those aspects of the water resource development program of the United Nations which fall within the common ground between meteorology and hydrology. A panel of experts established by the Executive Committee is preparing a program for WMO's international action. Furthermore, under a joint project with the United Nations Economic Commission for Asia and the Far East, efforts are being made to remedy the lack of hydrological data in the south-east Asian region.

INTERNATIONAL GEOPHYSICAL YEAR

WMO is participating in the preparations for the International Geophysical Year (1957-1958), one of the most ambitious scientific projects of our time. The main purpose of this period of intensified observation and study is to increase our knowledge of the phenomena observed, particularly in the tropical zone and in the upper layers of the earth's atmosphere. Priority has been given to problems fundamentally worldwide in character and calling for effective international collaboration.

OPERATIONAL AND TECHNICAL DEVELOPMENT FUND

This fund was created by WMO in order to encourage and support the development of activities of international meteorological importance, and to help remedy deficiencies in worldwide meteorology. Although the amount available is now limited, it is hoped that in time it will be expanded.

TECHNICAL ASSISTANCE

All those who work under the changing skies—the farmer, the aviator and the sailor, for example,—realize how their lives depend on the weather. But not so well known is the importance of the knowledge of weather in the economic life of a country. Sudden disasters resulting from storms and floods retard economic advancement. The existence of a national weather service and its proper functioning are of great importance to the development of the economy of a country. Many countries wishing to establish meteorological services, or to improve or to increase the application of meteorology to their projects of economic development, have requested technical assistance in meteorology from WMO.

Under the United Nations Expanded Program of Technical Assistance, these countries receive missions of experts, fellowships or scholarships. Such technical assistance was given in 1955 to 23 countries, which received 22 missions of experts and 31 fellowships. The projects concern mainly the agricultural, maritime and aeronautical applications of meteorology and hydro-meteorology.

CARIBBEAN HURRICANE SEMINAR

Under the technical assistance program, WMO, together with the United Nations Technical Assistance Administration, organized a regional seminar on Caribbean hurricanes. The purpose of the seminar to be held in February 1956 was to review, on as comprehensive a scale as possible, all meteorological knowledge and experience in connection with the development and behavior of hurricanes. The review was to be conducted by means of lectures and discussions. Eighteen experts from ten countries were invited, and in addition 22 governments were asked to designate qualified meteorologists to attend the seminar. It was hoped that as a result of this seminar more effective warning systems would be developed, with a consequent improvement in the protection of life and property.

ARID ZONE AND HUMID TROPICS RESEARCH

In these two fields, WMO collaborates with UNESCO. WMO has established a separate panel of experts for each of the two subjects. Because of its importance to the development of arid zones, the study of such problems as the uses of natural energy resources (wind energy, solar energy) and artificial precipitation is a part of the technical program of WMO.

WORLD THUNDERSTORM MAPS

Information about the mean monthly, seasonal and annual frequency of days of thunderstorms has been collected from Meteorological Services, and maps showing the worldwide distribution of thunderstorm activity have been prepared. The results of this work are being set out in a technical publication of WMO.

TECHNICAL REGULATIONS

Technical Regulations were adopted by the Second World Meteorological Congress which was held in Geneva in April–May 1955. They deal with all branches of meteorology, and include regulations concerning observing stations, observations, telecommunications, forecasting and climatological practices, and services for shipping and agriculture. A separate volume contains international regulations referring to aeronautical meteorology.

CLIMATOLOGICAL ATLASES

Meteorological services in various countries are preparing and publishing national climatological atlases. WMO has recognized the need for a certain degree of uniformity in these publications. A Working Group has therefore been set up to draft suitable specifications and to make proposals which might lead ultimately to the preparation of a World Climatological Atlas.

LIST OF SELECTED SHIPS MAKING WEATHER OBSERVATIONS

Practically all weather information obtained from the sea is provided by voluntary observers on merchant ships. The ships are supplied with instruments by the meteorological services, and report regularly by radio to the nearest coastal station.

There are at present about 2500 observing ships on the oceans (as well as thirteen stationary ocean weather ships). The first edition of an international list of the voluntary observing ships recruited from about 30 different countries was issued in 1955; it indicates the call sign, route and instruments used by these ships.

ARTIFICIAL PRECIPITATION

In view of the economic and social benefits which could result from successful attempts to induce rain or snow artificially, and because of a desire to control and modify precipitation, developments in artificial precipitation have been watched with great interest by scientists and laymen alike.

A working group set up for the purpose of studying this question submitted a report outlining the background knowledge of cloud physics, and summarizing the present state of development.

The report concludes that investigation and meticulously planned and analyzed seeding experiments will be needed over a period of at least several years before a reliable assessment of the economic potential of seeding operations can be made.

STANDARDIZATION OF METEOROLOGICAL INSTRUMENTS

To obtain homogeneity in the records of atmospheric pressure, the mercury barometers used at meteorological stations are generally compared, either directly or indirectly, with a national working standard barometer. These national working standards are compared from time to time with regional absolute standard barometers, if such exist in a particular region.

The results of an inquiry regarding the type and place of regional standard barometers were distributed to WMO members, and a set of standard forms was issued so that WMO's Secretariat might be notified of any future international comparisons of barometers.

In 1956, WMO was to organize for the second time a world comparison of radiosondes. The radiosonde is a balloon-borne instrument which measures temperature, humidity and pressure as the instrument rises in the atmosphere. The measurements are transmitted by an automatic device to ground stations. World comparisons are intended to obtain accurate data on the functioning of the various types of instruments under similar conditions.

METEOROLOGICAL TELECOMMUNICATIONS

One of the primary needs in meteorology is an uninterrupted and effective international exchange of weather observations. These observations, made all around the world at identical hours, are transmitted 24 hours per day by all modern means of telecommunication. The weather reports thus broadcast are the basis for the weather charts which in turn serve for forecasting purposes. This international exchange requires constant examination and review. In particular, teletype networks are being introduced to replace the less dependable wireless broadcasts. Agreements on plans of broadcasts and of networks, hours of observation and of transmission, etc., fall within the province of WMO, and are part of its routine duties. Another important problem is the development of facsimile apparatus for the transmission of surface and upper-air weather charts. The International Telecommunication Union is consulted on various aspects of these telecommunication problems.

Publications

WMO *Bulletin*. Information about the work of the Organization is given in the quarterly WMO *Bulletin*, the first number of which was published in April

1952. In addition to reports on meetings and the activities of the various constituent bodies, the *Bulletin* contains occasional articles on recent scientific developments in meteorology.

Other publications of WMO fall into three main categories:

(a) Basic Documents of WMO, published in the four official languages (English, French, Russian and Spanish), contain information on such subjects as the WMO Convention, the General Regulations, and the Technical Regulations.

(b) Final Reports of Meetings of WMO, which are published in English and French.

(c) Technical Publications, which include Technical Notes, Guides and Nomenclatures. The WMO Technical Notes, dealing with a variety of technical subjects, are published in one of the official languages only, but contain a summary in the other three official languages. WMO Guides and Nomenclatures are published in English and French.

INTER-GOVERNMENTAL MARITIME CONSULTATIVE ORGANIZATION (IMCO) (Not yet functioning)

Functions

The Inter-Governmental Maritime Consultative Organization, when it comes into being, is:

to provide for inter-governmental cooperation concerning regulations and practices relating to technical matters affecting international shipping;

to encourage the highest standards of maritime safety and efficiency of navigation;

to promote the availability of shipping services to the commerce of the world without discrimination; and

to consider unfair restrictive practices by shipping concerns.

Origin

The United Nations Transport and Communications Commission, after reviewing international organizations in its field, considered that a permanent central maritime agency should be established through which information could be exchanged, and maritime agreements and conventions adopted or revised. Such an agency, it was felt, could also deal on behalf of shipping with organizations in such related fields as telecommunication and aviation. Accordingly, on March 28, 1947, the Council asked the Secretary-General to call a conference to consider the establishment of an inter-governmental maritime organization. The Secretary-General was requested to invite to the Conference all Members of the United Nations and in addition Albania, Austria, Bulgaria, Finland, Hungary, Ireland, Italy, Jordan, Portugal, Romania, Switzerland and Yemen (with the exception of Switzerland, all these States later became Members of the United Nations).

The United Nations Maritime Conference met in Geneva from February 19 to March 6, 1948. It was attended by representatives from 32 countries and by observers from four other countries and nine international organizations.

A draft convention concerning the scope and purpose of the proposed organization, prepared by a temporary maritime organization, the United Maritime Consultative Council, was discussed by the Conference.

On the basis of this draft, a Convention on the Inter-Governmental Maritime Consultative Organization was drawn up by the Conference and opened for signature on March 6, 1948. IMCO will come formally into existence when 21 states, of which seven must each have a total tonnage of at least one million gross tons of shipping, have become parties to the Convention. By December 31, 1955, eighteen States had ratified the Convention. They are: Argentina, Australia, Belgium, Burma, Canada, the Dominican Republic, Egypt, France, Greece, Haiti, Honduras, Iceland, Israel, Mexico, the Netherlands, Switzerland, the United Kingdom and the United States.

In the meantime, a Preparatory Committee is functioning, composed of representatives of Argentina, Australia, Belgium, Canada, France, Greece, India, the Netherlands, Norway, Sweden, the United Kingdom and the United States. It will make the necessary preparations for the first session of the Assembly of IMCO.

Organization

As provided by the Convention, IMCO will work through an Assembly, a Council, a Maritime Safety Committee, and a secretariat.

The Assembly, consisting of representatives of all members, is to meet every two years. It will be the policy-making body of the organization.

The Council will be composed of sixteen members, of which eight will represent countries having an interest in providing international shipping services, and eight will represent countries having an interest in international seaborne trade. Between sessions of the Assembly, it will perform all functions of the organization except that of recommending to members the adoption of maritime safety regulations.

The Maritime Safety Committee will consist of fourteen members elected by the Assembly from among member nations having an important interest in maritime safety, of which at least eight are to be the largest ship-owning nations.

The secretariat will comprise the Secretary-General, a Secretary of the Maritime Safety Committee, and such staff as the Organization requires.

Activities of the Preparatory Committee

The Preparatory Committee of IMCO met for the first time in Geneva on March 6, 1948. At its second session, held at Lake Success on November 30 and December 1, 1948, it drew up a provisional agenda for the first session of the IMCO Assembly. It also prepared a proposed budget for the first two years of IMCO in the amount of £ 20,000, taking into account that the Organization's headquarters will be in London, and adopted a resolution concerning contributions by members to the budget.

The next meeting of the Preparatory Committee will be called prior to the first session of the IMCO Assembly, when IMCO comes into being, unless some important questions arise which make it necessary for the Committee to meet earlier.

INTERNATIONAL TRADE ORGANIZATION (ITO) (Not yet established)

Origin and Background

In the nineteen-thirties, when the world was suffering from an intense economic depression, many governments attempted to shelter behind various kinds of protective trade barriers such as high tariff protection, quota restrictions on imports and exports, and exchange controls. It became evident during the Second World War that these restrictions might become a permanent fixture in the world, unless an attempt was made to reestablish as soon as possible the pre-depression pattern of multilateral trading between nations. The General Agreement on Tariffs and

Trade (GATT) is today the major result of the efforts which were made in this direction.

The wartime allies in the Atlantic Charter and in the Lend-Lease Agreements bound themselves to seek together a world trading system based on non-discrimination, and aimed at higher standards of living to be achieved through fair, full and free exchange of goods and services. In pursuit of this aim, long before the end of the war, the United States, the United Kingdom and other important trading countries among the United Nations, discussed the establishment of international organizations to tackle the postwar problems of currency, investment and trade. The International Monetary Fund and the International Bank for Reconstruction and Development were established as a result of the Bretton Woods Conference which was held before the end of the war. But for various reasons, including its wide range and its complexity, the Charter for the International Trade Organization, which was intended to be the third agency to operate in a specialized field of economic affairs, was not completed until much later.

In 1946, the United Nations Economic and Social Council resolved to convene an International Conference on Trade and Employment, and established a Preparatory Committee to prepare for the consideration of the Conference a draft convention for an international trade organization. A draft Charter was adopted by the Preparatory Committee in August 1947, and formed the basis for the work of the United Nations Conference on Trade and Employment, held in Havana from November 21, 1947, to March 24, 1948. That Conference drew up a Charter for an International Trade Organization (known as the Havana Charter), and established an Interim Commission for the International Trade Organization (ICITO).

The main task of the Interim Commission was to prepare for the first session of ITO, including a plan of work for the first year of the proposed Organization. This task, so far as events could be foreseen, was completed in 1949, and since that time, the secretariat of ICITO has been occupied with the performance of duties for the Contracting Parties to the General Agreement on Tariffs and Trade (GATT).

By the end of 1950, the Havana Charter had been accepted unconditionally by only one country, namely Liberia; and in December of that year the United States Department of State indicated that it would discontinue its efforts to obtain the approval of the United States Congress for the Charter. It subsequently became evident that the establishment of ITO would be indefinitely postponed.

The General Agreement on Tariffs and Trade (GATT)

While the Charter for ITO was in course of preparation, the members of the Preparatory Committee decided to proceed with tariff negotiations among themselves instead of waiting for the Organization to come into existence, thereby promoting one of the most important objectives of ITO. The Preparatory Committee also sponsored the discussions which led to the formulation of the General Agreement on Tariffs and Trade (GATT). The tariff negotiations were held at Geneva from April to October 1947, when the 23 participating countries signed a Final Act which authenticated the text of GATT.

The Geneva tariff conference was the first of three main tariff conferences which have been held under GATT auspices. The fourth tariff conference was to convene in Geneva on January 18, 1956. The two others took place in 1949, at Annecy, France, and in 1950–1951, at Torquay, England. The total result of the first three of these conferences is that the rates of customs duties on about 60,000 items entering into international trade have been reduced or stabilized. All the countries adhering to GATT have taken part in these tariff negotiations: in fact it is a stipulation that a country wishing to join GATT should undertake to reduce the level of its own customs tariff through negotiation before it can be admitted. On January 1, 1956, there were 35 Contracting Parties (member countries) to GATT, and their combined foreign trade represented about four-fifths of total world trade.

STRUCTURE AND FUNCTIONS OF GATT

GATT is an international trade agreement, and its terms are set out in a series of articles. First there are the articles dealing directly with tariffs—Article I with the Most-Favoured-Nation obligation and Article II, the basic tariff article, incorporating the schedules of tariff concessions resulting from the tariff conferences. Article III provides agreed rules regarding the application of internal taxes, guaranteeing that foreign goods will be given equal treatment with domestic products. Articles IV to X—known as the technical articles—are general rules and principles relating to transit trade, to anti-dumping duties, to customs valuation, to customs formalities, and to marks of origin. Articles XI to XV deal with quantitative restrictions on imports and exports: Article XI formally outlaws quantitative restrictions; the remainder of these articles are qualifications to this general rule where balance-of-payments difficulties make necessary such departures. There are further articles dealing with state trading, subsidies and assistance for countries in early stages of economic development. Finally, there are provisions for joint discussion and settlement of differences.

Such is the structure of GATT. In fact all its provisions are linked to and stem from the tariff concessions, because these tariff concessions would be of doubtful value if the parties to the Agreement were to have their hands free in all other fields of commercial policy; for, given such freedom, it would be possible entirely to nullify the benefits accruing from concessions made in tariff rates. The result has been to create a code of trade policy rules governing the commercial relations of the countries which adhere to GATT.

SESSIONS OF THE CONTRACTING PARTIES

Under the terms of GATT, the Contracting Parties are required to meet from time to time to give effect to those provisions which require joint action. Up to the end of 1955, ten sessions had been held. The general practice is to hold one session a year, lasting about six weeks, at GATT headquarters in Geneva. The sessions are broadly concerned with items which arise out of the operation of GATT, or which are brought up as complaints of violation of GATT rules of fair trading; or matters may be put on the agenda by member governments as being appropriate for discussion in the GATT forum. The tenth session held in October-December 1955 may be taken as an example. The regular business of that session included: (a) consultations with Contracting Parties which are obliged, for safeguarding their balance of payments, to maintain discriminatory import restrictions, contrary to the general undertaking in GATT; (b) annual reports from certain governments on waivers from GATT obligations granted to them at earlier sessions; (c) new requests for waivers: in one important case Belgium undertook to eliminate all quota restrictions on imports of agricultural products before the end of 1962; and (d) complaints regarding breaches of GATT obligations.

The settlement of complaints that benefits afforded by GATT are being nullified or impaired is a significant aspect of the work of the Contracting Parties. A technique for dealing with complaints has been established by which a panel of neutral assessors, that is, representatives of countries which have no direct interest in the case, examine all aspects of the complaint impartially and report their findings and recommendations to the Contracting Parties. Not all the complaints reach the point of being brought before a session, because they may be settled "out of court", so to speak, through direct consultations between governments either during the session, or through normal diplomatic channels.

Great and small countries have been involved in these applications, both as complainants and as defendants. For example, in 1950 a complaint was made to the Contracting Parties that the British system of purchase tax so operated as to discriminate in favor of domestic products and against similar imported goods. The United Kingdom Government admitted that the tax did have this discriminatory effect, though unintentionally. They agreed to amend the system so as to eliminate the element of discrimination, and thus bring the operation of the tax into conformity with the obligations of the United Kingdom under GATT. In 1952, this pledge was fulfilled. In another case, the United States and Canada complained that Belgium was imposing discriminatory import restrictions aimed against imports requiring payment in dollars, although Belgium was not in balance-of-payment difficulties. Belgium undertook to eliminate this discrimination, and reported in 1954 that all exchange restrictions on dollar imports had been abolished. Complaints by Chile against Australia, by Norway against Germany, and by the United Kingdom and France against Greece have been successfully dealt with. In 1952, India brought before the Contracting Parties a complaint against Pakistan about the levying of discriminatory taxes on exports of jute to India. The Contracting Parties felt that this question might be more easily resolved if it were considered together with other trading difficulties between the two Governments, including the conditions under which coal was supplied by India to Pakistan. Therefore they invited the two Governments to consult together with a view to finding a solution along these lines. These consultations were concluded successfully when the two Governments signed a long-term trade pact, and agreed to drop the discriminatory levies in question.

Other complaints successfully dealt with include the suppression of a discriminatory tax levied on imports by the Belgian authorities, and the lessening of restrictions on American coal imported into Germany. In another type of case, Sweden undertook to remove the cause of a complaint by Italy that Swedish anti-dumping duties on Italian nylon stockings were being applied unfairly. In another, following a complaint by Czechoslovakia, trade between that country and Peru, which was previously stopped by the Peruvian Government, was restored. In 1955, it is significant to note, a number of the complaints which were put on the agenda were settled—or postponed for further discussions between governments— without resort to the complaints machinery.

REDUCTION OF ADMINISTRATIVE BARRIERS TO TRADE

For the past six years the Contracting Parties have been tackling customs formalities and various administrative barriers to trade, stage by stage. In 1950, they drew up a code of standard practices for the administration, by governments, of imports and export restrictions and exchange controls. In 1952, they adopted a code of standard practices for documents which are required for importation, and they made several recommendations which envisage the elimination of consular visas and formalities as soon as possible. They also drew up and opened for signature the International Convention to Facilitate the Importation of Samples and Advertising Material, the broad purpose of which is to minimize the costs and reduce the formalities and delays which traders and merchants have to face in sending samples and advertising material from one country to another. Following the adherence of fifteen governments, this Convention entered into force in November 1955. The Contracting Parties are also studying the possibility of drawing up uniform rules for the nationality of imported goods, and at the tenth session in 1955, they formulated a draft of a resolution which recommends governments to eliminate measures in the field of transport insurance which have a restrictive effect on trade.

REVIEW OF GATT IN 1954—1955

In the course of the ninth session, the Contracting Parties undertook a comprehensive review of GATT in the light of seven years' experience. The major results of the review of the Agreement may be indicated as follows: (a) reaffirmation of the basic objectives and obligations, including the principle of non-discrimination in trade and the general prohibition (with specified exceptions) to the use of quantitative restrictions on imports, which have guided the Contracting Parties in their commercial relations since 1948; (b) the drawing up of a renewed undertaking to prolong the firm validity of the tariffs bound under the Agreement to December 31, 1957, and thereafter to extend automatically the assured life of the Tariff Schedules by periods of three years; (c) the provision of suitable procedures for dealing with the problems of countries in early stages of development; and (d) the introduction of new provisions relating to export subsidies.

The amendments to the text of GATT, resulting from the review of GATT, were embodied in protocols which were opened for signature in March 1955. At the end of 1955, these protocols had not received the number of acceptances required for the amendments to enter into force.

ORGANIZATION FOR TRADE COOPERATION

During the review of GATT, the Contracting Parties decided to provide an organization which will administer GATT and establish the secretariat on a permanent basis. They drew up an Agreement, which, when it comes into force, will establish the Organization for Trade Cooperation (OTC). The Agreement contains the basic provisions relating to the structure and functions of the Organization. There would be an Assembly, an Executive Committee, and a secretariat headed by a Director-General. The main function of the Organization would be to administer the General Agreement. In addition, the Organization would be able to sponsor international trade negotiations, and to serve as an inter-governmental forum for the discussion and solution of other questions relating to international trade. The Agreement will enter into force, among the governments that have accepted it, after it has been accepted by governments whose territories account for 85 per cent of the total external trade of the territories of the governments which comprise the Contracting Parties.

It is stated in the Agreement establishing OTC (Article 11 G), that the Organization "may, by an agreement approved by its Assembly, be brought into relationship with the United Nations, as one of the specialized agencies referred to in Article 57 of the Charter of the United Nations".

SECRETARIAT

The GATT secretariat consists of a small number of specialists under the direction of the Executive Secretary, Eric Wyndham White. The secretariat offices are in *Villa le Bocage*, which adjoins the *Palais des Nations*, Geneva. The operation of GATT is financed through payments by governments which are Contracting Parties. The scale of contributions is assessed in accordance with their percentage share of the total trade of the Contracting Parties.

CHARTS

ORGANS OF THE UNITED NATIONS

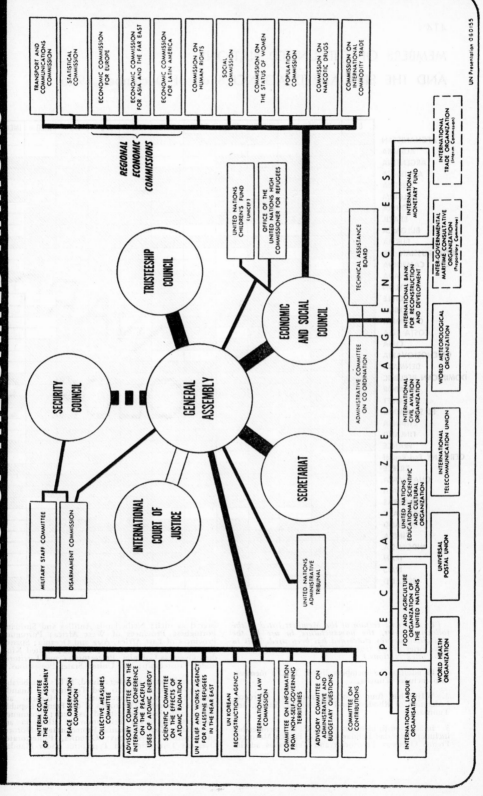

UN Presentation 050155

MEMBERS OF THE UNITED NATIONS
AND THE SPECIALIZED AGENCIES as of December 1955

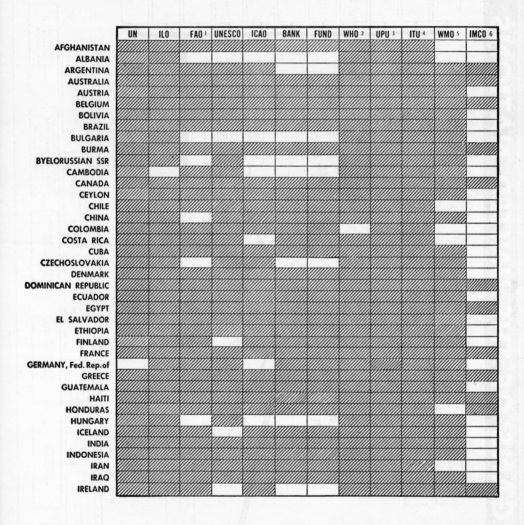

Columns: UN | ILO | FAO[1] | UNESCO | ICAO | BANK | FUND | WHO[2] | UPU[3] | ITU[4] | WMO[5] | IMCO[6]

Countries listed:
AFGHANISTAN, ALBANIA, ARGENTINA, AUSTRALIA, AUSTRIA, BELGIUM, BOLIVIA, BRAZIL, BULGARIA, BURMA, BYELORUSSIAN SSR, CAMBODIA, CANADA, CEYLON, CHILE, CHINA, COLOMBIA, COSTA RICA, CUBA, CZECHOSLOVAKIA, DENMARK, DOMINICAN REPUBLIC, ECUADOR, EGYPT, EL SALVADOR, ETHIOPIA, FINLAND, FRANCE, GERMANY, Fed. Rep. of, GREECE, GUATEMALA, HAITI, HONDURAS, HUNGARY, ICELAND, INDIA, INDONESIA, IRAN, IRAQ, IRELAND

(To designate certain of the Members listed in the following notes, the nomenclature in use by the specialized agency concerned has been used. This in some cases differs from the official nomenclature of the United Nations.)

1. In addition to members listed, FAO's membership includes Tunisia.

2. WHO has four associate members: Morocco, Federation of Rhodesia and Nyasaland, Sudan, and Tunisia.

3. In addition to members listed, UPU's membership includes: Algeria; Belgian Congo; French Morocco; French Overseas Territories and Territories administered as such; Netherlands Antilles and Surinam; Portuguese Provinces of West Africa; Portuguese Provinces of East Africa, Asia and Oceania; Spanish Colonies; Spanish Morocco; Tunisia; United Kingdom Overseas Colonies, Protectorates and Territories under Trusteeship; and United States Possessions.

4. In addition to members listed, ITU's membership includes: Belgian Congo and Territory of Ruanda-Urundi; French Protectorates of Morocco and Tunisia; Overseas Territories of the French Republic and Territories administered as such; Portuguese Overseas Provinces; Federation of Rhodesia and Nyasaland; Zone of Spanish Protectorate in Morocco and Spanish Possessions; Colonies, Protectorates, Overseas Territories and Territories under Mandate

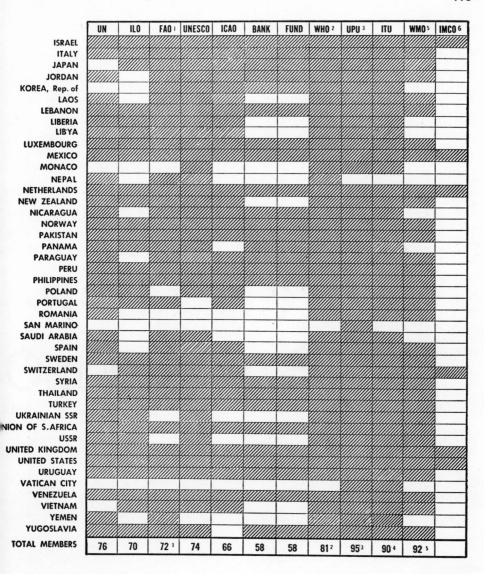

	UN	ILO	FAO¹	UNESCO	ICAO	BANK	FUND	WHO²	UPU³	ITU	WMO⁵	IMCO⁶
ISRAEL												
ITALY												
JAPAN												
JORDAN												
KOREA, Rep. of												
LAOS												
LEBANON												
LIBERIA												
LIBYA												
LUXEMBOURG												
MEXICO												
MONACO												
NEPAL												
NETHERLANDS												
NEW ZEALAND												
NICARAGUA												
NORWAY												
PAKISTAN												
PANAMA												
PARAGUAY												
PERU												
PHILIPPINES												
POLAND												
PORTUGAL												
ROMANIA												
SAN MARINO												
SAUDI ARABIA												
SPAIN												
SWEDEN												
SWITZERLAND												
SYRIA												
THAILAND												
TURKEY												
UKRAINIAN SSR												
UNION OF S. AFRICA												
USSR												
UNITED KINGDOM												
UNITED STATES												
URUGUAY												
VATICAN CITY												
VENEZUELA												
VIETNAM												
YEMEN												
YUGOSLAVIA												
TOTAL MEMBERS	76	70	72¹	74	66	58	58	81²	95³	90⁴	92⁵	

or Trusteeship of the United Kingdom; and Territories of the United States. (The Netherlands includes Surinam, Netherlands Antilles and New Guinea. The Union of South Africa includes the territory of South West Africa.) ITU has five associate members: British West Africa, British East Africa, Bermuda-British Caribbean Group, Malaya-British Borneo Group, and Somaliland under Italian Administration (Trust Territory of).

5. In addition to members listed, WMO's membership includes: Belgian Congo, Bermuda, British Caribbean Territories, British East African Territories and Indian Ocean Islands, British Malaya-Borneo Territories, British West African Territories, Federation of Rhodesia and Nyasaland, French Cameroons,

French Equatorial Africa, French Oceania, French Somaliland, French Togoland, French West Africa, Hong Kong, Madagascar, Morocco (French Protectorate), Netherlands Antilles, Netherlands New Guinea, New Caledonia, Portuguese East Africa, Portuguese West Africa, Spanish Protectorate of Morocco, Spanish Territories of Guinea, Sudan and Surinam.

6. Indicates States which have become Parties to the Convention on IMCO or are members of the Preparatory Committee. The twelve members of the Preparatory Committee are: Argentina, Australia, Belgium, Canada, France, Greece, India, the Netherlands, Norway, Sweden, the United Kingdom and the United States.

INDEX

INDEX

UNITED NATIONS REVIEW

The *Review*, an illustrated magazine published monthly by the United Nations, is designed to aid public understanding of the various aspects of the work of the Organization. The world-wide activities of the United Nations and its specialized agencies are objectively reported with a depth and perspective which only a magazine devoted wholly to the United Nations story can give.

Informative articles, illustrated features and objective appraisals of particular developments provide the current knowledge essential to a real grasp of the Organization's aims and problems, its operations and their scope.

•

Annual subscription:
$4.50; 22/6 stg.; 18 Swiss frs.

Individual copy: $0.40; 2/– stg.; 1.50 Swiss frs.
or equivalent in other currencies

Published in English, French and Spanish editions.

Obtainable from sales agents for United Nations publications throughout the world.

YEARBOOK OF THE
UNITED NATIONS, 1955

The most comprehensive account of the work of the United Nations and its Specialized Agencies during the year published in one volume. The *Yearbook* provides a permanent reference for public officials, scholars, diplomats, writers, teachers, librarians, students and others concerned with international affairs.

The tenth anniversary celebrations, sixteen new Members, the International Conference on the Peaceful Uses of Atomic Energy, and the first plebiscite under United Nations auspices to determine the future of a Trust Territory—these are a few of the developments of the year dealt with in this ninth *Yearbook* in the series.

The first part of the volume presents a documented account and review of United Nations work on political, economic and social questions, Non-Self-Governing Territories and International Trusteeship, legal, administrative and budgetary matters. The second part surveys the work of each of the Specialized Agencies.

U.N. Publ. Sales No. 1956.I.20
568 pages, clothbound

$10.50; £3/10/— stg.; 42 Swiss frs.
or equivalent in other currencies

Obtainable from sales agents for United Nations publications throughout the world.

UNITED NATIONS SALES AGENTS

ARGENTINA: Editorial Sudamericana S.A., Alsina 500, Buenos Aires.

AUSTRALIA: H. A. Goddard, 255a George St., Sydney; 90 Queen St., Melbourne.
Melbourne University Press, Carlton N.3, Victoria.

AUSTRIA: Gerold & Co., Graben 31, Wien 1.
B. Wüllerstorff, Markus Sittikusstrasse 10, Salzburg.

BELGIUM: Agence et Messageries de la Presse S.A., 14-22 rue du Persil, Bruxelles.
W. H. Smith & Son, 71-75, blvd. Adolphe-Max, Bruxelles.

BOLIVIA: Librería Selecciones, Casilla 972, La Paz.

BRAZIL: Livraria Agir, Río de Janeiro, Sao Paulo and Belo Horizonte.

CAMBODIA: Papeterie-Librairie Nouvelle, Albert Portail, 14 Avenue Boulloche, Pnom-Penh.

CANADA: Ryerson Press, 299 Queen St. West, Toronto.

CEYLON: Lake House Bookshop, The Associated Newspapers of Ceylon, Ltd., P. O. Box 244, Colombo.

CHILE: Editorial del Pacifico, Ahumada 57, Santiago.
Librería Ivens, Casilla 205, Santiago.

CHINA: The World Book Co., Ltd., 99 Chung King Road, 1st Section, Taipeh, Taiwan.
The Commercial Press Ltd., 211 Honan Rd., Shanghai.

COLOMBIA: Librería América, Medellin.
Librería Buchholz Galería, Bogotá.
Librería Nacional Ltda., Barranquilla.

COSTA RICA: Trejos Hermanos, Apartado 1313, San José.

CUBA: La Casa Belga, O'Reilly 455, La Habana.

CZECHOSLOVAKIA: Ceskoslovensky Spisovatel, Narodni Trida 9, Praha 1.

DENMARK: Einar Munksgaard, Ltd., Norregade 6, Kobenhavn, K.

DOMINICAN REPUBLIC: Librería Dominicana, Mercedes 49, Ciudad Trujillo.

ECUADOR: Librería Cientifica, Guayaquil and Quito.

EGYPT: Librairie "La Renaissance d'Egypte", 9 Sh. Adly Pasha, Cairo.

EL SALVADOR: Manuel Navas y Cía., 1a. Avenida sur 37, San Salvador.

FINLAND: Akateeminen Kirjakauppa, 2 Keskuskatu, Helsinki.

FRANCE: Editions A. Pédone, 13, rue Soufflot, Paris V.

GERMANY: R. Eisenschmidt, Kaiserstrasse 49, Frankfurt/Main.
Elwert & Meurer, Hauptstrasse 101, Berlin-Schoneberg.
Alexander Horn, Spiegelgasse 9, Wiesbaden.
W. E. Saarbach, Gereonstrasse 25-29, Köln (22c).

GREECE: Kauffmann Bookshop, 28 Stadion Street, Athènes.

GUATEMALA: Sociedad Económico Financiera, 6a Av. 14-33, Guatemala City.

HAITI: Librairie "A la Caravelle", Boîte Postale 111-B, Port-au-Prince.

HONDURAS: Librería Panamericana, Tegucigalpa.

HONG KONG: The Swindon Book Co., 25 Nathan Road, Kowloon.

ICELAND: Bokaverzlun Sigfusar Eymundssonar H. F., Austurstraeti 18, Reykjavik.

INDIA: Orient Longmans, Calcutta, Bombay, Madras and New Delhi.
Oxford Book & Stationery Co., New Delhi and Calcutta.
P. Varadachary & Co., Madras.

INDONESIA: Pembangunan, Ltd., Gunung Sahari 84, Djakarta.

IRAN: "Guity", 482 Avenue Ferdowsi, Teheran.

IRAQ: Mackenzie's Bookshop, Baghdad

ISRAEL: Blumstein's Bookstores Ltd., 35 Allenby Road, Tel-Aviv.

ITALY: Libreria Commissionaria Sansoni, Via Gino Capponi 26, Firenze.

JAPAN: Maruzen Company, Ltd., 6 Tori-Nichome, Nihonbashi, Tokyo.

KOREA: Eul-Yoo Publishing Co. Ltd., 5, 2-Ka, Chongno, Seoul.

LEBANON: Librairie Universelle, Beyrouth.

LIBERIA: J. Momolu Kamara, Monrovia.

LUXEMBOURG: Librairie J. Schummer, Luxembourg.

MEXICO: Editorial Hermes S.A., Ignacio Mariscal 41, México, D.F.

NETHERLANDS: N.V. Martinus Nijhoff, Lange Voorhout 9, s'-Gravenhage.

NEW ZEALAND: United Nations Association of New Zealand, C.P.O. 1011, Wellington.

NORWAY: Johan Grundt Tanum Forl g, Kr. Augustsgt. 7A, Oslo.

PAKISTAN: The Pakistan Co-operative Book Society, Dacca, East Pakistan (and at Chittagong).
Publishers United Ltd., Lahore
Thomas & Thomas, Karachi, 3.

PANAMA: José Menéndez, Plaza de Arango, Panamá.

PARAGUAY: Agencia de Librerías de Salvador Nizza, Pte. Franco 39-43 Asunción.

PERU: Librería Internacional del Perú S. A., Lima and Arequipa.

PHILIPPINES: Alemar's Book Store, 749 Rizal Avenue, Manila.

PORTUGAL: Livraria Rodrigues, 186 Rua Aurea, Lisboa.

SINGAPORE: The City Book Store, Ltd., Winchester House, Collyer Quay.

SPAIN: Librería Bosch, 11 Ronda Universidad, Barcelona.
Librería Mundi-Prensa, Lagasca 38, Madrid.

SWEDEN: C. E. Fritze's Kungl. Hovbokhandel A-B, Fredsgatan 2, Stockholm.

SWITZERLAND: Librairie Payot S.A., Lausanne, Genève.
Hans Raunhardt, Kirchgasse 17, Zurich 1.

SYRIA: Librairie Universelle, Damas.

THAILAND: Pramuan Mit Ltd. 55 Chakrawat Road, Wat Tuk, Bangkok.

TURKEY: Librairie Hachette, 469 Istiklal Caddesi, Beyoglu, Istanbul.

UNION OF SOUTH AFRICA: Van Schaik's Bookstore (Pty.), Ltd., Box 724, Pretoria.

UNITED KINGDOM: H. M. Stationery Office, P. O. Box 569, London, S.E.1 (and at H.M.S.O. shops).

UNITED STATES OF AMERICA: International Documents Service, Colombia University Press, 2960 Broadway, New York 27, N. Y.

URUGUAY: Representación de Editoriales, Prof. H. D'Elía, Av. 18 de Julio 1333, Montevideo.

VENEZUELA: Librería del Este, Av. Miranda, No. 52, Edf. Galipán, Caracas.

VIET-NAM: Papeterie-Librairie Nouvelle, Albert Portail, Boîte Postale 283, Saigon.

YUGOSLAVIA: Cankarjeva Zalozba, Ljubljana, Slovenia.
Drzavno Preduzece, Jugoslovenska Knjiga, Terazije 27/11, Beograd.
"Prosvjeta", Izdavacka Knjizara, No. 5, Trg. Bratstva i Ledinstva. Zagreb.

Orders and inquiries from countries where sales agents have not yet been appointed may be sent to: Sales and Circulation Section United Nations, New York, U.S.A.; or Sales Section, United Nations, Geneva, Switzerland.

56-01128—22½ M—Sept. 1956